Melodrama Unbound

FILM AND CULTURE SERIES

FILM AND CULTURE
A SERIES OF COLUMBIA UNIVERSITY PRESS

EDITED BY JOHN BELTON

For a complete list of books in this series, see pages 407–410.

MELODRAMA UNBOUND

Across History, Media, and National Cultures

EDITED BY
CHRISTINE GLEDHILL
AND LINDA WILLIAMS

Columbia University Press
New York

Columbia University Press
Publishers Since 1893
New York Chichester, West Sussex
cup.columbia.edu
Copyright © 2018 Columbia University Press
All rights reserved

Cataloging-in-Publication Data available from the Library of Congress
ISBN 978-0-231-18066-5 (cloth)
ISBN 978-0-231-18067-2 (paper)
ISBN 978-0-231-54319-4 (electronic)

LCCN 2017044006

Cover design: Milenda Nan Ok Lee
Cover image: © Shutterstock

To all melodrama lovers, everywhere

Contents

Prologue: The Reach of Melodrama ix
CHRISTINE GLEDHILL

Acknowledgments xxvii

Introduction 1
CHRISTINE GLEDHILL AND LINDA WILLIAMS

PART I: MELODRAMA'S CROSSMEDIA, TRANSNATIONAL HISTORIES

1. Unbinding Melodrama 15
   MATTHEW BUCKLEY

2. The Passion of Christ and the Melodramatic Imagination 31
   RICHARD ALLEN

3. Boucicault in Bombay: Global Theater Circuits and Domestic Melodrama in the Parsi Theater 49
   KATHRYN HANSEN

4. Global Melodrama and Transmediality in Turn-of-the-Century Japan 69
   HANNAH AIRRIESS

5. Transnational Melodrama, *Wenyi*, and the Orphan Imagination 83
   ZHEN ZHANG

6. Performing/Acting Melodrama 99
   HELEN DAY-MAYER AND DAVID MAYER

7. Melodrama and the Making of Hollywood 115
   HILARY A. HALLETT

8. Modernizing Melodrama: *The Petrified Forest* on American Stage and Screen (1935–1936)   135
MARTIN SHINGLER

9. One Suffers but One Learns: Melodrama and the Rules of Lack of Limits   151
CARLOS MONSIVÁIS (TRANS. KATHLEEN M. VERNON)

10. World and Time: Serial Television Melodrama in America   169
LINDA WILLIAMS

11. Melodrama's "Authenticity" in Carl Th. Dreyer's *La Passion de Jeanne d'Arc*   185
AMANDA DOXTATER

PART II: CULTURAL AND AESTHETIC DEBATES

12. "Tales of Sound and Fury . . ." or, The Elephant of Melodrama   205
LINDA WILLIAMS

13. Repositioning Excess: Romantic Melodrama's Journey from Hollywood to China   219
PANPAN YANG

14. Melodrama and the Aesthetics of Emotion   237
E. DEIDRE PRIBRAM

15. Expressionist Aurality: The Stylized Aesthetic of *Bhava* in Indian Melodrama   253
IRA BHASKAR

16. The Sorrow and the Piety: Melodrama Rethought in Postwar Italian Cinema   273
LOUIS BAYMAN

17. Costumes as Melodrama: *Super Fly*, Male Costume, and the Larger-Than-Life   289
DRAKE STUTESMAN

18. Melodrama and Apocalypse: Politics and the Melodramatic Mode in *Contagion*   311
DESPINA KAKOUDAKI

19. Even More Tears: The *Historical Time* Theory of Melodrama   325
JANE M. GAINES

Bibliography   341
Contributor Biographies   367
Index   371

Prologue: The Reach of Melodrama
CHRISTINE GLEDHILL

A meaning only reveals its depths once it has encountered and come into contact with another, foreign meaning.

... We raise new questions for a foreign culture, ones that it did not raise itself; we seek answers to our own question in it; and the foreign culture responds to us by revealing to us its new aspects and new semantic depths.

(Mikhail Bakhtin 1986, 7)

This prologue returns to the history of late eighteenth/early nineteenth-century theatrical melodrama, not to seek more accurate definition based on supposed origins but to probe melodrama's past practices for its significance to contemporary cinema: in particular, to the formation of the cross-generic modality that we argue infuses mainstream media fictions. This entails not only crossing disciplinary boundaries to investigate Victorian theatrical practices but to take seriously plays largely ignored as naïvely sentimental, morally simplistic, aesthetically excessive, and narratively incredible. But could our grandparents and great-grandparents have been so simple-minded and ideologically gullible as this stereotype implies? Moreover, how can claims for the modernity of cinema and its relation to melodrama be reconciled with such limited perceptions? If engagement with melodrama's past can now uncover "new aspects and semantic depths" in modern arts and entertainments, the relation between ideology and aesthetic experience may be reoriented, and critique redirected. Here I ask not what melodrama is—a taxonomic question—but what it did and does—aesthetic and cultural questions. Drawing on Mikhail Bakhtin's theory of genre (1986) and Raymond Williams's concept of "structure of feeling" (1973), I argue first that melodrama's aesthetic reaches beyond the limiting concept of representation, even as it commands referential recognition. Second, that in materializing the fusion of individual and society, melodrama reveals the work of emotion and personality in social and political processes—insights germane to the global political scene today.

HISTORICIZING MELODRAMA

Melodrama's role in the changing practices of European theaters from the seventeenth century into the nineteenth engaged shifting "structures of feeling"—the concept through which Raymond Williams (1973) rethinks culture as an everyday "felt sense of life." "Feeling" captures how individuals apprehend their world and their place in it; "structure" recognizes relations of concordance or dissonance between beliefs, values, institutional rules, professional practices, and daily life habits (63, 65). In Williams's later perspective (1997), historical change emerges as different structures of feeling interact: *residual* structures from the past persist into the present; *dominant* structures operate within social institutions and prevailing consciousness; *emergent* structures struggle against both to effect change (40–45). By definition a "felt sense of life" cannot be systematically located, but cultural institutions and forms, operating as sites of public discourse and practice, reveal traces of residual structures and signs of emergent structures resisting or contesting the dominant.

Melodrama arises as part of a broader shift from structures of feeling invested in hierarchic social formations—organized according to the authority of church, king, and aristocracy—to those supporting slow processes of individuation and democratization that would release the intellectual, entrepreneurial, and revolutionary energies of an evolving modernity. With this release, however, came all the existential ambiguities, social and interpersonal conflicts, and losses of belonging and community that such changes entail. The irony, not lost in melodrama, is that the newly forming, discrete individual becomes as mired and imprisoned as under previous hierarchies in the by now abstracted economic and political forces that justify inequalities and inequities in the name of personal freedoms.

In *Modern Tragedy*, Williams (1966) describes structural changes registered in the passage from tragedy to bourgeois tragedy to sentimental drama—changes significant for melodrama. In London, after twenty years of Puritan suppression, royal patents granted in 1662–63 led to the theatrical monopoly of Drury Lane, Covent Garden, and, later, Haymarket (for the summer season). This monopoly initially produced the aristocentric culture of Restoration tragedy and comedy, the elitism and license of which was gradually eroded during the eighteenth century under rising middle-class influence and the theater managers and playwrights who sought to serve it. In London, as in pre-Revolutionary Paris, aristocratic control had legally restricted theatrical growth through a licensed repertoire, defined by the spoken word, which was officially prohibited to "illegitimate" entertainers. Significantly, the officially sanctioned drama in Britain and France contributed to a shift in the meaning of "individual" from its earlier conception, defined by Williams (1988) as "indivisible"—part of a whole—toward its modern sense of unique singularity (161–65). Thus, the dramatic role of tragic hero changed from its centrality to a socioreligious hierarchy on which the fate of the state depended, to the tragically divided individual whose inner flaws led to personal downfall, and, in modern times, alienation from society altogether (Williams 1966, 36, 49). The tragic stance of the Restoration or neoclassical hero was vested in aristocratic codes of decorum, upheld through noble endurance of fate (26). However, while the moral dimension of decorum and the notion of individual error could appeal to a growing bourgeois audience, investment of tragic value in persons of rank ran counter to socioeconomic pressure for democratic enlargement. Aristocratic characters continued to people the eighteenth-century stage and nineteenth-century melodramas, but they operated in an increasingly bourgeois milieu, rubbing shoulders with "ordinary" citizens and subjected to middle-class values of moral worth, demonstrated by individual industry, sobriety, and piety.

The displacement of rank as dramatic source of moral authority reoriented the focus of tragedy from the idea of fate and heroic endurance toward "poetic justice," a new ideal consonant with Protestant morality, based in private, individual conscience, demanding virtue be rewarded and misdeeds punished. Such shifts in social perception and aesthetic practice gave a new moral mission to theater, appealing to middle-class notions of respectability. From the eighteenth century on, alongside Shakespeare and neoclassical tragedies, London's patent theaters staged new forms of sentimental drama that sought to restore a moral economy suited to mercantile enterprise, turning on individual energy, capital accumulation, social respectability, and familial stability. These goals merged social, personal, and moral conflict in a way that would eventually support melodrama. George Lillo's *The London Merchant* (1731, Drury Lane)—featuring an upright apprentice, George Barnwell, led by a sexually alluring and gold-digging prostitute, Millwood, into robbing his employer and murdering his uncle—is a standard example of sentimental dramaturgy harboring proto-melodramatic enactments straining at their moral leash. Whereas George's acts are followed by bitter repentance, arrest, and condemnation to the gallows, the spirited and acerbic Millwood generates greater frisson than the play's deserted heroine. Similarly, hugely popular adaptations of sentimental dramas by the German August von Kotzebue foreshadowed the moral sensationalism of later domestic melodrama. *The Stranger* (1790; 1798 in England and USA) and *Child of Love* (1780, revised 1798 by Elizabeth Inchbald as *Lovers' Vows*, the cause of familial contention in Jane Austen's *Mansfield Park*, 1814) tackled emotionally gripping, if eventually moralistically resolved, situations: respectively the covert return of an adulterous wife and the reunion of a father with his till then unknown illegitimate son.

However, sentimental fiction and drama were challenged almost immediately from within by the rise of the Gothic arts. Horace Walpole's *The Castle of Otranto* (1764) inaugurated gothic fiction shortly before publication of Oliver Goldsmith's *The Vicar of Wakefield* (1766), which, focusing on the felicities and trials of a country vicar and his family, was counted the "first genuine novel of domestic life" (Mack 2006, ix). If eighteenth-century sentimental drama found in the private bourgeois family a source of moral and social order, the family itself came under increasing social pressure. With industrialization and urban living, it was both separated from productive and communal relationships and psychologically central to the reproduction and maintenance of individual well-being. In retrieving the trappings of medieval demonology, the Gothic opened up a psychosexual dynamic, recasting the moral tenets of sentimental fiction's private conscience as the emotional and moral sensations of publically broken taboos. Moreover, it melded elite with popular traditions, spectacle with the domestic, facilitating the intersection of cultural boundaries important to melodrama. "Monk" Lewis's *The Castle Spectre: A Dramatic Romance* was staged at the legitimate Covent Garden in December 1797, and the play first advertised in Britain as a "melo-drama"—Thomas Holcroft's gothic-inflected but domestically oriented adaptation of Pixérécourt's *Coelina*, retitled *A Tale of Mystery*—appeared there in 1802.

More important, however, to an emerging melodrama was an impetus coming from quite another direction, indicated by *A Tale of Mystery*'s advertised subtitle: "consisting of dancing, speaking and pantomime." In England, the rise with the Industrial Revolution of an urbanized working class, now separated from home and rural communities in factories and fast-growing cities and joined by a growing army of lower-class bureaucrats and business agents, offered new market opportunities to entrepreneurial entertainers. In France, the combined pressure of a suppressed bourgeoisie and peasant immiseration led to political Revolution. In both cases, cultural monopoly was challenged by socioeconomic expansion requiring a widening public sphere. In eighteenth- and early nineteenth-century London, growth of theatrical entertainment combated legal restrictions on venues and repertoire. In Paris, Revolution had dramatically democratized the theaters, overthrowing the dominance of neoclassical drama and introducing the newly named "melo-drame." This term, according to Shepherd and Womack (1996, 194), was brought back in 1802 from the post-Revolutionary stages of Paris to England by Henry Harris, son of the new type of theatrical manager on the lookout for material to fill Covent Garden.

"Melo + drama"—music and drama combined on equal footing—signaled a new way of merging aesthetic practices. Music had been common in previous theatrical and operatic genres, and mid-eighteenth-century French and German romanticism had experimented with new ways of combining music with drama. Jean-Jacques Rousseau's often cited *scène lyrique*, *Pygmalion* (1762/1775) alternated speech with sequences of mime to music, seeking to communicate the verbally inexpressible. However, in little else was it what became known as melodrama (Branscombe 2001, 360–62). The role of music in urban entertainments and illegitimate theaters was generated by different conditions and driven in a different direction. As noted, British and French theatrical licensing permitted the spoken repertoire only to the patented theaters. Despite such restriction and official harassment, "illegitimate" entertainments-performed in temporary "pop-up" venues, in circus amphitheaters, and in a growing number of minor theaters—flourished. Initially they drew upon nonverbal, music-based and visual forms of folk tradition and urban entertainment practices: harlequinade, acrobatics, dumb show, pantomime, clowning, and dance. Mime and spectacular emblems—meteors, rainbows, lightning strikes, specters, flaming crosses, rising tombs—helped retail their narratives (Brooks 1976, 63–64). Soon, however, demographic pressure and economic opportunism led to ingenious methods of incorporating verbal language into the show, whether written on banners and signs, sung in emotion or narrative-expanding lyrics, or, as soon appeared, spoken dialogue (Moody 2000, 24–27).

From conditions of legal constriction, a heteroglossic method of play production arose: expressive cadences of speech interacted with musical underscoring; visual spectacle alternated with personal crisis; gestural modes of performance and choreographed movement carried emotion; and songs and dances were dispersed throughout. Providing a visceral dimension lacking in sentimental drama, melodrama infiltrated the patent theaters as their managers poached repertoire, star performers, and playwrights from illegitimate competitors. Thus, out of its hybrid sources and appeals, the newly named stage melodrama effected a temporary convergence between dominant middle-class and emerging proletarian structures of feeling. The 1814 staging of *The Woodman's Hut* at Drury Lane suggests the degree of institutional breakdown between legitimate and minor theaters. In addition to the abduction of the hero through the back of a grotto and the heroine's feisty handling of his captors, this "New Melo-Dramatick Romance" featured the destruction of the heroine's cottage by a thunderbolt, a forest fire, and the collapse of a burning bridge over a raging river, which defeated the couple's pursuers.

The unstoppable growth of the minor theaters and consequent relaxation of controls fostered programs mixing diverse entertainment forms. Shakespeare and the neoclassical repertoire played alongside pantomimes, extravaganzas, farces, and melodramas—to the complaints of many critics fearing for the cultural canon. In the absence of copyright laws, melodrama multiplied through translation, adaptation, and piracy, further encouraging generic hybridity and intertextuality. Literary and dramatic classics, popular fictions, newspaper reports and topical events, police journals and penny dreadfuls, narrative paintings and engravings, popular songs and street ballads all provided material for melodrama (Booth 1965, 50–51; Moody 2000). Like Hollywood's front office in the next century, theatrical managers and publicists exploited such mixed sources and modalities to maximize appeal. Examples of advertising for Coburg productions in 1828 include posters for *St Valentine's Eve; or, The Fair Maid of Perth*, a "Melo-Drama entirely New, Grand, Historic, Romantic founded on Scott's new and very admired novel"; and *The French Buccaneer; or, the Rock of Annaboa*, a "Nautical serio-comic Melo-Drama." Based on commerce rather than cultural monopoly, such generic hybridity and mixed programming, drawing together gothic, sentimental, folk, and urban working-class traditions, helped consolidate a flexible melodramatic mode capable of generating and shaping a diversity of theatrical subgenres. Melodrama, then, even on the nineteenth-century stage, never existed as a singular generic form. In Britain, we find gothic, oriental, nautical, historical, military, domestic, romantic, cape-and-sword, temperance melodramas, and so on. In the United States, amongst subgenres imported from Europe, nativist forms included frontier, backwoods, western, civil war, and antislavery melodramas.

Melodramatic specificity, then, lies in its operation as modality: as a mode of aesthetic articulation distilled from and adaptable across a range of genres, across decades, and across national cultures. Rather than defining content, *mode* shapes different materials to a given end. This end—what melodrama does—distinguishes melodrama from other modes—realism, romance, comedy—which it nevertheless draws on according to subgeneric need. Thus, melodrama thrives on comic counterpoint, may site its fateful encounters in romance, and, to ensure the authenticity of its claims and the recognition of audiences, keeps pace with changing conventions of verisimilitude (what is taken as true) and the expanding boundaries of realism (enlarging representation). If melodramatic modality is recognized by its effects, then its structural devices and dramatic mechanisms for achieving such ends shift according to the needs of evolving subgenres, changing historical circumstances, and specific national-cultural environments. Thus, the Victorian theater's motive-revealing aside disappears, and others—the climactic exposure or self-declaration of the villain or the last minute rescue (see *Way Down East* 1920; *Coma* 1978)—are adapted to new genres and media.

MELODRAMA AND MORAL FEELING

Converging cultural traditions, embracing both sentiment and spectacle, recalibrated the aesthetics of moral feeling. If it sometimes appears to reinforce "old-fashioned" Victorian "morals," melodrama served also as conduit for shifts in ethical perception underpinning the emerging relations between individual and society that would characterize modernity: for example, the successive transformations of those episodes of *The Vicar of Wakefield* that recount the seduction of the Vicar's beloved daughter. In 1800, Amelia Opie published a prose tale, *The Father and Daughter*, focusing on the daughter's downfall. Whereas Goldsmith has his Vicar attempt by gently ironic reasoning to rehabilitate his daughter, Opie intensifies and moralizes her years of expiation, struggling to support her illegitimate child and grief-maddened father. At the same time, her extreme suffering enables Opie to excoriate the unbending attitudes of local neighbors.

This story is incorporated into Marie-Thérèse Kemble's 1815 French masquerade comedy, *Smiles and Tears*. Lady Emily is reproved by her uncle for declaring the daughter's moral downfall "interesting." To his later admiration of her devotion to her demented father, Emily replies, "And may I not call that creature *interesting*? But what were . . . her father's *sensations* when he first beheld her?" (Act V, Scene 1, my emphasis). This move from the moral to the interesting to the sensational is key to the perceptual shifts that underpinned the formation of melodrama. Emily's desire to justify her use of "interesting" registers a shift from the medieval legal or financial meaning of "interest" to its signification within a newly emerging emotional economy, emphasizing identification with socially and morally different others (see Williams 1988, 171–73). However, as Peter Brooks suggests, a tension arises between the "interesting" located in the everyday and the "exciting" supplied by gothic sensationalism and minor theater spectacle (1976:64). In 1820, William Moncrieff adapted Opie's tale for the Coburg stage as *The Lear of Private Life; Or, Father and Daughter*, advertised as a "Premier Domestic Melo-Drama of Interest." In both tale and play, elision of "interest" with "sensation" peaks traumatically when penniless Agnes crosses storm-wracked woods seeking to return home, only to encounter her father who has escaped from an asylum and is searching for her grave. Fearing potential capture, her father threatens Agnes with a cudgel. But his bitter response to her plea to spare her baby underlines the pathos of their mutual situation: "A child! Strangle it, kill it . . . I had a child myself, but she is dead." If derangement justifies his violence, Agnes is its appalled and guilt-stricken spectator. But her tears forestall his turbulence as he feels another's sorrow: "Tears! in tears, poor thing, poor thing—don't cry, don't cry! . . . Come, come, come, you will not leave me, will you?" (Act II, Scene 3). Across these transformations, "sensation" adds to "interest" an emotional supplement, grounding *empathy* as a new site of social cohesion for a society based on economic individualism. "Feeling" supersedes abstract morality. How situations *feel* to the protagonist is what "interests" the audience, and the most acute feelings are those that are morally ambivalent or perverse. This new emotional freight appears in the repeated use of "interesting"—"of intense" or "peculiar" interest—in play advertising throughout the century.

"Sensation," then, points in two directions: to bodily thrills of specter-haunted dungeons, forest or house fires, explosions and drownings on stage; and to extreme states of personal being, appealing to an audience's recognition of, or curiosity about, hidden areas of life known to exist in private and vicariously sought in the theater. This shift from awe at tragic downfall toward empathy with emotionalized characters in extreme situations makes possible expanded social sympathies. In his preface to *Luke the Labourer; Or, The Lost Son*, D—G., citing pressure to appease not classical gods but those seated in the upper galleries of Covent Garden and Drury Lane, argues the democratization of recognition: "The public have no relish for magnificent woe . . . in blank verse . . . It is scenes of everyday life as approximating to *our own* condition, that affect us most . . . without being a farmer's servant . . . we cannot but commiserate with Luke the Labourer" (1828, 5 emphasis in original).

CULTURAL-CRITICAL DIVISION

By the mid-nineteenth century, London theatrical life was burgeoning. The relentless proliferation of minor theaters and the collapsing boundary between "legitimate" and popular entertainment had ended theatrical monopoly in 1843. The possibility of respectability and higher-paying middle-class audiences encouraged construction of smaller theaters, refurbishment of existing ones, and realignment of theatrical hours and programming to suit middle-class and professional timetables. Producers, writers, and performers of stage melodrama gradually refined its practices, integrating its visceral excitements more fully into domesticated scenarios, recasting the "poor and unfriended" as the respectable poor and sometimes fallen middle classes who nevertheless encounter their share of sensation and spectacle enacted in tenement fires, criminal threats, and hair-breadth escapes.

While mutating and proliferating, melodrama brought into play a sharper critical boundary between a growing mass culture of content- and affect-defined subgenres, and high cultural classifications—drama, poetry, prose—which provided the unity, coherence, and verisimilitude valued by the intelligentsia. Melodrama's detractors, from the moment it appeared, feared its threat to the established dramatic canon and health of national culture (see Moody 2000; Shepherd and Womack 1996). Whereas melodrama's early supporters had declared its emotional truth, later middle-class audiences and intellectuals, seeking greater self-recognition, made new claims on the "natural." George H. Lewes, influential philosopher and theater critic, declared that in *The Day of Reckoning* the reformist actor-managers, Madame Vestris and Charles Mathews, were:

> natural—nothing more, nothing less. They were a lady and gentleman such as we meet in drawing-rooms, graceful, quiet, well-bred, perfectly dressed, perfectly oblivious of the footlights. He is a polished villain—a D'Orsay without conscience, and without any of the scowlings, stampings, or intonations of the approved stage villain. There are scoundrels in high life—but they are perfectly well-bred . . . In every detail of dress, in every gesture, and in every look, I recognized an artist representing Nature. (In Rowell 1971, 206)

Smaller theaters with electric lighting and darkened auditoria centered the star actor, enabling the "colloquial" bodily movement and vocal delivery that Lewes claimed as "natural" and is described by Helen Day-Mayer and David Mayer in chapter 6. These changes refocused audience attention on dialogue, permitting literary dramatization. Melodrama's *coups de théâtre* became integrated as the *scènes à faire*—emotionally logical climaxes—of the Well-Made Play and New Drama. However, such changes, occurring across Western dramatic production from Ibsen to Belasco, can be discussed equally as naturalism or melodrama. The forces that drive characters, situations, and climactic encounters derive from the melodramatic mode, but the reformed drama's minutely realistic sets, more integrated crises, and underplayed or restrained acting enabled middle-class audiences to recognize lives lived within emotionally intense situations. In the British context, restraint equaled power. Thus J. T. Grein, advocate of the New Drama of Ibsen, Chekov, and Shaw, singled out John Martin Harvey's performance of Sidney Carton in a popular adaptation of Dickens's *The Tale of Two Cities*, renamed *The Only Way*: "When the last hour had sounded and Carton forfeited his life to save her whom he loved, Mr. Harvey made a great impression, but now it was by his composure, by the sobriety of his words and the suppression of his emotions" (as quoted in Rowell 1971, 221).

If, however, reform contributed to loss of the term, melodrama's sensational forms continued in working-class urban districts, provincial theaters, traveling companies, and early cinema into the twentieth century, when it inspired modernist theater and filmmaking alike (see Shepherd and Womack 1996, 243–45; Doxtater, chapter 11). Theatrical history, then, reveals not the displacement of one form by another—the "baton" model of history as David Mayer (1997) describes it—but an interaction or "oscillation" in which melodrama, because of its hybridity, could pivot in many different directions, toward sensational action, heartrending pathos, or avant-garde iconoclasm. If critical investment in realism eclipsed melodrama's name, it did not curtail its affective modality nor its core function—the aesthetic realization of social forces embodied in individual energies, released through and into modernity.

MELODRAMA AND CINEMA

Whereas it is a truism among film historians that silent cinema drew on melodrama both for narrative material and, in the absence of recorded speech, gestural techniques of story-telling, the desire of early film critics and later academics to establish cinema's credentials as a unique art contributed to melodrama's long relegation as old fashioned and "stagy." Yet, as Nicholas Vardac (1949) demonstrated, nineteenth-century stage practices prefigured many cinematic devices, including tracking shots, fades, dissolves, and parallel actions, achieved by ingenious stage machinery and lighting, including complex systems of traps, bridges, moving scenery or stage structures, rolling panoramas, and multiple sets. The pictorialism of the nineteenth-century stage produced what were effectively "moving pictures" (Meisel 1983; Booth 1981), with character expressed in costume, makeup, physical type, and bodily movement (see Stutesman, chapter 17). The introduction of the proscenium arch in 1880 and gas, then electric lighting, working in collaboration with scenery and actor, merged the theatrical and pictorial. Reinforced by the development of photography and reproductive technologies, the proliferation of scientific and leisure uses of proto-filmic devices and the rise of shopping arcades as commercial visual culture (Booth 1981), nineteenth-century pictorialism has helped characterize both melodrama and cinema as essentially visual forms. However, restriction of the word in the emergence of melodrama was short lived—more honored in the breach than the observance—and even though, for narrative reasons, the dumb character became a frequent figure in melodramatic dramaturgy, the force of the word and rhythms of the voice, along with music and sound effects, were as crucial to melodrama as was visual staging (Day-Mayer and Mayer, chapter 6; Bratton 1994; Shepherd 1994). Melodramatic modality, then, as a mode of auditory, visual, and verbal expressiveness was fully available to cinema, whether silent or sound.

AMERICANIZING MELODRAMA

Daniel Gerould (1983) notes that "the United States and melodrama came into existence at almost the same time—the late eighteenth century—and for much the same reason—the democratic revolution in thought and feeling." European imports during the early nineteenth century represented "a practical, non-elite art form" (7). Dramatizing an egalitarian ethos, and endlessly adaptable to local conditions, melodrama suited the entrepreneurialism and technological ingenuity of a young republican culture. David Grimstead (1971) suggests that melodrama's stress on feeling as an index of moral and social value functioned for American nationalism as a "great equalizer," bypassing inequalities of class and education (88). Having no landed aristocracy, Americanization recast class oppositions in terms of democratic values in a struggle with old Europe: life on the western frontier opposed to east coast cities, harboring old world decadence or reemerging divisions between rich and poor.

Linda Williams (2001), however, argues a deeper historical disturbance: the contradiction between egalitarian ideals and slavery. Both Williams and Gerould find in Harriet Beecher Stowe's *Uncle Tom's Cabin* (1852) the seminal catalyst for specifically American melodrama. As Gerould (1983) notes, it "used only indigenous material—Southern planters, Blacks, Yankees. . . . There was no European model or precedent for such a radically American work" (14). According to Gerould, it is the story of Eliza and George's escape to Canada rather than Uncle Tom's martyrdom that embodies the drive of Americanization: for the principle of equal opportunity and belief in the power of self-help identified virtue less with stoic endurance of misfortunes than with a willingness to "fight back, get to work, start a new life" (11). This reorientation to the future despite, as Williams argues, the continuing grip of a disavowed racist past, would be important to Hollywood's cinematization of melodrama.

American acting theory also contributed to this forward drive. Contrary to English critical values, the idea of the "natural" was grounded not in middle-class drawing rooms but in the "natural laws of man's heart" (Poe anthologized in Moses and Brown 1934, 60). Masculinization of melodramatic feeling, rather than class restraint, constitutes the modernizing value. Nym Crinkle (anthologized in Moses and Brown 1934) writes of Steele MacKaye's *Paul Kauvar: Or, Anarchy* (1887) that it represents "the protest of a vigorous masculine talent against . . . aesthetic inanity," which he equates with feminizing social etiquette (136–38). Masculinization defines a manly energy rather than the social refinement and restraint praised by Lewes and Grein. Identification of masculinized expressiveness as "natural" would be crucial to the forward momentum of Hollywood's largely action-based genres and the division of gendered labor within its star system.

Subsequent accounts have suggested that the worldwide appeal of Hollywood arose from the cultural fracture that Americanization performed for traditional societies. In different ways, Miriam Hansen (2000) and Laura Mulvey (1996) argue that American popular culture, representing "the modern," challenged established critical values, class-bound tastes, and traditional social mores. For societies in the throes of modernization, Hollywood offered, in Hansen's terms, a form of "vernacular modernism"—cultural and aesthetic experience distinct from art-gallery modernism, produced out of and for quotidian modern experience that eventually would lead to postmodern dissolution of the boundary between art and popular culture. Hansen, drawing her conclusions from silent cinema's international circulation, focuses less on melodrama than on the anarchism of slap-stick and screwball and of the multimedia context of early film exhibition. But if there is a synergy between visceral practices of shock, surprise and mayhem, and melodrama's spectacle and sensation—along with the melodramatic exploits of serial villains, detectives, and queens (see Singer 2001)—the lengthening of the feature film drew on melodramatic structuring of conflict, crisis, and resolution, while incorporating spectacle, comic side-kickery, and pathos. What emerged was a cinematized melodramatic modality that generated Hollywood's infinitely diversifying genres.

In Linda Williams's account (2001), however, American culture deploys melodrama not only for its generic fertility but for its capacity to replay, while attempting to anneal the underlying scar of slavery in U.S. history. Here it is melodrama's opposition between the perpetrator's guilt and suffering innocence that, recalling the past, is replayed across Hollywood's genres. Thus victimized heroes displace and appropriate to themselves black suffering as a means of regaining the lost innocence of America's foundation. If this scenario can be traced through race movies, war films, westerns, horror films, American gothic, and film noir, its emphasis on past guilt operates in tension with the optimism, individual striving, and "can-do" orientation to the future that Gerould and Hansen in different ways suggest made Hollywood's use of melodrama so universally appealing. We see here a cultural oscillation as melodrama is pulled in different temporal directions between past and future and toward different generic configurations and emotional scenarios for differently situated audiences. It seems clear, however, that melodrama's aesthetic history and ideological proclivity enabled American culture to combine individualism and melodramatic emotion in a forward trajectory capable of relating to the past in ways that could appeal worldwide.

MELODRAMA AND HOLLYWOOD'S SYSTEMS

Critical resistance continues to the idea that Hollywood works within a melodramatic aesthetic. One objection arises from the identification of melodrama with only one of its genres: the family melodrama. A more persistent objection, discussed by Linda Williams in chapter 12, is the influential categorization by Bordwell, Staiger, and Thompson (1985) of Hollywood's mode of narration as "classical." Ravi Vasudevan (2010, 26–28) points out that this conception focuses not only narration but *production*, linking the streamlined efficiency of Hollywood's compartmentalized studio system to narrational norms of consistency, clarity, and credibility, which are essential to audience comprehension. To this, the audiovisual expressiveness and convoluted plotting of melodrama is seemingly antithetical.

How, then, can melodrama's explosive devices be reconciled with Hollywood's smooth-running machine? In the first place, production of nineteenth-century melodrama already operated—much like Hollywood's studios—as a commercial genre-producing system, frequently initiated by an appealing title, poster, star actor, or special effect, which the writer then filled out. More important than the playwright were the scenery and costume designers and composers of musical accompaniment, all prominently publicized at the expense of the playwright (see figure 0.1). Second, plays established place and time, recognition of character, and forewarning of coming turns of plot as carefully as any Hollywood studio film. Theatrical programs spell out precisely the location of each scene, advertising their variety as key attractions. Costume, actor's physique, performance, and speech patterns indicate character traits, and musical cues establish character types, anticipate unwelcome or desired entrances, as well as coming mood changes or plot twists; notoriously, asides reveal duplicitous intentions or inner conflicts (see chapter 6). Melodrama's supposedly "excessive" emotion-producing devices—*peripetia* (reversal), *anagnorisis* (recognition), coincidence (fate), *coup-de-théâtre* or *scènes-à-faire*

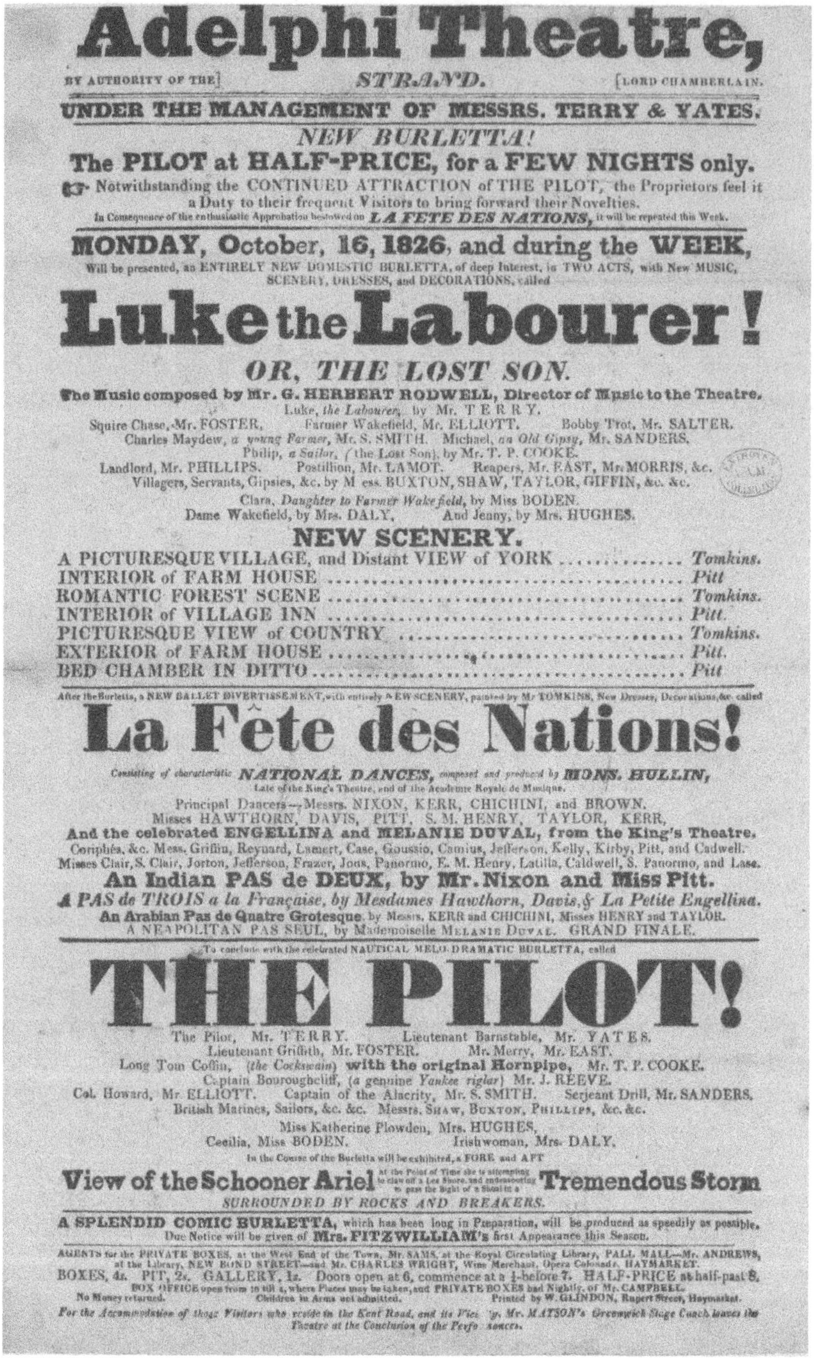

Figure 0.1 Adelphi poster for *Luke the Labourer*, advertising "new music, scenery, dresses and decorations" plus scene descriptions but no mention of the playwright, J. B. Buckstone. © Victoria and Albert Museum, London.

(explosive climaxes)—do not occur haphazardly but need dramatic preparation. There is little incompatibility between melodramatic dramaturgy and Hollywood's production or narrational systems—an assumption arising from the critical equation of melodrama with Sirkian stylistic "excess" that is presumed antithetical to efficient delivery of narrative. Indeed, Pixérécourt (2002) claimed that his plays observed the classical unities—except of place, which he thought "boring and monotonous" (317).

In Bordwell's model (1985, part one), *causes* constitute the logic of character motivation, itself key to narrative development and resolution. But from melodrama's perspective, dramatic emphasis shifts from cause to consequence. The consequences of an action outrun its causes, flowing into new situations only marginally connected to the initiating cause, opening up areas of feeling unanticipated by character or audience. Whereas for Bordwell, all other filmic elements are subordinated to the causal logic of narrative, when viewed as melodrama, such elements—interaction of gestures and eye-lines; the heightening effects of mise-en-scène, camera movement, and sound design—function as conduits for characters' emotional actions and reactions. As Deidre Pribram (2012) argues, the protagonists' emotions, rather than narrative logic, drive the drama.

RETHINKING PERSONALIZATION

Neo-Marxist criticism of the 1960s and 1970s argued that melodrama's focus on the individual, like the novel, displaces "real" social and economic problems into secondary personal and familial matters (Althusser 1969; Kleinhans 1978; Elsaesser 1987). In contrast, Peter Brooks (1976) suggests that melodrama recognizes a release of individual energy that is both product and generator of socioeconomic forces that power modernity. Melodrama materializes their fusion with the emotionalized, interpersonal identities of its protagonists. The nineteenth-century "realist" novel creates a reflective relationship between individual and socioeconomic context, in which the latter explains the former and grounds its claim to realism, whereas melodrama fuses individual and social as codependent. Action is generated by emotion as realized social force (see Pribram, chapter 14). Thus villains and victims are not moral abstractions but embody the energies of the newly authorized individual or suffer consequent injustices released into the new social order. Sometimes villain and victim may be one. Melodrama's protagonists embody and enact—rather than represent—socioethical values.

From another perspective, Matthew Buckley (chapter 1) questions the significance of nineteenth-century melodrama's presumed moral substrate. This, he argues, functioned as pretext for, rather than presumed core of, its spectacular and sensational appeals. However, melodrama's recalibration of moral feeling discussed above—suggesting less discordance than convergence between spectacle and the "interesting"—depends for the dramatic frisson of conflict on something being at stake. Excitement and suspense depend on our involvement at some level—of sensation, of empathy—in the contest between malevolent power and those struggling for survival or for justice. However, melodrama is not tied to any particular moral system, for *any* body can fill the place of victim or oppressor: the contest between them can be played out in innumerable ways.

Melodrama's elision of the personal and social is effected not only through characters' emblematic identities but through a "nonclassical" dramaturgy often derided as contrived. However, coincidence, circularity, chance, repetition, and deus-ex-machina interventions enact the malevolence of circumstances (too late) or the fortuitous happenstance of good luck (in the nick of time) precisely because of their incredibility. They materialize unfathomable and uncontrollable forces working through and around individual lives. To this end, the dramatic blockage and misrecognition that Peter Brooks argues underpins melodrama's expressive rhetoric mediates the tension between supposedly gratuitous sensation and the critical search for meaning. Excess functions not merely as negation of a norm—by which it would then be defined—but as a release of signification into theatrical or cinematic realization. This is not necessarily a matter of specific meanings, or only, as Brooks says, of "moral legibility" but of the dramatic energy and excitement of significance itself—assuring us that things matter, feel "real," and justify existence. Meaning is not a nugget of moral truth but a felt affect, the aesthetic-emotional experience that lifts audiences—as do music and dance—but that, in critical emphasis on social meaning and ideology, is denied to theatrical or cinematic drama. To experience empathy with victims and the frisson of villainy suggests not Sunday school morality but the way melodramatic modality can inhabit diverse moral, religious, and political systems to generate its aesthetic-emotional experiences. You don't have to believe to be moved by the Passion of Christ. Whether as pure spectacle or heart-rending pathos, melodrama's genres respond aesthetically to conditions of a modernity based on deracinated individualism, driven by the abstract instruments of global capitalism too often devoid of existential purpose (see Singer 2001).

Richard Dyer (1991) provides yet another approach to the "personal." Noting anxieties about the centrality and integrity of the individual provoked by late nineteenth-century theorists—Freud, Darwin, Marx—Dyer argues for a compensatory shift in moral evaluation from "general criteria governing social behaviour" to the identity of its performers; from "whether the performance is well done to whether it is . . . 'true' to the 'true' personality of the performer" (132–40). Arguably, melodrama's fusion of the social and personal was already working on the fractures opened up by such theories. A major problem for modern readers or viewers of melodrama is the assumption that its characters lack psychological depth or authenticity, especially when compared to the novel or short story, Bordwell's model of psychological causation. However, the novel's understanding of the human psyche and its motivations is itself based on conventions. In place of the novelistic narrator's character analysis, melodrama employs the visceral language of embodiment, gesture, and vocal delivery, initially considered more authentic than the dissembling word (Brooks 1976). Paradoxically, this was then codified in acting handbooks as a learnable language of emotional expression, which in a circular turnabout fueled the idea of the divided and dissembling self (see chapter 6).

In *Lady Audley's Secret* (1863 Royal Victoria), Lucy Audley warns her elderly husband, "We may read faces but not hearts." He gallantly asserts that *her* face is "index to the mind," to which in a wry aside she comments: "We may have two faces" (Act 1, Scene 1). Melodrama, then, developed its own means of staging psychology, putting considerable demands on the actor. As Dion Boucicault advised in *The Art of Acting* (1926), the actor must encompass within his character three roles, sometimes simultaneously: "Man by himself . . . the inner man; the domestic man as he is to his family . . .; and man as he stands . . . in society" (50–52; see also Brooks 1976, 201–2).

Ambiguity about selfhood was intensified in early cinema by the rising star system, which elided stars' fictional roles with their "real" lives, an elision magnified by the interaction of star and camera. Thus melodrama's personalization of the social is replayed in star images that bypass the novel's conventions of psychological interiority and embody social experience in physical type and personality (Dyer 1979). The star combines recognition of individuality and a socioethical emblematic function characteristic of melodrama. At the same time, Dyer suggests, the value given to spontaneity, intensified by the camera's capture of the star's every involuntary gesture, appears to undercut distrusted star hype, much as gesture and inarticulate cries were thought more authentic than words. During the early decades of cinema, the idea of "personality" was increasingly embedded in film stardom as a modern source of knowledge (Gledhill 2011). Belief that the camera gives access to the star's person not only authenticates the values they embody, but, in an echo of the nineteenth century's pursuit of the "interesting," fulfills our curiosity—our desire to feel what it is like to be a particular kind of person in a particular situation. Such curiosity is essential to the production of empathy and intersubjectivity as a new, virtual form of collectivity in a society of increasingly atomized individuals.

BAKHTIN AND THE GENERICITY OF EMOTION

Mikhail Bakhtin's work on genre suggests how melodrama's protagonists become embedded within "structures of feeling" as conceived by Raymond Williams. Bakhtin (1986) argues that because communicative forms emerge from *social use*, they must utilize shared conventions. Therefore, all such forms are generic, whether linguistic, gestural, literary, or performed in practical life or in the specialized functions of creative production. Any new work will carry the imprint of past uses: "Our speech—all our utterances—is filled with other's words, varying degrees of otherness and our-own-ness" (89). To make an utterance "our own" involves reaccenting, inflecting, or contesting past uses and meanings that any particular generic form brings with it. Use of languages, cultural forms, and aesthetic practices grounds us within the social. Melodrama's fusion of the social and individual embodies the sociality of personal consciousness. Its genres carry with them the structures of feeling within which they have emerged and which they enact. In Williams's terms (1997), residual, emergent, and dominant structures are inevitably at work in them: these are the materials out of which dramas are made.

Bakhtin (1986) extends the dialogic process: not only do we encounter others' uses in communicative forms but, in articulating our own thoughts, we negotiate or seek to control our interlocutors' anticipated responses, whether actual or imaginary. Although Bakhtin does not address emotion directly, it is carried in communicative forms, including gesture and tone, which nineteenth-century acting manuals attempted to codify. Emotions are deeply generic, acculturated, and historical. Significant for melodrama, Bakhtin's conception of the "otherness" we meet and struggle with in dialogic exchange opens the prospect of misunderstanding and of emotional cross-purposes, where an emergent feeling or perception is blocked by the perspectives and manipulations of others, by constraints of social codes or the inadequacy of available socioexpressive forms. Melodramatic crisis—its apparent excess—emerges out of such a breakdown or blockage. Misrecognitions—often deliberately engineered by perpetrators but as often due to misconstructions of what is overseen or overheard—foreground the difficulty of knowing the truth in a world of discursive overdetermination and connivance, leading to the struggle for public recognition of guilt and innocence.

MELODRAMA, IDEOLOGY, AND CRITIQUE

Melodrama's genericity—its repetitions, intersecting genres, and recombinations—make movements in structures of feeling and cultural imagining accessible. However, aesthetic practice constitutes a distinct realm of human experience, neither divorced from nor subsidiary to the social. To go *with* melodrama's modality demands that we refigure the critical relationship between its aesthetic dynamics and the cultural materials and ideologies it draws into its operations. Rather than taking ideology as the *endpoint* of critique—whether represented, disrupted, or naturalized—the relationship can be reversed. Ideologies, structures of feeling, social conventions, and cultural stereotypes are *themselves* the materials out of which new melodramas are engineered. Driven by circuitous plotting to clarify the identities of their oppositional protagonists, melodrama's frissons and astonishments make visible emerging feelings and perceptions. Yet melodrama also ensures that their aesthetic impact is felt *only in relation* to that which it is pushing against: residual and dominant structures of feeling. Thrilling and suspenseful feelings that we may recoil from politically, but without which there would be no dramatic conflict or outcome, can be vital to cultural understanding. In this respect, melodrama's genres—theatrical and cinematic—are, as Jane Gaines (2012) suggests, repositories of emotional knowledge, telling us what exhilarates, awes, melts, terrifies, repulses, or raises us to sublimity. Melodrama feeds off the haptic, often toxic, intersubjectivity of its protagonists' confrontational exchanges and its audiences' responses, in which eye contact and gesture, rhythms of body and camera movement, edited cuts and juxtapositions, supported by musical underscoring, engage the unspeakable that subtends what can be said. Recognizing melodramatic modality forestalls reduction of such aesthetic productivity to social or cultural reflection. Melodrama's genres offer insights that negotiate the positions and feelings of the others already present and *anticipated* in its historical genericity—to which audiences respond in different ways in their own times and contexts.

Critique asks what is in play at particular points in a work's history of textuality and circulation. The materials for critique are in the work. We may see *in it* the forces of change and reaction in process, but this does not mean the *text itself* operates critique. Raymond Williams and Bakhtin both argue for the "inside-outside" nature of critique in its relation to the past and future of the work. The presence of residual, emergent, and dominant feelings requires contextual sensitivity on the part of the critical analyst looking for movements of change. However, as Williams and Bakhtin argue, the analyst can never recoup the fluid, lived moment of the relations out of which the work emerged, and only partially, how it was received in its own time and contemporary contexts. For Bakhtin (1986), the "outsideness" of critique is less a restriction than a source of "creative understanding." Because we now occupy the future ahead of the work, if not the one it imagined, or a cultural location outside the work, and one it did not acknowledge, we are able to ask of the work "questions . . . it did not raise itself" (7). But these questions, if drawn from our time or social location, should not demand the work replicate our present critical perspective; rather, they seek what the work now reveals of the stakes of its own changes. This process may throw back to us perceptions we had not anticipated; it may access feelings and impulses we thought we'd left behind. The reintroduction of aesthetic feeling into this critical dialogue, together with the current reorientation to melodrama and thinking about emotions, offers new pathways to critique that may engage not only cultural meaning but movements of emotional attachment and repulsion, opening onto newly forming affective and imaginary territory.

Many thanks to our contributors from whose work this Prologue has benefited and to the Department of Cinepoetics, Freie Universität, Berlin, for a fellowship that gave me opportunity to bring together my thinking about genre, aesthetic affect, and melodrama.

Acknowledgments

This book would not have happened without the inspired collaboration of Columbia University and New York University in mounting the joint conference, "Screen Melodrama: Global Perspectives," co-convened by Richard Allen (NYU) and Jane Gaines (Columbia) in March 2013. Many of the participants in that conference have become welcome contributors to this volume. The opening night roundtable at Columbia, where a clash of melodrama cultures was clearly evident, convinced us that an anthology on melodrama was sorely needed to map out new crossmedia, transnational understandings of melodrama as a mode of literature, theater, film, radio, and television rather than the narrow film genre that continues to dominate film studies. Although such respected figures in the field as Thomas Elsaesser and Peter Brooks had offered important historical approaches to melodrama, it became clear that the mode needed to be "unbound" from a series of solidifying clichés if film melodrama scholarship was to progress. The anthology that has emerged is based on the proceedings of the conference but extends beyond its papers, both historically and transnationally. We are indebted to Richard Allen and Jane Gaines for their support, to all the conference contributors, and to those who have since joined the volume, expanding on its initial premises. We are grateful to three anonymous readers of the manuscript to John Belton, series editor, and Philip Leventhal, Senior Editor at Columbia, for the opportunity to produce this large compendium, and to Miriam Grossman and Ben Kolstad for shepherding the volume through its stages of production. Last, we owe gratitude to Luke Collins for help with the illustrations.

Melodrama Unbound

Introduction

CHRISTINE GLEDHILL AND
LINDA WILLIAMS

PROMETHEUS, AND MELODRAMA, UNBOUND

Prometheus, the Titan who gave fire to humankind, was punished by a jealous Zeus. Bound to a rock, his liver was pecked out each day by an eagle, only to have it regenerate each night for more painful pecking. This image of the bound Prometheus has survived in Greek tragedy as an emblem of heroic suffering, but the story of Prometheus did not end on that rock. Piecing together surviving fragments of other plays, classicists have shown that *Prometheus Bound* was followed by a sequel that greatly appealed to a later romantic imagination. In *Prometheus Unbound* the Titan hero was freed from his chains by Hercules, who killed the liver-pecking eagle. And in yet a third play, forming a trilogy, Prometheus is finally reconciled with Zeus and celebrated for his feat of stealing fire for humankind.

It is the *unbinding* of Prometheus that inspires this volume. Melodrama, like the Prometheus plays in toto, is more various than any singular image of suffering. Critics of melodrama have been so obsessed with this suffering side of the mode, at the expense of its exciting sensational actions, romantic thrills, or even its frequent comic undercurrent, that, as with the blind person and the elephant (chapter 12), they have missed many of its important characteristics. Prometheus is more than an eternal victim, he also is a bold action hero, the stealer of fire, a buddy of Hercules, *and* is even reconciled with Zeus in a happy ending. Ever since melodrama was named by linking the Greek word *melos* (music) with the Greek word *drama* (action), it has wormed its way into the most fundamental aspects of modern life and feeling. The melos of melodrama is not simply the addition of music to drama but what that music represents: the opening up of drama—on stage, in fiction, then in film, radio, and television—to waves of feeling that would have been unthinkable in Greek tragedy. Indeed, the very notion of the power and value of feeling is a sign of the pervasiveness of melodrama in contemporary life. In its long history since emerging in the late 1790s as a named theatrical form, melodrama has never been limited to the isolated genre of antirealist excess supposed by film studies; it demands understanding as the most prominent of modern cultural forms.

By unbinding melodrama from many critical misconceptions, we do not, however, suggest *everything* is melodrama. Comedy, romance, and realism are equally distinctive modes that frequently mix with melodrama as well as with one another. However, melodrama is crucial to understanding popular dramatic fictions in modernity. By freeing it from narrow generic definitions, we are able to show how melodrama, as part of an evolving modernity, emerged as a distinct mode that changed the course of dramatic and media histories.

THE UNBINDINGS

Our primary goal is to free melodrama from numerous misconceptions about its origins, nature, and function in order to stake out the claim that in mainstream cinema and much television the central aesthetic is melodrama, not something called "classical cinema." As many of our contributors show, melodrama is a protean form that leaps from one medium to another in the many cultures of a globalizing world. The "unbindings" our contributors undertake stem in part from a growing concern to historicize melodrama in relation to its past intermedial forms and diverse cultural contexts. Our volume divides these unbindings into two complementary, but intersecting, clusters: part one, "Melodrama's Crossmedia, Transnational Histories," focuses on institutions and practices, and part two, "Cultural and Aesthetic Debates," emphasizes questions of melodramatic textual practice, interpretation, and cultural-critical theory. Because our unbindings connect history with specific cultural and aesthetic questions, we detail the main topics of both parts of the volume here.

PETER BROOKS

There is no doubting the importance of Peter Brooks's 1976 study, *The Melodramatic Imagination: Balzac, Henry James, Melodrama, and the Mode of Excess*, in countering the patronizing and largely ignorant stereotypes of melodrama as an old-fashioned, simplistic, and moralistic form of outdated Victorian culture. Brooks's distillation of a melodramatic mode of imagination gave it cultural gravitas, enabling modern critics to take melodrama seriously as an aesthetic of intense emotionality that recalibrated morality as feeling and empathy, endowing ordinary lives with significance.

However, Brooks's ultimate purpose was to explain the fiction of Balzac and Henry James, not melodrama more broadly. His focus on a narrow thirty-year span of French post-Revolutionary melodrama and these two novelists allowed neither for the diversity of melodrama's national-cultural roots nor its commercial production practices arising from that other—Industrial—revolution, nor for its later role in the emergence of a mass popular audience and modern mass media. These practices of production and circulation are crucial to understanding melodrama's global travels and significance.

Opening part one, Matthew Buckley offers a far-reaching historicization of melodrama's sources, in the process unbinding it from two widely held myths about its origins and purpose. He begins with its supposed origin in the French Revolution, arguing that when it emerged as a named form at the beginning of the nineteenth century, melodrama was "a cosmopolitan hybrid, composed entirely of parts, techniques, emphases, and aims already developed in earlier, often pre-Revolutionary work produced all over Europe" (chapter 1). With deep roots in England and Germany as much as in France, and with distinguishing elements already well established and well mined by the rising tides of late eighteenth-century sentimental drama, opera, gothic literature, and popular spectacles of all kinds, it is not possible to claim, as Brooks does, that melodrama emerged spontaneously in response to the sudden end of the *ancien régime*.

Buckley's second myth is that melodrama is a drama of morality. In Brooks's argument, the Revolution overthrew a hierarchical social framework based in the authority of church and king, which had been invalidated by the loss of the "traditional Sacred" and its commanding form, tragedy, whose goal was to reconcile the individual to higher powers. Melodrama arose to fill the gap created by multiple and ongoing cultural disruptions, seeking to recover and make palpable the continuing but occulted presence of ethical forces at work in the world. Buckley argues instead that melodrama, arising in a theater increasingly commercially driven, lays only "superficial claim to be moral" drama, because its economic success is dependent on audiences for whom the "criterion of feeling and emotional affect—the demand that we be moved, not instructed"—was paramount (chapter 1). This does not mean that the category of virtue, so important to melodrama, must be discounted; however, one of its most perennial stereotypes—its moralism—is often secondary to its investment in sensation and spectacle, for which the conflict between "good" and "evil" serves as pretext.

A further challenge to Brooks's paradigm is taken up from a different direction by Richard Allen (chapter 2), who questions not only the argument that the French Revolution marked "the final liquidation of the traditional Sacred" (Brooks 1976, 15) but that this was followed by the triumph of secularism. Allen shows that from the Middle Ages onward the traditional Sacred had been adapting to a new, incipiently modern sense of selfhood within a continuing religious framework. He studies medieval painting and sculpted representations of the Passion of Christ, observing the shift from Christ as Godhead to Christ as human body, subjected to extreme suffering. He notes also the importance of the surrounding witnesses to this suffering—in particular the three Marys and St. John—whose agonized gestures and postures prefigure the gestural repertoire of melodramatic performance. In the shift from transcendental awe to personal empathy, Allen draws on art history to suggest a realization of the "Christianity of Pathos." In this new form of pathos, melodrama does not *replace* "the Sacred," nor is Christian morality "occulted"; rather, it is realigned with a newly emerging humanism that would eventually support the socioeconomic forces of a nascent capitalist order based on the individual.

This recalibration of Christian sources helps explain melodrama's persistence and proliferation. It is all the more crucial to understanding twentieth-century cinematic melodrama in South European or Latin American Catholic rather than North European Protestant countries, not to mention East and South Asian countries rooted in different religious formations. Louis Bayman (chapter 16) focuses on postwar Italian cinema, for example, demonstrating just how intertwined in a Catholic ethos and dramaturgy were both neorealist films and popular melodramas. For a country emerging from fascist rule, characters established within a Christian ethos of humility, poverty, and contact with the land provided signs of melodramatic virtue based in authenticity against the excesses and artifice of a regime given over to ostentatious wealth, corrupt political and business practices, and violent oppression. In a similar vein, extracts from the writings of the Mexican critic Carlos Monsiváis, translated by Kathleen Vernon (chapter 9), address the role of Catholicism in a different elaboration of the melodramatic aesthetic as it intersects with other entertainment traditions in Mexican popular culture and cinema from the 1930s through the 1960s.

Attempts to understand the transnational travel of melodrama outside the boundaries of Western thinking, when it meets with other cultural practices and religious traditions, makes the notion of a "loss of the Sacred" even more tenuous. Ira Bhaskar (chapter 15) argues that in Indian cinema of the 1930s and 1940s, the Sacred intertwines with the stylization of a transformed German expressionism to realize a modernizing subjectivity, calling on a combination of diverse religious and aesthetic traditions including, in particular, Sufi poetry and song. As in Catholic countries, the experience of the Sacred is not lost but ever present in everyday life and culture.

MODE, GENRE AND GENDER

One of the most important concepts Brooks has offered film studies is that of melodrama as a flexible *mode* of aesthetic perception and affect that could travel from stage to screen, from the nineteenth to twentieth and twenty-first centuries, and, as is now apparent, across national cultures. We define mode as a general form of expressiveness using the drama of light and dark, staging, color, music, speech, intonation and, importantly, plot. Brooks's description of familiar dramaturgical motifs of melodrama—the opening garden of innocent pleasure, the moment of the villain's self-nomination, the role of recognition—had already implicitly challenged film studies' displacement of melodramatic expression from plot into a subversive mise-en-scène. Through its neglect of interdisciplinary study, born of the need to establish cinema's own unique institutional status, film melodrama appeared to be a new discovery in the 1970s, detached from work already developing in theater studies. Narrowly defining it in its Sirkian manifestation as a form of ironic ideological subversion, or as a late addition to the successive mapping of Hollywood's genres in only one generic form, the family melodrama of the late 1940s and 1950s, film studies missed the pervasive cross-generic *modality* of melodrama.

Feminist film scholars also defined melodrama too narrowly as part of women's culture under patriarchy, focusing in particular on the emotional, personal, and psychosexual problems of the Oedipal family. Whereas many of Hollywood's other genres were granted the dignity of masculine and "classical" labels—western as epic, gangster as tragic hero—melodrama's emotional effects were siphoned off into a separately gendered genre, precluding consideration of melodrama's broader significance across popular cinema's genre systems. However, as Christine Gledhill's Prologue shows, theatrical melodrama never existed as a singular genre. Rather, through its popularity, voracious adaptation of diverse sources, and competition to win or amalgamate different audiences—male and female, working and middle class, and in the United States, white, African American, and immigrant European—melodrama generated a diversity of subgenres.

Never itself a singular genre, melodrama as a pervasive mode has functioned historically as a genre-generating machine. Moreover, to the development of Hollywood's genres, theatrical melodrama contributed not only a series of generic types but an organization of theatrical production that prefigured the studio system. Constituting an expressive mode of aesthetic articulation that shapes the operation of generic worlds, melodrama does not determine the specificity of locale, character type, décor, or situation that characterizes specific film genres. In a concept we retain from Peter Brooks, the most central function of the mode of melodrama lies in its recognition of the personalized virtues and vices of characters whose actions have consequences for others. The contest between them is not played out according to fixed moral values; rather, it enacts a struggle for a felt sense of justice that operates differently within different generic worlds. The point is that although conflict between perpetrator and victim is shared across genres, any *body* can fill these positions, and conflicts can be played out in innumerable ways.

The modality of melodrama thus enables interchange and overlap between genres, and between other modalities such as realism, romance, and comedy, as well as between different media, historical moments, and national-cultural contexts. Such interchange has been crucial to melodrama's role in modernity and to modernizing the dramatic functions of gender, class, and race. As Hilary Hallett (chapter 7) points out, at the turn of the nineteenth century, women as stage actresses, playwrights, and theater managers and in cinema as scriptwriters and film stars—and, we add, as film company owners and producers—contributed to modernizing popular culture. Hallett demonstrates the mutually productive interaction between melodramatic scenarios and popular cross-dressing actresses on stage and emerging film stars such as Mary Pickford and the serial queens. As melodrama transitioned into twentieth-century popular culture, its production of convention-challenging heroines contributed to the establishment of Hollywood as a worldwide entertainment form, making the "modern American girl" a driver of social change. At the same time, Hallett underscores the modernizing role of gender change as women journalists and publicists contributed to the travel of melodramatic scenarios from stage to screen to newsprint, magazines and back to films.

The failure in film studies to discuss the relationship between the melodramatic mode and genre has been particularly problematic for the introduction of melodrama into television studies, which perhaps, like film studies before it, is still preoccupied with establishing its own intellectual credentials. Linda Williams (chapter 10) outlines the history of melodrama's serialities across nineteenth-century fiction into early film fiction, radio, and television, and reappearing now with the flowering of multiseason serials on American television. She explores the way serials have melodramatized television fiction and even documentary, suggesting that the impediments to the recognition of this process lie in film and TV studies' investment in the assumed integrity of—and often critically masculinized—self-contained, discrete genres, especially when opposed to the pejorative feminization of serialization under the label of soap opera.

EXCESS

Both Thomas Elsaesser and Peter Brooks, writing in the 1970s, deemed excess to be melodrama's most distinctive feature. For Elsaesser, the excess of characters' emotions—siphoned into an orchestration of flamboyant color, baroque set design, strident music, expressive camera movement and performance—worked to critique the middle-class ideologies underpinning their narratives. For Brooks, excess was less a matter of ironic subversion than an inherent feature of the stage melodrama's "text of muteness," in which characters rendered mute by the machinations of the villain's plotting or by the inadequacy of language itself nevertheless found new, often corporeal, forms of expression. For both these foundational thinkers, melodrama was more than mere theatrical hyperbole; in an era of psychoanalytic fascination with forms of repression, excess took on new meaning and significance.

As long as melodrama was defined as, and confined to, familial or romantic dilemmas, excess appeared to have found a legitimate outlet, seemingly justified by the feminization of the domestic sphere. But once the argument was made for extending melodrama as mode across Hollywood's genres, its association with emotional or stylistic excess cut across their assumed gender specialization and rubbed up against a new paradigm of Hollywood cinema as a "classical" form of narrative. Within this paradigm, all other dimensions of film—genre, spectacle, and theatrical affiliations—were supposedly subordinated to the efficient, linear, psychologically motivated norms of classical narration. We argue instead that melodrama is not the always-exceptional excess to Hollywood's presumed classical narrative norms. Rather, it fulfils other normative expectations; for example, that Hollywood films will supply spectacle, excitement and pathos as well as recognitions of villainy and virtue.

A number of our contributors challenge the "excess" with which melodrama has been identified. For theater historians Helen Day-Mayer and David Mayer (chapter 6), what is perceived by later generations as excess conforms to melodrama's development within conditions of theatrical performance, dramaturgy, and musical underscoring that demanded of actors an expressive use of the body and voice. They explain how reliance on the static poses illustrating actors' handbooks underpins a common but mistaken conception of melodramatic acting as "exaggeration" that neglects the flow of movement between gestures. Moreover, they show how such practices evolved with changes in theater construction and lighting, in audience demographics, and in new codes of naturalism that influenced acting theory and practice. Thus in its first decades, cinema drew on a diversity of acting styles according to character type or dramatic moment, including performance traditions now felt to be alien as well as those then being recognized through the power of cinematography as a new modern.

From a perspective rooted in cultural studies, Deidre Pribram (chapter 14) releases the notion of emotional expressiveness from its initial limitation in film studies as object of irony or distanciation. For Pribram, taking emotions seriously means undoing the binary that opposes emotion to reason and feeling to thinking. Not only does emotion fuel thought and reason run through feeling; the intertwining of thought and feeling manifests the sociality of emotion and the individual as a "socioemotional" being. Whereas melodrama's personalization of the social is often critiqued as a displacement of the political, Pribram argues that emotion is both generated by and channeled into social discourse and practice. Far from excessive, the reason of emotion recalibrates the so-called cause-and-effect logic of Hollywood narrative and television serial drama within an emotionalized aesthetics of melodramatic expressiveness that should no longer be identified as excess.

WESTERN FILM THEORY AND TRANSNATIONAL MELODRAMA

Expanding interest in the category of melodrama in film studies coincided with the exploration of transnational cinemas, especially those of China, Japan, India, and Latin America. Drawing indigenous traditions of art, religion, and entertainment into new cinematic practices, these cinemas have challenged the application of concepts developed to explain Western forms. To Western eyes, the seeming exoticism of these moving-image cultures—complexities of plotting, intensity of emotional incident, and often seemingly unmotivated outbursts into expressive song and dance or violent action—appeared to warrant their description as melodrama, even if they were not so named in their home cultures. Such observations raise questions about whether melodrama is a universal mode of imagination or an import from the West and the North via colonization, modernization, or, more recently, corporate globalization.

Film studies has predominantly viewed melodrama as a product of Western modernity, formally established with the twin revolutions of the late eighteenth/early nineteenth centuries—French and Industrial. However, the new histories of European melodrama, offered not only by Matthew Buckley and Richard Allen but by other contributors charting its emergence in the southern and eastern hemispheres, foreground the different temporal-geographic and religious contexts in which melodrama has been formed and, upon traveling, reformed. Thus, another key unbinding challenges the automatic application of Western concepts. Several of this volume's chapters detail not only how theatrical and cinematic melodramas circulated between the West and countries distant from it but explore what happened to them as they encountered indigenous cultural practices and critical traditions, producing hybrid forms that only in retrospect and through different aesthetic lenses can be understood as performing the functions of melodrama in modernizing societies.

Kathryn Hansen (chapter 3) traces the history of a traveling theatrical troupe, who, following early careers as childhood entertainers in England, became established in Australia and from there took popular plays to emerging entertainment markets in China and India. Using Dion Boucicault's well-loved Irish melodrama, *The Colleen Bawn* as case study, Hansen shows how in Parsi theater it became *Bholi Jan*, adapted to the social, aesthetic, and cultural horizons of its spectators. Although never called melodrama, it was recognized in the 1870s as belonging to a new dramatic category. Breaking away from popular mythological plays about gods and demons to concentrate on social problems enacted on and through familial relationships, and later transitioning into cinema, this new genre became known as the "social." Kathryn Hansen's conclusion "that melodrama is a living organism that mutates to survive . . . and, in turn, creates conditions for its own evolution and metamorphosis" illustrates the power of melodrama to travel into local contexts and make a new home through cultural change (chapter 3).

Chinese culture, similarly, had no term for melodrama. In a Shanghai fraught with processes of modernization coming from different political directions—including the circulation of American culture through imported films—Zhen Zhang (chapter 5) shows how "Griffith fever" merged with the form known as *wenyi*, already constituted as a vernacular cultural genre that absorbed foreign content (Japanese, American, and European) as part of its appeal. Focusing on the pathos of broken love matches and families, Zhang shows how the figure of the orphan and abandoned woman, common to nineteenth-century and early film melodrama across different national cultures, serves as potent trope for the deracination of modernization and colonization, and thereby a powerful tool for transnational and cross-cultural analysis.

Conversely, emphasizing difference rather than shared tropes, Panpan Yang's case study (chapter 1) of Chinese cinema's response to Hollywood's *Gone with the Wind* (1939) and *Waterloo Bridge* (1940) draws on the romantic dimension of *wenyi* to offer a transnational address to the problem of melodrama's identification with excess, demonstrating how one culture's excess may be another's aesthetic normal, born of native sociocultural traditions.

The intermedial dimension of such transnational travels is emphasized by Hannah Airiess (chapter 4) in her examination of the convergence of English melodramatic fiction with traditions of Meiji-era serial literature in turn-of-the century Japan. She argues that the transition from feudal hierarchy to specifically Japanese forms of modernization was being processed before Hollywood's arrival in popular vernacular forms such as *shinpa* drama and *ninjōbon* novels, a process further intensified in the cinema.

Tracing similarly transnational and cinematic conjunctions across Indian cinemas of the 1930s and 1940s, Ira Bhaskar (chapter 15) explores how the cinematographic practices of German expressionism merged with the sacred musical and poetic traditions of *Bhava* to produce a distinctively Indian form of melodrama.

Taking human emotion as melodrama's central core, Bhaskar shows how Indian cinemas merged sacred feeling with personal dilemmas of modernization through the use of music, and especially the song, giving emotion both amplified form and social force in a distinctively Indian articulation of melodramatic aesthetics.

These contributions demonstrate that melodrama's global circulation is never a matter of a single European or Hollywood source, nor is the resulting melodrama the same as the "original" imports. In all these examples, we see how interactions between traveling cultural artifacts and existing practices and traditions generate new forms of melodramatic possibility.

"CLASSICAL" NARRATIVE CINEMA

The terms "classical realist" and "classical Hollywood cinema" reference historically contradictory ideas. In post-1968 thinking, classical realist narrative often meant an ideologically bourgeois form, representing the height of false consciousness, which only the avant-garde or countercinema could rupture. More influential today is Bordwell, Staiger, and Thompson's *The Classical Hollywood Cinema: Film Style and Mode of Production to 1960* (1985), which borrows terms from art history and André Bazin to argue that American film from 1917 to 1960 had reached the classical harmony and fullness of causally motivated, linear narratives.

Linda Williams (chapter 12) argues against the odd reversal that makes the classical—in art and theater history associated with earlier traditional forms—the exemplar of modern media and melodrama—which was actually born and so named with the rise of modernity—the exemplar of the old-fashioned. This wildly ahistorical deployment of both terms is entirely too static, whether concerning melodrama as the atavistic throwback to an older medium of theater—as if theater too were not capable of change—or taking "classical" cinema as the modern to melodrama's archaisms. In contrast, we encourage the kind of provocative investigation begun by Jane Gaines (chapter 19) that shows the way melodrama invokes relations between different experiences of time. Introducing the notion of three different modes of *historical time*, Gaines addresses the asymmetry of the relations between past, present, and future in the pathos of melodramatic timing. We are also struck by Martin Shingler's finding (chapter 8) that, despite its by then frequent pejorative connotations, both stage and film critics could positively apply the term *melodrama* to *The Petrified Forest* both as Broadway play (1935) and Warner Bros. film (1936). Whether in praise or contempt, this usage demonstrates that circa 1935–1936 the term was far from discarded and retained relevance at the height of Hollywood's supposed classical maturity. From such fluctuations in its use, Shingler suggests that melodrama has long been engaged in a continual process of renewal, adapting to cultural and technological changes. By unbinding melodrama from its identity as oppositional "other" to the classical's harmony and linearity or to realism, we begin to discover more fully what melodrama is and what it historically has been.

MELODRAMA OPPOSED TO REALISM

To touch its audiences' lives, melodrama has to command recognition, whether of human feeling, social experience, or moral dilemma. Recognition is essential to melodrama's ends: for suspense or pathos to work, we have to feel for characters and recognize the forces at work in situations they may not understand themselves. Here it is useful to recall the distinction between verisimilitude—that which is accepted as true—and realism, which appeals for the recognition of classes of people, of social conditions, or of areas of life hitherto unrepresented. Such expansion of the range of representation is often a matter of contesting the codes of verisimilitude and thus changing the way reality is perceived and understood. Melodrama is, then, not the opposite of realism but in ongoing engagement with it.

The history of melodrama's evolution across the centuries and across media, from nineteenth-century popular entertainments to cinema and television, can be traced through shifting conceptions of realism concomitant with changing production conditions, audience demographics, and performance practices. Louis Bayman's discussion (chapter 16) of Italian postwar cinema shows how melodrama, emerging from opera and later *verismo* forms in a culture steeped in Catholicism, cannot but inhabit frames of both verisimilitude and a realism expanding to meet the political crisis of the times. In the context of the United States in the 1970s, Drake Stutesman (chapter 17), describing the costuming of the black male hero of *Super Fly*, argues the melodramatic power of a tuck, hem, or material texture, of the flair or swing of a garment, to express metaphorically an emerging African American refusal of socioeconomic marginalization and political repression. In her concentration on costume, Stutesman both foregrounds a means of contemporary cultural recognition and directs our attention to neglected languages of melodramatic expression.

Conversely, Despina Kakoudaki (chapter 18) contrasts the generically spectacular qualities of the disaster melodrama with the chilling realism of Steven Soderberg's *Contagion*, which presents the threat of a global pandemic in tones that downplay thrills and excitement. Yet despite its almost clinically detached style that eschews emotion, Kakoudaki shows that the film starts and ends with family relationships as ground zero and ultimately produces melodramatic victims, villains, and heroes. The presence of melodrama in such an extreme realist text indicates that we need to articulate more complex relationships between the modes of melodrama and realism, without which we cannot understand the way melodrama and its various subgenres have adapted to changing conditions of the twentieth century, nor how they have remained central to contemporary popular culture.

MELODRAMA OPPOSED TO ART

If, as Martin Shingler (chapter 8) suggests, appreciation of melodrama was still available to theater and film critics in the 1930s, the new century, seeking to free itself from its Victorian moorings, frequently rendered melodrama a source of parody (Day-Mayer and Mayer chapter 6). However, melodrama continued under other names not only to generate the Hollywood genre system but also to inspire avant-garde producers of theater and film. The speedy transition of *The Petrified Forest* from stage to screen suggests how a melodrama of ideas could be created from the encounters of opposing personality types and performers embodying action and pathos. Understanding the reach of melodrama across conventional divisions between popular culture and art, Amanda Doxtater (chapter 11) enlarges the reputation of Carl Dreyer by tracing the productive presence of melodramatic practices in his work, which he had absorbed in his early years working for the Danish film industry. These practices, she argues, are at work in that definitive art house movie, *La Passion de Jeanne D'Arc*.

These examples suggest ways in which melodrama, under pressure from new aesthetic, social, and technological circumstances, transitioned from the cultures of the Victorian stage and adapted to processes of cultural modernization and transnational circulation. Melodrama may have lost its relative theatrical coherence and its name, but it continues to inhabit contemporary aesthetic forms worldwide in a diversity of ways. Despair is often expressed at the difficulty of pinning melodrama down in modern cultures. As we and contributors to this volume suggest, however, the need now is to identify not a singular generic form but elements and practices through which film and television activate the significance and power of the melodramatic mode.

The unbindings discussed here are not definitive. Our aim has not been to eliminate Peter Brooks's influence on melodrama studies. Nor have we sought to reduce the importance of gender within genres, or the perception of melodrama as heightened expression. Even notions of the classical will undoubtedly continue to denote the efficient operation of melodramatic production of the kind shared by nineteenth-century theater and twentieth-century film studios because the two categories are not antithetical. Similarly, we traverse the boundaries between melodrama and realism while claiming melodrama as a form of art. If this anthology opens the way to the possibilities of such unbindings, then our victimized yet heroic Prometheus will be a little less stranded on his rock, his unbinding rendering the real power and endurance of the melodramatic mode.

PART I

Melodrama's Crossmedia, Transnational Histories

1

Unbinding Melodrama

MATTHEW BUCKLEY

INTRODUCTION: MELODRAMA'S REVOLUTION

Until about a half-century ago, melodrama was generally understood to be a crude, excessive, irrational, naïve, superficial, marginal, and finally insignificant type of modern drama—a "minor" form, best exemplified by a handful of cheap, primitive, and ephemeral genres of the popular stage and screen, that had long since been superseded, on the modern stage as on the modern screen, by the more complex, controlled, rational, reflexive, substantive, and historically significant forms of realism and modernist aesthetics. These, it was generally assumed, were very obviously modernity's central and definitive dramatic modes: beside them, mere melodrama, however interesting as a transitional or liminal form, paled to insignificance. Melodrama scholarship, though growing and already challenging these traditional judgments and ideas, remained sparse, isolated in separate disciplines and—like melodrama itself—both marginalized and generally ignored. Historical and cultural comparative research was just beginning, and melodrama's extensive global history—including nearly the entirety of its history as a televisual form—remained almost entirely unmapped and thought, in general, deservedly neglected.

Today, after five decades of revisionist scholarship in theater, film, and television studies, and particularly in the wake of the now widespread study of melodrama's ongoing global history as a transcultural and transmedial aesthetic, it has become disconcertingly obvious that everything about this traditional view of melodrama's character, history, and place in modern culture is not simply distorted and biased but strikingly delusory, and in fact very nearly the opposite of anything one might call a rational view. In the most basic sense, such work has made it abundantly clear that melodrama has been Western modernity's dominant, even definitive dramatic form. Far from having faded or been forced into obsolescence, melodrama, we now recognize, has been produced in ever-greater quantities and consumed by ever-growing audiences from its origins to the present day, despite continual critical hostility, derogation, and disregard. Far from having been marginal, characteristically "low," or limited to its most clichéd, nominative forms, melodrama, we now see, expanded its range and register continuously from its moment of birth, spinning off into an ever-growing host of subgenres and variant forms—including those from which realism would arise—and crowding out, or "melodramatizing," alternative modes.

It is now clear, too, that melodrama—as a style and a set of conventional dramatic expectations—has long since reshaped not only drama but narrative of nearly all kinds, from the novel and the news to reality television and computer games, as well as the whole range of the musical, visual, spectacular, and performance arts, from opera and pop songs to propagandist display and public demonstration. In the past decade, as the vast ocean of melodrama's global, intermedial history has begun to emerge, it has become starkly evident that the production of melodrama around the world has so thoroughly dominated the mass-cultural histories of modern theater, film, and television drama (indeed, of modern narrative) that all other dramatic genres, modes, and styles—including dramatic realism and modernist aesthetics—seem, ironically enough, marginal, ephemeral, and arguably obsolete. Comparative work built on these recovered histories is now robust and advancing at speed, and among melodrama's many manifestations and across its varying styles and modes we are beginning to discern striking formal continuities and regular patterns of growth and change. Its many national and medium-specific traditions have begun to gain evident coherence as a complex, closely interwoven, single history of cultural and medial expansion, migration, and adaptation. The history of melodrama, we now realize, is not only that of a dizzyingly complex, dynamic, and variegated form of drama: it is that of a viral aesthetic, expanding continuously and in all directions from its birth through the present in a process of cultural transmission that most closely resembles contagion.

As this history has been uncovered, we have come to see too that melodrama's impact on cultural thought and consciousness has been profound. As an extensive body of interdisciplinary scholarship has made evident, melodrama's conventions, assumptions, and imperatives have shaped the structure of modern political discourse, given form to modern social and domestic ideologies, and conditioned the modern world's active structures of feeling, apprehension, and perception, penetrating and suffusing the consciousness of those cultures in which it is produced and consumed. Peter Brooks (1976) first caught this discursive aspect of melodrama's life a half-century ago when he described it, with some precision, as a "central poetry" of the nineteenth-century world. Today we have begun to see melodrama as a kind of affective meme, a self-replicating pattern of sensation and feeling that moves successively from the surface of culture to the subtending structures of social and individual life, and from there to the behavioral patterns of the body and mind. In this view, modern culture hasn't merely adopted melodrama, it has become melodramatic.

Taken as a whole, such research has overturned not only traditional views of melodrama but traditional views of the developmental trajectory of drama in modernity and of the modern era itself. What had been seen as a progressive march away from affective sentiment, naïve spectacle, and romantic distraction and toward presumably more self-reflexive, objective modes such as realism and modernist aesthetics—a process in which melodrama served as the naïve, hackneyed, overemotional "other" against which truly *modern* drama was defined—seems now just the opposite: a progressive triumph of those affective-spectacular modes, and a process in which melodrama occupies such a central position that seemingly resistant phenomena such as dramatic realism and avant-garde aesthetics seem mere eddies in an overpowering tide.

Such recognitions have profound implications for scholarly understanding of the modern critical tradition that constructed and maintained that mythic view—and of the narrative of modern art and culture that tradition constructed, professed, and passed down to us. What had seemed a rational, responsible, objective narrative of realism's inexorable rise and melodrama's obsolescence and demise, an account that itself testified to an advancing state of self-awareness and the triumphant progress of critical reason, looks now very much like a profoundly irrational, irresponsible, and finally unsustainable fiction—a myth, maintained almost reflexively for two hundred years, that seems to testify to nothing so clearly as an implacable, deep-seated desire to disown, deny, downplay, and ignore melodrama's steadily expanding presence in modern art, culture, and the mind.

Such an extraordinary revision of scholarly perspective, the fruit of decades of intensive work on popular culture in several different disciplines and many fields, seems nothing less than revolutionary. With it, we have not only recovered a long-repressed history of form but become aware, in so doing, of one of modernity's most persistent and most misleading myths about its own art and culture—able to see, for the first time, the modern era's aesthetic history and fundamental character as they unfolded, to borrow ironically from Wordsworth (1905), "not in Utopia . . . but in the very world" (36–38). Nowhere else, perhaps, does one find such a powerful illustration of the implications and accomplishment of the past half-century's scholarly turn to popular and mass-cultural study, and of the force and depth of its challenge to traditional accounts of the modern era. Indeed, critical recognition of melodrama's place in the culture of the modern era may turn out to be a marker of that era's end—a moment in which its self-spun mythos ceases to inspire blind belief and we begin to gain a more detached and more rational view of that time.

But this revolution is troubling, too, and there is good reason to suspect that we are not nearly so liberated from the modern critical tradition's distorted views of melodrama and the era of its rise as we might think, for the biases of those views are woven into the very fabric of our work, and they continue to condition, inflect, and inform what we do, how, and even why we do it in fundamental ways. From that modern tradition we have inherited our disciplinary formations, our critical practices and methodologies, our understanding of artistic production and traditions and of genre, style, and mode—even our foundational premises and assumptions about what modern art is and does, and about what modernity itself means and is. We may have come to recognize melodrama's historical significance and interest, but we have done so using critical theories, perspectives, methods, and practices not only poorly fitted to that task but in many respects designed to deny and to impede just that recognition: to draw attention elsewhere, valorize and foreground all that melodrama is not, and define modern art and its study in terms that would enable, justify, and sustain its critical exclusion, derogation, and dismissal. Melodrama scholarship may have carried out a revolution against the modern critical tradition, but it has done so in a language countervalent to that revolution at every level and with an outlook still shaped and driven by that tradition's ideas.

With such deep structural impediments and biases in mind, it is no surprise that even the most radically revisionist scholarship on melodrama from a few decades ago had such difficulty escaping an apologetic attitude toward melodrama's status as an art, or why it has taken so long—and still proves so difficult—to understand melodrama's fundamentally multimedial formal development as a commercial and popular art. It is difficult to articulate the intermodal aesthetic and discursive history of melodrama as a style, mode, rhetoric, ideology, and poetry and to describe its transcultural impact on modern art, aesthetics, and consciousness. By training and tradition, our gaze inclines away from such admixtures and border-crossings, placing them, almost instinctively, at the margins of those normative histories of discrete generic forms, specific aesthetic modes, and particular historical contexts and linguistic cultures that define our areas of study and determine the kinds of objects we seek to explain and exalt. Within such a framework, melodrama seems continually blurred and incomplete, a nonnormative construct, a thing slipping always out of view, across boundaries, and, almost necessarily, a "mode of excess."

Scholars have begun in recent years to address these now-pressing conceptual problems: in film studies, where such efforts are most advanced, melodrama scholarship has challenged the construction of film history's "tradition" as well as the conceptual basis, structure, and status of its genre systems and begun to develop a critical practice in which melodrama, and not realism, forms the primary and normative aesthetic ground. This important, urgently needed work lends impetus to related efforts to recognize—finally—melodrama's foundational generic position in the formal histories of other mediums and modes (such as musical theater, for example, or the novel).

However, revising our understanding of modern genre systems is only a beginning. Most obviously, we have yet to overcome, despite having now seriously challenged, the biases and obstacles imposed by the modern critical tradition's disciplinary separation of music, drama, theater, and film, and of the performative and plastic and literary arts, which still fractures approaches to melodrama as a historical and formal object of study. Less obviously, we have yet even to question many of the modern critical tradition's methodological tendencies and conventions, including not only its historiographic privileging of exceptional individual works and its valorization of canons constituted by such works but—more crucially—its referential association of the artwork with an individual medium and a single authorial creator. Such biases remain deeply inimical to the analysis and comprehension of a form that is from its inception multimedial and mass-cultural, thoroughly commodified and collectively produced on an industrial scale—a form whose history is constituted not by any canon but by the tidal movements of broad fields of commercial production, and whose works—in a manner that highlights their modernity—are created not by individual artists but the corporate work of many. Least obviously, we have yet even to notice, much less to question or challenge, many of that tradition's basic assumptions about modern art and culture, including not only the conventional notion that modern art is distinguished by its pursuit of realism or formal self-reflexivity but the underlying presupposition that it adopts a critical stance toward tradition, and even the subtending belief that modernity itself marks a decisive break with the past. Until we unbind ourselves from these fundamental practices, conventions, and assumptions, and not simply from the narrow realist narrative of modern art that they produced and supported, there is little doubt that we will continue to see the vast ocean of modern melodrama, and the broad global currents of cultural modernity, in a profoundly limited, distorted, and inaccurate way.

Freeing ourselves from these binds will take a long time, but one way we might advance that process now is to reconsider two foundational, still largely unquestioned conceptions of melodrama's origins and character—conceptions that are consonant with the past half-century's great revolution in perspective, but which are in fact myths, rooted in the modern tradition, that continue to distort and limit our understanding of what melodrama is and what it means. My aim is not to derogate or dismiss these conceptions, for like all compelling myths they illuminate as well as obscure the history they describe and tell us much about the modern culture and the fascinating critical history from which they arise. More crucial is to indicate the ways in which these myths have both shaped and obscured our view and to delineate something of the history of melodrama, and of modernity, that becomes visible once we set them aside.

THE MYTH OF MELODRAMA'S REVOLUTIONARY BIRTH

The first of these myths, most influentially advanced in our era by Peter Brooks but set out by Charles Nodier within a generation of the genre's rise, is the still widely accepted idea that melodrama is a product of the cataclysmic changes that accompanied the French Revolution. As Brooks famously put it almost a half-century ago, "The origins of melodrama can accurately be located within the context of the French Revolution and its aftermath . . . the moment that symbolically, and really, marks the final liquidation of the traditional Sacred and its representative institutions, the shattering of the myth of Christendom, and the dissolution of an organic and hierarchically cohesive society" (1976,14–15).

It is from this Revolutionary origin story, more than from any other source, that we derive the now commonplace assumption that melodrama is the drama of a "post-Sacred" world. In a more indirect way, we also derive from this account our sense of melodrama as the natural expression of a popular culture—*any* popular culture—that has, through the cataclysms of modernity, lost or been freed from traditional structures of religious and social order. Perhaps most fundamentally, this narrative of a form born from cataclysm inclines us to look upon melodrama's emergence as a spontaneous reaction to epistemological need, or an unmediated manifestation of popular feeling. Such a naturalizing perspective finds its strongest articulation in the years just preceding Brooks's work, the era of modernist certainty—or perhaps existentialist extremity—when Eric Bentley (1964) and Robert Heilman (1968) suggested that melodrama might best be understood as an immanent imaginative mode and an intrinsic facet of human consciousness—not a form at all, but a primal "version of experience" and a perspective of mind theoretically available at any time.

The explanatory value of this conception of melodrama's origins has been considerable, both for traditional and for revisionist scholarship. For both, the idea of a revolutionary origin offers a compelling rationale for melodrama's expressive extremity, its archetypical focus on victim-heroes, and its hyperbolic engagement with moral feeling, emotion, and sensation. It also provides a coherent explanation for melodrama's seemingly disorderly, almost primal structure of action, its pointed, relentless engagement with trauma, and its displaced "naturalism of the dream life" (Bentley 1964, 205). For traditional scholars and critics pursuing the effort to write a triumphant history of realism, this revolutionary origin narrative offered a compelling rationale for what was then seen as melodrama's brief, epiphenomenal life—the precondition, soon overcome, for a more sober, realistic drama of modern existence, a drama no longer caught in terror and its dreams.

For revisionist scholars and critics, including myself, that same revolutionary origin narrative offered a powerful rationale for melodrama's viral success in the modern era, insofar as that era is understood to be marked by the onset and spread of conditions of persistent crisis, continual change, and prolonged epistemological conflict and collapse. As such, it has provided a strong argument for melodrama's historical novelty and significance. From this narrative, more than from any other source, derives the redemptive perception of melodrama as a popular poetry—as *the* popular poetry—of the modern era, a poetry galvanized and made manifest (not incidentally) by the cataclysm of the French Revolution, that popular upheaval which serves, more than any other, as revolutionary modernity's own foundational event. If one is looking for good reasons to acknowledge the seemingly definitional significance of melodrama in modern times, to appreciate its extraordinary appeal and resilience, and even to account for its pandemic migration across modern cultures as they encountered the disruptive, violent transition to global modernity and embraced the popular revolutionary traditions of collective, free expression, there they are.

Unfortunately, nearly everything about this narrative of melodrama's origins is untrue, and the distortions it has produced in our understanding have been, and remain, considerable. Perhaps the most evident blurring of the truth is found in its most basic and concrete historical claim, that "the origins of melodrama can accurately be located in the French Revolution and its aftermath" (Brooks 1976, 14). Certainly, it is true that the first appearance of theatrical melodrama as a nominate dramatic genre of the popular stage—of "melodrama" in the specific modern sense of the term—occurred on the boulevard stage of Paris in the last years of the 1790s, and that the final development of this nominate genre was shaped and catalyzed by the events and context of the French Revolution and its aftermath. As Brooks (1976) rightly points out, that genre's particular formula—a distinctive admixture of tragedy, comedy, pantomime, and spectacle, accompanied by music and intended for a popular audience, peopled most prominently by villains and victim-heroes, propelled by pathos and suspense, coincidence and fate—arose directly from experimentation made possible by the Revolutionary liberation of the popular French stage and was paradigmatically established only in 1800, with the premiere of Guilbert de Pixérécourt's explosively successful *Coelina*. Moreover, Pixérécourt's "recipe," as Frank Rahill (1967) aptly described it, produced an *effect* that was not only revolutionary but exemplary of the unprecedented excitement of the Revolutionary era itself and the new structures of feeling it had engendered. Specifically, it catalyzed not only sensational arousal and emotional absorption, effects much sought and fairly commonly pursued by the sentimental and Gothic drama of the preceding era, but also a kind of affective intoxication of feeling—an irresistibly pleasurable, unifying, cathartic surge of sensory and emotive excess—that had distinguished the violent, traumatic political theater of Revolutionary action and, with melodrama, was transferred to the stage. In this sense, then, melodrama does seem indeed to be a product of the Revolution and its aftermath.

Yet entrances are not origins, if by the latter term we mean where something comes from and from what it emerges and not—or not only—where it first appears, fully developed and explicitly named. And it is not at all true, if we speak of origins in this sense, that melodrama's origins are to be found either in the late 1790s or on the boulevard stages of Paris, that they are fundamentally related to the French Revolution and its aftermath or, more generally, that they reflect or express cataclysmic crisis and change.

First, as theater historians have long recognized, *Coelina* achieved a new effect, but it was by no means a novel or unconventional play, nor one of a type exclusive either to Paris or to the post-Revolutionary age. To the contrary, Pixérécourt's landmark work is in formal terms both exceptionally derivative and wholly conservative. It is a cosmopolitan hybrid, composed entirely of parts, techniques, emphases, and aims already well developed in earlier, often pre-Revolutionary work produced all over Europe, and is unremarkable even in its reliance on that synthetic technique. Its formal character, that is, is not new but conventional in the extreme. By the 1780s, in fact, every one of the ostensibly distinguishing elements of melodrama that this origin myth attributes to the Revolution's cataclysmic effects—from its emphasis on extreme emotion, its mixture of diverse dramatic genres and theatrical modes, and its sentimental and spectacular appeals to its polarized morality and heightened, often monopathic, dream-image version of character—were not merely transnational commonplaces but nearly normative assumptions, both well-established and well-mined by the rising tides of late eighteenth-century sentimental drama and opera, gothic literature and plays, and popular spectacular entertainment of many kinds.

Even melodrama's primary nominative feature, its supposedly distinctive use of music to subtend action and galvanize feeling, had by 1800 a long, diverse, and culturally vital history in multiple arenas, from illegitimate theater and pantomime to spectacle and opera, including in the 1780s several different genres of music drama and at least one form of stage drama on the boulevard itself that took the same generic name. Indeed, one finds well before the French Revolution a rising tide across Europe of mixed, musically accompanied spectacular drama and theatrical entertainment, much of which resembles the formula of Pixérécourt so closely as to be almost indistinguishable from it. Such "near-melodrama" experienced similarly notable success, if not quite the mania that his formula would enjoy.

In the end, the single quality that in aesthetic terms distinguishes *Coelina* from precedent is its degree of formal distillation. The effect it achieved was distinctive and certainly new, but it is an effect that had been pursued for some time and by many, and its achievement marks rather a convergence and the crossing of a threshold than the expression of anything like a rupture or fall. Pixérécourt got there first, but as Frank Rahill (1967) pointed out decades ago, had he never existed it seems certain that melodrama would have been achieved by someone else quite soon, and very possibly not in France at all.

Second, it is apparent, too, once this convergent current comes into view, that the arrival of melodrama marks the culmination, not the beginning, of a sustained movement toward affective aesthetics that can be traced through the mainstream of drama, theater, and music—indeed, through the arts generally—at least as far back as the Reformation, and which accompanies the rise of modern culture as it is most broadly conceived. French efforts to produce heightened affective responses through the use of powerful emotion and spectacular thrill are found not only in Diderot and Rousseau but also in Racine and Corneille. In England they are evident in Lewis and Lillo and in Webster and Ford; and in Germany in Schiller and Lessing as well as in the *trauerspiel* drama that so fascinated Walter Benjamin. Efforts to forge a "mixed" genre that would synthesize and intensify diverse forms, drawing their disparate appeals together in a new, "modern" form, are a hallmark of the entire late eighteenth century and a central feature of dramatic innovation as far back as Dryden. Melodrama's use of music to heighten emotion and subtend action is regularly traced to Rousseau's *Pygmalion* (1762) but is more clearly the successor to widespread developments in comedy, opera, popular music, and illegitimate drama that span the whole of the eighteenth century and played a leading role—as a legal basis for genre-based reportorial control—in defining the social and political history of those forms. By the latter part of the eighteenth century at the latest, these diverse formal experiments had accelerated and begun to converge. By the 1780s one finds not only advances in each of these several areas but an evident and conscious trend toward the radically combinatory, synthetic, and distillate logic that melodrama exemplifies. Indeed, as Jules Marsan (1900) argued over a century ago, melodrama's formula is so clearly, closely, and long anticipated by the broad theatrical currents and innovations of the preceding era that it is unquestionably more accurate—if, we now understand, still too restrictive by far—to see its realization as the "logical outcome" of "the entire history of the eighteenth-century stage" (196).

As this revised narrative implies, the distortions produced by the myth of melodrama's revolutionary origin extend well beyond the question of timing. By locating melodrama's origins in Revolution, that myth severs melodrama's connection to the longer history of form and forecloses, at a stroke, serious consideration of its position and significance in the extended history of the arts. Melodrama becomes a phenomenon to be understood and studied not as a product of formal innovation within the *long durée*, but as the *sui generis* offspring of a culture stripped by catastrophe of belief, returned to a state of nature, making drama anew, in shock and need, amid the ruins—an orphaned art for an orphaned age. The melodramatic inflection of such a mythic view is extreme, and its emotional attractiveness has no doubt formed a great part of its redemptive appeal for revisionist scholars. By rescuing and redeeming melodrama, we rescue and redeem our history and ourselves. Extreme too, however, is the inflection in this Revolutionary origin myth of the modern critical tradition: melodrama's position is still, perhaps, that of the naïve, broken precursor to a subsequent, rational, realist art through which bourgeois culture would overcome its traumatic condition and once more develop a more mature, reflexive, and reasonable art. Perhaps most balefully, we find in this myth the strongest basis for the presumption—which has long bedeviled even revisionist scholarship—that melodrama is an excessive, uncontrolled, irrational, and crude form of art, a form born of chaos and fear, and not, as we have become increasingly aware—and as this revised, nonmythic history is intended to make evident—a finely-honed, keenly synthetic, often coldly logical art of excess, developed slowly over centuries by the combined efforts of all manner of affective arts.

THE MYTH OF MELODRAMA'S MORAL FOUNDATION

The manner in which this myth of melodrama's Revolutionary origins has distorted critical understanding of melodrama as a form is not limited, however, to the ways in which it has elided melodrama's relation to earlier developments in the arts and occluded its position and participation in a longer and broader cultural history. By deriving melodrama's origins from a moment defined, as Brooks (1976) put it (echoing Nodier), by the "the final liquidation of the traditional Sacred and its representative institutions, the shattering of the myth of Christendom, and the dissolution of an organic and hierarchically cohesive society," it has also given rise to a second and no less misleading myth: the idea that melodrama takes form from a crisis and collapse of traditional belief and as a new "drama of morality" fitted to a "post-Sacred" age (14–15). As Brooks puts it, "melodrama starts from and expresses the anxiety brought by a frightening new world in which the traditional patterns of moral order no longer provide the necessary social glue" (20), and restores faith in a common humanity and lends meaning to life by programmatically making visible and substantiating the operations of that moral order in human action. Seen through the lens of this epistemological origin myth, melodrama's cultural function becomes quasi-religious: what Nodier (2002), defending Pixérécourt's drama, described as melodrama's singular ability to stand in for a "silent pulpit" (xi), or what Ben Singer (2001) aptly describes as its capacity to provide "a compensatory faith that helped [and helps] people deal with the vicissitudes of modern life" (135).

The influence and apparent explanatory value of this second myth has been considerable for both traditional and revisionist scholarship. It has offered a compelling rationale for melodrama's emergence and growth within and alongside that of secular modernity, for its particular appeal among displaced and disrupted populations, and even for the ritualistic character of its cultural consumption. It has provided, as well, a coherent explanation for melodrama's seemingly rigid, even fundamental adherence to structures of moral polarization, conflict, and resolution. For scholars and critics pursuing the traditional effort to write a triumphant history of realism, this view of melodrama as a drama of morality born of cataclysm strengthened the notion that melodrama was a marginal, transitional drama. In its light, melodrama became not only a rude formal product of aesthetic collapse but the crude cultural product of epistemological trauma—a naïve, faith-driven precursor to the more sober, reflective, objective, and fully secular drama of realism, in which the transition to a post-Sacred world is completed and existence within the new age finds its appropriately self-reflexive form.

For revisionist scholars and critics, on the other hand, this view of melodrama as a drama of morality that accompanies the transition to a post-Sacred modernity has strengthened recognition of melodrama's vital function as a privileged mode in the modern, popular expression of collective belief, heightening understanding of its unparalleled, seemingly universalist power as a discourse of modern social and political change. One can see very well, from such a perspective, how melodrama engages with, plays upon, and articulates changing social beliefs, why it so programmatically—and pragmatically—endeavors to fit real events and experiences into its moral frame, and how its production and consumption participate in the public negotiation of modern community. In this view one finds ample reason to assert melodrama's central importance in the history of modern culture, to appreciate its extraordinary appeal and resonance, and to account for its pandemic growth in and alongside global modernity. In fact, one would be hard pressed to find a better basis for melodrama's critical redemption than the claim that it is a drama of morality fitted to a post-Sacred age, for such a claim seems to satisfy, with a *popular* form, a demand made of legitimate drama since classical times, not only redeeming melodrama's role in modernity but ratifying its position in the longer history of the theatrical arts.

Yet, despite its undeniable attraction, this view of melodrama's origins is also a myth—and one that has distorted our understanding of melodrama's character and aims no less profoundly than the myth of melodrama's Revolutionary origins has distorted our comprehension of melodrama's form and source. Once again, the myth captures the narrowest view of melodrama's early history. It is unquestionably true that the nominate form of melodrama that Pixérécourt devised by 1800 was not only moralistic but was celebrated by popular audiences as a new, or at least revitalized, drama of morality, and for its first decade at least—however odd it might seem from this side of history—was lauded even by critics as legitimate and even classical on this very basis. Moreover, Pixérécourt's own intensively and explicitly moral melodramas, as Nodier rightly observed, exemplified such claims and ruled the stage for thirty years. In fact, it is impossible to understand the quasi-religious adulation "the father of melodrama" received throughout his career without recognizing the force of such claims, the strength of Pixérécourt's commitment to the creation of moral drama, and the sincerity of his belief that melodrama's capability *as* a drama of morality constituted the primary achievement of the form he devised. It is true, too, that insofar as melodrama received its paradigmatic form in Pixérécourt's work, a great deal of subsequent melodrama has been produced and received, often legitimately, as a drama of morality, that most of melodrama has laid at least a superficial claim to be moral, and that nearly all melodrama thereafter, insofar as it enlists that Pixérécourtian recipe's morally polarized character structures, shares a basic trajectory of moral crisis and redemption and appeals to a shared popular-collective moral imagination, has been moralistic.

Yet, as even a glance at the dense, extended pre-Revolutionary genealogy of melodrama offered here should make evident, such moral structures, qualities, and aims were, by the time of *Coelina*, hardly new, nor confined to the theater of France. To the contrary, efforts to achieve a moral drama of this kind, and to do so through the stimulation of sympathetic emotion and pathos, the exploitation of polarized moral valences, the dramatization of moral crisis and redemption, and the affective appeal to a shared popular-collective morality, even as an "occult" rendered legible in action and ratified by feeling, had been pursued for decades by Mercier, Diderot, and Rousseau; by Benda, Florian, and Sedaine; by Lessing, Kotzebue, and Schiller; and of course by Beaumarchais; and in Britain appear even earlier, as in Lillo and Gay. In fact, as discussion of melodrama's early modern precedents makes equally evident, neither this traditional concern with the development of an effective drama of morality nor the turn to affective means to achieve it are unique to the eighteenth century: to the contrary, that concern defines, as a primary criterion of legitimacy, the entire history of premodern cultural debate about the value of the drama, from Plato through Tertullian, Corneille, and Moliére to Rousseau, and that affective turn is found over and over again, from Euripides on, though it takes hold and spreads only in the modern era.

Moreover, with even such a limited history in view, or even after a pause to recollect the broad outlines of the eighteenth century, it becomes difficult to find in the Revolutionary era anything like the collapse of "traditional patterns of moral order" that Brooks describes (1976, 20). In the culture of sympathy at large, and particularly in the theatrical arts, there is a rising, finally overwhelming emphasis on moral feeling, an emphasis that extends at least as far back as the reaction against Restoration-era libertinism (in which one *does* find a crisis of the traditional moral order). By the time of the Revolution, this impulse forms part of a sustained, self-conscious effort to invoke the authority of shared private belief—of a common moral order—as a counterweight against the rapidly disintegrating structures of institutionalized public behavior, or what we would rightly describe as a collapse of the collective *ethical* order. By the latter decades of the eighteenth century and well into the nineteenth, as industrialism's sharpest impact was felt, it was institutions, public traditions, conventional rules of conduct, and relations of social hierarchy and power—ethical structures, not moral ones—that "no longer provide[d] the necessary social glue" and so came to seem arbitrary, restrictive, and obsolete (Brooks 1976, 20). Again, the impression produced is not of rupture, or even novelty, but of convergence, synthesis, and consolidation: the formation of melodrama marks not a loss but a ratification of morality's presence and force and its integration—as a set of elemental conventions—into a larger aesthetic.

Melodrama's role as a modern drama of morality may, then, have coincided with the French Revolution and the crisis of belief in traditional order that it articulated, but its origins cannot accurately be located there, nor do they express an ostensible collapse of the moral order. To the contrary, Pixérécourt's effort to establish melodrama as a drama of morality is perhaps best understood as the most conservative, traditionalist aspect of his art, a marker not of its novelty but of its indebtedness to premodern expression and pre-Revolutionary values and concerns. Support for such a view is lent not least by the recognition that, if Pixérécourt's emphasis on melodrama's capability as a drama of morality served effectively as a *carte d'entrée* to the legitimate stage, satisfying tradition's most long-standing demand of the dramatic arts, it was almost without question the single most rapidly abandoned element of the recipe he devised. Even by 1805, the great wave of cape-and-sword plays, lurid gothic extravaganzas, and exotic/romantic adventure fantasies produced by Pixérécourt's imitators made it all too evident, as we know well today, that melodrama's engagement with morality can—like that of any genre—be exploited, rendered ironic, or simply pushed into the background as a slight gesture in more sensational fare. By 1810, melodramatic burlesques offering farcical dismissals of these work's stilted, still strongly aristocratic moral registers had become commonplace. Critical opinion had begun to swing against the genre as a whole, and notions of melodrama as a revived drama of morality, and even as a moral drama, clearly struck many, if not most, as naïve.

Such claims would be reasserted by 1820, as the appeal of such spectacular works waned and melodrama became both more domestic and more closely engaged with everyday life, but even then morality could—and often did—become mere moralism or simple exploitation of moral feeling. Perhaps most significantly, even domestic melodrama had by the mid-1820s begun to discard or even to critique the class-based moral order to which it initially adhered, and in the working-class and crime melodrama that emerged in the late 1830s that order is set in tension against—or even ridiculed by—the more difficult ethical orders that structure cultures of poverty, criminality, and exploitation in an immoral, or perhaps amoral, world. Morality is not abandoned, and in fact retains its force where it appears and is applied, but its authority no longer governs melodrama's world and no longer serves as the drama's aim or guarantee. By the time of Nodier's (2002) hagiographic portrait of Pixérécourt, the genre's early reputation as a revived drama of morality hung in tatters, and the socially conservative father of melodrama himself had come to condemn much of the drama that his recipe had enabled as "evil, dangerous, and immoral" (318). Perhaps most telling, melodrama had by then long since abandoned Pixérécourt's claims, as it has largely abandoned them ever since, and with melodrama's success as a mass-cultural form so too has the criterion of morality as a measure of artistic legitimacy declined and largely disappeared from view in critical debate, as in cultural evaluation at large. What has replaced it, and what distinguishes melodrama, is rather the criterion of feeling and emotional effect—the demand that we be moved, not instructed.

This is not to assert, of course, that melodrama was not or is not a drama of morality: it was and often is, and the form's appeal is often derived from that capability. It is, however, not always or fundamentally so, and its use and treatment of morality neither distinguishes melodrama historically as a form nor originates in an epochal collapse of the moral order, but emerges from a sustained aesthetic history and serves as one among its many sources of aesthetic force and affective appeal. Melodrama is also a drama of sentiment, of sensation, of ethics, of horror: it is the distillate, intoxicating effect, the catalyzation of an extreme physical and affective response, and not any one of its parts, that serves as the distinguishing imperative of its poetics.

Just as the distortions produced by the myth of melodrama's revolutionary birth extend beyond our apprehension of the genre's moment of origin to our recognition of its relationship to the longer history of form, the distortions produced by the myth of melodrama's moral foundation extend beyond our apprehension of the genre's fundamental character to our recognition of its relationship to the larger history of modern culture. By binding melodrama's origins and its goals to a cataclysmic crisis of belief, this myth again detaches melodrama's emergence from the history of the theatrical and spectacular arts, but now in such a way as to occlude—in complementary fashion—its more complex and more morally and ethically indeterminate history as a technical, industrial, and commercial art. Through it, melodrama becomes, as it becomes in the Revolutionary origin myth, a phenomenon to be understood and studied as an unmediated cultural articulation of collective suffering, fear, and desire, and an expression of popular faith—and not, or only incidentally, as a profoundly mediated outcome of modern aesthetic and cultural production, a memeplex *techné*, developed over decades, to appeal to such experiences, feelings, needs, and beliefs, and a primary expression of the historical development of modern, mass-cultural art. In the latter view, melodrama may seem diminished, but in fact it becomes enlarged, and the complexity of its historical engagement with collective life, and with morality, begins to emerge.

Perhaps more damagingly, the conception of melodrama as a drama of morality also blinds us to the range and complexity of its affective engagement with understanding and belief—to the many ways in which the moral solicitations and the claims of melodrama are set in relation to, rather than merely naïvely underpinning, governing, or grounding, the claims of other, often less abstract registers of feeling and thought, including not only social and personal ethics but the entire range (and variety) of interpersonal understanding, emotional, and sensational apprehension. Moral feeling occupies one end of that spectrum, and visceral shock the other, but they delimit an entire field of feeling and apprehension by which melodrama—like all drama—does its work. Indeed, the limitation of the emphasis on morality, and the manner in which it diminishes our idea of melodrama, emerges most forcefully perhaps if we recognize the immediacy with which we would rule out any similarly reductive conception of the fundamental concerns and operations of tragedy, comedy, farce, burlesque, or even medieval morality plays.

THE MYTH OF REVOLUTION

Casting aside these two origin myths seems at first glance to reveal a view of melodrama and its history that is, if anything, more rather than less revolutionary than that which they provided. What we see is not merely a new form but a new kind of form, and one produced not by crisis, cataclysm, or collapse, but by convergence, synthesis, and progressive strengthening over time. This form marks not a break with the past but rather its logical outcome and determinate aim: the achievement of a compressive, distillate form for a world of intensified, continual, accelerating change. Melodrama does not find its origins in the French Revolution or on the popular stage of post-Revolutionary Paris: rather, it is first achieved there, catalyzing a process of contagion, both aesthetic and experiential, through which both art and perception are, in a kind of phase shift, updated and transformed. This view of melodrama—as a viral vehicle or procedure whereby aesthetics and apprehension are adapted to a world of more intensified, more collective, more deeply imbricated, more continually negotiated experience—seems more full of implication for our understanding of art and culture, not least because it resonates so powerfully with modernity's most revolutionary artistic claims. Indeed, melodrama seen in this way finds its closest modern descriptions in Wagner's conception of the total work of art, Benjamin's characterization of the work of art in the age of mechanical reproduction, or, even more provocatively, in Artaud's radical vision of theater as plague. It is tempting to set melodrama forward as something like the realization, if unacknowledged, of the modern art forms they envisaged.

Yet to do so would be premature. If this revised view unbinds us from the myths of melodrama's Revolutionary origins to make visible its far larger and longer evolution in time, it also challenges modernity's own revolutionary claims about itself and its art—the ideas, implicit in the work of Wagner and Artaud and of Benjamin as well, that the modern era and its artistic creations are fundamentally new and different from the past, and that they are so because they articulate revolutionary change. The view of melodrama's history offered here suggests that these claims are anything but realistic, and that the formation of modernity and its art, and not simply of melodrama, is not revolutionary but evolutionary, not a radical departure from the past so much as a continuation of it, and not the product of rupture but of incremental, convergent processes of change that extend far back into the long durée, as artistic culture and form adapt to the gradual concentration, intensification of lived experience in an emerging modern world. Far from seeming revolutionary, melodrama seen in this light looks natural, conservative, and almost predetermined—nothing more (or less) than the inevitable concentration and distillation of traditional narrative form in response to the intensification and acceleration of modes of existence and structures of consciousness over time.

Such a radically expanded view makes more evident the foundational challenge that melodrama scholarship now poses to traditional critical histories of modern art and culture. Rather than simply calling into question modernity's derogation and neglect of melodrama, or merely forcing us to discard its realist/modernist aesthetic myth, it forces us to question as well modernity's differentiation and separation of itself and its culture from the past, and its claim to represent, embody, and emerge from revolutionary change. Like the development of melodrama, that of modernity seems in this perspective less the expression of a violent rupture than the product of a natural phase shift, a continuation and outcome of the past it succeeds. Such a radically expanded view also makes evident, however, the degree to which melodrama scholarship itself—by casting our own critical history as a Promethean unbinding of chains—remains caught up in that mythic modern perspective and bound, still, by its insistent desire for liberating narratives of revolutionary change. Put in slightly different terms, the challenge melodrama scholarship now faces may not be that of completing its revolution against the modern tradition, nor of demonstrating in convincing terms melodrama's radical novelty, but of unbinding itself from the constraints of a revolutionary perspective and working, as I've tried to work here, toward a history of melodrama that highlights its continuity with the past.

2

The Passion of Christ and the Melodramatic Imagination

RICHARD ALLEN

We have inherited from Peter Brooks's seminal work, *The Melodramatic Imagination* (1976), the assumption that melodrama emerges from the collapse of the traditional Sacred. According to Brooks, quoting Clifford Geertz, the traditional world of the Sacred yields an "intrinsic obligation: it not only encourages devotion, it demands it; it not only induces intellectual assent, it enforces emotional commitment" (18). Brooks claims that the collapse of this order was completed by the social and moral upheaval of the French Revolution. In the process of disenchantment that followed, "the explanatory and cohesive force of Sacred myth lost its power, and its political and social representations lost their legitimacy" (15–16). In place of the traditional Sacred, "the individual ego declar[ed] its central and overriding value, its demand to be the measure of all things" (16). Yet "some version of the Sacred" was needed to re-create a sense of moral order within the newly secular realm, and melodrama emerged as a rhetorical and dramaturgical form to fill the moral void. It dramatized the recovery of a domain of "operative spiritual values" a "moral occult" that both indicated within and masked by the surface of reality (5). This new moral order was conceived in terms of the individual: "melodramatic good and evil are highly personalized: they are assigned to, they inhabit persons who. . . have no psychological complexity but who are strongly characterized" (16). It was revealed through a highly expressive mode of dramaturgy that focused on the cultivation of pathos and the "aesthetics of astonishment." For Brooks, melodrama is a mode of representation and dramaturgy devoted to making individual virtue legible through a hyperbolic rhetorical appeal, through the senses, to sentiment.

Modern scholars of melodrama tend to historicize Brooks's account of melodrama by arguing that it is mainly salient to the early corpus of French provenance on which it is based. "Brooks may be read for his analysis of early melodrama," writes David Mayer (2004), but "as melodrama begins to alter in the late 1820s, the accuracy of his description is less sure, and his authority recedes" (154). Although certain critics, such as Matthew Buckley (2006), question the idea that melodrama has any relationship to the "traditional Sacred," most simply assume the "post-Sacred," or secular, character of melodrama as a mark of its modernity and move on from there. However, in this essay, I seek to rethink, rather than either assume or discard, the relationship between the "Sacred" and melodrama suggested by Brooks.

Following Charles Nodier (2002: xv), Brooks (1976) conceives the emergence of melodrama, quite plausibly, in relation to the official abandonment of Christianity during and after the French Revolution. However, although the French Revolution may have made a radical break with religion, the traditional Sacred had, by the time of the Revolution, already given way to a new, incipiently modern sense of selfhood that emerged within a broadly religious framework. The stark opposition drawn by Brooks, on the basis of the Revolution, between the idea of a traditional Sacred and modern "man as the center of all things" is not tenable. The new understanding of Christianity that emerged in the Middle Ages represented Christ as a suffering human being and a source of empathic identification, prompted by the emotional responses of the Virgin Mary and Mary Magdalene in ways that resemble the rhetorical strategies of melodrama. In 1908, French art historian Émile Mâle (1986, 450) described this new religious formation as the Christianity of Pathos; modern scholars use the term "affective piety," which can apply also to other religions. At the same time, melodrama itself is not without its appeal to transcendent value. As Louis James writes (1976), in melodrama "religious significance" is "close to the surface," and the gesture of the suffering innocent who looks or raises her hands toward heaven is "quasi-theological" (87). That is, it is at once emotional and spiritual; it intimates the appeal of Christ to God or Mary to Christ. Brooks's concept of the "moral occult" fails to account not only for the way the capacity to nominate virtue and vice is common currency in the period he discusses, and the occlusion of the moral domain is at best only skin deep, but also for the extent to which the nomination of this moral domain bears the traces of a theological understanding.

In summary, the melodramatic imagination does not emerge fully constituted in postrevolutionary France, as Brooks suggests; rather, it is recovered or rediscovered from an earlier melodramatic imaginary that was initially constituted from the reconceptualization of the Passion of Christ within medieval Christianity as a mise-en-scène of empathic suffering. The drama of affective piety is repurposed and reconceived in the context of a secular society; it is transposed from the relatively impersonal domain of the Sacred to the individualized domain of everyday life, where an echo of the Sacred remains.

Let me be clear. I am not arguing that the medieval Christianity of Pathos, which centers on the representation and enactment of Christ's Passion, somehow *is* melodrama, as we understand the modern form. Still less do I contend that the Christianity of Pathos explains all the kinds of theater and film melodrama that have evolved in the last 200 years. Yet, although the Christianity of Pathos cannot simply be identified with melodrama, it nonetheless yields forms of representation and dramatic enactment that can, with historical hindsight, be termed melodramatic where that adjective serves to denote many of the attributes we find in the modern mode, such as heightened emotional expressivity, the idealization of virtue, the pathos suffering virtue solicits, sensationalized tableaux of astonished recognition, and suspense. Indeed, the melodramatic attributes of the Christianity of Pathos encourage us to think of the ways in which, for the medieval spectator, the pleasures of text, pictorial representation, or dramatic enactment far exceeded the spiritual payoff that the church fathers sought to elicit, which is one of the reasons the Catholic church remained suspicious of, and eventually, at the Council of Trent, clamped down upon, the permissible kinds of representation and enactment of the Passion.

Conversely, an understanding of the idea of "the Sacred" in terms of the material practices of Christian affective piety promises to cast fresh light on our understanding of nineteenth- and twentieth-century European and American melodrama, especially upon the figuration and emplotment of unjust suffering as the paradigmatic signifier of human virtue and the solicitation of tears in response to that suffering. Melodrama, no doubt, has antecedents in classic drama (Heilman 1968), and perhaps also in the iconography of human suffering inscribed on Roman sarcophagi, but the story of Christ's divine incarnation and the profound historical influence of that story in shaping Western subjectivity gives it a unique influence.

This Christian framework is evidently not a universal one. The influence of Christian missionaries in Western colonialism should not be underestimated, but other religions and cultures have their own highly influential traditions of affective piety that bear comparison with, though also differ from, the Christianity of Pathos, in their emotional and spiritual contours. Two traditions stand out here. One is the *Vaishnav bhakti* tradition of Krishna devotion that is modeled on the ecstatic love-in-separation of the female devotee, Meera, whose significance for Indian cinema has been explored by Ira Bhaskar (2012; see also chapter 15). The other is the Sufi tradition, canonically embodied in the story of Laila-Majnun, which dramatizes the exquisite suffering-in-separation of the male poet-lover who is exiled from his beloved and assumes a canonical importance in popular melodrama from Turkey to South Asia.[1] Comparative melodrama studies must take into account the distinctive traditions of affective piety and their divergence and convergence in different film cultures.

The Christianity of Pathos also gives rise to more particular Christian themes, iconography, and allegory in melodrama in a manner that is mediated by the institutional and cultural history of the Christian Church. For example, Louis Bayman (2015; see also chapter 16) has recently shown how Italian melodrama of the immediate post–World War II period is infused with the practices, rituals, and belief systems of Catholicism, which is scarcely surprising in a country in which 60 percent of the people were practicing Catholics. Although the link forged here between melodrama and Catholic affective piety is historically contingent—melodrama is not necessarily religious—it is not accidental, for Italian melodrama here draws upon forms of religious life, feeling, and expression that have inhered in the Catholic tradition from the medieval period onward.

In northern Europe, the Protestant Reformation brought an end to the practice of performing acts of penance for personal sins through the doctrine that

Christ's death atoned for the sins of mankind. It thus undermined one of the main rationales for the Christianity of Pathos that ennobled immersion in Christ's suffering and pain as the path to repentance and redemption. However, the Counter-Reformation of the sixteenth century and the Catholic tradition it sustained preserved the core ideal of penance and the tradition of affective piety in religious ritual and the art that supported it, even as it prescribed and codified in the Baroque period the ways art could express emotion. It is this continuity of tradition that allows writers of melodrama in Catholic countries to so readily invoke affective piety. However, Catholicism is not the only Christian tradition of affective piety. The transdenominational tradition of Evangelical Protestantism, which developed in the United States in the nineteenth century and burgeoned in the twentieth, places at the center of religiosity the emotional power of conversion, a kind of once and for all repentance of sins that frames Evangelical Protestantism as a "religion of the heart" (Hart 2002:189). This tradition informs many of the affiliations between melodrama and religion in the American context, from *Uncle Tom's Cabin* (2005) to the films of D. W. Griffith.[2]

The centrality of the female witnesses in the Christianity of Pathos, the Virgin Mary and Mary Magdalene, is important for contemporary debates about melodrama. The ennoblement of their role recast centuries of denigration of female emotion within the church. How emotions associated with women were to be represented remained contested during the medieval period in ways that find their echoes in contemporary debates about realism and melodrama and in the identification of melodrama as a woman's genre. Feminist critics in the 1970s saw melodrama as a specifically female form dealing with female problems and issues (see Introduction). However, within the culture of affective piety, the female spectator and her emotions take on a certain normative status for both genders, even though at the same time the paradigmatic suffering body is a male one. This at once confirms and upsets assumptions about the alignment between gender, melodrama, and emotion. Although the history of affective piety suggests that women are aligned with emotional expression in a manner that is deeply culturally entrenched, at the same time, the centrality of female experience within affective piety as a path to moral understanding has a cultural normativity that subsequent formulations of the relationship between women and melodrama belie.

THE CHRISTIANITY OF PATHOS

In the Middle Ages, the idea of the traditional Sacred as an all-encompassing transcendental myth that hierarchically ordered social life began to be eroded within the framework of Christian society, in which a new, incipiently modern, sense of selfhood was emerging. Charles Taylor (2007) has called this new sense of self the "buffered" self: a self no longer directly subject to the invasion and control of supernatural beings and the subject of social and political rights. Evidence for this historical transformation lies in the fact that in much of western Europe from the fourteenth century onward, the supernatural authority of the kings of Europe and the Pope was being curtailed in favor of a more secular, juridical understanding of their powers (Southern 1953). Although this new sense of self could be called "secular" in its opposition to the all-encompassing hierarchical authority of the traditional Sacred, it nonetheless emerged within a religious framework in which, between the tenth and thirteenth centuries, a revolution took place in understanding Christ's incarnation and the function of religious art.

In the liturgy and art prior to the medieval period, Christ was a transcendent figure of awe and authority, a God enthroned in his majesty as judge of man even as he appeared on the Cross: a distant figure to be worshipped and praised. Before the Middle Ages, the Passion of Christ was essentially a contest between God and the Devil over the fate of humankind, which had a big stake in the confrontation but no role to play in it. Humankind, by sinning, had committed to the Devil. Through his incarnation as Christ and Christ's triumph over death, God defeated the Devil and rescued humanity (Southern 1953). However, beginning in ninth-century Byzantium, and then developed in the doctrines of leaders of the new monastic orders, the figure of the all-powerful Christ-God was transformed into the figure of the God-man, whose unjust mental and physical suffering at the hands of his persecutors called upon the witness to empathically suffer and grieve with him. The metaphysical struggle between good and evil receded, and the Passion of Christ became a direct address between God and humankind: Christ's suffering had a purpose—to lead the witness to God.

Between the tenth and the fifteenth centuries, the story of Christ was dramatized anew in meditation, liturgy, and *laude* in a manner that greatly intensified the emotional stakes of Christ's Passion for the devotee. Leaders of the new religious orders created prayers and primers that encouraged the meditant to imagine the scenes of Christ's human suffering as a prompt to emotional identification with that suffering, and thence to spiritual enlightenment. The *Meditations on the Life of Christ*, the most influential of these primers, dates from the early to mid-fourteenth century. It outlines in vivid and meticulous detail a mise-en-scène of pathos, sensationalized suffering, and lamentation. "With total absorption," the *Meditations* enjoins, "place yourself in their presence and observe carefully all the atrocities committed against your lord, as well as all that is said and done by him and through him" (Caulibus 2000, 252). At the scourging, "from all parts of his body the royal blood flows everywhere," and the thrashing only stops when both torturers and witnesses are exhausted (247). At the Crucifixion, "streams of his most sacred blood flow on all sides," and he "endures the sharpest pains, and he suffers anything that can be said or thought" (253–54), while the witnesses, most of all Mary Magdalene, are "shaken with sobs," their grief increased by each "outrage" (255).

These texts, and the religious practice they informed, influenced spheres of representational art and dramatic enactment in both northern and southern Europe to create a broad culture of affective piety. In the early Middle Ages, the function of art was to make the divine present in a particular place. Cultic legend ascribed to icons supernatural origins, the cultivation of visions, and miraculous powers (Belting 1994). In the Christianity of Pathos, the purpose of artistic representation or dramatic enactment changed. It was now designed to elicit an imaginative and sensory engagement with the suffering body of Christ as the path to emotional identification and spiritual enlightenment. As artistic practice began to take as its subject matter images of Christ's suffering on the Cross and Mary's Lamentation, it also began to develop the richly varied and expressive vocabulary of lifelike human representation that we associate with the Renaissance (Freedberg 1989), although what counts as lifelike is historically contingent and variable. For example, the northern tradition often represented a battered and bloodied Christ as opposed to the more refined, idealized body that is often found in the Italian tradition. It seems inconceivable that the development of lifelike representation and the Christianity of Pathos are causally unconnected: artists were prompted toward increasing lifelikeness to meet the needs of the devotional consumer. Hans Belting (1981) explains it this way: "The viewer tried to assimilate himself to the depicted person and demanded back from the latter the quality of aliveness which he himself possessed" (58). The image of Christ thus at once reflects and helps to bring into being a new sense of self: "In the conception of God as a crucified man, the viewer found the image of his own ideal; he found not a likeness of a triumphant God, but of a suffering God as a model," and "this was indicative of a new self-consciousness on the part of the individual, which was completely independent of social position and theological education" (147).

This new idea of the human being had more emotionally accessible and proximate representatives within pictures and dramas of the Passion in the figures of the Virgin Mary, the mother of Christ, and Mary Magdalene, who were privileged witnesses to Christ's suffering. In the Gospels, Mary is passive and stoic, and she witnesses the Passion only in the Gospel of John (19:25). However, from the tenth century on, the portrayal of Mary's maternal grief begins to assume center stage. Magdalene, too, emerges during this time as a composite figure of three Marys who, in addition to the Virgin, are mentioned in the Bible. In contrast to the Virgin Mary, who, given her divine purity as Christ's mother, could be understood as accepting his suffering, Magdalene was all too human, a reformed prostitute and a "penitent sinner," whose virtue was achieved through repentance rather than given (Jansen 2001). Her demonstrative displays of grief were a mark of her contrition and a model for all penitent sinners. The grief of both Magdalene and the Virgin Mary provided a vehicle through which the newly apprehended humanity of Christ was understood, and they became, to some extent, substitutable figures. The Virgin Mary, through allegorical interpretations of the *Song of Songs*, was also cast as Christ's beloved, whereas Magdelene's renunciation of her past life validated her underlying virtue or purity of heart. Individually and together, they at once served to model the witness's responses as a kind of spectator-in-the-text and became figures of empathic identification for the witness in their own right.

It is also during the Renaissance that the imagery of Christ's Passion is codified in lamentation scenes that display the grief-stricken reaction of the Marys and John the Apostle to the dead body of Christ, and in the aptly named "Pietà," a scene that portrays Christ as a prostrate figure lying in the lap of the Virgin Mary, at once man and child. In Italy, artists as early as Ciambue and Giotto (figure 2.1) developed a vocabulary of expressive gestures, drawing on both acts of everyday mourning and the codified gestures of classical sculpture, which heightened the shock and astonishment at Christ's suffering and death in order to prompt the audience to feel pathos (Barash 1976). We see these gestures and mises-en-scène taken up in the bronze reliefs of Donatello (figure 2.2; see Darr and Bonsanti 1986), the engravings of Andrea Mantegna (figure 2.3; see Martineau 1992), and in the extraordinary terracotta lamentation of Nicolo' dell'Arca (figure 2.6) that spawned a whole tradition of *compianti* or lamentation groups (see Klebanoff 2000). They are evident, too, in the northern tradition, in the limewood reliefs of Riemenschneider and his followers (figure 2.4; see Baxandall 1980). These works crystallize a mise-en-scène of pathos, of pity and despair, in response to unjust suffering. The willingness of Christ to tolerate and accept unjust suffering is an index of his purity of heart, his essential, divine virtue, which is recognized through the empathic response of the helpless onlookers whose suffering mirrors Christ's own and with whom the viewer is aligned.

Figure 2.1 Giotto di Bondone. *Lamentation* (1304–1306). Scrovegni Chapel, Padua. Courtesy of the Scrovegni Chapel, Padua.

Figure 2.2 Donatello. *Lamentation over the Dead Christ* (1455–1460). Victoria and Albert Museum, London. © Victoria and Albert Museum, London.

Figure 2.3 Andrea Mantegna. *Entombment* (1465–1470). National Gallery of Art, Washington, D.C. Courtesy of the National Gallery of Art, Washington, D.C.

FROM CHRIST'S PASSION TO MELODRAMA

I have argued that the Christianity of Pathos develops a melodramatic imaginary around the representation and narration of Christ's suffering. However, how can one plausibly derive, if only partially, a modern secular theatrical genre from the medieval religious imagination? The challenge is both conceptual and historical. The conceptual challenge lies in the objection that the nature of Christ's suffering and the pathos it elicits cannot provide a framework for demotic melodrama because Christ is divine and his omniscience undermines the meaning of his suffering. Within the world of melodrama virtue lies unacknowledged; knowing no self-interest, vanity, social machination, or pretense, it is inarticulate in its own defense and, perceiving only goodness, it is innocent of social injustice, to which it is therefore subject. However, the reader or spectator is given privileged insight into the forces of social injustice, personified as evil, that range against the innocent protagonist whose fate we therefore anxiously anticipate (Elsaesser 1987; Shepherd and Womack 1996). The story of Christ seems to preclude such (melo)dramatic irony, for Christ is an all-knowing figure whose aspiration is to die to save man from his sins.[3] He seems to orchestrate the events of which he is the protagonist rather than act as a victim of circumstances beyond his control. Furthermore, in the light of divine teleology, the struggle against injustice in this world pales in the face of the redemption that is promised in the next; evil is, in effect, overcome only in death, which is a happy ending only for those who believe. However, even if this theoretical objection can be overcome, it remains to be seen how, historically, the theological tradition of affective piety helps to inform and shape the secular tradition of melodrama.

To argue that Christ's divinity precludes a connection to melodrama misunderstands the central theological and rhetorical import of the Passion story as it is reconceived within affective piety where Christ is *both* man *and* God. The Christian formula "Son of God" separates the dramatic roles of Christ and God in a manner that creates our identification with Christ. In the Gospels, Christ is shown to have foreknowledge and acts upon it. The conceit of the Passion, however, is that Christ submits to God's will like a human being and suffers as fully as a human being suffers, indeed, infinitely more so because he is the perfectly sensitive man. The Passion story is narrated and experienced as if Christ is not in control of the events that he is subject to, otherwise his final dying words on the Cross would not make sense: "My God, My God why hast thou forsaken me" (Matthew 27:46). Like the witnesses at the foot of the Cross, we weep for Christ, the suffering man, and despair at his death until our wish that his fate might somehow be avoided is rewarded on Easter Sunday with his resurrection, when the mystery of God's plan to conquer death is revealed. Indeed, if we take the divine agency from Christ and place it all in the hands of God, God himself appears as the orchestrator of a grand melodrama in which Christ's suffering and persecution is calibrated in just the right way to elicit pathos and thereby to cement the admiration and allegiance of his human audience.

Melodrama is centrally concerned with social injustice, and it dramatizes that injustice through a rhetoric of muteness that invests "that which is seen and made visible with a moral power which far outweigh[s] that of words" (Moody 2000: 88). Christ is the victim of social injustice, is subject to abusive interrogation by the high priests and Herod, and is absolved by Pilate only to become the victim of mob rule. Already in the Gospels, Christ's rebuke to that injustice is registered through his silence. Matthew and Mark state that Christ "held his peace" in front of the high priests (Matthew 26:63; Mark 14:61), and Luke reports that Herod "questioned with him in many words; but he answered him nothing" (Luke 23:9). In the text of the *Meditations*, as Christ is taunted by his accusers, we are told that "he remained silent and mute" (Caulibus 2000: 248). Christ's silent rebuke to his accusers testifies more eloquently than words could say to the inherent innocence of the divine made flesh and provides an exemplar for the rebuke that in melodrama is meted out by innocence to injustice.

If we think of Christ wholly as a divine agent, he *chooses* martyrdom; however, if we think of him as the human victim of injustice, his martyrdom models the passive "martyrdom of virtue" that often defines the protagonist of melodrama.[4] Consider an early melodrama such as Pixérécourt's *The Dog of Montargis or The Forest of Bondy* from 1816 (Gerould 2002). The dumb, innocent, falsely accused Florio is sent to the gallows, framed by the villain for a murder he did not commit. His plight is staged in a manner that recalls the Passion of Christ; as he is led away, the heroine, Lucille, at once a mother figure to him and an innocent childhood sweetheart, cries like Mary as she looks upon his unjust suffering and faints as he draws near to the gallows. This kind of martyrdom is equally evident in *Uncle Tom's Cabin* (2005). The steadfast, stoic, forgiving Uncle Tom suffers intolerable abuse from his white persecutors. His death at the hands of Legree is explicitly analogized to Christ's own martyrdom. The martyrdom of virtue pervades Griffith's melodramas too. For example, when the heroine of *Way Down East* (1920) is cast adrift after the loss of her child, we are informed that she wears "upon her back the age-old cross" that is the stigma of the fallen woman, even as she remains pure of heart. Then, at the film's denouement, cast out again, she lies prostrate on the ice flow at the lip of the precipitous waterfall and is saved from her Calvary in the nick of time by the hero, David, who bears her to safety in his arms, figured as in a Pietà.

I have suggested how Christ's Passion is conceptually compatible with melodrama. The historical connection with melodrama is established when the divine story is retold within medieval theater. From the ninth century on, the church developed traditions of theatrical performance by the clergy that included Passion plays (Young 1933). However, alongside and growing out of these religious performances, a vernacular tradition emerged that flourished from the thirteenth to the sixteenth century. This theatrical tradition of Christ's Passion brings us much closer to melodrama because it is designed to entertain the broad, unlettered public in a way that works of art, commissioned by and large by wealthy patrons, were not. Vernacular theater "humanized" the drama of Christ's Passion with everyday language, foibles of character, and social conflicts that resonated with the populace at large. Above all, it reintroduced the Devil into the story of Christ's Passion, whose role had been marginalized by the Christianity of Pathos.

Virtually all writers on melodrama agree that the figure of the villain is central to melodrama. However, in Renaissance pictorial tradition, the role of the villain is less evident because the human story of Christ's Passion displaced the traditional emphasis upon God's triumph over the Devil at Calvary. The Devil is depicted only in those biblical situations in which he is explicitly invoked, such as the Temptation of Christ and the Last Judgment. However, in other scenes of Christ's torture, the ordinary evil of abusive men is indirectly linked to the agency of the Devil by making the torturers physically grotesque. These figures are especially present in the northern tradition and introduce a certain "carnivalesque" quality of mockery to the sensational scenes of Christ's suffering, as in the small *Crucifixion* woodcut by Riemenschneider's pupil Peter Dell the Elder (c.1528, figure 2.4). Yet they also occur in the southern tradition in the large-scale works of the Sacri Monti that

Figure 2.4 Peter Dell the Elder. *Crucifixion* (1528) (detail). Skulpturensammlung, Staatliche Museen zu Berlin. Courtesy of Skulpturensammlung und Museum für Byzantinische Kunst, SMB/Jörg P. Anders.

Figure 2.5 Tabacchetti and Giovanni d'Enrico. *Christ on the Road to Calvary* (1599–1600). Sacro Monte di Varallo, Italy. Courtesy of the author.

began construction in the sixteenth century (figure 2.5), in which scenes of the Passion are given "lifelike" realization in a manner that borrows from theatrical staging via the tradition of compianti or sculptural lamentation groups (Gentile 1989).

In the fourteenth- and early fifteenth-century mystery plays, which embed the Christianity of Pathos within the older metaphysical framework of God's struggle with the Devil, a villainous Devil and his minions assume a more central role. What is most salient from the standpoint of melodrama is the fact that, as John Cox (2000) has shown, the Devil is explicitly cast in class terms as a mendacious, scheming aristocratic figure who is aligned in attitude and deportment with the duplicitous Jewish elders and contrasted with the "landless peasant" Jesus and his followers. In other words, in the mystery plays, the story of Jesus became at once a metaphysical battle between good and evil and the expression of a struggle for social justice that directly addressed the concerns of the public for whom the plays were performed. The Christian story became an allegory of social injustice by casting the figure of the Jew, already a social outsider in feudal England, as someone who is allied to or even embodies the source of aristocratic feudal power and greed, aligned with the Devil. This helped to fuel virulent forms of anti-Semitism.

In melodrama, Moody (2000) writes, "the possession or loss of language often functions as a sign of evil or innocence respectively. Rhetorical skill and linguistic power tend to connote duplicity and deceit, a sophisticated tangle of words which—like the law—the poor and the wronged struggle to unravel" (88). The mystery plays provide a model of this, for Christ's silent virtue is dramatized as a weapon of the weak against the powerful, who wield language as a form of social domination. For example, in the *Wakefield Buffeting* (mid-fourteenth century), as David Bevington (2012) argues, Christ is provoked by two kinds of rhetorical assault. While Caiaphas rants and raves like a buffoon, the "smooth-tongued" Annas seeks to trick him into admitting that he is the son of God (537). Christ's response is to remain silent for the whole play, save for four lines; indeed, as Bevington notes, he actually speaks less in the play than the Gospel of John authorizes (John 18:20–23). Clearly the author is seeking to emphasize the rhetorical power of Christ's calm and silent presence as a rebuke to the profane verbal abuse that he endures.

Thus, as the Christianity of Pathos entered into the vernacular theatrical tradition, it rejoined older, but still popular ways of conceiving Christ's Passion in terms of the eternal struggle between God and the Devil. It is within this fusion of traditions that Christ's Passion begins to assume the ligaments of melodrama. In the mystery plays, a mise-en-scène of pathos combines with the personification of evil and the dramatization of social injustice, which together come to define the later, theatrical genre of melodrama. I am not, of course, claiming that the mystery plays are identical to modern melodrama, but rather that one can legitimately seek the origins of modern melodrama in them and discern a historical connection between modern melodrama and the Christianity of Pathos that goes beyond a common rhetoric of pathos.

WOMEN, EMOTION, AND EMPATHY

The role of the Virgin Mary and of Mary Magdelene as models for empathic identification are central to the Christianity of Pathos. Lines of lamentation spoken by Mary at the foot of the Cross are found in the liturgy as early as the ninth century, and soon thereafter the *Planctus Mariae*, a laud in which Mary laments Christ, was established as a separate devotional hymn performed on Good Friday. In its detailed evocation of Mary's distress at the suffering of her son, the *Planctus Mariae* provided an inspiration for devotional meditations that were often written for and sometimes by women (McNamer 2011). Furthermore, congruent with the drive to interpret the New Testament as a fulfillment of the Old, leading intellectuals of the new monastic orders, such as Bernard of Clairvaux, reinterpreted the passionate and erotic book of the Old Testament, *Song of Songs*, as a song of devotion of Mary to her Lord, recasting Mary as both a mother and a bride of Christ. This new devotional role allotted to Mary in texts of meditation provided scripts for nuns and monks to model their own devotion to Christ (Fulton 2002). They were often sung in a way that amplified their emotional resonance. Meanwhile, Mary Magdalene (from whom, it should be noted, the term "maudlin" is derived) also assumed central importance as a model of empathic identification (Jansen 2001). It is she who is the privileged witness at the tomb to whom the risen Christ appears as she copiously weeps, and she is invariably placed in the scenes of lamentation, anointing the feet of the dead Christ with her oils and her tears.

Sarah McNamer (2011) establishes the centrality of gender to the development of the Christianity of Pathos. Tradition conceives the development of Christian affective piety as a top-down process, doctrinally driven by the great male monastic leaders, but McNamer argues convincingly that it was a bottom-up process shaped by the demand of female meditants who wished to prove their devotion to Christ. Because the marriage of a nun to Christ was consummated only in heaven, how was she to prove herself worthy of his love? Only by cultivating what in medieval law was termed *maritalis affectio*—that is, by showing devotion to her loved one. Nuns proved their love by joining Christ empathically upon the Cross, and male writers wrote scripts that would enable them to fulfill their acts of devotional piety.

Patristic fathers of the early church, inheriting the Platonic suspicion of emotions as inimical to reason and self-control, associated women with emotion in the light of theories of the gendered body and denigrated women for their excessive displays of emotion, especially in mourning. For example, as early as the fourth century, John Chrysostom, Archbishop of Constantinople, fulminates against immoderate female mourning as a "disease of women," which denies the truth of the Resurrection and must be corrected by a masculine response that is both measured and philosophic (Lansing 2008:101). These views were sometimes echoed by secular authorities, who sought to control the behavior not only of women but also of men who needed to be trained not to fall into womanish ways. Although the Christianity of Pathos did not counter the underlying view that defined women by their emotions, it gave women credit for the very thing for which they were maligned. Passionate emotion was now something to be embraced.

McNamer (2011) plausibly argues that whether works of affective piety are created for man or woman, they invariably invite us to assume the impassioned, empathic gaze of a female devotional meditant. The connection between female devotee and male respondent is powerfully enacted in the emotive fifteenth-century lamentation group of Niccolò dell'Arca, which was commissioned by a confraternity of flagellants who practiced self-inflicted flagellation to experience Christ's suffering (figure 2.6). Here is an artwork in which the female witnesses model the response of emotional shock and astonishment at Christ's suffering and death, most probably in order to inflame a male audience to flail their bodies to the point of bloody exhaustion (Klebanoff 2000).

How might we understand the significance of the gendered practice of affective piety for nineteenth- and twentieth-century melodrama? In the nineteenth century a social ethics, led by women, emerged out of affective piety that was manifest in, among other areas, the cause of emancipating African American slaves. As Jane Tompkins (1985) and Ann Kaplan (1987, 1992) have argued, in Harriet Beecher Stowe's *Uncle Tom's Cabin*, the figure of the woman as mother, in her capacity for empathic understanding and practical wisdom, is a source of moral superiority in an unfeeling world of men that reduces human beings to commodities. Stowe creates sympathy for the cause of black emancipation by casting her central protagonist, Uncle Tom, as a Christ-like figure of humble, selfless virtue who submits to every injustice and ultimately death itself through an unshaken conviction in God's will and purpose. Our tears for Tom (that is the tears of the "white race"),

Figure 2.6 Niccolò' dell'Arca. *Lamentation over the Dead Christ* (1463). Church of Santa Maria della Vita, Bologna. Courtesy of the author.

modeled upon Mother Mary's tears at the foot of the Cross, are designed to lead us to contrition and repentance so that just as "we" come to recognize our responsibility for Christ's death through our sin, and are inspired to do good in Christ's name, so "we," who are responsible for Uncle Tom's death and, by extension, the institution of slavery itself, will seek to abolish it in the name of establishing God's Kingdom on Earth.

I have focused, thus far, on Christ's suffering as a template for melodrama, with the female spectator as witness. However, given the ennoblement of the Marys within the Catholic tradition, their story becomes as important for the Christianity of Pathos as the story of Christ. The Passion of Christ is also the passion of Mary, weeping for her son/lover at the foot of the Cross, who undergoes intolerable separation and loss and pays what is, for a mother, the ultimate sacrifice. In the Catholic tradition, Mary is the object of pathos as much as its subject. Similarly, Mary Magdalene becomes the center of her own story as the reformed prostitute whose perfumes are transformed into the oils with which she anoints Christ. The Magdalene embodies the paradox of the virginal "prostitute," the unchaste woman who remains pure. Her sexual love is sublimated into a spiritual love that is expressed in her copious tears, and as Katherine Jansen (2001) has shown, so total is the Magdalene's penitence that she actually becomes identified in both her underlying virtue and her love of Christ with the figure of Mary herself.

The story of this composite Mary becomes the model for the "fallen woman" melodrama, where due to circumstances beyond her control or simply by following her desire, a woman of essential virtue has sex out of wedlock and conceives. In an "old-fashioned" melodrama such as *Way Down East*, she is tricked and ensnared into sex because she is naïve. In a more modern melodrama such as Raphael Matarazzo's *Nobody's Children* (1951), the heroine gives in to spontaneously passionate desire. Either way, through no essential fault of her own, she is cast as a woman who, though pure of heart, has fallen from virtue. She gives birth to a child from whom she is often destined to be separated. The child might die, as in *Way Down East*, or be taken from her, as in *Nobody's Children*. Either way she suffers the grief of Mary and the "martyrdom of virtue." Her rebirth takes different forms. In Matarazzo's Catholic melodramas, the heroine is led to renounce the world and assume the nun's habit. But she is also, commonly, "rescued" by the love of a good man, as in *Way Down East* in which, having been punished for and cleansed of her putative sin by immersion in icy torrents, she is metaphorically taken down from her cross and reborn in the arms of the hero (Williams 2001).

Medieval affective piety, as we have seen, accords a normative role for both men and women to women's emotions as the conduit toward empathic understanding. This might lead us to question the assumed alignment between melodrama and gender in modern spectatorship. Pam Cook (2012) has argued that there is no reason to assume in theory that identification in the cinema must be gender bound (the audience, here, has more imagination than the film theorist!), and there is no evidence to support the idea that only women watched "weepies," even if the majority of the audience were women. Following Christine Gledhill, Linda Williams (2001) has suggested that far from being adequately viewed as simply a woman's genre—a domain of emotional excess that is marginal to the normative framework of Hollywood realism—melodrama must be understood as the default mode of Hollywood cinema.[5] We might conclude from this argument simply that Hollywood melodrama, thus liberated from the "ghetto" of the woman's film, is not gender bound. Or, we might instead note the universalization of women's experience of feeling in affective piety and emphasize the extent to which Hollywood film has successfully modeled for everyone structures of feeling and empathic response traditionally associated with women. Rather than contributing simply to the reproduction of gender ideologies, as in the orthodox view, Hollywood cinema, indirectly drawing upon the tradition I have described, may well also have contributed, in the twentieth century, to their transformation.

I have argued that we must rethink the relationship between melodrama and religion as it has been conceived by Peter Brooks and passed down into melodrama studies. Brooks's account is predicated on an oversimplified understanding of the relationship between the traditional Sacred and the secular. It ignores the way the traditional Sacred had already been displaced by an idea of selfhood that emerged within the framework of the Christianity of Pathos. Secular melodrama rediscovers rather than invents the relationship between a mise-en-scène of unjust suffering and emotional empathy that was earlier constituted within the Christianity of Pathos, while having analogues in other traditions of affective piety (Bhaskar, see chapter 15). As a result, a theologically informed understanding of good and evil lies much closer to the surface of melodrama than Brooks's conception of a moral occult allows: it is readily deployed and readily understood. I have suggested, further, that the historical form in which the Christianity of Pathos first directly engages with the social function of melodrama is the mystery play, the first secular form of the Passion play. The Christianity of Pathos gives a normative role to the experience of women in their capacity for empathy, and I hope my argument will contribute to renewed discussion of the relationship between women and melodrama. Finally, I hope that this essay will support greater attention in melodrama studies to those contexts, whether Catholic or Protestant, Sufi, or Hindu, in which melodrama readily appears as the shadow cast by affective piety upon secular dramaturgy.

NOTES

I am indebted to Christine Gledhill on melodrama, Isabelle Frank on art history, and Ira Bhaskar on the rich tradition of affective piety in Indian cinema. Thanks also to Liz Helfgott, Peter Nelson, and Linda Williams.

1. On the influence of Laila-Majnun on the Turkish "Arabesk" tradition of melodrama, see Dadek (2015).
2. Mel Gibson's melodrama of affective piety, *The Passion of the Christ* (2004), is Catholic-inspired but appealed equally to Protestants. See Stevenson (2013, 3).
3. This objection was suggested to me by Linda Williams.
4. Williams (2001) shows how the protagonists of melodramas such as *Uncle Tom's Cabin* and *Way Down East* go beyond a passive stance and assume agency against social injustice, but this does not gainsay the central role played in these melodramas by silent rebuke and the "martyrdom of virtue."
5. Williams (2001) argues that this conception of Hollywood film as melodrama challenges the idea of classical Hollywood cinema as it has been conceived by David Bordwell and Kristin Thompson. However, the relationship between melodrama and classical cinema does not have to be an either-or proposition. It can be a both-and proposition if the claims are made at different explanatory levels.

3

Boucicault in Bombay

Global Theater Circuits and Domestic Melodrama in the Parsi Theater

KATHRYN HANSEN

In 1887, the *Times of India* welcomed a new production to the Gaiety Theatre in Bombay, "a Parsee adaptation of Boucicault's COLLEEN BAWN." *Bholi Jan* (*Innocent Belle*), the Gujarati version of *The Colleen Bawn*, was greeted enthusiastically (*Times of India*, February 12 and 19, 1887). *Bawn* had long been a hit in India, but the site was now the "native stage," the Indian-language sphere of hybrid theatrical practices and large commercial companies. With this crossover, Boucicault's work was recast. Transformed into Parsi theater, *Bawn* ushered in a different kind of cultural production, which was to have a long afterlife in South Asian popular culture.

In the nineteenth century, dozens of melodramas—the same titles popular in England—were carried to India and performed in colonial playhouses. Texts, impresarios, actors, musicians, and scenarists crossed the seas, popularizing the latest genres and styles. Certain dramas were adapted for production in Indian languages, much as Shakespeare's works were. The majority belonged to the category of domestic melodrama. This genre, which arose in England in the 1820s, embraced an enormous body of literature concerned with family, gender, class, and racial matters (Williams 2012, 200). Most frequently performed in colonial India were the domestic melodramas of Dion Boucicault, Augustin Daly, Edward Bulwer-Lytton, and adaptations of Ellen Wood's *East Lynne*.

The circulation of melodrama around the world occurred amidst a plethora of political, technological, and artistic developments. In this chapter, I focus on domestic melodrama's adaptation to Indian theatrical practice through the case of *The Colleen Bawn*, one of Dion Boucicault's most successful creations. I trace the play's entrance into India via one particular global theatrical circuit, the Lewis Dramatic Troupe, established by George B. W. Lewis and directed by his wife, née Rose Edouin. Perhaps surprisingly, this circuit originated in Australia, moving north and west from there to China, Southeast Asia, and India.

British theatrical families who had relocated to Australia comprised some of the most robust troupes of the period, but to the story of Indian theater the Lewis Dramatic Troupe was of particular importance. Mimi Cooligan's 2013 monograph on the Lewises and Desley Deacon's work (2008) on Australasian theatrical circuits allow their tours of India to be mapped. To these sources, I add my store of advertisements, notices, and reviews culled from historical South Asian newspapers.

BOUCICAULT AND THE COMING OF SENSATION DRAMA

During Queen Victoria's long reign, theatrical production attained unprecedented levels of popularity. Dion Boucicault (1820–1890) was the period's most prolific and celebrated playwright, as well as being a successful actor, director, manager, and producer (figure 3.1). He composed *The Colleen Bawn* in 1860 at a turning point in his career. Although born and raised in Ireland, Boucicault had not tackled Irish subjects before, and this was the first of his celebrated "Irish dramas" (Cullingford 1997, 290). Boucicault himself termed the play a "sensation drama," gesturing to the violent attempt to drown the heroine and to her heroic (and secret) rescue.

Boucicault flourished within a global circuit, the transatlantic network connecting the Anglophone world through a common language and entertainment economy. He wrote *Bawn* while living in New York, and together with his wife, Agnes Robertson, he first starred in it there. The drama played to full houses for six weeks before traveling to England. In London at the Adelphi Theatre, it became the longest running show to date. Queen Victoria saw *The Colleen Bawn* at least three times. Next the play moved to Dublin, where it was ecstatically received as a long-awaited national drama of Ireland (McFeely 2012, 28). It became the inspiration for the opera *The Lily of Killarney* and several films and continues to be performed today.

The Colleen Bawn combined a crime plot with class conflict, romantic intrigue, ethnic humor, and a picturesque setting. It was based on the 1829 novel, *The Collegians*, by Gerald Griffin, which was itself based on the factual murder of a young woman near Limerick, Ireland. Poverty-stricken Eily O'Connor, the "colleen bawn" (the fair-haired girl of the title), is secretly married to Hardress Cregan, a man of property. The couple conceal their union to avoid his widowed mother's disapproval. Hardress's servant Danny, realizing Hardress half regrets his impulsive marriage, decides to eliminate Eily so his master can make a better match with Anne Chute, an heiress and the "colleen ruaidh" (redhead). Danny lures Eily into a boat, then throws her into the water. Danny is immediately felled by a gun blast from the shore, fired by Eily's rejected lover Myles-na-Coppaleen, who was in pursuit of an otter. Eily is assumed dead but is rescued from the water and secreted away by Myles. Eventually the married couple is reunited and the Hardress family fortune restored.

Interwoven with these events, a mortgage plot links two sets of characters. Hardress's widowed mother is beset by a mortgage debt held by a conniving attorney, Corrigan, who pressures her to marry him in return for its cancellation. To retain the family property, she wants Hardress to marry Anne, who is in love with Kyrle

Figure 3.1 Dion Boucicault (1820–1890). Sarony (photographer), n. d. TCS 1.3259, Harvard Theatre Collection.

Daly, her cousin. These characters are landed gentry or bourgeoisie, Anglophile and sophisticated; Hardress and Kyrle are college-educated. As members of the Anglo-Irish ruling class, this grouping represents the British colonial presence and long history of domination of Ireland (Cullingford 1997, 291).

The second set, centered on Eily, are marked as Irish: Father Tom, a priest; Danny, Hardress's servant; Sheelah, Danny's mother; and Myles-na-Coppaleen, a horse-thief. They are of the peasantry or lower class, simple and old-fashioned. Living in a lakeshore cottage, Eily is a border figure, unsophisticated and pure at heart, yet striving to become a suitable wife for Hardress by dropping her brogue, avoiding Irish songs, and improving her domestic habits. Danny, too, hovers in between. Raised with Hardress and accidentally maimed by him in childhood, Danny has internalized the values of his master and his class. A third group represent law and order: a magistrate, a corporal, and six soldiers. They appear in the finale to investigate the murders and bring about justice.

Conventions of melodrama—formulaic plot structures and recurring themes—pervade *Bawn* (Howes 2011, 84–85). The action is driven by deception, disguise, conspiracies, schemes, and misunderstandings, with coincidence prevailing. Only in the reconciliation scene are true relationships unveiled and secrets revealed. Binary oppositions dominate the moral and social landscape: good versus evil, rich versus poor, town versus country, Irishness versus Englishness. The struggle between these dualities is given shape through the expression of heightened emotions, especially by ordinary people (McWilliam 2000, 59).

THE LEWISES: AUSTRALIAN AGENTS OF CHANGE

Full-length performances of *Bawn* in India began in the late 1860s with Lewis's Dramatic and Burlesque Company. George B. W. Lewis (1818–1906) and his wife Rose (1844–1925) introduced Victorian popular drama to China, Southeast Asia, India, and Ceylon. Their theatrical tours originated in the port city of Melbourne. During the gold rush of the 1850s, Australia became the entertainment metropole for the Pacific and Indian Ocean region, its economy largely independent of London (Deacon 2008, 81.6–81.7). The Lewises and other family groups became agents of cultural change throughout the Asia-Pacific area.

George Lewis and Rose Edouin (figure 3.2) were economic migrants, drawn to Australia to better their lot. Both had been child entertainers in London, from poor families that put their offspring to work. George Lewis arrived in Australia in 1853 and joined the circus, touring the goldfields (Colligan 2013, 15). Rose emigrated with her parents and five siblings in 1857 when she was thirteen. Within a month the children were dancing in the Theatre Royal in Melbourne. The Edouins toured the gold rush towns in a horse-drawn van with "The Celebrated Edouins" painted on its side. Quite independently, George Lewis presented hippodramas in the same locale, extravagant shows featuring horsemanship combined with popular melodrama. The motives that led Lewis to Australia—the search for new markets and greater earnings—propelled him

Figure 3.2 Mrs. G. B. W. Lewis, née Rose Edouin. Photograph album of Australian actors and actresses (c. 1870–1900). Gordon Ireland (compiler). State Library of Victoria, Melbourne, Australia.

toward China and then India. In 1860, the year that *Bawn* opened in New York, Lewis first visited Calcutta, performing equestrian acts. Four years later, he took his theater company back to China. Regular tours to India began in 1867, with the Lewis company residing for long periods in Calcutta. A bold visionary, Lewis established the Lyceum Theatre on the Maidan and later the Theatre Royal on Chowringhee Road in the heart of the city.

Rose Edouin was similarly ambitious. With only a year's schooling, she made her stage debut at age six. By eleven she gained notice as Puck in *Midsummer Night's Dream* (Colligan 2013, 22). A precocious actress, she was drawn to Lewis's Australian company for more mature roles and wider exposure. Rose and George became romantically involved, and the couple married in Shanghai in 1864. After several seasons in Calcutta with summer tours across northern India, Lewis's company ventured to Bombay in 1872. They played at the Grant Road Theatre, and Boucicault's melodramas figured prominently. The artistry and leadership of Rose, the company's "directress," were essential to their success (figure 3.2). She was the life-blood of the company, especially of *The Colleen Bawn*.

Through its strength in numbers, Lewis's company could handle the large casts and staging complexities of domestic melodrama. The 1867 tour to Calcutta included twenty-one artists from Melbourne (Colligan 2013, 84). The souvenir program for Sheridan's *School for Scandal* in 1869 listed twelve male and five female roles. During the 1872 tour to Bombay, the company—like British theaters—advertised its scene painter, here Maurice Freyberger, alongside the mechanist, properties manager, and musicians. Freyberger is known to have designed the sensation scenes for Boucicault's melodramas in India (Mehta 1960, 176). These may have imitated the paintings of scenes from *Bawn* by Egron Lundgren (figure 3.3).

Actors on tour had to withstand many challenges. Rose acted, sang, and danced night after night, switching repertoire every two shows. She was constantly pregnant and giving birth, though most of her children died young. The climate and environs in India posed additional hazards. After grueling winter runs in Calcutta and Bombay, the troupe undertook difficult travels during the hot season. They covered thousands of miles by train, performing across the plains and in hill stations. On one trip, Rose's brother Charles died of heat exhaustion. Willie Gill, a company member, described the incident:

> We started from Calcutta March 28th [1869] and since then have played at Jamulpore, Dinapore, Benares, Allahabad, Cawnpore, Lucknow and Agra . . . traversing altogether a distance of 1,700 miles. . . . We play a week in each place and give twelve pieces during it. . . . One of our members was lost while traveling between Cawnpore and Simla—poor Charles Edouin! He died in a railway carriage at 7pm on the night of 9th May last. He had no illness to speak of, though for a few days he had been complaining of the heat. Apoplexy was the cause of his death. . . . Our carriage was shunted off at a station called Etawate, and next morning he was buried. (Gänzl 2002, 45–46)

The family system provided support through these vicissitudes, and it helped actresses like Rose maintain respectability. "Mrs. Lewis," a title that signaled her status and domesticity, was a versatile performer. The company's repertoire included seven Boucicault plays in which Rose starred: *Octoroon, Colleen Bawn, Arrah-na-Pogue, London Assurance, Rip Van Winkle, The Shaughraun,* and *Led Astray*.

Figure 3.3 Painting by Egron Sellif Lundgren (1815–1875) of sensation scene (Act II, scene 6) from *The Colleen Bawn*, showing Eily attacked by Danny Mann. Courtesy Royal Collection Trust. © HM Queen Elizabeth II, 2016.

She excelled at strong female roles (*East Lynne, Colleen Bawn*), male roles (*Hamlet, Romeo and Juliet*), and ethnic others (*Leah the Forsaken, Octoroon*). Rose's star caliber and directorial expertise enabled British melodrama to flourish in India.

RECEPTION BY THE PUBLIC IN INDIA

The Lewises dedicated nine years to their India tours. They introduced *Bawn* to Simla in 1869 and Calcutta in 1871 (Gänzl 2002, 49; Colligan 2013, 103). The tour to Bombay in 1872 brought *Bawn* to wide notice—and into the orbit of Parsi theater. They carefully constructed their run to build a wave of excitement. The Irish-themed *Bawn* was preceded by a night of Irish comedy, followed by three nights of Boucicault's *Octoroon*. Finally: "Mr. Lewis has much pleasure to announce the truly characteristic SENSATIONAL 'IRISH' DOMESTIC DRAMA, THE COLLEEN BAWN, OR THE BRIDES OF GARRYOWEN" (*Times of India*, September 7, 1872).

The drama and the entire tour were well-received. The company returned, reprising *Bawn* in 1876. After the Lewises' departure, the drama was frequently performed. The Norvilles presented it at the Grant Road Theatre in 1879 (*Times of India*, May 6, 1879). Following the opening of the Gaiety Theatre, *Bawn* often played there (*Times of India*, February 5, 7, and 11, 1881; November 28 and 30, 1882; December 21, 1885; June 1, 1886; November 30, 1891). The operatic version, for which Boucicault cowrote the libretto, enjoyed a successful Bombay season under Madame Tasca (*Times of India*, January 28, 1878).

Through these iterations, *Bawn*'s scenes and tunes stayed alive among audiences. Who made up these audiences? Traveling companies such as Lewis's sought the patronage of British officials, civilian and military. They gravitated toward urban centers where administrators and the army concentrated. Outposts near railway junctions or garrison headquarters also attracted them. Jamalpore (Jamalpur) in Bihar was connected by rail to Calcutta and Delhi, and nearby Munger Fort housed a regiment. Rose's second child, Lucy May Lewis, was buried there in 1868, attesting to a visit from the company. The audience in such out-stations comprised colonial officials and subordinates, army brass and rank-and-file, and local Indian viewers.

The most prestigious shows were graced by rulers and royalty. A playbill for Lewis's Lyceum Theatre from 1869 celebrates the presence of the Earl of Mayo, Viceroy of India. Indian nobles often accompanied Raj dignitaries to the theater. On opening night in 1871, the house was again graced by Lord Mayo, with two grandsons of Tipu Sultan and various native princes (Colligan 2013, 97). Alongside these elite patrons, most playgoers were ordinary two-rupee ticket-holders. British soldiers formed a significant constituency. Lewis's company offered them military-themed fare: Boucicault's *Jessie Brown, or the Siege of Lucknow* and Tom Taylor's *Up at the Hills* (Colligan 2013, 92–93).

Middle-class Indians indubitably came to see Lewis's company. Among the curious was Girish Chandra Ghosh, legendary Bengali dramatist. Ghosh (1844–1912) managed several professional companies and authored eighty plays. Mrs. Lewis became his friend and mentor. Attending Lewis productions enabled Ghosh to absorb the conventions, dramaturgy, and staging techniques of Western-style professional theater (Chatterjee 2007, 134). The audience for the Lewises in Bombay included three groups of Indians: Parsis, Hindus, and Bhatias (merchants). Parsi women and girls attended a benefit for Mrs. Lewis (*Times of India*, September 24, 1875). Of the Indian admirers who contributed to the Lewises' success, some retained impressions and memories, tastes and habits, that soon found a hospitable home in the Parsi theater.

PLAYHOUSE PIONEERS: KABRAJI AND BALIVALA

Parsi theater originated in the 1850s with educated young men who were drama buffs. Parsis are Zoroastrians, a community long acclimatized to India; they migrated from Iran around 900 CE. Many Parsis moved from rural Gujarat to Bombay in the eighteenth century, seeking fortunes as bankers and traders. Social ties with colonial elites led to exposure to the theater, and soon Parsis organized their own dramatic productions (Hansen 2011, 3–25). Parsi theater was not defined by language, region, or ethnicity. Many companies operated under Parsi management, yet actors, writers, musicians, and painters were Muslims, Hindus, and Jews. Parsi theater made an impact through its wide circulation. Traveling troupes put on plays across the subcontinent, molding local theater forms wherever they went. Parsi theater also ushered in India's early cinema, with genres and stylization that had pan-Indian appeal. In 1872, when the Lewises brought *Bawn* to Bombay, Parsi theater was expanding as its early phase of amateurism yielded to professional companies. Foremost was the Victoria Theatrical Company, established by K. N. Kabra (honorific, Kabraji) in 1868. The legendary K. M. Balivala, who debuted as an actor in 1871, became the Victoria's long-reigning director in 1878. These two pioneers were the masterminds behind importation of *The Colleen Bawn* into Parsi theater.

Kabraji (1842–1904) was a prominent social reformer and journalist as well as a theater innovator. Born into humble circumstances, he was educated on scholarship but left school early to work (*Times of India*, March 26, 1891, April 26, 1904). From 1861 to 1902 he edited *Rast Goftar*, the reform-oriented newspaper founded by Dadabhai Naoroji (Palsetia 2001, 193). He also held the editorship of *Stree Bodhe (Stribodh)*, one of the first magazines directed toward women readers (Shukla 1991, WS-64). He studied classical music and founded the Gayan Uttejak Mandali, an association for music promotion and education among Bombay's middle class, including Parsi women (Rosse 1995, 64–95). In later years, he was active in public life, serving on the board of the Bombay Corporation, as justice of the peace, and as a fellow of Bombay University. Kabra wrote some of the first plays performed by the Victoria Theatrical Company. These included a trilogy about ancient Iran based on Firdausi's epic, the *Shahnama*. Later, he established another drama company, Natak Uttejak Mandali, for which he adapted Hindu mythological tales such as *Harishchandra*. Of his dozen published plays, three besides *Bholi Jan* were based on English works.

K. M. Balivala (1853–1913) also grew up in modest surroundings. He entered the printing trade as a compositor and then became an actor (Gupt 2005, 116). He was expert in both female and male roles and proficient in Gujarati as well as Urdu. He steered the Victoria company for thirty-five years, maintaining its stature in the Parsi theater world until his death. Known for his courageous actions, Balivala admitted actresses to his company before others were willing to do so. He toured with the large ensemble up and down the subcontinent and then voyaged to Singapore, Burma, and Ceylon. His trip to London, England, earned Balivala notice in *The Tatler* and *The Sketch* (Yajnik 1934, 220–21).

The positive reception accorded *Bholi Jan*, the Indian avatar of *Bawn*, grew from Balivala and Kabra's artistic collaboration. Kabra was at the height of his dramaturgical powers and had already adapted several Victorian tales into successful dramas. For Kabra, the Queen's Golden Jubilee celebrations held in 1887 increased the project's appeal. His Gujarati version of "God Save the Queen" was well-known. At *Bholi Jan's* debut, it was sung before the curtain rose (Rosse 1995, 78). One of *Bholi Jan*'s main protagonists, Hijo, was played and sung by Balivala, and he surely influenced the construction of his star vehicle. As artistic director, he made casting decisions, directed music, lighting, and other aspects of stagecraft, and supervised publicity and relations with dignitaries. Balivala may have aided Maurice Freyberger in designing the panoramic set of the river spanned by Hope Bridge as well as the interior scenes, the rustic hut of Dhan (the Colleen), and the opulent salon of the Bakhtiarjis (the Hardress family).

METAMORPHOSIS OF MELODRAMA

Bholi Jan closely follows Boucicault's *Bawn* in dramatic structure and cast of characters. Both plays consist of three acts with the same number of scenes in each. The characters and their relationships are comparable. Even the sobriquets, *bawn* and *jan*, rhyme with each other in Parsi-inflected Gujarati. *Bholi* was variously spelled *bholee, bholie*, or *bhollee*, resembling *colleen*.

Bhollee Jan	*The Colleen Bawn*
Dhan, the heroine	Eily O'Connor
Jahangir, Dhan's husband	Hardress Cregan
Baiai, Dhan's mother-in-law	Mrs. Cregan
Edal, a moneylender	Mr. Corrigan
Bhuliyo, a boatman	Danny Mann
Shirin, Jahangir's cousin	Anne Chute
Hijo, Dhan's cousin	Myles-na-Coppaleen
Bahman, Shirin's cousin	Kyrle Daly
Tehmuldaru, a Parsi priest	Father Tom
Jeevi, Bhuliyo's mother	Sheelah

Boucicault reworked the theme of culture wars between urban and rural society by depicting premodern Ireland as the heartland. He wrote into his play nostalgia for the countryside and the good humor of simple folk, interpolating spectacular scenic effects, extensive passages in dialect, and songs based on Irish ballads. He invented the comic figure of Myles-na-Coppaleen ("of the ponies"), who carried the day as the clever, courageous Irishman. A goodly part of the play's power lay in its pastoral vision, its evocation of "a past that was not really the past" (Daly 2007, 5).

In *Bholi Jan*, the location shifted to Surat in Gujarat, a port city on the banks of the Tapti (or Tapi) River. For Bombay audiences, particularly Parsis, many of whom hailed from the region, Surat conjured sentiments of yearning and nostalgia. The setting was a useful cognate for Boucicault's Irish landscape and appropriate to showcase virtues of simplicity and purity. A further division within the play set the city of Surat against the rural districts surrounding it. The river became a pictorial point of reference within the frame of the proscenium stage. It effectively divided the landscape: the Bakhtiarji family mansion (*haveli*), emblem of wealth and urban decadence, towered on one side, and Dhan's humble hut in the sand stood on the other. Kabra further worked in the element of regionalism by styling Dhan as *noshakari*—a resident of Navsari to the south of Surat—and Edal (the moneylender) as *ankalesariya* and *bharuchi*, a man from Ankleshwar in Bharuch (Broach) to the north.

Even as he constructed a folkloric past through brushstrokes of village speech and manners, Kabra inserted signs of modernity. The painted backdrop featured

Hope Bridge with its imposing steel girders. The historical original was erected by the British across the Tapti in 1877. Its citation by Kabra and Balivala was a remarkable addition, echoing the geographical imagination of Boucicault's theater that utilized stage technologies to highlight modern communication and transportation systems (Howes 2011, 96). That the Surat area was under colonial governance also emerges through back stories invented by Kabra. Tehmuldaru is a Parsi priest (*mobed*) who once made a living selling toddy. The Abkari Act, an unpopular measure passed in 1878 to regulate and tax liquor sales, ruined him. The character Bahman (Kyrle Daly) goes to England for education and finds employment as an army surgeon, reentering the family as Shirin's (Anne Chute's) prospective husband.

Boucicault's *Bawn* focused on two abiding concerns: the plight of the innocent heroine and the dilemma of a lost family fortune. Although preservation of the virtuous Eily is at the play's center, class and gender create a broad canvas for the heroine's distress. The mortgage melodrama, as a narrative type, highlights threatened dispossession, leading to the struggle for recovery of lost or estranged property, but the notion of mortgage regularly extends beyond the economic to the sexual and personal. Ancestral lands may have been alienated but so may be the heart's affections. The restoration of the protagonist's ownership—of a marriage partner as much as an estate—becomes the driving motive (Howes 2011, 86). Thus *Bawn*'s ending entails a double recognition—of Eily as Hardress's lawful wife and of Corrigan as a false claimant and wrongdoer.

In Kabra's adaptation, the economic dislocations of colonial modernity are acutely felt by the Bakhtiarji family. Its indebtedness is attributed to the deceased patriarch's "improper expenditure" (*khoto kharcho*). Although the play does not detail the vices usual to melodrama such as gambling, drinking, and keeping company with courtesans, this phrase suggests such conduct. As in *Bawn*, the focus is on the expiation by the children, not on the sins of the father. Both Jahangir and Dhan struggle to uphold ideals of their time, echoing agendas of social and moral reform. Although Jahangir keeps his marriage secret from his mother, he insists to her that love (*pyar, mohabat*) be the precondition for matrimony, not only on his side but on his future bride's. The priority he places on individual desire brings him into conflict with his mother when he rejects her proposal that he marry Shirin to restore the family's fortunes.

Dhan meanwhile strives to become a reformed woman (*sudhareli*) by learning to read, write, sew, and sing—domestic accomplishments required in bourgeois companionate marriage. These goals are soon overshadowed by the acts of self-sacrifice demanded of her. It is her "wealth" (*dhan*) that saves the family, not in the form of dowry as imagined by her mother-in-law but the wealth of chaste service to the husband—*pativratya*—the patriarchal gender ideology enjoined upon devoted wives.

Bholi Jan necessarily offered its audience a musical experience quite distinct from its English antecedent. Kabra included ten songs: *ghazals*, *thumris*, *garbis*, and *lavanis*. Although they are indicated to be sung to specific ragas (Khamach, Desh, and so forth), this does not preclude possible folk origins or a folk tenor, paralleling the Irish ballads in *Bawn*. It is not known whether live music was performed during the dialogue portions of *Bholi Jan*. However, musical underscoring played a large part in creating atmosphere in Boucicault's plays. Handbills for *The Colleen Bawn* specify fourteen Irish melodies by name; most were worked into the orchestral score rather than sung (Pisani 2014,187–88).

Dance, too, undergoes cultural translation. In *Bawn*, the final scene is set in a ballroom. When the curtain rises, the guests are dancing in male-female pairs. In Kabra's text, the guests are seated watching professional female dancers in the manner of a nautch. The dancers sing an Urdu ghazal, "There's no escape from the prison of my love's coiled locks" (*Zulf-e pur pech men dil aisa giraftar hua, chhutna dushvar hua*) (Kabraji 1888, 73).

In *Bawn*'s famous sensation scene (Act 2, Scene 6), Myles dives headfirst into the waters to save Eily. Boucicault positioned this action within an elaborate set: "A Cave; through large opening at back is seen the Lake and moon; rocks—flat rock; gauze waters all over stage; rope hanging. Enter MYLES singing, top of rock" (Boucicault 1987, 229). The moonlit tableau of Myles supporting Eily, her red cloak trailing in the water, appeared again and again in print art, as on the cover of sheet music for Browne's "Galop" (figure 3.4).

The corresponding scene in *Bholi Jan* is closely patterned on Boucicault. Bhuliyo/Danny throws Dhan/Eily into the river and tries to drown her. Hijo/Myles fires a shot at Bhuliyo/Danny. Then Hijo/Myles discovers Dhan/Eily.

Bholi Jan

Hijo: Oh! Oh! Who's that? That clothing belongs to Dhan! Oh Dhan, my Dhan, my dear sister Dhan! How did you get here? I'm coming to save you.

(Dives headfirst from the island into the river. He is seen swimming. He bobs up and down. Taking Dhan in one hand, he swims toward the island. He catches onto the shore with one hand, while in the other he holds Dhan to his chest; she is in a dishevelled condition. The curtain falls.) (Kabraji 1888, 55)

The Colleen Bawn

Myles: What's this? It's a woman—there's something white there. (Figure rises near rock—kneels down; tries to take the hand of figure.) Ah! that dress; it's Eily. My own darlin' Eily. (Pulls off waistcoat—jumps off rock. Eily rises—then Myles and Eily rise up—he turns, and seizes rock—Eily across left arm.)
End of Act Two (Boucicault 1987, 230–31)

Subtle cultural cues distinguish the Gujarati and English versions. In Kabra, Dhan is Hijo's "dear sister," whereas in Boucicault she is his "own darling." Kabra replaces Myle's otter with a human thief as Hijo's target. The main difference is that Kabra elongates Act 2, Scene 5—a brief soliloquy by Myles—to two and half pages and extends Act 2, Scene 6—the sensational drowning scene—with dialogue. Building a mood of foreboding, he adds thunder and lightning effects throughout. Dhan's apprehension grows; she expresses fear of crossing

Figure 3.4 Cover illustration of sheet music, "The Colleen Bawn Galop" (1861). T. Browne (composer), T. Packer (artist). Courtesy Calthrop Boucicault Collection, Special Collections and Archives, University of Kent, UK.

the river in a storm. The atmosphere is eerier and the sequence leading to her murder more suspenseful.

Fear haunts Eily too: the rock in the lake reminds her of a tomb. Yet the underwater cave, although foreshadowing death, saves Eily's life. Kabra translates Boucicault's mix of moods—the threat of death in a pastoral setting—into Indian terms. Stormy weather is a trigger for romantic love in Indian poetry. In painting, lovers often venture forth amidst a torrential downpour. Fording a river is another Indian trope; it may symbolize death or spiritual release. Kabra, exchanging the lake for a river and turning a full-moon night into a dark and stormy one, preserves the juxtaposition between barely repressed sexuality and full-blown dread that afforded Boucicault's scene its heightened measure of "sensation." The conjunction of erotic tension with danger and distress, concentrated in the heroine, was successfully transcreated.

SCRIPTS IN CIRCULATION

Bholi Jan is by no means a word-for-word translation of *Colleen Bawn*. With Boucicault's penchant for dialect, slang, and humor, a literal rendition in any language is unimaginable. Kabra grasped the components of melodrama and found correlates within the social and aesthetic horizons of his spectators. The conformity of his play to the original prompts questions about the process of translation. (I make no rigorous distinction between translation and adaptation for present purposes.) Where did the Kabra-Balivala team encounter the English play? Did they work from a printed script? How could they comprehend the conventions of melodrama when it was so very new?

Kabra and Balivala certainly had opportunities to view *Bawn* on stage. As noted, the Lewises and the Norvilles performed it on Grant Road in the 1870s, and other companies staged it at the Gaiety in the 1880s. Both venues offered a mix of Italian circus, English opera, Parsi theater, and Gujarati and Marathi plays. It was no oddity for an Indian viewer to attend an English play or an Englishman an Indian one. After seeing the play, a printed copy must have come into Kabra's or Balivala's hands. The match between components of the English and Gujarati texts is so precise that this seems essential. Printed English dramas were available from Bombay booksellers. They were purchased and consumed much like novels and also used as scripts for theatrical performances. *The Colleen Bawn* was published in 1860 by Thomas Hailes Lacy in London and Samuel French in New York. Lacy's editions of Victorian plays were offered for sale in Bombay by Thacker & Co (*Bombay Times and Journal of Commerce*, June 8, 1859). Another possibility is that Balivala purchased the playbook while in London. In 1885–86 he led the Victoria Theatrical Company to England. Taj (1969, 5) claims that copies of English dramas traveled with the company back to India and were given to staff playwrights for adaptation.

Translation also required knowledge of how melodrama worked. Kabra had been grappling with the form of melodrama for some years. In 1879, he published

Vinash Kale Viprit Buddhi, a three-act adaptation of Henry Milner's domestic melodrama, *The Gambler's Fate*. His 1884 comedy, *Sudhi Vachche Sopari*, was based on Elizabeth Inchbald's *Wives as They Were, and Maids as They Are*. Although not a melodrama, this play employed motifs of familial debt, imprisonment, and lost parents (Nicoll 1955, 145–46). Most important, Kabra began serially publishing his adaptation of Ellen Wood's melodramatic novel *East Lynne* in 1880. His translation had at least two spinoffs in the Parsi theater. The first, *Dukhiyari Bachu*, was by Edal Mistri. The second, *Bholi Gul*, was by B. N. Kabra, K. N. Kabra's younger brother. First performed in 1892, *Bholi Gul* was popular well into the twentieth century (Marfatia 2011, 230).

Kabra's prior engagements with Victorian melodrama had prepared him to translate *Bawn*. Public receptivity also smoothed the path. Domestic melodrama appealed over older Indian dramatic art in offering intricate plotting, suspense, and a rapid pace. It challenged actors and spectators to greater levels of emotional involvement. It deployed new kinds of speech such as asides and soliloquies that created multiple perspectives. And it showcased social problems, giving shape to the everyday experience of its viewers. By the time of *Bholi Jan*, audiences were increasingly drawn to the pleasures of this new art form.

Curiosity about any translation begins with its relationship to its source. I have suggested how Boucicault's melodrama was copied and amended as it moved across linguistic and cultural boundaries. *Bholi Jan* may even have exceeded its model in the display of modern science and engineering with Hope Bridge as backdrop and in the heightened pathos of Dhan as a poverty-stricken *pativrata* (devoted wife). But a translation stands on its own as well. It is an artifact; it brings newness into the world. *Bholi Jan* interacted with its literary and theatrical surroundings on its own terms, quite apart from its ancestry. In the next section, I explore how melodrama was naturalized in the Indian environment and evolved into the genre known as "the social."

MODERNITY AND THE INDIAN "SOCIAL"

Although *Bholi Jan* was advertised as adapted from Boucicault, it was neither introduced to Bombay as "melodrama" nor as "sensation drama." These terms are missing from publicity and reviews and absent from histories of Parsi theater and Gujarati drama. Instead, the play was termed a *samsari khel*, literally "worldly play," or social drama (*Kaisar-i Hind*, February 6, 1887). *Samsari* plays were a new category. *Samsar*, the earthly world, contrasted with other worlds inhabited by gods and demons in Hindu cosmology or fairies and *jinns* in Islamicate lore. The term indicated a class apart from older strains of theatrical entertainment: mythological plays (*Shakuntala, Harishchandra*) based on tales from the epics and the Puranas, and Indo-Muslim romances (*Gul-e Bakavali, Indar Sabha*) stemming from the Islamicate narrative genres *dastan, qissa* and *masnavi*. In the early Parsi theater, these two types had prevailed; a third category, historical drama, was coming into vogue.

By contrast, the social drama was concerned with humans living in present time and space. *Samsar* embraced material acquisitions and pleasures: wealth, property, reputation, family, marriage, domesticity, love, and sex. In the Parsi theater, *samsari* plays focused on the social worlds of designated communities. They dwelled on the web of relationships within the family, on the profound sociality of everyday existence. Engaging with distinctions of ethnicity and class, they looked to servants and outsiders for examples of difference. The *samsari* play illustrated a new kind of self-reflexivity, an interest in examining social embeddedness. Later, *samajik natak* became the common equivalent for "social drama," replacing *samsari khel* with no significant change in meaning.

"Melodrama," as it entered English parlance in the early nineteenth century, meant drama interspersed with songs and underscored by music, from *melos* (Greek, song) plus *drama*. This concept had little purchase in India because virtually all drama was already musical. Traditional theatrical forms such as Jatra and Nautanki were operatic in structure, featuring sung dialogues, solos, recitatives, and orchestral accompaniment. A number of early Parsi plays were billed as opera after the visits of European opera companies. Even the *Indar Sabha*, the celebrated pageant of song and dance, was considered by some to be a descendant of Western opera, although its genius lay in blending traditions of *masnavi, ghazal,* and *mujra*. The fondness for frequent interludes of song and dance continued into the Indian cinema. *Indrasabha* (1932), made by Madan Theatres, famously contained seventy-one songs.

The Victorian domestic melodrama at mid-century was more complex than the equation of *melos* plus *drama* suggests. Regardless, the term was rarely used for the works that proliferated in India. Instead, they were absorbed into the new genre of social drama. The socials that followed *Bholi Jan* produced multiple takes on the triangle of mother/son/daughter-in-law, the obsession with money and its loss, the conflict between arranged marriages and love marriages, the clash of old ways and new. These socials highlighted the advance of modernity in lifestyles and institutions. Figures such as the police, detectives, lawyers, and magistrates; settings such as the coffee house, the tavern, and the ballroom; and illicit activities such as horse racing and gambling came within the narrative compass for the first time.

Socials decisively placed female characters at the center, not appending them to men's stories as the mythological, romance, and historical had done. The title of a social often consisted of a woman's name (*Bholi Gul*, "The Innocent Gul," *Nek Parveen*, "The Good Parveen"), or it referred to the virtuous wife (*Pati Bhakti*, "Worship of the Husband," *Patni Pratap*, "The Splendor of the Wife"). Female roles increased not only in scope but in number. *Bholi Jan* was typical in contrasting two young women of different temperaments or fates, usually sisters or cousins. The presence of an older woman, generally the mother-in-law, expanded the canvas of domestic relationality.

Socials were the first plays in which actresses rather than female impersonators played women's parts. A few women had entered the acting profession earlier, but prejudice against them remained (Hansen 2011, 14–17). The first major actress of the Parsi theater was Mary Fenton. Fenton was advertised as "the English actress," although she was India-born and the daughter of an Irish soldier. She never set foot in England. She took the name Mehrbai when she married actor Kavasji Khatau, but her "Englishness" was too valuable an asset to be erased from public memory. Between 1887 and 1895, she starred in a series of social dramas that brought her wide celebrity. Her embodiment of Indian styles of femininity helped define new norms just as women entered public spaces and gained visibility (Hansen 1999). Most of the socials that starred Fenton were written by B. N. Kabra, K. N. Kabra's prolific younger brother. His theatrical version of *East Lynne*, titled *Bholi Gul*, played in the Novelty Theatre for a long time. Equally successful was *Gamreni Gori* ("The Village Beauty"). From an unknown English source, the plot revolved around the rural belle Gulbanu and her marriage to the orphan Jahangir. B. N. Kabra went on to write *Kal Jug*, *Dorangi Duniya*, and *Bap na Shrap*.

The social had a long historical arc. In western and northern India, commercial theater in Gujarati, Urdu, and Hindi flourished even as a new industry—cinema—took birth. Social dramas were written anew, addressing changing conditions and an emerging national consciousness, and old material was reworked for its perennial appeal. Socials provided star vehicles for the final generation of female impersonators, particularly Jayshankar Sundari and Bal Gandharva, and served as platforms for the first goddesses of silent cinema, Patience Cooper and Sulochana. Important agents of the social's circulation were playwrights who went to work for film companies, adapting their stage works into screenplays.

After the Kabras, many Parsi playwrights composed social dramas in Gujarati. Jahangir Patel "Gulfam" wrote ten plays; *Fankdo Fituri* was often performed. The play became a silent film starring Thelma and Yvonne Wallace in 1925 and was remade with sound in 1939. Jahangir Khambata, a well-known actor-manager, wrote *Juddin Jhagro* and half a dozen plays based on Parsi social mores. Ardeshar Patel "Adna" composed the very popular *Aslaji*, based on Moliere's *The Miser*; it starred Mary Fenton. Pherozeshah Marzban "Pijam," Ratanji Faramji Shethna, and others carried the genre into the twentieth century (Shastri 1995, 244–54).

Meanwhile, companies specializing in Gujarati theater diverged from Parsi-owned troupes in Ahmedabad and Mumbai. Mulshankar Mulani created powerful social dramas that starred the magnetic Jayshankar Sundari. In *Jugal Jugari*, Sundari played the ideal wife Lalita, whose husband ruins their marriage through gambling. Nrusingh Vibhakar wrote six dramas, most dealing with nationalism and social reform (*Sneh Sarita*, *Sudhachandra*); Sundari played the female leads.

In Urdu, social dramas were penned by Ahsan, Talib, Betab, and Agha Hashr, among others. These authors from the United Provinces joined the Bombay companies as staff writers, introducing into the social Urdu-Hindi dialogue and north Indian settings. Betab began his career with *Qatl-e Nazir* (1901), based on the murder of a courtesan in Lahore. His *Kasauti* (1903) was an adaptation of B. N. Kabra's *Dorangi Duniya*. Betab's most successful drama of this period, *Zahri Samp* (1906), starred the dynamic Amritlal Keshav Nayak.

B. N. Kabra's *Dorangi Duniya*, Betab's *Kasauti*, and Ahsan's *Chalta Purza* were made into both silent and sound films. So was Betab's *Zahri Samp*: the 1933 film featured Patience Cooper and Kajjan. In the 1920s, Hindi socials played well in the Parsi theater, notably Radheshyam Kathavachak's *Parivartan* (1925; film versions from 1929 on). Harikrishna Jauhar, writer of detective novels and romances, produced a hit play in *Pati Bhakti*. He penned the screenplay for the silent film with Patience Cooper (1922), creating a foundation for socials such as the Gohar starrer, *Gunsundari* (silent 1927; sound 1934, 1948).

Above all, Urdu playwright Agha Hashr made a lasting impact. Among his thirty-plus dramas, several adapted English sources, including *Nek Parveen or Silver King* (original by Henry Arthur Jones). His most powerful melodrama, *Yahudi ki Larki*, yielded several film versions (Hansen 2009). He often turned his socials into screenplays: *Ankh ka Nasha* (1928), *Asir-e Hirs* (1931), *Khubsurat Bala* (1927). Through setting, costume, and language, especially use of the Urdu *ghazal* and Hindustani music, Hashr's distinctive approach anticipated Muslim social films of the 1940s and 1950s (Bhaskar and Allen 2009).

The social in the Indian context thus developed out of Victorian domestic melodrama, subsuming an infinite variety of familial, societal, and national topics. It dwelled in the modern world, apart from the realm of gods and heroes. Yet melodrama was not so neatly contained within one genre. Socials were meant to reform and educate; historicals to instill national pride; mythologicals and devotionals to inspire religious fervor. Even so, purposes converged and stylistic practices grew together. Melodramatic modes of narration and enactment came to dominate the popular aesthetic regardless of genre.

Whereas domestic melodrama evolved into a distinct correlate—the Indian social—melodramatic conventions more broadly diffused among all types of productions, theatrical and cinematic. Spectacular confrontations between good and evil forces, or miraculous interventions by gods and goddesses, already commonplace in historicals and mythologicals, acquired layers of emotionality and social signification overlaid with the palette of melodrama. Tableaux became popular in mythological and devotional narratives, congruent as they were with Hindu iconography. Betab's Parsi theater *Mahabharat* culminated in a tableau representing the goddess Ganga (the river Ganges) piercing her Untouchable devotee's chest to reveal the Brahminical sacred thread hidden within (Hansen 2006, 4988). This moment of climax collapsed the hierarchy of caste even as it enunciated the victory of righteousness (*dharma*). Betab's toolkit of melodramatic devices enabled him to combine a radical social message with acute elevation of feeling. The potential of melodramatic form to heighten theatrical experience was not limited by content or genre.

CONCLUSION

In this chapter, I have tracked the migration of domestic melodrama during its travels from the Anglo-Atlantic world to Australia to South Asia. The circulation and mutation of *The Colleen Bawn* was a multistage process dependent upon many agents. Playwrights, producers, performers, patrons, and the public were essential to passing the drama along, enabling it to flourish in exceedingly varied environments. The collective actions of these various groups, fortuitously, left traces in the historical record. Newspapers from the time preserve daily notices of public entertainments, but until recently this archive was rarely tapped because microfilm—the common medium for preserving historical newspapers—is difficult for researchers to use. Accessibility of the *Times of India* altered dramatically in 2010 when the academic publisher ProQuest made the entire run of the newspaper available in digital format.

Nonetheless, the vast majority of dramatic works from the nineteenth century remain cloaked in obscurity. Many of these are domestic melodramas. The data on Boucicault's play, its Indian translation, and the networks around it are exceptional in their clarity and availability. Using these clues, scholars of Victorian popular theater, Australian local history, South Asian theater, and global film studies have begun to investigate the systems in which theatrical melodrama circulated. This project has reimagined geographically isolated but culturally interconnected systems as subsets within a global circuit. I have examined points of contact and convergence to understand the boundary crossing that led to productive transformations. The analysis brings out differences that separate cultural productions in distinct contexts, shedding light on similarities and parallels previously occluded. Melodrama is a living organism that mutates to survive in the conditions in which it finds itself and, in turn, creates conditions for its own evolution and metamorphosis.

4

Global Melodrama and Transmediality in Turn-of-the-Century Japan

HANNAH AIRRIESS

Peter Brooks's *The Melodramatic Imagination* (1976) has had an immeasurable impact on studies of melodrama that look beyond genre.[1] Brooks states that melodrama was constructed as a "peculiarly modern form" that functioned to assert an ethical sense as social institutions that enforced a pre-Enlightenment morality unraveled (14). He specifically grounds his argument in the post-French Revolution era, and this era constitutes the origin point of melodrama in much subsequent scholarship. Histories of European and American melodrama in its various forms have been traced using this formulation of melodrama's emergence, but can we understand its transnational presence beyond the West in the same terms? If so, how might that history be constituted?

In this chapter I pursue these questions through an analysis of the field of studies focused on Japanese melodrama. By constructing a transmedial history of melodrama in Japan beginning at the turn of the twentieth century, I hope to set up a framework for understanding Japanese melodrama as a global phenomenon tied to the transnational circulation of discourses on modernity.

Excellent work on Japanese literary and theatrical melodrama has been done in the last fifteen years, but English-language studies on Japanese film have historically focused on specific cinematic genres such as family melodramas and the woman's film. Conversely, literary scholarship, such as Jonathan E. Zwicker's (2006) *Practices of the Sentimental Imagination: Melodrama, the Novel, and the Social Imaginary in Nineteenth-Century Japan* and Ken K. Ito's (2008) *An Age of Melodrama: Family, Gender, and Social Hierarchy in the Turn-of-the-Century Japanese Novel*, has addressed the emergence of sensational melodramatic narratives of the Tokugawa and Meiji periods, and M. Cody Poulton (2001) and Inuhiko Yomota (2001) have focused on literary and theatrical melodramas written by Izumi Kyōka in the early 1900s. However, much of this work employs film scholarship by Thomas Elsaesser, Christine Gledhill, Linda Williams, Ben Singer, and others to explain the cultural work performed by the melodramatic mode as far back as the beginning of the nineteenth century. By crossing back and forth between literature, theater, and film, this scholarship provides outstanding examples of a transmedial investigation that not only expands the framework of melodrama but facilitates its transnational circulation. Scholarly work on Japanese cinematic melodrama benefits from considering its intimate links to earlier transnational melodramatic forms present in literature and theater. Doing away with medium-specific parameters helps establish what melodrama historically accomplishes as a significant mode of cultural mediation.

Christine Gledhill (2002) emphasizes the need to historicize melodrama across media and argues that in eighteenth- and nineteenth-century theater melodrama became "a site of generic transmutation and 'intertexuality' . . . melodrama multiplied through translation, adaptation, and, in the absence of copyright laws, piracy" (18). Daniel C. Gerould (1983) has similarly made a claim for the adaptability and proliferation of the mode across cultural contexts, claiming simply that "melodrama has always been an art of wholesale borrowing" (10). Beginning with melodrama's prominence in literature of the late Meiji era (1890–1912), I pursue this understanding of melodrama as continuously adaptive and fundamentally transmedial and transnational, expanding the position of melodrama in Japanese film studies beyond its present parameters. I also demonstrate the transnational circulation of melodrama across different media as it surfaced in different cultures. At the turn of the twentieth century, melodrama functioned to construct enduring cultural narratives that engaged with the contingencies of modernity in late modern Japan.

HISTORICIZING MELODRAMA: JAPAN'S MELODRAMATIC IMAGINATION

The attempt to theorize melodrama's presence in Japanese film studies has proven to be an especially challenging task. Two methodological tendencies are apparent in these studies: one that overdetermines history and another that underdetermines it. Mitsuhiro Yoshimoto's influential 1993 essay, "Melodrama, Postmodernism, and Japanese Cinema," demonstrates the former. It examines postwar melodrama within the context of Japan's fraught geopolitical relationship with the United States. It begins with a chronological explication of Japan's "fundamental aporia of modernity," a crisis that remains unresolved to this day. Here Yoshimoto traces three key moments in the history of modernity in Japan: Commodore Matthew Perry's arrival in the mid-nineteenth century (the first encounter with modernity), the 1920s Taisho era (the emergence of mass media), and the postwar period. It is within this third moment that melodrama emerges as a dominant articulation of the persistent crisis of modernity in Japan, and more specifically of the "disparity between modernity and modernization, whose 'synchronic uneven development' had been the sociocultural strain on Japan for more than a century" (103–7).

Yoshimoto's historical framework provokes several questions. If melodrama is an articulation of an ever-present crisis of modernity—in Japan's case an aporia that came to port with Perry in 1852—why is it only in the postwar period that it assumes critical prominence as a form of mediation? Furthermore, if we are to resituate what Yoshimoto designates as Japanese postwar melodrama in a more expansive history of the form, would this entail a reformulation of melodrama as a mode of negotiating modernity in terms other than a symptom of ideological crisis?

Although Yoshimoto importantly calls for rigorous historicization of melodrama in the Japanese context, his essay presents a history of modernization that spans more than a century but offers an examination of melodrama only as a response to shifts within the postwar period. He briefly references "prewar melodrama," but its mediating function in that era and its relationship to postwar melodrama is not addressed. Yoshimoto points to the emergence of melodrama in Europe as being rooted in the development of the bourgeoisie and consequent class conflict, presumably referring to its presence in the wake of the French Revolution. The terms of melodrama's development in Japan are never clearly set, however. Is it possible to trace consistencies between Japan's different epochs and sites of melodramatic production?

Using Frederic Jameson's formulation of melodrama as an "ideologeme," Yoshimoto argues that melodrama "support[s] the social formation of postwar Japan" and acts as a constant reminder that Japan was (and continues to be) "trapped in the geopolitical space of Western hegemony" (105–6, 108).[2] In that modernity in Japan signifies domination by Western powers, melodrama constitutes a negative subject position in which the protagonist (as Japan) is continually acted upon rather than acting. Although this fraught geopolitical relationship remains active, Yoshimoto argues that melodrama stopped functioning as an ideologeme by the end of the 1960s.

It is imperative to recognize the ways imperialism and occupation are inscribed in Japanese mass media. However, it is equally necessary to recognize how uneven power relations play out in different ways according to specific historical circumstances, and how media responds to such historical conditions beyond mirroring or perpetuating the effects of the power relations under which they are produced. Yoshimoto's theorization of melodrama, and indeed modernity, leaves no opportunity for reflexivity on the part of Japanese cultural producers and the public. The claim that "melodrama is created through the repression of an assertion of self" in postwar Japan, and that such repression is symptomatic of an anxiety about Western hegemony that has existed for more than a century, forecloses the critical potential of melodramatic narratives (108).

More recent writing by Aaron Gerow (2010) frames modernity in Japan within a contradictory impulse to "both catch up to the West by emulating it, and establish a nation-state based on difference" (31). Gerow understands early film as a way to work through the contradictions of modernity as it was popularly experienced and perceived. This model recognizes the fraught status of modernity in Japan in relation to the West while conceiving of ways in which popular narrative modes can be deployed to articulate new cultural forms of awareness. Understanding melodrama and other cultural media forms within an overdetermined historical framework, as Yoshimoto does, fails to account for the complexity of different modes of expression that can be traced throughout the development of Japanese modernity. An investigation of the reception and adaptation of melodrama over the last century and a half reveals a more complicated negotiation of modernity within popular melodramatic modes and cultural production at large.

The underdetermination of history in studies of Japanese filmic melodrama is another persistent perspective that takes up a Brooksian formulation of melodrama that separates it from the historical context. This framework, rooted in the emergence of melodrama in the wake of the epistemological rupture of the French Revolution and its search for a "moral occult," has been employed frequently to advance arguments that neglect a broader history of melodrama. Catherine Russell's (1993) essay, "Insides and Outsides: Cross-cultural Criticism and Japanese Film Melodrama," attempts to account for the enduring prominence of melodrama in Japan. Russell maps Brooks's concept of the "moral occult" on the opposing concepts of *giri* (obligation) and *ninjō* (emotion) to establish melodrama's continual presence from Chikamatsu Monzaemon's eighteenth-century Bunraku and Kabuki plays to Mizoguchi Kenji and Ozu Yasujiro's films (146). Although Russell usefully expands melodrama's position in Japanese cinema studies, suggesting its persistence as a "metagenre" akin to its role in American narrative film, melodrama as a moral occult is presented as a form always already present rather than as a historical configuration with concrete genealogy in Japan or globally.

In "Unbinding Melodrama," Matthew Buckley (chapter 1) makes an important intervention in Brooks's formulation of melodrama. He argues that Brooks's thesis neglects the literary and theatrical practices occurring before the French Revolution that anticipated the birth of melodrama. The aftermath of the French Revolution is in no way the point of origin for melodrama but instead a moment of melodrama's "consolidation" from different theatrical forms, albeit shaped by the trauma of the period. Buckley proposes a model of thinking about melodrama as a "distillate form," or a concentrated combination of elements from different genres and forms that long predate the French Revolution. In other words, rather than speaking of melodrama's emergence from "crisis, cataclysm, or collapse," the contours of melodrama are shaped by a logic of synthesis. This notion of melodrama as a distillate form is useful both as an account of melodrama's development in France and elsewhere and as a way to understand the history of melodrama's presence and circulation in Japan.

Buckley urges a reevaluation of our historical understanding of melodrama, without which melodrama easily becomes a generic narrative of rupture amidst social change. Both over- and underdetermination inhibit attention to historical specificity and thus miss how melodrama is a valuable heuristic tool for understanding modernity in a Japanese and transnational context. To grasp the value of melodrama as a category requires understanding the mode historically, which crucially entails an examination not only of its "origins" and "influences" but also an exploration of its multidirectional movements, translations, and transformations.

In her recent essay "Transplanting Melodrama: Observations on the Emergence of Early Chinese Narrative Film," Zhen Zhang (2012, 28) asks, "If melodrama is quintessentially 'Western' or 'American,' how might we reconcile the claim that melodrama is fundamentally a cultural form of modernity and different cultures and cinemas may engage in parallel or alternative forms of its melodramatic imagination?" This is precisely the question we must ask to explain melodrama's global circulation and its production beyond its European and Anglo-American articulations. To fully account for melodrama's presence in Japan is to understand its status as a distillate form, incorporating characteristics drawn from both Japanese sentimental literary and theatrical forms and elements of European melodramatic texts produced in a near-contemporaneous period. The vast number of melodramatic adaptations and translations traced between Europe and Japan are crucial in expanding an understanding of melodrama's function as a tool by which to navigate modernity across cultures. Such an endeavor provisionally positions melodrama as a "Western" form, entrenched in a specific European history, but it subsequently works toward decentering Europe in favor of a model of melodrama as a global phenomenon rather than being unidirectional in circulation. The work of translation, as a larger cultural phenomenon linked to the global struggle for modernity, should be understood as a "translingual practice" with the potential to reterritorialize in multiple directions (see Liu 1995).

Furthermore, to gain a fuller sense of the network of melodramatic exchange occurring in the decades surrounding the turn of the twentieth century requires an understanding of melodrama as a necessarily transmedial mode. Analysis of the history of melodrama's adaptations across media illustrates the inadequacy of focusing on a single medium. Melodrama benefits from a consideration of past iterations across different media as it challenges contemporary understandings of what medium, form, and content constitute melodrama. I consider these past forms in the next section.

A MELODRAMATIC HISTORY OF TURN-OF-THE-CENTURY JAPAN

The year 1868 marked the transition from the feudal rule of the Tokugawa Shogunate to the Meiji Restoration, a period defined by the consolidation of power in terms of the Japanese nation-state under the rule of Emperor Meiji. At the end of a long period of isolationist policy, both government and economic moves were made to establish Japan's position on the global stage and its identity as "modern." The Meiji Constitution (1890), the Imperial Rescript on Education (1890), and the Meiji Civil Code (1898) were drafted to cultivate modern national subjects. The Rescript on Education, in particular, initiated a total transformation of what constituted civic morality and subjectivity in Meiji-era Japan. Carol Gluck's (1987) study, *Japan's Modern Myths: Ideology in the Late Meiji Period*, characterizes the Rescript as a product of a "process of collective reinterpretation," combining ideologies and interests from figures ranging from "Court moralists" to "Western-oriented educators." The Rescript reflected the multiplicity of competing discourses around family, education, and nation at the end of the nineteenth century (103).

To understand Japanese melodrama as a historical form tied specifically to the transformations of the modern era requires a consideration of the contested location of modernity in Japan. In *Overcome by Modernity*, historian Harry Harootunian (2000) presents an enlightening account of the participation of Japanese modernity within a global process of modernization. Rather than using models such as "retroactive" or "alternative" modernity, which inevitably frame Japanese and other non-Western country's modernization in reference to a normative "base timeline" dictated by the West, Harootunian understands Japan and other non-Western countries as possessing a "co-eval modernity," implying that modernity occurs contemporaneously in different locales but necessarily adopts different forms. In other words, "whatever and however a society develops, it is simply taking place at the same time as other modernities" (xv–xvii).[3] Although certain formulations of modernity in other locations can be located earlier than the Meiji period, the model of co-eval modernity assists in emphasizing contemporaneous resonances between Japanese modernity and other national contexts. This is useful in contextualizing melodrama's rapid circulation within a global network of exchange with countries similarly engaged in the projects of industrialization and nation-building.

In *An Age of Melodrama*, Ken K. Ito (2008) argues that as the nineteenth century was nearing its end and nearly every dimension of life found itself subjected to changes from contesting value systems and ideologies, melodrama surfaced in Japan as a prominent mode within serialized popular fiction. This wildly popular body of melodramatic fiction articulated new individualized frameworks of moral legibility that responded to the assertion of modern value systems established by Meiji ideologues in conjunction with the influence of foreign cultural production.

From 1897 to 1903, Ozaki Kōyō's *Konjiki yasha* ("The Golden Demon") was serialized in the *Yomiuri* newspaper, becoming one of the most important novels of the late Meiji period and retaining mass popularity for decades after publication ended. The story centers on a young couple named Kan'ichi and Miya. Engaged as teenagers, Miya later decides to break off the engagement to marry a wealthier man of higher cultural status. Heartbroken, Kan'ichi severs all ties and begins a new life as a loan shark, which is morally degrading yet highly profitable. Although his work hardens him, Kan'ichi eventually recovers his sense of sympathy and care for others through an encounter with two young lovers. Furthermore, Miya realizes her mistake in rejecting Kan'ichi and is consumed once more by her love for him. Kōyō summarized the trajectory of his narrative as "the battle between love and gold," which Ito (2008) explains as a "binary designation of 'love' as virtue and 'gold' as vice" that evokes the search for "moral certitude" during the rapid growth of industrial capitalism in the 1890s (3, 88). Kōyō died at age thirty-seven, leaving his story unfinished, but *Konjiki yasha* nonetheless remains one of the most significant examples of literary melodrama and a foundational articulation of the cultural milieu of the late Meiji era.

Melodrama was not a term frequently used in the Meiji period, but because of shared formal elements Ito posits melodrama as a useful concept for understanding cultural production in turn-of-the-century Japan.[4] In fact, Ito, Jonathan E. Zwicker, and Mark Anderson all present close textual readings of *Konjiki yasha*, reading the narrative in terms of melodrama but using different frameworks for the concept. Anderson (2009) advocates for the term *shinpa* as synonymous to melodrama. Shinpa, as I detail later, is a term used specifically for melodramatic theater and its subsequent cinematic adaptations. Anderson's inclination to find a term that encompasses many different forms of melodrama is significant, but shinpa's meaning as "new school" drama and its historical parameters complicates its potential utility as a term for a transmedial mode that possesses the potential for broader historical usage in earlier and later epochs. Therefore, I believe Ito's use of the term *melodrama* is valuable in that it does not favor any one particular medium. Citing Linda Williams, Ito (2008) points to the "simultaneous presence of pathos and action" and "recognition of virtue" that dominate these narratives and help establish a new moral legibility in a moment when older, feudal ethical systems were overturned for modern egalitarian values (55, 82). *Risshin shusse*, or "self-advancement," is a theme that emerges in these narratives and endures in subsequent media articulations (39, 92). This previously unavailable form of upward mobility, along with the drama of recognition and spectacular action and violence, were crucial components to the fabric of late Meiji melodrama.

Although Ito employs a Brooksian formulation of melodrama, considering these serials through Buckley's (see chapter 1) argument for melodrama as a distillate form is particularly appropriate for turn-of-the-century Japan. Melodrama in the late Meiji period can be understood as a product animated by the social transformations of early modernity and as an amalgam of generic elements from earlier sentimental literary forms, including imported literary melodrama. In *Practices of the Sentimental Imagination*, Zwicker (2006) provides a comprehensive account of nineteenth-century literature that predates Meiji serials, noting a shift away from eighteenth-century aesthetics into a "fiction of sentiment" (9). Although these sentimental tales of the period are not pure melodrama—as he finds in them elements of other forms, such as tragedy—he importantly initiates a longer historical view of melodrama in which we see its development arising from different literary forms, ranging from romantic tales in *ninjōbon* novels to imported Victorian literature.

The global circulation of nineteenth-century melodramatic literature highlighted by Zwicker plays an important role in the production of these late Meiji narratives. Ito (2008) surveys four authors who produced the most popular serialized melodramas at the turn of the century, all of whom were avid readers of English-language fiction. Ito notes the importance of Charles Dickens for these authors—specifically for Tokutomi Roka, who based *Omoide no ki* ("Footprints in the Snow") on *David Copperfield*—but the most interesting element of this influx of European literature was the massive numbers of noncanonical popular melodramatic fictions that were translated and read. Kikuchi Yūhō, for example, noted his indebtedness to Bertha M. Clay's 1880 novel *Dora Thorne*, which formed the basis of his *Chikyōdai* (Ito 2008, 17, 146). Clay was the pseudonym of Victorian author Charlotte M. Brame, and Keiko Hori (2000) demonstrated the similarities between her novel *Weaker Than a Woman* and Ozaki Kōyō's *Konjiki yasha*.

How to characterize influence is a particularly vexing issue. It is important not to overstate the influence of this body of French and English melodramatic fiction on the content of these turn-of-the-century Japanese texts. Indeed, Jonathan Zwicker and others demonstrate the nineteenth-century serials' participation within a broader history of Japanese sentimental fiction. However, it is crucial to recognize the significance of the appeal of this now largely forgotten body of translated melodrama and genre fiction to a large readership and that a massively popular text such as *Konjiki yasha* found its basis in a near-contemporaneous English melodramatic text. In her analysis of early Chinese cinema, Miriam Hansen (2000) notes its relationship to Hollywood cinema as one of influence, but not imitation; rather, films such as Sun Yu's classic *Daybreak (Tianming,* 1933) "achieves translation, hybridization, and reconfiguration of foreign (and not just American) as well as indigenous discourses on modernity and modernization" (19). If we are to posit melodrama as a mode of negotiating the modern, Hansen's framework enables us to understand the importance of *Konjiki yasha*'s position as a "reconfiguration" of *Weaker Than a Woman* alongside its Japanese literary antecedents in the formation of Japanese iterations of melodrama.

Late Meiji serial fictions such as *Konjiki yasha* evoked their historical moment through both their narratives and their mode of distribution. As is typical with serials, readers did not simply consume the stories as published but profoundly shaped the narratives through reader response columns published in the newspaper alongside the story. Hajime Seki's (1997) impressive archival research demonstrates the way a community of readers was constructed through *Konjiki yasha*'s mode of publication: its serialization alongside the reader's column produced both a relationship between readers and a new kind of relationship between author and audience. By creating an opportunity for the readers to shape the text, Seki observes that the dynamic of *Konjiki yasha*'s serialization produced a narrative that we can read as more directly negotiating the social and ethical coordinates of the public in the late Meiji period. Furthermore, as *Konjiki yasha* was being published, scenes from the narrative were depicted and circulated as illustrated prints and picture books, and episodes from the story were staged in theaters. Their reception, in turn, had an impact on the narrative content of the ongoing newspaper serialization of the story. The feedback loop present in the formation of serials such as *Konjiki yasha* demonstrates the importance of transmedial exchange and the mode of publication in the development of Japanese melodrama.

In *Playing the Race Card*, Linda Williams (2001) cites Henry James's reference to *Uncle Tom's Cabin* as a "wonderful 'leaping' fish," referring to its enormous popularity and its " 'leaps' into new forms of media" (45). The extent to which the most popular literary melodramas pervaded different media forms during the late Meiji era is staggering. Like *Konjiki yasha,* many of the serials were adapted for the stage, often as they still were being serialized and had yet to conclude. In the late Meiji era, popular theater was undergoing vast transformations, with different schools reacting against each other to form new and distinct styles of performance. The serialized melodramas were staged as shinpa performances, a style that was a reaction against kabuki, and significantly included narratives staged in contemporary times. English-language scholarship on shinpa tends to refer to this theatrical style as "shinpa melodrama," occasionally with denigrating implications, but often referring to the plays' foregrounding of the recognition of virtue as a narrative focus and the combination of pathos and action that Ito has observed in the novels on which the plays were based.

The adaptive potential of Meiji melodramatic narratives did not stop at shinpa productions; they found a home in the growing realm of silent film as well. Yomota (2001) notes that early cinema borrowed heavily from shinpa storylines, dialogue, and its "melodramatic imagination" (402). When shinpa plays proved successful, those stories were reanimated in film, often adapted multiple times over. Like the shinpa performances that formed one component of larger popular programs, early film was included in such live stage performances as *rensageki*, or "chain dramas." Specific scenes from popular shinpa melodramas, usually the most well known and sensational, were filmed and interspersed within a staged performance of the entire play (Iwamoto 1998). As technology developed and the plays could be filmed in full, production companies continued to produce *saieiga*, or remakes, at an astounding pace.

Konjiki yasha became a shinpa play while still being serialized, and in 1911 it was made into a film; by 1954, nineteen versions had been produced. Kikuchi Yūhō's *Chikyōdai* moved through all three media incarnations in only six years. Another of his popular titles, *Onoga tsumi* ("My Sin"), was made into a new version every year from 1912 to 1922 (McDonald 2000, 6). Although most of the film adaptations of Meiji melodramas are no longer extant, a few have survived, primarily as feature-length adaptations produced in the late 1920s and 1930s. Shimizu Hiroshi directed a 1937 version of *Konjiki yasha*, and Mizoguchi Kenji directed versions of *Onoga tsumi* (1926) and adaptations of work by Izumi Kyōka, a student of *Konjiki yasha*'s author, Ozaki Kōyō.⁵

Izumi Kyōka's work often has been studied through the lens of melodrama. Japanese-language scholarship by Yomota and Ayako Saitō, for example, have provided excellent work on adaptations of Kyōka's writing, revealing the significance of these transmedial narratives.⁶ Saitō (2011) focuses on *Giketsu Kyōketsu* ("Loyal Blood, Valiant Blood"), one of Kyōka's most famous novels. *Giketsu Kyōketsu* began publication in the *Asahi* newspaper in November 1894. It was adapted for the theater by Otojirō Kawakami, a founder of the shinpa style, at the end of 1895 under the name *Taki no shiraito* ("The Water Magician"), equaling its already momentous success as a serialized novel (42–46, 57).⁷ The first film adaptation was produced in 1912 (McDonald 2000, 9). The play was initially advertised as an adaptation of a "Russian novel," which scholars suggest may be related to its similarities with Leo Tolstoy's *Resurrection* (Poulton 2001, 33). Although *Giketsu Kyōretsu*'s 1895 publication date precedes the 1902 translation of *Resurrection* in Japanese, the advertisement is of note in considering the global contemporaneity of these similar melodramatic narratives.⁸

Mizoguchi's 1933 adaptation of *Taki no shiraito* centers on a traveling performer named Tomo and her relationship with a law student named Kin'ya. Kin'ya comes from noble blood but after his father's death is reduced to driving a horse drawn carriage. He aspires to attend law school but is unable to afford it. Upon meeting Kin'ya, Tomo pledges to provide him with money so he can move to Tokyo and attend school. She continues to send money until her performance troupe lands on hard times. Determined to provide for Kin'ya, she borrows a large sum of money from a loan shark named Iwabuchi. In one of the most suspenseful scenes, six men sent by Iwabuchi surprise her and rob her at knifepoint. They hold her down, pulling her coat off and grabbing the money out of her robe. She chases after them, brandishing one of the attacker's knives, but she is pushed back down at the base of a bridge. The robbers get away, jumping over her collapsed figure.

Realizing what Iwabuchi has done, Tomo returns to Iwabuchi's house, entering knife first. He attacks her, dragging her along the floor. It is implied that he is going to rape her, but while still on the ground she jabs her arm upward, stabbing him as she looks away. He dies, and when she is eventually arrested and put on trial, Kin'ya—now a successful young lawyer—is assigned to prosecute her. He tries Tomo at her insistence, as it fulfills her original aspirations to see him succeed. She is sentenced to death, and he commits suicide shortly after.

The film was a hit. Saitō (2011) cites a 1933 article in the film journal *Kinema junpō* that states even though it had a long run people were still lining up on the last day to see it. The article's author comments that *Taki no shiraito* continues to have a deep-rooted attraction for audiences, presumably speaking to the narrative's multiple articulations across media (65). Its transmediality points beyond an understanding of melodrama as a "woman's film" or "family drama" to a broader mode that addresses the fraught status of modernization and modernity. However, like Yoshimoto's configuration of postwar melodrama as a narrative of victimhood, Tadao Satō (1982) reads the film as a story of the "unfortunate woman." He argues that Kin'ya "not only fails to acknowledge the sacrifices of the heroine but also condemns her to death" (79). Chika Kinoshita (2005) argues, however, that rather than framing Tomo within the terms of self-sacrifice and victimhood, her story can be understood as a failed attempt at gaining upward mobility, or *risshin shusse* (107).

Whereas Satō's understanding of *Taki no shiraito* ignores the complexities of the intersections of modernity and gender in the film, and the opportunities afforded to women at the time were extremely restricted, Kinoshita (2005) suggests it is possible to understand the narrative as Tomo's attempt at risshin shusse by "investing" in Kin'ya's success with her capital, under the assumption they would marry (107). Rather than framing *Taki no shiraito* and the conventions of melodrama as that of victimhood, Kinoshita's work on the film demonstrates a formulation of melodrama as a matrix for experiencing the strains of modernity, specifically through the negotiation of gender roles, social mobility, and romantic life.

A history of *Taki no shiraito* also emphasizes crucial aspects of the narrative that would otherwise be ignored in favor of the "suffering woman" paradigm. Just as Ben Singer (2001) has stressed the importance of sensationalism and action in American melodramatic theater at the turn of the century, late Meiji melodramas found popularity because they featured violence, passion, new technologies, and spectacle. M. Cody Poulton (2001) describes the novel as such:

> [*Taki no shiraito*'s] coach race that begins the novel is brisk and exciting, the murder scene is reminiscent of kabuki at its bloodiest, or of the most lurid Meiji crime fiction, the courtroom scene is full of suspense. . . . The story is in turns spectacular, romantic, and violent, with a clearly delineated conflict between two opposing ethical choices—in other words, pure melodrama. (32)

These claims for the allure of the spectacular are no less true for Mizoguchi's film, as we see in the above scenes. The significance of risshin shusse, the emphasis on virtue and recognition, as well as the prominence of spectacle and violence, generates an expanded frame for our understanding of Japanese cinematic melodrama. *Taki no shiraito*, *Konjiki yasha*, and other Meiji melodramas similarly constitute texts that moved between media and even nation with an amazing fluidity, informing cultural narratives that lay at the foundation of modernity in turn of the century Japan.

MELODRAMA AS GLOBAL VERNACULAR

As noted earlier, Gerould (1983) claims that melodrama is an "art of wholesale borrowing." In the introduction to *American Melodrama*, he demonstrates this by detailing the histories of translation, appropriation, and copyright infringement that shape each play included in the volume. His history of the "Americanization" of theatrical melodrama in the second half of the eighteenth century begins with the importation and localization of French and British plays into the context of American urban centers. He then importantly demonstrates that the circulation of these plays was not unidirectional, for these adapted plays were subsequently exported back to the United Kingdom (10).

Gerould refers to these melodramas as "relocatable theatrical commodities." They possessed a localized appeal based on different translations in different regions, as well as a broader transnational appeal in the way their core melodramatic narrative remained the same. This historical model is not radically different from the relationship between Meiji serials such as *Konjiki yasha* and European melodramatic literature. This connection is particularly appropriate when considering that the circulation of melodramatic texts was not limited to importation from Europe into Japan. Both *Konjiki yasha* and *Hototogisu* were translated and published in English in 1905, just a few years after their serialization in Japan. Although it is unclear if they were widely read, the translation of these narratives emphasizes the multidirectionality of the global circulation of melodrama at the turn of the century, and the ways in which melodrama generated local articulations of broader concerns of modernity and modernization in that era.

Zhen Zhang (2012) also contributes to establishing the global circulation of melodrama through her work on the influence of D. W. Griffith on 1920s Shanghai melodramatic cinema. Rather than constructing a framework of cultural circulation using totalizing regions of "East" and "West," Zhang breaks down the network of influence at two levels: between Europe and the United States and between the United States and China. She creates a parallel between Griffith's debt to European melodrama and the influence of his films on the development of *wenyi*, a "native" genre akin to melodrama (29, 35). In both instances, melodrama forms the key mode by which to delineate moral and ideological contestations in moments of great social instability.

Zhang adopts the term "vernacular melodrama" as a way to describe the subsequent production of melodrama and wenyi films in response to the popularity of Griffith and other melodramatists. Vernacular melodrama is one articulation of Miriam Hansen's (1999) broader concept of "vernacular modernism," which Hansen establishes as a realm of cultural practices that "register, respond to, and reflect upon processes of modernization and the experience of modernity." Such practices range from photography and radio to architecture and advertising. "Vernacular" holds myriad meanings, implying "discourse, idiom, dialect, with circulation, promiscuity and translatability" (60). Considering the position of melodrama as a mode that reflects upon modernity, as well as a form that, as we have seen, is defined by its translatability, localization, and promiscuity, melodrama functions as an exemplary practice of vernacular modernism.

Zhang's vernacular melodrama offers an excellent model for the negotiation of the mode in its various sites of reception, the way it changes according to the local culture, and the potential for change incited by melodrama's appearance there. However, I would like to push Zhang's terminology further. Rather than understanding melodrama as an object amongst many others in mass culture subject to vernacularization, I suggest it is a preeminent mode of vernacular modernism, functioning as an early global vernacular that emerges prior to Hollywood cinema's position as the first "global vernacular," which Hansen (1999) cites as a "cultural practice on par with the experience of modernity" (65)

If melodrama is not limited to a single genre or medium but is the production of transnational and transmedial cultural narratives, as discussed in this essay, melodrama's worldwide presence around the turn of the century undoubtedly positions it as a global vernacular mode. However, the flexibility and diversity of melodrama's articulations necessarily assumes the model of vernacular modernism on qualified terms. In her essay on early Chinese cinema, Hansen (2000) argues that the films she addresses function as vernacular modernism on two levels. The first is the aesthetic sensibility of the film: its presentation of a specific kind of "imaginary space" with a "modernist look that could be copied, mass-produced for wider consumption and more ordinary, everyday usage." The second is the structural level, in which the films "respond to the pressures of modernity in their thematic concerns, through particular oppositions and contradictions that structure the narrative and inform the constellations of characters" (14). Melodrama, when understood with the historical breadth I have outlined, registers at the level of content and narrative and maintains a modernist aesthetic in many—but not all—of its global manifestations. However, melodrama's function and appeal through the second level, as a thematic and narrative response to the experience of modernity, is unequivocal. Considered on these particular terms, Hansen's (1999) elegant summation of the capabilities of "classical" Hollywood cinema speak to melodrama's global status as well:

> If classical Hollywood cinema succeeded as an international modernist idiom on a mass basis, it did so not because of its presumably universal narrative form but because it meant different things to different people and publics, both at home and abroad. We must not forget that these films, along with other mass cultural exports, were consumed in locally quite specific, and unequally developed, contexts and conditions of *reception*; that they not only had a leveling impact on indigenous cultures but also challenged prevailing social and sexual arrangements and advanced new possibilities of social identity and cultural styles; and that the films were also changed in that process. (68)

Although Hansen's argument focuses on a later stage of modernity than that of the turn of the century Japanese literary serials, reading Hansen's explication of cinema's flexibility with Meiji melodramatic narratives in mind allows us to conceive of melodrama as a form of global vernacular modernism. It frames melodrama as an earlier vernacular form that precedes cinema, that "registers, responds to, and reflects upon modernity" through different media forms in the decades surrounding the turn of the century (60). Tracing the presence of melodrama in Japan both beyond the framework of the nation and across different media illustrates the breadth of its capacity as a mode, engaging with issues far beyond the terrain of the woman's film and bourgeois family melodrama with which film studies began their interest in melodrama. Melodrama's exceptional transnational and transmedial circulation demonstrates that far from being a peripheral genre or form, melodrama can act globally as a matrix for the experience of modernity.

NOTES

1. For example, in Christine Gledhill's (2002) essay, we can conceive of a history of melodrama that travels across media, illuminating its pervasiveness and redefining our understanding of its contemporary manifestations.
2. Yoshimoto (1993) argues that an "ideologeme can become either a set of abstract philosophical propositions or value system on the one hand, or a diachronic process of transformation in the form of a proto-narrative" on the other (105–6). Postwar melodrama, he writes, can be understood in both terms.
3. Harootunian (2000) argues that although the Meiji period, beginning in 1868, signaled the beginning of the process of capitalist modernization, it is not until after World War I that Japan moved from light to heavy and capital industries. It is within this latter moment of economic development, the further rise of mass culture, and political crisis that Harootunian locates modernity through contemporary critical discourse. I do not refute the assertion that the period following World War I functions as the dominant

phase of Japan's cultural modernity, but late the Meiji period marks the introduction of foundational changes that established Japan as modern.

4. It is worth noting that once the term *melodrama* (translated as *merodorama*) started growing in usage in Japan in the twentieth century, it was assigned different meanings in different historical periods. In short, as in other cultural contexts, the term was not static. Building upon Ito's formulation, however, I believe utilizing melodrama as a framework is helpful because it emphasizes lineages and consistencies across media and regions.

5. In particular, *Nihonbashi* (1929) and *Taki no shiraito* (1933).

6. Yomota (2001) further argues that Kyōka's literary and theatrical fiction profoundly informed subsequent twentieth-century theater and film in East Asia, temporally and geographically expanding the influence of shinpa theater from an influential precursor of early cinema to a foundational presence in East Asian cultural production (402, 406, 409).

7. Saitō (2011), among other scholars, points out that Kōyō made such heavy revisions to Kyōka's text that *Giketsu Kyōketsu* cannot be understood as simply Kyōka's. Instead, the novel should be understood as a product of both authors.

8. Mizoguchi Kenji, who directed a 1933 adaptation of Kyōka's work, allegedly claimed that "all melodrama is based on *Resurrection*." This anecdote is related in Shindo Kaneto's 1975 documentary *Aru eiga kantoku no shōgai—Mizoguchi Kenji no kiroku* ("Kenji Mizoguchi: The Life of a Film Director"). Screenwriter Yoshitaka Yoda says that Mizoguchi made the above statement as Yoshitaka was writing the screenplay for the 1937 film *Aien kyo* ("The Straits of Love and Hate"). Notably, he uses the word "melodrama" (*merodorama*).

5

Transnational Melodrama, *Wenyi*, and the Orphan Imagination

ZHEN ZHANG

The figure of the orphan is ubiquitous in oral, literary, and theatrical storytelling worldwide. As part of modern experience, cultural imagining around orphanhood intensified in the wake of the Industrial Revolution, colonial and capitalist expansion, and parallel movements of nationalism and decolonization. As a specific strand within the melodramatic mode that has salient global appeal, orphanhood has facilitated melodrama's transnational applicability in modern times. The emergence of narrative cinema as an intermedial synthesis of existing cultural and aesthetic forms helped usher the orphan onto the big screen for mass identification, modeling her as a quintessential modern individual embodying the struggle for freedom and autonomy, often entailing sacrifice and suffering, in the search for new forms of belonging and attachment.

In film history, Griffith's *Orphans of the Storm* (1921) is paradigmatic as an early feature-length American film melodrama capitalizing on the orphan figure sourced from the French Revolution (see Mayer and Tsivian 2006, 116–37; Brooks 1994, 11). His *Way Down East* (1920), used by Linda Williams (1998) as an exemplary text to demonstrate the basic components of melodrama, features orphanhood embodied by the heroine (Lillian Gish) as a multiply abandoned woman. Beguiled and betrayed by a lady's man of considerable means and schemes, the fatherless and poverty-stricken Anna loses her baby as well as her mother in the first part of the narrative, but fortunately meets a young man who falls for and rescues her in an ice storm, before a happy ending marked by matrimony.

Significantly, one of the earliest—and highly popular—Chinese feature-length narrative films, *Orphan Rescues Grandfather* [孤儿救祖记] (Zhang Shichuan and Zheng Zhengqiu, 1923), also places an orphan at the narrative center. But it frames the male child in a uniquely Chinese patrilineal family structure. An affluent household suddenly loses its male heir. At the insinuation of an ill-intending relative, the patriarch banishes the widow, unaware of her pregnancy. Assuming his mother's maiden name, and thanks to his mother's sacrifice and a charitable educator's support, the grandson grows into a studious and courageous adolescent. He rescues the patriarch from danger, leading to the revelation of true identities and family reunion. The patriarch gives the entire family fortune to the widow, who in turn donates half to a school for poor children (Jiecheng and Jianyun 1923, 6–8; Zhang 2005, 127).[1] Orphanhood, as the ten-reel film's selling point, is encapsulated in this newspaper advertisement:

> A child who is an orphan, the pity!
> A grandfather to be rescued, the danger!
> A child who rescues his grandfather is an orphan, how strange!
> A grandson does not know his grandfather and the grandfather does not know his grandson, how entangled!
> The orphan's mother, a young widow who has been slandered, the injustice![2]

In the early 1920s, "Griffith fever" swept over the Shanghai film scene, spurring hybridized adaptations of his films. One of them, the 1929 *An Orphan* [雪中孤雛]—literally "Orphan Chicks in the Snow"—grafts the same Chinese title used for *Orphans of the Storm* onto a Sinified version of *Way Down East*, complete with the requisite snowstorm rescue, boldly scrambling motifs from the two Griffith films into a new Chinese film. For moviegoers in subtropical Shanghai, the neighboring Jiangnan region, as well as for the diaspora in tropical Nanyang (Southeast Asia)—where Shanghai films were popular but snowstorms nonexistent and feared—the frigid mise-en-scène of this film would have had an extra compelling effect as an instrument of orphan-centered ordeals. Yet above and beyond Griffith as a particular source and moment of influence, a review of Chinese film history reveals the centrality of the orphan figure as an integral part of a transnational melodramatic mode and of a global vernacular articulating the modern experience.

Examining Chinese film historiography in relation to melodrama and orphanhood enables us to examine broader questions. In what ways do different film traditions reshape or invent anew this age-old figure in overlapping or divergent visions of enlightenment and modernity? For instance, why would *Orphan Rescues Grandfather* focus so strongly on the cross-generational child-widow/mother-grandfather kinship relation and filial piety? I hope discussion of the intertwined nature of the orphan imagination and cinematic storytelling will be meaningful for the broad agenda of reconceiving melodrama studies transnationally. The history of Chinese-language narrative cinema from the 1920s onward is populated by orphans of various kinds, a phenomenon more pronounced in periods of dramatic social and political upheavals, and reconfigured in the post-World War I era when the family-state [*guojia* 国家] of "China" was cruelly divided by ideological differences and divergent paths through modernity (Zhang 2010). Using Griffith fever as a historicizing starting point, I retrace the relationship between the inception of narrative cinema in 1920s Shanghai and melodrama film studies in the West. To enable comparative and transcultural connection with the Western term *melodrama*, I reassess the genealogy of the concept *wenyi*, which several Chinese scholars have championed as a culturally distinctive practice migrating from translated literature to theater and screen. I argue that the two terms are historically bound together and better seen, following Kathleen McHugh (2005) on postwar Korean melodrama, as a kind of "transnational familiar."

The orphan-centered films foreground creative engagement with existing melodramatic elements and those transplanted from different languages, media, and reception contexts. Orphan melodrama is a subset of melodrama understood as both a transmedial and transgeneric mode, forging a global vernacular shared by storytelling traditions concerned with remaking the individual and family under modern conditions. Inspired by Matthew Buckley's notion that melodrama (from theater to screen to politics) functions "as a kind of affective meme" (chapter 1), adapting and transforming itself in an unremitting, viral process of self-replication, I argue that the orphan is both a transcultural, archetypical protagonist and an emblematic "meme" of modern times in which "homelessness" is the quintessential human condition and mode of consciousness (Lukács 1971).

The orphan figure serves as a unique meeting point between various crisscrossing melodrama traditions, enabling understanding of melodrama as a transnational vernacular that shapes competing mass-mediated sensorial cultures and modern subjectivities on and off the page, stage, and screen. Here I extend and modify a thread in Miriam Hansen's (my late advisor) and my own work on vernacular modernism and early cinema (Hansen 1999, 2000, 2010; Zhang 1998, 2005, 2012). A cluster of melodramatic tropes centered on the "modern girl" or the "fallen woman" exemplifies the contradictions of modernity—promise of liberation as well as the "disposability of human beings" (Hansen 2000, 2010, 292). Arguably, the fate of the orphan—often in affinity with the fate of woman in modernizing societies, exemplified by both *Orphans of the Storm* and *Orphan Rescues Grandfather*—gives rise to a more concentrated and dynamic melodramatic register in transnational film history.

On one hand, connoting trauma and independence, rootlessness and new attachment formation, the orphan tale inspires a melodramatic imagination of the modern nation built on an admixture of old and new sociocultural forms and ethnopolitical values. The orphan's precarious life in times of war and other catastrophes, and her provisional membership in transitional socioeconomic and political systems, foreground the failure of these institutions to shelter and nourish their members and provide equal access to material and intellectual resources, affecting in particular those who are historically marginalized. These include women; ethnic, racial, and sexual minorities; children; migrants or immigrants from lower classes or colonized nations; and political or economic refugees. A focus on orphanhood also unbinds melodrama studies from perspectives specific to the West that are predicated on individualism and psychoanalysis, thus enabling attention to broader, deeper, and transnational social and cultural forces in the making of modern personhood and citizenship.

Thus the orphan figure presents a poignant embodiment of melodrama broadly defined as a "transcultural mimetic form" (Taussig 1993), acquiring expressive urgency in transitional sociocultural structures and world orders. The relevance of this figure and the notion of orphanhood to the shared yet variable experiences and consequences of two world wars, and to the worldwide movements of nationalism, decolonization, migration, and modernization offers potent imagery to popular political agendas and cultural formations, including modern drama and national cinemas—albeit with different intensities and within different historical trajectories. Poised on the threshold between oppression and liberation, dependence and autonomy, devolution and evolution, the orphan—often a picaresque figure subject to pathos and action-loaded peregrinations—invokes situations and feelings of victimization, loss, and nostalgia as well as possibilities for redemption. This figure traverses a force field constituted by the universal and the singular, the ideological and the psychic, the social and the affective, the normative and the transgressive. The collision of these forces produces an implosive energy, exposing the orphan condition as the locus of modernity's contradictions and the limits of cohesive national or cultural identity. The orphan imagination, hitherto underexplored in cinema studies, contributes to rehistoricizing and transnationalizing the "melodramatic imagination"—Peter Brooks's famous term that has dominated melodrama studies in the West since 1976.

MELODRAMA VERSUS *WENYI*: THE TRANSNATIONAL FAMILIAR

It is well established that the "rediscovery" in the 1970s of *All That Heaven Allows* (1955) and other films in Douglas Sirk's Universal cycle galvanized Western film studies' interest in melodrama. In its opening sequence, Jane Wyman's character, widowed Carey, meets her new gardener, Ron (Rock Hudson), and invites him for lunch in her yard full of fall foliage, thus initiating their fateful romance. The gardener demonstrates his earthy origins and worldly knowledge about trees and flora by pointing to the Golden Rain tree nearby, an "exotic" species from China. He cuts a branch to show her its "rain" splattered leaves. Carey is enthralled. This particular branch introduces a cluster of striking images and colors that make up Sirk's signature "ironic mise-en-scène," said to subvert bourgeois culture. My focus here is the relationship between Anglo-American melodrama studies spurred by that rediscovery and non-Western traditions that might be named melodramatic. Indeed, how long have cinematic melodramatic tales been staged in China under "Golden Rain" trees or other native or imported species? If melodrama is to be envisioned as the "forest" rather than the "trees," as Linda Williams (1998) has imaginatively put it, then it is imperative that we attend to specific cultural-ecological systems that have nourished long-standing aesthetic species as well as transplanted or hybridized kinds.

The relationship between this body of scholarship and national cinema studies has remained problematic for "cross-cultural" analysis and more recent transnational studies (see Kaplan 1991; Yoshimoto 2006). Although much Anglophone melodrama scholarship centered on American and West European traditions has been barely concerned with the "rest" of the world or simply assumed its own universal applicability, studies of national and regional cinemas have tended to gravitate toward a culturalist view that trumpets native categories while dismissing "melodrama" and other Western originated terms outright as irrelevant. In his introduction to *Melodrama and Asian Cinema*, Wimal Dissanayake (1993) argues that "melodrama" is a Western category for which there is no synonym in Asia. If vague equivalents of "recent vintage" can be found, they mobilize particular "deep-seated cultural psychologies"—as if these were timeless properties and thus fundamentally contradistinctive to those of the West (3–4). In this generic mapping along a clichéd East–West axis, intra-Asia cultural variations and historical differences are subsumed under a homogenous Asian culture as a magnified "national" space vis-à-vis the hegemonic West. The articles in Dissanayake's anthology offer disparate, largely textual case studies of postwar and contemporary films, without historically tracing their respective traditions and the way these may function in their own terms as melodrama or how they interrelate with traditions of the West and elsewhere.

More recently, Western revisionist melodrama scholars such as Christine Gledhill, Linda Williams, and Ben Singer, among others, have moved beyond psychoanalytically inflected and narrowly periodized "genre" studies, ushering in broader historical and cultural perspectives. Linda Williams's seminal article, "Melodrama Revised" (1998), proposes a radical reorientation in melodrama studies, charging the idea of the melodramatic mode with new rigor and opening with this daring assertion:

> Melodrama is the fundamental mode of popular American motion picture; it is not a specific genre like the western or horror film; it is not a "deviation" of the classical realist narrative ... melodrama is a peculiarly democratic and American form that seeks dramatic revelation of moral irrational truths through a dialectic of pathos and action. It is the foundation of the classical Hollywood movie. (42)

In restoring melodrama's centrality to American cinema, Williams's project significantly rewrites American film history through an expanded viewfinder, and admirably repositions American cinema as a national cinema tradition produced by the ferment of its struggle for independence from the "Old World," its particular realization of modernity, and—given the history of slavery and waves of immigration from all over the world—its continued, tension-ridden quest for national identity based on a problematic multiracial and multiethnic foundation. However, how is the notion that melodrama is quintessentially "Western" or "American" to be reconciled with the claim that melodrama is fundamentally a cultural form of modernity? Moreover, this form has functioned as a keynote in numerous national or regional cinemas worldwide, especially in the aftermath of momentous historical ruptures such as struggles for independence or decolonization and revolutions, whose historical geneses, scales, and legacies are not dissimilar to those of the French Revolution and the American War of Independence. Rather, we need a concept of melodrama through which different cultures and cinemas may engage in parallel or alternative forms of melodramatic imagination.

In "The Melodramatic Field," Christine Gledhill (1987) argued not only for the transgeneric properties of melodrama but for its dependence on translation: "Based on commerce rather than cultural monopoly, melodrama multiplied through translation, adaptation, and, in the absence of copyright laws, piracy" (18, see also 28). This observation may be stretched further to account for the transnational proliferation and modernization of melodrama as a form of global mass culture, especially in the wake of industrial capitalism and attendant colonial or semicolonial modernity in the era of mechanical reproduction and uneven development.

The question how distinctive cultural or national contexts "translate" melodramatic idioms or grammars from external sources while reenergizing local or regionally grown forms is central to moving revisionist melodrama studies toward genuine comparative studies of both melodrama and modernity. In the Chinese context, *wenyi* [文艺], a modern Chinese literary and aesthetic sensibility that has seeped into popular as well as art cinema, forming an evolving and widening tradition, has been at the focal point of scholarly attention in the last two decades. Taiwan film critic and script writer Cai Guorong describes wenyi as having two strands: "those works that deal with family relationships and ethics, and those that depict romances," both often set in the recent past or contemporary period (cited in Law 1997, 15).[3] Two of the earliest feature films, *Orphan Rescues Grandfather* and *Sea Oath* [海誓]—a.k.a. *Swear by God* (Dan Duyu, 1921)—are often cited as initiating this twin-genealogy, but these two strands may interweave (Zhang 2012). Stephen Teo (2006) observes that the wenyi genre—which he terms "an enigmatic nomenclature"—encompasses "a broad spectrum of melodrama including the romantic film or love story, the 'woman's picture' or the literary adaptation" (203); yet he anchors its maturation and proliferation in the postwar period, particularly in the suffering heroine-centered and emotion or "sentimentality" infused melodramas made in Hong Kong (204). Emilie Yueh-yu Yeh (2009) offers a more ambitious attempt to uncover wenyi's conceptual and historiographic distinctiveness, "bypassing translation and making Chinese terms keywords" in order to trace an alternative tradition within non-Western practice and theory that cannot be easily subsumed by the term *melodrama* (443). She rightly locates the term's provenance in the 1910s and 1920s when it was first introduced from Japanese *bungei* [文藝] into modern Chinese vernacular, especially with reference to literature and drama translated or adapted from foreign sources. This trend of Sinicizing foreign literature (novels and plays in particular) quickly extended to other modern arts including cinema, especially as the Chinese film industry and its narrative cinema were fast emerging and thirsty for inspiration in both content and form.

Yeh's more recent article, "*Wenyi* and the Branding of Early Chinese Film" (2012), draws on a wealth of primary sources to reinforce or revise four previous conceptions. First, at its formative moment and in its initial uses, *wenyi* refers to the import of Western literature and its Chinese translations that were integral to "Mandarin Ducks and Butterflies" [鴛鴦蝴蝶] fiction, popular from the late Qing to the early Republican period; here the term was associated with "taste, refinement and cosmopolitanism" (72), which later helped to elevate cinema's social and artistic status. Second, early wenyi film as a genre also refers to screen adaptations of foreign literature (and its Chinese translations or versions).[4] Third, as a contentious concept and practice, wenyi "served stakeholders of diverse interests" from the "right" to the "left," thus articulating competing interpretations of humanism, equality and freedom (75). And fourth, as a historically evolving complex "metagenre," wenyi could serve as a more "intrinsic and illuminating term" for studying Sinophone film history in and outside of Mainland China, replacing the default Western term melodrama (77). Yeh's observations are well-grounded and provocative. From translation of foreign novels and plays, and domestic popular romance fiction and film, to articulations of social ethos and political aspirations, wenyi has left pervasive imprints on the production and consumption of a particular transplanted and transmedial modern sensibility or "structure of feeling" across the Chinese-speaking region and diaspora.[5] Beyond mere influence, literal translation, and imitation, the emergence of wenyi as a cultural assemblage underscores the productive process and complex nature of cultural circulation, incorporation, and invention.

Yeh insists on wenyi's unique cultural and linguistic identity and distinction from melodrama. Yet the bulk of wenyi films produced for most of the twentieth century, including the examples she cites, chime with elements described as melodrama. Rather than consigning wenyi entirely to a national or Sinophone framework, Yeh's methodology and argument contain possibilities for engaging with melodrama's transnational circulation. Her deeper investigation and wider definition of wenyi resonate with similar scholarly attempts in the West and elsewhere to unbind melodrama from its "default" Westernized myths and definitions (such as excess in mise-en-scène, hyberbolic emotion, and Manichean moral opposition), identifying melodrama's heterogeneous histories both as distinctive local or national experiences and as part of the global circulation of mass cultures. Its unruly "evolution" and shifting and expanded valences across generic and geographic borders have shaped wenyi into a category akin to modality or register now also associated with melodrama. Indeed, what's most revealing about the etymological source and semantic amplification of wenyi is its original reference to Western texts' circulation, domestication, and transmediation in East Asia. This revelation acknowledges the instrumental role of translating or transplanting Western modern letters and arts, often via Japan, during China's tortuous transformation—in the wake of industrial capitalism, colonialism, and attendant wars and revolutions—from a feudal, patriarchal cultural and political order to a fledgling modern nation-state. Various interpreters and practitioners of wenyi, with diverse cultural missions or political agendas, have generated under this rubric a cultural apparatus that is also integral to the production of vernacular modernism embodied by early Shanghai cinema (see Zhang 2005). Its porousness and open-ended nature has allowed it to flourish into forests of similar or related generic species, spreading across Chinese cinematic climates of Shanghai, Hong Kong, Taiwan, and the diaspora over different periods of time—wherever and whenever the geopolitical and other "ecological" conditions proved receptive and favorable for its rooting, growth, and transformation.

Like melodrama in the West, wenyi is an elastic category with a rich and complex history, borne out of the ferment of mass culture under industrial and capitalist modernity, and baptized by revolution and progressive movements in recent world history. Each iteration of wenyi bears distinct cultural-linguistic clues as to the crisscrossing routes it has traveled. Rather than a fixed category or obvious generic label, the diverse forms of wenyi have meant different things for different publics at different times. It parallels, intersects with, and sometimes reroutes melodrama's transnational circulation. Certainly, Chinese critics and audiences in cosmopolitan Shanghai were also aware of the usage of "melodrama." Critic Yao Sufeng, for instance, used the term in 1934 to describe Zheng Zhengqiu's films, such as *Orphan Rescues Grandfather* (cited in Huang 2014, 176).[6] The term was more commonly used in Hong Kong under British rule, as seen in the English translation of the Chinese title for the 1986 Hong Kong International Film Festival's annual retrospective, "Cantonese Melodrama 1950–1969" (with melodrama standing for "wenyi film"; Li 1986).

At the core of each term—wenyi and melodrama—and their respective practices lie a number of basic attributes and qualities that have undergone intensive rehearsal and consolidation within a specific period of time, forming a more or less discernible body of works that serve as reminders of the chronotopes of their respective emergence. These include stage melodrama in France and England in the years preceding and following the French Revolution, the complex genesis and spread of Parsi theater in India in the mid-nineteenth century (Thomas 2006; Vasudevan 2010; Hansen, chapter 3), as well as in China; the screen adaptations of the Civilized Play 文明戏 (a kind of modern spoken drama); and Mandarin Ducks and Butterfly fiction of the 1910s and 1920s (Zhong et al. 1997; Zhang 2005).[7] Yet beyond these compressed periods of genre formation, both melodrama and wenyi have functioned as a crucible for the conception, dissemination, proliferation, and multiplication of melodrama as a global vernacular, with kaleidoscopic articulations over a very long period of time. These, along with other forms and names of melodrama, are interconnected in a larger constellation of parallel or competing vernacular modernisms and attendant production of affective-sensorial structures.

What discussion of wenyi has not substantially embraced is the role theater played in its formation. It was indeed the playful synthesis of a range of literary practices and theater reformations that nurtured the nascent electric shadowplay [影戏] in China, especially in early narrative films with foreign sources and more prominent wenyi characteristics. Many early screenwriters who came from Mandarin Ducks and Butterfly literature and pioneer filmmakers such as Zheng Zhengqiu and Hong Shen were deeply involved in the theater world—particularly the Civilized Play and New Drama [新剧] (which were closer to modern Western spoken drama and Japanese *shinpa* theater), and Peking opera or other Chinese regional opera forms. Zheng Zhengqiu, for example, was an avid Peking opera aficionado and critic as well as a pioneer in the Civilized Play movement (Zhong et al. 1997; Zhang 2005). Borrowed from Japanese *bunmei*, the Chinese terms *wenming* [文明]—"civilized" or "civilization"—and wenyi are products of the same historical moment, connoting on one hand emulations of modern European letters and arts and post-Meiji reform Japanese culture (along with the social mores and political visions they represented) and, on the other, efforts at reengaging with existing or evolving cultural practices. Thus early modern Chinese theater and early cinema are suffused with a number of compound cultural symbols, storytelling forms, and linguistic registers—a mixture of classical Chinese and the new vernacular, deploying bilingual titles in pidgin or elegant English prose.

The transplantation of *East Lynne*, a Victorian novel, to *Konggu lan* [空谷兰] ("Orchid in an Empty Valley"), a 1926 Chinese "tragic love film" (*aiqing pian* [哀情片]), written by Bao Tianxiao and Zheng Zhengqiu and directed by Zhang Shichuang, is an exemplary case in point. Published in 2014, Xuelei Huang's extensive research uncovers a tangled and cumulative history of textual travel and transformation: from the "rewriting" in English of Ellen Wood's bestseller shortly after its 1861 publication as *A Woman's Error*, one of the many romances catering to the "lower classes" by Charlotte Mary Brame, through an expanding "melodramatic repertoire" including many stage and screen versions crisscrossing the Atlantic, to its serialized Japanese version *No no Hana* ("Flower of the Wilderness") by the prolific translator Ruiko Kuroiwa around 1900, then to Bao Tianxiao's Chinese translation and newspaper publication of Kuroiwa's version, followed by its adaptation as a "Civilized Play" directed by Zheng Zhengqiu and his New People Society, and eventually to Bao's 1925 screenplay, commissioned by Mingxing company and developed with Zheng Zhengqiu and Zhang Zhengqiu. These triangulated transnational and translingual crisscrossings culminated in the Chinese sound remake that traveled to the 1934 Moscow film festival and elsewhere in Europe, bringing the zigzagging exchanges full circle (157–75).[8] Huang concludes, "the European genre of melodrama, Hollywood cinema, Japanese *shinpa* drama, the Chinese New Play, and the tragic love film were all interlinked, sharing overlapping territories of styles and sources" (163). What Huang aptly calls a "long chain of cultural production" (163), involving numerous agents and forms of transmediation over large swaths of time and space, testifies not only to the fecund, multilayered terrain of wenyi but also to its incessant cross-pollination with various kinds of melodrama "inside the global mediascapes" (141–42).

PERMUTATIONS OF THE ORPHAN DRAMA

In this context, a nascent yet highly volatile and competitive film industry provided basic infrastructure for the production and distribution of a domestic narrative cinema appealing to a widening audience in China and Nanyang (the diaspora in Southeast Asia). The flourishing publishing industry supplied a wealth of source materials ready for stage and screen, including often very liberal translations of foreign literature and adaptations of plays through the synergy of wenyi and melodrama.

A crucial catalyst for the quick growth of feature-length Chinese narrative film was the popularity of a variety of early American, French, and other imported films in varying subjects, genres, and styles. The ones that attracted the Chinese audience most often contain action, spectacle, cliffhangers, gags, emotional upheavals, and ethical dilemmas involving family and romance, with many plot twists and turns. Many of D. W. Griffith's films exhibited in Shanghai, and widely admired by Chinese filmmakers and audiences alike, combined such elements. According to

Zheng Junli (1936), a well-known director, actor, and critic, Griffith fever gripped Shanghai following the 1924 success of *Way Down East* (1920) and the reexhibition of his earlier films including *The Birth of a Nation* (1915), *Intolerance* (1916), *Broken Blossoms* (1919), and *Orphans of the Storm* (1921).⁹ However, Jianhua Chen (2009), consulting newspaper advertisements, has established May 1922 as the first Shanghai screening of *Way Down East*, followed by nearly ten other Griffith films through to the spring of 1924, which contributed to what Chen describes as the "historical discursive environment" that ignited a spurt in the growth of Chinese narrative cinema. Thus the Chinese reception of Griffith, the alleged "father" of American narrative film—specifically melodrama—functioned as a "nodal point" in a web of sentiments, debates, and film practices informed by "nationalism and cosmopolitanism, race and gender, visual culture and literature" (250–51). Griffith fever, compounded by the great popularity of Mandarin Ducks and Butterflies literature by writers such as Bao Tianxiao, Zhou Shoujuan, and Zhu Shouju, who were recruited by the Mingxing company and other studios, spurred the proliferation of a variety of sentimental tales revolving around family and romance. By 1926 the number of films in this body of wenyi melodrama took up more than half the total output, although almost all have been lost or are yet to be found (Li and Hu 1997, 148).

Films adapted from sentimental popular fiction recycling the age-old "beauty and scholar" formula appear predominantly concerned with individual desire or "free love," for example *Jade Pear Spirit* [玉梨魂] (Zhang Shichun and Xu Hu 1924).¹⁰ However, the lovers usually find themselves torn between love and duty, personal freedom and kinship ties. The temptation as well as the high price of "free love" given up for duty is often made analogous sacrifice for to revolution, winning "national sympathy" in cultural production and intellectual discourse in this period (Lee 2006). Nevertheless, reform of the old Confucian extended patrilineal family and promotion of mass education offered social and narrative options for marginalized groups and new generations of different relevance—witness the popularity of *Orphan Rescues Grandfather* and similar films among women and less-educated classes. Zhou Jianyuan (1923), manager of the Mingxing company, argues that the film, with its focus on "love for children" [qingzi zhi ai] rather than "love among the couple" [fufu zhi ai] catered to a sensibility that befitted this reformist Chinese cultural context.¹¹

Relevant to the early twentieth-century Chinese context, Griffith's *Orphans of the Storm* had inscribed the entwined tropes "orphan" and "storm" within the French Revolution. However, aside from Adolphe Dennery and Eugène Corman's 1874 *Les Deux Orphelines*, Griffith's freely adapted source, melodrama in France and England had been rehearsing the motif of the orphan for some time. Significantly, Guilbert de Pixérécourt's paradigm-setting *Coelina* (1800; *A Tale of Mystery* in Thomas Holcroft's 1802 adaptation) is about an orphaned child, adopted by a kindly uncle but threatened with marriage to the son of the villain. She is eventually reunited with her lost father, earlier made dumb in a murder attempt. The play's theatrical spectacle, enhanced by suspense, shock, pathos, and horror was key to its sensational success. Griffith was indebted to this early history of stage melodrama and its trans-Atlantic crossings, but used cinematic means—in particular temporal manipulation through editing—to orchestrate the dialectic of pathos and action, exemplified by the "last minute rescue" and redemption of innocence. The orphan tale involving adoption and disability (blindness or dumbness) appears centrally in the development of nineteenth-century melodrama, providing dramatic possibilities for maximizing the dialectical interplay between separation and reunion, pathos and action, kindness and villainy. The orphan embodies melodrama as meme—"a self-replicating pattern of sensation and feeling that moves successively from the surface of culture to the subtending structures of social and individual life" (Buckley, chapter 1)—speaking in both aesthetic and social terms to the stressful transitions of industrialization and modernization. These "stormy" moments uproot people and destroy families, producing horrific suffering as well as tales of survival and the formation of new kinship and community. The refitting of Guilbert de Pixérécourt's orphan tale in the aftermath of the French Revolution to a proliferating stage genre brought melodrama across an "affective threshold" to meet a wide mass audience, anticipating moviegoers on the global horizon of the twentieth century.

The Shanghai filmmakers drew on both the energies and despair generated by the Republican Revolution and the May Fourth "new culture movement," as well as on newly emerging Euro-American-Japanese literary, dramatic, and cinematic forms, to create a domestic wenyi melodrama in the contradiction-ridden context of China's postdynastic, quasi-secular, semicolonial modernity. The broad transnational "melodramatic imagination," amplified by Griffith fever, appealed to writers and filmmakers across a wide political and aesthetic spectrum. Although less sympathetic to domestic commercial cinema, May Fourth writer and critic Tian Han openly expressed his admiration for Griffith and his "literary" approach to developing a cinematic language, using "close-up," "fade-in," and "fade-out" (Chen 2009, 253). Griffith's films raised the bar for filmmaking as a distinctive storytelling form on a par with the older sister arts.

Comparisons between Griffith and Zheng Zhengqiu, the "father of Chinese cinema," by critics then and scholars now are legion, largely because of their shared pioneer spirit and interest in social and ethical crises of modernity, their ability to arouse the emotional responses of a wide audience through elaborate plots and intelligible cinematic storytelling, although with divergent outcomes circumscribed by respective historical conditions. In the post-Opium wars context, Zheng focused on the social and affective structure of the extended patrilineal family caught in the painful transition from a largely agrarian country under dynastic rule, entrenched in age-old beliefs including Buddhism and Confucianism, to a fledgling secular republic with aspirations for national sovereignty, modernization, democracy, and individual freedom.

The synergy between Griffith fever and a nascent domestic film industry, however, produced more varied experiments in melodramatic expression. Indeed, it was the wide thematic spectrum of Griffith's melodramas that excited the Chinese filmmakers and critics, who in turn found in traditional and new vernacular resources the inexhaustible possibilities for cinematic storytelling. Some directly transplanted

Griffith's signature elements, especially the hero-rescues-beauty sequence and the requisite parallel editing building toward a spectacular climax, whereas others tinkered with narrative techniques for plot construction and moral lessons appealing to Chinese moviegoers. *Orphan Rescues Grandfather*'s success was owed largely to its "intricate plot" [情节曲折] and effective orchestration of "grief and joy, separation and union" [悲欢离合], elements ingrained in traditional and modern vernacular Chinese fiction and drama.[12]

Spearheaded by *Orphan Rescues Grandfather*, a stream of family ethical melodramas depicted the deep bonds of the extended family broken by modernity and capitalism, often anchoring the pathos of innocence wronged in either the orphan [*gu'er* 孤儿] or quasi orphan, or in the widowed mother [*guamu* 寡母]. Looked down upon as "small people" or children [小人], women, particularly widows who could neither remarry nor go back to their natal family, had even lower social status than a male child. A woman's subaltern status is at once more abject and less recognized. Orphanhood and motherhood are thus interconnected through not only their biological ties but also their shared social semantics. Thus the widow in *Orphan Rescues Grandfather* would stay chaste and devoted to her son (the titular character) after her husband's death and during her long separation from the rich family she was married into but who misjudged her (see figure 5.1).

The figure of the child, an orphan in particular, although as vulnerable and isolated as the widow, sidesteps the taboo issue of sexual transgression and presents a socially more acceptable and open horizon in terms of both narrative development and social change. The voluminous representations of orphanhood in the late Qing and early Republican period were also intimately connected to a larger

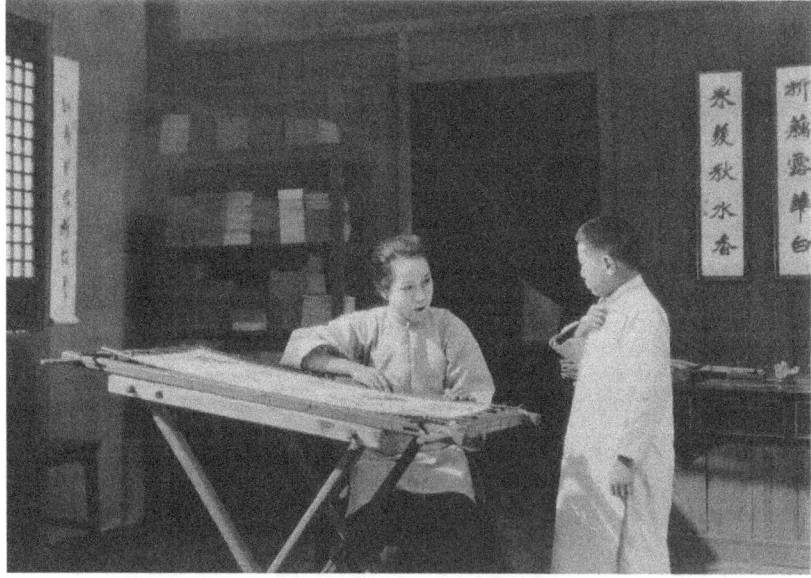

Figure 5.1 *Orphan Rescues Grandfather* (1923). Courtesy of China Film Archive.

intellectual and public discourse on "saving the children," on developmentalism and national strengthening (Jones 2011). This melodramatic template vacillating between varying degrees or combinations of orphanhood and widowhood is also evident in *Abandoned One* (Dan Duyu, 1923; see Zheng and Liu 1996, 45), made in the same year as *Orphan Rescues Grandfather*, and followed by *The Poor Children* (Zhang Shichuan, 1924), *A Blind Orphan Girl* (Zhang Shichuan, 1925), *A Little Friend* (Zhang Shichuan, 1925), *The Student's Hard Life* (Guan Haifeng, 1925), and *Who's His Mother?* (Gu Wuwei, 1925). The extant film, *Mother's Happiness* [儿孙福] (Shi Dongshan, 1926), focuses on a widowed mother whose love and sacrifice go unappreciated by her ungrateful children. The languid narrative rhythm, metaphoric mise-en-scène and vernacularized allusions to classical poetry (such as a broken pottery pot, emptied-out home, fallen leaves) yield maternal drama as an allegory for the birthing pain of a new social order. A decade later, Zhu Shilin (1899–1967) remade the film into a talkie, *Song for a Mother* (1937).[13] The same story was given a new interpretation in *A Mother Remembers* (Chun Kim, 1953), a Cantonese melodrama set in postwar Hong Kong, demonstrating the enduring appeal of maternal sacrifice as the linchpin of fragmented kinship and community in times of sociopolitical chaos and moral confusion.

In sum, the historical circumstances of China as "the Sick Man of Asia" and an underdeveloped nation provided unique conditions for selectively absorbing Griffith fever, giving birth to its own various "orphans of the storm" who would "rescue" China and its fledgling film industry. As Shanghai cinema, along with its exhibition and distribution sectors, became quickly established as a viable national cinema, and when Chinese filmmakers and audiences alike were exposed to more varieties of imported films, Griffith fever dissipated. However the orphan imagination ignited by both *Orphans of the Storm* and *Orphan Rescues Grandfather* continues to prove enduring and generative as a persistent melodramatic register in Chinese-language cinemas.

THE ORPHAN IMAGINATION AS A GLOBAL VERNACULAR

To recapitulate, the prevalence of the orphan figure in melodramas worldwide allows us to track a unique transnational genealogy, opening new pathways for exploring particular national cinemas and storytelling forms without becoming trapped in either cultural essentialism or false universalism. As a transcultural "meme" crossing many film traditions, it enables us to approach melodrama as a transnational mode more historically, moving away from previous fixations on heterosexual romance, the Oedipal complex, and "women's pictures," defined under the mantle of ideological critique of capitalism and bourgeois patriarchy mostly in Western terms.

Orphan imagination, as a form for critical and comparative film historiography within the larger framework of modern world history, provides an analytical thermometer for measuring the fantasies and ideals invested in cinema, the competing or complementary ways of envisioning and embodying different ways of becoming independent and modern in the world for the self as well as for a community, and in relation to local "blood" cultures as well as neighboring ones or those of strangers. The orphan's precarious and adaptable status in traditional kinship patterns and in forms of subordinate or quasi citizenship makes her readily responsive to diasporic and cosmopolitan callings, even though she also may question them and retain her ambivalent attachment to her real or imagined origins. We see this, for example, in Bruce Lee's films and the cultural orphanhood his transnational stardom embodies. The orphan imagination is invested in this sense of alterity to one's own community and culture, and to the status quo that makes up the social and ethical norms governing a national or a transnational entity that more often than not reproduces inequity on a large scale.

The transcultural as articulated in the orphan imagination is thus not just about interaction or translation between nations or cultural forms on an empirical level; it also refers to the combined transformative power of the cinematic medium and the melodramatic mode within any given culture. It acknowledges the coexistence of, and tension between, competing claims (including disclaimers) to the nation within a "cosmopolitical" framework, in which subnational, seminational, or nonnational sociopolitical forms and cultural formations—as distinct from those authorized by the sovereign nation-state—are accorded recognition and legitimacy (Cheah and Robbins 1998). At the same time, as Bruce Robbins reflects, cosmopolitical thinking and feeling do not subscribe to an abstract universal reason divorced from the nation as a lived reality (12–13).

In this respect, the orphan imagination—on and off screen—introduces a range of gender, sexual, generational, and ethnic relationships within or between different social and cultural contexts as comparable objects of study, requiring excavation of melodrama's heterogeneous origins and transcultural careers. The orphan figure, invoking journeys and transpositions between different homes, languages, and genres, shows how the drama of family, kinship, and community is played out in a broad landscape of global modernity.

NOTES

A National Endowment of the Humanities Summer Grant, a faculty fellowship at New York University Humanities Center, and a University Fellowship at Hong Kong Baptist University supported my research. Many thanks to Karen Beckman, Tim Corrigan Jane Gaines, Andrew Jones, Adam Knee, Abé Mark Nornes, Amy Villarejo, Kristen Whissel, Lanjun Xu, Emilie YY Yu, Yinglin Zhang, and Kiki Tianqi Yu for hosting my talks and offering helpful comments, and to Christine Gledhill and Linda Williams for their inspiring work and editorial support.

1. The film is considered nonextant. Discussions are based on print material, stills, and secondary literature.
2. The ad was published in, among other places, *Sheng Bao*, December 28, 1923. Translation by Xuelei Huang (2014, 293).

3. Cai is also one of the screenplay writers of Ang Lee's *Crouching Tiger, Hidden Dragon* (2001), hailed as a perfect blend of martial arts and wenyi film.
4. This is clearly stated in one of Yeh's main sources, Xu Zhuodai's *Yinxi xue* [Photoplay] 1924. See also my discussion of Xu's book in *An Amorous History of the Silver Screen* (Zhang 2005, chapter 5).
5. Wenyi's status and influence was significantly diminished in the People's Republic of China after 1949, especially during the Cultural Revolution when Euro-American cinema and literature were largely off limits.
6. Many educated people in Shanghai during the Republican period spoke or understood English (among other foreign languages). Modern Shanghaiese contains pidgin vocabularies and terms. See my discussion of "Yangjingbang style" (Zhang 2005, chapter 2).
7. On the intimate kinship between Civilized Play, Mandarin Ducks and Butterflies fiction and early cinema in China, see Zhong et al. (1997) and Zhang (2005, chapter 3).
8. Huang points out that the 1931 U.S. sound version was released in China under the title *Konggu lanxun* ("Scent of Orchids in the Empty Valley"), recalling in the audience's mind the hugely successful *Konggu lan* only a few years earlier in 1926.
9. The films were widely known and reviewed in film-related publications by their Chinese titles: *Way Down East* (*Laihun* 赖婚), *Orphans of the Storm* (*Luanshi guchu* 乱世孤雏), *Birth of a Nation* (*Chongjian Guangming* 重见光明), *Broken Blossoms* (*Canhua lei* 残花泪), and *Intolerance* (*Zhuanzhi du* 专制毒); see Zheng (1936, 38–39).
10. This is another typical case of wenyi transmediation and melodramatization of a "tragic love story" from fiction to screen. Authored by Xu Zhenya, the "father" of Mandarin Ducks and Butterfly fiction, the novel, written in rather arcane classic prose, was first serialized in *Minqian Bao* in 1912 and had dozens of book editions through the 1940s. In 1924 Zheng Zhengqiu adapted the fiction to a screenplay, with significant changes that made the film more accessible to middle-brow taste and in tune with May Fourth ideas about social reform.
11. Zhou (1923) also stresses that the new film form, *zhengju*, or formal drama, departs from the company's earlier farce and comedy productions as well as so-called reality drama [*shishiju*]. *Zhengju* seeks to generate affective audience response and sympathy through fictional realism, or turning "ideals into reality."
12. From advertisement and review of the film in *Sheng Bao*, December 1923. Cited in Huang (2014, 192–93).
13. The source material is allegedly an American silent film, *Over the Hill to the Poorhouse* (Harry Millarde, 1920). For a perceptive reading of Zhu's film in particular and the ethic/aesthetics of his work as a whole, see Li (2006, 79–90).

6

Performing/Acting Melodrama

HELEN DAY-MAYER AND DAVID MAYER

SQUIRE . . . I tell ye! I want no supper of *her* gettin'! (Anna *stops arranging the dishes and . . . staggers backward up stage*) And the sooner she goes the better . . . My son marry this . . . beggar without a home or a name? (Anna *stretches out her hands towards him*) . . . You've . . . struck me in the heart! . . . Go! Out o' thet door, and never let me see your face again! (*Turns away R.*)

DAVID Take care—father! . . . you are insulting the woman I want for my wife! (*Takes* Anna *in his arms*)

SQUIRE (*drawing back*) The woman ye want fer yer wife 'n' what is she? . . . Ask her about the child, 'bout the child that's buried in Beldin churchyard—(Anna *totters toward Squire, imploringly; sinks at the feet, back to audience.*) . . .

ANNA You found out so much! . . . Did you find out also that I had believed myself to be an honorable wife? That the father of that child was a wretch who betrayed an ignorant girl through a mock marriage—. . . (*impatient gesture*) You have been hunting down the defenseless girl who only asked to earn her bread in your house. There is a man, an honored guest at your table—why don't you find out what his life has been? For he (*pointing to Sanderson*) is the father of my child—he is the man who betrayed me!

(Act III, *'Way Down East*, by Lottie Blair Parker, 1899)

In 1919, Lottie Blair Parker's drama, including this scene, was filmed by D. W. Griffith, with her stage dialogue repeated in the film's intertitles.

How do we imagine actors performing this melodramatic scene? What performance skills and techniques were, and still are, necessary to transfer Parker's words and stage directions into vivid drama? How is this scene translated into film? There are further questions. What characteristics distinguish stage and film acting in the latter part of the nineteenth and early twentieth century? Can we distinguish melodramatic acting from the more general characteristics of acting in this period?

We rarely encounter stage melodramas today, but, if we do, we are prepared for acting that is gestural and not altogether naturalistic. We may think melodrama unfashionable and dated. We may know that melodrama has had a bad press and that its detractors such as George Bernard Shaw (1932), William Archer (1923), and an earlier generation of American critics and academics denigrated melodrama in order to draw favorable attention to the "new" dramatists and to Naturalism.[1] However, our problems as spectators begin with our first viewing of silent film melodrama, or indeed with silent film.

Prior experiences of spectatorship stand in our way. Conditioned to performance through our twenty-first century experience of what we view as more or less realistic acting within a more or less realistic mise-en-scène, we are hesitant to accept early actors' work as effective means of explicating narrative, clarifying character relationships, expressing appropriate or valid emotion, or providing aesthetic pleasure. We are conditioned to the camera as an instrument for recording truth and the actor's performance as a means of validating that truth.

The silent film actor, particularly the film actor working before 1915, cannot be depended upon to fulfill the same function.[2] Rather, as the camera ventures out of doors to a "location" and places the actor in an actual townscape or countryside or finds the actor in a studio setting displaying—as much as preorthochromatic film will allow—the late-Victorian scenic artist's skill in representing realistic interiors, we see the actor gesticulating and posing in a manner recognizably discrepant to what, at worst, is perceived as scenic backdrop or, at best, environment. Against this would-be realistic background, the actor explicates prior conditions or events, current narrative, and changing emotional states through bodily stance, broad and numerous gestures, and—to the extent that these are visible to a camera lens at some distance from the performer—large facial expressions.

This disjunction is troubling. To the twenty-first century spectator, particularly those who live in Western societies where Protestant inhibition and self-restraint have long been equated with decorum, the actor does too much—perhaps because audiences demand too much. Full gesture is used alike for intimate domestic moments and emotionally fraught situations—even to convey abstract or conceptual information (deity, sanctity, wickedness, ethnicity)—with an apparent frequency and intensity that by modern standards seems inappropriate. We read such elaborations of stance and gesture as florid, overemotional, and excessive, particularly to the degree and distance that gesture is carried away from the body in a series of seemingly random gesticulations suggesting extremes of passion and emotion, which either fail to clarify or overstate their case.

How do we reconcile ourselves to these performances? How can the nature of the actor's performance be explained? Can we discern in apparent excess—what modern observers describe as a lack or loss of control—a method and an aesthetic, or, to be more exact, methods and aesthetics? Are movements toward realism (or Naturalism) the only valid criteria for measuring and assessing early silent film performance? Can generalities cover all instances within the considerable expanse of film acting?

Theater historians are aware that elements of melodrama are timeless. Although the term *melodrama* didn't appear until the last decade of the eighteenth century, the theatrical canon abounds in dramas dealing with serious subjects in which leading characters face physical and moral peril; where moral character is visibly divided between the upright and honorable and those tainted with evil and cruelty; and serious dramas intentionally or ironically conclude with a "happy ending." Melodramatic form was employed by Euripides (performed in a festival given over to tragedy), favored by Jacobean dramatists, revived in literary and dramatic forms in Germany by Lessing, again in France, where it was finally named *melo-drame* by Renee Charles-Guilbert de Pixérécourt, developed by Alexandre Dumas père, by Victor Hugo, and in England by authors as unalike as Hugh Walpole and Charles Dickens. It was carried to America by numerous European actors and dramatists and there found such diverse—almost antithetical—exponents and interpreters as Edwin Forrest and Edwin Booth, Walter Hampden and Fanny Davenport. However, our concern here is with melodramatic acting within a specific Western framework—the latter half of the nineteenth century and the early decades of the twentieth. We therefore draw upon stage and film drama that operated within this designated locus and temporal envelope.

As theater historians, we understand melodrama as a theatrical or literary response that points to potential chaos in a world that emerged with industrialization and revolution in the 1790s and continued well into the twentieth century. It emerges from societies where things go wrong, where ideas of secular and divine justice and recompense are not always met, where suffering is not always acknowledged, and where the explanations for wrong, injustice, and suffering are not altogether understandable. Melodrama responds with emotion rather than intellect, and answers to a world in which explanations of why there is pain and disruption and discord are flawed or deeply and logically inconsistent and in which all too visible discrepancies are readily observed between calamities and palliative answers. Melodrama provides an emotionally intelligible picture of the world to deracinated Western cultures, frayed or severed by science and technology from former religious and spiritual "truths." Melodrama also speaks to audiences and readers feeling their way in an urbanizing environment in which no one is visibly accountable for the failure of public services, for unpredicted hazards, or for inadequate civil protection. It has the capacity to offer these audiences emotional satisfactions and emotionally validates the world as they experience it. For such spectators, it is helpful and reassuring to depict a world that may be explained in comparatively simple terms of good and evil. Melodrama depicts a Manichean world wherein forces of wickedness and goodness are in constant contention and there is little place for characters who are neither wholly good nor altogether bad.

Such sharp divisions between suffering goodness and active malevolence give rise to melodrama's principal characters—villain, hero, heroine—the first unambiguously wicked, the latter two morally uncorrupt and incorruptible. Identifying these characters and making them visible to the drama or film's audiences is one of the chief endeavors of melodramatic acting. However, against later caricatures of melodrama, it must be insisted that such acute distinctions are chiefly associated with melodrama's early years and are less marked, if still present, by the 1860s and after.

Both theatrical and filmic melodramas demanded—and received—concessions from their audiences. Audiences accepted the theater and cinema as spaces of simulation and imagination. They knew that scenery was made up of canvas, paint, and wooden frames that, when assembled and properly lighted, depicted places and environments but were not really those places. They knew actors were enacting a made up narrative and speaking or miming words that had first been imagined by someone else. And they knew that actors were conspirators in a plot—in which they, the audience, shared—to tell a story and convince them of the truth of that story, no matter how outlandish.

The casting of actors for melodramatic stage and film roles assumed that skills of voice, posture, and gesture, when shared with the audience—sometimes through the agency of direct address or "asides"—communicated a character's moral status. These endeavors were supplemented (and indeed led) by effective dramaturgy—dialogue or intertitles—by costuming and hand properties, and by the judicious use of accompanying music that could imply a range of moral and emotional states. Important also for both the Victorian spectator and the modern student is awareness that the actor performs a stereotypical role. In a standard stock, repertory, or "combination" company of a dozen to fifteen actors, many specialized in a particular "line," or role, consistent in character and dramatic function from melodrama to melodrama. Indeed, so stereotypical and morally defined were such roles that they could be burlesqued.

When a melodrama was translated from the stage to film or when an original movie melodrama was cast, the full range of such stereotypical roles was less likely to be utilized for a variety of reasons. For economy's sake, it was cheaper and faster to employ fewer actors. A two-hour drama abridged to as few as two reels focused on the vicissitudes of the principal characters and only brought in subordinate roles when necessary. In addition, except in long shot, a full Victorian cast of actors could not be accommodated. Both stage and film melodramas were often structured to advance their plots at such an accelerating tempo that audiences were denied any adequate opportunity to question inconsistencies or anomalies or moral ambiguities. As well as a director's or an author's task, it was also the actor's problem not merely to maintain the tempo but to approach his or her role with utmost sincerity, identifying with the play and the emotional truth of the role. Once an actor signaled to the audience that the drama might be viewed ironically or parodied, the power of the melodrama was sabotaged.

In mounting a melodrama, the villain's part was the first role cast. Although the actors playing hero or heroine might be better known to the public and admired for their looks and previous reputations in dramas in which they had overcome villainy, the villain was chosen who could best enact the crime that subsequently ensnared them. Additional casting determined the villain's associates and those who aided the hero and heroine. Villains were supported in their dramatic endeavors by henchmen and women of dubious virtue; the hero and heroine were assisted by a range of servants, friends, family members, and associates who were largely virtuous but often comically down to earth.

Melodrama depended on the abilities of the audience to recognize evil and to distinguish it from good. The conventions of this genre were there to assist, and actors played to these conventions. Melodrama's trouble usually arose from two sources. The first was a recognizable social problem that was likely to affect all the drama's characters: war, military or naval service and the harsh regulations governing lower ranks, economic depression, agricultural blight, disruptive industrialization, urban distress or isolation with attendant unemployment or poverty, the vicissitudes of life in foreign lands with a restless or hostile native population. But none of these genuine sources of difficulty was sufficient to drive the plot.

The plots of melodrama have a further propelling force—villainy—and its performance is the engine of melodrama. The villain, for reasons personal to him and altogether reprehensible, instigated an action that destabilized the hero and heroine and placed their lives, fortunes, livelihoods, good names, social relationships, and romantic intentions in grave jeopardy. Having been abruptly extruded from stability and comfort by the villain—whose machinations the hero and heroine initially fail to recognize—these leading characters must struggle to reclaim lost ground. Abetted by their friends and associates, often comic and of a lower social status, the heroine and hero discover the nature of their peril, and, recognizing that they are the victims of combinations of malice, avarice, lust, envy, and cruelty, they identify and expel the villain from his place of power. With the villain thus identified and his power nullified or destroyed, the initial source of stress (which had become the background problem) vanishes. And, crucially, the audience has not been allowed time to note that a serious and major problem—the immediate social background to this drama—has been abruptly dispelled. With the happiness and security of the hero and heroine restored, society appears briefly healed. This villain, then, had a further function, which helps to explain why audiences found melodrama a continuous source of pleasure. By fusing his identity with the underlying social problem, he (rarely, she) helped to disguise unresolvable contradictions and conspicuous incongruities between the actual world and the world as depicted in the theater that the drama papered over. Melodrama exacts no toll on the "good" characters who emerge unscathed; they have grown wiser in the ways of the world—wiser, but not cynical. Further, as they have only naiveté to lose, they are still innocent. They have briefly suffered physical and emotional hardships and may have been threatened with permanent social ostracism, poverty, ill-health, and even death, but their fresh accumulation of wisdom has cost little.

As the nineteenth century progressed, melodrama became deeply interesting when the moral clarity of hero and villain became blurred through their fusion into one character, when the very self of a role was deeply divided. From the 1860s onward, a leading character emerged whose multiple identities were concealed from the play's other characters. Drama has always been a medium that enables the performance of multiple layers of character, exposing fissures and slippages in identity. Now, with successive advances in neurological science and emerging ideas about the unconscious, it was more widely recognized that beneath outward character a second—hidden—identity lurked that might be exposed and liberated. Neuroscientists such as Mesmer, Charcot, and Freud foresaw healing properties in liberating this twin; showmen and artists—people of a vivid and theatrical imagination—saw the liberated twin as a danger. Henry Irving specialized in melodramatic roles in which the seemingly "good," innocent outer character was tormented by his guilty inner self and, in one notable instance, Charles Reade's *The Lyons*

Mail (1854), Irving enacted a double role, playing an innocent husband and father as well as a murderous but physically identical criminal. Both British and American actors performed a Dr. Henry Jekyll, who uncontrollably turned into a monstrous Mr. Hyde before audiences' eyes. Numerous temperance melodramas dramatized the benign father turned into a monster at the domestic hearth and depicted the struggle to return the alcoholic monster to his former self. The actors who essayed such double roles required the physical skills and knowledge to perform as both villain and hero, and they required audiences to willingly accept the half-fiction of a dual identity and the plausibility of the inner, as well as the outer, self.

The question, now, is how did actors address these needs? What tools had they at their disposal? The answer is, first, their voices, second, their bodies: their characters and situations expressed through stance and gesture and movement. We acknowledge, but intentionally elide, what was generally regarded as the melodramatic actor's most important skill—a dramatically effective speaking voice. Virtually every book or manual that instructs the would-be actor refers to the necessity of vocal work—projection, modulation, enunciation, and timbre—to convey thought and express emotion. Melodramatic stage acting necessarily expects and demands the use of the audible, clear, expressive voice. It demands the capacity to convey texts—play scripts—intelligently and with appropriate emotion. Melodramatic texts are among the most demanding for stage actors, who must convey a range of emotions without suggesting that the written rhetoric may appear excessive—beyond the vocabulary and the emotion of everyday speech.[3] But because this volume leads from the live stage to the silent screen, we recognize that the turn of the century actor was summarily deprived of his voice, which was both a loss and a vastly compensatory gain, prioritizing gestural vocabularies. It is the physically pliant, gesticulating melodramatic actor who concerns us in this chapter.

The Victorian melodramatic actor's voice is almost beyond recovery, but the existence of both acting manuals and early films in which professional actors—sometimes stage-trained and stage-experienced—perform offers physical evidence. Although we can view drawn and lithographed images of live Victorian stage performance, we can only attempt conjectural interpretation of unverifiable simulacra. Further, we can observe a handful of classical ballets whose aestheticized gestural codes derive from the ballets d'action that first made their appearance in the second half of the eighteenth century (see Noverre 1760). But it is difficult to connect these danced narratives and their prescribed gesticulation to theatrical or early screen performance.

Gesture, together with stance and movement, lie at the heart of this essay; these elements help differentiate the performance of melodrama from other theatrical and filmic genres. The origins of late-eighteenth- and nineteenth-century gestural acting—and by extension, twentieth-century melodramatic film—are found in two congruent theories of the Enlightenment. First, the idea of gesture as a signifier of emotional and, to a lesser degree, conceptual meaning can be traced back to Jean Jacques Rousseau. To account for the origin of languages, Rousseau (1791), drawing on anthropological beliefs, argued an imagined era before there was recognizable speech or language, when people everywhere communicated by gestures that were universally read and understood.

The second idea was that the body and mind together formed and powered a living machine. Given the identical emotional stimulus—pain, fear, hunger, desire, wrath, distain, mirth—it was thought that this human machine would always mechanically and automatically reproduce gestures appropriate to these impulses and that these automatic gestures were instantly readable. These theories were compromised by lapsarian philosophy: removed from their original primitive Edens, over the centuries mankind (and consequently gestures) became corrupted. Formerly instinctive gestural meanings were dissipated and lost and were replaced by local, personal, and idiosyncratic gesticulation. In consequence, many theories of acting are about recovering and reactivating in the actor's mind and body these universally understood gestures so they again become innate. At their extreme, the actor was encouraged to shed individual traits and to acquire a standard, but aestheticized, gestural vocabulary imagined to be close to this lost universal gestural vocabulary.

The theatrical world in the nineteenth and twentieth centuries saw many changes: technical advances altered the nature of pictorial representation, melodrama spread from Britain's "Minor" theaters into the Patent House and beyond to the theaters of North America, and acting styles favored by the public changed. Despite these numerous developments, acting manuals addressed to would-be performers between the arrival of melodrama in the 1790s and the consolidation of the silent motion picture industry in the 1920s changed little in the advice they offered.

Each manual uniformly addresses the actor's need to be effectively (that is, emotionally tellingly) visible on the Georgian and Victorian pictorial stage. Each manual emphasizes the expressiveness of the actor's physical body and assigns to the actor's stance, gesture, facial expression, and motion meanings that define the role's moral character and her or his immediate emotional and psychological state. Many credit the physically expressive actor with the capacity to convey basic abstractions (such as deity, justice, and forgiveness), as well as to argue, debate, or conduct everyday, romantic, business, or criminal transactions, and they further credit the actor with a conspicuous artistry that falls pleasingly within the range of current aesthetic tastes. We cite five examples that parallel the evolution of melodrama. In most instances, these manuals should be regarded as describing the author's ideal actor rather than depicting or describing individual actors. Garcia is the exception, with illustrations depicting recognizable performers.

Henry Siddons's *Practical Illustrations of Rhetorical Gesture and Action* (1807) is the earliest of these works. Adapted from a German source, the male and female actor's body as it interprets emotions and abstract states is illustrated in several dozen plates, depicted at full-length, with no separate renderings of hands or facial expressions. Siddons explains the psychological processes that lead to and govern the actor's attitude. Significantly, Siddons thinks in terms of tragedy, comedy, and domestic dramas that have not yet evolved into melodrama, but he clearly distinguishes between rectitude (the upright body) and villainy (the body bent, off-center, the shoulders at uneven levels).

Other manuals were addressed to the aspirant actor throughout the century, but none depict known performers until the publication of Gustav Garcia's *The Actor's Art* (1888). Addressed to "Artists, Students and Amateurs," Garcia, a former operatic baritone who taught singers at London's Guildhall School, illustrated his book with vignettes of unnamed but recognizable actors performing in role: each gesticulating, each deploying facial expressions, each illustrative of a passion. Separately Garcia includes telling facial expressions and depictions of actors' hands—convulsed, relaxed, open, flexed, balled into fists, and other expressive states—that further illustrate how the actor's face, limbs, and body can convey emotion. Thus, for the first time, melodramatic performance is subject to pictorial analysis coupled with advice on its execution.

An approach to physical acting promulgated by François Delsarte came into practice first in France in the 1860s, and then moved avidly into America. Strongly influencing mid- to late-Victorian melodramatic performance, it had a similar impact on early film melodrama. Delsarte never published a manual of instruction, but his methods were seized upon and first published by Genevieve Stebbins and the American stage artist Steele MacKaye (1997). Their work was not illustrated, but other practitioners and teachers of acting quickly brought out manuals that pictured draped models—not actors—depicting the passions. Typical of these was a manual for schools, the anonymous *Home and School Speaker* (1897). The melodramatist and actor Dion Boucicault opened a New York school in which he offered acting instruction based on his own interpretation of the Delsarte system.

Delsarte and his subsequent interpreters recognized scientific descriptions of the body (by, for example, Charles Darwin) as programmed to respond to intellectual, environmental, and emotional stimuli in certain predictable—mechanical—ways, via gestures and bodily movements. But Delsarte also observed that individuals acquire many personal traits and unconscious gestures that become habitual and are deployed to express emotional states or to assist transactions that are understandable only by those closest to the user and are to others (theater audiences) altogether unreadable. Victorian teachers of acting believed, as did Rousseau, that in automatic movements and gestures lay a universal alphabet, and the aspirant actor was expected to shed personal idiosyncratic gestures and to acquire this vocabulary of stance, gesture, and movement.

Delsarte divided the actor's faculties into body, soul, and mind, describing each function as vital, emotional, and intellectual. The body itself was further divided into zones of expressiveness. Thus the origin of the gesture (in the limbs or chest or abdomen) further defined meaning. Delsarte training, therefore, was devoted to making these natural movements that reveal the passions so automated that corrupting gestures were eliminated and replaced with those supposedly natural and innate. However, reacting against the possible mechanization of movement, with every actor moving exactly alike, some Delsarte practitioners sought to make actors' movements "biological"—sinuous and vinelike—emphasizing the actor's grace, balance, force, and energy as expressed in the term *élan*.

Delsartian acting was better illustrated—and simplified—by the London actor Henry Neville, who, like theatrical professionals Steele MacKaye and Dion Boucicault in New York, ran an acting school in London from the early 1880s. All three offered a version of the Delsarte system. Neville's system—explicated in his 1895 text aimed at platform reciters, amateurs, and professional actors—implies a distinctly *fin-de-siècle* aesthetic. In this system, the once upright stance associated with the idealized, admirable character of eighteenth-century theater, known as the *crux scenica*,[4] now, nearly a century later, bends in sinuous curves, and gestures follow ovals and arcs. We can witness such movements in early film. Victoria Duckett (2015) links Sarah Bernhardt's "spiraling," vinelike turns and gestures in her films to the aesthetics of *art nouveau* (8–9).

Neville describes a 180-degree, multidimensional range of gesture and movement that can be asymmetrical rather than formally balanced. He designates three different bodily levels—the abdomen, the chest, and the limbs—for three different groups of gestures: epic, rhetorical, and colloquial. The colloquial represents the everyday gestures that carry information or relate to everyday transactions and etiquette. The rhetorical gestures convey conceptual thought, bring emotions into play, and express a thinking process. Epic gestures express high emotion and lofty sentiments and ideas. Even colloquial gestures are large, with limbs away from the body, describing circles, parabolas, and arcs, and so seem distant from today's notion of the "realistic." There's clearly a concern to match levels of emotion with levels of gestures—from waist to chest to above the head. It's a form of visual volume control, with the gesture rising and expanding as the emotional and moral volume increases. When schematized in guide form, this inevitably appears formulaic and, in this respect, is not indicative of actual practice. However, it demonstrates the desired plasticity of the actor and the multidimensional nature of the gestures that the actor might achieve. The manual format, however, is unable to indicate the flow of one movement into another or the nature of that motion in terms of speed, dynamics, and quality of movement.

Finally, well into the twentieth century, when silent films had reached feature length and audiences were fully attuned to film performance, Charles Aubert (1927) published *The Art of Pantomime*, returning even at this late date to the idea of gesture as an innate universal language. Addressed to actors, dancers, artists, and sculptors, the book is heavily illustrated with numerous stick figures posed to represent emotional and mental states. Schematic renderings of facial expression, hands, eyes, lips, and angles of the head are emphasized as parts of the performer's expressive and physical armory.

Naturally, there were arguments about gesture. Not everyone agreed. The notion of the universality of gesture is contradicted, for example, by Guido Lambranzi, who, citing the specific gestural sign language used by residents of Naples and Genoa, insisted that gesture is local and particular to a culture (as cited in Winter 1975, 93). Those claiming that gestures originally constituted a transcultural and transnational language, applied and understood by primitive peoples, faced the problem of what gestures become when that language is lost or corrupted. Do they still provide a vocabulary that conveys meaning? And if not, can they form the actor's alphabet? The evidence is contradictory. In American and British silent film acting, we sometimes witness performances in which the actors appear to be working within an effective self-contained communications system with well-timed gestures pertinent to the moment, subject matter, and period, neither excessive nor too few. But we also see the opposite: actors working to their own private system of gestures, gestures sparse or excessive and badly timed. Therefore, *some* gestures *sometimes* have meaning, but we also see gestures applied inappropriately. When gestures are divorced from an emotional context, when they are used heartlessly and excessively, when the same gesture is used repeatedly, when the use of gestures delay actions that the drama demands, they are devoid of meaning and are visibly ridiculous. This emptying of meaning is intentionally made evident in the 1908/1912 parody of stage melodrama in the film *Why Girls Leave Home* (see Mayer 2006). Here skilled actors pretend to be members of an incompetent touring troupe, exhibiting and reveling in the tired clichés of the touring actor's repertoire, mechanically repeating the same gestures and delaying plot elements until these moments become more vacuous—and funnier—with each heartless repetition.

One of the more pertinent approaches to nineteenth-century gestural acting was expressed in 1892 by Percy Fitzgerald, Henry Irving's literary adviser. Fitzgerald notes that gesture is most effective when it precedes speech and is used with restraint.

> Gesture . . . is nearly as potent a medium of expression as the voice itself; in many cases it is more subtle, swift, and comprehensive. There is a language in gesture, with innumerable shades of meaning. It will convey everything . . . with many more delicate emotions for which words are too formal, and too slow. There is one method of great force, and which is used to enrich the dramatic expression . . . This is the anticipation of the utterance by the gesture. . . . The body seems to run eagerly forward, in advance of the mind. The dramatic result, which has extraordinary effect in the way of riveting attention, seems to work in this fashion. The anticipatory gesture is made. . . . Then a second or two of suspense follows; all is finally satisfied by the utterance itself.
>
> There are other devices—the suspended or intercepted gesture . . . the attempt at self-mastery; and what is more effective than the simple gesture of despair, without a single word being spoken, and which conveys so much? . . . The tendency, therefore, of gesture is in the direction of reserve, and economy of motion. . . . The more we multiply gestures, the more we make them insignificant. . . . Gesture is a language to express ideas *that are not written* . . . for which words are too coarse and inefficient. (50–59)

Fitzgerald's recognition that the timing of gestures and the actor's self-restraint enhanced performance coincided with a technical development that further influenced melodramatic acting: the introduction of electric stage lighting. Prior to the 1870s, theaters had been illuminated, first by candles, then by gaslight, but throughout the eighteenth and first three-quarters of the nineteenth century, theater auditoria remained fully illuminated. There was little difference between light levels in the auditorium and on the stage, necessitating large gestures to render the actors fully distinct. Then, in the 1870s, as electric stage lighting was introduced, auditoria were darkened. The pictorial stage and its actors became more distinct to audiences seated in darkness. Gradually actors accepted that being visible didn't necessitate large gestures (see Mayer 1997).

Gestural performance cannot be considered complete without the presence of an element central to the dramatic event: the almost continual presence of incidental music in stage plays, at silent film showings, and during much of the filming itself. Victorian and Edwardian stage performances and their reception depend upon the close lamination of many discrete theatrical elements: script, mise-en-scène, acting, spectators. The unifying bonding element, above all others, is music. Music reaches into the auditorium to underline dramatic action and enclose the audience within an aura of sound. Often intertextual, quoting bars of familiar airs, hinting at musical styles or genres, or signifying through key and modal changes, incidental music teaches the spectator how, in moral and emotional terms, to interpret character and behavior.[5] Imparting an external dynamic to the action, music quickens or slows the spectator's pulse. Further, music supports the physical and emotional work of the actor. Gestures seen in total silence may seem excessive, vacuous, or grafted on as an afterthought; when fully supported by musical accompaniment, gestures sustained by the actor seem altogether plausible to the audience.

When we examine acting manuals such as Henry Neville's and the pictorial evidence of plays and motion picture frame enlargements, we see actors caught in extreme poses—"attitudes"—at the full extent of a gesture. We see these same attitudes in Victorian sculpture and in much narrative painting of the period (see Meisel 1983) and are properly encouraged to consult this anecdotal material to gain a clearer understanding of how telling gesture defined the key moment of these frozen narratives.[6] A gesture, however, is far more than these discrete extremes of attitude.

Despite illustrations that imply otherwise, a stage gesture is not an isolated moment, unless the end of a scene or a key moment in that scene has been intentionally selected to form a momentary "picture" (the theatrical term for *tableau*). Rather, within and around any gesture are innumerable permutations of movement—all at the discretion of the actor, the demands of the role, and dozens of other variables. As several actors may be sharing a scene, gestures constitute part of the exchanges between them and express the unspoken subtext of the theatrical moment. Part of the problem is what these manuals and pictorial resources less successfully tell us, if at all, about *how* the actor negotiates the intermediate stages of the gesture to reach its limits or *how* the actor makes effective transition from one gesture to another or *how* these gestures work with music.[7] Yet it is these very negotiations that are vital to gauging the dramatic power and fluency of performed gesture.

Here again, music assists the transitional process, not only sustaining gesture as it travels from the actor's trunk into limbs, joints, wrists, hands, and extending or curling fingers, but also hinting at a shifting or intensifying emotional climate between gestures and, concurrently, setting the groundwork for the gesture to follow. As when music conveying one emotional climate may segue into altogether different music, so gesture can segue into gestures that elaborate or contradict. The actor's gestural vocabulary may initiate entire sentences of gesture that parallel, amplify, and communicate the content of the dramatic text. Sometimes music initiates the gesture; sometimes dialogue or thought or emotional impulse drives the gesture, and music follows; sometimes gesture initiates further thought, and again music follows. At other times gesture, impulse, and music appear to begin together. There is no fixed running order. And all the while the audience usually remains unaware that music has served the drama and its performance so well. If the spectator is too aware of music, the illusion is less than perfect.

Thus music is to the stage or silent film actor what water is to the swimmer. Music, emotionally and imaginatively drawing in the audience, buoys up and physically supports the actor, and although thought—particularly verbs that shape the intellectual and emotional content of spoken text—provides the impulse for gestures, music acts as the supporting medium, furnishing tempo, orchestral coloring, tonality, rhythm, direction, and force. Music, like water, is the medium of support, propulsion, and resistance, and the actor or swimmer continually moves with and against its currents and density.

Music is inseparable from melodrama. Returning to the third act scene from Blair Parker's 1898 *"Way" Down East*, imagine the following exchanges heavily informed by forceful, pertinent gesture and telling movement. Words, actions, and gestures alike are bound closely together by orchestral music:

SQUIRE . . . I tell ye! I want no supper of *her* gettin'! (Anna *stops arranging the dishes and . . . staggers backward up stage*) And the sooner she goes the better . . . My son marry this . . . beggar without a home or a name? (Anna *stretches out her hands towards him*) . . . You've . . . struck me in the heart! . . . Go! Out o' thet door, and never let me see your face again! (*Turns away R.*)

DAVID Take care—father! . . . you are insulting the woman I want for my wife! (*Takes* Anna *in his arms*)

SQUIRE (*drawing back*) The woman ye want fer yer wife 'n' what is she? [. . .] Ask her about the child, 'bout the child that's buried in Beldin churchyard—(Anna *totters toward* Squire, *imploringly; sinks at the feet, back to audience.*) . . .

ANNA You found out so much! [. . .] Did you find out also that I had believed myself to be an honorable wife? That the father of that child was a wretch who betrayed an ignorant girl through a mock marriage—[. . .] (*impatient gesture*). You have been hunting down the defenseless girl who only asked to earn her bread in your house. There is a man, an honored guest at your table—why don't you find out what his life has been? For he (*pointing to* Sanderson) is the father of my child—he is the man who betrayed me!

Here, as was typical for plays of the late Victorian era, is an exchange rich in specified action, in stage effect, and in movement and gesture. Here is an instance of the melodramatic actor in synchronicity with the total mise-en-scène. Evidence from numerous theatrical promptbooks and actors' manuals suggests that music works with and through these elements, supporting searing, expansive gestures—the Squire's dropped head, upstage arm pointing. Sanderson, the villain, at first sprawling comfortably in his chair, seemingly aloof from the conflict, then, quietly agitated, sitting upright, finally turning away in confusion and shame. Music supports Anna's stretching hands and the Squire's shuddering withdrawal as his son clasps the woman his father would drive from home. And again, music underlines Anna's question: "There is a man . . . why don't you find out what his life has been? For he (the questioning upturned wrist and palm now turning to stage floor and *pointing to* Sanderson) is the father of my child—he is the man who betrayed me!" Music enables, indeed encourages, gesture to be checked, to work with or against the tempi of speech, to be elaborated, modified, turned, "stretched," supported, and fluently segued from one gesture to another.

When this scene was filmed by Griffith in 1919, Blair Parker's words, spoken but inaudible, and now largely repeated in intertitles, the confrontations, passions, and gestures of Burr McIntosh as Squire Bartlett,[8] Lillian Gish as Anna, and Richard Barthelmess as David remain as emotionally charged and, at times, as physically large and, fortunately, as dramatic as ever. Lillian Gish, concurrently, fills in with emotionally intense and intimate "pocket gestures." Close-up shots and two-shots, the intensity of gesture now intercut with a matched intensity of rapidly changing facial expressions, space out the frequency of big moments filmed as long shots. Intense emotions are not constrained nor gestures fettered. The actors' vocabulary of stage gesture is still employed, but film allows the range and scale to vary from large and expansive arm-extending thrusts, driving forcefully away from the actors' trunks, to intimate, less obvious, small-scale stress-displacing—yet fully observable—movements. These small gestures intentionally leak the character's covert thoughts and emotions. There is no sense in which these gestures are artificial, practiced, and simply applied. In a performance of lesser quality, the gestures would appear to be superficially grafted on and become a stiff and clumsily obtrusive distraction—a poor example of melodramatic acting, merely serving to sabotage the effectiveness of the drama and its emotional content. Here they work.

To drive Anna from his home, the Squire approaches the door, turning the knob with his right hand, his left pointing first to the threshold. He then swings his extended right arm upward in an arc and jabs in the direction of the as yet unseen snowstorm. All the while, his left hand is balled tightly into a fist. Three more times, each with increased fury, the expelling jab is repeated until the jabbing hand turns into a fist. The fists tighten. Anna, meanwhile, at first dumbfounded and stepping sideways, makes small self-comforting gestures, running her hands down the sides of her apron. As she turns, she puts on a cloak, and only then unties her apron strings and pulls it off. As the Squire confronts her, she folds the apron over one wrist to release her hands and then gestures with both wrists flexed, palms facing outward toward the Squire in part as a plea, in part as a defensive shield. Then, as David hears of her baby and she is unable to deny her past, she anxiously clutches the apron and drops her head in defeat. The apron, its strings untied, hangs limply, mirroring Anna's sense of hopelessness. She then returns the apron that gave her status and a role in the family home, gently draping it over a chair back as she moves behind the Squire to take her imposed leave of the family. David angrily smashes the plate that his father only moments before had angrily rejected, and Anna, as she reaches the door, turns back to face the family. Her tearful face hardens, and she fixes her gaze on Sanderson. In a series of three staccato arm's length piercing jabs that mirror and answer the Squire's previous thrusts, she demands, "There is a man, an honored guest at your table—why don't you find out what his life has been?" She strikes the table with her fist and, again and again, jabs and scolds with her pointed finger: "For he is the father of my child—he is the man who betrayed me!" The gestures here are simultaneously appropriate, furious, and domestic, with the gestural style growing organically from the characters' emotions. And none seem out of place or excessive in a realistic New Hampshire farm kitchen.

Acting manuals merely offer the rudiments—the merest vocabularies of such performances. Films, however, closely analyzed, fill in, elaborate, and make visible melodramatic gestural performance. They sometimes lead us (as in the case of Joseph Byron's 1899 photographs of "*Way*" *Down East*) back to the original stage performance through which we can discern a commonality in approach and emotional and gestural intensity between Phoebe Davis, the original Anna, and Lillian Gish's equally nuanced film Anna.

Music also unites past and present. We know that many silent film directors used accompanying music to assist their actors performing before the camera. Photographs of Alice Guy filming on an interior set show a string trio providing music that is inaudible to the cinema audience but nevertheless allowed her actors to find and hold and build appropriate emotive gesture. It was essential, not alien, to performance. For the spectator, as well as the actor, music remained an interpreter of and an essential performer in the melodramatic event.

In this chapter, we have indicated the outer—essential—lineaments of melodrama performance. These constituent elements—voice, stance, facial expression, gesture, movement, all surrounded by accompanying music—were tools at the disposal of the Victorian stage actor and, voice excepted, the early film actor. What the actor contributed to melodrama beyond these basics was her and his mental resources: intelligence, quickness of thought, imagination, and integrity, the latter a fixed belief in the truth of the role undertaken. No role was complete without these further resources brought into play and orchestrated into a coherent and expressive whole that fully engaged spectators' emotions as well as their suspense and credulity.

Today, more than a full century after such overt bodily skills and accompanying mental resources were practiced, Victorian melodrama's visibly physical approach to acting may be alien to us. Although the actor's mind and body are still the required tools of the profession, the movie camera and a more naturalistic stage have reduced the size and frequency of gesture. Consciously observing and then accepting such performances on early film can be hard work, sometimes distancing us from dramas we had hoped to enjoy. We sometimes have to take on faith that the melodramatic actors' work was effective and accepted, indeed often praised. It has stood the test of time. Looking closer at the filmed performances we are fortunate to recover, we can begin to understand why.

NOTES

1. Thomas Postlewait (1996) offers the best account of the denigration of melodrama and its rationale.
2. The standardized technologies and common industrial and commercial practices of a world cinema were in use by 1910. It is nearly five years later, however, before there is some agreement about acting technique.
3. It is still possible to experience the Victorian melodramatic actor's voice via the Internet. The most accessible Victorian actor is the silent cowboy, William S. Hart. (Google "William S. Hart's farewell.") Hart speaks in the cadences and vocal inflections of the Victorian stage actor.
4. Relaxed body upright, arms similarly relaxed to gesture easily, knees slightly flexed, heels together, toes apart at a ninety-degree angle—the first position of ballet. The posture implied control, denying or subduing unruly and antisocial impulses. Departures from this position enabled actors to define and audiences to infer character.
5. Earlier in the nineteenth century, characters were identified by musical signatures that heralded or accompanied each character's entrance. By the 1880s this practice was largely abandoned. See Pisani (2014), Marks (1997), Robinson (1990, 1995), and Mayer and Scott (1983).
6. Some histories improperly describe nineteenth-century acting as a sequence of fixed attitudes or gestural units: see Booth (1991, 120–25) and Brewster and Jacobs (1997, 79–137).
7. Throughout the nineteenth century, actors were praised for their fluency and eloquence, or criticized for the shortcomings of their "transitions."
8. From the original 1898 stage production.

7

Melodrama and the Making of Hollywood

HILARY A. HALLETT

Melodrama has had almost no purchase with historians of the United States. Despite its ubiquity in other disciplines and regions of historical study, few who write histories of the American scene have explored what the melodramatic mode, and the cultural forms it shaped, has to say about the nation's encounter with an emerging mass culture. Lacking familiarity with the vast scholarship on melodrama in other fields, U.S. historians employ a static, reductive definition of the profoundly mutable, slippery form that emerged in eighteenth-century Europe and Britain in response to the crumbling of hierarchically organized, "sacred" orders (Brooks 1976; Gledhill 2002, 14–20). Historians of American culture mostly understand melodrama only as a formulaic story of good and evil, in which a virtuous heroine, "helpless and unfriended," patiently waits for the hero to rescue her from the villain's dastardly plot (Grimstead 1968; McWilliams 2000).

Yet a diversity of melodramatic expressions dominated American popular-cum-mass culture after the Civil War, reflecting the shift in moral perspectives demanded by the new nation's democratic experiments. As the United States rapidly industrialized, its expanding entertainment industries imported, modified, and embellished European melodramatic conventions in plays variously labeled apocalyptic, heroic, problem, nautical, sensational, immoral, domestic, horse, and frontier melodramas (Bank 1982; McConachie 1992; Hall 2001). All variations dramatized the struggles of ordinary women and men rather than describing the unfolding of a "classical" hero's fate as with premodern tragedies (Braudy 1997, 125–26). All employed an emotional register and beautifully executed stagecraft to produce heretofore unimaginably realistic spectacles (Gledhill 2002, 34–35). Melodrama then, in Linda Williams's words, enlisted "realism to generate outrage against realities that could and, to its creators, should be changed" (chapter 12, "Melodrama and Justice"). Paradoxically, melodrama celebrated the individualism advanced by Western mass society and acted as an antidote to its isolating effects. Melodrama drove the plots and characterizations employed not just in many plays but in the novels, inexpensive, nationally syndicated newspapers, and early story films aimed at, and purchasable by, all Americans. By the 1920s, the sociologist

Robert Park (1925) asserted that a melodramatic rhetoric had been transferred from stage to newsprint to film. But this observation failed to spark further reflection as the histories of the press, theater, and film developed separately, despite their obvious intertwining and interdependence.

In this chapter I sketch a still too little recognized arc in melodrama's translation from stage to newsprint to screen: its production of ever-more sensational and "immoral" melodramas focused on female characters whose grit, initiative, and moral complexity challenged respectable middle-class gender morality. This process began during the mid-nineteenth century on the "legitimate stage" as it grew due to the new patronage of women from the burgeoning urban middle class (Johnson 1984; Ryan 1990; Dudden 1995). Many of these fans preferred "sensation" and "immoral" variants that used melodrama's intense emotional register and artful stagecraft to encourage audiences' identification with powerful heroines whose trials and tribulations led them to jettison strictures about "true womanhood" as necessarily passive (Welter 1966; Cott 1978). The intense action and suspense of sensation melodramas helped to justify their heroines' active role in the villain's defeat. The first American female theater star, Charlotte Cushman, rose to fame playing sensationally "manly" heroines, or by literally assuming the power of the hero in "breeches roles." In contrast, immoral melodramas, initially adapted from French plays, focused on the "erring woman's" relationship to society. Even the more moralizing Anglophone translations of these plays explored the psychological motivation of their female characters with a depth that encouraged sympathy and understanding (Eltis 2013). By 1900, a sensational-romantic type of melodrama tracking the exploits of a strong-willed young woman trying to make her way in the world gained popularity. Charting a heroine's path to maturity, it required physical comedy, emotional pathos, and derring-do—often abruptly concluding with her clasped in the "right man's" arms. Yet, as romances in the nineteenth-century Anglo-American chivalric sense, these tales of love and adventure left stereotypes about respectable Anglo-American women's sexuality largely unchanged.

This complex melodramatic culture—with its iconoclastic heroines and female stars—fueled the American film industry's development into "Hollywood" by creating the frisson that sparked global interest in its products. Like the stage before it, the American film industry aimed to please the female trade as it became big business during the 1910s. As Ben Singer (2001) has shown, sensational-romantic serials were geared toward a female audience. They were also favored by influential early film stars and their exploits used in the era's burgeoning fan culture. Interviews and press publicity explained the genuine "masculine" courage required by the professional feats performed by actresses such as Pickford and serial queen Pearl White, while still depicting them as attractive "girls." As a consequence, the "Pickford Revolution"—producer Benjamin Hampton's (1971) shorthand for the star system's emergence in film—relied on melodramas that featured independent, adventurous, and, at times, "immoral" young women who resisted the villain and challenged society's mores. These damsels might suffer distress, but they endured their trials with grit and typically triumphed in "The End."

Viewed from abroad as a "quintessentially American" type, the early film industry's first stars were predominately young women, a point Richard de Cordova (1990) notes in passing in his oft-cited history on the star system's emergence (72; see also Schneider and Schneider 1994, 16). These "girls" became emblematic of modernity's dangers and enticements in much public discourse around the world because, as Miriam Hansen (1983) argues, "resistance to the cinema's path to cultural respectability (and thus acceptance into the public sphere) was sexual and gender related, rather than primarily class related" (173–74; see also Sanderson 1998; Gledhill 2011; Gaines 2016). The timing of the star system's emergence partially explains the symbolic baggage these heroines shouldered. Hollywood became a widely shared "social imaginary" after the end of World War I just as America's role as a global leader became impossible to miss (Taylor 2002, 90). In this volatile nativist climate, Hollywood embraced a European brand of passionate melodramas that threw sexual respectability for women to the wind. Personalities such as Alla Nazimova, Pola Negri, Gloria Swanson, and Rudolph Valentino offered glamorous instruction in the behavior necessary to perform these passionate melodramas. Publicity about Hollywood's first stars and studios used a similar mode, depicting residents as living in a western American bohemia where the girls were equal partners in rebellion with the boys (Cooper 2010; Hallett 2013). With both anti-Semitism and nativism on the rise, Henry Ford and others attacked "degenerate" movie producers for using passionate melodramas and their stars to encourage ordinary "movie-struck girls" down the path of sin (Stamp 2000; Lindemann 2000; Baldwin 2001). Many believed that the threat this un-American "Movie Menace" posed to so-called native American womanhood warranted government regulation of the industry. Hollywood's birth depended upon diverse melodramatic forms that dramatized the destruction of the "West's" once seemingly stable gender order.

MELODRAMATIC WOMEN ON THE NINETEENTH-CENTURY STAGE

The immoral melodramas produced after 1850 helped theatrical producers target women patrons from the swelling middle class for the first time. These plays descended from the grandmother of all immoral melodramas, *La Dame aux camélias* (1852), which first questioned the morality of the sexual double standard. Over fifty years after its 1853 debut, it remained among the two most popular plays performed in the United States (Hamilton 1910; Stanton 1957). It also provided the signature role for the late-nineteenth century's greatest international star, Sarah Bernhardt (Brandon 1991). Following Bernhardt's lead, every great actress demanded to assail the role of Marguerite, the courtesan whose self-sacrifice for her lover demonstrated that even a prostitute could attain virtue. Even the Anglophone world's more sexually sanitized versions of the melodrama—performed as *Camille* (1853) in the United States and as *Heartsease* (1875) in the United Kingdom—prompted an outcry among theater critics as a "deification of prostitution" (Dudden 1995, 228 nt.22).

But the play's popularity with actresses and women audiences spawned a host of imitators that explored the erring woman's relationship to society, even if, to avoid charges of "French immorality," Anglophone versions had to refrain from openly critiquing social morality (Vicinus 1989; Eltis 2013).

Camille showed how female characters could drive a plot, and such plays were often written, adapted, or commissioned by women (Gledhill 2002, 34; Hyslop 1985). This trend prompted critical concern that the "morbid fictions" of a "herd" of female playwrights threatened to force Shakespeare, Scott, and Dickens to the theatrical margins (Dudden 1995, 229). Their innovative stock types, plot devices, and active heroines starred in stories in which chance and responsibility factored into judgments about their character. Threats to a loved one's virtue often justified these heroines' exercise of daring-do, explaining how a heroine executed the first rescue of a victim strapped to railroad tracks in Augustin Daly's *Under the Gaslight* (1867). After the rescue, the near victim remarks, "And these are the women who aint to have the vote" (Act IV, Scene II; see Bank 1982, 242). Women's patronage of these plays made the stage—previously off-limits to the "ladies" because of its reputation for immortality and the presence of prostitutes in the theater—the first den of male sociability to succumb to sexual integration (Ryan 1990, 76).

"I feel much better about womankind," playwright Julia Ward Howe wrote to Charlotte Cushman after her conquest of New York in 1857 (Leach 1972, 278). Like her great rival Edwin Forrest, Cushman repeated the same roles, using a physical and emotional expressivity that British critics considered characteristically American. Cushman had triumphed in her first London season of 1856, before bringing the imprimatur of British approval home to certify her reputation as America's first great dramatic actress. Her performances exhibited melodrama's support of a new kind of heroine whose "manly" freedoms must have appeared as antidotes to women's typically unacknowledged frustrations with their limited lives in America's much-vaunted democracy. "Her style was strong, definite bold and free: for that reason observers described it as 'melodramatic,'" recalled critic William Winter (1906, 151), suggesting the mode's ability to license women's exercise of virtues long reserved only for men. "The woman . . . assumes all the power and energy of manhood" was how one critic described her type ("Charlotte Cushman" 1874). Credited with bringing breeches parts into American vogue, the tall, powerfully built, husky-voiced actress playing Romeo accentuated his aggressive charms, depicting him as "a militant gallant, a pugnacious lover, who might resort to force should Juliet refuse to marry him" (Abbott 1912; Wallen 1998; Dudden 1995, 92–99). Contemporaries marveled at the passion with which the cross-dressing actress fought duels and made love to other women on stage, notably her sister Susan in adaptations of Shakespearean tragedies that stressed their melodramatic aspects (figure 7.1). Consequently, Cushman became renowned in theatrical lore for her virility. "When a fellow in the audience interrupted the performance" of *Romeo and Juliet* one night, "Miss Cushman in hose and doublet strode to the footlights and declared: 'Someone must put this person out or I shall be obliged to do it myself.'" Thereafter, "all honors that a player might win were hers" (Abbott 1912).

Melodrama and the Making of Hollywood 119

Figure 7.1 Charlotte and Susan Cushman in *Romeo and Juliet* (1860).

To achieve such renown, the first female stars like Cushman required modern methods of publicity to convey information about their private lives that helped to smooth the flouting of respectability that their melodramatic performances entailed. New genres like biography and autobiography explained this private self. As carefully stage-managed as anything she did, publicity about her decorous domestic "real" life contradicted the sensational gender-bending aspects of her work onstage. These stories explained her Puritan pedigree, the collapse of her father's business, and her turn to the stage to support her family. Ever her own best publicist, Cushman initiated this presentation in a story she sent to *Godey's Lady's Book* in 1836, just weeks after landing her first acting job. Titled "Excerpts from My Journal: The Actress," the story prodded readers to recognize that acting offered many worthy women their best financial alternative when forced to fend for themselves. Cushman also publicized her tender feminine side by making much ado of a decision to forgo marriage after the end of a "tragic love-affair" with a never identified "young gentleman of a Presbyterian family." The gentleman reportedly broke their engagement after finding Cushman "being entertained by some of her theatrical friends and mates at a rather lively supper party" ("Miss Cushman" 1876). Indeed, one biographer speculates that her preference for intimate relationships with women made it easier for her to present an image of ladylike decorum in her private life by removing the threat of sexual scandals with men (Merrill 1999, 205–42). Since the *Odyssey*, stories in the Western tradition about famous individuals—always men of noble birth—emerged from the hero's seemingly authentic personification of fame's "one essential ideal:" a display of "fearless faithful manhood," following the decrees of fate on the public stage of life (McConachie 1992, 88; Braudy 1997, 95–96). In contrast to the seeming elision of male actor and role, Cushman celebrated her ability to act like figures she was not, making her success a performance that signaled the crumbling power of sexual difference to define individual achievement and desire.

After Cushman retired in 1874, women's importance as theatrical stars and patrons increased alongside the growth of commercial entertainment. Between 1880 and 1900, the number of shows touring the country jumped from 50 to more than 500. By 1900, popular-priced seats in Chicago, Denver, Philadelphia, New York, and elsewhere outdistanced population growth by four to one (Nasaw 1993, 174–78). Women's work on stage soared along with the proliferation of playhouses. Employing almost entirely men in 1800, performance became one of the largest professions for women a century later (Hill 1970, 42). The stage offered the best chance for both self-support and social mobility for women with the fewest resources. Only as performers and writers did women earn the same, or greater, wages as men for equal work (Johnson 1984, 39; McArthur 1984, 12–13). Theater directors were typically less important than the divas and handsome matinee idols whose preening sparked the interest of "matinee girls." And as lionized actresses outnumbered their male counterparts and took their shows on the road, the stage offered a singular arena to exhibit a woman's ability to compete equally with a man (Dudden 1995).

By 1900, the dramatic growth in the number of female performers and fans supported melodrama's evolution into a mode that sensationalized the dangers, attractions, and moral ambiguities engendered by women's increasingly independent confrontations with the conditions of modern life. The success of theatrical impresario David Belasco, whom Pickford (1954) called the "wizard of the modern stage," captured melodrama's dramatization of tensions related to the emergence of modern gender roles (55–56). By 1907, when Mary Pickford made her Broadway debut with Belasco, the wizard had built an unrivaled following among women theatergoers with sensational romantic and immoral melodramatic plays. Noteworthy modern immoral melodramas written by Belasco include *Madame Butterfly* (1900), *Du Barry* (1901), and *The Girl of the Golden West* (1905); he staged many others. Hugo Munsterberg (1971), the Harvard professor and author of an early theory of film spectatorship, was one of many leading fin-de-siècle intellectuals who argued that these melodramas, and the feminized audience who supported them, spelled cultural calamity. Such patrons, he wrote, could not "discriminate between the superficial and the profound." Their influence thus "militate[d] against the home and the masculine control of high culture" (139). A 1910 survey of theatrical producers and critics found that women composed between two-thirds and three-quarters of the audience even at night (Eaton 1910, 79). The next year a critic at Columbia University summed up the results, writing, "every student of the contemporary theatre knows that the destiny of our drama has lain for a long time in the hands of women," making the theater "the one great public institution in which 'votes for women' is the rule, and men are overwhelmingly outvoted" (Hamilton 1911, 34).

SENSATIONAL MELODRAMAS AND THE ROMANCE OF EARLY AMERICAN FILM

Like no other industry of its day, the early American film industry publicized the accomplishments of women in sensational-romantic melodramas on and off screen. As with Cushman earlier, the fame of these women dramatized their ability to exercise qualities long reserved for heroic men. But unlike Cushman, the first movie stars were marketed as glamorous young women who—though still sexually respectable—exhibited in "real life" many of the same arresting, gender-bending aptitudes, interests, and abilities as the fictional characters they played on screen. The seeming truthfulness of the cinematic experience intensified this development by taking theatrical melodrama's increasingly realistic stagecraft to new heights of verisimilitude. The process transformed the heroines of the Victorian stage into figures audiences recognized as "genuinely" *The Girl of the Golden West* modern and new. By the time Mary Pickford (figure 7.2) incorporated United Artists in 1919, her persona was equal parts "America's Sweetheart"—a romantic, spirited ingénue who politely called for women's rights—and "Bank of America's Sweetheart," as her competitor and colleague Charlie Chaplin (1964) called her—a skilled businesswoman who became the highest-paid woman in the world. Her star image contained two contrasting elements: one a perennial youth involved in perpetual re-self-definition; the other a trailblazing professional endowed with a stature reserved for "the daddy of the family," as early press stories continually called her. In this way, sensational romances about the exploits of stars such as Pickford on and off screen contributed to the "grounding of modern feminism" (Cott 1987, 7–9; Glenn 2000, 2–8).

As the film industry shot up to become America's "fourth or fifth" largest industry, a 1920 survey by First National of more than 10,000 movie exhibitors confirmed that female-centered melodramas best attracted the audiences who fueled the conversion of stage venues into movie houses ("Motion Picture Industry" 1921;

Figure 7.2 Magnet Pickford looking after "Little Mary."

"Jazzy, Money-Mad Spot" 1921; " 'Movie' as an Industry" 1917).[1] The chattering classes held a dim view of these melodramas and blamed the poor aesthetic quality of movies on women's preference for them. The *Atlantic Monthly* was grimly steadfast about what women wanted to see: romantic, thrill-driven melodramas focused on "the inevitable idealization of the heroine" (Gerould 1921, 22–30). A *Nation* editor lamented the results: "The popular film 'drama of heart interest' is the lineal descendant of the cheap stage melodrama of a dozen years ago, and it is the contemporary relative of the fiction of our popular magazine" ("Morals and the Movies" 1921). The *New Republic* agreed: "The morals of the movies are also the morals of the popular magazine," a critic declared, citing "Fanny (*sic*) Hurst" as the best example of an author who succeeded in both mediums ("Movie Morals" 1917). The reporter proved prescient. In 1921, *Photoplay*'s mostly women readers selected *Humoresque*, a film based on Hurst's maternal melodrama, for the magazine's gold Medal of Honor, the equivalent of the first Academy Award ("Announcing the Photoplay Magazine Medal of Honor" 1921).

From the start, Pickford capitalized on the interest fans showed in her rapscallion ingénues in romantic-sensational melodramas that used suffering to justify the heroine's extraordinary action to ameliorate things for herself and others. This allowed Pickford to escape playing the "wishy-washy," suffering victim heroines in the melodramas, often starring Lillian Gish, still preferred by D. W. Griffith (Pickford 1954, 73). With Famous Players she played three sharp-witted scamps of humble origins in the sensational romances, *The Bishop's Carriage* (1913), *Caprice*

(1913), and *Hearts Adrift* (1914) (see Whitfield 1997). Although these films are lost, the traces that remain exhibit the imprint of the classic Pickford screen type: a fearless, funny, lovely guttersnipe whose poundings by fate rouse her to thrilling action that elicits sympathy, respect, and love (see Gledhill 2011). In 1914, Pickford's role in *Tess of the Storm Country* crystallized the appeal of heroines in romantic melodramas. Tomboy Tess proved so popular that Pickford remade the film as an independent producer at United Artists in 1922. Tess's father is a fish poacher who is framed for murder. While he languishes in jail, Tess fights off the true killer's attempt to force her into marriage, rescues an unwed pregnant girl, delivers her baby, agrees to raise it, and confers grace upon the dying child when a minister refuses. The film's end features Tess reuniting with the wealthy beau she spurned earlier because of his doubts about her moral character.

Sensational-romantic melodramas such as *Tess* allowed actresses to portray psychologically complex roles: in this case a virtuous rascal, a hoyden of preternatural self-control, and a young woman whose mane of golden pre-Raphaelite curls telegraphed her sensuality and grace. The extraordinary daring-do and moral clarity exhibited by these seemingly ordinary young female heroines in the face of sensational dangers prompted admiration and amazement in their audiences. Pickford's sexually uncompromised Tess also offered a more optimistic spin on Thomas Hardy's suffering fallen woman in *Tess of the d'Urbervilles* (1891). Griffith adapted Hardy's novel—faulted by critics at the time for challenging the era's sexual morality—into the immoral melodrama *Way Down East* (1920), featuring just the kind of heroine that Pickford abjured. The opening credits of Pickford's *Tess* highlighted the difference: "Daniel Frohman Presents America's Foremost Film Actress, Mary Pickford, in the famous tale of woman's heroism, 'Tess of the Storm Country' by Grace Miller White" (Pickford Core Clippings). The credits also emphasized the film's debt to White's best-selling novel to attract the large fan base for "growing girl" stories. Future Pickford movies turned the strategy into a formula, as in *Rebecca of Sunnybrook Farm* (1917), based on Kate Douglas Wiggin's 1903 novel. In these sensational-romantic films, Pickford played independent and spirited young women struggling to find happiness and restore order in a chaotic world (Tibbetts 2001).[2]

Publicity about Pickford strove to associate her with the stars of the cliff-hanging serials often set in the modern American West (Hallett 2011). Serial stars Ruth Roland, Helen Holmes, and Pearl White had to both wield and tolerate pain to prove their valor, long a hallmark of America's western heroes. Silent western films exaggerated, and then spread around the world, the association between modern "Americanism" and its sensationally mobile men and violent action. The longest-running silent film serial, *The Hazards of Helen* (Kalem 1914–1917), illustrates how the genre promoted a similar vision of modern American women. *Hazards* displays the mise-en-scène of a modern western, as giant locomotives, fleet horses, speedy motorcycles, and rifle-toting good and bad guys track back and forth across the dusty California landscape. Helen, the sole female in this Wild West, rides, shoots, rescues, and is rescued. Publicity about Helen Holmes—the first and most iconic actress to play *Hazards*' lead—emphasized her identity as a genuine westerner (figure 7.3). Born in "her father's private car somewhere between

Figure 7.3 Helen Holmes (c. 1912).

Chicago and Salt Lake," Holmes had been raised in "railroad yards" throughout the American West (Holmes Collection 1915). A "slim, seductively rounded young woman with luring lips and 'come-hither' eyes," Holmes "looked to be a most dangerous person," but was really the good wife of the serial's director, J. P. MacGowan, and mother to an adopted baby girl (Holmes Collection 1915).

Publicity about Pearl White promoted her as another "peerless fearless girl" who invited her fans to identify with a female protagonist liberated from many of the customary restraints that economic dependence and the cult of domesticity placed on women. "You know my adventurous spirit and desire to live and realize the greatest things," White reminds her crest-fallen suitor, after rejecting his marriage proposal so that she can gather material for the novel she wants to write ("Through Fire and Air," Pathé 1914). White's off-screen persona was pure New Western Woman, as an Ozark-raised, former circus performer turned globetrotting cosmopolitan who sought European "pleasure jaunts" and "beef-steak [automobiling] and aviation" for fun. "Oh for a girl that could ride a horse like Pearl White," swooned one young male fan (Jowett, Jarvie, and Fuller-Seeley 1996, 263). Pickford also called herself "a devoted fan" of White and claimed to have encountered her on a train bound for Los Angeles in 1914. "In awe I watched her enter the club car, light a cigarette, and in the presence of all these men, raise a highball to her lips" (Pickford 1954, 99). The publicity surrounding Pickford's last stint on Broadway in Belasco's *A Good Little Devil* (1913) advertised her association with these western romantic melodramas: "You have seen her rough riding on the western plains. You have watched her during thrilling moments on runaway motorcars and flying machines" (Belasco 1912).

Blending social reality with desire, the press depicted female stars of western melodramas as enjoying unrivaled opportunities for adventure and professional satisfaction in "real life." This shift—from emphasizing conventionally domesticated off-screen lives to more unconventional behavior—intensified the ability of these stars to promote the liberation of their sex (White 1919). Ruth Roland's popularity was second only to Pearl White. Both women were actress-writer-producers who became famous working with Pathé. Between 1911 and 1915, newspapers credited them with being the only women to rank with male actors in popularity contests of western stars, a budding genre then, considered targeted at boys (Roland Core Clippings n.d.; Smith 2003). Eight of the eleven serials that made the San Francisco native Ruth Roland a star were westerns that showcased her equestrian skills riding her horse Joker (figure 7.4).[3] Roland also created her own production company, writing, producing, and starring in western serials including *The Timber Queen* (1922). As far away as China, advertisements trumpeted her American athleticism: "Riding on a furious horse, climbing the cliff as if walking on flat land, her talents are unsurpassable"—suggesting the appeal of modern Americanism and its "girls" across lines of sex and nation (Bao 2005, 200).

As with stage melodramas during the previous century, these cinematic western melodramas had a symbiotic relationship with the press. By the time William Randolph Hearst coproduced *The Perils of Pauline* (1914), he and Joseph Pulitzer had already reengineered the purpose, look, and tenor of national news. Using

Figure 7.4 Ruth Roland (c. 1912).

bold headlines, illustrations, cartoons, and a narrative style that some called melodramatic and others simply sensational, the papers with the biggest circulation repackaged themselves to entertain as much as to inform. This motivation transformed the newspaper into "an urban institution" that, "like the department store, the vaudeville theatre, and the amusement park, transcended traditional categories of class, ethnicity, occupation, and neighbourhood" (Nasaw 2000, 53). The use of syndication services exploded after 1900, turning newspapers into national institutions. By 1920, the same melodramas filled many minds across the country and, with silent film, around the world. E. W. Scripps, a pioneer in syndication services, summed up his formula for creating reproducible news: "Whatever else it is, our newspaper must be excessively interesting, not to the good, wise men and the pure in spirit, but to the great mass of sordid, squalid humanity. [Humanity] is passionate," he reminded his editors; "therefore the blood that runs in our veins and in our newspapers must be warm" (as cited in Lee 2000, 10). Next to production values, Scripps and Hearst placed the key melodramatic convention of polarization—between corruption and innocence, rich and poor, male and female—at the center of their circulation building style. By World War I, Hearst's newspapers, magazines, and movies displayed the rage for female protagonists who hurled themselves into the fray. Even if Pauline often relied on Harry's last minute help, the *Literary Digest* still declared her "the apotheosis of the old-time melodrama heroine," who would have "perish[ed] ignominiously if faced by half the perils that surround her more advanced sister of the screen" ("Real Perils of Pauline" 1921).

The celebrity reporting of early film publicists such as Louella Parsons also employed this melodramatic mode to create western myths about these stars and their role in the development of Hollywood (Fahs 2011; Hallett 2013). The "moving picture has opened a great new field for women folk," where her "originality," "perseverance," and "brains are coming to be recognized on the same plane as [a] man's," declared Gertrude Price, one of several prominent female "moving picture experts" (Abel 2006, 247). These journalists often told stories that flipped the traditional immoral melodrama of sexual danger on its head, by breezily describing the City of Angels as an urban El Dorado for intrepid female migrants. After 1915, as the industry settled around Los Angeles, Parsons and other publicists reworked the era's popular frontier mythology in ways that encouraged women's migration west. A piece about scenarist Josephine Quirk's move from New York to Los Angeles resurrected Horace Greeley's old advice for feminist ends: "When Horace Greeley penned those immortal words, 'Go West, Young Man,' he failed to reckon with the feminine contingent. That of course was before the days of feminism," Parsons (1920) explained, declaring, "In the present day, if milady goes west she travels not to sew on buttons or do the family washing, she goeth to make her own fortune." In describing single young women as the key adventurers, such melodramas depicted the industry as a release for feminist, rather than working-class male, ambitions and unrest.

POSTWAR MELODRAMAS OF PASSION AND THE MAKING OF HOLLYWOOD

The industry's use of sensational-romantic melodramas may have succeeded too well, and single young women seeking work in the picture business became an unusually visible eddy in the wave of native-born midwesterners who washed up in southern California during the 1910s (Thompson 1955, 48–51, 88–89; Beach 1969, 25–28).[4] "There are more women in Los Angeles than any other city in the world and it's the movies that bring them," one shopkeeper bluntly asserted ("Confessions of a Motion Picture Press Agent" 1918). This development was at odds with the development of other western American boomtowns such as San Francisco, which had long been dominated by single young men. A remarkable number of over twenty-five-year-old women were also widowed, divorced, or single and worked outside the home (Hill 1970, 270–76; Thompson 1955, 89–93). Los Angeles's economic base of real estate, tourism, and motion pictures created the service and clerical jobs that drew wage-earning women to Los Angeles, women who benefited from California's 1911 passage of female suffrage and jury service, and its legislation establishing the eight-hour day (1911) and a minimum wage (1917) (Mead 1998, 2004). By 1920, Los Angeles had become the only western boomtown where women outnumbered men.

After the war, a wave of more risqué melodramas and the promotion of non-Anglo, daringly erotic personalities contributed to mounting anxiety about the moral danger the movie industry posed to young women in Los Angeles and around the world. Ernst Lubitsch's *Passion* (1920) illustrated the threat these foreign melodramas posed to American values. One of the first films imported from Germany after the Treaty of Versailles, *Passion* packed movie houses and drew critical hosannas throughout 1921 (" 'Passion' Sets Record" 1921; "Menace of German Films" 1921; Scaramazza 1974, 15). The fanfare focused on Pola Negri's performance as Madame Jeanne du Barry, the last mistress of Louis XV (who had also been the subject of Belasco's eponymous great immoral melodrama). "Pola Negri and a cast of 5000 people in Passion," promised ads (figure 7.5). Negri's

Figure 7.5 Pola Negri fan card (c. 1920).

orientalized glamour licensed her star image's startlingly direct projection of sexual need (Howe 1922, 38; Negri 1970, 180–85). "This is a story of a wonder woman—the world's most daring adventuress" (Basinger 2000). To ensure that American audiences understood the nature of the heroine's conquests, producer Jesse Lasky changed the title, *Madame du Barry*, to *Passion*. A country girl who heads to Paris to find her fortune, Jeanne follows "adventure, siren fingered" into the arms of a succession of men. In a burlesque of past melodramatic conventions for representing female sexuality, Jeanne playfully acts a naïf one minute, a dominatrix the next. Her plea while waiting to lose her head—"One moment more! Life is so sweet!"—emphasizes pleasure rather than repentance. Although du Barry pays for her wicked ways, her actions revised the conventions established by prewar Anglo-American melodramas that often treated overt eroticism as separating bad women from the good.

Publicity in the 1920s about Negri and her great American-press rival, Gloria Swanson, tracked the personal and professional exploits of these sophisticated, globetrotting cosmopolitans, whose conduct illustrated their sexual emancipation. In Hollywood, Negri also made passionate melodramas, including *Bella Donna* (1923), which had given Nazimova a Broadway success in 1912; and *A Woman of the World* (1925), in which she literally whips the hero into line. A Pole, Negri had already divorced a Russian count before moving to Los Angeles where she took a series of high-profile lovers, including Charlie Chaplin and Rudolph Valentino. Both Swanson and Negri would divorce their way through the twenties; Swanson's third husband made her the first American star to marry into the European aristocracy in 1925. Both women also worked with Ernst Lubitsch, who directed some of the era's boldest sex comedies. Swanson caught audiences' eyes in six films, variously called "marriage-and-divorce pictures" or "sex pictures," directed by Cecil B. DeMille between 1919 and 1921. Her first starring vehicle was the British writer Elinor Glyn's melodrama of passion, *The Great Moment* (1921). Publicity advertised the film as "the vivid drama of a society girl with a gypsy's heart, and the romantic adventures into which her untamed nature led her" ("Great Moment" 1921). Despite her American roots, Swanson came to exude a European chic under the tutelage of Glyn, becoming the "Prototype of the Glamour Queen" (St. Johns 1969, 103). Mary Pickford later emphasized the difference between her homespun appeal and those of the "foreigners" who were making such waves in early Hollywood. "Now of course, [Lubitsch] understood Pola Negri or Gloria Swanson, that type of actress, but he did not understand me because I am of course a purely American type" was how Pickford explained the trouble that occurred in 1923 when they worked together on *Rosita* (Pickford Oral History Transcript: 2733–2743). Pickford claimed her decision to have Lubitsch direct her as the Spanish street singer was a disaster, but in actuality *Rosita* succeeded in its day, suggesting the astute businesswoman understood the commercial appeal of European melodramas of passion after the war.

These melodramas pressed hard against the boundaries of the sexual order, prompting alarm about their influence on the "flapper fans" the industry targeted during the 1920s (Howe 1924, 7). As a result, industry insiders imagined their ideal spectator as a young white woman eager to identify with role models who, however fantastically, reflected the changed conditions under which they worked, played, and dreamed. It is little wonder that these "un-American" melodramas of passion also helped to reinvigorate the film censorship movement (Hallett 2013). By 1920, proposed movie censorship legislation and public debate over movie morality spiked, focusing on the industry's influence on the morality of young women. Critics created powerful melodramas of sexual danger about Jewish producers' control over the most powerful culture industry ever seen. Funded by Henry Ford, these critics charged that a "Hebrew Trust" created stories and stars that enticed white womanhood, the fount of America's racial purity, into degrading themselves (*International Jew* 1920, 48).

The press also created passionate melodramas about the environment inhabited by movie colony residents, describing this first Hollywood as a Bohemia that nurtured women's personal, professional, and sexual freedoms (Hallett 2013). Such stories often featured an "extra girl" who put her quest for artistic success and individual fulfillment first, exhibiting the bohemian commitment to passion, play, and self-actualization. The first article in *Photoplay* to use "Hollywood" to stand in for the movie colony offered readers a virtual tour that claimed young single women dominated its scene. "Women can—and do—what they like," for "they work, play, love, and draw their pay checks on exactly the same basis as men," the reporter explained (Winship 1921, 111). A photograph depicted the abode of one epicene, dark-haired extra girl in orientalized garb. "The rough board walls, the phonograph, the Chinese housecoat, are absolutely typical of the mountain colony extra girls. How'd you like to live here?" invited the picture's caption.

The "extra" in the picture resembled Alla Nazimova, whose persona exhibited qualities prized by these passionate melodramas. "A hint of the Slav, a hint of the Oriental, a hint of the Parisienne, a hint of the woman of the theatre," described Nazimova's appeal ("Hedda Gabler" 1907). A classically trained actress, Nazimova had studied under Stanislavski at the Moscow Art Theater before coming to New York where she helped to change producer Charles Frohman's opinion about what audiences wanted to see. Previously Frohman declared the "erotic and the decadent" had no place in the American theater. Nazimova's star turn on Broadway in the incendiary melodrama *Bella Donna* (1912) convinced him that "sex conflict" was the order of the day ("Hedda Gabler" 1907). Metro's head scenario writer and producer, June Mathis, sought to associate her protégé, Rudolph Valentino, with Nazimova's brand of passionate, continental artistry. A devotee of European art, Mathis had already adapted Vicente Blasco Ibanez's internationally best-selling novel of the Great War, *The Four Horsemen of the Apocalypse* (1919). Passionate melodramas such as the *Four Horsemen* and *The Sheik* (both 1921) presented Valentino as a distinctly foreign lover (figure 7.6). His appeal emphasized the seeming impossibility of Anglo-American lovers following their erotic passions within the context of Western civilization. Mathis convinced Nazimova to cast Valentino as Armand, the male lead in their *Camille* (1921). "Why not a *Camille* of today?" asks the opening intertitle of this "modernized version" of the immoral melodrama that made women's erotically daring performances of womanhood possible.

Figure 7.6 Swanson and Valentino in *Beyond the Rocks* (1922).

Fear over this immoral influence drove the eruption of the movie industry's first so-called canonical scandal, which arose after "starlet" Virginia Rappe died following a hotel party hosted by the slapstick star Roscoe Arbuckle in rollicking San Francisco over Labor Day in 1921. The sensational reporting throughout Arbuckle's arraignment and trial for manslaughter first circulated the term *Hollywood* to a broad audience.[5] The press shaped a succession of melodramatic narratives out of witnesses' contradictory and changing testimony, in the process grappling with the industry's influence on American culture. The first story offered a sensational-romantic melodrama gone awry. Here Rappe was cast as a plucky, virtuous heroine whose ambitions were successfully preyed upon by the villainous Arbuckle.

The second made room for imagining the event as a passionate, consensual "orgy" and blamed middle-class parents for allowing their daughters to imitate these heroines out west. Ultimately the story that won out reverted to a most traditional immoral melodrama that cast Rappe as a fallen woman and Arbuckle—and by extension Hollywood—as the villain responsible for her fall. These narratives demonstrated melodrama's diversity by 1920, which allowed it to convey contradictory points of view. Even more significant, they emphasized melodrama's power to transform the subjects and topics it touched. Here Arbuckle—a heretofore rotund comedic star widely idolized by young children—became almost instantly a ghastly beast.

Standing in as modernity's scapegoat, Hollywood represented the most powerful threat confronting the "millions of pretty girls" who turned "their faces to the gilded west" ("A Star at Last" 1921). The *Literary Digest* asserted this verdict before the trial began, declaring, "what the demand for censorship has been unable to accomplish . . . the revelations of the Arbuckle case most thoroughly accomplished" ("Time to Clean Up the Movies" 1921). A cartoon summed up what a "clean up" of "movie morals" entailed. In the foreground, a matronly "ma" confided, "Oh, pa, Tilly has given up wanting to be a movie star." Meanwhile her daughter, tucked in the kitchen in the image's background, lightened a load of dishes by singing a song. Here lay the message of the scandal's melodrama, "The Good That Comes From Evil," as the cartoon declared. No longer would the industry spin such unabashedly optimistic tales about female migrants who triumphed over all the conventions that had composed respectable femininity in this new west (Hallett 2013). The Hays' Code, instituted in the wake of the scandal, aimed to do just that.

Although the Hays' Code would make enforcing the sexual double standard on film one of its particular obsessions in the decades to come, Hollywood never stopped holding out the lure of sexual adventure to women. Like so much of mass culture, the film industry continued to favor sensational, romantic, and passionate melodramas in telling tales about its celebrated inhabitants. And these melodramas often served to dramatize one of the twentieth century's most distinctive story arcs: the unraveling in democratic societies of stable notions about gender difference that had long prevented women from taking center stage. To understand this process, we should recall melodrama's central role in making women, doing once unimaginable things, a part of the ordinary dreamscape of audiences around the world.

NOTES

I offer my sincere thanks to Christine Gledhill and Linda Williams for their astute editorial suggestions. With their help, this essay surfaces an argument implicit in my 2013 book about how diverse melodramatic forms, preoccupied with modern young "girls," fueled Hollywood's birth.

1. "First National Completes Interesting Survey." *Wid's Daily*, October 18, 1920. Estimates of theaters showing only movies usually hovered around 15,000. Feature films

specifying "female stars" totaled 43.8 percent of programs screened; "male stars," 6.01 percent, "all-star," 19.39 percent. Categories without stars included two-reel short slapstick, 9.9 percent; rural comedy drama, 7.98 percent; feature-length slapstick, 6.25 percent; adaptations of comedy stage successes, 6.01 percent; feature-length "stunt" comedy, 5.4 percent.

2. Pickford remained a child or adolescent throughout a film only in *The Poor Little Rich Girl* (1917, Artcraft), *Rebecca of Sunnybrook Farm* (1917, Artcraft), and *The Little Princess* (1917, Artcraft).
3. *The Red Circle* (1915, Balboa), Hands Up (1918, Pathé), *The Tiger's Trail* (1919, Pathé), *The Adventures of Ruth* (1919, Pathé), *Ruth of the Rockies* (1920, Pathé), *The Avenging Arrow* (1921, Pathé), *White Eagle* (1922, Pathé), *The Timber Queen* (1922, Pathé), *Ruth of the Range* (1923, Pathé).
4. In 1920, Los Angeles's sex ratio was 97.8 female to 100 male.
5. "Hollywood" first appeared in the *Readers' Guide to Periodical Literature* (Minneapolis: H.W. Wilson Co.) with "In the Capital of Movie-Land," *Literary Digest*, November 10, 1917, 82–89. The term appeared regularly only after 1922. In *ProQuest Historical Newspapers*, "Hollywood" was first used as something more than a location in "Hollywood Is Interested," *Atlanta Constitution*, July 3, 1921. The usage proliferated during 1922.

8

Modernizing Melodrama

The Petrified Forest *on American Stage and Screen (1935–1936)*

MARTIN SHINGLER

In January 1935, Robert E. Sherwood's play *The Petrified Forest* began a lucrative six-month run at the Broadhurst Theater in New York at 235 West Forty-Fourth Street. The play received rave reviews in the press and a nomination for a Pulitzer Prize. Within months of closing, the leading members of the cast reprised their roles at the Warner Bros. film studio in Los Angeles. The film version, released February 6, 1936, at Radio City Music Hall in Manhattan, corresponded closely to the stage production, enabling millions of moviegoers to see what fewer than 250,000 theatergoers had seen the previous year on Broadway. Because the New York drama critics used the term *melodrama* to describe both the stage play and the film, *The Petrified Forest* provides contemporary scholars with an opportunity to consider the state of melodrama in the 1930s. As explained in more detail in this chapter, *The Petrified Forest* also suggests that melodramas that combined philosophical dialogue with action and pathos could transfer readily from stage to screen, appealing to patrons and critics of Broadway theater *and* Hollywood cinema.

Investigation into the reviews of stage and screen versions of *The Petrified Forest* highlights how critical appraisal of melodrama varied from one critic to another. In 1934 melodrama was deemed unworthy of praise, but the following year this particular melodrama was lauded for its intelligent script and fine acting. This raises some important questions about melodrama's ongoing process of rejuvenation. As this popular dramatic mode evolved, some critics recognized, embraced, appreciated, and celebrated transformations in the style and content of melodrama, and others persisted in condemning it for what it was considered to have been rather than what it was becoming. Understanding precisely what melodrama is at any one time has clearly been a challenge for theater and drama critics throughout the twentieth century and remains equally challenging for theater and drama historians in the twenty-first century.

A DRAMATIC MODE SUBJECT TO CONTINUAL REDEFINITION

Melodrama's continual process of renewal is based in part on its propensity to transmute, adapting to wider cultural changes, technological innovations, and aesthetic trends. Michael Walker (1982) writes that the "melodramatic tradition was itself continuously developing, with new forms being produced through dialectical interaction with historically evolving generic groups" of films (35).[1] Meanwhile, Christine Gledhill (2002) describes how melodrama reinvented itself for modern audiences through its relation to changes in realism:

> melodrama re-enacts for contemporary society the persistent clash of moral polarities by exploiting its shifting relations with . . . realism; for it deals in conditions of personal guilt and innocence which can be established in relation to discourses that demarcates the desirable from the taboo. Thus if the good and evil personifications of Victorian melodrama no longer provide credible articulations of conflict, modern melodrama draws on contemporary discourses for apportioning respectability, guilt and innocence—psychoanalysis, marriage guidance, medical ethics, politics, even feminism. (32)

In so doing, melodrama has retained its relevance for successive generations of theater and movie audiences and remains, as Linda Williams (1998) writes, "the dominant form of popular moving-image narrative," one that "consistently decks itself out in the trappings of realism and the modern" (58). Williams explains how film melodrama generates "sympathy for a hero who is also a victim" across a wide range of genres, invariably culminating in "a climax that permits the audience, and usually other characters, to recognize that character's moral value."

> This climax revealing the moral good of the victim can tend in one or two directions: either it can consist of a paroxysm of pathos (as in the woman's film or family melodrama variants) or it can take that paroxysm and channel it into the more virile and action-centered variants of rescue, chase, and flight (as in the western and all the action genres). (58)

Although this might suggest an "either-or" of pathos and action, for Williams it is the combination of pathos and action that is a defining feature of melodrama, both of which are marshaled for the purposes of moral legibility. As she observes, "As American melodrama developed from stage to screen, and from silence to sound, it frequently instituted more realistic causations and techniques for the display of both pathos and action, but it never ceased to serve the primary ends of displaying both" (59).

The scholarship of Walker, Gledhill, and Williams has established how melodrama maintained its popularity and potency by successively shedding one skin in favor of another to rejuvenate and win favor with new generations. If melodrama can be compared to a snake, however, it would need to be a most unusual one, because, with each shedding of its skin, it would reemerge with a distinctly new appearance. Although still the same snake in essence, it would be transformed visually to better assimilate to a new environment. The usefulness of this analogy is that it highlights the necessity for considering melodrama in terms of not only what changes occur with each transmutation but also what remains essentially the same (that is, beneath the surface).

The propensity for melodrama to transmute has produced major problems in defining precisely what the terms *melodrama* and the *melodramatic* mean. Numerous scholars have observed that these terms have been applied to different kinds of drama over time; most notably, Russell Merritt (1983), Steve Neale (1993), and Rick Altman (1998) have problematized these concepts. In some cases, it has been argued that melodrama never existed as a coherent dramatic category and that the term *melodrama* has been "hopelessly blurred and debased by popular mis-use" (Merritt 1983, 25).[2] In other instances, it has been claimed that the American film trade press used the terms *melodrama* and *meller* between 1938 and 1960 mostly to describe thrills and spills of action movies aimed at a predominantly adolescent and male audience, rarely applying them to romantic dramas aimed at mature women (Neale 1993, 74). In another instance, it has been countered that these terms were applied equally to male-oriented action genres and female-oriented domestic dramas by critics and publicists within the same historical period, for example, Altman on the 1950s (1998, 23). Consequently, it is important to establish the meanings and applications of *melodrama* at play within given historical moments, as used by different types of cultural commentators, which is no easy task because contradictory usages occur within any particular period. Rather than a singular definition fitting a singular practice, I suggest the meaning of melodrama is contingent, subject to change or renewal. Rather than fixed meanings, what I pursue here are the issues and values embedded in the discourses that work to establish particular definitions among certain 1930s American theater and film critics: in their case, concerning action melodramas involving romance.

ONE CRITIC'S ASSESSMENT OF THE PROBLEM WITH MELODRAMA

On June 3, 1934, Elinor Hughes, film critic for the *Boston Herald*, made revealing comments when assessing Bette Davis's performance in the adventure crime caper *Fog Over Frisco* (William Dieterle, 1934). In an article headed "Bette Davis at Last Shows She Is Learning How to Act," Hughes was surprised to find a good performance in "a picture so filled with action that it might well have been just another melodrama, and melodramas, unless exceptional, give but little opportunity for good acting to stand out." Thus this American film critic in 1934 associated melodrama with action movies and understood these to be vehicles for audience thrills and excitement rather than the display of acting skills.

Hughes continues that *Fog Over Frisco* "is one of the most entertaining pictures of its kind that we've seen for some time. Not clever and witty . . . it sticks grimly to the main purpose of capping one thrill with another and keeping the audience guessing until the very end." She adds:

> action melodramas of this sort are one of the most fruitful and least exploited fields of the movie picture industry. This may seem an unreasonable statement in view of the many melodramas that do get produced, one after another, but almost all of them suffer from certain faults that prevent them being favourably received and worthy of praise.

Accounting for melodrama's faults, Hughes noted four major deficiencies associated with this dramatic mode:

> one common failing is that they are deadly inconsistent; another, that they ask entirely too much of the powers of observation of the spectator; a third, that they leave many, too many questions unanswered and wind up with a burst of shooting that is supposed to settle everything satisfactorily or at least make the audience forget to ask anything more; a fourth, that the characters are uninteresting and implausible stock types.

Although a singular example, this review indicates a conception of melodrama, dominant among some leading American film critics, that failed the criteria of coherent narrative logic, dialogue over spectacle, conclusive endings that resolve issues raised in the plotting, and psychologically realist protagonists with whom audiences could identify.[3]

Elinor Hughes's conception of melodrama may well conflict with that held by generations of film scholars since the 1970s, given the different criteria they used (see Altman 1998, 24–33). However, along with others in the early to mid-1930s she contributed to a derogatory conception of melodrama, distinguishing those that conformed to criteria of credibility (as many undoubtedly did) as "exceptional" rather than representative. On the other hand, even though the reviews of the stage production of *The Petrified Forest* provide little indication of whether the New York drama critics judged it to be exceptional or representative, they do clearly indicate appreciation of melodrama as a dramatic mode.

A PHILOSOPHICAL CRIME THRILLER AND TRAGIC ROMANCE

The Petrified Forest as both play and film is a rather slow-paced crime melodrama featuring short bursts of action. The story centers on a group of people held captive by a gang of mobsters and features a tragic romance in which a young woman falls in love with an older and more sophisticated man who is shot dead during the final moments of the play. According to realist criteria, it features a highly improbable sequence of actions, involving a cast of remarkable and contrasting characters, and culminates in an astonishing event—an assisted suicide. This appears to conform to Hughes's conception of melodrama. The characters are thrown together in an isolated roadside diner and fuel station in the Arizona Desert. The Black Mesa Bar-B-Q is owned and run by the Maple family, the youngest member of which is Gabby (Gabrielle), a dreamy and creative young woman who longs to join her estranged mother in France and pursue a career as an artist rather than serve coffee and hamburgers in the family diner. Into her life one day come two extraordinary men. The first is Alan Squier, a disheveled and penniless novelist and former gigolo who is tramping his way across the USA toward the West Coast. The second is the notorious gangster Duke Mantee, a killer on the run after a killing spree in Oklahoma City. Within the space of a few hours, these men bring romance, excitement, and tragedy into Gabby's otherwise humdrum existence.

Shortly after meeting Squier, Gabby offers to share her life savings with him if he will help her get to a Bohemian life in France. Some hours later, however, he dies in her arms, having been shot at his own request after bequeathing the proceeds of his life insurance policy to the young woman, thereby giving her the means to move to Europe. This scenario provides the audience with romance and tears, as well as the spectacle of a thrilling shootout toward the end, when the local sheriff and his men encircle the diner and attempt to flush out Mantee and his armed gang.

On making his entrance in the play, the main character Alan Squier is described as "a thin, wan, vague man of about thirty-five" who is shabbily dressed and has the appearance of being "condemned" (Sherwood 1962, 16). This term is used again later to describe Duke Mantee on his first appearance (37). Both men, therefore, have an aura of death or doom hanging about them (see figure 8.1 from the film).

Figure 8.1 Confrontation between intellectual Alan Squier (Howard) and man of action, Duke Mantee (Bogart), men who nevertheless share a brooding disposition.

Purportedly based on the real-life criminal John Dillinger, who was shot down in Chicago by police and federal agents in July 1934, Mantee is withdrawn and intense. A philosophical nature lurks beneath his taciturn veneer, in addition to a world-weary cynicism and a brooding disposition that link him closely to Squier. In this way, the two men—one an intellectual and the other a man of action—appear to have much in common, and, consequently, they quickly reach a mutual understanding.[4] It is by acting in unison that they provide Gabby with the means to achieve her freedom and independence.

Gabby is pretty, youthful, and dreamy, but she has a core of strength to her character that attracts and impresses Squier. The intellectual is struck not only by her youth and beauty but also by a picturesque quality born out of her ruggedness, which includes the coarseness of her language, her strange naivety, the primitivism of her paintings, the fierceness of her desires, and her impulsiveness. Despite her dreaminess and romanticism, Gabby is also a pragmatist, which lends her a psychological complexity. There is little to mark Gabby out as conventional or traditional. Indeed, by the standards of 1935, she is a modern woman whose aspirations lie in self-fulfillment rather than duty, servitude, or virtue. There is even a degree of amorality about her as well as a sexual assertiveness that seems to speak of a more feminist than feminine attitude. Interestingly, Gabby makes no effort to become modern or transgressive. She simply *is* modern and transgressive.

Gabby bears many similarities to the heroine of David Belasco's most acclaimed western melodrama, *The Girl of the Golden West*, first staged in New York in 1905. This play, which Daniel C. Gerould (1983) argues modernized melodrama for American middle-class audiences, featured a new and distinctly American heroine, "frank, open, unconventional," described by Belasco as "a child of nature." As Gerould writes in *American Melodrama*, "A product of the frontier and gold rush, the Girl is naturally independent and self-reliant, with a strong sense of her own worth as a human being. Innocent but not ignorant" (25).

Gabby appears to have been conceived by Robert Sherwood along similar lines to Belasco's famous heroine, his play bearing further resemblances to *The Girl of the Golden West*, which was, as Gerould observed, "one of the new villainless melodramas" in which "the villain—that indispensable driving force of earlier melodrama—fades away," replaced by a "divided hero" and a "vestigial villain." Gerould notes that part of the modernity of Belasco's western melodrama in 1905 lay in "changes in the simple classifications of hero, heroine, villain and in the moral underpinnings of these types" (25). Consequently, the complex characterizations of Gabby, Squier, and Mantee and their inherent moral ambiguities were less features of modernized stage melodrama than established tropes by 1935.

This further suggests that Elinor Hughes's "implausible stock types" (1934) belong to an earlier perception of melodramatic film, distinct from practices circulating on the mainstream American stage during the first three decades of the twentieth century. Gerould (1983) writes that the "stereotyped characters of the mid-century melodramas were no longer acceptable in the 1890s" and that Belasco was part of a group of American playwrights who "modernized melodrama by reducing its sentimentality and wooden rhetoric, limiting violence (chiefly to act endings), making its plots more coherent and its characters and themes more serious and intellectually respectable." He adds that Belasco's plays were "intended for literate Broadway audiences" and that "the new wave of melodramas showed the impact of realism and its more rigorous standards of verisimilitude" (23). Gerould observes that the modernity of *The Girl of the Golden West* lay specifically in three factors: (i) greater narrative unity and simplicity of action; (ii) colloquial, off-hand, ironic dialogue, close in tone, syntax, and rhythm to American regional speech; and (iii) smaller and subtler gestures by the cast, concentrating impact on small lifelike details. Judging by the reviews in the New York papers, the same features could be seen thirty years later in Sherwood's *The Petrified Forest* on stage at the Broadhurst.

A SENSITIVE, LITERATE, CANDID, AND SUBTLE MELODRAMA

The Petrified Forest is the work of the playwright Robert Emmet Sherwood (1896–1955) whose familiarity with Broadway theater and Hollywood cinema made him the perfect candidate to create a melodrama that could work as effectively on stage as on screen in the mid-1930s. After studying at Harvard University, Sherwood began his professional life as a film critic for *Life* magazine in the early 1920s, becoming a screenwriter at Famous Players-Lasky and a member of the exclusive Algonquin Round Table in New York City (Atkinson 1970, 280). After the success of his first play, *The Road to Rome*, in 1926, he rose to prominence as one of Broadway's leading playwrights and subsequently scored a series of hits; most notably, *The Queen's Husband* (1928), *Waterloo Bridge* (1930), and *Reunion in Vienna* (1931), all of which had been made into Hollywood movies by 1934.[5]

As Sherwood rose from obscurity to fame and fortune between 1920 and 1934, the actor Leslie Howard (1893–1943) similarly carved out a highly successful career on Broadway and in Hollywood.[6] In 1931, he starred in three MGM movies before appearing on Broadway in Philip Barry's *The Animal Kingdom* in 1932. The following year, Howard starred in Warners' *Captured!* (Roy Del Ruth, 1933), as well as making movies at Fox, RKO, Columbia, and MGM, although his greatest success proved to be the British swashbuckling adventure comedy *The Scarlet Pimpernel* (Harold Young, 1934).[7]

For Howard, Sherwood created a leading character that exploited both the star's image and acting style. By 1935, Howard was well known to British and American audiences as a stage and screen star who projected sensitive masculinity (Eforgan 2010, 52). As Jeffrey Richards writes in the foreword to Estel Eforgan's *Leslie Howard: The Lost Actor* (2010), Howard "represented an archetype not generally held to be popular with the mass audience—the intellectual." He adds that Howard's "sensitive features and blond good looks . . . cultured speaking voice . . . slightly absent-minded air . . . dreamy-eyed abstraction offset by the dry, donnish wit—all combined to give the appearance of the 'absent-minded professor' of popular myth" (xiii). Although Howard's character in *The Petrified Forest* was not a befuddled don, he nevertheless possessed many of these traits, being intellectual, whimsical, sardonic, and vague.

Just as Alan Squier proved to be the perfect role for Howard, Humphrey Bogart proved to be the perfect actor to play the gangster Duke Mantee, and young Peggy Conklin was well cast in the role of the love-struck, life-starved Gabby Maple.[8] In *The Petrified Forest*, Bogart and Conklin both matured as actors in theatrical roles that impressed the New York critics (see Mantle 1935, 39). Just as convincing was Leslie Howard as Alan Squier, for whom the actor utilized his skills for subtle underplaying. Here, as elsewhere, Howard employed what Jeffrey Richards describes as "such economy of gesture and expression that he appeared not to be acting at all" (Eforgan 2010, xiii).

After the play's first night, Howard received the lion's share of the critical adulation. Burns Mantle (1935) observed that the actor can "inspire more interest and express more drama by letting those around him do most of the talking" (39). Similarly, Percy Hammond in the New York *Herald-Tribune* for January 8, 1935, stated that Alan Squier is the "ideal Howard hero," noting that "under violent circumstances he maintains his well known calm, and surmounts the numerous crises with his irresistible smile," giving a "powerful performance" that bore no trace of "an actor's oil." The critic also observed that the first night audience "was stormy in its approval and even the coolest of us grew excited and clapped our hands." Evidently, Howard's subtle underplaying proved highly effective in stimulating a rapturous response among his audience.

Describing it as a "candid and subtle melodrama," Percy Hammond noted the play's "shrewd and literate combination of the fanciful and the substantial," heartily recommending it to "every wise drama-lover." Similarly, Burns Mantle (1935) declared *The Petrified Forest* to be "the most exciting philosophical melodrama the stage has presented in a considerable stretch." After describing the scenario, he stated, "Now this sounds a good deal like a shooting melodrama" but for most of the time "the characters sit about and discuss life and love, passion and crime, the American Legion and foreign gangsters. Discuss them in some of Mr. Sherwood's most effectively worded phrases" (39).

These reviews reveal New York drama critics' understanding of *melodrama* as an action genre associated mostly with thrills and spills. However, if Hammond's "candid and subtle melodrama" implies the play is an exception to the rule and his use of "literate" values dialogue over action and spectacle, Mantle's "exciting philosophical melodrama" suggests a profound and thought-provoking work. Despite being widely touted as a melodrama, the play was nonetheless considered a vehicle for fine acting, marking a significant shift from the critical discourse employed by Elinor Hughes the previous summer and a less derogatory view of melodrama. Mantle and Hammond indicate that stage melodrama could appeal to "wise" or discerning drama lovers able to appreciate a combination of the whimsical and fantastic with the serious and profound. There is no suggestion here that the play was best suited to working-class audiences with a taste for heightened emotionalism, fantastically contrived plots, or sensational set pieces. Expressions such as "exciting philosophical melodrama" suggest a dramatic mode capable of engaging audiences on both emotional and intellectual levels, and praise for the play's "effectively worded phrases" highlights literary merits—its poetic qualities—suggesting a significant achievement in terms considered artistic.

Melodrama emerges from these reviews as a dramatic mode combining elements of fantasy and realism that provided audiences with opportunities to both think and feel about various aspects of contemporary American life: that is something sophisticated, versatile, and multidimensional. Such reviews also contradict claims by twentieth-century scholars that melodrama had become a moribund and devalued form by the 1900s (see Pearson 1992, 21). On the contrary, they prove that melodrama remained vital and popular as a dramatic form for middle-class audiences and critics, among others, and that it flourished at premier Broadway theaters during the 1930s.

More broadly, the reviews of *The Petrified Forest* in the New York papers demonstrate a critical view of melodrama in the USA in the mid-1930s that was neither uniform nor fixed. Rather than being uniformly negative, contradictory critical evaluations and conceptions existed alongside each other. Although dismissive opinion circulated in the Boston press, more positive opinion was expressed regarding stage melodrama on Broadway in the New York theater reviews. Meanwhile, the New York film reviews of *The Petrified Forest* published in February 1936 indicate that, contrary to Elinor Hughes's opinions, film critics also held more positive views of melodrama.

THE DESTINY OF ALL GOOD PLAYS

Archie Mayo directed *The Petrified Forest* at Warner Bros. between October 14 and November 30, 1935 (Sikov 2007, 75). On this occasion, Peggy Conklin's role was performed by Bette Davis, who had caught the attention of film critics in 1934 as a vibrant new acting talent when appearing with Leslie Howard in RKO's *Of Human Bondage*, directed by John Cromwell (Klaprat 1985, 357). Joining the cast of *The Petrified Forest* after completing work on her own star vehicle *Dangerous* (Alfred E. Green, 1935), Davis experienced a dramatic change of pace in a part strikingly different from her previous roles. Indeed, The *Petrified Forest* provided Davis with the chance to reveal the quieter side of her persona. To perform Gabby Maple, Davis reigned in her histrionic skills and performed without the hysterics audiences and critics had come to associate with her. The role called for a quiet and charming innocence, albeit one that hints at a more ambitious, independent, and coarser personality beneath the surface. It also demanded that the actress hold the attention of the audience without detracting from the subdued performance of the leading man and yet without receding so far into the background that the character's significance within the plot is lost.

When released in Manhattan at the beginning of February 1936, Warner Bros.' movie version of *The Petrified Forest* was greeted with almost unanimous praise from the New York film critics. Eileen Creelman announced in the *Sun* on February 7, 1936, that "here's another play returned from the Hollywood studios even more effective than when it left Broadway," pointing out that "Warners, who can make gangster films just a bit grimmer and more realistic than anyone else, have bravely resisted any temptations to concentrate on that angle, or even to change the ending." Here and elsewhere, *The Petrified Forest* was regarded as a prestige picture, several critics noting that it bore a strong resemblance to the stage production in plot and setting, having a screenplay that "stuck closely to the legit script" (Anonymous, *Variety*, February 12, 1936). On February 7, 1936, reviewers noted that Howard gave "the same quiet, compelling performance of the quixotic Alan Squier which he gave on the stage" (Cameron, 1936); Bogart equaled "his superb interpretation in the theatre of the gangster character" (Crewe, 1936).

Critics of the film version raved over the fine and literate script, as well as Archie Mayo's artful direction. "Fulfilling the destiny of all good plays, Robert Emmet Sherwood's lusty stage melodrama 'The Petrified Forest' is now decked out as a motion picture at the Radio City Music Hall," wrote William Boehnel in the *World-Telegram* on February 7, 1936. The critic added that "the whole thing is played so richly, so rightly that the film emerges as a work of distinction." Echoing these sentiments in the *American* on the same day, Regina Crewe (1936) announced that "a fine literate play becomes an intelligent motion picture," calling *The Petrified Forest* "a production of highest class and most distinguished calibre." Similarly, Kate Cameron (1936) noted in the *Daily News* that "Robert Emmet Sherwood's philosophical, melodramatic play, 'The Petrified Forest,' in which Leslie Howard starred last Winter on the New York stage, has been transferred by Warner Brothers into a thrilling and absorbing screen play." She further stated that "the picture retains all of the poetic appeal of the original without sacrificing any of its excitement."

When reviewed in the trade paper *Variety* a few days later (February 12, 1936), it was predicted that the film would "draw critical raves for its all-around quality, its fine adherence to mood and its blending of haunting melodrama with philosophic discourse." The anonymous reviewer, however, expressed doubt as to "whether the picture's box-office reaction will parallel its artistic success," suggesting the film was highbrow fare rather than popular entertainment. For William Boehnel (1936). *The Petrified Forest* was not only a "beautifully written, superbly acted, robust, brutish melodrama" but also presented "a truthful picture of contemporary American life, manners and character."

"Beautifully written" and "superbly acted" suggest something stylish, artistic, polished, even refined; hence, more likely to be judged at this time as having both female and middle-class appeal. Meanwhile, the terms "robust" and "brutish" provide a counterpoint to the play's beautiful writing and superb acting (that is, its artistic merits), grounding these in something realistic, solid, forceful, even tough; something, that is, more likely to be deemed masculine and appealing to working-class moviegoers. The combination of these terms suggests a critical judgment of *The Petrified Forest*'s cross-class and cross-gender appeal.

Whereas William Boehnel largely ignored the tragic romance at the heart of this scenario to appreciate its more "masculine" qualities, others emphasized the importance of the doomed love affair. For instance, Kate Cameron (1936) stated that "there is something heart-warming and appealing in the sudden love which develops between Gabrielle and Alan." Although hinting at the improbability of the "sudden" love scenario, Cameron nevertheless implied that this relationship was emotionally satisfying. Although these male and female critics highlighted different aspects of *The Petrified Forest* for their respective readers, both Boehnel and Cameron clearly regarded the film as praiseworthy. For the former, the drama was laudable for its realism (and contemporary social significance), and for the latter, the drama's chief merit appeared to lie in its ability to *touch* or *move* an audience at an emotional level. Together these reviews suggest that the power and appeal of *The Petrified Forest* in the mid-1930s, whether play or film, lay in its capacity to make audiences think *and* feel.

A VEHICLE FOR FINE AND VIRTUOSIC PERFORMANCES

Although in July 1934, Boston film critic Elinor Hughes expressed surprise at discovering a fine performance by Bette Davis in the action melodrama *Fog Over Frisco*, the New York film critics appear to have taken it for granted that Davis could display her acting skills to advantage in Sherwood's "brutish" melodrama. The film version of *The Petrified Forest*, like the recent stage production, was widely accepted as a showcase for fine acting involving subtle, realistic, and measured or precise performances, building on a tradition that David Belasco helped to establish some thirty years earlier.

As a playwright, producer, theater manager, and acting tutor at the New York School of Acting (which became the American Academy of Dramatic Arts in 1892), Belasco was instrumental in melodrama's ongoing transformations during the late nineteenth and early twentieth centuries, helping to modernize melodrama to meet the demands of an upwardly mobile and increasing professional and managerial Broadway audience (Schwarz 2009, 23–32). Having dispensed with convoluted plots and declamatory speeches in his plays, Belasco demanded subtlety and naturalism from his actors. In *Before Stanislavsky*, James McTeague (1993) shows that many features later associated with method acting in the mid-twentieth century were introduced to students at the New York Acting School between 1885 and 1891, for example, the development of characterization through detailed script analysis (52). Students were also encouraged to use their imagination and discover the "imaginative truth of the play," drawing on memories of their own life experiences as a source for imaginative feeling (58). As McTeague writes, "The imaginative act eliminated the actor as a person with an identity: in theory, at least, the actor is the character, feeling as the character might feel in the same situation" (59–60). Teaching drama students to feel the emotions being portrayed ensured that actors developed a close psychological bond with their characters. Consequently, this meant that characters in modern melodramas of the period acquired an emotional integrity and psychological complexity beyond any "implausible stock type."

Many of these same principles were carried forward into the teaching at the American Academy of Dramatic Arts, where generations of American stage and screen actors (for example, Edward G. Robinson and Spencer Tracy) were taught the "think the thought" approach to acting (McTeague 1993, 63). Despite placing greater emphasis on gesture and physical expression than diction, academy students were instructed to employ their imagination and intellect, using their brains "in terms of the character's needs" and never for an instant thinking a thought other than what his or her character would be thinking. McTeague notes that this approach bore "a strong resemblance" to Stanislavsky's system; however, it was "an organic and practical approach that constitute[d] a viable prescriptive acting theory, years before Stanislavsky's influence appeared on the scene" (64).

Graduates of the New York Acting School in the late 1880s and the American Academy of Dramatic Arts from 1892 were well placed to perform in the modern melodramas of David Belasco and his counterparts. By the 1890s, as Christine Gledhill (1991) has observed, the "more literary, analytical and naturalist bent [of stage melodrama] and the influential growth of psychology and related disciplines . . . defined a shift in character construction and performance mode" (219). Consequently, characters "referred less to pre-existing types" as actors "strove for the illusion of random individuality." Meanwhile, a "new set of techniques based on psychology and observation from life, valued restraint, underplaying and subtlety and sought to displace what seemed now the limitations of pantomimic ritual and rhetorical dialogue in order to convey the inner life and private personality of the characters." Gledhill further notes that this shift instituted changes in "American melodramatic production which were crucial to the transfer of the melodramatic imagination from stage to screen" (221).

The performances of Leslie Howard and Bette Davis in *The Petrified Forest* appear to belong to this tradition of modern melodramatic acting, indicating the persistence of this style and approach some forty years after it was first instituted on the American stage. The subtlety and precision of their gestures and vocal inflections are certainly on full display in their final, most dramatic and emotionally charged scene together. Here, after Alan Squier has been shot by a departing Duke Mantee, Gabby cradles him like a baby in her arms, the pair sitting on the floor beside a bullet-riddled wall (figure 8.2). Squier's death takes a few minutes and is filmed entirely in a medium close shot with both characters facing the camera and unable to see each other's face. Initially, the pair adopt forced smiles in an attempt to be brave for each other, but as Squier slips quietly into death, his speech slows and fades away and his face and body relax, sinking toward the young woman holding him. Meanwhile, Davis's large and liquid eyes register her anxiety and distress as Gabby feels the dead weight of Alan's body.

At one point, Davis's eyes roll from side to side in their sockets as though, without daring to move her body and thereby disturb the man dying in her arms, she searches around in vain for a way out of this situation.[9] Yet, after a short struggle for breath, during which only the sound of the desert wind can be heard howling in the background, she cradles the dead man's head in her hand and explores his face for signs of life.[10] Calling his name has elicited no response, and once resigned to the fact of Alan's death, Gabby assumes a fixed and determined smile. Davis's

Modernizing Melodrama 147

Figure 8.2 Gabby cradles dying Alan.

facial muscles tighten as she grimaces, evoking her character's effort to hold back tears and, once again, put on a brave face.

This is a big scene played with subtlety and presented with a great deal of intimacy, and viewers are closely bound up with these two characters in the final moments of their relationship. In this way, the audience is invited to perceive the characters' confused thoughts and feelings through slight changes in the actors' breathing, facial tension, and intonations. Clasped together and fixed into a seated position on the floor in the corner of the room, their body movements are restricted to head and neck. Attention therefore remains focused on the actors' faces and voices. Breathing takes on a crucial role here. Having been shot in the lung, Squier appears to gradually expire as Howard takes shorter breaths. He speaks more softly and in shorter segments, repeatedly pausing and eventually expiring halfway through his final line. Gabby also struggles to breathe due to her shock, fear, and panic but her inner strength is revealed through the way she persists in remaining calm and collected so as not to disturb the man ebbing away in her arms. Slight gasps for breath and a voice that noticeably rises in pitch and volume betray her true feelings, and the tension in her face proclaims her determination to master her emotions and remain in control.

With the exception of Davis' "eye-rolling," there is little here that conforms to the critical stereotype of melodramatic acting, one that equates it with histrionics and excess, emphatic gesturing, and exaggerated facial grimacing, physical posturing, rhetorical flourishes, and florid movements that embody hyperbolic and sententious dialogue in what Peter Brooks described as the "plastic figurability of emotion" (1976, 47). On the contrary, the methods employed by Howard and Davis throughout this scene seem particularly well suited to the understated nature of the drama (minimizing high-octane action in favor of philosophical and poetic dialogue) and the intimate presentation (framing in a medium close shot). They also conform to some extent with British traditions of acting, perhaps as a consequence of Leslie Howard's role as the film's star. In *Reframing British Cinema, 1918–28*, Christine Gledhill (2003) argues that most leading actors in British films of the 1920s lent their characters an emotional intensity through intimations of feelings that remain largely unexpressed (62). Consequently, emotional continence became a hallmark of British silent film acting of this era. In the 1920s, Gledhill observes, many leading actors in British films pitched their performance between restraint and passion (62–63). This partly resulted from middle-class codes of decorum, but it was also a consequence of a belief that "passion is powerful only if generated against a counterforce of outward control" (63).

The performances of Leslie Howard and (to a lesser extent) Bette Davis during this death scene conform to a British model of underplaying. For all its understatement, however, this scene is highly charged in terms of emotion due to the intensity of the acting and the focus throughout on inner thoughts and feelings. Intense actor identification with the characters here replaces either a grand display of outward emotion or a cathartic outpouring of grief. The keynote remains restraint. Indeed, the heroism of the characters lies precisely in their ability to master their feelings and preserve emotional continence. Here, sensational excitement has been replaced by an exciting serenity. This, moreover, is achieved by the production of a calm exterior that belies a high degree of internal agitation. Furthermore, this stimulates a heightened emotional response from the viewer, who is invited to experience the emotions that the character appears to be repressing.

CONCLUSION

In 1967, Frank Rahill described *The Petrified Forest* as a brilliant attempt "to construct a play of ideas on the cadre of the Western" (239). Since the 1970s, however, most critics have dismissed this film as stagey, pretentious, and dull. Charles Higham (1981), for instance, described it as a "typical mid-thirties melodrama," stating that the "writing was heavy and pretentious" (104). Similarly, Alexander Walker (1995) criticized the film for its pious adaptation of a stage drama, with characters that "engage interminably in the sort of matinée philosophizing that passed for seriousness in its day and with its middle-brow audience" (75). For Walker, the assumption that the film was aimed at a middle-class audience was clearly part of the problem. Elsewhere, he criticized Howard and Davis for their performances. For Walker, Howard is not so much naturalistic and charming as "soft," being "too intent on playing to *his* sort of audience." Meanwhile, Davis is dismissed on account of her "pseudo-poetic breathiness" and her "nasal whine." Only Bogart receives praise here, Walker stating that he "alone manages to kick it into occasional life" (77).

These statements stand in marked contrast to those of the New York film critics in 1936, who praised the film for its blend of haunting melodrama and philosophic discourse (*Variety*), its truthful picture of contemporary American life (Boehnel), its heart-warming and appealing romance (Cameron), its fine phrases and penetrating philosophies (Crewe), and for being simultaneously poetic and profound, exciting and moving. Sharing the fate of many popular melodramas, *The Petrified Forest* was eventually seen by critics and historians as old-fashioned, artificial, unrealistic, and theatrical. In the process, its rich hybridity, realism, intelligence, and ability to make audiences think and feel have been ignored in order to render it a melodrama typified by the genre's later stereotypical critical conception.

Along with its literate, poetic, and philosophical script, the moral ambiguities and complex identities of its principal characters brought home to critics that even the most brutish action melodrama could be adult, intelligent, and sophisticated. These qualities also rendered both the stage play and the film version well suited to both male and female audiences, as well as to both upmarket middle-class audiences (prepared to pay a higher price for their entertainment at New York's Radio City Music Hall and other first-run cinemas) and working-class audiences (more likely to see the film version in second- and third-run cinemas across the USA). These same qualities, however, led to the film being devalued by later generations of critics and historians. Consequently, the critical history of *The Petrified Forest* reveals not only how much tastes (and cultural conventions) change over time but also, more specifically, how the ongoing modernization of melodrama—which ensures the longevity of this prevalent dramatic mode—renders individual melodramatic plays and films "old-fashioned." As melodrama reaches out to new generations by incorporating new aspects of realism, many melodramas will inevitably share the fate of *The Petrified Forest*. It would therefore seem that the fate of all good melodramas is to become obsolete even as melodrama itself rejuvenates, evolves, and continues to thrive. Of course, what was once rejected also can be recuperated. A film combining the artistry of fine phrases, emotionally exciting performances, sardonic wit, thwarted romance, the moral ambiguities of assisted suicide, a thrilling shootout, and the combined star power of Bette Davis, Leslie Howard, and Humphrey Bogart is unlikely to remain in a state of critical or cultural obscurity forever.

NOTES

1. Never a single genre, melodrama incorporated westerns, crime thrillers, social problem dramas, historical biographies and costume dramas, romantic dramas, and dramas of maternal separation and self-sacrifice, to name just a few.
2. Similarly, Roberta Pearson (1992) writes in *Eloquent Gestures* that the term *melodramatic* has "been so indiscriminately applied to such greatly diverse theatrical styles and performers as to lose any precise meaning" (8).
3. See John S. Cohen Jr.'s comments on the Douglas Fairbanks Jr. picture, *Parachute Jumper* (Alfred E. Green, 1933), in the New York *Sun*, January 26, 1933. Describing the film as an "inconsequential but passable enough little program melodrama," he notes that "there are loose ends galore in the plot, which is so inconsequential that it doesn't matter much."

4. Duke Mantee stands out from the rest of his gang of mobsters. Although ruthless, he is not malevolent. At no point, for instance, does he threaten Gabby with physical or sexual abuse, as might be expected from a hardened criminal fresh out of prison. Throughout the drama, Mantee remains patient and calm, as much a witness to the unfolding events as a participant. Awaiting the appearance of his girlfriend Doris, he is even prepared to compromise his gang's safety, refusing to leave when there is a clear chance of escape. This suggests that he is essentially a romantic, like Squier.
5. *The Queen's Husband* (1928) became the basis for RKO's *The Royal Bed*, directed by and starring Lowell Sherman. James Whale directed *Waterloo Bridge* for Universal Pictures in 1931, and Sidney Franklin directed *Reunion in Vienna* for MGM in 1933.
6. Having begun his acting career in London in 1914, Leslie Howard achieved greater success on Broadway in such plays as A. E. Thomas's *Just Suppose* (1920), Sutton Vane's *Outward Bound* (1924), Michael Arlen's *The Green Hat* (1925), Jacques Deval's *Her Cardboard Lover* (1927), John Galsworthy's *Escape* (1927), and John L. Balderston's *Berkeley Square* (1929). In 1930, he became a major film star after appearing alongside Douglas Fairbanks Jr. in a Warner Bros. production of *Outward Bound* (Robert Milton). He was later nominated for an Oscar for his performance as Professor Henry Higgins in *Pygmalion* (Anthony Asquith and Leslie Howard, 1938) and, famously, played Ashley Wilkes in the multi-Oscar-winning box office smash *Gone with the Wind* (Victor Fleming, 1939).
7. Sherwood had been hired by producer Alexander Korda to adapt Baroness Orczy's swashbuckling comedy into a movie vehicle for Howard and outlined ideas for *The Petrified Forest* to Howard on board ship en route to England (see Eforgan 2010, 99). It is likely that their conversations continued during production at Denham studios. Howard was so enthusiastic that he not only agreed to star in Sherwood's play but also to coproduce it on his return to the USA.
8. By 1935, Humphrey Bogart and Peggy Conklin were well known to Broadway audiences. Bogart had been the romantic leading man in a succession of lightweight comedies between 1923 and 1933 (Kanfer 2011, 20-28). Peggy Conklin, meanwhile, had graduated from the chorus line of a musical comedy in 1928 to named juvenile parts in comedies in the early 1930s, enjoying major success in *The Pursuit of Happiness* (1933).
9. Bette Davis's emphatic eye movements here may seem dated to some contemporary viewers who consider "eye-rolling" to be a defining feature of overacting. It may well be that even in 1936 some viewers judged moments such as this to be histrionic, an example perhaps of the actress's bravura style, designed to draw attention to the fact that she was visibly acting. Davis still had much to prove at this time and was intent on impressing the New York critics with her acting skills. After winning her first Oscar for her role as a stage actress in *Dangerous* in March 1936, Davis had less need to draw attention to her dramatic artistry, although this never prevented her from producing some highly visible performances (for details, see Shingler and Gledhill 2008, 68).
10. No music is used throughout this scene to underscore the emotions of the characters; in other words, no dramatic underscoring, so often associated with melodrama (Brooks 1976, 48). Consequently, the task of conveying and stimulating emotion is left entirely to the actors.

9

One Suffers but One Learns

Melodrama and the Rules of Lack of Limits

CARLOS MONSIVÁIS

*NOTE ON THE AUTHOR AND THE TRANSLATION

Carlos Monsiváis (1938–2010) has been celebrated in Mexico and beyond as that nation's most lucid and influential cultural, social and political observer. A prolific essayist, he is credited with the reinvention of the Latin American genre of the crónica (chronicle) which, in his hands is a blend of immersive reporting and allusive and aphoristic reflection. Monsiváis also wrote widely on cinema, with a special focus on the films and key figures of the Mexican Golden Age of the 1930s to 1950s. The essay included here is an edited version of a longer piece that was originally published in the large format book, A través del espejo. El cine mexicano y su público, *under the dual authorship of Monsiváis and Carlos Bonfil. The book is comprised of an introductory history of Golden Age cinema, written by Bonfil, and Monsiváis's extended essay on Mexican melodrama, accompanied by a wealth of full color reproductions of film posters of many of the films mentioned in the two texts. The piece's original title, "Se sufre pero se aprende," has multiple resonances. A saying in Mexico passed on from parents to children, the maxim appears in a sign affixed to the bumper of a truck driven by the hero of the film,* Nosotros los pobres, *described in this essay by Monsiváis as a melodramatic "classic of classics." It also is the title of a bolero, first recorded in 1951, by Mexican composer Federico Baena Solís.*

Monsiváis's writing on film has been embraced, and much cited, by scholars of Mexican and Latin American cinemas. His essays aim at a broader public and generally eschew the critical and bibliographic apparatus associated with academic work. Building on partial and incomplete citations included in the original, I have compiled a list of references that identify the works in question. I have also provided a small number of explanatory footnotes. Omissions from the original text are indicated by ellipses. Translating Monsiváis is not an easy task and relatively little of his writing has been translated into English. Linda Egan, the author of the only full-length English-language study of his work, describes his style as a matter of "thoughts pirouett[ing] from his imagination with lyric grace." It is my hope that this translation captures both his thoughts and some of that poetic grace.

Kathleen M. Vernon

Why is such importance accorded to a genre that originates in the theater and the serial novel only to spread to the novel, cinema, radio, and television? And what is meant by the term *melodrama*? The dictionary offers two definitions: "drama with occasional musical accompaniment" and the more recent sense of "work that emphasizes the sentimental and pathetic in detriment of good taste." In the Latin American context, melodrama has revolved around the disjuncture between happiness and tragedy for the individual, the couple, or, more commonly, the family. The outline is simple: melodrama begins with a sudden storm of bad luck, assures that its characters are rewarded with a compensatory outpouring of laughter and affection, entrusts its message to the noble sentiments of the spectators, and then heads toward the happy resolution of misfortune. As for the characters, they exist primarily as emblems of a series of feelings: compassion, pain, arrogance, evil, innocence, coquetry, cowardice, irresponsibility, resentment, generosity. Consistent with this schema, all that remains is to deliver the proper dosage (parceled out in time and space) of amorous suspense, extreme situations, emotional blackmail, and last minute salvation or perdition.

In Mexico and Latin America, melodrama was rooted in the (slow) process of secularization during the nineteenth century and the partial transfer of religious feelings to private life. A direct antecedent of melodrama is the *folletín*, or serial novel, in which, week after week, overwhelmed by the accumulation of eventful actions, readers came to hate the villains, idolize the unlucky heroines, and vow to aid the heroes. As a rehearsal for the melodramas to come, the folletín lay the groundwork for the techniques that would make theater audiences shudder with emotion.... The immediacy of live theater heightened the spirits of the audience, and melodrama secured a hold on the public caught up in the (then genuine) moral dilemmas they posed. The basic plots and situations established infinite variations, and their formative effects were endless. The vitality of the genre even seemed to contaminate the classics—hence those who find Shakespeare's tragedies "melodramatic" and see in melodrama the outlines of a popular pedagogy. One goes to the theater to learn how to react in the face of misfortune, to memorize phrases and expressions of dignity or resignation that provide consolation in the face of humiliation, to defend what is one's own, and to resist the lure of worldly temptations—and finally, on death's door, to utter suitable last words.

In a certain sense, classic melodrama of the late nineteenth and early twentieth centuries in Spanish and French theater recasts the Christian catechism in secular terms as it reworks behavioral archetypes. Wielding a model of the moral ideal that is materialized in cries and sobs, accusatory and guilty silences, the Soul (Family, Woman, Man) confronts its enemies: the World, the Flesh and the Devil.... This is religion immediate to the sufferings of the everyday.... During the era that ended in the 1930s, melodrama reaffirmed its techniques of containment and self-control.

A catechism for the modern age, it dramatized the moral ills of the century and mined the moral risks at the edge of the abyss that are conjured in the dim light of cinema and theater stalls.

Why such a direct link between religion and melodrama? The obvious reason is that Christianity continues to provide the primary source for models of sacrifice, from divine punishment to posthumous forgiveness. In addition, during the golden age of melodrama, the language of the emotions owes much to the New Testament preaching of the parish priest. Amidst the sighs and eyes welling with tears, the paradigm shifts. Not only does God incarnate give his life for his fellow man and through his death on the Cross pay for the sin of transitory happiness. Human beings, too, thinking and suffering reeds, have thrust upon them an implacable geography: heaven and hell, limbo and purgatory. Christian symbology manifests itself in the supplicating gaze of the sick mother, the newborn abandoned in the vestibule of a church, the face of a man in the prime of life suddenly aged by the news of family dishonor. The moral universe is defined by a set of perennial oppositions: sanctity/prostitution, faithfulness/adultery, fertility/sterility, faith/blasphemy, good fortune/bad luck. In melodrama hell is deviation from the path of the straight and narrow, sobbing erupts as a form of absolution, virtue produces paradises, and miracles multiply like the loaves and fishes of the New Testament.

THE AESTHETICS OF CONSOLATION

The task of doing away with the impetus to tragedy and satire falls to melodrama, the secret and public source of family orthodoxy. The message is this: we are born to wander through the Valley of Tears, and our greatest boon is suffering tempered by self-pity. Sadness and affliction offer momentary relief from the weight of moral squalor, and to suffer or to contemplate suffering is a heroic undertaking. Who but a pure soul feels solidarity with those mothers of unending generosity, the adulteresses ennobled by suicide, the romantic idylls cut short by family rivalries? What other recourse exists in societies defined by patriarchal norms, lacking in literacy, and having little use for books? Melodrama—the restricted setting of family relations—is also a request for membership in a community (*I wish to cry in order to belong*) and a condition of *maturity*, as conceived by that compendium of talents and renunciations called society.

From the late nineteenth to the first half of the twentieth century, melodrama is the stage upon which the features of traditional morality are accommodated and ennobled. Extreme emotion is identified with the sublime: to pity the rich, to forgive the sinner, and to welcome poverty as a divine gift. Forbidden to look at anyone outside of one's own social class, one accepts that the dark color of one's skin is a curse and offers up hopes to a spirit of conformity. Melodrama bestows specific modes of behavior, desperate words on stormy nights, and steely convictions appropriate for family scenes that combine stony faces and agonized gestures.

In the face of an unending set of problems without solutions, the spectator (reader) opts for aesthetic persuasion. If the beautiful is a variant of the ineffable, then beauty also resides in forgiveness obtained half a minute before the curtain descends. Thus the aesthetics of suffering in some way compensate for the inexorable logic of moral distinctions. In terms of *aesthetics*, what could be more beautiful than the repertory of facial expressions of fear, sorrow, and shame? In terms of *ethics*, is there a scene more pleasing to the Lord than that of the woman who submits to divine judgment, especially if her acts of penance are for sins she has not committed? Bypassing the limits of the plot, one genre alone affords its spectators the great gift of sentimental identity. Neither comedy, adventure, or terror plumb the depths reached by that cauldron of self-destructive passions and self-consuming lives.

. . . .

THE SECULARIZATION OF TEARS

With the Mexican Revolution a new morality emerged, a relativism born of acts of great violence: "If I am to be killed tomorrow, let me sin first." Add to this the effects of technology, the growing electrification of the country, expanded communication provided by the railroad, the telephone, the cinema—everything that consolidates the new "Religion of the Century"—the acceptance of scientific and industrial wonders whose functioning only a few understand. Traditional moral controls are loosened and a phenomenon E. M. Cioran (1995) has called *the secularization of tears* develops, in which religious awe inflects the quotidian and its cathartic effects. Silent film, in the absence of the exaltation of the word, fashions a gestural language of suffering and exasperation. Arms are raised to the departing lover, toward the heavenly heights of anguish, grasping curtains whose touch conveys the experience of romantic agony. For audiences denied access to the Porfirian era theater,[1] film melodrama proposes an equitable distribution of its stone tablets-of-the-law to former peasants and aging landowners alike: there is no exploitation of workers but instead the shared and infinite suffering of the dispossessed; there are no class divisions but rather fateful behaviors determined by one's social origins (the right or wrong side of the tracks); God does not forget his children but tests them to better reward them in the hereafter. . . . Italian divas and Hollywood vamps lend a different dimension to the feminine image, and melodramatic plots take on a tragic cast in the films of Murnau, Von Stroheim, Von Sternberg, King Vidor, and especially D. W. Griffith. Among the swirling storms of hatreds and misfortunes, *Broken Blossoms* (1919), *Orphans of the Storm* (1921), *Way Down East* (1920), *The Last Command* (1928), *Tabu* (1931), *Sunrise* 1927), *The Big Parade* (1925), and *Greed* (1924) confirm the nobility that melodrama also commands. The great directors transcend the limits of the genre without abandoning its strategy of catastrophic misfortune. The narrative spirit is undoubtedly tragic, but the storytelling mechanisms are melodramatic. . . .

In its passage from theater to film, classic melodrama expands its audience and sets in motion the beginning of its own demise. Although the flights of pain and passion are apparently preserved, the new medium imposes its own rules.

Spectators may accept the dictates of nineteenth-century morality, but in their fervored responses they consign it to the past. . . . The defense of honor at the point of a gun is no longer persuasive, nor does the mere mention of adultery produce revulsion. Likewise, the idea of sex for money fails to provoke moral indignation. As the old certainties of tradition disappear, so too do long-standing moral lessons; ambition reigns, driven by cynicism and lechery. The wages of sin are no longer death.

BEWARE OF WORTHY SENTIMENTS

The great laboratory that is cinema glories in the anachronisms that are the foundation of social consensus but does not leave them intact for long. In the darkness of the cinema, and with total seriousness, popular audiences endorse certain forms of behavior and discard others as antiquated. The best example is *Santa* (Antonio Moreno, 1931), based on the novel by Federico Gamboa. This drama of a young "fallen woman" brings together two of the key attractions of melodrama: the power and potency of film and the love song. Audiences embraced the film as they had done for the novel and would do for the subsequent 1943 version directed by Norman Foster.

What was the basis of *Santa*'s success? Among various hypotheses one stands out: the notion of melodrama as a contact zone between traditional morality and morbid fascination, or more accurately, morbid fascination as an instrument of traditional morality. The young, debased Santa becomes the most solicited prostitute and figures as the emotional center of the brothel. A certain social realism takes precedence over didactic moralism, and Santa is transformed from the sacrificial victim of the original novel to an unfortunate migrant to the Mexican capital, the bearer of a cautionary tale expressed in a conveniently idealized vision of the prostitute. The culmination of her transfiguration is found in the bolero of the same name by Agustín Lara: "Santa, my Santa/ you who illuminate my existence/ Santa, be my guide/ and shine your light upon my heart." Here we have the central metaphor of the melodrama: the prostitute motivated solely by altruism as the guiding light of the soul-blind (*ciegos del alma*). This marks the appearance of the "long-suffering Mexican woman" who leaves behind the immigrant slums for houses of ill repute, and who will come to populate the early morning streets of the city in the impossible search for noble passions. Santa anticipates and explains a whole series of filmic prostitutes to follow. Their sin confers on them a capacity to fascinate spectators that is denied to their virginal sisters.

SELLING PLEASURE AND BUYING SELF-DESTRUCTION

In 1933 Arcady Boytler directed *La mujer del puerto/* The woman of the port, one of the first classics of melodramatic excess. Rosario (Andrea Palma) has sexual relations with her boyfriend. Her father, don Antonio, is seriously ill, and there is no money for medicine. Basilio, Antonio's boss, pursues Rosario, and she discovers that her boyfriend is cheating on her. When Antonio goes to confront the boyfriend, the latter throws him down the stairs. Rosario has managed to acquire the medicine by promising to pay later, but when she gets back, her father has died. As she returns from his grave, a carnival scene erupts around her. Years later, a sailor, Alberto Venegas (Domingo Soler), arrives in Veracruz on a Honduran ship. Rosario is seen in the street, leaning on a lamp post. As she walks and smokes, Lina Boytler sings: "I sell pleasure to men who come from the sea/ and who depart at dawn/ what good would it do me to love?" Alberto rescues Rosario from a drunk in a seedy bar, and they return to her room where love making ensues. A shocking revelation is soon to follow: Alberto and Rosario are brother and sister! She commits suicide by throwing herself into the sea....

Take it or leave it: industrialization, technology, and the growth of urban populations erode the dominance of traditional morality. The time has come to exploit the visual potential of sin and sexual desire. The question becomes how to elevate poverty as a supreme good without undermining the value of individual effort. Melodrama offers one response: providing scenarios in which suffering is the highest expression of morality, and, indeed, its ultimate justification.

In the cinema of the 1930s, melodrama competes with films centered on the Mexican Revolution that find their cathartic impact in the historical record, in a battle from which neither combatant would emerge unscathed. Revolution themed films, following experiments with the epic mode (as in Fernando de Fuentes's *El compadre Mendoza* / Godfather Mendoza [1935] and *Vámonos con Pancho Villa* / Let's go with Pancho Villa [1936]), are faced with the obvious fact that growing censorship leaves only one option, melodrama. The other option—the celebration of the people in arms, the stories of heroism and betrayal—is perceived as provocation once the Revolution is institutionalized by the ruling party.[2]

A CLASSIC: *CUANDO LOS HIJOS SE VAN*

In Mexican cinema, melodrama comes to dominate in both quantitative and qualitative terms for reasons of "moral proximity": it is the genre that confers the greatest "intimate prestige." If not the most popular (comedy offers the idea of a world turned on its head, and adventure and horror films as well as the western entertain without the need for injecting so much guilt into the proceedings), melodrama is the genre that sets the stage for dinner table discussions and a life philosophy without which the family might lose it way. Intimate prestige, in this context, has to do with the sense of immediacy, of being there, in the theater seat, defending sacred values: love for the fatherland, the mother, the family, the children, honor, personal identity....

The story of *Cuando los hijos se van* / When the children leave home (1941) is simple, as summarized by its director, Juan Bustillo Oro: "It is nothing more than the tale of the breakup of a happy family, with the children grown and suddenly buffeted by new winds blowing through society." The father, José Rosales

(Fernando Soler), is a fair and honorable man who nevertheless commits a grave injustice against his younger son, Raimundo (Emilio Tuero). The mother, Lupita (Sara Garcia), is pure self-abnegation, and the other two children are selfish and cynical. The daughter (Marina Tamayo) marries an older man for money, and the older son (Carlos López Moctezuma) is a scoundrel who is only redeemed by Raimundo's death. The film begins a few days before Christmas, with the family together, followed by a second Christmas celebration attended only by the parents and an old family friend, and ends with a third Christmas Eve observance with the whole family in attendance except for the recently murdered Raimundo.

. . . .

Reacting to the film's reputation as a work "capable of wringing tears from a stone," Mexican producer Gregorio Wallerstein made a fifty-peso bet with Bustillo Oro that he wouldn't cry while watching the film. He lost the bet. Bustillo Oro tells of going to watch the film in the Cine Alameda in Mexico City where the majority of the audience was seen wiping away tears and an occasional sob was heard. The actress Sara Garcia recounts a trip to Cuernavaca where she was approached by a man in front of the Hotel Español who asked if he could give her a hug. He told her he was the owner of the hotel and had recently seen *Cuando los hijos se van* after which he wrote to his mother in Spain with whom he had not been in contact for three years. Two days before his meeting with the actress he received his mother's tear-stained letter in reply. Actors such as Garcia were themselves works of melodrama, institutions for the exchange of blame and forgiveness, tragicomic beings with faces prepared to project at a moment's notice expressions of surprise, suffering, repentance, and the blessings of compassion. Such actors and actresses were the perfect mirrors of the public that they represented on screen.

. . . .

IMITATION AND SINGULARITY

In Mexican melodrama the keyword was *excess*—the absence of limits on what was said and what was experienced. During the period 1931 to 1955, the Mexican cinema bested Hollywood's competition when it comes to excess, at least in terms of the number of tragedies visited on a single individual or family, the intensity of the tears, the abundance of inconceivable situations resulting from misunderstandings or too much understanding, and the pronouncements evocative of gravestone inscriptions. If not on the basis of its artistic virtues, Mexican film melodrama stand out, along with Argentina and Brazil, for its exaltation of the disastrous in nearly all its forms. Although Hollywood melodrama had staked out a dominant position worldwide, during two decades the Mexican variety held its own, spreading its addictive power rooted in its singular methods of suffering. The strength of Mexican melodrama lay in its contiguity, its audience's familiarity with what is seen and heard: scenes of family life, the sounds of the city and the countryside, the immediate comprehension of the dialogue. But the influence of Hollywood was everywhere; it provided an impossible yet no less desirable model to which to aspire.

Despite the foreignness of the situations, settings, and dialogues American films proposed, they inspired an anxious voyeurism and unconscious imitation among Latin American spectators. Particularly important was the balance achieved by Hollywood between lavish production values and the tortured trajectory of the family and the couple. Prime examples are *Gone with the Wind* (Victor Fleming, 1939), which extends an epic reach to melodrama, or *Casablanca* (Michael Curtiz, 1942), in which the star-crossed lovers Humphrey Bogart and Ingrid Bergman encounter the definitive obstacle to their romantic union: World War II. And the new role for women, at once modern and timeless, embodied by performers such as Bette Davis, Joan Crawford, and Barbara Stanwyck, provided the inspiration for scriptwriters around the globe.

This play of influence and impersonation is central to the dialectics of national cinema, in which slavish imitation leads to the development of personal style and reverence toward genre conventions represents the first step in their parodic transformation or naturalization as Mexican. For example, Emilio Fernández, a great admirer of John Ford and his re-creation of North America's heroic past, achieves dazzling moments through his embrace of melodrama, not of Mexicanness, as he had hoped, but for the invention and projection of a popular imaginary in a poor country. At the other extreme is the director Juan Orol, an avid fan of the gangster film, from Howard Hawk's *Scarface* to the films of Humphrey Bogart, Edward G. Robinson and James Cagney. Orol made shameless use of melodrama with unintentionally comic results.

THE CLASSIC OF CLASSICS: *NOSOTROS LOS POBRES*

More than half a century after its release, *Nosotros los pobres* / We the poor (Ismael Rodríguez, 1948), featuring the archetypal couple Pepe el Toro (Pedro Infante) and la Chorreada (Blanca Estela Pavón), continues to figure as the quintessential melodrama. Everyone has seen it, it resides in collective memory, wrapped in a protective irony. It plays a key role in the social construction of a myth: "the culture of poverty" and its concatenation of tenderness, family devotion, and solidarity that not only finds compensation but also its source in material scarcity and neglect. The opening images of *Nosotros los pobres* show the film emerging from the grimy pages of an illustrated book rescued from a trash can by a pair of street urchins. Orchestral accompaniment ensues as the pages reveal the credits and a "Warning" [Advertencia] to viewers: "In this story you will encounter crude and unvarnished language and audacious situations. But I trust to your broad-mindedness. . . . To these good and simple people, whose only sin is that of being born poor, I dedicate my efforts."

Beginning with this opening epigraph, Rodríguez and his screenwriters extoll a series of melodramatic expressions, characters, and situations. The first scene depicts a multitude of neighborhood denizens, carpenters and rag pickers, bakers, milkmen, and drunks, housewives without a house to care for, who intone a hymn to the spirit of the community, "¡Ay, qué rechula es la mujer!" ("How lovely is woman"). Workers and lumpen sing and dance in ordered harmony, and suddenly, from the heights of idealized movie musical unreality, we tumble into an abundance of suffering. To summarize the plot is a nearly impossible task. Pepe el Toro lives with his mute and paralyzed mother and his daughter Chachita (in reality his sister's child); her mother (Carmen Montejo) fell from the straight and narrow and worked as a prostitute, and Pepe refuses to forgive her for the suffering she caused their mother. Celia, the "Chorreada," the neighborhood "good girl," is the object of Pepe's honorable intentions, and Celia, as payment for such good fortune, is obliged to put up with her weak and indecisive mother's love for her vile and marijuana smoking stepfather (Miguel Inclán). Pepe is robbed by the evil stepfather and is forced to borrow money from a money lender with designs of her own on Pepe. When the money lender is murdered, suspicion falls on Pepe, and he goes to jail. While there, his mother is attacked and beaten by the thief. Pepe fights in prison with the money lender's murderer, putting out his eye, and the latter confesses. Pepe rushes to the hospital where fate in its melodramatic irony has ordained that his mother and long lost sister coincide on their deathbeds. The last words, uttered at graveside, fall to Chachita, having found her mother at the moment of losing her, where she celebrates finally having a proper tomb to mourn.

. . . .

In *Nosotros los pobres* plot dominates above all other elements, and plot is the stuff of life itself for spectators of the late 1940s. Conflict follows upon heartbreak in an unending stream of misfortune, broken only by an occasional joke or song, in a confirmation of the nature of Mexican melodrama. . . . Everything is what it seems and as it is presented: virtue, defenselessness, immorality, generosity, romantic love, corruption. Immersed in the stories, the audience shares in the characters' errors and confusion: a sense of collective identity is born in the movie audience precisely at the moment when individualism becomes established, pushing aside traditional culture. Country values (dignity, truthfulness, sacrifice) are celebrated amid the clamor of urbanization that fails to take them into account. Family honor is extolled at the same time that moral relativism shapes the standards of accepted behavior.

Drawing on "typical" characteristics rooted in (more or less) real life experiences, *Nosotros los pobres* fabricates a notion of *poverty* in which the poor themselves believe, however irrational that belief might appear to us today. Why would they not attend to a consciously articulated version of their own existence projected on screen? Why would they not wish to consider their reflection in a heroism and urban romanticism that although lacking in prestige have their rewards? Smiling through their tears, the masses allow themselves to be persuaded and accept their reinvention at the hands of Rodríguez and his collaborators, complete with wardrobe, customs, the joy of a privacy-free life, a sing-song way of speaking, and an unrefined vocabulary. Thanks to its persuasive energy, the urban slang dreamed up by the director and scriptwriter Pedro de Urdimalas invaded the speech patterns of actual urban dwellers, although certain expressions would require translation today.

. . . .

The director, Ismael Rodríguez, is blunt about his goals: "When I made [*Nosotros los pobres*] neorealism was popular. Using our characters and setting I tried to make a neorealist film, experimenting with what was known as dramatic chiaroscuro, the mixture of tears and laughter" (cited in García Riera 1971). To guarantee the laughter and tears, Rodriguez is faithful to the then dominant code of values: machismo is the supreme principal; to women belong the monopoly on emotional blackmail; suffering is the best proof that one is alive; misfortune is a normal part of life among the poor.

. . . .

The lasting popularity of *Nosotros los pobres* (and its sequels, also directed by Rodríguez, *Ustedes, los ricos*, "You the rich" [1948] and *Pepe el Toro* [1953]) provides evidence of the efficacy of the film's enactment of the replacement of class consciousness by a confused mix of social resentment and emotional blackmail. Its repertory of characters and themes is a formula for box office success: an old woman in a wheel chair, a money lender, an unjust accusation of murder, the simple-minded but faithful friend, the neighborhood as microcosm of a larger social universe, the crudeness and generosity of neighborhood gossips, the prostitute with a heart of gold, dramatic moments, a timely joke, buckets of blood. And finally, in an intensely hierarchical society, *Nosotros los pobres* gives expression to a delirious and visceral cinema that is poised on the knife edge between a brutal realism at the limits of what censorship allows and the plausible representation of tenderness.

THE UBIQUITY OF MELODRAMA

In the period from the 1930s to the 1950s Mexican melodrama reached its high point, making its presence felt in film, radio, theater, civic discourse, the teaching of history, nationalist rhetoric, the bolero, and the *canción ranchera* (cowboy song).[3] The song repertory of Agustín Lara is, among other things, melodrama rendered in the language of late romanticism: "The love that caused my life to wither/ the love that was my undoing/ . . . where can that love be?/ May the Virgin grant/ that you bless the memory of my kisses/ that you reserve for me a tiny piece of your heart/ The love that destroyed my life/ where can that love be?" Melodrama is indispensable in the long journey toward modernity. What other narrative mode systematically glorifies self-destruction as a requirement of the human condition? And what other genre naturalizes forms of behavior that seem scripted by the lyrics of a bolero? To wit: "I don't know if this love is a sin/ that requires punishment/ if it transgresses the laws of man and God/ I only know that it turns my life upside down/ like a whirlwind/ that sweeps me off and carries me into your arms/ with blind passion." Excess is normalized, and to be melodramatic is to recalibrate emotions in the context of the culture industry, confirming the move from the genuine to the convincing. Thus the *canción ranchera* leaves behind its idyllic rural pretensions and nostalgic complaints and opts for a compressed form of melodrama, as expressed by composers such as Manuel Esperón (and his lyricist

Ernesto Cortázar), Tomás Méndez, Cuco Sánchez, and, of course, José Alfredo Jiménez: "I grew tired of begging her/ I grew tired of telling her that without her/ I'd die of suffering/. . . . The mariachis stopped playing/ and my drink fell from my hand without my noticing/ she wanted to stay/ when she saw my sadness/ but it was already written/ that this night I would lose my love.". . . . The *canción ranchera* is gloriously incontinent: "If cry I must/ I will cry for her my whole life long.". . . And thus the hidden and the surreptitious reveal their mysteries; for its practitioners and consumers, melodrama is a guide to happiness, to the sensual upheaval that gives order and meaning to what otherwise would be the sad experience of a humdrum existence. By this way of thinking, and feeling, harmony arises simply from a belief in the inevitable: "It is not for lack of love/ I love you with all my heart/ and in the name of that love and for your own good/ I say goodbye." But much is changing with the shift from the emotional climate of the late nineteenth and early twentieth centuries, in which there is no distance between the reigning moral standards and behaviors of the public and the codes of melodrama, and the atmosphere of the 1940s, in which traditional values have become alien to the lived reality of the majority of spectators, despite the melodramatic vestiges still present in many of their cultural responses (a taste for high-flown final words, gestures of sadness and defeat) but now disconnected from "the obligations of honor." The "theology" of melodrama comes apart under the stresses of modernity, and desperate emotions are increasingly less likely to be translated into actions.

From a prime ethical referent of urban society, melodrama devolves largely into a form of aesthetic expression rooted in the past while subject to the modifications of the present. Its continuing hold on the public derives from the energy invested in imagining a multitude of unending complications and situations without resolution, a source of pleasure for those who know the sum of so many misfortunes is a consolation if it obeys the formal requirements of the genre. The result points ahead toward the ascendance of camp and kitsch. In the rest of Latin America, Mexican soap operas exercise a powerful fascination among audiences—as attested to by everyday fans and highbrow authors alike—who suffer along with the characters and situations and delight in the excess of the genre. So prestigious is melodrama that it draws free from its original contexts and becomes, for many, a source of independent and autonomous fantasies of suffering whose chief value lies in their lack of concessions to rational judgment.

. . . .

MELODRAMA: FEMMES FATALES AND THE TRAGIC CABARET

During the first decades of sound cinema in Mexico, female characters reflect the classic combination of archetype and stereotype. Everything happens to Woman (each character represents the species and a sector of the species): she lacks will; she is ennobled by love/passion; she is mistreated and humiliated because someone has to take upon herself the sins of the world; she is a harlot and a flirt, long suffering, good-natured, and vengeful. . . . Melodrama is the genre of expiation and atonement, its goal is to protect the family, reminding it of the dangers of secularism: adultery, the rebellion of sons and daughters against parental authority, the moral ruin brought upon those who succumb to seduction and greed, the destruction of traditional customs and values. This, on one hand, while on the other cinema singles out woman in previously inconceivable ways, drawing her out of the moralizing shadows and depositing her in a new "ecological niche," the close-up. The close-up certifies lust and beauty, it places the camera at the service of expressions of serenity or agitation and breaks the hold of women's enslavement to much proclaimed "moral" values. Film mistreats and minimizes woman while glorifying female archetypes.

During the so-called Golden Age of Mexican Cinema, the industry imitates Hollywood with respect to genres, styles, formats, formulas for box office success, and the attempt to create a home-grown star system. It does so as well, to the extent possible, in the vision of woman. *To the extent possible*, Mexican machismo is more forceful than the American variety, at least when it comes to verbal expression.

. . . .

There are few equivalents in Mexican cinema for the independent characters one associates with Katherine Hepburn, Rosalind Russell, Joan Crawford, or Jean Arthur. Dolores del Río, lovely and ethereal, is sublime beauty perfected by humiliation. In her Mexican films, whether the revolutionary epics of Emilio Fernández or the archetypal melodramas directed by Roberto Gavaldón (*La otra* / The other one (1946), *La casa chica* / The love nest (1950), *Deseada* (1951), *La selva de fuego* / Jungle fire (1945),[4] her characters lack a will of their own. Del Río, the supreme model of femininity, entrusts the meaning of her existence to other forces: social convention, the lover blinded by responsibility, a patriarchy determined to snuff out any sign of personal autonomy. Hence her limitations in melodramatic roles: beyond her acting skills, her beauty condemns her to an endless round of psychological submission. For her part, María Félix, in films such as *El peñón de las Ánimas* / The rock of souls (Miguel Zacarías,1943) or *La diosa arrodillada* / The kneeling goddess (Roberto Gavaldón, 1947), takes full advantage of the power and privileges accorded by the genre to villainy; she achieves, in the space generated by the fascination she exercises over others, mastery of herself and the haughtiness and withering gazes that sap the will of those that are their object. Femininity, thus "virilized," can enable an attitude of conquest, whether that of the local tyrant (*Doña Bárbara* [Fernando de Fuentes, 1943]) or the *demi-mondaine* who insists on luxury because she needs it and because luxury is another element of seduction. The demanding and destructive woman is mysterious: her "ambiguity" derives from the failure to comprehend the extent of her demands. She will not give herself to her lover until he has submitted to her will. Melodrama, in opening such a zone of exceptionalism, undergoes an unexpected transformation.

. . . .

In melodrama, the cabaret functions as a kind of "open society" in the horizon of repression, the place where archetypes are registered and recertified and stereotypes run rampant. Each dance dramatizes the stages of sexual pleasure (and the punishment that prolongs it), and amid the clamorous intensity of tropical percussion the climax achieves an act of "unipersonal coitus" (a yet uncataloged Koan that condenses for spectators all the fantasies of sexual satisfaction forbidden by the censors). Here the rumba is a "crime of nature" and the exotic female dancer lends a face, torso, and shaking hips to the expression of individual and collective desire, and to the hunger felt by each and all (cannibalism is born and perfected in the look). Through dance and the *danzón*, bodies come together and long-held taboos are erased.[5]

Censorship—both external and internal—drives spectators toward fetishism (I use the word here in the popular sense of the term), and fetishism consolidates the impact of melodrama. Audience and the industry agree upon a pact that celebrates the virtues of repression while (not so surreptitiously) embracing voyeurism. In accordance with Judeo-Christian morality, irresistible female beauty is to be destroyed, but through the sense of sight it is preserved and treasured. Banned from the screen are portrayals of the sexual act and frontal nudity, and dialogue is kept decent through high-flown "poetic" language. Offered in compensation to family men and their unmarried peers is the contemplation of articles of clothing, legs, breasts, and the adventures of moist and mobile lips (another occasion of unipersonal coitus). Whereas women—chaste by virtue of their repression—find in the faces projected on screen (and in the image of "virile maturity," whatever that may be) the meaning of desire, men, whether from the emerging urban middle class or the mid-twentieth-century proletariat and rural zones so resistant to and yet so desirous of modernity, settle on one or several filmic presences and transform them into fetishes by means of vertiginous ceremonies that include photographs, accumulated reveries, and apparitions of the Virgin in the land of Onan.

During a period of several years, melodrama offers a prodigious source of fetish objects available for veneration: the raven tresses of María Félix, the white telephones that attest to wealth and status, the Afro-Carribean costumes of María Antonieta Pons, the hats of "First Lady" Gloria Marín, Dolores del Río's "bird of paradise" dress from the brothel scene in *Las abandonadas*, Columba Domínguez's shawl in *Pueblerina* (Emilio Fernández, 1949), Blanca Estela Pavón's simple percale dress in *Nosotros los pobres*, Esther Fernández's braids in *Allá en el rancho grande / Out on the Big Ranch* (Fernando de Fuentes, 1936) and Marga López's chaste and sorrowful expression in *Salón México* (Emilio Fernández, 1949). Without fetishism, melodrama would lose its bite and thus, with time, the fetishistic mind-set seemingly takes over entire plots in films with names such as *Vagabunda* / Tramp (Miguel Morayta, 1950), *Trotacalles* / Streetwalker (Matilde Landeta, 1951), *Aventurera* / Adventuress (Alberto Gout, 1950), *Mujeres sacrificadas* / Self-sacrificing women (Alberto Gout, 1952), *El puerto de los siete vicios* / The port of the seven vices (Eduardo Ugarte, 1951), *La hija del penal* / Born in prison (Fernando Soler, 1949), *Hipócrita* / Hypocrite (Miguel Morayta, 1949), *Coqueta* / Flirt (Gernanda A. Rivero, 1949), *Sensualidad* / Sensuality (Alberto Gout, 1951), *Amor y pecado* / Love and sin (Alfredo B. Crevenna, 1956), *La carne manda* / The flesh commands (Chano Urueta, 1948).

Fetishism brings about a new way of relating to melodrama and to fashion itself. Skirt lengths go up and necklines descend, the focus shifts from a wistful glance at a woman's ankles to the open contemplation of her legs. And fetishism guides and confirms shifts in moral standards and behaviors in the cinema and beyond. By the 1950s, Mexican spectators are no longer willing to accept suggestions and partial views. . . . Family fare loses its dominance, and there is an increase in the production and circulation of films for male audiences or "broad minded" couples. Prudishness is out, and without taking into account the difference between sensuality and eroticism, tastes demand a shift from the always implicit to the nearly explicit, a change that erodes the laws of melodrama from within.

The other fetishism, that which projects an image of Mexicanness, lasts a few decades before descending into parody. Jorge Negrete's embroidered *charro* (Mexican cowboy) hats, the baggy zoot-suits of underclass gigolos Victor Parra (*El suavecito / The Ladies Man* [Fernando Méndez. 1951]) or Rodolfo Acosta (*Salón México*), Pedro Armendáriz's fulsome mustache and spurs, the sweetly seductive voice and dandy-ish mustache of Emilio Tuero are key items in the wardrobe of Mexican melodrama, fetishes beloved by one generation while considered picturesque, amusing, or ridiculous by the next. In their heyday they provide the cornerstones of the film industry. As objects of near religious devotion, they are venerated simultaneously in makeshift rural projection halls, first run cinemas, and urban neighborhood flea pits.

. . . .

"IF NOT FOR YOU MY SUFFERING WOULD MAKE NO SENSE"

Melodrama remains the dominant genre into the early 1960s, its persistence perhaps best represented in the alchemical figure of the ouroboros, the serpent that eats its own tail, tracing the same movement over and over. Suffering is a synonym for expiation and death a sublime form of forgiveness. And the romantic couple, more often than not, can be said to exemplify Elias Canetti's aphorism: "She fears him as if a God; he despises her as he does himself." Nevertheless, by the late 1950s melodrama has begun to lose its ability to unite audiences across class and generational lines, its influence weakened by the growth of youth culture, a desire for stories with greater narrative complexity, and the exhaustion produced by repetition. Rendered superfluous for many sectors of the population by the advancing tide of cultural change, melodrama loses its adherents, those whose actions and attitudes had been shaped by its inexorable logic. What remains of its influence owes less to its moral structure, derived from religion, than to melodrama's displays of verbal eloquence and poetry of circumstances.

What was the basis of melodrama's power? Its secret heart and the source of all the plot complications and shocking revelations, according to Jesús Martín Barbero, are found in a handful of primordial certainties (the family, Catholic values, the intrinsic nobility of the victim, confidence that the truth will win out).

"The thing that turns all of human existence—from questions of disputed paternity to cases of unknown brothers and sisters and hidden twins—into a struggle against appearances and deceptions, into an act of decryption. This is what constitutes the true motor of the plot: the movement from *ignorance* to *awareness*, and *recognition* of identity, 'the moment at which the moral takes hold.' "[6]

. . . .

"I DON'T LIKE TO BEAT MY HUSBAND"

The 1960s also bring a change in melodramatic themes rooted in a revolution in social behaviors and attitudes not recognized as such at the time—a new idea of woman. How to continue to insist on the subjection of women, the basis of (Mexican) melodrama, in the face of the "feminization" of the economy and the entry of women into the industrial workplace, higher education, and positions of professional responsibility? Who would put up with the torrents of tearful submission when, for example, on the U.S./Mexican border large percentages of women have assumed the role of family breadwinner? And, as divorce rates rise, who will indulge the demonization of adultery? Various factors contribute to this process of (silent) democratization from below: rising literacy levels among women that surpasses by far the increase among men, the disintegration or realignment of the tribal family, and the decline, at least in urban areas, of the mystical cult of virginity (that fortress of dreams). Add to the list the dissemination of studies of human sexuality; radical theories of class, race, and gender; critical and revisionist analyses of national traditions; the vital presence of (primarily) American, French, English, and Italian literature and film; and the confirmation of the absurdities of machismo.

Overall, the movement (the cause) that links and structures the vision of reality is feminism, a force that to different degrees influences the behavior of millions of women and their perspective on society. The point is not that actresses, screenwriters, directors, and spectators have knowledge of the development of feminist theory. What is most important is the impact, however fragmentary and distant, of certain arguments about bodily autonomy, patriarchy, domestic slavery, and social and labor discrimination. The phenomenon has a measurable effect on language use and vocabulary. Beginning in the 1970s, a form of "unisex" speech dismantles the gendered ghetto of "dirty words" and "bad language" and recalibrates, thanks to its expressive effects, the distinction between hypocrisy and candor.

These changes are concretized in the emergence of new female characters, whose roles respond to the conflicting demands of generic obligation and a push toward individualization. The Long Suffering Mexican Mother finds herself replaced by characters indifferent to the pleasures of self-pity. The emblematic icon of the all-sacrificing mother, Sara Garcia, is supplanted by the wily and willful mother of *Doña Herlinda y su hijo* who turns a blind eye to the homosexual "perversions" of her son while assuring that he remains in the (mutually) protective confines of the closet. In another vein is the character played by María Rojo in *Danzón* (Maria Novaro, 1991), an *aventurera* (adventurer), who, unlike her predecessor in the film of the same name,[7] doesn't need to sell her love in order to invest her experience with an independent character.

Traditional melodrama relies on starkly defined psychologies, in which doubt was the prerogative, not of individual characters, but of the moral code to which their anguish and afflictions pay tribute. The regimentation of behavior (determinism) reaches such a point as to establish the types of divisions found in Greco-Roman theories of temperaments: sanguine, phlegmatic, choleric, or melancholic. But by the 1970s the exhaustion of melodramatic moral imperatives produces a search for alternatives and in the pursuit of continued survival, the Mexican industry abandons the punishments and scolding and embraces the spectacle of the "distortion of consciences." What was once the hell of societal disapproval (the eye of God) is now amorality, the result of confusion and misapprehension. Cast into the domain of the unconscious, duplicitous and unexpected, dramatic expression is at pains to provide order and understanding.

. . . .

From the world as it should be, if it were not for suffering, to the world as it would be if not for social conformity. In its decline and fall, traditional melodrama carries with it the family audience for cinema. Machismo continues to be present in diminished form but has lost its hold on much of the public. If the idea of the heroine makes less and less sense, the antiheroine is also on her way out, and female characters are "normalized" in their infinite variety. The mothers and wives reduced to tears by their inability to find the words to express their thoughts and feelings do not disappear entirely from the screen, nor do the prostitutes whose obscene language offends (the remaining) tender ears, but traditional values have lost their internal coherence.

The public, if it does not flee the cinemas entirely, ends up fragmented into generational niches. Few, if any, taboos remain, and moral censorship has lost its teeth. The number of women film and video directors climbs, and to the extent possible they make use of the opportunity, previously unavailable, to choose themes and approaches without having to justify themselves. Their films address the feminine condition by means of individual stories and through the analysis of rituals, social formations, and an apprenticeship in survival. The characters who prosper are neither liberal nor traditional, and a cinema of everyday lives replaces one that enshrined domestic mythologies.

. . . .

NOTES

1. General Porfirio Diaz served seven terms as Mexican president, from 1876 to 1911, when he was forced from office by an armed rebellion that became the Mexican Revolution. Theater during the *Porfiriato* was characterized by a mix of serious and popular genres, but audience access was restricted by class and geography.
2. The Institutional Revolutionary Party (Partido Revolucionario Institutional, or PRI) has dominated political life in Mexico for more than eighty years, since its founding in

1929 as the National Revolutionary Party with the goal of consolidating the gains of the Revolution and putting an end to a period of strong man rule. The continuous PRI control was broken in 2002, but the party regained the presidency in 2012.
3. An essential complement to Monsiváis's writing on film melodrama is his writing on the bolero. See his essay "Bolero: A History," included in the collection *Mexican Postcards* (1997).
4. *La selva del fuego* was in fact directed by Fernando de Fuentes.
5. With roots primarily in Cuba, the music and dance form known as *danzón* has long been popular in Mexico. The *danzón* is a slow partner dance that requires patterned footwork set to a syncopated beat. Although *danzón* may appear overly formal to contemporary viewers, with its contained movements and highly prescribed footwork, the dance was initially regarded as scandalous, due both to the close bodily contact between partners and the opportunity it provided for economic and racial "mixing."
6. Monsiváis is citing Martín Barbero's *De los medios a las mediaciones: comunicación, cultura, hegemonía*, published in English as *Communication, Culture and Hegemony: From the Media to Mediations*.
7. The reference is to *Aventurera* (Alberto Gout, 1950) and its star, Ninon Sevilla, the protagonist of several of the films mentioned here by Monsiváis as examples of the role of fetishism in Mexican melodrama. In a passage from the original essay, not included in the present text, Monsiváis (1994) describes the Cuban born Sevilla as melodrama's "first modern character": "she transforms *femininity* into a show that demands its own rewards, she interprets femininity" (187).

10

World and Time: Serial Television Melodrama in America

LINDA WILLIAMS

> Had we but world enough, and time,
> This coyness, Lady, were no crime
> We would sit down and think which way
> To walk and pass our long love's day ...
>
> Andrew Marvell, "To His Coy Mistress"

What is it about contemporary American serial television that has made it some of the most compelling popular art of our time? In this chapter, I argue that the contemporary form of serial television that has recently out-produced and, for many, out-classed Hollywood is fundamentally melodrama, although it is an incarnation of this mode that manages its "world" and "time" in a different way from that of previous serials. Because these serials are often admired, critics are tempted to make exalted comparisons to Victorian novels (many of which were originally serialized), to Greek tragedies, or to anything other than the lowly medium of fictional television, not to mention melodrama. I insist, however, that the three main terms of my title—seriality, television, and melodrama—describe the particulars of these works that so fascinate television audiences today, so I begin with a brief history of each.

SERIALITY

The first known use of the word "srial" was in 1840, appropriate for an industrial era beginning to *mass produce* parts. The first listed meaning was adjectival: "relating to, consisting of, or arranged in a series, rank or row"; the second is "appearing in successive parts or numbers <a *serial* story>." Two slightly divergent meanings appear in two later definitions: "*a*: performing a series of similar acts over a period of time: a: <a *serial* killer>," and "*b*: occurring in or involving such a series <a *serial* murder>" (Merriam-Webster online).

To a culture that values originality, serial repetition is often linked to rote, compulsive, or criminal repetition. Serials, when graduated to noun form, seemed debased. Because serial stories can go on and on, and repeat themselves with only small differences, they are deemed inherently unoriginal. Yet it is precisely the ability to build upon these repetitions, which bring back the same or similar characters, the same or similar situations, the same credit sequences, the same music—in short the same *world*—that mark the originality of the television serials that enthrall viewers today. Serials, as opposed to series, hook us on repetitions that can make change seem earth-shaking. Many novels now considered "great" once appeared in serial form. Unlike television or radio, these stories were not disrupted by commercials, but they were inherently "interrupted" insofar as they were published in discrete parts.

In nineteenth-century Britain, readers who could not afford to buy a whole novel were able to purchase monthly one-schilling "parts" of what would eventually become the full work (Patten 1978, 60). In France, serials were associated with newspapers: popular serials by Eugène Sue and others filled their bottom quarter. The lurid, continuing tale of a father's search for his "fallen" daughter, *Les Mystères de Paris* (extended over three thousand pages between June 1842 and October 1843), attracted a readership that, as Peter Brooks (1984) notes, had never before felt the need for a newspaper (146). Charles Dickens and Sue's publishing careers demonstrate that it was seriality itself—ongoing stories with a wide range of interconnected worlds—that popularized the novel for mass market readers.[1]

Once readers were hooked on early parts, they were able to defer the pleasure of narrative resolution. Indeed, in the case of *The Pickwick Papers* (1836), getting hooked did not happen until the fifth installment, when Dickens responded to letters encouraging him to develop a couple of working-class characters who would eventually become central to the narrative (Hayward 1997, 24). Postponement permitted an indulgence in ever-more complex subplots. As Jennifer Hayward stresses, seriality simultaneously compresses and expands the temporal experience of a text. Doled out in short, segmented parts—shorter than the potentially many chapters a novel reader might consume in one sitting, albeit helped by illustrations—and enforcing pauses of as much as a month or as little as a day between "doses," the serial novel encouraged an unprecedented degree of growth and change among its characters. Paradoxically, then, the reliance on the short "part" permitted the creation of characters that might endure over longer periods of reading (25–83).

Whereas most writers have time to prepare and revise, the "periodical writer," as Dickens calls him, "commits to his readers the feelings of the day, in the language which those feelings have prompted" (Patten 1978, 102). The serial novel is also more responsive to the moments of its creation than are single works, and it can include timely social and political allusions. Experience of a serial offers an immediacy denied to works previously dominated by the "circumspection of him who has had time to prepare for a public appearance" (Dickens as cited in Hayward 1997, 25–83). Precisely because it must find its way as it goes, the serial novel can be more alive and connected to the white-hot time of its pressurized creation. Thus, although initially regarded as a crassly unoriginal and commercial form, seriality became highly valued, partly because of the narrative effects of its commercial, temporal pressures.

It may go without saying that the novels of Dickens, Sue, and others were melodramatic in form. Like the plays that preceded them, they offered tales of high emotion and sensation, with pronounced victims and villains. But the question of how and why melodrama and seriality so often combine is yet to be plumbed beyond the conventional devaluation of both as "cheap."

MELODRAMA

> It is the custom on the stage: in all good, murderous melodramas: to present the tragic and the comic scenes, in as regular alternation . . . The hero sinks upon his straw bed, weighed down by fetters and misfortunes; and, in the next scene, his faithful but unconscious squire regales the audience with a comic song. We behold, with throbbing bosoms, the heroine in the grasp of a proud and ruthless baron: her virtue and her life alike in danger; drawing forth a dagger to preserve the one at the cost of the other; and, just as our expectations are wrought up to the highest pitch, a whistle is heard: and we are straightway transported to the great hall of the castle: where a grey-headed seneschal sings a funny chorus with a funnier body of vassals. (Charles Dickens, *Oliver Twist*, 1837)

Dickens is here making fun of a "preposterous" theatrical form that was already subject to ridicule and parody in some quarters, and which was already itself capable of self-irony. Yet Dickens is also acutely aware that in his own literary practice he, too, alternates overwrought "tragedy"—actually melodrama—with comedy. Dickens enjoys his parody but ends it with a virtual defense of melodrama: it is not preposterous at all; it resembles real life. "The transitions in real life from well-spread boards to death-beds, and from mourning weeds to holiday garments, are not a whit less startling," writes Dickens in this narrator's aside. And in his own reinvention of melodrama from stage to page, Dickens finds a new, novelistic rhythm for the "good, murderous stage melodrama."

In this passage, we encounter two constants in the reception of melodrama: the critique of yesterday's unrealistic, excessive, over-the-top kind; and a replacement that might eschew the term for an ever-more modern and "realistic" present. Melodrama, like seriality, is a product of a mass market era of serial production, manufactured parts, stereotypes, and popular formulas. And in modernity, nothing dates like yesterday's melodrama (or yesterday's serial). From melodrama's wildest popularity on the Parisian boulevard stage (1800–1820) to the inevitable backlash, most subsequent melodramatic works pointedly stressed their rejection of its clichés, but only, as Dickens, to reformulate them for a new era or a new medium.

A key source of this failure to recognize melodrama has been its supposed lack of realism, as if realism and melodrama could not coexist. But as Christine Gledhill (1987) has long argued, keeping up with realism is the way melodrama modernizes. Since its inception, melodrama has addressed timely social problems and controversies of the kind never treated in tragedy. As Dickens well knew, and demonstrated in *Oliver Twist*, melodrama enlists realism to generate outrage against realities that could and, to its creators' minds, should be changed.

Today, common usage points to two diametrically opposed conceptions of melodrama: (1) old-fashioned, "blood-and-thunder" melodramas found on the nineteenth-century French, English, and American stage and continued in early film serials, and (2) "domestic," "family," or "women's" melodramas that, as off-shoots from Victorian melodrama's many domestic varieties, continued into twentieth-century fiction, film, and radio. This opposition between seemingly masculine and female forms has made the genre term *melodrama*, as this volume argues, especially incoherent because the latter meaning has tended to replace the former. For many film scholars today, melodrama still connotes a story of a suffering woman in a domestic context. In contrast, contemporary action or superhero films, together with their television variants, are identified by their various genre names, omitting the melodramatic glue of pathos *and* action that holds them all together.

Perhaps understandably, in discussion of contemporary serial television, the word "melodrama" is rarely used. To many critics and reviewers, melodrama implies a negatively archaic and excessive form. The works seem too "good" to warrant it. The result is that we recognize cop shows, westerns, sci-fi films, or series and serials as discreet genres with different histories, iconographies, and even types of mises-en-scène. We can recognize slight shades of difference between a private eye and a cop genre, or between horror and sci-fi, but we fail to identify the skeletal modal structure that holds them all together.

As Rick Altman (1999) noted of film genres, they are open to invention. Indeed, he argues, it was feminist film critics who began *retrospectively* to identify as a "genre" the 1940s and 1950s woman's films. Yet Mary Ann Doane (1987), who wrote the most complete study of such films in *The Desire to Desire*, hesitated to call them a genre "*precisely because she was in the process of changing [the] status*" of those films (75). The only way feminists could make the woman's film a genre was through a redefinition of melodrama as "family melodrama," linking the two forms through their common address to a female audience. "Only when this connection took place," writes Altman (1999), "would the woman's film abandon its quotation marks in favor of full generic status" (76–78).

By giving over the once broad term *melodrama*—encompassing both so-called female-centered pathos and so-called masculine adventure and action—to a narrow genre encompassing only women and family, feminist critics, myself included, too hastily severed women altogether from action itself, thus denying the very female agency that is one of feminism's primary demands. By severing melodrama from what on the stage was a mixture of pathos and action—in which women frequently acted as heroic rescuers, and men were in need of rescue (most familiarly in Augustin Daly's 1867 *Under the Gaslight*)—feminist critics ignored the many possibilities of female action.

Melodrama at its most basic should be understood as the mode that once organized both the popular nineteenth-century stage and, *mutatis mutandis*, most mainstream Hollywood movies. It is what makes the latter "Hollywoodian" in the first place. The mode manifests in the extra emotion that music can bring and the larger-than-life excitement of the film medium itself. It is certainly not the same as nineteenth-century stage melodrama. The form has mutated, but Hollywood at both its most vulgar and popular is encapsulated in the very word "melodrama." The idea of a basic syntax once named melodrama, until recently lost as a named entity, is a natural starting point for understanding melodrama as the foundation of what Miriam Hansen (2000) has called Hollywood cinema's "vernacular modernism" (see Gledhill, "Prologue"; Williams, chapter 12; Airiess, chapter 4). Of course, in traveling from the nineteenth into the twentieth century, melodramatic character development transformed under the increasing pressure of "realism," which the vast expansion of world and time made possible with seriality.

SERIAL TELEVISION MELODRAMA

Serial (melo)drama flourished in all forms of media, especially when these media were new: newspapers in the 1830s, film in the 1910s, radio in the 1920s. All these flourishings seem to bear out Roger Hagerdon's thesis (1995) that new media turn to serial narrative to promote the medium itself. "Once attracted" and "hooked" on the serial narrative, "that audience is then available and predisposed to consume other texts the particular medium provides" (29). By the end of 1914, no less than twenty film serials had been developed in conjunction with newspapers (33). By 1920, as Ben Singer (2001) writes, more than sixty serial films had been made, comprising about 800 individual episodes. Singer reports that these films resisted the growing standardization of the stand-alone feature length film (63). In the 1930s, Hagedorn (1995) notes, the new audiences brought to film were children, through the appeal of such serials as *Flash Gordon* (1936) and *Dick Tracy* (1937), themselves often based on previous newspaper strips.

Much the same process occurred with the innovation of radio in the late 1920s. As Michele Hilmes (1997) notes, by the early 1930s, radio was a thriving entertainment industry offering daily, fifteen-minute formats, many later lengthened to thirty minutes. Soap operas aimed at women coping with depression era problems monopolized the afternoons, selling soap and beauty products. Romance or domestic dramas included titles that became some of the longest running soaps: *The Guiding Light, The Edge of Night*, and *Stella Dallas*, which in later episodes had the long-suffering Stella suffering less and solving mysteries. In the evenings, a wide range of generic serials flourished in the mid- and late 1930s—sci-fi (*Buck Rogers*), westerns (*The Lone Ranger, The Cisco Kid*), soap operas, and private eyes (*Richard Diamond*)—offering continuing stories, clear oppositions between good and evil, pathos and action: all popular genres, but also forms that were recognizable as melodrama. Many of these would be continued into the new medium of television.

With the move to television, however, situation comedies (*I Love Lucy*, CBS, 1951–1957) and episodic *series* (*Gunsmoke*, CBS, 1955–1975), not serials, became more popular. Even if originally serialized on radio, a program only survived the transition to television by producing individual episodes with strong closure.

At this point, television seemed to be more interested in the new worlds it could create than in the continuous stories generated out of this world's temporal unfolding. Only the daytime soaps survived in true serial form after their slow death on radio, thus relegating all continuous narrative seriality to the lower regions of the critical spectrum and, as previously noted, to a genre deemed to have special appeal to women. There seems to have been no obvious commercial reason to abandon serials in prime time, thus questioning Hagedorn's thesis that new media always turn to serials. Possibly the prestige of the unique live teleplay made the originally short-segmented serials seem outdated, paradoxically reinscribing an old-fashioned concept of classical unity and theatrical status into these "events." Perhaps also, as a new medium, television needed to disassociate itself from the still quite recent "old" medium of radio and its continuing narrative serials.[2]

At any rate, television reinvented many of the old radio serials as series in prime time, and relegated continuing serials to daytime, leaving only the more female-addressed form of "soap opera" to proliferate on afternoon TV, until television itself began to reinvent prime-time seriality in the late 1970s. Soap opera, however, should not be immediately conflated with melodrama, whose commercial beginnings were more vested in appeals to the everyday lives of women (see Gledhill 1994). Melodrama's long history of perseverance has been forgotten, and the more recent, better remembered but equally derided history of soap opera has fostered this conflation, especially given the reduction of melodrama to women's culture.

Soap opera, unlike melodrama, *was* originally created for women, developing a pace attuned to housework and women's time. Also unlike melodrama's inception, it had roots in women's domestic fiction, which, Nina Baym (1978) argues, treated domestic ideology "realistically" as a realizable social program for human betterment. The value for female audiences of suffering self-sacrifice found in soaps, and later in "women's pictures," offered practical ways of dealing with men and a world with few expectations for women (Gledhill 1994, 130). In domestic fiction, as in soap opera, conversation—not action, pathos, thrills, and suspense—dominates. A drama of conversation certainly appealed to the new medium of radio, but it appealed much less to the visual media of film and television.

Thus, if not initially tuned into melodrama, the afternoon serials were, as Gledhill (1994) notes, "prone to melodramatization" as they carried on over time (124). Without "seasons," and with "no end in sight," these extreme instances of ongoing narrative carried on striving to generate and regenerate interest, in the process becoming ever-more melodramatic. In contrast, prime-time melodrama emerged in the new series format, of which *Gunsmoke* (CBS, 1955–1975) is emblematic. It had already existed on radio (also as a series rather than a continuing story). It grew in this form from half-hour episodes to an hour. Noted, even when on radio, for its exceptional realism, the series was nevertheless melodramatic in its stark moral oppositions and action-based climaxes. It was the series, then, not the serial, that came to be the dominant form of narrative television from the 1960s to the 1980s. These series were also short-form melodramas (shorter than feature movies, longer that the low-budget adult and children's serials previously shown at the movies).

Some critics have called the series a form of "amnesia television" because there was little continuing memory of what had transpired from one episode to the next. The ongoing situation—for Pa, Hoss, Adam, and Little Joe on the Bonanza Ranch—would remain stable, while new characters played by guest stars temporarily altered this situation for one episode. The next episode would reset, with no memory of the previous one. Thus a series could spin endless stories from its basically stable situation without having to keep track of the past. As Jeffrey Sconce (2004, 97–98) notes, the series could build enduring diegetic worlds to which audiences would gladly return week after week, with tidily resolved individual episodes and yet a basic ongoing situation (world).

ACCUMULATION: SERIALS RETURN TO PRIME TIME

In the late 1970s, however, some qualities of serialization began to sneak back into prime-time network television. Borrowing his term from Horace Newcomb (1974), Sconce (2004) describes certain "cumulative" effects that could accrue to a series narrative as it matured over several seasons. Sconce's example is *ER* (1994–2009), which usually featured a range of related crises: "bus crash on the turnpike, hospital power outage, liver transplant . . . interwoven with long term storylines that may or may not receive attention that week or even that season (Doug and Carol's romance, Peter's deaf son Reese, Weaver's personality conflicts)" (98). Over a number of seasons, a narrative could "accumulate" and lead to powerful outcomes rather than reverting, as had Pa, Hoss, Adam, and Little Joe, to the same stable situation on the Bonanza Ranch. Sconce cites *Magnum P.I.* (CBS, 1980–1988) and *Hill Street Blues* (NBC, 1981–1987) as among the most cumulative. It is perhaps not surprising that these "accumulations" gathered around the same familiar genres that were once serialized in radio: private eyes, westerns, and hospitals.

At the same time, however, a more prestigious form of television began to present new stand-alone serial formats. Indeed, the first prime-time serial fictions (in the broad sense of being longer than the usual half-hour or hour-long segments and continuing over days or weeks) were advertised as quality cultural "events," adapted from popular historical sagas in the new form of the miniseries. Miniseries were not serials in the Dickensian sense of not knowing where they might end up, but continuing stories with a predetermined end. In 1976, a televisual adaptation of Irwin Shaw's 600 page novel, *Rich Man, Poor Man*, aired on ABC every Monday night for six weeks, with each segment lasting two hours, offering a continuing six-part series. The prestige of a movie (for which one bought a ticket, versus a television show, paid for by commercials) was thus combined with the prestige of the long saga of a German immigrant family over two generations of recent U.S. history. The following year a serial adaptation of Alex Haley's *Roots* also aired on ABC, this time for eight *consecutive* nights. This miniseries virtually paralyzed the nation, closing restaurants and movie theaters while, for the first time, American audiences viewed black history, from slavery through emancipation, as the "Saga of an American Family."[3]

Both of these serialized adaptations were critical and popular successes, offering up history in the form of multigenerational family "sagas" or "epics" in high-end productions that combined history with "adult" themes: alcoholism and adultery in the first; slavery, rape, and miscegenation in the second. These serials seemed too serious, too "realistic," and too thematically important to be placed in the same category with either series "horse operas" or serialized soap operas. Yet, by this time, even the soaps were more like melodrama in their inclusion of exciting incidents, moral dilemmas, quests for justice, colorful characters, and strong emotions.

Scratch the surface of either the "accumulative" series or the miniseries, however, and melodrama is evident, in ways now informed by its domestic and family variants. In each, the workplace—whether slave fields or cabin, police station, hospital, or private-eye office—expands into a kind of surrogate home. The miniseries with its multiple "parts" and literary origins lent these first television prime-time serials a special aura of importance. Presented as hyped television "events" rather than part of the regular television schedule—with grandiose music, suspenseful arcs across episodes, and the usual staples of long-suffering heroes and heroines—these were prestigious historical melodramas with abundant pathos and action.

One doesn't even need to scratch, however, to recognize the melodrama in the next serial wave to crash over television. Beginning in the late 1970s and throughout the 1980s, "prime-time soaps"—*Dallas* (CBS, 1978–1991), *Dynasty* (ABC, 1981–1989), and *Knots Landing* (CBS, 1979–1993)—gained enormous popularity. Their subject matter was also similar: family intrigues, nefarious business deals, scheming ex-wives, multiple characters, and narrative convolution. Often scoffed at, but enormously popular over the entire decade, these programs could be quite playful with their seriality. One entire season of *Dallas* turned out to be a dream. But these prime-time soaps—whose very name intimated a will to imitate the capricious plotting of actual soaps—also diverged from them in production values, pacing, and their focus on families rather than women.

By the late 1970s and early 1980s, seriality, in the form of domestic melodrama, was to be found in abundance on television. Even the perennial sitcoms began to become more serious and serial,[4] although it is more difficult for a comic situation to continue in serial form because its very existence *as comedy* requires strong closure.[5] By the year 2000, seriality had become the new norm for television. It is possible that with the advent of cable and digital technologies, seriality once again became a crucial way to "hook" audiences onto particular programs in the face of an otherwise bewildering choice of channels. At any rate, as Sconce (2004) notes, by this time the existence of an entirely stand-alone episode with no loose threads or ongoing arcs was practically unthinkable.

CONTEMPORARY SERIAL TELEVISION MELODRAMA

The reason many media scholars have declined to use the term *melodrama* to describe today's serial television is the more difficult-to-address question of "quality." To some, melodrama may seem an appropriate enough term for nostalgic or condescending discussion of old radio or old TV, or even prime-time soaps, but wrong for "quality" works such as *The Sopranos* (HBO, 1999–2007), *Six Feet Under* (HBO, 2001–2005), *Mad Men* (AMC, 2007–2015), *The Wire* (HBO, 2002–2008), *Battlestar Galactica* (Sci-Fi Channel, 2004–2009), *Breaking Bad* (AMC, 2008–2013), and the new kinds of serials produced by the likes of Netflix and Amazon: *House of Cards* (Netflix, 2013), *Transparent* (Amazon, 2014–ongoing).

Quality TV is a problematic term. It implies that television still is the "vast wasteland" it was once dubbed, to which *this* TV program is the exception. Jason Mittell (2015), however, is justifiably reluctant to "map a model of storytelling tied to self-contained feature films onto the serial television" (17–18). One good reason for this is that the rhythm and beat structure of television drama is entirely different from that of the art film. Another reason is that the storytelling of televisual serial poetics cannot be reduced to the stylistic marks of an auteur, as recognized in cinema. This is not simply because television is "not a director's medium," as many recognizable film auteurs have gravitated to it.

Although we may think we know it when we see it, quality is a matter of aesthetic judgment, combined with significance of theme. It is hopelessly subjective. Both Jason Mittell and Jeffrey Sconce have proposed the alternative notion of "Complex TV"—Mittell (2015) in a book by that name, and Sconce less definitively in his 2004 article. For both, serial, or strongly "cumulative" TV, is necessarily more complex than series TV, but the very term *complexity* cannot avoid implying judgment. Complex is the positive that refutes the older negative judgment that TV is a simplistic wasteland.[6] Mittell (2015) attempts to avoid judgment when he states that continuous storytelling is a "multifaceted variable" with a wide range of possibilities, from entirely contained episodes to extreme ongoing seriality that itself can vary between high degrees of self-reflexivity and more straight-forward storytelling. However, there is no avoiding his inference that serial complexity is better than a single-episode series. This is not to say that the more intense and cliffhanging the plotting the better. Nevertheless, the stronger the serialization—for example, in *Lost* (ABC, 2004–2010) or *24* (Fox, 2001–2010)—the more overt the melodrama.

The melodrama of a serial feels stronger when there are suspenseful gaps in time—whether the gap occurs between an episode of old-time film serials from one Saturday afternoon to another, between episodes of weekly serial television, or even the gap a commercial makes from one narrative "beat" to another. Time suspended, time resumed, time manipulated are all basic ingredients of the strong emotions generated by melodrama because melodrama, most fundamentally, wants us to care for its protagonists. The more we invest our time in their worlds and their changes, the more we care.

Serial time often seems synonymous with melodrama time because there are so many ways it can be parceled out: the long parts of nineteenth-century serialized fiction, the shorter parts of early twentieth-century serial films that often backtracked in time at the beginning of a new episode and thus could cheat the clock, and the slow-paced melodrama of soap operas that savored a slow burn reaction to news of an illegitimate pregnancy or divorce before going to the inevitable commercial.

Serials, by their very nature, seek to expend an abundance of time in their narration. Most fundamentally, however, the abundance of time provides opportunities for characters from different story worlds, over time, to interact. This observation may take us to the very root of serial melodrama's special connection with time in the medium of television. In 1974 Horace Newcomb wrote: "With the exception of soap operas, television has not realized that the regular and repeated appearance of a continuing group of characters is one of its strongest techniques for the development of rich and textured dramatic presentation" (54). Is it possible, then, that television has simply begun to make better use of the abundance of time it has always had at its disposal? According to Mittell (2015), the complex serial poetics of the new television serials redefines the older episodic forms of television narrative under the influence of serial narration (18). This seems to me irrefutable. However, Sean O'Sullivan (2010) contributes an important observation: what serial television has invented is more than a transformation of series into serial; it has invented an entirely new measure of narrative time—the season. The old seasons of episodic series television were so numerous that they were not felt to be narratively distinct. Before 1999, O'Sullivan argues, a television season was only recognized as a system of production. It did not yet measure a narrative unit. But with *The Sopranos* and the advent of cable programming, seasons became much shorter, usually thirteen, sometimes twelve episodes (versus the twenty-two or twenty-four-episode runs of series dispersed over thirty-six weeks). Shorter seasons of digestible narrative units, run over twelve or thirteen continuous weeks on cable networks and subsequently released on DVD with different covers for each season, were then consumed as chunks of narrative (as in "I binged the whole season in one night!").

As O'Sullivan's argument reveals, a season is unique to contemporary television serials and is not comparable to the chapters of a novel. "The thirteen-episode uninterrupted complete season provided for the first time in American television history, a distinct narrative form, one that was large enough to occupy significant time and space, but not so large as to turn into vague sprawl" (68). The key ingredient at work in "complex/quality" TV is thus time itself: narrative time in an abundance that only television can offer, but still a small enough chunk of narrative that it can be absorbed and digested rather than the endlessness of soap opera. If the goal of seriality is that most commercial one—to continue a story over time to encourage consumption—then in moving-image culture this will-to-continue began most visibly with the "serial queen" films of the 1910s, the radio serials of the 1930s and 1940s, and the Saturday afternoon movie serials of my own youth in the 1950s (*Fu Manchu, Flash Gordon*). However, the afternoon soap operas of the 1960s through the 1990s, which are now slowly dying off, were transformed into the prime-time soaps (*Dallas, Dynasty*, and so on) of the 1980s, and more recently into the hour or half-hour serial television melodramas in thirteen, twelve, and currently only ten weekly installments. The new commercial model of all-at-once release through online streaming offers a more binge-friendly, less regularly experienced "dosage." This was always possible with finished serials, but it now works against the commercial logic of purchasing one part at a time unless, of course, it is now the season that is considered the most relevant part!

Whatever we say about these contemporary serial melodramas, complexity may not be their most important hallmark. What they all share, as melodramas and as serials, is both an abundance of world and an abundance of time that differs radically from the efficient, tidy, well-motivated resolution concluding a series episode or a feature film. Complexity may imply diegetic worlds with lots of time for plot twists, reversals, even alternate universes (as in *Lost*), and I have already suggested that this counters the simplicity of the single episodes of series; however, in serials this complexity might also be called "convolution" (as in soaps, as in *Dallas*, as in *Lost*). *The Sopranos*, *The Wire*, or *Breaking Bad* might be deemed complex, but not in the fashion of a novel because their rhythms are uniquely televisual.

TELEVISUAL TIME / SERIAL TIME

"Beat" is a term used in film and television and other time-based arts to refer to timing or pace. In a screenplay, it is often used to indicate a pause in dialogue, but as commonly used by television writers, it refers to any change in scene that creates a particular rhythm.[7] For reasons having to do with the presumed attention span of prime-time network audiences, scripts rarely allow a beat of more than two and a half minutes (O'Sullivan 2006, 117). When writers create a television script for any network television single-episode series, their first task is to "break" the story into a moment-by-moment outline (or "beat-sheet") constituting a series of moments that yield a typical rhythm of six beats before each commercial. A beat is thus a short, continuous unit of space/time that has no real equivalent in the conventional novel, and which in the single-episode series generally emphasizes only one narrative spatiotemporal cluster at a time rather than the rapid "juxtaposition of several" moments typical of most contemporary televisual serials.

Beat structures—alternating pulses of short units of space/time—provide the central, though variable, rhythm of television's serial narration, adapted from the network series episode. Today a season of cable drama is typically composed of ten to thirteen, or for networks, twenty-two to twenty-three episodes, and each episode comprises between thirty and forty beats. An episode is too short a time to "get into" a serial, so a season is the more conventional measure of its worth. What, then, do we mean by a whole television serial?

The one thing the beat structure of television serials does not let us talk about is the forward moving efficiency of Hollywood narrative, or that of a single episode in a series. Neither a season nor the serial's single episode mirrors the Hollywood format of strong beginnings, slightly meandering middles, and definitive ends. It resembles, rather, the greater subplotted coincidences and collisions familiar to nineteenth-century stage and fiction melodrama. Serial melodrama rarely focuses on a single hero and the completion of his or her goals, and often explores the longest, rather than the shortest, distance between two plot points.[8] Of course, stage melodrama never possessed the vast dimensions of world and time of either the nineteenth-century novel or today's serial television. However, it did expand upon the causalities of neoclassical tragedy, adding comic characters and multiple subplots. We find, then, a range of different combinations of world and time in a range of different types of melodrama.

Series television melodrama, for example, gives plenty of world but very little time in the sense of duration and change. With the advent of greater narrative accumulation, time became a factor in the "world building" of contemporary television. Seriality, like melodrama, is a form easily derided for its potential excesses: too long, too complex/convoluted, too emotional. But as Deidre Pribram (chapter 14) notes, "understanding the processes of emotionality within the specific traditions and parameters of melodrama allows us to retain a sense of characters as culturally embedded beings." One of her examples is Walter White's crisis in *Breaking Bad*. After a lifetime as a dutiful high-school teacher, husband, and father, and learning that he is dying of cancer, White feels betrayed, economically and ideologically. The emotional roller coaster of his relationship with Skyler, his wife—eventually played out over a primary visceral attachment to their newborn baby—is strong melodrama, made possible by a serialization that, as Pribram notes, offers scant equilibrium of the sort found in series episodes or feature films. Serial melodrama's narrative "results from accumulated emotional states . . . lodged in fluctuating twists of temporary amelioration and newly encountered harm." Thus what seriality affords is the ability to produce "multiple versions of what an emotional act—betrayal, trust, fidelity—might or ought to be, rather than presuming a taken-for-granted, self-evident notion of what constitutes 'betrayal' or any other emotion" (chapter 14).

The space and time that seriality gives to such emotional shifts cannot be reduced to reputedly femininized excesses. Mittell (2015) argues against conflating soap opera and melodrama and concurs with my own argument that much contemporary serial television operates within the melodramatic mode (244–45). However, I do not follow Mittel's adoption of Robin Warhol's gendered terms: "effeminate" to describe genres that veer toward the sentimental, and "masculinist" to those veering toward traditionally male values (248–49). Melodrama has too long a history to fall into such gendered dichotomies. Consider the recent serial *Transparent* (2014–ongoing), whose transgendering, transparent hero/ine may be in the process of proving how archaic such polarizing terms have become.

O. J. REDUX

Serialization itself may subvert familiar binary oppositions, whether between male and female genders or black and white races. In the spring of 2017, two serialized versions of the O. J. Simpson double murder trial converged on television. Both are in the form of miniseries; both revisit a trial that itself played on television at a glacial, soap opera-ish pace. The trial itself was understood by many viewers to be a serial answer to an earlier trial of Los Angeles policemen caught on videotape beating African American motorist Rodney King. The verdict of both trials was a galvanizing experience for a racially polarized America because there was no race neutral or gender neutral—in short no *unmelodramatic*—way to experience them. Morally and emotionally, white or black, one had to put one's finger on the scales and decide who was the victim and who was the villain of these racially saturated scripts. This is not to say, however, as many critics of the Simpson verdict have said, that an objective, "colorblind" justice was perverted by the calculated invocation of racialized ways of seeing; there had been little evidence of colorblind justice in Los Angeles in its previous history.

"Playing the Race Card" was an accusatory phrase used by the prosecution in the Simpson trial when the defense team introduced detective Mark Furhman's past racist use of the word "nigger." With this incendiary word, as prosecutor Christopher Darden explained, "the entire complexion of the case changes. It's a race case then. It's white versus black" (Bugliosi 1996, 66). And indeed it was.

Like the mode of melodrama itself, the race card has been vilified as an archaic evil, a throwback to a distant era beyond which modern U.S. citizens have long since "progressed." And yet, again like melodrama itself, the race card finds unsuspected relevance and appeal with each new configuration of racial victims and villains, and each new stage of American racial politics. In the painfully long and slow movement toward and beyond Civil Rights, and no matter how each "bad" old melodrama is vehemently rejected by either whites or blacks, these two central and opposed "moving pictures"—the vision of a black man beaten by white slave drivers or cops, or the "counter" vision of the white woman endangered by the emancipated and "uppity" black villain—have driven the dialectic of American racialized culture (Williams 2001).

The only way to understand these dual lenses is to take the long view and consider the entire history of American race relations going all the way back to slavery. The first work to elicit (white) sympathy for suffering slaves (the serialized novel, *Uncle Tom's Cabin*) and the "anti-Tom" works (such as Griffith's galvanizing *The Birth of a Nation*) that "answered" it help explain how the nonacquittal of the police involved in the beating of Rodney King informed the acquittal of Simpson in his trial for murder (Williams 2001). Now, twenty years after that trial, these two works have replayed the stories as serial television melodrama. One is fact-based fiction, Ryan Murphy's *American Crime Story: The People vs O. J. Simpson*, which originally aired on the FX channel in six slightly less than hour-long episodes. The other is a documentary, Ezra Edelson's O. J: Made in America, which originally aired on ESPN over five nights for a total of seven and a half hours, but also was released, minimally, as a day-long film. Both unpack the racial logic of the original Simpson verdict by giving it sufficient "world and time" to explain its complex, black and white, masculine and feminine, emotions.

In Ryan Murphy's *American Crime Story*, we see Defense Attorney Johnnie Cochran humiliated before his young daughters by Los Angeles police who throw him onto the hood of his car. In *O. J.: Made in America*, Edelman's more expansive documentary, we understand better how Simpson himself was "made" in (a racist) America when he became the darling of the very white USC campus, and later forged friendships with white celebrities as well as many white Los Angeles policemen. Turning away from his San Franciscan inner-city Portrero Hill neighborhood and the antiracist activism of fellow black athletes of the time, we understand how Simpson came to see himself as not raced. Upon returning home to his Brentwood mansion to surrender to police after the "run" in the white Bronco, he asked why there were so many "niggers" in his neighborhood. These were many of the very same people who would later acquit him in his murder trial. In both miniseries, but especially in Edelman's, the perspectives of black protagonists—black defense lawyers, black prosecutors, black onlookers who cheered the white Bronco—were inscribed in the very fabric of events. Perhaps for the first time in the history of American entertainment, it became possible for opposed "black and white" perceptions to resonate simultaneously in one (serial) melodrama.

Though both television programs correspond to the format of a television miniseries and obey the rhythms of contemporary serial melodrama previously described, the Oscar nomination of Edelman's documentary, based on the fact that it had been screened in at least some theaters as a day-long "movie," permitted it to receive the kind of attention that only Oscars can give. My point is not the unfairness of a documentary of seven and a half hours competing with those of mere feature length. Rather, it is the fact that serial television melodrama has made such a day-long "film" possible by giving sufficient world and time to weighty topics that go to the heart of American identity: race, celebrity, media, and, ultimately, justice itself. Powerful, racialized feelings circulate around these issues. In another earlier and even more extended serial (sixty plus hours), *The Wire* (HBO 2002–2008) broached many of the same fundamental issues, minus celebrity, and could dig even deeper (Williams 2014). Serial presentation, whether six hours, seven and a half, or 60 plus, has made possible the kind of storytelling that black and white races just might watch together with some understanding, and without losing civility. Unlike the original trial, whose televised verdict only served division and in many cases could not be countenanced by racially mixed groups, now, with twenty years distance and the affordance of serial melodrama, it is possible for this highly volatile melodramatic material to do what Deidre Pribram argued of *Breaking Bad*: enact "multiple versions" of the kinds of betrayals white viewers saw in the Simpson acquittal, and the kinds of betrayals black viewers saw in the verdict that acquitted the police in the beating of Rodney King. With the greater world and time of serial television melodrama, neither verdict could be viewed as a self-evident truth.

It is no longer possible for people without televisions to brag that they don't "waste their time" with the medium. But scholars should beware of assuming that something entirely new has occurred. Serial television melodrama organizes our time in different ways than the melodramatic stage, feature films, movie serials, soaps, or television series. That organization—the very feeling of time—often causes us to spend more and more time watching serials. Sometimes these serials are a complete waste of time; sometimes, as in these examples, they are well worth our time. Mass market modernity has long understood that by keeping us coming back to ongoing stories it will continue to generate our purchase of its commodities. Our relation to seriality can resemble an addiction. But this addiction is not to something that should be called complex TV. It is, and should be called, serial television melodrama.

NOTES

1. This is also true of novels by Wilkie Collins, George Eliot, and Harriet Beecher Stowe (see Payne 2005).
2. Live teleplays were first presented in anthology formats, such as *Playhouse 90* (CBS, 1956–1960), *The Philco Television Playhouse* (NBC, 1948–1955), or as "one off" productions; and later in prerecorded programs such as *Alfred Hitchcock Presents* (NBC, CBS, 1955–1965) or *The Twilight Zone* (CBS, 1959–1964).
3. See my discussion of this series as racial melodrama in *Playing the Race Card* (Williams 2001, 220–21).
4. As Jane Feuer (1986) notes, when sitcoms become serial, they also tend to move away from comedy and toward melodrama. Most commentators on comedy have observed that the mode stresses both the integration of a community as well as firm closure (usually through the expulsion of a blocking character, and most conventionally in marriage).
5. Thanks to Katherine Guerra for this insight.
6. Mittell (2015) writes, "One reason why television's formal narrative properties have been so ignored is the assumption that television storytelling is simplistic . . . [however] new developments over the past two decades have led to the rise of a particular model of narrative complexity on mainstream commercial American television, one that is unique to the medium and thus must be examined on its own terms" (4).
7. See Michael Z. Newman's (2006) discussion of prime-time serial rhythm.
8. Jennifer Hayward (1997) writes, "Serial fiction structurally encourages a large cast of characters and multiple story lines and therefore subverts the conventional narrative focus on a single hero and heroine" (33). I would add that it thus structurally encourages the plot structures of melodrama.

11

Melodrama's "Authenticity" in Carl Th. Dreyer's *La Passion de Jeanne d'Arc*

AMANDA DOXTATER

My film about Jeanne d'Arc has unjustly been called an avant-garde film, which it absolutely is not. It is not a film intended for film theorists, but rather a film of universally human content, intended for a broad audience and with a message for any open human mind.
—Carl Th. Dreyer, introducing the film at the Danish Film Museum, 1950[1]

The immolation with which Carl Th. Dreyer's *La Passion de Jeanne d'Arc* (1928) culminates is one the most remarkable sequences of pathos to be captured on film. We witness in graphic detail the climactic results of Jeanne's (Maria Falconetti) trial as she is bound to the stake to burn. Sweetly complicit, she bends over to pick up the rope that has slipped down. As the flames rise, Jeanne's discomfort becomes palpable; she coughs and sputters, her nostrils flaring as if actually struggling not to breathe in the smoke. At her last breath, her head falls limply and fire engulfs her body. Flesh melts away beneath a ravenous wall of flame. Interspersed with shots of Jeanne's suffering are other graphic shots of onlookers moved by her suffering. A sympathetic Massieu (Antonin Artaud), whose empathy sets him apart from his fellow churchmen, implores her to be brave and offers a crucifix to embrace for comfort. We catch glimpses of officials at the trial slowly realizing that their persecution of the young woman has backfired disastrously. And most vividly, the frenetic lamentation of spectators running in every direction is captured in Eisenstein-like montage and wild camera angles. Violent, almost manic editing combines pans of weeping peasants, the close-up of a baby startled from the breast, a child wailing over its dead mother to convey a mass public on the verge of revolution. Jeanne d'Arc's martyrdom is proclaimed through exquisite pathos and the eruption of action, both portrayed with unbridled cinematic prowess.

Flash back now to "Lydia," a scenario that Dreyer wrote some ten years earlier while employed in Denmark at Nordisk Films Kompagni (Nordisk) and eventually filmed as *Lydia* by Holger-Madsen in 1918. A heady tale of overlapping love triangles, forgery, murder, suicide, and scenes of debauched theater life, "Lydia" also culminates in a woman's spectacular death by fire. In the scenario, Karl Fribert

(Valdemar Psilander) is an average man who becomes blinded by his love for the eponymous stage diva (Ebba Thomsen). Fribert's consuming passion for Lydia drives him to commit forgery and murder the cad playboy who has impregnated her. Ultimately, overcome by remorse, he decides to turn himself over to the authorities and goes to see her perform one last time. Fribert informs her of his plan backstage. That evening, Lydia is fatefully slated to perform the world premiere of her death-defying "fire dance" (*Ilddans*), described in the film's program as a ritualistic "adoration of fire" (*en Tilbedelse af Ilden*). As she dances, she steps into the flames, committing suicide on stage. From the audience, Fribert eventually comprehends that her performance has become real, and he lunges toward the stage to intercede. His struggle to reach her through the chaos of a burning theater is in vain.²

At first take, the two immolations seem incompatible, their audience address radically different. The pathos of *Jeanne d'Arc* is laced with reflection brought about through estrangements and camera disorientations, whereas Lydia's posturing traffics in cheap thrills and overidentifications of the kind of popular culture Dreyer himself would disparage as inartistic.³ According to conventional film criticism, *Jeanne d'Arc* embodies a modernist, realistic, and authentic innovation of cinema art, whereas *Lydia* displays the clunky, filmed-theater aesthetic of a primitivism that cinema has long outgrown. Although Holger-Madsen's version of the woman's immolation no longer exists, production stills suggest that Fribert's deciphering of Lydia's performance was likely conveyed through cross-cut frontal reaction shots: the stage from Fribert's point of view (POV), positioned in the audience (figure 11.1) alternated with a shot of his reaction seen from the POV

Figure 11.1 Lydia's firedance, seen from Fribert's POV.

Figure 11.2 Fribert, an enthralled spectator in *Lydia* (1918)

of stage center (figure 11.2). The sequence would have been a far cry from *Jeanne d'Arc*'s pyrotechnic ending.

And yet significant parallels connect the two scenes. Each revolves around the spectacle of a female body being destroyed by fire before spectators (diegetic and otherwise) who watch and respond to it. Both performances blur the boundaries between entertaining spectacle and ritual sacrifice, in effect raising ethical questions about consuming pathos.[4] Fire, in both instances, forces spectators to confront the materiality of a performing body. In each scene the spectacle of an actress's flesh in harm's way tests the ontological conditions of mimesis, the boundary between acting and nonacting. Each asks spectators to decipher "authentic" suffering from feigned. Fribert charges the stage when he understands that, *actually*, Lydia's flesh will burn. A similar deciphering occurs in *Jeanne d'Arc* (albeit in reverse) as the cinema spectator ponders in which shot Falconetti's body has been replaced by wax that will *actually* burn. Recognizing suffering sparks revelation in each sequence. Fribert's realization is echoed in the shout from the crowd in *Jeanne d'Arc*: "You've killed a saint!" Different spectators, in each instance, represent different investments in the spectacle. Massieu's reaction differs from the soldiers or the peasants watching. Fribert's reaction, signaled by his heavily made-up face, sets him apart from his fiancée beside him, or the naturalistically represented audience members behind him. And each scene dramatizes the transformation of spectator from passive consumer of spectacle to active participant, charging into the fray. Fourth-wall voyeurism gives way to an enlivened, articulated space of cinematically coded performance.

Uniting *Lydia* and *Jeanne d'Arc* is a prominent iteration of the melodramatic mode at Nordisk that I call *varieté melodrama*.[5] Although Denmark could not claim to have the same robust tradition of Boulevard theater that England or France did, images of the theater and the *varieté* abounded in Nordisk's melodramatic imagination. The *varieté* depicted underworlds filled with seedy criminals, unscrupulous cads, burlesque dancers, circus sideshows, exotic dancers, and musical acts. Invested in the space of live theater, *varieté melodrama* exploited play-within-the-play situations and scenes of performance both on and off the stage. It featured actor-characters, nonperformers compelled to act, as well as other characters engaged in the dramatic manipulation of makeup, costuming, and disguise. It delighted in contriving scenes of dramatic irony in ways that set identities and identifications into play, making it proto-modernist and fully melodramatic.[6] This iteration of melodrama at Nordisk provided Dreyer with a rich cache of mediations surrounding performance and pathos with which to engage and create *Jeanne d'Arc*.

Dreyer's engagement with this form of melodrama was neither easy nor fully conscious. *Jeanne d'Arc* comes into being through Dreyer's deep attraction-repulsion to the melodramatic mode.[7] In my reading, Nordisk's stigma as producer of melodrama provided Dreyer with the impetus to reimagine it as its dialectical opposite, authentic cinema. "Authentic" was a self-evidently positive, if ultimately ambiguous, term used by Dreyer and his critics to describe his ambitions for film. Throughout, I keep the term in quotation marks to gesture toward its rhetorical association with nonmelodrama even as the *Jeanne d'Arc* project helps articulate it more concretely *within* melodrama: as the opposite of feigned, as moments when acting is suspended, and actor and spectator experience strong, sincere pathos.[8] Yet I see Dreyer's very negation of *varieté melodrama* as itself a melodramatic innovation of the mode. In what follows, I briefly outline Dreyer's early career at Nordisk to show how melodrama and the desire for "authenticity" form the backbone of his artistic persona. I then sketch the contours of *varieté melodrama* with the help of Dreyer's scenario "Esther," adapted from Honoré de Balzac's novel *Splendeurs et misères des courtisanes* (filmed as *Den hvide Djævel / The Devil's Protegé*, Holger-Madsen, 1916). Against this backdrop, I analyze *Jeanne d'Arc*'s engagement with the core thrills of *varieté melodrama*, including its spectacle, aesthetics, and fascination with suffering. From production to final cut, the *Jeanne d'Arc* project reimagines the space of the *varieté* and the body of the *varieté* star, transforming *varieté* spectacle into show trial. I take *Jeanne d'Arc*'s epilogue—"We are witness to an amazing drama: a young, pious woman confronted by a group of orthodox theologians and powerful judges"[9]—as an invitation to analyze Dreyer's fascination with dramatizing pathos. "Authenticity" alone doesn't suffice to read what is arguably Dreyer's most masterful depiction of female suffering; we need the melodrama of the *varieté*.

SHAPING DREYER'S PERSONA: MELODRAMATIC NEGATION AND "AUTHENTICITY"

Dreyer learned to make film during what has come to be known as the "Golden Age of Danish Melodrama" at Nordisk, the company that would become synonymous with early Danish cinema. Between 1910 and World War I, the company made approximately 2,000 features and short films. Working at Nordisk from 1913 to around 1920, Dreyer garnered experience writing intertitles, adapting scenarios, editing, and eventually directing. Although Nordisk films initially enjoyed a reputation for high production values and compelling, sensational drama, eventually "melodrama" would be blamed for the company's failure to compete globally.

Dreyer's elevation as an artistic director is predicated explicitly on his break with Nordisk and its melodramatic output. Citing artistic differences, Dreyer left the company after completing his second and last feature there, *Leaves from Satan's Book* (1921).[10] Historical accounts of the break solidified the company's reputation for melodrama and effectively ensured that, during his lifetime, Dreyer would never openly embrace the mode. Dreyer was acutely aware of the way his *oeuvre* was being incorporated into Danish cinema history. His contemporary and friend, Ebbe Neergaard, who wrote the first authoritative book on Dreyer in 1940, would write, referring to *The President* (1919), "Even by his first film, Dreyer had achieved results that corrected exactly what would come to be Nordisk Films's weak point. Melodramatic style. Through his work with *milieu* as it is characterized by decor, minor characters, and extras, he sought to create the first foundation for filmic *authenticity*" (19, emphasis in the original).[11] Neergaard's book on Dreyer, translated into English in 1950, was instrumental in establishing Dreyer as an international *auteur* who overcame his early years at Nordisk.[12] Reviewing a reissued version of Neergaard's work in 1964, Danish author and critic Klaus Rifbjerg (1964) would continue to echo antimelodramatic rhetoric: "It can't be put in a more simple and banal way. The reality that Dreyer brought to film by cleaning up all of the melodramatic hocus pocus, by stylizing and at the same time guiding *reality*, the authentic milieu, the 'actual' people, into film has brought the art from cheap sideshow performance (*gøgl*) to a point where today, it to some extent feels its most vital" (67).[13]

Danish film history and Dreyer scholarship alike have continued to rehearse a familiar denigration of Nordisk melodrama as unrealistic, theatrical, artificial, spectacular, and commercial, whereas Dreyer was tragic, realistic, sincere, austere, and "authentic."[14] The rhetoric of "authenticity" reverberated through Dreyer's career, reaching a fever pitch with *Jeanne d'Arc*. In his article "Realized Mysticism," published shortly after the film's release, Dreyer (1964) describes a project of presenting truth by breaking with tradition (banishing makeup and filming in sequence) and "renouncing methods of 'beautification'" (31).[15] This rhetoric of purification, combined with the many production accounts attesting to the film's austerity, established the notion that in *Jeanne d'Arc* Dreyer purged any trace of what might be called melodramatic excess or theatricality to make film of a higher order.

But Dreyer's relationship to Nordisk melodrama and the rhetoric of "authenticity" is more complex than this trajectory would have it. For one thing, Dreyer's Nordisk scenarios reveal him to be an accomplished practitioner of melodrama. His early scenarios are at once quintessentially Nordisk and quintessentially Dreyer. In contrast to many of the company's early scenarios, which are skeletal outlines for shooting containing little or no dialogue, character description, or anything that might eventually be included on an intertitle, most of the scenarios attributed to Dreyer include extended, often quite literary passages that flesh out *varieté melodrama* in wonderful ways. He was clearly also imagining how his scenarios might eventually be shot (if ultimately by another director) as he often included suggestions for camera set ups, notes on shot scale, prop choice, visual effects, and mises-en-scène uncommon in Nordisk scenarios. Dreyer clearly possessed an intimate understanding of melodramatic conventions at the company.[16]

Looking at dramatic sensibilities that recur throughout Dreyer's *oeuvre* further unsettles the idea of a decisive break with Nordisk melodrama. Even a cursory glance reveals a wealth of the dramatic spectacles, plays-within-the-play, and performer characters that animated the *varieté*. The dramatic irony of such situations of performance allowed Dreyer to stimulate audiences by exploring his career-long preoccupation with female suffering.[17] *Mikaël* (1924) features a deliberate play-within-a-play scene when those embroiled in a love triangle attend the opera only to watch another love triangle performed in the ballet, *The Black Swan*. Eponymous divas such as Lydia and Esther and concert musicians performing with cursed violins in "Guldets Gift" (*The Temptation of Mrs. Chestney*, Holger-Madsen, 1916) foreshadow the ensemble of performer characters in *Gertrud* (1964). A dramatic urge animates the disguising and unmasking of arch criminals and detectives pursuing them (often in front of boudoir mirrors that resemble backstage dressing rooms) in Dreyer's scenario "Rovedderkoppen" (*The Spider's Prey*, August Blom, 1916). And in "En Forbryders Liv og Levned" (*A Criminal's Diary*, Alexander Christian, 1916) an escaped criminal elegantly steals back the proplike paraphernalia of his criminal persona on display at a nearby museum. Performance in Dreyer's *oeuvre* could also be comical or farcical, as in one of his earliest surviving Nordisk scenarios, "Elskovs Opfindsomhed" (*Love's Ingenuity*, Sofus Wolder, DK, 1913), in which an actress character cross-dresses as a young suitor to charm an older woman, or in "Hans rigtige Kone" (*Which is Which?* Holger-Madsen, 1917), a play of mistaken identities featuring another actress character. Dreyer's interest in theatrical performance also could be straightforward, as demonstrated by the many play texts he adapted, including *Ordet* (1955) and *Gertrud* (1964), and the theater reviews he wrote for Copenhagen newspapers (Dreyer 1964).

VARIETÉ "AUTHENTICITY": STAGE SPACE AND PERFORMING BODIES

Varieté melodrama at Nordisk already incorporated notions of "authenticity" upon which to draw. Disparaging Nordisk as exclusively producing artifice underestimates how its plots depended structurally on establishing worlds and moments coded as more real, more "authentic." Making artifice legible as such required making "real" pathos legible through contiguous, nontheatrical interactions. In what might be called *dramas of authentication*, *varieté melodrama* modulated the relationship between "authenticity" and artifice by exploring the spectrum of states between performance and reality. As seen in "Lydia," this form of melodrama delighted in self-reflexively undoing the fourth-wall realist theater with its clear distinctions between performer and spectator, actor and nonactor. In spectacularly corporeal moments such as Lydia's fire dance, Dreyer used performing bodies (whether performer characters or nonperformer/spectator characters suddenly thrust into performance situations) to blur the boundaries between performer and role, feigned risk and "authentic" harm.

Spatially, the *varieté* exploited every inch of the house to generate encounters between performing coded as real life and performing coded as performance. Actors pulled audience members onstage, and audience members in turn dramatically interrupted performances with real life proclamations intended for actors on stage. Off stage spaces also provided important opportunities for drama. Rivals challenged each other backstage, in the wings, or from the audience; the drama of the theater flowed in every direction. The camera was positioned everywhere: in the balcony, in the orchestra pit, on stage, or in the wings. The cinematic performance space of the theater expanded to include the dressing room, with frequent shots of actors putting on makeup or disguises in mirrors and could be opened up through editing (shot-reverse shot) or through longer takes that exploited depth (Bordwell 2006, 82–83). The alternations between "authenticity" and artifice at Nordisk produced thrills of immersion and reflection for diegetic audiences and cinema spectators alike. Repeatedly filming the titillating spaces of "live" drama demonstrates Nordisk's awareness of the ontological differences between theater and film and its desire to exploit them.

DREYER'S "ESTHER" SCENARIO

Reading Dreyer's "Esther" scenario shows how, in the *varieté*, performance added layers of signification to melodrama's core ambition—recognizing (authentic) pathos in another—through embellishment, costuming, and makeup.[18] In "Esther," Dreyer changes Balzac's courtesan-with-a-heart-of-gold into a *varieté* starlet performing to support herself and her brother, Lucian. The orphan siblings struggle to make a better life for themselves in Paris but ultimately fall under the malign influence of escaped criminal Jacques Cellin.

Dreyer sets Esther up as a true-heart character enduring the adversity of a shoddy theatrical world epitomized by the costuming she is forced to wear. In naturalistic strokes, his scenario conveys the discord between an essential sincerity and the theatrical exterior she presents.

> She's a young and healthy woman, who, despite having earned a livelihood for herself and her brother by performing in varietés on the outskirts of town, has in no way been infected by the vice (*last*) surrounding her for so long. On the contrary, the impoverished, feigned elegance in which she is dressed betrays (*røber*) her profession. Her essence is absolutely sympathetic. (Dreyer 1915)

The artifice of the *varieté* milieu disguises the true heart and creates the preconditions for her virtue to be perceived by the rich Baron in the audience who will fall for her. Here, onstage artifice and offstage "authenticity" coexist and reinforce each other in juxtaposition.

But onstage performance could also heighten pathos represented in the offstage, naturalistic world of the film. Dreyer writes a climactic scene in which "Esther" performs the spectacle of "Marguerite and the Golden Calf" (*Marguerite paa Guldkalven*). Although Dreyer's scenario doesn't provide detail about how this scene was to be shot, Charles Gounod's opera *Faust* (1859) included an extravagant scene in which Marguerite is held in a prison for the murder of her child amid an orgiastic Wallpurgis night gathering of witches and courtesans. Mephistopheles tempts her with the promise of forgiveness, but she steadfastly refuses, opting instead to mount the scaffold and commit her fate to God. At the last moment, a chorus of angels triumphantly announces her salvation. Although we can only speculate how the filming of this play-within-a-play scene might have depicted the relationship between the performed scene of Marguerite's virtuous rejection of temptation on the scaffold and Esther's "authentic" suffering in her self-sacrifice for her brother's livelihood, Marguerite's endurance of cosmological torture on stage would have amplified and articulated the pathos of Esther's plight in real life. The spectacle of this last-minute salvation might also have ironically compounded the pathos of her suicide later—from which no chorus of angels will ultimately save her.

Dreyer also parallels Esther's onstage performance with a Faustian scene involving Lucian, her brother who succumbs to temptation, selling his soul to Jacques for riches. Here, theatrical spectacle and its more naturalistic iteration coexist and inform each other. In the case of "Esther," Dreyer's melodramatic imagination even exceeded Nordisk's. In Nordisk's filmed version, Dreyer's eponymous heroine and pillar of virtuously performed sacrifice has been deleted entirely. Program and stills reveal Dreyer's love quadrangle (culminating in a double brother and sister suicide) was reduced to a more conventional triangle of exploitation in which a destitute Lucian dies a pitiable victim-hero. *Varieté melodrama*, in other words, took as much pleasure in reading and deciphering the ironic misprisions made possible by *staging* innocence, guilt, or suffering as it did in seeing virtuous suffering rewarded. Gesturing toward a proto-modernist notion of self, this iteration of melodrama did not necessarily establish stable identities and often invested more in exploring the ethical implications of performance than in moral polarization. More interesting than the revelation of Esther's innocence (in fact, she becomes complicit in the plot to swindle the Baron) is the fact that innocence and suffering are put on stage to be experienced and deciphered by diegetic spectators like the Baron, the audience, and then ultimately the film spectator. In short, Nordisk melodrama provided Dreyer with rich imbrications of "authenticity" and embellishment.

JEANNE D'ARC: GALVANIZING PERFORMANCE SPACE IN THE *VARIETÉ*

In his critical rhetoric, Dreyer differentiates cinematic "authenticity" from the theatrical using spatial metaphors of proximity and distance that map onto his attraction-repulsion to melodrama. Though drawn to melodrama, he must deny it. In his 1933 article, "The Real Talking Film," Dreyer aligns the theater (a ready substitution for *varieté*) with inauthentic, exaggerated representation at a distance, the cinema meanwhile becomes "authentic" through its proximity to the spectator and ontological "being."

> A theatrical performance is a picture seen from a distance. In order for the overall effect to be life-like, it has to be painted with a coarse brush—the paint must be applied in thick dollops. All details must be made coarse and enlarged—exaggerated. In the theater everything is inauthentic, and everything depends on bringing inauthentic details into such an agreement with each other, that altogether it produces a colorful illusion of reality, while film presents reality itself in a rigorous black and white stylization. . . . The distance between theater and film amounts to the distance between *representing* and *being*. (Dreyer 1964,32, emphasis in the original)

Although Dreyer's claims to "authenticity" seem to privilege the ontology of cinema over the theatrical, in *Jeanne d'Arc* he continues to reimagine the distance between the two. Dreyer's fascination with the ontology of live performance (the theater) cannot be underestimated, as his extensive (and expensive) production experiment with *Jeanne d'Arc* makes clear. Constructing a small city-set of Rouen for actors to inhabit and shooting the film in sequence so that his cast could *relive* the trial effectively turned the project into an immersive performance event. Dreyer remained fascinated by (and dependent on) the material *being* of acting bodies—an actual presence taken for granted in the theater—as the means to achieve any cinematic stylization of reality.

With *Jeanne d'Arc*, Dreyer's attraction to melodrama allows him to reconceive *varieté* as a *show* trial by exchanging a diegetic proscenium stage for the courtroom. This veils *varieté* space in naturalistic garb while continuing to cultivate the drama of its live interactions. The opening of the film proper, which irises into the courtroom, establishes it as a theater space. The camera tracks down the length of the courtroom amid an audience of ecclesiastical spectators eagerly anticipating the performance about to begin. The camera's POV situates the film spectator as an audience member amid the silhouetted rows—the front of the house. In the illuminated stage space before them, stagehands scurry to arrange stools and props in preparation for the spectacle. POV shots from the back rows of the theater can be found at Nordisk, but in *Jeanne d'Arc*, editing galvanizes this *varieté* space, heightening its ontological claims to liveness. The rapid camera movements of the interrogation—tilts, swish pans, zooming close-ups, its wildly interspersed high and low angle shots, placement of action at the edge of the frame, disjointed editing, abstract mise-en-scène, and lack of establishing shots—all work to blend performance space with space of spectatorship. A dramatic zoom into the face of a judge collapses the distance between spectator and stage. The complete spatial disorientation that Dreyer brings about by abandoning eye-line matches reimagines cinematically the fluid performance space in Nordisk films. Like *varieté* characters, whose complete disregard of proscenium boundaries means they regularly find themselves onstage in the middle of the action, one judge suddenly appears on stage beside Jeanne, close enough to spit on her cheek. The cinematic virtuosity of the interrogation sequences utterly deflates any fourth-wall voyeurism in the diegetic realm of the film.

Dreyer also uses editing and variation of shot scale to emulate the sensation of physical presence in a space of live performance; he stages melodramatic suffering at a micro level. Quick microflashes and extreme close-ups highlight performing bodies: the twitch of a cheek, a tiny smirk, a raised eyebrow, the flare of nostrils, or the unsavory swabbing of an ear. Bodies fill the theater space and the frame; the grotesque physiognomy of the judges writ large conveys intimate immersion. The dramatic space that emerges through this phenomenological attention reverberates with the emotions and reactions—felt and perceived—of those present to Jeanne's suffering. Dreyer thus presses upon film to overcome its inevitable ontological absences, making it an experience along the lines of what Erica Fischer-Lichte (2008) calls a performative event. Performance, in Fischer-Lichte's theorization, is predicated on the phenomenological feedback loop between performer and spectator.[19] Live performance, whether between individuals or on the scale of mass religious ritual, avant-garde performance art, or circus sideshow, has the potential to transform its participants.[20] It is this unmediated, transformative power of performance that Dreyer tries to elicit via *Jeanne d'Arc*'s galvanized chaos of micro perceptions.

Jeanne d'Arc's iconic use of the extreme close-up (a framing impossible to replicate in the theater) is often enlisted as evidence that the film transcends melodrama.[21] The film's repetitive, emphatic, almost percussive (over) use of this larger-than-life framing, however, particularly in conjunction with its lack of establishing shots, comes close to enacting the theater's quality of the "inauthentic." Their stylization functions like Dreyer's "thick dollops of paint." But most important, the close-up allows Dreyer to convey tears, orchestrating a profusion of pathos for both diegetic and cinema audiences to negotiate. Too small to be legible in the theater, the tear becomes a metonym for melodramatic emotion in the cinema. Dreyer pushes *varieté melodrama* into film. Tears also provide a quintessential exteriorization of suffering—a kind of ontological proof of internal experience. As Steve Neale (1986) theorizes, tears in someone watching suffering also authenticate being moved by another's suffering. Tears in *Jeanne d'Arc* communicate important shared experience: the peasants witnessing Jeanne's immolation weep, and Jeanne's suffering moves at least one of her judges to tears. Put in terms of the *varieté*, the tear affords important confirmation of affective interaction between performer and audience.

Eyewitness accounts of the filming (put into circulation by Dreyer and his cast and crew) constituted them as on set spectators, a proxy audience for the cinema spectator. Shared tears make the cinema spectator "present," in a sense, to Jeanne's suffering. Costume designer Valentine Hugo's account of the scene in which Falconetti's head is shaved is particularly vivid in this regard:

> In the silence of an operating room, in the pale light of the morning of the execution, Dreyer had Falconetti's head shaved. Although we had lost old prejudices [against

short hair on women], we were as moved as if the infamous mark were being made there, in reality. The electricians and technicians held their breaths and their eyes filled with tears. Falconetti wept real tears. Then the director slowly approached her, gathered up some of her tears in his fingers, and carried them to his lips. (Bordwell 1973, 19)

Dreyer's gesture—which replicates Massieu's wiping away of Jeanne's tears in the diegesis—performs a symbolic blessing of Falconetti's suffering performance and the tears of the assembled audience attest to its affective, even transformative, potential. These accounts that document actual, on set pathos crucially exceed the final cut of the film, further suggesting that Dreyer envisioned cinema as an interactive, immersive, and potentially transformative performance event. Luis Buñuel's (2000) description of tears in *Jeanne d'Arc* encapsulates this desire. He writes, "We have kept one of her tears, which rolled down to us, in a celluloid box. An odorless, tasteless, colorless tear, a drop from the purest spring" (122). A tear rolling down into the audience provides the most exquisite proof of film's capacity for pathetic communication, the perfect transformation of film into live performance. With *Jeanne d'Arc*, Dreyer catches *varieté melodrama* in a celluloid box.

DENUDING THE *VARIETÉ* ACTRESS: FALCONETTI'S BODY AS SITE OF "AUTHENTIC" MELODRAMA

Like the space of the *varieté*, Dreyer reinvests the body of the *varieté* actress as a site of pathos and "authenticity." *Jeanne d'Arc*'s purported eradication of melodrama (accomplished diegetically and extra-diegetically) is a drama that takes place on the body of Falconetti, a *varieté* actress herself. As Neergaard (1960) puts it in his history of Danish cinema, "Dreyer had chosen the *varieté* actress (*varieteskuespillerinden*) Marie Falconetti for the role of Jeanne d'Arc. When liberated from make-up, she became capable of displaying the naked, soulful face that Dreyer wanted" (126).[22] Dreyer's strict prohibition of makeup on set attracted the attention of many contemporary critics and contributed to the project's "authenticity." But this stripping of embellishment actually reiterates and magnifies melodrama's dialectic of artifice and "authenticity." The *varieté* actress is elevated to tragic actress, but only by the kind of disclosure and recognition of suffering that is a part of all melodrama.[23]

Dreyer's casting of Falconetti provides the cornerstone upon which *Jeanne d'Arc*'s extra-diegetic claims to "authenticity" are built. Dreyer first discovered the young actress of the Comédie-Française one evening while she was performing in the light comedy *Lorenzaccio*, in Paris. From his seat in the audience, he recognized some aspect of Falconetti's humanity in spite of (or because of) her thick costuming and makeup. In a scene that uncannily rehearses the scenes of *varieté* enthrallment and recognition in "Esther" and "Lydia," consuming and deciphering the embellishment of Falconetti's performing body marks the precondition for Dreyer, as spectator, for recognizing her "authentic" suffering. Drum and Drum

(2000) invest the encounter with a kind of mystical, wordless transmission between performer and spectator: "How Carl Dreyer was able to see beneath that surface to something deeper and more profound, was able to strip away the makeup, the urbanity, the sophistication and see the simple power and intensity of Joan, no one can say, not even Dreyer" (128). When Dreyer then invites Falconetti to his apartment wearing no makeup, extra-filmic accounts of this greenroom encounter function as a naturalistically coded performance between actress and spectator that structurally reinforces the film's "authentic" suffering. Dreyer authenticates Jeanne's suffering by referring to the traces of actual suffering inscribed on Falconetti's face, in an earlier drama that has occurred, offstage.[24]

Jeanne d'Arc itself relates the story of a saint and a *varieté* star similarly disrobed. Falconetti plays the role of the true-hearted *varieté* performer persecuted and redeemed through the making of the film. In the guise of a nakedness equated with "authentic" human experience, flesh becomes the most perfect exteriorization of interiority (soul, feeling). In his 1950 introduction to the Danish Film Museum screening of the film, Dreyer describes wanting "to strip (*afklæde*) Jeanne d'Arc of her halo and formal accoutrements of a saint and find a way into the actual little woman-child, who suffered death at the stake for her faith."[25] Dreyer cloaks the melodramatic desire for revelation and recognition within the rhetoric of nudity. He may stylize costuming or evoke beautification rather than show it, but he retains melodrama's insistence on reading through and deciphering bodies. Legibility is introduced in the film's opening intertitles where, interspersed with authenticating shots of the trial document, the spectator is tasked quite literally with *reading* a humanity obscured by a soldier's costuming: "Reading it, we discover the 'real Joan' not in armor, but simple and human" (Dreyer 1999).[26] Dreyer's preoccupation with reading the body emerges again in sartorially focused dialogue from the trial that draws attention to clothing and hair while evoking naked bodies beneath. A volley of questions about Jeanne's visions and her own ability to recognize a saint—essentially by differentiating between costuming and the body underneath—demonstrates the desire and inability of Jeanne's judges to read her. They demand to know how St. Michael appeared to her: "Was he wearing a crown?" "Did he have wings?" "Was he dressed?" "How did you know if it was a man or a woman?" and the ultimate question, "Was he naked?" Jeanne's brilliant rejoinder, "Do you think God was unable to clothe him?" draws further attention to the film's hyper-awareness of corporeality as requiring decipherment. Dreyer uses the question of how one recognizes the flesh of an angel or its equivalents—goodness, innocence, sainthood—to substitute for *varieté melodrama*'s fascination with whether a performer is performing on stage or performing an identity coded as naturalistic. Each articulates melodrama's core humanist ambition to recognize suffering in another.

When one monk questions Jeanne's ability to recognize Saint Michael, asking "Did he have long hair?" and Jeanne responds, "Why would he have cut it?" her response foreshadows the film's climactic moment of "authenticity" by denuding her. The ultimate stripping of the *varieté* actress in *Jeanne d'Arc* will be cutting her hair. In the uncomfortable proximity of the close-up, the barber's insistent shears reveal strip after strip of her scalp. Shreds of hair cling to Jeanne's tear-stained cheeks as she stares upward in exhausted submission. This iconic sequence of the film accomplishes her corporeal *coup-de-theatre*: the tortured change of heart by which she retracts her confession, sending her to the stake. Agony plays across Jeanne's face in minute detail: quivering lips, the tears that dangle precipitously off her chin, the dry lips that bite nervously at trembling and despairing hands.

The haircut scene elicits pathos by exploiting audience awareness that Falconetti's hair was *actually* being cut. The pressure that the haircut puts on Falconetti and the material conditions of filming are reminiscent of avant-garde performance artists putting their bodies in harm's way.[27] Though many critics viewed Falconetti's haircut as further proof of Dreyer's unrelenting commitment to a kind of "authenticity" through realism (Drum and Drum 2000, 139), this in no way precludes its being melodramatic. The haircut's conflation of actress and role (representing and being) also echoes traditions of extreme realism in spectacular stage melodrama in which heroines and heroes could risk being cut in half by an actual log saw, trampled by real horses, or crushed by actual locomotives on stage. The pathos and thrill elicited by these scenes activated concern for the actor's body that could rival identification with a fictional character.[28] As Ben Singer (2001) writes, "They feared for the actor's flesh, not the protagonist's. This form of spectacular realism shifts the frame of attention from a believable diegetic realm, the frame one would expect realism to foster, to the material circumstances of the theater. Indeed, this is the precondition for the spectacle's effectiveness as a thrill" (185). This kind of corporeal spectacle, like Jeanne's haircut or the fire dance in "Lydia," melodramatically heightens vacillations common to all mimetic performance—alternations between reading the phenomenological body of the actor and the semiotic body of the role she is playing.

Dreyer's melodramatic "authenticity" enacts these vacillations spatially, as reflective distance and the proximity by pathos. The haircut sequence thus intercuts intimate interior shots of Jeanne with exterior shots of sideshow spectacle; interior pathos is interspersed with exterior action. Outside, the camera pans over circus sideshow performers entertaining the masses. A dancer prances in tights with a trained dog, contortionists wrap legs and arms behind their necks, and a sword-swallower plunges a sword down his throat. As these shots demonstrate, melodrama's *gøgl* (the circus sideshow that Rifbjerg argues Dreyer had eradicated) quite literally and vibrantly persists. Sideshow performance here fully conflates representing and being; one cannot represent a contortionist without being one. Inside, Falconetti's luminous face, present in close-up and mid-shot (figure 11.3), is both juxtaposed and elided with the spectacularly pliant bones and flesh of the sideshow performers (figure 11.4), bodies revealed at a greater remove, in long shot.

Here are dual and interrelated "cuts": the hair*cut* and the inter*cut*.[29] The hair*cut* is so striking because of its ontology. Falconetti's hair signals the material limits of the performing body on stage. Had something gone awry, Dreyer would have had to wait months to reshoot. As film spectators, our pathetic response to Jeanne's experience is enmeshed in living Falconetti's sacrifice with her, in the real time of its performance. But also present is the quintessentially cinematic inter*cut*, which creates a simultaneity of experience by editing disparate experience

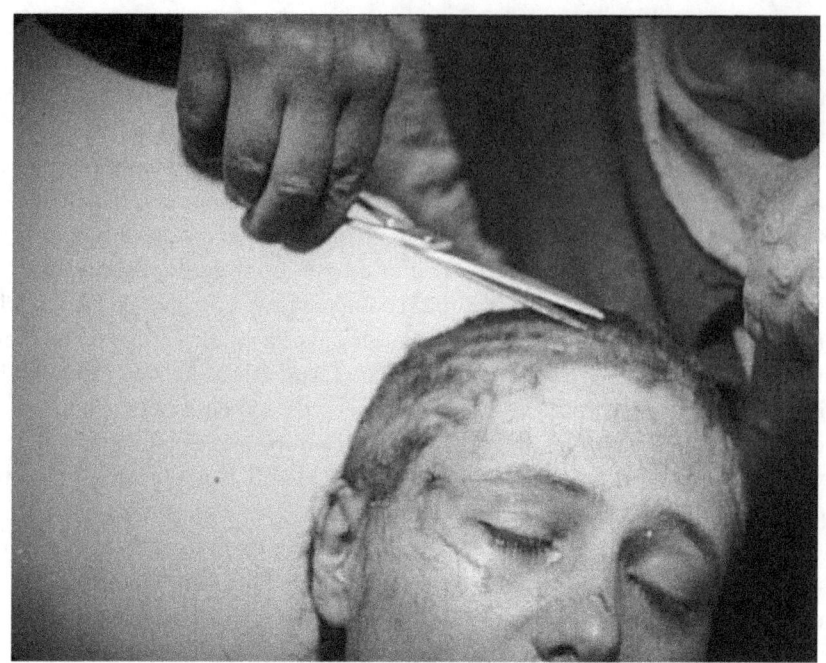

Figure 11.3 Falconetti's haircut in *La Passion de Jeanne d'Arc* (1928).

Figure 11.4 Circus sideshow performer in *La Passion de Jeanne d'Arc*.

(the circus sideshow and the jail) together. Again, seemingly antithetical sensibilities (cinematic and theatrical) coexist, feeding and informing one another in an intricate dialectic. The one begets and encompasses the other visually. The barber's scissors make graphic the cinematic cut even in the theater time of the cell, and the spectacle of sword plunging deep into a performer's body communicates the cinematic within the performance. Dreyer's mapping of proximity/distance, film/theater, being/representing onto interior/exterior, intimate scale/long shot, naturalistic performance/circus spectacle makes vivid the dialectical underpinnings of performance in *varieté melodrama*.

In attempting to eliminate melodrama and make "authentic" film, Dreyer interrogates the relationship between the two. His *oeuvre* contributes much to understanding melodrama's rather paradoxical development, as a mode both conservative and innovative. Seen through a melodramatic framework, Dreyer's almost obsessive return to the experience of a suffering female body—and corporeality in general—over the course of his career resonates with the concealments and revelations of Sergei Balukhatyi's *Poetics of Melodrama* (1926). Balukhatyi describes melodrama as a skeleton over which new, different flesh can be stretched to make it look like "higher" genres.

> In its 'pure' aspect, melodrama acts directly through its constructional and emotional forms, but melodrama can also be found in many other types of drama in which its 'pure, primordial' principles are masked, weakened, and complicated by other aspects, such as realistic portrayal, psychological motivation, or ideological dialectics . . . it is possible for a melodramatic skeleton to become covered with the solid flesh of realistic material and concealed beneath an elegant layer of psychology and ethical, social, or philosophical content. We thereby lose the feeling of melodramatic style and accept the play as a 'higher' genre." (as cited in Gerould 1991, 128–29)

With *Jeanne d'Arc*, Dreyer stretches new cinematic flesh on the skeleton of melodrama he encountered at Nordisk. Wrapping the bones of *varieté melodrama* in the flesh of "authenticity," Dreyer innovated melodrama through its concealment. At the same time, he stripped away that flesh to expose more "purely" a skeleton of melodramatic performance, effectively reimagining the relationship of skin to flesh, and flesh to bone. Reading *La Passion de Jeanne d'Arc* as both embodying and reacting to a melodramatic legacy yields new possibilities for understanding Dreyer as an uncompromising aesthete with popular culture ambitions.

NOTES

1. In Danish, the epigraph reads: *"Min Film om Jeanne d'Arc er med Urette blevet kaldt en Avant-garde Film, hvad den absolut ikke er. Det er ikke en Film bestemt for Filmteoretikerne, men en film af almenmenneskeligt Indhold, bestemt for det brede Folk og med Bud til ethvert aabent Menneskesind"* (Dreyer 1950). Unless otherwise indicated all translations are my own.

2. Fribert reaches Lydia in time to carry her expiring body up to the roof of the theater where she revives for a brief moment, asks for his forgiveness, kisses him, and then dies. Distraught, Fribert throws himself off the roof. Though most of the films resulting from Dreyer's scenarios are no longer extant, key scenes can be reconstructed by triangulating between scenario, the studio's published librettos (containing extensive plot summary), and production stills. Extant Nordisk films, of which there are about 150, also provide information as to how sequences might have been shot.
3. Dreyer participated vociferously in contemporary debates that disparaged Danish popular cinema (Nordisk melodrama) and once lamented that even Danish film posters stank (see Dreyer 1964, 15).
4. Dreyer's interest in the spectacle of sacrificial or persecuted female characters perishing by fire (*bål* in Danish) reoccurs throughout his *oeuvre*, both before and after *Jeanne d'Arc*. In *Day of Wrath* (1943), Herlofs Marthe will be tied to a ladder and burnt as a witch. Anne will face the same fate. And in *Leaves from Satan's Book* (1921), the Spanish Inquisition episode ends as the innocent Isabella is carried out in a swoon to be burned (a scene to which the audience is not actually privy).
5. *Varieté melodrama* is my term for an iteration of melodrama prevalent at Nordisk but never identified as such. Despite a proliferation of genre designations used in marketing and production materials at Nordisk during "The Golden Age of Danish Melodrama," the word *melodrama* is conspicuously absent.
6. This aligns with Christine Gledhill's (1989, 46) complication of melodrama's presumed overidentifications by considering dramatic irony and suffering. In a similar vein, Peer Sørensen (2009) explores pathos and irony in Danish author Herman Bang's literary melodrama. Bang wrote the novella "Michael" that Dreyer filmed in 1924.
7. Dreyer's attraction-repulsion to melodrama is reminiscent of initial feminist encounters with melodrama in the 1980s. As Linda Williams (1998, 45) discusses, feminist film scholars' emphatic aspersion of melodrama as sexist demonstrated simultaneously a fascination with its pathos and forms. Such fascinations have grounded subsequent feminist recuperations of melodramatic pathos.
8. My thanks to Sergio Rigoletto for bringing this point to my attention.
9. In French it reads, "*et nous sommes témoins d'un drame impressionnant–une jeune femme croyante, à une cohort de théologiens aveuglés et de jurists chevronnés.*"
10. Correspondence between Dreyer and Nordisk suggests that the break with Nordisk was accomplished with much less bravado than generally thought (Kau 1989, 392).
11. In Danish, "*Allerede med sin første film havde Dreyer nået resultater, der korregerede netop det, som skulle vise sig at være Nordisk Films svage punkt. Den melodramatiske stil. Gennem sit arbejde med miljøet som det tegnes gennem decoration og bipersoner og statister, søgte han at skabe det første grundlag for filmisk ægthed.*"
12. Neergaard also praises Nordisk cinema for its capacity for emotional expressivity, but not its melodrama. Neergaard wrote the first history of Danish cinema. Published posthumously in 1960, the volume included a preface by Dreyer about his friend.
13. In Danish, "*Mere banalt og enkelt kan det ikke siges. Den virkelighed Dreyer bragte ind i filmen ved at rydde op i det melodramatiske hokus-pokus, ved at stilisere og samtidig føre virkeligheden, det ægte miljø, de 'rigtige' mennesker ind i filmen, har bragt kunstarten fra det billige gøgl til et punkt, hvor den i dag i nogen grad føles som den mest vitale.*"

14. Nordisk has been recuperated by film scholars and historians, for instance, for its entrepreneurship (Thorsen 2009) and for its tableau aesthetic (Bordwell 2006). Engberg (1993) offers historical context for what she calls the company's "erotic melodrama," but no one has systematically analyzed melodrama at the studio.
15. In Danish, *"For at give sandheden renoncerede jeg på de 'forskønnende' midler."*
16. Dreyer was hardly a lone creative wolf at Nordisk. Work by Harriet Bloch and Robert Dinesen also displays the personal innovation of conscious stylists working within studio conventions.
17. Dreyer's interest in female suffering is well documented. When asked about "love" in *Gertrud* (1968), he responded modestly (in English) that although it may not have been intentional, he has "always been attracted to people's sufferings (*sic*) and particularly woman's suffering." (This interview is available online at http://www.mastersofcinema.org/dreyer/resources.htm.)
18. As Linda Williams (2001) writes, "sympathy for another grounded in the manifestation of that person's suffering is arguably a key feature of all melodrama" (16).
19. Fischer-Lichte (2008) redefines performance in terms of its phenomenology rather than hermeneutics, drawing a sharp distinction between film and performance; filming or otherwise recording performance negates it as performance.
20. As I have explored elsewhere, Dreyer's interest in extreme performance included traditions of mass spectacle such as the ritualized danger and beauty of the bullfight (Doxtater 2010).
21. Bodil Thomsen (2006) and David Bordwell (1981) both read *Jeanne d'Arc*'s naked physiognomy and close-ups as evidence that it is not melodrama. For Thomsen, the film becomes "real," haptic flesh. For Bordwell, the film's corporeality is trumped by psychology of an order supposedly incommensurate with melodrama. For Charles Affron (1982), the naturalism of the close-up is automatically incompatible with melodramatic type.
22. In Danish, *"Til rollen som Jeanne d'Arc havde Dreyer valgt varieteskuespillerinden Marie Falconetti, der befriet for sminke netop var i stand til at vise det nøgne, sjælfulde ansigt, som Dreyer ønskede."*
23. *Jeanne d'Arc*'s art cinema status has meant that the traditionally melodramatic aspects of its narrative (persecuted innocence and a virtuously suffering victim protagonist) have been recuperated as tragedy.
24. As Neergaard (1940, 50) relates the encounter, Dreyer intuited (*anede*) that Falconetti had experienced true adversity and suffering.
25. In Danish, *"at afklæde Jeanne d'Arc for hendes Glories og Helgenskrud og finde ind til selve det lille Kvindemenneske, der led Døden paa Baalet for sin Tros skyld."*
26. In French, *"à la lecture nous découvrons Jeanne telle qu'elle était—non pas avec casque et cuirasse—mais simple et humaine."*
27. See Fischer-Lichte (2008, 11–23) for a discussion of harm in work by Marina Abramović.
28. Nordisk achieved such spectacle through actual tightrope acts or Emilie Sannom's jumps from airplanes.
29. My thanks to SOCE for this formulation and for its enduring support. Thanks also to the Danish Film Institute for generously facilitating my research, and to Mark Sandberg and Linda Williams for feedback on early iterations of this work.

PART II
Cultural and Aesthetic Debates

12

"Tales of Sound and Fury..." or, The Elephant of Melodrama

LINDA WILLIAMS

In a 1972 foundational essay on film melodrama, Thomas Elsaesser (1991) observed that "in the Hollywood melodrama characters made for operettas play out the tragedies of mankind" (89). Elsaesser was writing about the 1950s *genre* of family melodrama by pointing to the pathos of mediocre human beings "trying to live up to an exalted vision of man but instead living out the impossible contradictions that have turned the American dream into its proverbial nightmare" (89). From his vantage point of the early seventies, Elsaesser was excited to describe a group of films that explored the way "melos is given to drama by means of lighting, montage, visual rhythm, décor, style of acting, [and] music" (78). His analysis helped ignite a whole generation of budding film scholars, myself included, who discovered in these films all the condensations, displacements, and sublimations of emotions that seemed "excessive" to a more "classical" Hollywood cinema.

Four years later Peter Brooks (1976) made a more sweeping claim for melodrama as a pervasive mode of modern culture. His groundbreaking book, *The Melodramatic Imagination: Balzac, Henry James, Melodrama, and the Mode of Excess*, enlarged the vision of melodrama, not as the failed tragedy of inadequate humans but as an imaginative mode and specific theater genre (15). In Brooks, melodrama was the quintessential response to a modernity that had "lost" the Sacred and could no longer produce tragedy. But in his case, melodrama was also viewed as a quest for a hidden moral legibility now "occulted" (4–5) in the modern, post-Sacred era. In the absence of a moral and social order linked to the Sacred, and in the presence of a private and domestic sphere that had increasingly become the entire realm of personal significance, a theatrical form of sensation developed that expressed "the domain of operative spiritual values which is both indicated within and masked by the surface of reality" (50).

For Brooks, the origins of modernity are located in the French Revolution and its dissolution of an organic and hierarchically cohesive society that invalidated the classical literary forms—tragedy, comedy of manners—and marked the beginning of an age of melodrama (15). To Brooks, melodrama and the Gothic novel are two popular early romantic forms that nourished one another. One offered a sentimental virtue, the other a purgative terror (18). Both have endured, outliving many other romantic forms. Though Brooks did not trace the evolution of melodrama into film, it was through his book that it became possible to understand the function of melodrama in an age of mass culture as well as to escape the narrow sense of it as simply a genre.

Elsaesser and Brooks have been the most influential pioneers of melodrama study for students of film and media. Brooks was interested in the logic of the abrupt post-Revolutionary shift to melodrama and then its "submerged" continuation in the realist novels of Balzac and Henry James, while Elsaesser explored a more evenly distributed "melodramatic imagination" across Western popular culture since the eighteenth century.[1] A great many studies have since extended the understanding of melodrama across many media in a wide range of directions. Nevertheless, in the wake of these two founding works, one pointing to melodrama as an excessive film genre responding to the senselessness of modern life ("tales of sound and fury . . . signifying nothing"), the other pointing to melodrama as a quintessentially modern worldview, the term *melodrama* has not been able to shake loose—to *unbind* itself—from the notion of stylistic excess and marginality.

But if we jump to a nearby field, where the grass can often seem greener, consider the words of drama historian Matthew Buckley (2012), who writes that melodrama has

> suffused the entire range of dramatic sub-genres and genres, migrated into other narrative modes, and adapted seamlessly to new media. Melodrama in this expanded, modal sense—as a distinctive 'drama of excess' organized around a strikingly formulaic set of affective techniques and conventions—appeared to dominate both the history of the Victorian stage and that of Hollywood cinema as well as of TV and to have played not a subordinate but a central role in modern narratives of all sorts, including those, like the realist novel or documentary film that were traditionally seen as having marked melodrama's demise. (429–30)

I applaud the leap that drama historian Buckley has made to the near ubiquity of melodrama in popular culture, and I naturally cheer that he goes on to validate it with my own idea that melodrama is what Henry James (1941), speaking of *Uncle Tom's Cabin* (novel and plays), called a "leaping fish"—a mode whose adaptive dynamism, transformational variation, and intermedia movement seems able to leap almost anywhere, even if it also "continually eludes our grasp" (156–60). However, I'm acutely aware that the field of film and media studies has not accepted this leap. Rather, film scholars have established a near consensus that the norm of Hollywood cinema should be called the "Classical Hollywood Cinema," with melodrama as a special, sometimes even subversive, genre that violates the norms of the "classical." I agree with Buckley about the prevalence of melodrama in mass media of all sorts, but I hope to convince the field of film and media of the modernity, pertinence, and pervasiveness of forms of melodrama. I furthermore want to challenge the assumption, held by many—Ben Singer, as well as Brooks and Elsaeser—that melodrama's excesses challenge the "classical." Is melodrama, as it first emerged and as we know it today, really so excessive?

EXCESS COMPARED TO WHAT? "CLASSICALITY" AS A CATEGORY IN FILM AND MEDIA STUDY

For Elsaesser and Brooks, a popular "nonclassical" form of drama—called melodrama—replaced an earlier classical theater and fiction. Most significant, it replaced tragedy, which had been used to signal a kind of artistic perfection and stability (whether in fifth-century Athens or seventeenth-century neoclassical France). Melodrama's seeming decline from neo-classical French drama needed explaining, because it was neither a "well-made" play nor possessed of the stability of the classical. Peter Brooks's characterization of melodrama as a new theatrical "mode of excess" seemed to sum it up. Historically, the perceived excess of melodrama has been measured against, and seen to follow upon, the loss of classical harmony and proportion.

Yet when we turn to the study of the emergence of the cinema as a new art form, a strange reversal occurs. Melodrama, which every Western theater historian knows *followed* the neoclassical theater, is treated in cinema studies as if it preexisted the emergence of what came to be called the "classical" cinema. It is as if melodrama were the original (theatrical) sin of which an emerging narrative cinema purged itself to gain the stability and art status of the "classical." Having purged itself, this Hollywood cinema has been able, at least according to its most influential scholars, to continue indefinitely.[2] It is as if the new art form did not want to show its indebtedness to the older theatrical one and thus needed to invent its own sense of the classical maturity of its art borrowed from notions of art history and literature. Instead of tracing the evolving forms of melodrama, and melodrama's own achievements of stability and endurance, cinema studies tried to rid itself of a seemingly "archaic" form. Thus the so-called classical cinema has seemed to ban one of the central forces of its very modernity to the periphery of its field, reducing it to a mere genre. Many scholars have acknowledged this dilemma, but they have not been willing to reconsider the whole catastrophe of what we do when we call the mainstream norm of cinema "classical."[3]

The adjective "classic" or *classical* applied to a work of art has long designated work of the highest quality or class. It might also be what is taught in a class, and perhaps not surprisingly the term's popularity roughly coincided with the rise of film studies in the classroom. In its noun form, a classic is something that by definition has endured through time to the point of seeming eternal. However, almost anything can seem to arrive at a moment of classical perfection. There is thus an inherent paradox in the very idea of the classic that Frank Kermode (1983), in his classic study, *The Classic*, calls the tension between permanence and change. In an era of increasingly relative values and divided subjectivities, we may be disinclined to think in terms of classics—the very notion can seem retrograde, anachronistic, unmodern, and, as Miriam Hansen (2000) once noted, an odd term to apply to a medium so recent as film (337).

In the mid-eighteenth century, Johann Joachim Winkelmann contributed to the rise of German neoclassicism by defining ancient Greek sculptures as having a "noble simplicity and a quiet grandeur" in their stance and expression. He believed that the only way his own generation could become great would be to imitate these Grecian qualities. He singled out Greek statuary as having a simplicity and humanity that earlier cultures did not have.

It was in specifying how classical Greek sculpture differed from the archaic that Winkelmann originated many of the terms used to define the classical in visual arts: terms such as natural, lifelike, realistic. Unlike the archaic, the classical style was close to nature, objective (oriented toward objects, not subjective feelings), with a harmony of proportion (but not mechanical regularity and absolute symmetry). These qualities are repeated over and over in formulations of the classical, in art, poetry, and fiction. And, of course, these are qualities posited in Bordwell, Staiger, and Thompson's encyclopedic 1985 tome, *The Classical Hollywood Cinema: Film Style and Mode of Production to 1960*. The appropriation of the term *classical* has as its root the idea of a brief harmony of measure and fullness that comes between an earlier archaic rigidity and a later baroque busyness wherein the "classical" loses its dominance.

Although the history of Hollywood cinema, as understood by Bordwell, Staiger, and Thompson, does not exactly correspond to this pattern—especially to the notion of a *short-lived* harmony of the classical because, at least for Bordwell, the classical Hollywood style has persisted from 1917 to the present—it has nevertheless been forced into something like this mold, with early cinema acting the part of the archaic past and so-called classical cinema enjoying an extraordinarily long-lived run, followed perhaps by a contested-postclassical cinema that is denied by Bordwell and Thompson but argued by some to be dominant today.[4]

However, we might ask why this model of cinema's style of storytelling has been constructed according to the aesthetic standards of a premodern era? The fact that from its very first exhibitions the cinématographe appeared to be the exemplification of the modern in its larger than life, sensational moving images means that much of what was put into early cinema was already formed by a popularized and recognizable melodramatic sensibility of music (almost always present in silent film) and drama (inherited from the melodramatic stage of sensation and spectacular effects). Rick Altman (1989), Ben Singer (2001), Ben Brewster and Lea Jacobs (1997), not to mention the earlier Nicholas Vardac (1949), have all shown, one way or another, that many of cinema's first story films were short, wordless adaptations of sensational preexisting stage melodramas, not the (classical) novels they often seemed derived from (see Altman 1989, 321–55).

Needing an archaic "before" the classical, and finding the archaic period of early cinema entirely too brief, Bordwell, Staiger, and Thompson (1985) cast the stage melodrama as the longer archaic "before" and the so-called "classical cinema" as the more modern "after." When cinema was seen to have achieved a smooth-functioning form of narrative, they called it the invisible classical style, as if the previous century's domination by stage melodrama was the long archaic period that cinema did not really have. The result has been to freeze the very idea of melodrama as that which could not itself "mature and ripen" but which could only, through its excesses, impede or subvert the maturity and realism of the classical.

Another problem of attributing the classical to cinema can be gleaned from the well-known story of Coca-Cola's flirtation with this term. "Classic Coke" was invented in 1985, the same year that *The Classical Hollywood Cinema, Film Style and Mode of Production* was published. Prompted by encroachments in sales from rival Pepsi, Coke had previously introduced a slightly new formula for its syrup and called it New Coke. However, the company didn't bargain on the attachment of Coke drinkers to the old formula, or at least to the old name. Although blind taste tests showed that most people actually preferred the new Coke to both the old Coke and Pepsi, these consumers didn't want to lose the *idea* of a traditional Coke. So the company marketed a variation on the old formula, which they called Coca-Cola Classic, thus reverting to a sense of the eternal value of Coke. If New Coke implied that there had been something wrong with the old, Classic Coke seemed to rectify that impression. The introduction of the term *classic* did not change much in the Coke product, but for a short time it lent a patina of age that counteracted the adverse reaction to new Coke. With time, however, Coca-Cola quietly dropped the name Classic and reverted to plain old Coke.

And this is what I propose the field of film studies do. Quietly drop the term *classical* and deal with what has actually persisted: the heritage of melodrama as a function of multiple styles eliciting different qualities and kinds of emotions—a melodrama that was itself an adaptation to modernity.

"CLASSICAL" HOLLYWOOD CINEMA: A FORGOTTEN HISTORY OF SCARE QUOTES

Hardly anyone spoke of a "classical" cinema during what many agree was its heyday.[5] The vast majority of early observers, especially the classically inclined French, admired the energy, speed, and dynamism of the cinema—attributes associated with modernity that seemed in direct opposition to what they observed in the classicism of art and drama. Abel Gance, D. W. Griffith, and even Carl Theodor Dryer (see chapter 11) were obvious masters of melodrama and were not ashamed of the term. What, then, is behind the history of the rise, fall, and rise again of the term *classical*?

Melodrama was the most common term for popular film until André Bazin used the term *classical* in his famous "L'Évolution du langage Cinématographique." But Bazin referred to the American and French sound cinemas of the 1930s as classical. He described a "well-balanced stage of maturity" attained by that cinema in an array of genres. And it is significant that Bazin named only genre films that had in previous criticism been described as subcategories of melodrama. These comprised comedies (*Mr. Smith Goes to Washington*), burlesques (Marx Bros.), dance and vaudeville films (Astaire/Rogers), crime and gangster films (*Scarface*), psychological and social dramas (*Back Street, Jezebel*—films that would much later be called woman's films), horror films (*Doctor Jekyll and Mr. Hyde*), and westerns (*Stagecoach*). As a complement to this American classicism, Bazin also cited the maturity of French film in its trend toward either "somber" or "poetic" realism. American cinema with its many genres, the French with its poetic realism offered signs to Bazin that the sound film, prior to World War II, had reached a maturity of both content and form.

This is how Bazin (2005) put it in Hugh Gray's English translation: "One has the feeling that in them an art has found its perfect balance, its ideal form of expression." Such films, he added, comprise "all the characteristics of the ripeness of a classical art" (29). Bazin's term has been deployed to justify renaming Hollywood cinema *in toto* as "classical"—from multiple types of melodrama to a more "mature" classicism. Unrepresented in this translation, however, are the scare quotes Bazin (2003) originally placed around the word: *"Bref, tous les caractères de la plenitude d'un art 'classique'"* (137). With these quotation marks Bazin acknowledged the very audacity of calling "classical" a medium so modern and so obviously grounded in such exclusively generic variants of melodrama, themselves the quintessence of popular modern entertainment.

In the decades following Bazin, as the term *classical* was "transvalued"—as Miriam Hansen (2000) so well put it—from a seemingly desirable maturity to a (sinister) ideological hegemony, these scare quotes would be entirely lost. And it was in this period of 1970s apparatus theory that the term *classical*—now a term of abuse, meaning without antihegemonic credentials—really stuck.

One example of this "transvaluation" can be found in the early pages of *The Imaginary Signifier*, in which Christian Metz (1982) writes of a "play of presence-absence, which André Bazin already foresaw in his notion of 'classical editing'" (40). Twenty pages later, however, the term is unmarked by scare quotes in the phrase: "This is the origin in particular of that 'recipe' of the classical cinema" (63). By the late seventies classical, again without scare quotes, would already be ensconced as a term to describe a mainstream, "normalized" Hollywood cinema that most critics had come to oppose rather than, like Bazin, to value. Its very harmony and simplicity was viewed as the process by which *discours* was transformed into *histoire*, and subjects of viewing were "sutured" into the text, unaware of how insidious visual pleasures were luring them into the acceptance of dominant ideology.

If the late 1970s turn against Bazin, also seemed to be a turn against the value of all that "ripeness and maturity," the subsequent rehabilitation of Bazin—whose idea of the classical is quoted as support at the very beginning of Bordwell, Staiger, and Thompson's 1985 book—left the field with a supposedly more neutral, value-free, and scientific observation of the classical's features. Thus, in the same year that Classic Coke was (re)born, Bordwell, in part one of the book wrote: "the principles which Hollywood claims as its own rely on notions of decorum, proportion, formal harmony, respect for tradition, mimesis, self-effacing craftsmanship and cool control of the perceiver's response—cannons which critics in any medium usually call 'classical'" (3).

Of course, Bordwell, like everyone else, dropped his own use of scare quotes three pages later in this 506-page book and never looked back. The term has been understood as signaling a mainstream popular cinema against which more challenging avant-garde, or art cinemas, could be opposed. Yet it is important to recognize how calcified became this once entirely provisional, scare-quoted term, which Bazin used to describe only a decade-long period of stability in film art before the challenge of *Citizen Kane* and neorealism in the 1940s. Why do so many of us keep on using it, when better alternatives have been proposed, either in the more general term "mainstream," or in Miriam Hansen's (2000) more pointed "vernacular modernism"? This last option is worth considering further.

Though Hansen offers an excellent critique of the flaws in the anachronistic idea of a "classical" cinema that is somehow also modern, she stops short of banishing the term from film studies. Rather, she reconciles herself to it by urging us to consider it not as a hard-wired universalist model for "classical" storytelling but as a metaphor for a new global sensory vernacular produced by the rise of Hollywood, for which slapstick is a paradigm. Although Hansen naturally wants the rise of Hollywood to correspond to the production of this new and more modern organization of the senses, she misses the fact that before the rise of cinema, popular mass-produced serialized melodramatic fiction and popular mass-produced stage melodrama (and even some popular mass-produced stage melodrama serials, see Airiess chapter 4) were already realizing the kind of shift in the modern sensorium that was continued by cinema's solidification under the supposed regime of the "classical" but which was very often a new, more cinematic form of melodrama.

Ben Singer's 2001 book, *Melodrama and Modernity*, had already made this argument about theatrical melodrama. But Hansen could not hear it because, as is evident in her two articles on vernacular modernism, she, like many other film scholars, already sees melodrama as a singular film genre, more in line with films of female suffering than as a broader force orchestrating the adjustment to the shocks and transitions of the modern. Thus, although she allows that certain *genres*—the musical, horror, *melodrama*—share with slapstick the production of a new sensory modern culture, she does not see that the very orchestration of feelings and sensations considered excessive in relation to "classical" norms were actually in the process of *becoming* the new norm. Reconnecting film melodrama with its nineteenth-century past enables us to see that, in its broadest sense, melodrama constitutes the ur-mode of popular (vernacular) modernism rather than a narrow genre; that on the stage it was already becoming the sensationalist mode par excellence; and that even before the invention of cinema, stage melodrama was already what Hannah Airriess (chapter 4) calls "an exemplary practice of vernacular modernism." As a mode that reflects upon modernity, a mode that "leaps" from one medium to another, and that translates from one culture to another, melodrama was already becoming a global vernacular modernism before the rise of film; it simply increased under the growing hegemony of Hollywood and many othe transmedial and transnational forms.

Film scholars need to learn that modernity, however defined, does not always coincide neatly with their chosen medium of study. Melodrama's modernity was already becoming global even before it moved into film. This modernity could mean, as Hansen (2000) notes of cinema's vernacular modernism, "many different things to different people and publics, both at home and abroad" (341). Similarly, while still on the New York stage, a play such as Boucicault's *The Poor of New York* could travel to Paris and be given an entirely different ending as *The Poor of Paris*, just as, later, Hollywood films in the sound era could be made for export with adjusted endings. Though it is tempting to make cinema itself the all-important vector of vernacular modernism, it was really melodrama—long before the term "classical" was imposed upon its cinematic manifestations—that was the true global matrix for the experience of modernity.

At the very least, then, the idea of a "classical" Hollywood cinema deserves to be treated as provisional. In imitation of David Bordwell's naming the radical changes claimed by many scholars to have been brought about by modernity the "modernity thesis," I propose that we call these claims about classical cinema the "classicality thesis."[6] And to this dubious thesis I would like to propose an antithesis: the elephant of melodrama.

THE ELEPHANT OF MELODRAMA

Melodrama is like the blind man and the elephant: it all depends on what part of the animal you first touch. In the 1970s, Thomas Elsaesser (1972) and Peter Brooks (1976), feeling the trunk, could only understand the "excess" of an exceedingly long nose. Feminists in the early and mid-1980s, feeling the wetness of the eyes, saw only the pathos of the woman's film (Kaplan 1983, 1985; Doane 1987; Mulvey 1989; Williams 1984). David Bordwell, Janet Staiger, and Kristen Thompson (1985) in the 1980s, feeling the wrinkles of the skin, discovered the archaic relic of the stage melodrama hardening into one of a few recalcitrant genres, and opposed to the "classical." Rick Altman (1989), writing at the end of the decade, felt the same wrinkles and called them archaisms "embedded" within more recent overlays of classical unity and efficient linear narrative. Tom Gunning (1986, 1989), smelling the sawdust of the circus attractions, sensed tamed attractions that were exceptions to a more "classical" norm. More recently, at the turn of the millennium, Ben Singer (2001), feeling the sparks of electricity with which Topsy—the supposedly disobedient but actually harassed Barnum elephant—was electrocuted, felt the energy of a sensational modernity at the low end of the cultural spectrum. At roughly this same time, I too groped and sensed the Elephant's African heritage and saw in it the quintessential American black and white melodrama of race (Williams 2001).

What all of us missed, with the single exception of Christine Gledhill's mapping of an entire "melodramatic field" in her introduction to *Home Is Where the Heart Is*, was the enormous size and variety of the entire animal. Gledhill (1987) was the only one in the 1980s and 1990s to perceive the elephant in the room and to name it melodrama:

> Melodrama exists as a cross-cultural form with a complex, international, and well over two-hundred-year history. The term denotes a fictional or theatrical kind, a specific cinematic genre or a pervasive mode across popular culture. As a mode melodrama both overlaps and competes with realism and tragedy, maintaining complex historical relations with them. It refers not only to a type of aesthetic practice but to a way of viewing the world. (1)

Gledhill saw that melodrama was more various than any single or even connected genre (whether woman's films and family melodramas or blood and thunder action). She also asked how tenable it is to construct melodrama in a critical, disruptive relationship to the classic, realist narrative text (13). Following Martha Vicinus and David Grimsted, she noted that melodrama does not so much confront how things are but asserts how they *ought* to be (16). Following Gledhill's lead, it is clear that as long as we think narrowly, and only in terms of the typical traits of genres, melodrama as a whole will only be partially glimpsed. However, the minute we begin to think of it as something larger and much longer lived, it begins to make more sense. This does not mean that melodrama is the only mode at work in cinema, just that most familiar genres often build upon the backbone of melodrama.

MELODRAMA AND JUSTICE

David Bordwell (1985) quotes Frank Borzage from 1922: "Today in the pictures we have the old melodramatic situations fitted out decently with true characterizations" (14). Notice that Borzage does not say that the true characterizations negate the old melodramatic situations; rather, the (always relative) "truth" of the more realistic characterizations contribute to the development of new kinds of melodrama. Bordwell, however, treats Borzage's statement as a judgment that old melodrama is negated by new classicism. Indeed, whenever Bordwell acknowledges the existence of melodrama, he finds its inherent lack of realism to be *generically* motivated by the fact that it is melodrama—perennially considered a holdover from the old, never a forward-looking development of the new.[7] Yet as Borzage plainly insists, melodrama grows and adapts in tension with new norms of what seems, or *feels*, true. To pose the problem in what may seem like melodramatic terms: melodrama's developing virtues go unrecognized in the dominant model of the "classical."

Film and media studies have readily recognized melodrama as a genre but have dubbed "the classical" the more pervasive and dominant form from which occasional genres—usually melodrama and film noir—deviate. In an era when cinema was gaining legitimacy as an art form and later as a legitimate field of study, melodrama became the scapegoat—the place where everything about cinema that seemed illegitimate, old-fashioned, and overwrought was lumped—unless, of course, it was ironically intended.

Yet we speak intelligently enough of modes of realism, or modes of comedy when we find them in drama, literature, film, television, or video games. We are not so naïve as to believe that realism as a mode does not work across and within many genres. Realism, as a mode, is broader than genre. By the same token, we should also speak of modes of melodrama that are broader than any genre. All of the literary genres—novel, non-nonfiction, tragedy, comedy—can exist in the mode of realism, just as all of the literary genres and all of the multifarious film genres—(musicals, gangster dramas, westerns, and so forth) can so exist as well. But what we too often forget is that any literary or filmic genre can *also, and at the same time*, exist in a mode of melodrama. The novel may be prone to operate in a realist mode, but modes of realism themselves change and a given novel might operate in both a mode of realism *and* a mode of melodrama. There are melodramas that emphasize pathos and melodramas that emphasize action, there are melodramas of repression and sublimation—all the genres that Bazin once praised for their "classical ripeness" exist in the mode of melodrama. There are also camp melodramas (Almodóvar) that still do the work of melodrama, the many varieties of Bollywood melodrama, and so on and so on . . .

Perhaps the real problem with thinking about melodrama as a mode with a range of specific genres is the concept, present in Peter Brooks's subtitle, of melodrama as "the mode of excess." This is where we have all gone wrong: the elephant is not a sign of excess but of expansiveness, many facets and pervasiveness. We might certainly argue that a given work is excessively comic (where does it really stand?) or too realistic (rubbing our noses in death or bodily functions), but we would not argue that comedy or realism are themselves inherently excessive. Why do so with melodrama? The reason, I believe, has to do with the tendency to view melodrama as old and regressive rather as an evolving medium that is still relatively new.

The "classicality thesis" has been popular because it has provided film teachers with an eminently respectable pedagogy, wedded to ideas of continuity, coherent space/time, and causality that certainly did emerge from the greater chaos and nonnarrative "attractions" of early cinema. But these stylistic qualities can carry the mode of melodrama every bit as well as they can carry the mode of realism or comedy. In the grand progression out of episodic attractions, to which the tableaux and spectacles of stage melodrama were once attached, it may once have been tempting to view Hollywood narrative as having aligned itself with a preexisting "classicality" translated into cinematic terms. But melodrama itself has learned to adhere to more coherent motivations and more complex psychologies; it should not be defined by qualities that are the opposite of the "well-made play." Ill-made plays can become better made and yet still do the work of melodrama; and it is to the nature of that evolving work that we must finally turn.

I venture to argue that the primary work of melodrama—in contrast to the work of the "classical" as in, say, classical tragedy—has fundamentally been that of seeking a better justice. Enlightenment values of freedom, equality, and justice, however perverted and corrupted, are most frequently invoked in melodramas of all sorts, as might be expected by a mode of drama related, as Peter Brooks argues, to the principles of the French Revolution. But even if melodrama can be seen forming throughout the eighteenth century in the music-drama of Rousseau, the *drame bourgeois* of Diderot, or the *sturm und drang* of Schiller, it is clear that emerging Western democratic values desiring a better justice for all supplant the more stoical and regressive political values of classical and neoclassical tragedy's reconciliation with harsh fate. Tragedy, as Robert Heilman (1968) writes, is not really about the plague in Thebes or any truly social problems (97). It is about fates that cannot be altered. Melodrama, on the other hand, modernizes drama by confronting new and seemingly intractable social problems, to the melodramatic end of recognizing virtue and in that act recognizing an ideal of social justice unimaginable in tragedy. Melodrama is the form by which timely social problems and controversies can be addressed. As Christine Gledhill saw, it is not opposed to what we recognize as realism. Rather, it enlists realism to generate outrage against realities that could and, to its creators, should be changed. Melodrama feeds upon the problem of these realities—the very injustice of them. To this extent, much melodrama is allied with dreams of revolution or at least the kind of change that might rectify the social injuries they diagnose.

The Wire (2002–2008), for example, is a contemporary serial television melodrama that offers the most thoroughgoing critique of neoliberal capitalism at every level of American society. Its creator, David Simon, has worked hard to convince viewers that it is an American version of Greek tragedy. In fact, it is an excellent serial melodrama (see Williams 2014). Melodrama has tended to be on the side of the oppressed, and thus, seemingly on the side of social change, even revolution. However, perceptions of justice and injustice will always be relative. It might be the injustice of slavery in one melodrama (*Uncle Tom's Cabin*), the injustice commited by former slaves in another (*The Birth of a Nation*) or, in yet another, the pathetic life of a drug addict and criminal informant (*The Wire*).

If we are not to fix it at some moment of its past history, we must consider melodrama's protean qualities even as we try to isolate some of them for scrutiny. Neither excessive music nor the defeat of evil by good is essential to melodrama. What is essential, I contend, is the dramatic *recognition* of good and evil and, in that recognition, at least the hope that justice might be done.

If the innovation of adding melos to underscore spoken drama once shook up and enhanced the expected emotional power of the melodramatic stage vis-à-vis the tragic stage, this does not mean that turning down the sound or the rhetoric makes realism. Rather, melodrama's conventions have continued to grow and change. Within thirty years of its initial sensation, as Matthew Buckley (2009) has shown, "when its popularity made it into a dominant form, melodrama had become Exhibit A in the degenerate decline of the drama" (176). Not surprisingly, many who continued to do melodrama did not call it so by name. However, as Buckley puts it, "no longer exiled from cultural history, melodrama seems now central to it, an essential thread in the warp and weave of global modernity" (176).

Consider the clichés of the contemporary blockbuster action film. These films are rarely called melodramas—more frequently they are named by their popular genres: action, adventure, thriller, etc.—but they are unmistakably structured in the mold of blood and thunder melodramas. It is typical in contemporary blockbuster films for action heroes to be recognized not only by their heroic actions but first and foremost by their suffering of some outrage to which they are not yet able to respond. The hero's suffering seems to earn him the moral right later to kill the enemy with impunity. Indeed, the pathos of the suffering victim turned righteous action hero is the curious and often suspect alchemy of much of contemporary melodrama's cultural power. To suffer and to be injured is, according to a certain Judeo-Christian framework that Nietzsche abhorred, to be empowered. The very injury that makes me see the evil in my injurer and the good in myself is the basis of a fundamentally resentful form of moralism—a Nietzschean *ressentiment*—at the heart of much melodrama (see Anker 2014).

It is the protean leaping fish of melodrama—as a mode working in relation to the other modes of realism, comedy, and romance and as the skeleton of all but the most nonnarrative forms of comedy—that emerged triumphant in Anglo-European modernity. It is melodrama that replaced the rules and harmony and unities of the ancient Greek or neoclassical French stage with large quantities of pathos and action in the service of discovering where goodness and justice lie. But if we approach melodrama only in terms of its clichéd, "old-fashioned" aspects—pounding music, victims tied to railroad tracks, villains twirling mustaches, rescues that happen in the nick of time—or if we look for it only in the familiar sentiments of the "woman's film and soaps" or, finally, if we find it only in the more recent conventions of action films, with victims locked in nuclear-armed trucks hurtling to destruction, then we may fail to see its more mutable contemporary forms and protean nature. Melodrama renews and modernizes itself by adapting the most recent awareness of social problems and failures of justice to melodramatic ends.

In American melodrama, the question of the viability of the American dream of liberal justice and opportunity for all is still at issue, but not because characters fail to live up to the "tragedies of humankind" (Elsaesser 1991, 89). The melodramatic experience is not a degraded, modern version of tragedy; nor must we think of it as the failure of inadequate or mediocre humans to play out tragedy. Rather, just as there are great tragedies, there are great melodramas, especially now that, with long-form television serialization, no single catastrophe or "happy end" need mark its conclusion. In *On The Wire* (2014), I have endeavored to show how television serial melodrama, at least in this one instance, has imagined a new kind of institutional as well as personal melodrama that no longer rests on the self-righteousness produced by one individual's personal injury but on the capability of institutions to do good or evil.

If, as I have been arguing, the mode of melodrama still holds us in its grip, we do well to recognize it, not only when it is familiar "over the top," overly coincidental "bad" drama but also, and perhaps especially, when it is "good." It is not "a tale told by an idiot." It signifies *something* much more in tune with who we are as a culture than the "classicality" thesis ever could—for better *and* for worse.

I end this chapter with a quiz. Before glancing at my final note, see if you can answer this question. Which famous filmmaker wrote the following?

> In real life, to be called 'melodramatic' is to be criticized. The term suggests behavior which is hysterical and exaggerated. [But melodrama] is the backbone and lifeblood of the cinema.... My own greatest desire is for realism. Therefore I employ what is called melodrama ... for all my thinking has led me to the conclusion that there [i.e., through melodrama] is the only road to screen realism that will still be entertainment.[8]

If we fail to recognize the author, perhaps we now need to rethink the way we categorize certain auteurs by genre and reformulate their expertise in the mode of melodrama.

NOTES

1. A much earlier work that also centers on the contrast between tragedy and melodrama is Robert Heilman's *Tragedy and Melodrama: Versions of Experience* (1968). Here, too, it is the contrast with tragedy that is central, although Heilman eschews any historical priority of one over the other.
2. Against notions of the "postclassical," both David Bordwell and Kristen Thompson have continued to argue that the classical American cinema endures. Thompson's *Storytelling in the New Hollywood* (1999) argues that narrative principles remain the same as in the 1930s and 1940s, and Bordwell's *The Way Hollywood Tells It* (2006) examines some new norms but claims they are mere variants of the older ones.
3. See Rick Altman (1989) and Miriam Hansen (2000). I have acknowledged the dilemma in a previous article, "Melodrama Revised" (1998) and in my book *Playing the Race Card* (2001). I can't say I have changed a lot of minds. Here, I take a different tack by addressing what I see as the problem of the "classical" in film.
4. See, for example, Angela Ndalianis's argument (2005) that the "postclassical" cinema and other forms of sensational "special effects" are a new form of the baroque.
5. Bordwell, Staiger, and Thompson (1985) mention Bardeche and Brassillac's exceptional reference to the classic period of the silent cinema; Renoir also used the term in 1926 to describe both Chaplin and Lubitsch.
6. See Bordwell's (1997) argument against this "modernity thesis" (136–49) and Ben Singer's (2001) answer (9–11, 101–30).
7. For example, Bordwell (1985) writes: "The melodrama genre often flouts causal logic and relies shamelessly upon coincidence." In other words, melodrama is a specific genre and, as such, "each genre creates its own rules" (20). Thus, as Bordwell puts it, genres have their own logic that is compatible with psychological causality or goal-orientation: the westerner seeks revenge, the gangster power and success, the chorus girl the big break. But as we can see, there is no single generic motivation to define melodrama.
8. Alfred Hitchcock in 1937 ("Why I Make Melodramas" in Gottlieb 2015, 76–78).

13

Repositioning Excess

Romantic Melodrama's Journey from Hollywood to China

PANPAN YANG

The truth lies not in one dream but in many.
—Arabian Nights *(Pier Paolo Pasolini, 1974)*

MELODRAMA AT THE CROSSROADS OF CULTURES

A notoriously slippery term, "melodrama" is opening new debates as it moves beyond a narrowly defined genre and is articulated as both genre and modality within a wider sociocultural embrace. The notion of modality "defines a specific mode of aesthetic articulation adaptable across a range of genre, across decades, and across national cultures" (Gledhill 2000, 229). When it is claimed that melodrama has traveled across national boundaries, studies of melodrama inevitably engage in cross-cultural analysis, which Kaplan (2006) suggests is always "fraught with dangers," if full of potential (151).

Many scholars have noted that there are no synonyms for melodrama in Chinese. Is melodrama a specifically Western form, or can it be found in Chinese dramatic and cinematic forms? Despite the claims made for Chinese melodrama in Anglophone academia (see Dissanayake 1993; Berry and Farquhar 2006; Zhang 2012; Ma 2015), aesthetic interrogations of melodrama have rarely been pursued in a cross-cultural context. Due to the untranslatability of the word *melodrama* and of related Western critical terms such as Peter Brooks's frequently quoted "moral occult" (1976, 20), Chinese scholarship has discussed melodrama using very different vocabularies and paradigms. What happens when we put the two bodies of knowledge into conversation?

In this chapter I offer a close-up on melodrama at the crossroads of two cultures, investigating how the melodramatic imagination of Hollywood film, particularly in its romantic streak, was woven into local film and theater practices in China in the 1930s and 1940s. Starting with the Chinese reception and remakes of *Gone with the Wind* (Fleming, 1939), I demonstrate the existence and evolving forms of melodrama in China, arguing that the expression "a beauty at a turbulent time"(*Luanshi Jiaren*)—the Chinese title of *Gone with the Wind*—sums up key aspects of all the exemplary romantic melodramas discussed here. My central concern, however, lies in the points where history and theory intertwine. How can the transnational encounters of Hollywood, and what I would like to call Chinese melodrama, shift the valence of critical concepts in a cross-cultural context, especially with regard to the notion of "excess"? If, as several authors in this volume argue, melodrama is intimately connected to the global processes of modernization, can we gain a better understanding of melodrama as an essential thread in the warp and weave of global modernity by foregrounding parallel or alternative forms of the melodramatic imagination in a non-Western context?

HOLLYWOOD DREAM IN THE ORPHAN ISLAND

From November 12, 1937 to December 8, 1941—the so-called Orphan Island Era [*Gudao Shiqi*] in Chinese film history, Shanghai was divided into three areas with different governments: the International Settlement, the French Concession, and the Chinese Municipality. The Japanese controlled the Chinese Municipality during this period, but the International Settlement and the French Concession remained exempt from Japanese rule and were, ironically, called "the free zone." Circled by the Japanese army, the free zone looked just like an "orphan island" in the sea of Japanese-occupied territory. The appellation Orphan Island Era therefore offers a topographical and political account of the city of Shanghai at a turbulent historical moment.

During the Orphan Island Era, Hollywood movies flooded into the free zone, and the film industry enjoyed a sort of monstrous prosperity. Hollywood dreams became even more seductive because they offered a momentary escape for audiences who witnessed Japanese atrocities and experienced bodily and psychological traumas. Their indulgence in Hollywood fantasy seemed the best way to forget about pain and shame in this war-torn city. Writing on the Chinese reception of Hollywood film during the Orphan Island Era, Daoxin Li (2006) observes that the emergence and popularity of a large number of fan magazines, most of which had "Hollywood" in their titles, demonstrates Chinese audiences' increasing curiosity about Hollywood. For example, a long-lived Shanghai-based magazine, *Hollywood* [*Haolaiwu*] published 130 issues from 1938 to 1941. In 1940, two new magazines, *Hollywood Film News* [*Haolaiwu Yingxun*] and *Hollywood Scoop* [*Haolaiwu Texun*], came to the fore. Reading the titles of Hollywood films distributed in China during this period, Li notes that Chinese distributors had a preference for the romantic genre. Unlike historical biopics and westerns, which required understanding a specific cultural background, the romantic genre was thought to be easily understood by audiences all over the world because romantic love was considered universal to humanity. Therefore, the romantic genre was believed to be the most appropriate for distribution in an international market.

GONE WITH THE WIND IN CHINA

It is against this historical context that Scarlett O'Hara traveled to China. The 1939 Hollywood melodrama *Gone with the Wind* premiered at Shanghai's Roxy [Dahua] Theater, and then at Beijing's Zhenguang Theater in 1940. The price for one ticket was 8 yuan, which amounted to two bags of imported flour at that time (*Three-Six-Nine Pictorial* 4, no. 10 [1940]: 16). Despite the never-seen-before high price, it enjoyed a five-week run at Roxy Theater. The title of the film was first translated literally as *Sui Feng Er Qu*, but was later changed to *Luanshi Jiaren* ("A Beauty at a Turbulent Time") at the premiere. The expression "a beauty at a turbulent time," as Nicole Huang (2005) points out, foregrounded the image of a beautiful woman against the wartime backdrop, easily reminding Chinese audiences of *Romance of the Western Chamber* [*Xi Xiang Ji*], one of the most renowned Chinese dramatic works written by Wang Shifu (1250–1337 CE), or *The Sea of Regret* [*Hen Hai*], one of the highly successful romance novels written by Wu Jianren during the first decade of the twentieth century. Blending the foreign with the indigenous, the expression "a beauty at a turbulent time" contributed to the success of the film in the Chinese market.

The Shanghai premiere also saw the emergence of eye-catching double-page ads (figure 13.1) and countless photos of Vivien Leigh on film magazine covers (figure 13.2). Audiences could also find out where to purchase Vivien Leigh photos "6 cents for one photo. Please come to Mingxing Photo Company, No. 131, Shanghai Museum Road" (*Hollywood* 81 [1940]: 1). This film attained unprecedented

Figure 13.1 Double-page ad for "Five-color Film *Gone with the Wind* in *Hollywood* (*Hao Lai Wu*), Issue 81, 1940. Chinese Periodicals Database for the Republican Period.

222   Cultural and Aesthetic Debates

Figure 13.2 Vivien Leigh, magazine cover from *Desert Pictorial* (*Shamo Huabao*), no. 43, 1940. Chinese Periodicals Database for the Republican Period.

popularity in Shanghai: "For Shanghai people, even if you have to eat less each day, you should save money and go to watch *Gone with the Wind*" (*Women's World* 3, no. 4 [1941]: 37–39). Like the female protagonist in Shi Jimei's story *Wild Grass* [*Yecao*], many Shanghai girls of that time were found holding a copy of the novel *Gone with the Wind* in public spaces such as in the library or inside a street car, apparently positioning themselves within the gaze of others—the best way to maintain their cultural look and identity as a modern girl. The name Scarlett

O'Hara lingered on everyone's lips. A 1940 review of this film described a "typical" conversation among female students in Shanghai:

> "Have you seen *Gone with the Wind*? Scarlett O'Hara! I love her so much!"
> "Oh no! How could you love her! She is so selfish!"
> "Selfish? Scarlett is courageous enough to pursue whatever she wants."

> (*Lian Sheng* 11 [1940]: 20–21)

It is the selfish, headstrong, greedy, controversial Scarlett that stirred up a big appetite for Western commodity culture in China, realized through purchasing film tickets, star photos, and novels. The international distribution of *Gone with the Wind* showed how Western commodity culture was being circulated and retranslated in the context of China's encounter with and response to such culture as an aspect of modernization.

MELODRAMA AND *WENYI* PICTURES

Among the film ads, the selling points of *Gone with the Wind* included its vivid colors, its four-hour-long experience, and *wenyi*, which literally means "letters and arts." Wenyi is a concept that first of all signals a cross-cultural conjunction (see Zhen Zhang, chapter 5). As Yueh-yu Yeh (2009, 2013) notes, the term *wenyi* was first borrowed in the early twentieth century from Japan by Chinese intellectuals to name translated fictions of Western origin. To win the hearts of more readers, Chinese intellectuals translated Western fictions that were very touching and centered on love stories. That is to say, in its initial stage, wenyi indicated at least three meanings: (1) Western origin, (2) refined taste and good quality, and (3) an appeal to emotion and romantic love. It was a commendatory term, carrying the aura of letters and arts. The second meaning noted here made wenyi a very different concept from melodrama within Western critical cultures. In a depreciative sense, the Oxford Dictionary, for example, defines "melodramatic" as "characteristic of melodrama, especially in being exaggerated, sensationalized, or overemotional." An issue worth drawing out here is that at different points in its history, melodrama, or its close equivalents, could be used as a term of wild praise, as a neutral descriptor of a film industry genre, or as a recoil at excessively bad taste. It is the protean and contradictory possibilities of melodrama that invite scholars to keep searching for a more historically informed perspective, capable of producing a more inclusive totality.

Indeed, neither melodrama nor wenyi are timeless concepts. Yeh (2012) elaborates how wenyi was utilized in the 1930s and beyond to brand film as a desirable, viable commodity in the marketplace of cultural consumption. In the database of the newspaper *Shenbao*, the expression "wenyi picture" [*wenyi pian*] is not prevalent until the mid-1930s.[1] By labeling Hollywood's *Gone with the Wind* as a "wenyi blockbuster" [*wenyi jupian*], Chinese advertisements used Margaret

Mitchell's 1936 Pulitzer-winning novel as a vehicle to ensure the quality of the film (see *International* 2, no. 2 [1940]: 2). However, during the Orphan Island Era, some films labeled wenyi pictures were explicitly based on ancient Chinese literary resources, whereas others had no Western or Chinese literary origins at all. Wenyi gradually lost its Western connotation but held onto the emphasis on emotion and romance. In this sense, wenyi picture largely overlaps with romantic melodrama, the subset of Western melodrama that gained great popularity in China. The expression wenyi picture opens up the specific nature of Chinese culture's mediation of Western melodrama—its special focus on romance skews melodrama toward an emphasis on what is only one of its dimensions and possible generic forms. In terms of academic discourse, Taiwanese scholars started to translate theories of Western melodrama into Chinese in the early 1980s, when Taiwan wenyi picture production was at its peak. This propelled some Taiwanese scholars to align wenyi pictures with melodrama.[2] The distribution of Hollywood pictures in the Orphan Island Era and scholarly translation of terms in the early 1980s come together to explain why, even today, some critics in Chinese-language circles seem to equate melodrama with the love story.

Literature helps to sell movies, and vice versa. Following the film premiere in Shanghai, several Chinese translations of Margaret Mitchell's novel appeared. An incomplete bilingual version was published in *English-Chinese Translation Serial* [*Yinghan Yicong*] in 1940. Fu Donghua's complete translation was finished a mere few months later and was warmly received by its Shanghai readers. An abridged version translated by Zhu Fan was published in *Wan Xiang* in 1944. Shorter versions of the story as tie-ins would also be handed to audiences before some film screenings to help them make sense of the film's narrative.

TYPES OF EXCESS

The concept of wenyi helps explain how the transnational travel of *Gone with the Wind*, or of Hollywood romantic melodrama in general, may aid rethinking melodrama theory in a cross-cultural context. In what follows, I attempt to investigate how "excess," a notion often associated with melodrama, means different things in the Hollywood and Chinese contexts. By repositioning the notion of excess, I underline the different cultural norms against which to measure different types of excess and argue that the perceptions of excess can even run in opposite cultural directions.

In the Western context, the many connotations of the word *excess* associated with melodrama include overwrought emotion, overblown visual aesthetics, overlong spectacles, exaggerated acting, overly contrived plotting, and so on—qualities deemed excessive by elite cultures and deemed potentially subversive by ideological criticism. As critics often talk about excess when they are actually talking about different things, we need to distinguish different types of excess before we can unbind or disentangle the different cultural and historical meanings of this notion.

The first type of excess I want to analyze is narrative excess, which refers to elements not fully contained by the framework of narration. When Kristin Thompson, for example, writes on excess in "The Concept of Cinematic Excess" (1986), she is actually talking about narrative excess. Her norm against which to measure excess is a model of orderly, goal-driven, causal narratives, the so-called classical Hollywood cinema defined by Bordwell, Staiger, and Thompson herself in their influential 1985 work. However, if following this norm, we shift our attention to the Chinese dramatic tradition, it becomes apparent that narrative excesses of Thompson's kind are much less noticeable in the Hollywood system than in the dramatic traditions of China. Chinese audiences do not try to find a narrative significance in every detail when watching a Chinese classical opera; instead, they enjoy the repetitive singing and arousing spectacles that are in excess of so-called classical narrative needs but contribute emotional significance to the story. Second, a problem with many Western critics' use of the "classical" model as a norm is that it relegates melodramatic elements such as spectacle, decor, and costume to mere extras, deviations from the narrative, and dismiss melodrama's coincidences and *deus-ex-machina* happy endings as overly contrived. These spectacular devices of plot and mise-en-scène, so often derided by Western elite culture, are actually well accepted as golden principles of dramaturgical construction in the Chinese tradition. For instance, the old Chinese saying "no coincidences, no stories" [*wuqiao buchengshu*] acknowledges their necessity in dramatic writing.³ In *Xian Qing Ou Ji*, a comprehensive book about dramaturgy, performance, cuisine, and other aspects of cultural life in seventeenth-century China, Li Yu (1610–1680) gives high praise to this plot device in Wang Shifu's *Romance of the Western Chamber* [*Xi Xiang Ji*].⁴ Zhang Sheng contacts his childhood friend General Du to help him drive away bandits, and they arrive at the last minute before their leader takes beautiful Cui Yingying as his consort—a typical deus-ex-machina happy solution. This breathtaking peripety is praiseworthy because it embodies the root impulse of drama—the need for dramatization. These golden principles of narrative construction in Chinese dramaturgical tradition, seen from a Western perspective, well deserve the adjective *melodramatic*. They throw the negative connotations of *melodramatic* into question and indicate the need to think through different lineages of dramatic traditions and performance types for understanding melodrama as not only transcultural but also crossmedia phenomena.

The second type of excess I want to discuss is bodily excess, which I define as the sexual display of an often-female body exceeding daily life expectations and breaking cultural norms. Arguably, in the historical context of the Chinese reception of Hollywood in the 1930s, audiences recognized as excessive the use of body or flesh in Hollywood romantic melodramas, even if this was part of the film's appeal. The perception of excess here runs in the opposite cultural direction than that associated in Western criticism with the needs of narrative.

Surveying Chinese film magazines and newspapers of the 1930s, we find that the word *rou gan*—which could be literally translated as "the sense of flesh" or "the fleshly," suggesting sexual excitement and rapture—was frequently used by Chinese critics to describe Hollywood pictures. For example: "In each Shanghai newspaper, there are always two large pages of film advertisements. . . . They are never-seen-before blockbusters. They are seductive, romantic, fragrant, erotic, fleshly, amorous and passionate" (Lu Xun, *Sprout* [March 1930]: 28). Lu Xun's adjectives could also be used to describe *Gone with the Wind*. For instance, during the rape, depicted as if it occurred against the burning of Atlanta, Scarlett's bare shoulders and the expression of ecstasy in Rhett's and Scarlett's faces conveyed a sexual excitement that was considered too bold, too direct, and too strong for an ascetic Confucian culture. Another example registering such bodily excess occurs in an anonymous article titled "I Love the Sense of Flesh," published in *Film Life* [*Yingxi Shenghuo*] in 1931, suggesting that a sense of flesh exceeding daily life expectation was the dominant feature of Hollywood pictures.

More needs to be said about the norm of an ascetic Confucian culture against which to measure what I call bodily excess. During the Song dynasty (960–1279 CE), Zhu Xi (1130–1200), the most important neo-Confucian thinker, offered a sophisticated cosmological account of human nature as inherently associated with the larger world. He saw desire [*yu*] as turbulent waves threatening to overflow the dam of ritual propriety. Although Zhu Xi discussed desire in a more general sense, at some points in his argument he did not consider it a force that must be always repressed. However, the often-quoted motto "hold onto the heavenly principle, eliminate personal desires" [*cun tianli, mie renyu*] was attributed to him, and the idea of reducing or even eliminating desires, especially sexual desire, was then amplified by his followers, becoming a slogan of Confucian asceticism. To be sure, the May Fourth generation's iconoclastic project of overthrowing Confucian thought had, since 1919, already put asceticism under attack. But the articles written and published by the May Fourth cultural elite did not have as powerful an impact on the illiterate or semi-illiterate mass as they hoped. The asceticism of Chinese Confucian culture, though put into question, was still a dominating force of the moral universe in China in the 1930s. In contrast to such an ascetic ethos, Chinese audiences at that time found a bodily excess—a sense of flesh exceeding the bounds of Confucian rules as well as their daily experience—in Hollywood melodramas such as *Gone with the Wind*, showing how the sensational side of film spectatorship could be experienced differently in different cultures.

Until recently, Western film studies have consistently characterized melodrama as a narrow genre and a particular exception to the idea of the "classical" norm popularized by Bordwell, Staiger, and Thompson. This supposed opposition between melodrama and a classically conceived Hollywood has colored Western perceptions of Chinese cinema as "melodramatic." Much to the contrary, however, if we put Chinese reception of Hollywood films in their historical context, we find cultural norms lead to different understandings of excess and the melodramatic.

Further, melodrama's journey from Hollywood to China requires a theorization of the notion of bodily excess that might enrich and dynamize our understanding of melodrama as a cultural form of modernity. According to Peter Brooks (1976), melodrama is a modern cultural response to moral insecurity, and excess is a route to the lost Sacred. The Christian idea of "the Sacred" should not be applied to the Chinese context without modification. However, the historical period of 1930s

China—when the iconoclastic project and a renewed thirst for moral values were simultaneously emerging, clashing, and negotiating with each other—resonates with Brooks's description of a post-Sacred era. The moral insecurity here manifested itself as a contest between "traditional Confucian" values and more recent "modern Western" ones. In one register, the norm against which excess was measured lay in an ascetic Confucian culture that emphasized the importance of the family and social stability by eliminating personal desires. Yet in another register, in Hollywood romantic melodramas, Chinese audiences witnessed the emergence of a modern cult of feeling and a new concept of personhood, in which heterosexual love and personal desire functioned as a measure of the individual. The notion of bodily excess thus underlined the contradictions and tensions of the two unsynchronized moral systems. At a politically, culturally, and morally volatile time, the reception of Hollywood romantic melodrama represented one of the most significant and deeply symptomatic ways Chinese audiences might negotiate moral feeling.

BANNED HOLLYWOOD, ORIGINAL REMAKES

In Chinese history, the period from December 8, 1941 to August 15, 1945, when the Japanese controlled all of Shanghai, is termed the "Fallen City Era" [*Lunxian Shiqi*]. Japanese colonial rule banned Hollywood films in Shanghai from the second half of 1942 to 1945. Shortly before and after the ban, *Gone with the Wind* and other commercially successful Hollywood romantic melodramas were "remade" into a range of highly original cultural products, including film, classical opera, stage, and radio drama.[5] "A beauty at a turbulent time" and the melodramatic imagination of Hollywood film persisted in China even when the actual Hollywood products were absent. Chinese remakes of Hollywood melodrama provide effective evidence against the assumption that there is no Chinese melodrama because there are no synonyms for "melodrama" in Chinese. At the same time, Chinese remakes provide an expanded viewfinder through which to examine Hollywood, an opportunity to see Hollywood from its outside.

Among Chinese film remakes of *Gone with the Wind*, it is worth mentioning the 1940 Huacheng Company version starring Chen Yunshang. In a rare instance, Zhang Shankun, the head of Huacheng Company, served as both scriptwriter and director for this picture. To avoid the Japanese censors, this film was set in ancient China (figure 13.3)—where the ongoing "war" would not be readily identified as the anti-Japanese war. Like the old South in the Hollywood version, ancient China in the Huacheng Company version—signified by windows with exquisite applique design, beautiful flower patterns on vases, and traditional Chinese musical instruments—became a space of innocence, a dream remembered, a civilization gone with the wind and, therefore, a locus of nostalgia. In addition, *Gone with the Wind* was remade into a Cantonese movie of the same title, produced by Huadian Company and directed by Mei Lingxiao. During its shooting, it stirred up a discussion in Hong Kong newspapers as to whether the trend of

228 Cultural and Aesthetic Debates

Figure 13.3 Chen Yushang in Huacheng Company's *Gone with the Wind* (1940) in *Beauty Weekly* (*Da Mei Zhoubao*), no. 54, 1940. Chinese Periodicals Database for the Republican Period.

remaking Hollywood films meant a lack of good original scripts in the Cantonese film industry (*Hua Zi Daily*, December 8, 1940).

The most celebrated theatrical remake of *Gone with the Wind* was led by Ke Ling and performed by the Kugan drama troupe. It enjoyed a one-month-long run at the Paris Theater in October 1943 (*Shenbao*, October 15, 1943). In Ke's version, Tara was a small village south of the Yangtze River and the ongoing war was the Chinese Civil War (1926–1929). Scarlett O'Hara was called Hao Sijia, the oldest daughter in the Hao family. Ke's choice not to set the story in the present—a strategy, as already noted, familiar to writers and directors in the "Fallen City"—successfully protected his work from the Japanese censors. "The spoken drama, *Gone with the Wind*, is so different from the Hollywood film," wrote a student who spent 10 yuan to watch it, this play bears no resemblance "in terms of form or spirit" (*Shenbao*, October 25, 1943).[6] Needless to say, this U.S.-China, screen-theater transplantation—echoing in reverse melodrama's passage from Europe to America, from theater to cinema—once again exemplifies melodrama not only as a transnational but also as a crossmedia phenomenon. The media and cultural interchange, however, does not change the core of the story that I call "a beauty at a turbulent time"—individual turmoil paralleling tribulations in the larger, national wartime background. Its mechanism of emotion—moving us to sympathy for the sufferings of the female protagonist—is perhaps the core operation of melodrama. A question raised here is whether the commercial success of the Chinese remakes should be partly attributed to the ban on Hollywood. If Hollywood melodrama, in its overwhelming triumph over the Chinese market, was thought disastrous for the

Chinese home industry during the Orphan Island Era, could we legitimately claim that banning Hollywood actually carved out space for the rebirth of local cultural practices in protean shapes?

The story of the Chinese remakes and reception of *Gone with the Wind* finds its double in the case of *Waterloo Bridge* (LeRoy, 1940), also starring Vivien Leigh. "A beauty inevitably becoming a fallen woman at a turbulent time," sums up the most important aspect of the film's narrative. During World War I, Roy (Robert Taylor), a captain, and Myra (Vivien Leigh), a ballerina, serendipitously crossing Waterloo Bridge during an air raid, meet and immediately fall in love. Roy has to go to the front soon after he proposes marriage. Myra, along with fellow dancer Kitty, loses her job and, believing her fiancé to be dead, is forced to turn to prostitution. While offering herself to soldiers on leave arriving at Waterloo Station, Myra catches sight of Roy, who is alive and still wants to marry her. Feeling guilty that she will bring shame to Roy's family, Myra takes her own life. This film was shown in Zhenguang Theater in 1941 and was praised for its capacity to resonate with the audience (*Desert Pictorial* 17 [1941]: 27). To be more precise, it was the film's emphasis on chastity and its antiwar consciousness that resonated with Chinese audiences of that time. According to an anonymous article, "when Yan Huizhu, a famous Chinese classical opera actress, was watching *Waterloo Bridge* in the movie theater, her fur coat was wet with tears" (*Three-Six-Nine Pictorial* 12, no. 17 [1941]: 22). By revealing an actress on the Chinese classical opera stage as a film fan in her real life, this article praised *Waterloo Bridge* for its capacity to touch even someone who had experienced countless dramas on stage and underscored the permeability between theater and film as a prevalent feature in the culture and art practices at that time. *Hunduan Lanqiao*, the Chinese title for *Waterloo Bridge*, also plays an active role in instilling the film with traditional cultural relevance for Chinese audiences. *Lanqiao*, a bridge located in Shanxi, China, recalls an ancient tale about keeping the promise of love. A man and a woman agreed to a date under this bridge. On that day, the woman didn't show up owing to a storm, but the man waited and waited until he was drowned in the rain. *Hunduan* literally means "one's soul is disconnected from the body" and is a euphemism for death. The Chinese title not only clearly states that this is a story about a failed love promise but also suggests the heroine's suicide at the end of the Hollywood film. Myra (Vivien Leigh) walks into the path of a moving truck on the Waterloo Bridge. Here comes the key "moving" device. In the pathetic scene of the death, the camera, in conjunction with the melody *Auld Lang Syne*, to which they once danced together, lingers on a good luck charm that she gave him. Their love promise, as evidenced by the good luck charm and the haunting melody, is now gone with the wind.

In the Chinese presentation of *Waterloo Bridge*, we again witness melodrama effortlessly flying from one culture to another.[7] Among the various Chinese remakes of the film, the most popular version was the Yihua Company's song-and-dance film *Huduan Lanqiao* (Mei Qian, 1941), starring Li Lihua (figure 13.4). The story was transplanted from Waterloo Station in London to beautiful West Lake in Hanzhou, China. Li Lihua drowns herself in the lake at the end of the film. The gendered asymmetry of the narrative structure—in which the woman dies to prove

Figure 13.4 Li Lihua in Yihua Company's *Waterloo Bridge* (1941) in *Three-Six-Nine Pictorial (San Liu Jiu Huabao)* 9, no. 9, 1942. Chinese Periodicals Database for the Republican Period.

her love and the man lives to tell their story—remained intact in the Chinese version. Also in 1940, a four-hour Yue opera version of *Waterloo Bridge* was performed in Carter [Kade] Theater (*Shaoxing Opera News* 66 [1941]: 3). Originated from Zhejiang province and known for its elegant and soft singing style, Yue opera had, since the 1930s, gained increasing popularity in Shanghai, where a group of Yue opera performers launched a movement to reform their operatic practice, including learning from Western cultures. Another subversive aspect of the Yue opera reform was its transition from a male-only opera to a female-only form. Under women's performances, the tender and gentle features of Yue opera became even more outstanding (see Chen 2012). The adaptation of a Hollywood film into a Yue stage opera marked a bold experiment in this reform. The experiment was successful. The new stereoscopic scenic designs employed by the Yue opera contributed to its modern look. A reviewer used the phrase "cinematic Yue opera" as a word of compliment, celebrating the marriage of two modes of representation (*Shaoxing Opera News* 65 [1941]). Hollywood romantic melodrama provided a moving story for operatic adaptation, and traditional Yue opera added to melodramatic technique, especially in the ways songs and storytelling were combined. In a five-minute Yue opera duet, two unemployed young women use their voices as a testament to suffering and pain, directly soliciting audience empathy. Inadvertently, this song sequence captures a historical moment when many unemployed young women in Shanghai had no options except joining female-performed opera classes as their livelihood. In the Hollywood version, the suffering of the female protagonist is largely a result of the long-time absence of the male protagonist, but in the Yue opera version, the fact that the cross-dressed actress, Li Yanfang, played the role of the male protagonist might suggest the permanent absence of the man and the inevitable disillusionment of the heroine's dream that he would come to save her. Costume was arguably the only sign that ensured Li Yanfang's male role. Her elegant and soft singing was unmistakably a display of her femininity. In addition, a spoken drama remake of *Waterloo Bridge* was performed in Xinguang Theater and broadcast by Shanghai Radio in 1945 (*Shenbao* July 22, 1945). Listening to radio melodrama foregrounded the importance of the melos in melodrama and, as I elaborate in the next section, opened up new sources of melodramatic perception.

To sum up this section metaphorically, I suggest that melodrama is represented by the fire in *Gone with the Wind*—it is eternally changeable, endlessly diverse, and ceaselessly mobile.[8] Like flame, melodrama rejects any once-and-forever allotted form and is ready to dynamically assume different aesthetic forms. As demonstrated by *Gone with the Wind* and *Waterloo Bridge*, to write the international history of Hollywood melodrama not only would point to Hollywood's global influence but would trace the diversity of forms Hollywood melodrama assumed in the local contexts of its reception. It is in such aggressive, productive ways that Hollywood's melodramatic imagination—crystalized in the image of a woman illuminated by the fires of war—was woven into the history of Chinese cinematic culture. Tracing romantic melodrama's journey from Hollywood to China does not mean that Hollywood is the only origin of Chinese romantic melodrama. Its multisource origin can be traced back to indigenous traditions, including Chinese fictions and dramatic works in the era before cinema (Yeh 2009; Zhang 2012). These traditions directly or indirectly contributed to the forms of metamorphosis that Chinese remakes went through.

MELOS, MELODRAMA, AND EXCESS

Although prints of Chinese remakes of *Gone with the Wind* and *Waterloo Bridge* no longer exist, some of their songs survive on vinyl records or as sheet music. In attempting to "reconstruct" these films without prints, I segue into the investigation of the melos in melodramas.

Hollywood's *Waterloo Bridge* features an old Scottish song, *Auld Lang Syne*, as *The Farewell Waltz*. The same piece from the Western score is used in the 1941 Yihua Company's song-and-dance *Waterloo Bridge*. And there is no doubt about the popularity of this song among Chinese audiences; its score was reprinted in a variety of Chinese magazines of that time. The 1941 Chinese version, however, supplies the Western score with new Chinese lyrics, written in the language of ancient Chinese poetry, with a certain degree of vernacular overlay (Wu 1997).

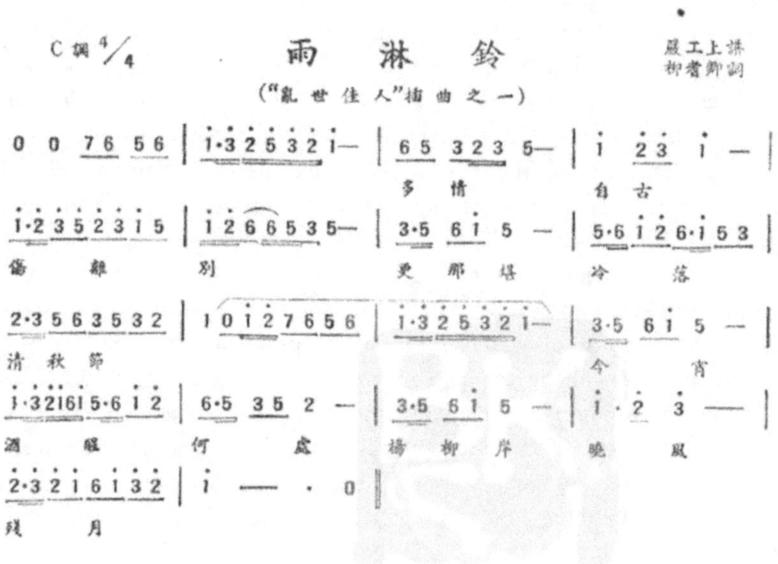

Figure 13.5 An interlude sung by Chen Yunshang in Huacheng Company's *Gone with the Wind* (1940) in *Silver Song Collection (Yin Ge Ji)* no. 1, 1941. Chinese Periodicals Database for the Republican Period.

Li Lihua, the luminous star and melodramatic heroine, sings the song. Another example of such transnational and temporal interchange is found in the still surviving score and lyrics for one of the interludes in the 1940 Huacheng Company's version of *Gone with the Wind*, sung by female star Chen Yunshang. One such lyric is *Yu Lin Ling* (figure 13.5), written by Liu Yong during the Song dynasty (960–1279 CE). One important aspect of Song dynasty lyric poetry [*Song ci*] is that a particular lyric or a plurality of lyrics was written for a specific tune, with set rhythm, rhyme, and tempo. The name of such a specific tune forms the title or the first half of the title for a particular work. However, over time the actual tunes seem to have disappeared. Here, we witness how a work of lyric poetry from the Song dynasty found a new tune of the 1940s as well as a second life in the Chinese remake of Hollywood melodrama.

At stake here is the oscillation of Chinese audiences between cultural identities: on one hand, those aberrant adaptations that claimed themselves "remakes" proved their incurable obsession with Hollywood; on the other hand, as the songs indicate, ancient Chinese culture retained a grip on film production of the early 1940s. This oscillation leads to a noticeable drift between old and new languages, archaic and contemporary sensibilities. It's also noteworthy to reiterate that, in both examples, a female film star, who plays the melodramatic heroine, sings the songs. The singing film star "anchors a representational system in which speech must periodically give way to song, allowing the female voice to come to the fore as a locus of dramatic and affective intensity" (Ma 2015, 6). Following the common tradition of various Chinese operas, the melodramatic heroine uses the device of singing, frequently in the first person, as an emotional outlet, a statement of feeling, a testament to her suffering and longing.

Song, a conjunction of lyrics, voice, and music, is often more powerful than words because music, as Peter Brooks puts it, "partakes of the ineffable" (1976, 75). The Chinese saying "when words are not enough, you sigh; when sighs are not enough, you sing" [*yanzhi buzu, gu jietanzhi, jietanzhi buzu, gu yonggezhi*] seems to offer an interesting parallel to Brooks's account.[9] Only music can achieve this effect of overwhelming contact with the unsayable: "Everything was said and nothing was said" (Lefebvre 2004, 64). It seems to activate the audiences' embodied engagement and cause immediate, direct, visceral, and emotional reactions, bypassing the film narrative. Like the movie star, a song is at once embedded in and spills beyond the framework of film narration. In this sense, songs in melodrama might be linked to Kristin Thompson's (1986) notion of excess—namely, narrative excess. Again, Chinese melodrama did not merely come from Hollywood. The preference for repetitive singing in excess of narrative needs and the device of female singing as an emotional outlet in Chinese melodrama can be read as traces of Chinese traditional opera carried forward into new cultural contexts and forms.

CHINA'S GONE WITH THE WIND

In the years following the Shanghai premiere of Hollywood's *Gone with the Wind*, it was common to see film advertisements such as "A Film comparable to *Gone with the Wind*: The Shooting Story of *Rebirthed Love*" [*Zai Sheng Yuan*] (*Three-Six-Nine Pictorial* 8, no. 13 [1941]: 30); "*Apricot Blossom* [*Xinhua Chuqiang Ji*], on a par with *Gone with the Wind*!" (*Mass Film News* 1, no. 30 [1941]: 240); or "*Since You Went Away* [*Zi Jun Bie Hou*]!The film compares favorably with *Gone with the Wind*!" (*Time Film* 1, no. 13 [1946]: 10). What is more, "a beauty at a turbulent time" continued to be a theme of many Chinese melodramas occupying Shanghai's film screens in the following years, the most salient example being Cai Chusheng and Zheng Junli's *The Spring River Flows East* [*Yijiang Chunshui Xiangdongliu*]. The two parts of this film, *Eight War-Torn Years* and *The Dawn*, were released one after the other in 1947. Even before *Eight War-Torn Years* finished shooting, film critics had described it as China's *Gone with the Wind* (*Cinematic World* 249 [1946]: 7). The label "wenyi blockbuster" [*wenyi jupian*] was also used in newspapers to market this film (*Shenbao*, October 2, 1947; *Shenbao*, October 17, 1947).

It might not be accidental that codirector Zheng Junli had played the male protagonist in Yihua Company's *Waterloo Bridge* (1941). The storyline of *The Spring River Flows East* covers a ten-year span. At the beginning of part one of the film, Sufen is a young working-class woman in a romantic relationship with Zhongliang. Ten years later, she will have experienced the Japanese invasion of Manchuria, the Second Sino-Japanese War (1937–1945), and the postwar depression. On a personal level, she will have experienced love, marriage, childbirth, poverty, job seeking, desertion, and betrayal by her husband Zhongliang, followed by suicide.

At first glance, the cross-cutting between the self-sacrificing wife's life of sorrow and scarcity in Japanese-occupied Shanghai and the dissolute husband's life of wealth and decadence in Chongqing makes palpable both the spectacle of the good person who suffers and the evil person who creates suffering. On a deeper level, Zhongliang's corruption—portrayed as a reluctant, gradual, and almost inevitable process—can be read as the fate of a helpless man engulfed by an evil world out of his control. Instead of failed love, as in *Gone with the Wind*, it is the upheavals of an era that betray the melodramatic heroine. The conflicts of modernity in China in that period are epitomized in the fate of the family and played out against an emotional backdrop of entrapment, destruction, and desolation. Indirectly echoing Yihua Company's *Waterloo Bridge*, Sufen drowns herself in the Yangze River at the end of the film. However, Sufen dies not to prove love but only to prove virtue. Melodrama does not necessarily guarantee the defeat of evil by good. What is essential to melodrama, as Linda Williams (chapter 12) accurately notes, "is the dramatic *recognition* of good and evil and, in that recognition, at least the hope that justice might be done" ("Melodrama and Justice"). In the case of *The Spring River Flows East*, if we say—as many critics did at that time—that the end of the film is too dark because Sufen's death means "no hope," we can still recognize the hope for justice in the film's subplot in which Zhongliang's brother Zhongmin joins the guerrillas to fight for a new modern China. That melodrama works to provide moral-affective signifiers at a time of moral chaos can be applied very well in the Chinese context. By recognizing the crisis of a turbulent era that needs to be ended as the real evil, rather than the moral status of an individual, Chinese cinema of this period acculturates social change through the capacity of melodrama to address modernity, incorporating it into China's revolutionary nation-building discourse.

In this sense, *The Spring River Flows East* testifies to the way Chinese melodrama modernizes by working hand in hand with realism rather than as its antithesis. Realism is a hotly debated term in modern China, as elsewhere. It is never a unitary style. In this context, I refer to revolutionary realism. Melodrama's realist power lies in its hope that audiences who have felt the pain of social injustice in the movie theater will "do the right thing" when they approach problems in their everyday reality. If the emotion *Gone with the Wind* (1939 Selznick; 1940 Huacheng Company) evokes is mainly nostalgia, which leaps backward into the past to rediscover and color it, the emotion *The Spring River Flows East* awakens is mainly indignation, which leaps forward into an imagined future to demand change. The Chinese phrase "igniting the fire of indignation" [*dianran nuhuo*] accurately describes how the sensation of the fire called melodrama is internalized in the spectator's body as "affection" and then bursts into action. The affection that I refer to here is no longer a personal feeling. Rather, it bears strikingly similarities to *L'affect* in a Deleuzian sense: as Brian Massumi put it in the translator's introduction to *A Thousand Plateaus*, "a prepersonal intensity corresponding to the passage from one experimental state of the body to another and implying an augmentation or diminution in that body's capacity to act" (Deleuze and Guattari 1987, xvi). This very notion of affection opens to the social, underscoring melodrama's role in acculturating and reinitiating social change.

In contrast to Thompson's model of narrative linearity, the narrative of *The Spring River Flows East* depends crucially on coincidences: in a coincidental fashion, the homeless and jobless Zhongliang discovers in a newspaper the address of old acquaintance Lizhen, who immediately gives him a place to stay at her house, soon finds him a job, and later becomes his second wife; also in a coincidental fashion, Sufen is forced to work as a maid for Wenyan, who ends up as Zhongliang's secret mistress in Shanghai. These coincidences can better be understood as praiseworthy in Li Yu's dramaturgy than excessive in Thompson's model. Moreover, it is clear that the introduction of the street singers' folksong about the moon hardly contributes to the film's narrative progression. Yet it is the repetition of the old pentatonic folk melody that prolongs a melancholy moment, unleashing temporal vertigo and making one of the most touching and unforgettable sequences of this film. Recognizing the significance in Chinese cinema of such seemingly excessive convolutions or interruptions to narrative progression not only asks for reverse comparison with Chinese perceptions of bodily excess in Hollywood's *Gone with the Wind* but also calls for a more nuanced reflection on these intersections of melos and drama arising from a non-Western lineage, a project that should not end here.

THE ELEPHANT OF MELODRAMA: A TALE OR AN IMPLICATION

To end this chapter, I'd like to tell a Chinese tale that parallels the analogy of Linda Williams (chapter 12) and might be called "the Chinese elephant of melodrama." General Cao wondered how heavy an elephant was, though no scales could hold this huge animal. His six-year-old son came up with a solution. He brought the elephant to the river and led it to board a boat. Then he marked on the boat the water level. The elephant was led back to the shore and stones were placed in the boat until the water reached the same level as when the elephant was on board. It remained an easy job to weigh the stones separately and add up the total—that was also the weight of the elephant.

And this is what I propose methodologically in this chapter: some issues raised by the elephant of Hollywood melodrama, such as its relations to excess, realism, and modernity, might be as intractable as how heavy an elephant is. Like weighing the stones, we can shift our attention to Chinese remakes of Hollywood melodrama—the remake of the elephant. In this expanded viewfinder, some intractable issues are clarified or, at least, gain some new perspectives. To put it more broadly, numerous stubborn assumptions and formulations about melodrama do not exist in theoretical traditions outside the Euro-American canon. Therefore, I propose investigating melodrama theory in a cross-cultural context as a way of unbinding melodrama. In studying romantic melodrama's journey from Hollywood to China, rather than trying to apply an already assumed understanding of melodrama to Chinese texts, let's open up the possibility of mutual imagining.

NOTES

I thank Zhen Zhang and Dana Polan for their conversations with me on *Gone with the Wind*, where this chapter began.

1. *Shenbao* was the most influential Shanghai-based newspaper, published from 1872 to 1949.
2. More recently some scholars in mainland China, such as Ning Ma and Chungeng He, use a coined Chinese word for melodrama, *Qingjie Ju*, which literally means "plot drama." I think this is a bad translation for it restricts melodrama to its narrowest definition and reconfirms melodrama's bad reputation, especially for its supposed artificial plotting.
3. One source of this old Chinese saying is the short story "An Oil Peddler Wins the Head of a Courtesan" in Feng Menglong's *Stories to Awaken the World* [*Xing Shi Heng Yan*], originally published in 1627.
4. The original story can be traced back to *Yingying's Biography* [*Ying Ying Zhuan*], a short story written by Yuan Zhen (779–831 CE).
5. Zhen Zhang touches on the issue of remake in her conference paper in 2013.
6. In part due to inflation, the price here was higher than a 1940 ticket for Hollywood's *Gone with the Wind*.
7. *Waterloo Bridge* (LeRoy, 1940) is in itself a remake of the 1930 American film also called *Waterloo Bridge*, adapted from the 1930 play of the same title.
8. I say this with a nod to *Eisenstein on Disney* (1988), in which the notion of cinema as fire is introduced. Also see Weihong Bao's (2015) *Fiery Cinema: The Emergence of an Affective Medium in China: 1915-1945*. As its title indicates, this notion is contextualized throughout the book.
9. One source of this saying can be found in "The Great Preface (to the Book of Songs)" [*Shi Da Xu*]. The authorship of the preface has been a matter of continuous dispute.

14

Melodrama and the Aesthetics of Emotion

E. DEIDRE PRIBRAM

Melodrama has long been associated with emotion, frequently in a pejorative sense due to its apparent emotional excesses. Conversely, scholars have argued that the melodramatic mode expresses "forces, desires, fears which . . . operate in human life," for which we have "no other language" (Gledhill 2002, 31, 37). In this chapter I explore how emotionality serves melodrama as an alternative "language" precisely to express forces, desires, and fears that operate beyond cognitive or ideological explanation.

Melodrama should not be viewed as an indication of narrative failure or weakness. Indeed, its apparent emotional "excess" can be conceptually reworked to recognize the mode's acknowledgment of emotions as a significant presence in our life experiences. What happens if we accept melodrama's commitment to emotionality not as excessive but as key to its aesthetic structure and cultural value? Such an undertaking necessitates developing ways to conceive and speak about emotionality in both aesthetic and social terms with greater range, nuance, and complexity than hitherto, so we can trace the processes, meanings, and social purposes of emotional life. This analysis of emotions augments ways of understanding melodrama as a dramatic narrative form, and melodrama becomes a means of exploring specific cultural conceptualizations and deployments of emotions. Expanding understanding of emotions as sociocultural phenomena retrieves a melodramatic vision focused on culturally embedded beings operating within or contesting social institutions and practices. Melodrama, therefore, provides an alternative to the focus on the internal psychology of characters, conceived largely as self-governing entities.

This discussion begins with an analysis of "affect" and "emotion" as formulated in current cultural theory. In cultural studies, emphasis has largely been placed on "the turn to affect," but I believe the neglect of "emotions" results in the loss of potentially significant theoretical paths forward. Next, I consider how emotionality surfaces in, and may be read from, historical accounts of melodrama. Emotions may have long been acknowledged as central to melodramatic aesthetics, but a historic shift occurs in Western thinking from the late nineteenth century onward, coinciding with developing concepts of psychological subjectivity, for which melodrama's use of emotionality is troubling. Finally, I address the role of emotions as they play out in the contemporary melodramatic format of dramatic serialized television, a popular and critically valued aesthetic development. I offer a discussion that indicates how the notion of an aesthetics of emotion proves helpful in interpreting the narrative and social worlds depicted in current television series or serials.

EMOTION AND AFFECT

The current turn to affect has largely been received as long overdue, with which I concur. However, in the recent emphasis on affect, emotionality is often tacitly overlooked or purposefully set aside. In the introduction to *Feminist Theory*'s special issue on feminism and affect, Carolyn Pedwell and Anne Whitehead (2012) argue that the affective turn has moved beyond a previous focus on text and language and toward a "vital re-centering of the body" that "cannot be reduced to either 'discourse' or 'emotion,' but exceeds these categories" in favor of the "material intensity" of "embodied encounters" (116). They note that not all feminists are comfortable with the affective turn, citing Ranjana Khanna's concern that "the idea of affect's movement beyond the subject, beyond expressiveness" is tantamount to a "suspicion of content" (118).

Nevertheless, a number of feminist scholars regard the affective turn as a way to preserve the recent extensive rethinking on the body (Gibbs 2002; Probyn 2004). Affect, here, serves as a corrective against a return to the invisibility of the body, subordinated to mind, culture, or ideology. Anna Gibbs (2002), for instance, resists the notion of the corporeal as "largely . . . a body of words, the sum of discourses about it" (336). Gibbs posits affect as inherent in the body and "outside of awareness," in contrast to "emotions" and "feelings," which are culturally constructed (337).

Feminist scholars are not the only theorists who seek to move beyond the discursive. Larry Grossberg (1997) locates the affective within a social formation composed of multiple economies (241). He believes cultural theory has narrowed such multiplicity to meaning and representation, with the result that some economies, including the affective, are reduced to subfunctions of ideology (97, 251). Grossberg (1992) defines affect as a form of energy, a motivating force or intensity invested in our experiences, practices, and identities (82). By disconnecting affect from meaning or ideology, Grossberg differentiates it from emotion, which he sees as mediating between affect and cultural signification. Thus emotion encompasses affect in its manifestation as immediate bodily sensation but also incorporates the cultural meanings we give to those affective experiences.

Likewise, in Brian Massumi's (2002) influential account of affect, emotion is identified as the quality or content of an experience, achieved through language, logic, ideology, structure, narrative, and other forms of signification (26–27). Emotion functions in the realm of meaning production through the "sociolinguistic fixing of the quality of an experience" (28). In contrast, affect is equated with intensity, vitality, and force in ways that are "irreducibly bodily and autonomic" in nature, manifesting primarily in the skin, "at the surface of the body, at its interface with things" (28, 25). Affect theory emphasizes the movement, indeterminacy, and life potential that exist before signification (7). In contrast, signification functions in ways that freeze mobility into fixed, socially determinate positions, just as thought "stops" an onrushing world in the attempt to explain something about it. In this conceptualization, affect is a nonconscious state that registers the intensity of experience in its strength and duration. Though affect may be qualifiable, that is, capable of transformation into an emotional state, Massumi cautions that there is no direct correspondence between intensity and quality, or between affect and emotion (26). Indeed, because the two "follow different logics and pertain to different orders," he argues the need to theorize them separately (27).

It is this division that I seek to challenge. To exemplify the "excess" that is affect—the surplus that lies beyond or outside signification—Massumi uses a twenty-eight-minute film, aired on German television in the 1970s, about a snowman, which has no dialogue or voice-over. It became the subject of an empirical study investigating child viewers' emotional responses to its effects (Sturm and Grewe-Partsch 1987). Massumi's (2002) description of the film reads as follows:

> A man builds a snowman on his roof garden. It starts to melt in the afternoon sun. He watches. After a time, he takes the snowman to the cool of the mountains where it stops melting. He bids it good-bye and leaves. (23)

Massumi contends that the children's powerful responses to the film, most notably fear but also pleasure, demonstrates *"the primacy of the affective in image reception"* (24, emphasis in original). His assumption is that once language as dialogue or voice-over is subtracted, what remains incorporates neither narrativity nor signification.[1] By disavowing a link between images and narrativity, Massumi makes this instance of "image reception" nondiscursive, nonideological, nonsignifying, and, therefore, an expression of unmediated affective intensity. In equating affect-in-image as that which "resonates to the exact degree to which it is in excess of any narration or functional line," Massumi believes he has located pure affect (26). Instead, I argue that what he has located, within the specific parameters of his own definitions, is *emotion*, precisely because he has not exhausted the narrative or signifying functions of the images.

The question then becomes how much do the film's "affects" depend on a basic awareness of what a snowman is? On recognizing that it is an anthropomorphized weather phenomenon (snow/man)? On understanding, in this context, that the snowman melting symbolizes death? Arguably, the ability to make this link accounts for the reports of frightened but pleasurably engaged child viewers. Rather than autonomic, meaningless affective responses, the children's reactions are emotional in that they rely on shared cultural and aesthetic knowledge.

By maintaining that affect, "disconnected from meaningful sequencing, from narration," is a-signifying, Masumi assumes it is asocial, confined to discrete, atomized individuals (25). Conversely, the moment we acknowledge the social, we come face to face with emotion as affective experience transformed through cultural engagement. In these terms, it resonates with all the splendid implications of communication, whether shared or contested, as the effect of meaning-producing communities existing within specific cultural contexts. And once the sociocultural is invoked, we are indeed in the realm of emotions. The advantage of affect theory rests in its engagement with the material, the visceral, and the embodied. Yet to neglect emotionality is to lose the considerable analytical productivity promised if we linger, for a time, in the company of emotions as felt experiences thoroughly entangled with the sociocultural.

Although affect theory has sidelined the study of emotions by limiting them to conscious, cognitive, articulated phenomena, emotions do not necessarily involve either conscious awareness or articulation. Given the diversity of ways we experience emotions, the notion of conscious awareness stands as a limiting threshold. Further, affect theory has tended to conflate articulation ("sociolinguistic fixing") with the entirety of meaning. Yet nonlinguistic systems of communication are meaningful in that they produce associations, representations, and narratives, even when they remain inarticulable—as melodrama demonstrates. Nonverbal communication occurs largely in bodily terms, including gestures, facial expressions, and appearance. Even when the human voice is involved in nonsemantic or "contentless" paralanguage, it remains thoroughly emotion-laden, conveying culturally contextual or contingent meanings. Any "body" can feel or gesture, but nonverbal communication, like emotions and images, emerge in the specific configurations that result from the work of human systems of meaning.

Considering the multitude of ways emotional relations are experienced and expressed in different sociocultural contexts is to address meaningfulness. By definition, forms of visual or nonverbal signification function on the edge of semantic availability rather than by means of linguistic articulation. As Gledhill (2002) reminds us, the emotional, visual, and performative practices of melodrama derive their cultural purposes and power, in part, through the ways they enable the recognition of, and put into dramatic motion, experiences beyond linguistic or ideological expression (31, 37).

EMOTIONS AND MELODRAMA PAST

Writing about melodrama's consolidation in the wake of the French Revolution, Matthew Buckley (2009) argues that the event produced, "not a widespread sense of newfound freedom but a terrible sense of loss" and "a seemingly unstoppable wave of retributive violence and mass execution" (179–80). In this respect, as Buckley and others have argued, French melodrama, rather than offering a utopian understanding of the world, emerged to deal with deeply dystopian circumstances.

Melodrama's morality has long been tied to its emotionality, in which melodramatic aesthetics and dramatic narrative structure use emotional means to arrive at moral legibility. Although a sense of a greater moral good has usually been understood as melodrama's central feature, Buckley argues that it is actually emotionality that defines the mode and its subgenres. Thus the aim of melodramatic tactics "was not moral didacticism, but emotional force and intensity of affect" (181). Emphasizing stage melodrama's relationship to audience awareness of a dystopian reality, Buckley believes that what it acknowledges is a desired world of "love, honor, and order" constantly "surrounded and threatened by irrational hatred, cruelty, and chaos" (186). To whatever degree melodrama's moral legibility offers consolation, such attempts are overwhelmed by the intensity of the contradictory, disturbing affects and emotions the social world generates. For Buckley, melodrama's most effective expression rests in allowing audiences to recognize their felt history and their felt experiences. By the 1840s in England, he argues, critical and public discussion made it clear that melodrama's emotional aspects accounted primarily for its popularity and had become the genre's most "enduring" feature (181).

Applying Carolyn Williams' description of Victorian melodrama as "an oscillating movement between absorptive, introverted moments of sympathetic identification and highly spectacular, extroverted scenes of shocking violence," Buckley depicts melodrama's aesthetic structure as grounded precisely in its deployments of emotion (182). Buckley's point is that melodrama's core structure is based on movement from emotion to emotion, swinging among opposing or contrasting emotional effects. This sharp oscillation structures melodrama's dramatic form, carrying us along through conflicting "scenes of fracture and reconciliation, flight and refuge, horror and comedic relief, and exilic loss and restorative justice" (182). The shock of contrast, which Buckley refers to as "compressive shock," also occurs between melodrama's characters whereby victims evoke "sympathetic pathos" and villains elicit "recoiling antipathy," often at the same moment (182). Melodrama's structure, lodged in unceasing emotional events both on stage and as audience experience, is described by Buckley as "a coherent aesthetic technique," which he labels "sensational expressionism" (181–82; 188).

In Buckley's argument, the terms *affect* and *emotion* often appear together, as if similar but not quite identical concepts, for example, in his reference to the appeal of melodrama's "affective and emotional sensations" (181). In this instance, the "sensational" of sensational expressionism appears to encompass both affective and emotional events. Yet, at another moment, in referring to "the genre's sensational and emotional solicitations," "sensational" replaces "affective" as if to equate the two, rendering "emotional solicitations" as an addition to, or beyond, sensational expressionism (181).

In analyses of melodrama, the sensational is often associated with physical action, the awe of special effects, and audiences' visceral responses. In film studies, such effects may be termed a cinema of sensations or attractions—replicating the shocks of modernity on the human senses. Such conceptions of visceral response correspond to current affect theory as sensory, autonomic, nonconscious, and a-signifying. Equally, melodrama's supposed lack of restraint—its emotions often appearing as a surplus beyond rational, ideological, or articulable explanation—may well be regarded as excessive. Yet this surplus is worth seeking out because in it are located some of the most meaningful, most moving aspects of the melodramatic mode. Tracing the emotional recognizes new dimensions in aesthetic activity, beyond those identified as either "cognitive" or "sensational"—dimensions that have enormous cultural significance.

In this respect, Buckley's positioning of melodrama as a named theatrical form within the aftermath of the French Revolution engages with emotions thoroughly entangled with the sociocultural. No doubt there were visceral responses to the French Revolution in melodrama and elsewhere. But to the degree that the Revolution was a shared, historical event of almost unfathomable political and social impact, responses to it were also decidedly socioemotional. Through recognition of emotions, we are able to acknowledge our history, our cultural experiences, and our felt existence. An audience's felt moments of recognition are acts of emotion stimulated by the aesthetic practices of melodrama and other popular cultural forms, arising out of shared, lived experience and knowledge. Such acts of emotion, when recognized, allow us to accept, appreciate, admit, or deny that which we suddenly apprehend as familiar. In these senses, melodrama can justifiably be viewed as grounded in an aesthetics of emotion.

Ben Singer's 2001 exploration of late theatrical and early cinematic melodrama locates the form in the larger circumstances of modernity as a whole. He returns to the question of excess: "melodrama . . . showcases emotional excess" from the rhetoric of the villain to the excess of "the spectator's visceral responses" (39). Generally using the term "visceral" rather than "affective," Singer sees melodrama's sensational effects as operating primarily on the sensate, material body, even when dramatizing situations of moral injustice (40). However, concepts such as justice and injustice cannot be solely visceral because they rely on social norms, expectations, beliefs, and traditions sustained through communally exercised behaviors and practices. Recognition of justice and injustice depends on various complex forms of acculturation, a process that combines social notions of morality and emotionality—how we ought to feel about and respond to events, for example—with outrage at acts of injustice. This is to say, our recognition of and reactions to depictions of morality and immorality are located in narratives of emotion.

While he identifies strong pathos and heightened emotionality as key constituents of melodrama (7, 44–45), Singer expands the commonly acknowledged range of emotions to include the "hatred, envy, jealousy, spite or malice" expressed by villains and the "hatred, repulsion, or disdain" felt by audiences toward them (39, 40). Recognizing other forms of melodramatic emotionality redresses the disproportionate critical attention devoted to pathos in melodrama. This is a compelling concern if we wish to approach melodrama as an aesthetics of emotion. For example, Singer notes of blood-and-thunder melodrama that veneration for the action heroine or hero may be a more appropriate description of audience attitudes than pity for those who are victimized (55–56). Melodramas also evoke fear, anger, anxiety, tension/suspense, admiration, exhilaration, and so on.

The pathos of a melodramatic situation calls on audiences (and, sometimes, characters) to respond to a wide range of socially induced or socially charged emotional states, including vulnerability, isolation, terror, panic, grief, and outrage.

Although felt by individual characters, such emotions are generated by the distressful or insurmountable social circumstances they face. In this sense, such depictions do not displace social issues into privatized or personalized concerns, as some critics have argued. Rather, they foreground the individual as "socioemotional." This concept is differentiated from both the visceral and cognitive being, so that specific characters embody or realize the effects of particular social conflicts, leading to audiences' feelings of fear, pity, anxiety, admiration, or outrage.

In the late nineteenth and early twentieth centuries, an alternative to melodrama's perceived heightened or overwrought emotionality took shape as dramatic realism, combining "ordinary quotidian reality, with an attempt to portray fully developed, psychologically multidimensional" characters (Singer 2001, 49). The focus on psychology as the basis of characterization contrasts with the concept of the socioemotional individual—of culturally embedded beings operating within or contesting social institutions and practices. The psyche emerges as a competing reality to socially located experience at the historical moment when the dominant notion of self, in the West, develops into the psychological individual.

This move accompanies the advent of psychology, psychiatry, and psychoanalysis as emergent scientific and professional disciplines (see Day-Mayer and Mayer, chapter 6). As a result, emotions retreat to the interior of the human subject to be experienced individually and privately, if consciously experienced at all, for emotions may well be hidden in the unconscious. Two competing conceptualizations of human experience come into existence in which the location of emotions proves key: expressionist, exteriorized displays of emotions versus notions of deeply internalized, private selves (see Pribram 2016, chapter 2).

Accompanying these cultural changes, an aesthetics of deep interiority takes critical precedence over a still ongoing aesthetics of emotional expressionism. Dramatic realism, influenced by new understandings of psychological being, rendered Victorian melodrama's narrative and performative techniques, and their associated audience responses, critically outmoded. However, as noted previously, melodrama's emotional functions were closely aligned with its moral purposes, in which the audience's strong emotional reactions to the narrative and its characters was key to the dispersal of its desired values. More than simply pleasurable releases, the experience and expression of emotions, such as tears, were signs of a person's capacity for deep feeling and, therefore, of his or her virtue (Gledhill 2002, 34; Hyslop 1992, 74).

In contrast, dramatic realism signaled a new set of techniques that encouraged audiences to focus more intently on "the inner life and private personality of the characters" (Gledhill 1991, 219). In northern Europe and the United States, a move in aesthetic values occurred from public sentiments—emotion aligned with morality—to psychology. Restrained performances and dialogue became critically respected above melodrama's physically and emotionally extroverted, gestural qualities. In contrast to melodrama's widely perceived lack of character development or depth, psychologically based characterization and narrativity was and continues to be viewed as capable of journeying to the interior of the individual heart and mind. In influential intellectual and artistic circles, and contemporaneous with the invention of the psychic subject, the psychological as source of "truth" displaces the social. The shift from sentimental morality to psychological interiority thus signals a moment of historical change in the understanding of emotional subjectivity. In the twentieth century, the prevailing notions of high art win over melodrama and emotion.

In melodrama, emotions and the public sphere are closely intertwined, in both textual content and social activity. David Mayer (1999) notes that the term *real* comes to be employed as a sign of critical approval only late in the nineteenth century (12). However, when "high art," in opposition to mass-produced popular culture, claims realism for itself, emotions shift from public manifestation to a more privately introspective or repressed mode. In this new organization, the psychological subsumes the emotional, and the public display of emotionality, for instance, tears, declines. Emblematic of this shift is the cessation of the earlier Victorian practice of viewing theatrical performances with full house lights on, enabling audience members to be seen as much as to see (Mayer 1997, 100). The dimming of house lights resulted in a more isolated, less communal viewing experience, in which the darkened playhouse, in psychoanalytic terms, could be said to represent the retreat into a private psyche.

Similarly, Singer (2001) contrasts the earlier "raucous interactivity between audience and stage" as "a ritual part of the melodramatic experience" (179). He quotes from a 1902 British theatrical review that speaks of modern drama as "the repressed quietude of realism" (50). Emotionality as repressed quietude was taken up as a new, middle-class, social and critical ideal and, at the same time, served to produce the supposed emotional excess of melodrama. A cultural reconceptualization of emotions creates altered circumstances in which externalized displays of emotion, along with melodrama in general, are increasingly considered overwrought or exaggerated.

Melodrama represents a pervasive narrative mode in which emotions are recognized and accepted as fundamental to its aesthetic functions. Yet melodrama's emotionality also rankles and disturbs, a discomfort that continues to the present day, too often resulting in accusations of excess or dismissive disinterest. However, melodrama's characters, widely viewed as lacking in psychological depth, often portray human subjects planted firmly in the difficulties and dilemmas of particular sociocultural contexts. In this sense, it can be argued that the specific traditions of melodrama and its emotional "excesses" retain characters and audience members as culturally embedded beings, operating within or contesting social institutions and practices. As such, melodrama's critical dismissal marks a displacement of emotions as sociocultural phenomena and the attendant loss of an aesthetics of emotional expressionism.

EMOTIONS AND MELODRAMA PRESENT

Linda Williams (2009) has argued that melodrama is the narrative mode that underpins most forms of American popular culture, including film and television (341).

If emotionality is melodrama's most central and enduring feature, we should expect to see emotions structuring melodramatic narratives over time and across media. At the same time, identifying changes in the mode of contemporary melodrama helps us see past the presumed emotional excesses associated with earlier performative and aesthetic techniques, allowing a clearer assessment of the role of emotionality in current depictions of the socioculturally entangled individual.

Writing in 1976, David Thorburn considers television melodrama to be one of the United States' most characteristic, complex, and serious aesthetic forms, operating across an accumulation of genres (legal shows, westerns, police and detective programs, medical series) in a manner comparable to a dramatic-narrative mode. Acknowledging criticisms of television melodramas' "fantasy of reassurance" through their "happy or moralistic endings" (78–79), Thorburn argues that this convention allows melodrama's narratives to encounter "forbidden or deeply disturbing materials: [representing] not an escape into blindness or easy reassurance, but an instrument for seeing" (80). This claim rests largely on melodrama's emotional elements and effects. Thorburn contends that TV melodrama's narrative structure follows characters' emotional responses and behaviors as they intensify over the course of an episode or series. Although melodrama's concentration and intensity of emotional events departs from reality, he maintains that the emotions themselves are not unreal (80). Quite the contrary, TV melodrama's "various strategies of artificial heightening permit an open enactment of feelings and desires" that largely remain unrecognized or unacknowledged in the ongoing rush or "muddled incoherence" of lived experience (84–85). Conversely, melodrama's viewers encounter a coherent narrative world in which "harm is the norm" (79).

Thorburn's description of TV melodrama anticipates Buckley's aesthetics of expressionism, but it has had little influence in current televisual narrative theory. Seemingly taking up Thorburn's perspective, Jeffrey Sconce (2004) argues that increasingly serialized (as opposed to episodic) shows have become popular because they provide "depth and duration of character relations, diegetic expansion, and audience investment," establishing whole, complex, narrative worlds that "viewers gradually feel they inhabit along with the characters" (95, 111). Yet Sconce locates the lauded "quality" of such narratives in structural ingenuity and self-reflexivity, and, for the most part, neglects just those serial elements he had previously noted (95).[2]

In similar terms, Jason Mittell (2006) suggests that innovative television series should be grouped together under the label "narrative complexity," which constitutes "a redefinition of episodic forms under the influence of serial narration" (29, 32).[3] However, he distinguishes the seriality of narrative complexity from melodramatic forms: "narrative complexity moves serial form outside of the generic assumptions tied to soap operas . . . rejecting or downplaying the melodramatic style and primary focus on relationships" (32).

To value recent serial dramas for plot and structure over character development and interpersonal relationships is highly questionable. Serial shows such as *The Wire* and *Breaking Bad* emphasize audiences' emotional investment in the development of characters and in their changing relationships. It is such changes that enable the expansion of their diegetic worlds (see Williams 2014). Of course, serials also involve intricate plots to achieve their aesthetic purposes, as well as stunning action sequences in a manner similar to early melodrama's spectacular exploits. But they do not do so to the exclusion of character relationships or the narrative role of emotionality.

Although Mittell (2015) recently acknowledged that "complex television dramas" deploy melodrama's emphasis on "relationships and characters' struggles" and rely on "affective morality," this admission simply supplements narrative complexity (241, 245). However, recognition of melodramatic aesthetics necessitates a more thorough reworking of the ways we make sense of contemporary television. In an era when television series, including shows associated with "quality TV," are moving from episodic-serial hybrids to full serialization,[4] understanding the fundamental difference serial melodrama brings to narrative processes is crucial. For instance, as Linda Williams (2012) notes, seriality entails movement over time—transformation—not an "it" moment of epiphany in which the "true" nature of a character or fictional world is revealed (531–33; also see chapter 10). The "truth" exists in the movement itself, through continuous alterations in situations. Thus we cannot say of *Breaking Bad* that one single moment depicts the "real" character of Walter White (Bryan Cranston). He exists as the accumulation of his interactions with others, the actions he takes, how he feels, and how we feel about him over the evolving, prolonged existence of the series. Seriality's meanings and emotional effects rest in its succession of moments, not necessarily significant in themselves but important in their accumulated relationality, and in the way they are gathered for audiences over narrative time. Whether presented in a structurally ingenious or a straightforward, linear manner, such emotional accumulation itself involves complex narrative processes.

In this regard, we can consider Preston "Bodie" Broadus (J. D. Williams) from *The Wire*, who appeared over a four-year period (2002–2006) as a secondary rather than central character. When we first encounter Bodie, he is sixteen or seventeen years old and involved in the drug trade in a low-level capacity. In Episode 12 of Season 1 ("Cleaning Up"), Bodie is ordered to murder his friend, sixteen-year-old Wallace (Michael B. Jordan). An endearing character, Wallace looks after a group of young children in the projects, living with them in a squat, feeding them and making sure they go to school, although he is little more than a child himself. As a viewer, I felt shocked when Bodie shoots and kills his unsuspecting friend, believing it unforgivable. Yet by Episode 13 of Season 4 ("Final Grades"), when Bodie meets his own demise, I found his all but inevitable death deeply moving. Over the course of four seasons, the nature of the audience's emotional engagement with the character may change in generative ways, in my experience, for example, through stages from anger to empathy.

Bodie's story is not a psychological account, focusing on the character's insights; nor is it about him and his individual flaws. We know relatively little about Bodie as an interiorized, private entity. He never experiences a moral epiphany, an "it" moment that results in his transformation. To the end, he remains a drug dealer who has only marginally made his way up the ladder. In his early twenties, when he is shot to death, Bodie seems like an old man of the streets, disturbed by the way the drug trade has changed.

Rather than vested in character interiority, the felt "moral legibility" in Bodie's story line belongs to audience members through their emotionally charged recognition of the economic and social conditions that determine his existence, meaning that Bodie cannot live his life differently. This is a *felt* recognition—not simply an intellectual judgment—one developed over narrative time and accumulating events. Bodie's function as a character is to lead us to care about him differently than at the outset of his story. As such, he functions as a socioemotional character in a narrative world in which "harm is the norm."

Certainly, audience members will not all follow the same emotional trajectories. But tracking various socioemotional arcs in response to melodrama's narrative techniques is productive. For me, Bodie's story, culminating in his death during a shootout he cannot win, feels simultaneously futile and oddly heroic. Futile because his attempt to protect the street corner on which he deals from encroaching, more hardened competition is a lost cause. But heroic, as well, in laying claim to his economic subsistence, trying to safeguard his livelihood and identity, represented by his corner, the sole location where he exists in the world. Melodramatic seriality enables increasing and changing emotional engagement through story expansion, so that we do not forget or negate the earlier Bodie; rather, we accumulate socioemotional nuances and complexities in our perceptions of the character and his circumstances.

The Wire has been heralded as exceptional, precisely because it encompasses the interior workings of a complex social world that constructs and constrains its denizens. Similarly, the socioemotional dynamics of *Breaking Bad* demonstrate melodrama's capacity to embed emotional stakes in social contexts. Consider, for example, Walter and Skyler's marriage crisis in Season 3, Episode 3 (April 4, 2010). The melodramatic aesthetic frames their story "socioemotionally" through feelings of betrayal that arise from the institutions of gender, marriage, and domesticity. Rather than offering introspection, the aesthetics of emotional expressionism reveal how Walter and Skyler (Anna Gunn) externalize their feelings in actions aimed at affecting or altering each other's emotions. Utilizing melodrama's performative "language" to express what cannot otherwise be articulated, the couple deploy extroverted gestures conveying emotional states. Rather than taking feelings of betrayal as self-evident, *Breaking Bad* uses melodrama's socioemotional aesthetic to dramatize a conflict over what betrayal means, asking who has the right to feel betrayed, to expect loyalty, on what grounds.

Walter's circumstances derive from his subsistence as an underpaid, undervalued high school chemistry teacher who, just as he turns fifty, learns he has lung cancer. Realizing that a dutiful life as husband, father, and teacher has failed to bring either financial success or respect, he turns his talents at chemistry to the drug trade. Skyler, having learned that Walter is involved in illegal activities and fearing for the safety of the family, demands that Walter leave home and begins divorce proceedings. Walter, growing increasingly angry at her refusal of reconciliation, breaks into the house. Following a failed appeal to the police, Skyler feels trapped in her own home by his imposed presence. Walter pressures Skyler to accept his drug money, insisting he has *earned* it—for the family's sake. He feels betrayed by Skyler's refusal to acknowledge that he is fulfilling his role as economic provider.

Skyler's sense of domestic entrapment is visualized when she barricades herself and her infant daughter in the master bedroom to escape Walter. One morning as Skyler slips out to work, a large duffel bag of cash obstructing her path makes Walter's economic point. Barring her way, he insists she listen to him without interruption, mistakenly taking her imposed silence for acquiescence. Later Skyler makes her own point of view felt through an action with enormous emotional reverberations. While he is fixing a hopefully idyllic family dinner, Walter is stunned when Skyler returns home to state just three words: "I fucked Ted" (referring to her boss and giving the episode its title, "I.F.T."). This gains both Walter's attention and his silence as Skyler stakes *her* counterclaim on the rights of marriage and family. She makes him pause in his own self-justification—but only when confronted with what appears as sexual betrayal. Now it is Walter who feels alienated in his claimed domestic space. In performing an act she understands Walter will feel as marital betrayal, Skyler *enacts* her own feelings of betrayal by Walter's failure to consult her over drastic changes to the circumstances of the family, which threaten both physical danger and emotional harm. Skyler conveys her sense of betrayal through an action she emotionally recognizes Walter will perceive as breaking trust. The emotions expressed and exchanged between Walter and Skyler are effective precisely to the degree that they link closely to the meanings and ethical values marital relations have for the characters, and for audience members (see Pribram 2014).

Walter's and Skyler's tribulations are not primarily a story about individual dissatisfactions; rather, they concern the social pressures and cultural expectations placed on husbands and wives in contemporary Western middle-class life. Primarily, Walter's anger is about the values of his era, his class and gender position having failed to deliver the rewards promised in return for his own commitments. Walter's and Skyler's roiling feelings and actions can only be understood within recognized cultural values—in this episode, concerning justice and injustice in terms of gendered marital relations. *Breaking Bad* foregrounds marriage as an emotional institution as well as an economic, social, and legal one. Walter's and Skyler's feelings are not private or only personal; rather, they engage in a high-stakes struggle, involving repeated acts of emotional contestation over the ethical meanings of, and their respective identities as, spouses and parents.

The realization of Walter and Skyler's relationship uses another facet of melodrama: an aesthetics of performance based on emotional expressionism. Their relational dynamic is not primarily self-reflective but a drive to communicate, as both attempt to affect the feelings and, so, the behaviors of the other. Over the course of these three episodes, their relationship plays out as a continually escalating series of emotional contestations. At one instance, when two police officers join the couple in the living room—Skyler having called them to complain that Walter is in the home against her will—their infant daughter starts crying. Skyler's fear for the baby has led her to physically separate the newborn from Walter.

But in the presence of the officers, Walter reaches the baby first, picking her up and soothing her as Skyler helplessly watches.

The baby, like the duffel bag of cash, becomes the material repository of their feelings, over which the two perform their competing claims against the backdrop of a familiar domesticity. The significance of the dramatic element, in this instance the baby, lies in the meanings and emotional valences each character attaches to her, meanings made available for audience recognition, whether conscious or not. The baby, for Skyler, is the being she most wants to protect, to make safe, over whom she has come to feel almost constant terror. For Walter, estrangement from his infant daughter is unfair because everything he has done has been for her sake. He believes he has acted to safeguard her future, in his eventual absence. The child embodies the couple's conflict, lodged in the incompatibility of what each feels most intensely about her well-being.

If we return to the climactic scene of the third episode, in which Skyler announces "I fucked Ted," the narrative's emphasis on emotional expressionism rather than psychic introspection becomes clear. We have witnessed Skyler's decision to have sex with her boss when, encountering him in the office's photocopier room, Skyler approaches Ted and kisses him. The scene then cuts directly to Skyler pulling into her driveway at home later that evening. None of the sexual activity between Skyler and Ted is shown, an unusual choice for contemporary programming. That the physical act is implied rather than visualized accords with Skyler's motivations; she is not driven by sexual desire or love for Ted. The significance of her act resides in the emotional impact it has on Walter. Thus the narrative dwells on the subsequent encounter between Skyler and Walter and the shock of her announcement. Theirs is not, as in psychological realist drama, a journey of self-discovery but a series of performative actions aimed at the other, as they fight over changing, emotionally charged situations, each infused with cultural values. Sometimes the characters attempt to articulate their positions in rational language, as Walter does around the cash-filled duffel bag. But the most gripping moments occur when the two express their feelings through actions intended to wound or defeat the other, as when Walter breaks into the house, refusing to leave, or when we grasp that Skyler has had sex with her boss in order to unnerve Walter.

Here, Buckley's description of melodrama's core structure, careening from emotion to contrary emotion applies. Melodramatic serialization offers scant equilibrium, as arguably occurs in episodic structures that regularly depart from, only to reinstate in circular fashion, a comforting status quo. In serialization, forward narrative movement results from accumulated emotional states, activated not in a steady linear progression toward improvement or decline but lodged in fluctuating twists of temporary amelioration and newly encountered harm.

Breaking Bad relies on melodrama's practice of producing multiple versions of what an emotional act—betrayal, trust, fidelity—might or ought to be, rather than presuming a taken-for-granted, self-evident notion of what constitutes "betrayal" or any other emotion. Melodrama's socioemotional trajectory demands exploration of the ways betrayal takes shape according to specific and varying contexts and characters. Besides offering narratives *about* emotion, televisual serial narrativity is structured by, in Buckley's terms, oscillating emotionality. *Breaking Bad* draws out a narrative of emotion; in this specific instance, a narrative about feelings of betrayal between spouses, between individuals and social strictures and, ultimately, through characters following different paths, which address the varying positions of different audience members.

The climactic finale of "I.F.T." provides a compelling example of how such narratives of emotion become operational. We recognize that Walter is stunned into silence by Skyler's declaration. Yet, in a dramatically effective sequence, the audience too feels shock in this moment, despite the fact that we already know Skyler has had sex with her boss. Audience shock cannot derive from surprise at Skyler's action, but must arise from its implications. Some will feel aligned with Walter, empathizing with his devastated sense of marital betrayal. Others may be startled because this is the first time they clearly recognize Skyler's motives: to turn against Walter her own sense of betrayal. Viewers in the former group may well be dumbfounded by the cold, succinct way Skyler informs Walter of her adultery, intended for maximum destructive impact. Viewers in the latter case, like myself, feel astonishment at Skyler's skillful recuperation of some feeling of control over her existence, even if limited and temporary. In all instances, audience members are left to determine whose feelings of betrayal they most sympathize with or respect. As befits the complexity of an emotional assemblage such as betrayal and the complicated circumstances surrounding it, that judgment may not be easy or consistent. Certain spectators may well be left with mixed emotions.

In the case of the conflict within the White marriage, a number of largely young male viewers vocally expressed on various Internet forums their antipathy toward Skyler (see Mittell 2015, 347–48). Despite Walter's numerous, highly questionable acts, affecting both his family and his moral status, these viewers blamed Skyler for refusing to stand by her spouse. Hers was the series' unforgivable, ultimate betrayal. In response, actress Anna Gunn (2013) wrote a much-publicized *New York Times* editorial, accusing Skyler-despising viewers of misogyny. In subsequent seasons, perhaps in response to objections on the part of an important viewing demographic, Skyler's character was altered so that she championed Walter, becoming complicit in his illegal pursuits, until his actions finally brought the family to ruin.

Reactions to Walter and Skyler's relationship illustrate the potential cultural impact of narrative depictions grounded in emotionality, and the multiple forces that play a part in the felt experiences available to audiences. Whether embedded in nonlinear or reflexive structural ingenuity or not, the constantly evolving and socioemotionally saturated relations portrayed in *Breaking Bad*, and other contemporary TV serials, offer astonishing narrative complexity at the emotional level. Pursuing an aesthetics of emotion requires tracking intricate deployments of a potentially extensive range of auditory, visual, and performative expressions to convey an equal diversity of emotions among an often large cast of characters sharing a narrative world. We can thus follow the drama of shifting emotions embodied by characters responding to varying social conditions. Such an analytical emphasis recognizes socioemotionality as an important facet of subjectivity, alongside rational, affective/visceral, or psychological being.

Emotions, in both narrative theory and cultural theory, have largely been ignored or, in the specific case of melodrama, treated as excess. Yet understanding the processes of emotionality within the specific traditions and parameters of melodrama allows us to retain a sense of characters as culturally embedded beings operating within the contexts of social institutions and practices; to appreciate the communicative, expressionist functions of emotionality; and to pay better attention to the narratives of emotion that surround us. Melodramatic modes of storytelling, grounded in emotions and felt recognition—involving us in perceptions of how we do, might, or ought to feel things—enable us to connect with and understand the narrative and social worlds we occupy.

One of the motivations for the development of affect theory has been to counter too-pat conceptualizations, lodged in rationality, provided in recent decades by linguistic, psychoanalytical, and ideological theories. However, turning to emotions addresses similar concerns without reduction to a largely neurobiological, autonomic version of human activity. Through emotions, as both sociocultural and narrative phenomena, we retain a sense of meaningfulness, without necessarily having to explain those meanings in cognitive or ideological terms. Critical scholarship, through the analytical, articulable means available to it, cannot provide an exhaustive account of the emotional expressions and experiences that are performed via narrative media, but we can do better in acknowledging emotionality's pervasive, vital presence in our stories and in our lives. Emotions, in their role in the circulation and expression of meaningfulness, in their centrality to human relations, and in their entanglement with the sociocultural, remain indispensable to the appreciation of the aesthetic structure and cultural value of melodrama.

NOTES

My heartfelt thanks to Christine Gledhill and Linda Williams for their challenging comments and insightful counsel.

1. I use "narrativity" as Massumi does, to refer to the broad activity of storytelling.
2. Sconce's list of innovative television series includes *Northern Exposure, Star Trek, Twin Peaks, Seinfeld, Xena: Warrior Princess, ER, Buffy the Vampire Slayer, Friends, The X-Files, The Sopranos*, and *The Simpsons* (2004, 95).
3. Mittel (2006) cites *Seinfeld, Lost, The West Wing, The X-Files, Twin Peaks, Alias, Malcolm in the Middle, Arrested Development, Veronica Mars, Firefly, The Sopranos, Six Feet Under, Curb Your Enthusiasm, The Wire, The Simpsons, Oz, Deadwood, My So-Called Life, Buffy the Vampire Slayer*, and 24.
4. For example, *The Wire, Breaking Bad, Lost, The Following, The Bridge, House of Cards, Dexter, Under the Dome, The Walking Dead, True Blood, Game of Thrones, Ray Donovan, The Affair, How to Get Away with Murder, Blind Spot*, and *Fargo*.

15

Expressionist Aurality

The Stylized Aesthetic of Bhava *in Indian Melodrama*

IRA BHASKAR

This chapter focuses on two ideas central to melodrama debates: emotion and the traditional Sacred. I argue that, arising from their encounters in the 1930s and 1940s with German expressionism and the new technology of sound, India's different cinemas developed a new aural and visual aesthetic as an expressive language for the articulation of *bhava* (emotion), itself a fundamental tenet of Indian aesthetics. Expressionist low-key, high-contrast lighting that molded mise-en-scène, a nonnaturalistic performance mode, and the use of music, in particular song, reinvented expressionist aesthetics, which resulted in the stylized orchestration of emotion that characterizes the Indian melodramatic form. At the same time, this coalescence of practices developed an idiom that was deepened in its connotative and communicative charge by an intersection with the Sacred. Contrary to Peter Brooks's position that melodrama uncovers the "moral occult" in lieu of a destroyed traditional Sacred, I have argued elsewhere that the Sacred has remained fully active in Indian cultures and has a fundamental and constitutive relationship to Indian melodrama (Bhaskar 2012, 172). The idiom of the Sacred here foregrounds a charged language of emotion as the affective drive of individual subjectivity; at the same time, it both amplifies and deepens the implications of the subjective in the social. The Brooksian idea of melodrama as a compensatory form for the loss of the Sacred certainly needs rethinking, not just in the context of Indian melodrama but, as this volume suggests, in other contexts as well (see chapters 2, 9, and 16).

GERMAN EXPRESSIONISM AND INDIAN CINEMAS

A preliminary question concerns the impact of German cinematic expressionism on Indian filmmakers. Its significance for Hollywood in the 1940s has been codified and critically canonized via the work of émigré directors such as Murnau, Lang, and others, particularly in the emergence of film noir with its expressionist lighting, split subjectivities, and ambiguous moral spaces (Thompson and

Bordwell 1994, 259; Schraeder1996). This direct link between the haunted screens of German expressionism and American film noir is now part of film history, but Patrice Petro (1989) offers another history of Weimar cinema. She rereads "Weimar's 'haunted screen' in terms of a 'melodramatic imagination'" (28). Noting that Lotte Eisner's description of the *kammerspielfilm* foregrounds its "intensity of expression," Petro comments that it is "marked by a slow and deliberate narrative pace, an excessive or overly emphatic visual style" exhibited particularly in those moments when the despair of the characters is expressed in the "incoherent sounds" and "mute voicing" described by Eisner. The kammerspiel film is, Petro suggests, a form that "anticipates Brooks's analysis of melodrama as a 'fundamentally expressionist drama'" (29). It is in this cinematic realization of melodrama's powerful articulation of the unsayable and the inexpressible that I see German expressionism's impact on Indian cinemas during the 1930s and 1940s, an influence that has yet to be explored and deserves to be understood. Taking a cue from Brooks's identification of melodrama as an expressionist form "in psychic, in ethical, in formal terms" (1976, 55), and from Petro's work on Weimar melodramas, I am interested in identifying and exploring how the emerging aural aesthetics of Indian cinemas' encounter with expressionist visual and performative forms developed the distinctive melodramatic modes and idioms of these cinemas, and how in turn this encounter redefined expressionism for Indian cinemas.

The story of Himanshu Rai and Devika Rani's connection with UFA in the 1920s is now well known, as is Rai's collaborative ventures with different international film companies, including Munich's Emelka Film Company with which Rai coproduced the 1925 silent *Prem Sanyas* (*Light of Asia*), directed by Emelka's Franz Osten and photographed by Josef Wirsching and Willi Kiermeier. Osten went on to direct other silent films for Himanshu Rai—*Shiraz* in 1928 and *Prapancha Pash* (*A Throw of Dice*) in 1929. When Rai set up Bombay Talkies in 1934, Osten moved to Bombay, where he directed several films for the company over the next five years before he was interned by the British in 1939 at the outbreak of World War II (Brandlmeier 1995). Wirsching, too, worked with Bombay Talkies, as did the set designer Carl von Spreti (Barnouw and Krishnaswamy 1980, 93–103). Wirsching continued to have a career in Bombay films until the early 1970s, photographing the classic courtesan tale *Pakeezah* (1971) toward the end of his career. Other German technicians and artistes also worked in Bombay Talkies, but the German connection is not limited to this studio. Mohan Bhavnani had been trained in UFA, and his Bhavnani Films employed two Jewish exiles: Walter Kaufmann, the music composer who wrote music for a number of the Bhavnani films (see Gangar 2013), and script writer Willy Haas, who had worked with directors Pabst and Murnau, writing *The Naked Truth* (1940) and *Prem Nagar* (*City of Love* 1941) for Bhavnani (see Gangar and Ungern-Sternberg 2005; Ungern-Sternberg 2005). It is likely that the presence of these and other personnel from the German film industry influenced the shooting and narration of the films they worked on through conversations and exchange of ideas. Both the look and concerns of Chetan Anand's 1946 *Neecha Nagar* (figure 15.1) suggests that the aesthetic discussions between

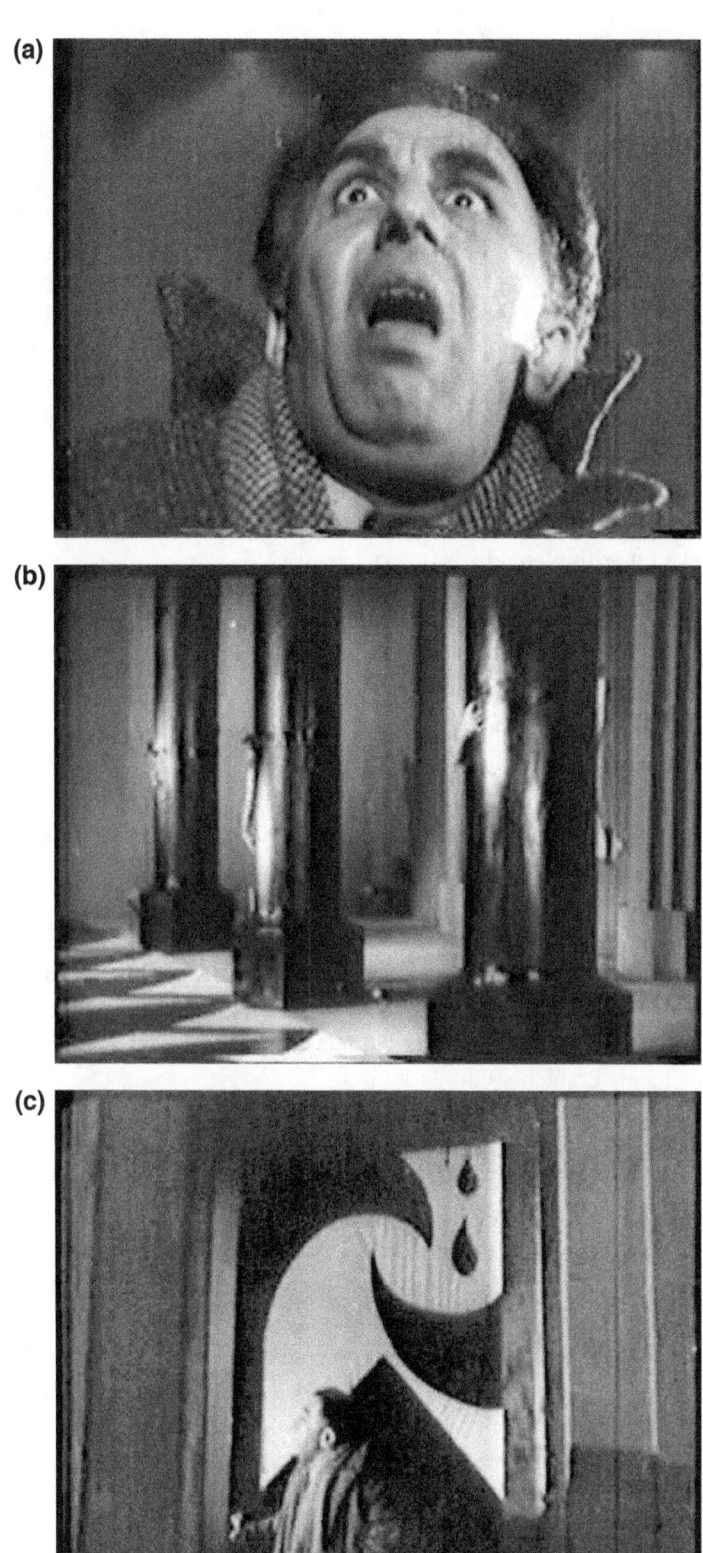

Figure 15.1a-c Neecha Nagar (1946, Chetan Anand). Expressionist lighting, shadows, and distorting reflections.

Willy Haas, Anand, and his wife Uma, who worked on this project, must have been significant for the resulting film (Ungern-Sternberg 2005, 45).

There are many other connections,[1] but for the purposes of this discussion the experience of V. Shantaram is exemplary. In a biography of her father, Madhura Pandit Jasraj (2015) narrates how in 1933 he went to Germany to print his and India's first color experiment with *Sairandhri* at the Agfa and UFA laboratories in Berlin and at Babelsberg (107–14). In his autobiography, Shantaram (1987) recounts that although the *Sairandhri* project was not successful, he spent a long time at UFA. At night he would make a note in his diary of everything that he saw during the day, including how difficulties were dealt with. He used these insights later when he returned to work in the new studio of Prabhat in Pune, increasing the quality of their films (167). While in Berlin, he often went to see films with his German assistant with whom he was very friendly.[2]

Disillusioned and depressed with the *Sairandhri* results, Shantaram recounts that he turned to thoughts of his next film. The idea of making a film that would critique obscurantist and inhuman ritual practices in Hinduism had begun to grow in his mind. The memory of a goat sacrifice witnessed in his childhood sharpened his focus, not only on the practice of animal sacrifices but also on the shocking presence of human sacrifice practiced by some cults. Obsessed with this idea, Shantaram decided to set his next film in medieval India, centering on the figure of a ritualistic priest serving a Chandika temple[3] whose power over the illiterate and blindly superstitious populace Shantaram wanted to image via the priest's powerful hypnotic look. He needed a telephoto lens for an immense close-up of the priest's eye, and Peterson, his associate at Agfa, took him to a lens manufacturer. Though the kind of lens he wanted was not available, he was assured that, with some changes, a 300-millimeter lens would be ready for him within a fortnight (172). Thus Shantaram's *Amrit Manthan* premiered in 1934, the first film made in the company's new Prabhat studio in Pune.[4]

Amrit Manthan opens onto a dark cavelike space with flickering lights and a moving camera tilting and panning over a cavernous dark area until it rests for a few seconds on a frontal close-up of a huge, ferocious-looking sculpted head with bulging eyes and protruding tongue. All the while, audible on the soundtrack is a hymn chanted to the Goddess Chandika. The camera moves back to reveal the face to be part of a huge statue of the Goddess. It begins to circle the space, now visible as a temple, in a low-angle semicircular tracking shot that reveals the cavernous space full of worshippers. A priest circles a large ritual plate holding auspicious oil lamps in offering to the deity as hymns continue on the soundtrack.[5] The tracking camera, which had begun its movement from beside the huge statue, circles the congregation at its periphery, revealing the sculpted and pillared architecture of the Goddess's sanctum. The group gathered in worship gazes at the Goddess, illuminated by oil lamps. A standing figure in the center is seen from the back. As the camera completes a semicircle and positions this figure in the center of a long shot, with the Goddess in deep space in the background, the film cuts to a huge close-up of a single eye (figure 15.2).

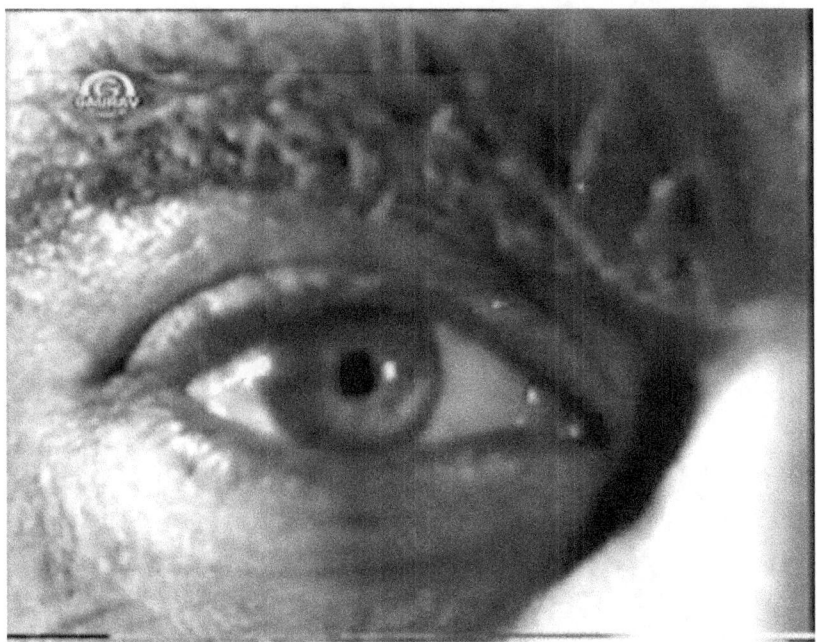

Figure 15.2 Amrit Manthan (1934, V. Shantaram). The Priest's commanding eye.

There is complete silence as the eyeball moves from right to left and back, surveying the group, while a sonorous voice addresses the crowd, asking whether they have heard King Krantivarma's new order that from that year, at the great *yagya* (celebratory ritual worship) of the Goddess Chandika, animal and human sacrifice will not be allowed. As the group starts in surprise, the huge eye squints, and the voice exhorts them to understand that the King's reform aims to uproot and destroy the mighty tree of religion and *dharma*. The face of the head priest making the announcement is not revealed in this scene. His authority seems to operate through his hypnotic look and the disembodied voice that blames the gathering for having given the King power to change tradition. The sequence continues to alternate the close-up of the priest's eye with expressionist compositions of the gathering, who demand that tradition be upheld with the death of the King (figure 15.3). The priest's voice assures them that it is the Goddess who has spoken through them and it is she who will now choose the King's assassin. The sequence ends with the Goddess's garland falling before a righteous noble, Yashodharma, who the priest announces is the chosen one. All the while, it is the eye that controls the proceedings that determine the death of the King.

The expressionist idioms of this opening sequence—deep shadows, semicircular tracking, flickering lights of the cavelike temple, the chanted mantras, and the close-up of the priest's eye—articulate the differing worldviews embodied in the two protagonists, the vile priest, Rajguru, and the off-screen, morally upright and humane ruler, Krantivarma, who has banned animal and human sacrifices. It sets

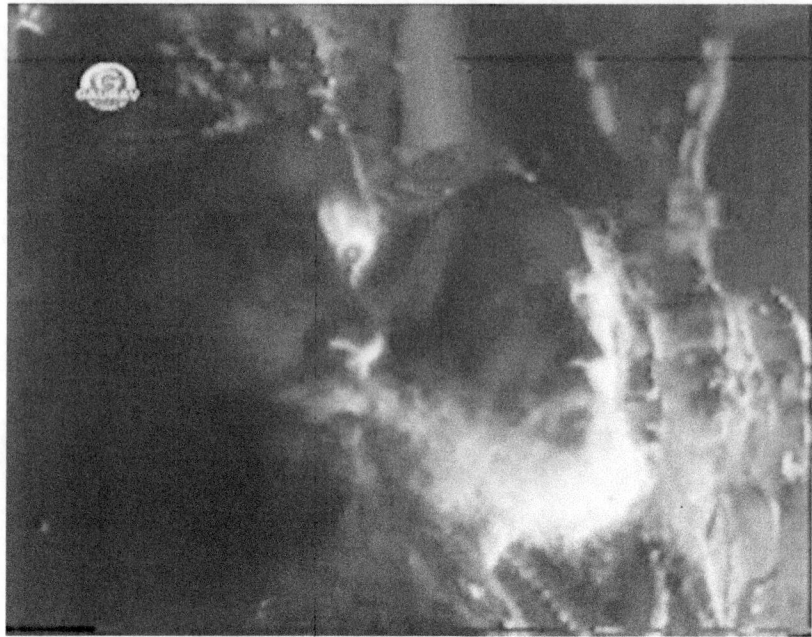

Figure 15.3 Amrit Manthan (1934, V. Shantaram). Expressionist low-key lighting and shadows on worshippers, conveying their investment in tradition.

the stage for the melodramatic conflict between polarized values: on the one hand, an overweening drive for complete control and destructive power, and on the other, a benign concern for the well-being of the people.

That expressionism provided Shantaram with a highly dramatic and expressive idiom to address social evils is evident both in this example and in his 1937 film *Kunku*, which critiques the practice of marrying young girls to older men. At a crucial moment in *Kunku*, after Neera, the young wife of the old ex-widower Kakasaheb, has refused the consummation of her marriage and unburdened her heart to his widowed daughter, he undergoes a critical confrontation with his alter ego. Having overheard the conversation between his young wife and his daughter, he is determined to prove them wrong that his marriage to a young woman was mistaken. As he climbs the stairs to his room, he is astonished to see that the wall clock has stopped. Angrily swinging the pendulum to begin the clicking of the clock, and throwing his cane away to prove he does not need it, he enters his bedroom and walks to the dressing table to look in the mirror. The image does not satisfy him, and he pulls out a bottle to dye his moustache black, only to be confronted with his image in the mirror asking whether the dyed moustache will make *his* heart young again and satisfy Neera's youthful heart. The image in the mirror calls him a monkey for having married a young woman. Annoyed at this criticism, Kakasaheb shatters the mirror, and from every shard now spread on the floor his other self laughs at him (figure 15.4). Alternating between close-ups of the recoiling Kakasaheb and his laughing image in the shards, the sequence foregrounds the

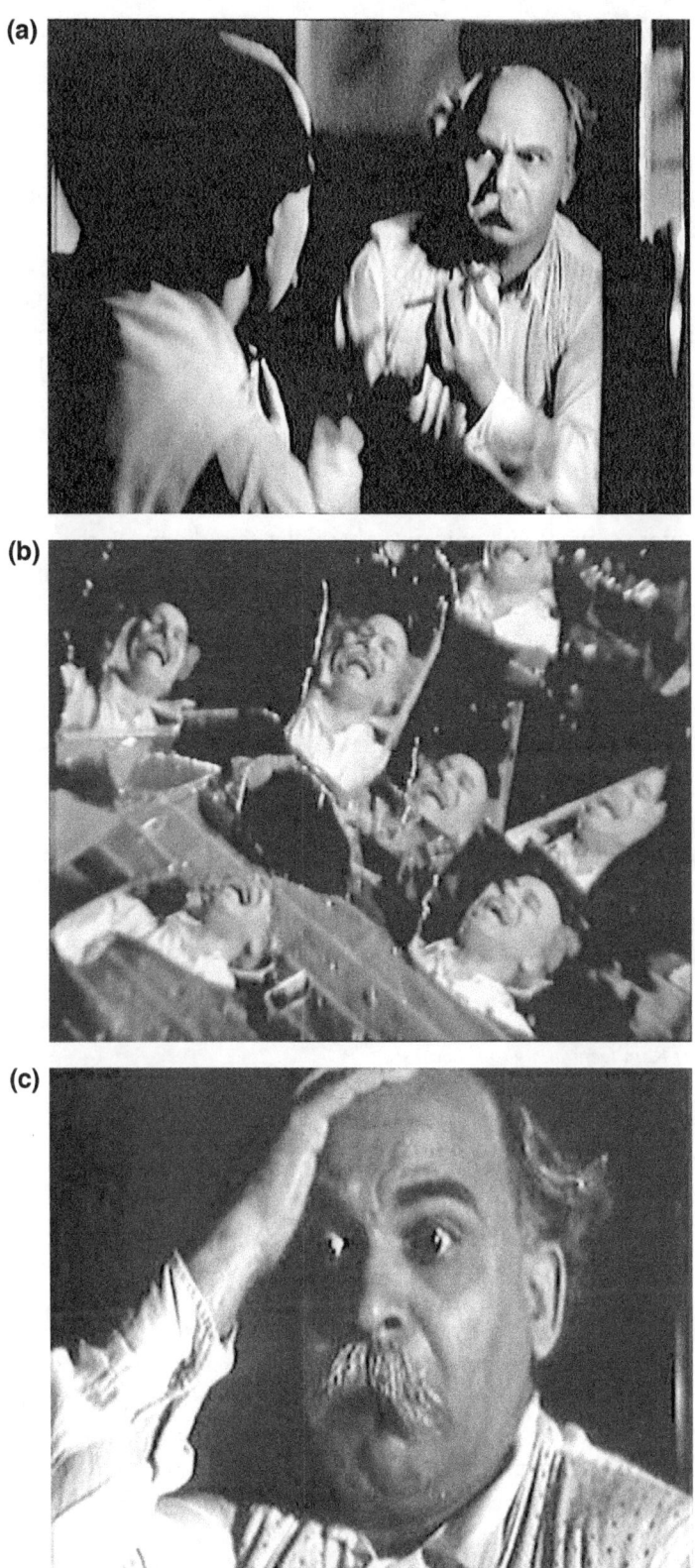

Figure 15.4a-c *Kunku* (1937, V. Shantaram). (a) Kakasaheb confronts his mirror image. (b) His reflection fractured in the broken mirror's fragments. (c) He recoils from his reflected images laughing back at him.

inner contradictions of the character. The splitting of the self between the drives of desire and reality and the use of angled and tilted perspectives are all familiar expressionist tropes that Shantaram uses here to foreground socially unjust and exploitative practices against women.

Expressionism enabled Shantaram to make pointed social critique in dynamic form. It also facilitated the psychologization of characters. As I have argued elsewhere, "in the expressionist foregrounding of emotion, melodrama also enacts subjectivization as the embodiment of the individual's most intense condition of felt selfhood" (Bhaskar 2012, 163). Shantaram's *Shejari* (1941) demonstrates this stylized orchestration of affect, embodied in the expressive language of *bhava* (emotion). Here the articulation of intense personal emotion is deepened in its connotative and communicative charge by the idioms of the traditional Sacred, abstracting the subjective within a larger social-historical-political matrix. Shantaram's narrative of Hindu-Muslim friendship and brotherhood figures a vision of communal amity in the fractious atmosphere of the 1940s, when violent sectarian conflict had driven the communities apart. At a critical moment, the intense suffering generated by the breakdown of the relationship between two friends, the Hindu Patil and the Muslim Mirza, is cast as the emotion of figures from the *Ramayana*—the grieving of Bharat for his banished elder brother Ram—in a language inspired by vernacular re-creations of the Sanskrit epic.[6] Stunned at the course of events and in a world of private anguish, Patil almost unwittingly begins reciting Bharat's anguish at the separation from his brother, Ram, and then asks his wife to sing the verses, thus giving voice to his feelings of bereavement at the decisive rupture of the relationship with his Muslim friend and brother:[7]

> *When Shri Ram went away to the forest,*
> *Bharat was engulfed in sorrow*
> *He fell and rolled on the ground, crying*
> *And cried out, O Ram, my beloved . . .*
> *I cannot bear this separation,*
> *How can I live separated from my beloved brother*
> *My breath's leaving me, come back . . .*[8]

There are different translations and transcreations of the Sanskrit *Ramayana* in Marathi, and it is likely that Shantaram, the lyricist Athavale, and the music director Master Krishnarao imagined this sequence from the way in which the Marathi *Ramayana* was sung and performed in Maharashtra, where it was popular and accessible even to the unlettered. The emotion of the vernacular *Ramayana*—its narrative, its everyday language used to express the heart-rending mourning song—evokes a mythic resonance in this separation of brothers. The poignancy and hopelessness of the moment is conveyed through the high-pitched timbre of Patil's wife's singing, the stylized gestures of their bodies stretched out in despair, the expressionist lighting, and, as the singing reaches a crescendo, Patil's inability to endure the burden of the song/recitation anymore (figure 15.5).

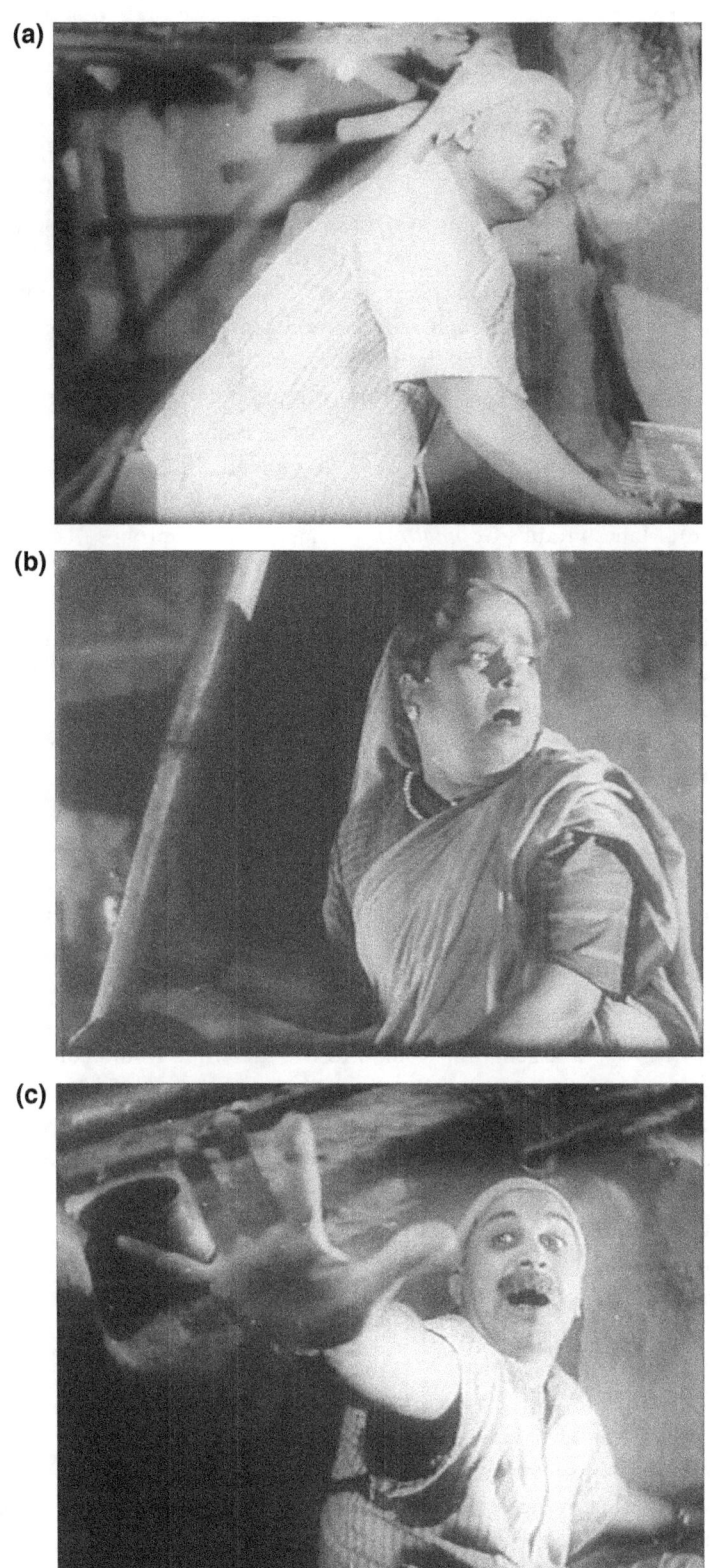

Figure 15.5a-c *Shejari* (1941, V. Shantaram). (a) The grieving Hindu Patil. (b) His wife singing Bharat's anguish. (c) Patil unable to bear the burden of the song.

EXPRESSIONISM, THE SONG, AND INDIA'S AURAL AESTHETICS

The film sequence just described is also an example, as we shall soon see, of the crucial features of the Indian melodramatic form that I have discussed elsewhere: "the privileging and amplification of emotion, [and] the centrality of music and the song as the vehicle for this expression, as well as the development of the song as the language of the ineffable" (Bhaskar 2012, 166). The exteriorizing and foregrounding of felt interiority, as a crucial function of the song, also represents the Indian reinvention of expressionist aesthetics. In the 1940s, expressionist idioms—lighting, composition, performance—were widespread. Mehboob Khan's *Aurat* (1940) and *Najma* (1943), Chetan Anand's *Neecha Nagar* and K. A. Abbas's *Dharti ke Lal* (1946), Mahesh Kaul's *Gopinath* (1948), and Kamal Amrohi's *Mahal* (1949), to name just a few films from the decade, clearly demonstrate the coalescence in Indian melodrama of visual expressionist idioms and the aural aesthetics of the song. In *Najma* this aesthetic articulates the containment of woman's desire (Bhaskar and Allen 2009, 252–53); and in Kaul's *Gopinath*, the denouement of a woman's faith and love is expressed in the devotional idioms of *Vaishnav bhakti* (Bhaskar 2012, 172–74).[9] Amrohi's expressionist *Mahal* (1949) instantiates the destructive power of woman's desire and embodies the new charged language of emotion as an alternative aesthetic that foregrounds the distinctiveness of bhava as the affective drive of individual subjectivity.

Mahal opens as a Gothic romance with the arrival at an isolated mansion, one rain drenched night, of the new owner, Hari Shankar. He is immediately introduced by the gardener to the tragic history of this abandoned monument to love on the banks of the river Yamuna. Forty years ago, the mansion had been built by a man who would arrive by boat every night to oversee its building. After it was completed, he brought a beautiful woman to live there. He would come by boat to see her every midnight and leave at the break of day. One stormy night, the boat was caught in a whirlpool and he drowned. But before he died, his voice rang out over the water saying to his beloved that she must not despair; he would definitely return. However, after waiting a few years, Kamini also drowned on another stormy night in the river. In every storm thereafter, the people of the area would sight a boat sinking in the river, after which the sobbing of a woman would be heard. Shortly after hearing this story, Shankar has a dramatic encounter with the portrait of the dead owner who looks exactly like him; the mansion resounds with a song in a beautiful female voice about the certainty of the return of the beloved; and as he follows the voice, he sees at a distance a mysterious woman singing the haunting song. A sense of apprehension and yet enticement is created through high-contrast expressionist lighting, fluid camera movements, a baroque mise-en-scène, and the haunting song. Drawn irresistibly to the voice, the song, the woman, Shankar comes to believe that she is the spirit of the dead Kamini, and he the reincarnated lover come to fulfill the love that destiny had sundered (figure 15.6). Every attempt by his friend and his family to convince him that he is hallucinating and that he is on the path to destruction proves futile; at the stroke of two every

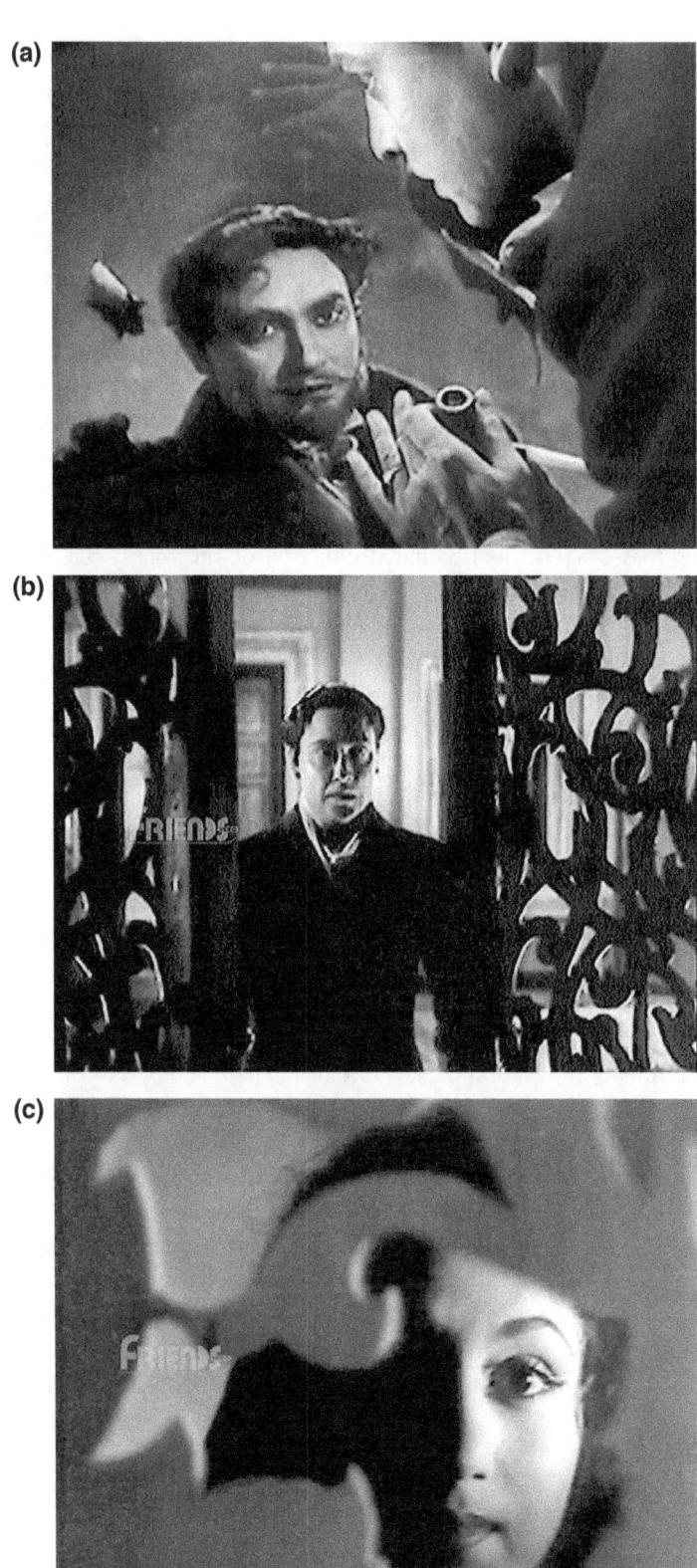

Figure 15.6a-c *Mahal* (1949, Kamal Amrohi). (a) Hari Shankar confronts the portrait of the dead owner that resembles him. (b) He is drawn to the woman's haunting voice. (c) The spectral woman returns.

night, wherever he might be, the haunting song returns, and Shankar becomes desperate to return to the mansion to glimpse Kamini.

Undoubtedly, it is Kamini's song, "*Aayega aanewalla*," that is the emotional fulcrum of this film. When Kamini sings "Oh yes, my beloved will return" or "how long will one suffer without hope, without support," in the different spaces of the mansion, the garden, or on the river, it is as if space itself were reverberating with her desperate faith and desire. This demonstrates an extremely significant feature of the Indian film song—the manner in which the individual and the environment, especially nature, are brought into resonance via the voice. These moments occur as here when the voice is thrown into the environment—when the mise-en-scène is soaked through with human desire, when the cosmos itself seems to reverberate with human emotion. However, it is not just the often invoked use of playback and dubbing that enables this peculiar disjunction of the voice from the human body. Rather, the amplification of emotion via the voice, penetrating, mapping, and dominating space, as in this case, suggests a crucial aesthetic principle that is central to the performance modes of the culture. One might say that the privileging of emotion, or bhava, points to a distinctive aesthetic aimed at evoking the appropriate *rasa* (taste, flavor, essence) as its goal.

It is perhaps not surprising that this film was shot by Josef Wirsching and that one can attribute its visual expressionist idioms to the creative interaction between Wirsching and director Amrohi. At the same time, it is the aural aesthetics of Indian cinemas that makes this film an excellent example of Brooks's idea that "in psychic, in ethical, in formal terms" melodrama is an expressionist form (1976, 55). What I am suggesting here is that the stylized amplification and exteriorizing of emotion via the song, combined with visual expressionist idioms, particularly the use of dramatic chiaroscuro lighting, created a cinematic grammar for a realization of interiority and the articulation of desire, in all its nuanced forms—whether as the enchantments and elation of new love or the pain and pathos of separation articulated in the literary and performing arts traditions as *viraha*.[10] As long as black-and-white cinematography lasted, this constellation of visual and aural style prevailed not just in the Hindustani cinema of Bombay but in India's other language cinemas as well. Examples abound throughout the 1950s and 1960s.

Guru Dutt's *Sahib Bibi aur Ghulam* (1962) was, according to credits, produced by Dutt and directed by its scriptwriter Abrar Ali. However, close attention to the choreography of the song sequence as well as film lore suggest it was directed by Dutt, a reputed master of "song picturization."[11] The film is also shot by his long-term cameraman and collaborator, V. K. Murthy, who had begun his career at Bombay Talkies and as a young man had worked with Wirsching on *Mahal*. All the film's songs deploy the idiom I have been explicating; for example, the song that Jaba, one of the two female leads of the film, sings at a critical moment in the narrative:

Meri baat rahi mere man mein
Kuch keh na saki uljhan mein

(My feelings remained unexpressed
I couldn't say anything in my confusion)

This is an expression of emotion that runs counter to her normal ebullient and teasing self. The gravity, the emotional intensity, the despair that is evident in both Shakeel Badayuni's lyrics and the high-contrast lighting and fluid camera movements are justified by Jaba's situation—her sense that she has lost the man she loves at the moment that she also realizes that she loves him deeply. The song precisely, but also evocatively, expresses all that Jaba could not say to him in the preceding scene. As an articulation of interior, inexpressible because ineffable, emotion, the Indian film song has a particularly weighty function.

This exteriorization and amplification of the character's emotion is also evident in Ritwik Ghatak's Bengali art film melodrama, *Subarnarekha* (1962), in which the protagonist Sita's song *Aaj ki Anando* ("such happiness today") begins in a high-pitched *aalaap*.[12] A low-angle, fast, circular pan commences from her figure and circles the trees of the forest in which she and Abhiram are standing, just after they understand that they have been in love for a long time. Her voice continues in a sound bridge to the next shot, another circular pan over the rocks and the river Subarnarekha. This shot finally rests, after completing its circle, in an extreme long shot of the two barely visible figures of Sita and Abhiram on a rock, almost at the point from which the circular pan had begun. It is only when the next shot frames the two characters in a three-quarter length shot that Sita's seated singing figure moves from the aalaap into the words of the song. The intensity of their emotion is articulated through camera movements over the landscape and exhibits once again the distinctive feature of the Indian film song discussed in relation to *Mahal*: the voice that inhabits the landscape, which then echoes with the characters' emotions—now amplified and resonant in the environment.

The aesthetics of the song sequences of *Mahal*, and particularly of *Aayega Aanewala*, also deeply influenced Vincent's 1964 Malayalam film, *Bhargavi Neelayam*. One of its key songs seems to quote *Mahal* even as its narrative cites the classic Amrohi film in its expressionist lighting, its spectral female protagonist, haunted house, and the song picturization of *Pottithakarnna Kinaavu* (*I made a silken swing with my shattered dreams*), in which the ghostly woman draws the stunned sympathetic male out of the house into different spaces of the garden and the surrounding environment.[13] Once again there seems to be a disjuncture between the voice and the body, with the voice inhering in the environment, which resounds with the emotions of the character. These characteristics, then, are not limited to the Hindustani cinema produced in Bombay. Neither are they exceptions; they represent the choreographic norm of song sequences articulating interior emotion, multiplied across India's different language cinemas from the 1940s to the 1960s. In what ways, then, can we understand this form and its aesthetics?

MUSICAL TRADITIONS OF SOUTH ASIA AND THE *NATYASHASTRA*

Recognizing the centrality of the song for the Indian cinematic form—its expressive functions, its articulation of a yearning for the beyond, its performative quality—directs us to its emergence from a different aesthetic sensibility and tradition. Focusing on expressionist aesthetics, I have only gestured toward the varied performance traditions that molded the aesthetic idioms and forms of Indian cinemas as they developed from the silent period into sound. The coming of sound immediately drew into cinema the diverse musical traditions of South Asia—*bhakti* (devotional) music, folk forms, popular performative and theatrical forms such as the *lavani*,[14] classical music as well as the semiclassical musical forms of thumris, kajris, dadras, and ghazals. The music of the kothas was a crucial element of this aural world as Yatindra Mishra (2009) points out: courtesans and singing women became the first stars of the 1930s, including Jaddanbai, Ameerbai Karnataki, Rajkumari, Kanandevi, Zohrabai, Gohar, and several others (46–47).[15] Cinema gave these singers a wider audience and a new world, while, along with musicians and music directors, they brought earlier musical traditions into film. But in that first decade a rapid transformation of music also took place, evolving and consolidating the contours of film music, and a filmic form in which that music, with the song as its centerpiece, had a central role.

If dialogue and dialogue writers became important in the early years of sound cinema, just as in film industries around the world, it is the abundance of songs in the films of the 1930s (with thirty a common number) that renders Indian cinemas distinct. Although the song was featured in other early sound cinemas, Indian film industries drew upon indigenous performative traditions in which musical dramatic form was common and to which song and dance was integral. In fact, drama was conceptualized and enacted in the classical period as dance-drama, with spoken and sung and danced passages alternating. Bharata's *Natyashastra* describes this form as one in which "speech is artificial and exaggerated, actions unusually emotional, gestures graceful" (Rangacharya 1996, 115). The Sanskrit word *natya* used for drama comes from the root word *nat*, which means dance and thus indicates drama, dance, and music functioning together (1). Furthermore, central to natya as performance is *abhinaya*—the use of the body, gestures, and facial expressions along with words for the enactment and expression of emotion (78). The very notion of drama, then, includes both enactment via dialogue and enactment via song and dance. Not only does the dramatic include song and dance, traditional drama could not be conceptualized without it. In this context, the *Natyashastra* says, "just as a picture without colour has no beauty, a drama without song has no charm" (294).

However, while the *Natyashastra* describes in detail different kinds of musical instruments, musical forms, and songs to be used in performances, it also states that speech, music, songs, and gesture should be used for the "expression of emotion." Precise description and classification of looks, expressions (both gestural and facial), and mime aimed to capture the nuances of human emotion (bhava) in the different situations elaborated. The myriad human emotions experienced in the course of life are categorized under eight or nine primary emotions or *sthayi bhavas* (love, mirth, anger, pity, heroic vigor, wonder, disgust, terror/fear, and calm). At the same time, a proliferating number of individual variations and resultant emotional conditions and states (*vyabhichari bhavas*) give a rich and textured quality to their representation in any performance. It is the transmutation of these emotions that a performance must achieve to create a more universal rasa (taste, flavor, essence) to be savored by audiences (52–77).[16] Thus the act of performance and representation simultaneously expresses emotion and distances it from the individual, attempting, through the stylization of performance, an abstraction and universalization of the emotion expressed.

Stylization is a key idea in the *Natyashastra*. Although it conceives a mimetic style based on the imitation of everyday human behavior—the *lokadharmi* (realistic) form—it is in fact the nonnaturalistic or stylized form, the *natyadharmi*, that is privileged by Bharata (115). It is this form that recognizes performance as performance, that foregrounds the performative, and that underscores the artistic/stylized nature of art as that which is not real life but a performance. Therefore, key to rasa aesthetics is the idea of stylization, the performative and the universalizing of individual emotion through its distancing effect. Once we accept the mode of stylization as a form of abstraction, it is not so difficult to accept the supposedly unreal quality of the Indian film song. The director Mani Ratnam once told me in an interview that for him the song was the space for abstraction, for going beyond the "literalism" that telling the story of recognizable characters and situations demands, and that with the song he could move into the abstract to give voice to that which he could not express otherwise. Such is the prime function that the song performs in Indian cinema.

As an aesthetic treatise, the *Natyashastra* was both descriptive and prescriptive. However, alternation of spoken word and song was characteristic not only of classical Sanskrit drama but also of a range of folk forms in different vernacular languages. Equally, the Islamicate[17] tradition of *dastans* and *qissas* used both speech and song in their oral narrations.[18] Moreover, the content of the songs and their modes drew from a variety of poetic traditions and sources. On the one hand, the Ras-lilas of Brindavan and the sensual Radha-Krishna poems embedded the idioms of the love song;[19] on the other Islamicate musical forms such as Sufi music, the *ghazal* form with Urdu poetry (*shairi*), and its repertoire of metaphors, idioms, and tropes subtended such content (Bhaskar and Allen 2009, 14–16). In addition, a host of musical idioms drew from classical and folk forms from different parts of the country. Thus, although the content of this semioperatic form of dramatic narrative varied, the basic contours and shape of its performative mode were the norm, as is evident in classical drama, folk forms, the Urdu Parsi stage, and the cinema. The coming of sound enabled the realization on Indian screens of a form that was already familiar, popular, and capable of articulating the bhavas so essential to the rasa experience. The audiences did not need to know rasa aesthetics to recognize and accept what this semioperatic musical drama was doing. It was always already a realized form infinitely pleasurable in its new avatar on the screen.

STYLIZED EMOTION, TRADITIONS OF THE SACRED, AND INDIAN MELODRAMA

I turn now to the connections between this stylized expression of intense emotion, the deep reservoir of indigenous images and myths they drew on, including

Bhakti and Sufi sacred traditions, and melodrama. These multiple traditions perform an amplification, elevation, and hyperbolic rendering of human desire that themselves represent Indian cinemas' reinvention of expressionist aesthetics, to which the song is central, and that I conceive as the orchestration of emotion in Indian melodrama. This can be explained through two song examples that reference Sufi cosmologies, structures of feeling, and poetic forms (see Shackle 2007). Like Bhakti, Sufi devotional poetry uses the language of love, drawing metaphors and images from ordinary experience and generating the emotional charge that has given Sufism its popular provenance. Mystical Islam inspired in Sufi poets and mystics a passionately intense love relationship with the Divine Being, often addressed as the Beloved or, when the poets took on a female persona, as the Lover. Central to Sufi philosophy is the idea of the phenomenal world as an expressive manifestation of the divine principle, the ultimate Reality, with Divine Love as the central essence of the universe (88). Furthermore, human experience is seen as a state requiring ultimate transcendence, rendering human love an affective condition that can both embody and lead to an ecstasy of union with the Divine. This is clearly indicated in a central Arabic phrase that, as Christopher Shackle points out, is often cited in Sufi thought: "*al-majaz qantarat al-haqiqa* (the 'Phenomenal is a bridge to the Real')." Moreover, Shackle notes, "the twin force of love as 'phenomenal love' (*ishq-e majazi*) and 'real love' (*ishq-e-haqiqi*) in which the human is seen as the mirror of the divine" offers the "prospect of bringing sexuality into full alignment with spirituality" (88). It is not surprising then that the vocabulary of human love bespeaks the divine in Sufi thought, with romantic emotional love, eroticism, and spirituality imbued with a feeling of ecstatic enchantment and total submersion of the Self in the Other. It is this inherent connection between the Sacred and the profane—the possibility that human "being" can be infused with divine essence—that underpins the appeal and power of Sufi thought, for human experience and emotion are then capable of a complete otherness of being.

Sufi poetry is sung in many different varieties, with the *qawwali* among its traditional expressions. As a devotional and spiritual musical form, the qawwali is performed at different holy shrines by one or two lead vocalists who are given support by a group of singers maintaining the rhythmic beat by clapping hands to induce a state of emotional heightening and exaltation. The *qawwals* sing the compositions of the Sufi mystics and poets; hence the mystical-poetic text has a privileged position in the qawwali repertoire (see Qureshi 1986). One of the most popular poets, whose practice the qawwals of the subcontinent have kept alive, is Amir Khusrau, the thirteenth/fourteenth-century poet and disciple of the Sufi saint Nizamuddin Auliya (see Sunil Sharma 2005).[20] Since his Hindavi works were composed in Brajbhasa, the vernacular of the Agra-Mathura region, it is not surprising to find associations with Krishna cultic and poetic practices. Khusrau's compositions are prolific and varied, as is the Khusrau tradition that has come down to us, but I focus here on the genre of *rang* (color) songs,[21] which have generated several popular qawwalis sung even today by different and very well-known qawwals. For example:

Aaj rung hai ri ma, rang hai ri	What gorgeous festivities we celebrate today
Mere Mehboob ke ghar rang hai ri	Yes, in my beloved's home is the festival of color
Mohay apnay hi rang mein rang le,	Dye me in your hue, my love,

And, of course, the well known

Chap tilak sab cheeni moh se naina milayeke	I have lost my sense of separate being in your love

which contains the lines

Apnisi rang deeni re, moh se naina milayke....	You have dyed me in your colors, once our eyes met....
Aisi rang do ke rang naahin chhutey,	Color me so that the color never fades,
Dhobiya dhoye chaahe saari umariya	Even if the washerman were to wash over a whole lifetime[22]

All these popular qawwalis of the rang genre are clearly responding to the charged eroticism of the Braj region, even as they use the idiom and metaphoric resonances of Radha and Krishna playing Holi in Brindavan that has been immortalized in so many songs of the *thumri* genres (see Rao 1990). At the same time, they express a key Sufi idea metaphorically—the experience of oneness of being in which the human is deeply imbued/colored by the divine. The soul wearing the colors of the Beloved metaphorically expresses the key conception of *Ishq* in Sufi mysticism: the merging of two bodies into one soul, the immersion of the Self in the Other. It is not surprising that the genre of rang songs continues to be extremely popular or that it is used and interpreted in the songs of Bombay cinema. For example, a central qawwali from *Tanu Weds Manu* (2011) uses the mystic Sufi worldview, with the Lord as Lover addressed as the ultimate dyer—*Rangrez*—and the lyrics exemplifying the amplified elevated articulation of human desire and devotion:

Aye rangrez mere, rangrez mere	Oh dyer of mine, Dear Dyer of mine,
Yeh baat bata rangrez mere	Please reveal your secrets divine,
Yeh koun se paani mein tune	What concoction have you created dear,
Kounsa rang ghola hai,	Of water and your amazing colors!
Ke dil ban gaya saudai,	That my heart yearns in love so profound,
Mera basanti cholahai,	My cloak's colored in deep yellow unbound...

The qawwali also marks a crucial turning point in the narrative, with the central female protagonist undergoing a heightened experience of her true love in a magical realization. Moreover, it is in the powerful use of spoken vernacular language, with its earthy and yet mystical metaphors, that this entire range of significations become clear.

With the advent of color, it is the soundtrack and song that take over the functions of black-and-white expressionist mise-en-scène to produce the saturation of emotion that characterizes the Indian melodramatic form. Another example, also a qawwali from the recent color film, *Veer Zaara* (2004), demonstrates how the song's intensification of emotion gives an intense charge to political and social issues, rendering them extremely personal. The setting is significant: the qawwali is performed at a *dargah*, a Sufi shrine that is a sacred space accessible to all believers, albeit of different faiths and gender. The dargah evokes a feeling relating to the granting of boons, and the qawwali articulates the faithful's yearning for the grace of the divine, together with the lover's yearning for the beloved. Working thus in a double register, as an expression of devotion to the Saint and to the Beloved, the lyrics announce the arrival of the devotee, the Lover, one who will immerse all of himself—his heart, his life—in love, consumed by it as the moth is by the flame. While the moth-flame imagery may be generic, it centrally evokes the affective and imaginary being of a lover/devotee, who the beloved recognizes and commits to. This qawwali narratively expresses the key ideas of *Ishq* (passionate love) as transcending all division. The integrity and honor of Ishq is a value unto itself,[23] incorporating the yearning for and the ecstasy of the union with the Beloved, ideas that are the core of mystical Sufi poetry and also of several iconic songs of Bombay cinema. In this case, it is mobilized to argue for new imaginaries of selfhood, constituted not by hardened and divisive ideologies of sectarian and national constitutions of the self, but by a liberated sense of love and devotion that refuses the boundaries set by society, religious communities, or nationality. The narrative drive of *Veer Zaara*'s fictional world is charged by a vision that recognizes the price that individuals have to pay for a devotion that challenges social norms. Here, the manner in which the Sacred is mobilized through the Sufi qawwali creates a charged emotional articulation that addresses the contemporary and its ideological fissures through its message of Love. The desire of the lovers is amplified and given a weight that not only drives the narrative but also speaks to the ruptures and fissures of the present. It thus radically challenges the national ideologies that cause these ruptures, highlighting the value of emotionality represented by the two lovers. *Veer Zaara* is a narrative that endorses spiritual and emotional belonging in the face of worldly severance and separation. It is deeply invested in overcoming boundaries, both geographical and psychological. It uses the spiritual conception of Ishq to do so, articulated forcefully in the central qawwali of the film.

As I have argued elsewhere (Bhaskar 2012), the Sacred is central to Indian melodrama's affective charge and to the manner in which it elevates and amplifies human emotion, which is itself the core of melodrama. As in the previous example, its deployment articulates key social political concerns as it contours the subjective and the individual. Here I have explicated key characteristics of a cinematic form that foregrounds bhava and that works with expressionist stylization and the performative to both express emotion and attempt, via the stylization of the performance, an abstraction and universalization of that emotion. We can now see how Indian melodrama developed its distinctive identity, even as it responded to a global aesthetic style such as expressionism, and its role in shaping cinematic melodrama. Indian cinemas reinvented those forms as they molded their own alternative melodramatic aesthetic around the centrality of a key concept in Indian aesthetics: bhava.

NOTES

1. Eleanor Halsall has recently completed a PhD on the subject of German personnel in the Indian Film Industry (SOAS, London). Its publication will contribute significantly to the scholarship on this period.
2. The only film he names is *Madame Butterfly*, the Paramount film directed by Marion Gering, released in the United States on December 30, 1932. Madhura Pandit Jasraj's biography of her father (2015) relates that its "tragic love story of an American soldier and a Japanese girl . . . was beautiful, but the tragedy only made his heart sink further" (113).
3. Chandika is a powerful Goddess in Hindu mythology. She is ferocious and destroys evil-doers mercilessly. She is often imaged as Kali the Goddess of Destruction, wearing skulls around her neck.
4. The Prabhat Film Company was founded in Kolhapur in Maharashtra in 1929 by V. Shantaram, V. Damle, S. Fatelal, K. Dhaiber, and S. Kulkarni. Prabhat made six silent films and then the first Marathi talkie—a mythological film, *Ayodhya cha Raja* ("The King of Ayodhya"), in two versions, Marathi and Hindi, and then India's first color experiment, *Sairandhri*. After Shantaram's return from Berlin, the partners moved to Pune and the production of *Amrit Manthan* began.
5. In all Hindu temples, when the ritual of worship is over, the *aarti* takes place, when the worshippers stand and a priest offers the ritual lamps, which stand on a large plate, to the idol. The priest circles the plate around the face of the idol. This is also the traditional form of welcome to the bride and groom when they first enter their married home.
6. One of the two great Indian epics, Valmiki's Sanskrit *Ramayana* inspired many versions in various Indian vernacular languages, including Marathi, the language of *Shejari*. A well-known Marathi Ramayana is the sixteenth-century *Bhavartha Ramayana* by Saint Eknath. Among other famous *Ramayana* re-creations is the *Rama-Charita-Manas* by the Rama devotee Tulsidas. Composed between 1574 and 1577 in Awadhi, one of the languages of the north Indian state of Uttar Pradesh, Tulsidas's text circulated widely through folk music, theater, and narration. It is still sung all over north India. See S. P. Bahadur's *Ramayana of Goswami Tulsidas* (1972).
7. In the Hindi version of *Shejari*, titled *Podosi*, this is sung in language that suggests the Bharat Vilap (lament) sequence from Tulsidas's *Rama-Charita-Manas*.
8. As sung by Muliya, Patil's wife, inspired by vernacular Marathi *Ramayana* performance traditions, and translated from the subtitles of the DVD released by the Prabhat Film Company.
9. Vaishnavism was a movement of Krishna *bhakti* (devotion) that was extremely popular in North India and took an intense form through several sixteenth-century Saint poets and singers. It is rooted in the bhakti of Krishna and Radha, immortalized in

Jayadeva's *Gita Govinda*. This tradition provided the emotional and imagistic reservoir for the poetic efflorescence associated with the vernacular literatures of Krishna devotion (see Bhaskar 2012, 175).

10. In Sanskrit, *viraha* connotes the condition of separation from the beloved and the yearning for union. In the Indic traditions, *viraha* is considered integral to love and has been a rich source of poetry, for example, Jayadeva's *Gita Govinda* (see Miller 1977).
11. *Song picturization* is a term popular in the Bombay film industry, signifying the realization of the song on the screen, implying every stage from planning to the finished sequence, including choreography, camerawork, and editing.
12. In North Indian classical music, the *aalaap* is the opening section in which a melodic composition introduces the structure of the raga.
13. Thanks to Veena Hariharan for the translation from Malayalam.
14. *Lavani* is a traditional folk form of song and dance with a powerful rhythm from Maharashtra performed with percussion instruments. Combining eroticism with sharp political and social satire, it became extremely popular in Marthi urban theater and films.
15. Kothas were the salons where courtesans sang, danced, and entertained their patrons.
16. Chapters VI and VII of Bharata's treatise on drama, the *Natyashastra*, detail its aesthetic theory of *bhava* (emotion) and *rasa* (essence, taste, pleasure). See also Richard Schechner (2001) on "Rasaesthetics." He argues that an aesthetic founded on "rasa" is essentially different from the one "founded on 'the theatron,' the rationally ordered, analytically distanced panoptic" (29).
17. In *Islamicate Cultures of Bombay Cinema*, Richard Allen and I, following Marshall Hodgson as quoted by Mukul Kesavan (1994, 246), define the term *Islamicate* not as referring to Islamic religion per se "but to the social and cultural complex historically associated with Islam and Muslims, both among Muslims themselves and even when found among non-Muslims." Thus it denotes the "expressive and social forms associated and identified with Muslim culture, and their impact on the Hindustani cinema produced by the Bombay film industry" (Bhaskar and Allen 2009, 3).
18. Philip Lutgendorf (2006) describes the transformation of the narrative traditions of the "medieval Perso-Arabic and Turkic-speaking world" in their interaction with Indic narrative traditions in South Asia. Oral storytelling "remained a popular entertainment form in Islamicate South Asia," continually renewed by "Persian-language traditions" (246).
19. The cosmic dance of Krishna and Radha and their followers is celebrated even today in Brindavan, Mathura.
20. Khusrau is also spelled Khusraw. He is believed to have created the *qawwali* form, and a number of his compositions are still sung by qawwals today.
21. The *rang* songs are inspired by the Festival of Colors or Holi that marks the end of winter and the onset of spring and is celebrated with great enthusiasm across north India. Khusrau interpreted the festival in mystical terms, so his rang songs are erotic, spiritual, and mystical.
22. All these popular qawwalis have been sung by the most well-known qawwali singers of the subcontinent: Nusrat Fateh Ali Khan, the Sabri Brothers, Abida Parveen, Rahat Fateh Ali Khan, and others.
23. The honor of *Ishq* is not to be measured by any societal yardsticks other than commitment of the lovers to each other and to their love.

16

The Sorrow and the Piety

Melodrama Rethought in Postwar Italian Cinema

LOUIS BAYMAN

Melodrama addresses itself to the emotions: virtue rewarded, Gothic fervor, blood and thunder, serial queens, weepies, opera, soap opera, *The Oprah Winfrey Show*. Melodrama assumes, and helps create, a spectator who measures the success of the drama by the feeling it elicits. From musical accompaniment, to breathtaking action in coups de théâtre, to the diva performances of the late Victorian stage and the early feature film—and alongside affective markers such as sobbing, screaming, swooning, oaths of revenge, bloodlust, rage, or fear—melodrama makes expressivity itself the spectacle.

Italy may be considered a wellspring of such spectacular feeling. Its city spaces are designed to offer public stages to a people for centuries characterized (or caricatured) as naturally passionate and habitually histrionic, linking irrepressible emotionality with ostentatious display (see Champagne 2015, 8–9). Attention to Italian culture demonstrates the limitation of understanding melodrama using assumptions more specific to Protestant bourgeois cultures: for example, the notions that melodrama enacts a victory of excess over repression, is defined in opposition to realism, and presents moral predicaments that compensate for the absence of the "traditional Sacred." Italian melodrama is, instead, informed by the Catholic belief that reality is itself infused with the divine, and it employs emphatic, even operatic expressivity as the vehicle for realist depictions of lower-class life. Investigating Italian melodrama helps us open up different perspectives on the nature of melodramatic representation.

THE BASES OF A POPULAR FORM

Although melodrama in Italy spans theatrical, musical, literary, pictorial, and other forms—perhaps also its architecture, politics, religious practices, and style of communication—in this chapter I limit my focus to cinema in the first decade after 1945. The reconstruction of Italian cinema following its near-destruction during the war occurred thanks to melodrama. *Catene* / *Chains* (Raffaello

Matarazzo) broke the box office records for 1949, the year that confirmed the reinstitution of Italian cinema as a popular entertainment industry. It tells the story of the emigration and clandestine return of a husband and father of two (wartime film hero Amedeo Nazzari), after shooting dead a gangster in a crime of passion. *Anna* (1951, Alberto Lattuada) was the most successful film at the domestic box office of the 1945 to 1960 period; it tells the tale of a novice nun who works in a hospital where by coincidence her ex-fiancé is sent after an accident. She remembers how she betrayed him with a nightclub barman whom he shot, leading her to enter the sisterhood. The top box office successes in the years of the industry's rebirth, 1950 to 1954 (Casadio 1990, 23), include melodramas such as follow-ups to *Catene* (using the same stars and crew), *Tormento* (1950, Raffaello Matarazzo), and *I figli di nessuno / Nobody's Children* (1951, Raffaello Matarazzo). Other high-ranking box office successes of the period include the romantic crime dramas *Core 'ngrato / Ungrateful Heart* (1951, Guido Brignone), *Sensualità* (1952, Clemente Fracassi), *Perdonami! / Forgive Me!* (1953, Mario Costa), *Chi è senza peccato . . . / Who Is Without Sin?* (1953, Raffaello Matarazzo), and *Mambo* (1954, Robert Rossen), which reunited the stars of *Anna*, Silvana Mangano and Vittorio Gassman. *La nemica / The Enemy* (1952, Giorgio Bianchi) and *Maddalena* (1954, Augusto Genina) represent equally successful maternal melodramas; at the same time opera-citing nineteenth-century costume dramas *Senso* (1954, Luchino Visconti) and *Casa Ricordi* (1954, Carmine Gallone) also triumphed at the box office in this period.

Cinema was the foremost popular form during the country's transformation from a regionally fragmented, agricultural society into a mass urbanized one (see Forgacs and Gundle 2008). The postwar melodrama boom provides evidence of the industry's success in connecting with a mass audience by giving new life to a richly varied, shared cultural heritage following the shocks of war (see Bachman and Williams 2012). *Catene* was initiated by the founder of the production company Titanus, Gustavo Lombardo, a veteran of early 1920s Neapolitan cinema. He employed Raffaello Matarazzo, since the early 1930s a successful journeyman director of diverse genres. The film took its title from a story in a 1947 early edition of *Bolero*, which belonged to the Italian postwar boom in *fotoromanzi*, magazines made up of photo-stories. The title of the *Bolero* story is itself an allusion to *Anime incatenate* (*Chained Souls*), from the first edition of the best-selling *fotoromanzo* out the previous year, *Grand Hôtel*. Exemplifying further intermedial circulation, *Grand Hôtel* is the magazine that Silvana, the lead character in the neorealist melodrama *Riso amaro / Bitter Rice* (1949, Giuseppe De Santis), habitually reads—a film partially reprised with the same principal leads as the huge commercial success of 1951, *Anna*. *Catene* is a film adaptation of a *sceneggiata*, a Neapolitan stage form popular since the interwar years that adapted songs into (typically highly conventionalized) musical dramas. The source song for the *sceneggiata* on which *Catene* is based is "Lacreme napulitane" ("Neapolitan Tears"), written by Libero Bovio in 1925 and performed in the film by Neapolitan singer Roberto Murolo. His lifetime project was to record the entire repertoire of Neapolitan songs, including "Torna!"—the name given to the film's color remake, again directed by Matarazzo in 1954—which is played at several important points in *Catene*, including in alternation with "Lacreme napulitane" over the film's opening credits.

Notably, in such a rich interweaving of popular cultural artifacts, these melodramas also take on their diverse properties, becoming operatic, musical, iconic, and theatrical. The bold, self-consciously dramatic aspects of Italian melodrama elicit recognition as part of a heritage of heightened drama going back to the nineteenth century and before. These films had obvious mass cultural appeal, typically combining romance, family strife, musical performance, local color, and crime drama. Although the reference points may include nineteenth-century bourgeois culture, the postwar melodrama boom has been described as the last expression of a peasant culture in Italy (Baldelli 1999, 131; Morreale 2011, 3) largely because its outlook exhibits a shared sense of helplessness in the face of a chaotic universe and a tendency toward antimodern conservatism. Family exists at the center of their cosmos (simultaneously idealized and the site of disappointment or catastrophe), whereas cities are impersonal and vice-ridden, and the rich are scheming exploiters.

As in other cultures, "melodrama" does not represent a specific genre in postwar Italian cinema. Rather, Italian film genres are constituted as melodrama*tic* according to any of five axes, along which will be plotted the analysis that follows:

Sentiment: empathic feeling is a primary force within the lives of the protagonists, and it is confronted with the destructive impulses of villainy and the ruthless denial of sympathy wrought by unfeeling social structures or blind fate.

Lyricism: the expression of sentiment is a guiding principle of the drama, especially strong affective elements grounded in the body—often in the form of gestures, cries, nonverbal articulation, tears, drawn breath, and stasis or collapse. This overwhelming, yet fragile, bodily expressivity is made lyrical in its appearance alongside indicators of a different register, removed from the immediate realms of setting and action, but privileged as expressing a more intimate condition, in particular through the musical soundtrack but also via lighting, editing, and composition.

Action: the industry of this period produced many films about gangsters, racketeering, urban decay, crimes of passion, and war and spying. Melodrama inheres in both action and pathos, which are combined in these films: even misdeeds often are explained through victimhood, resulting from poverty, corruption, the violence of war, or the bleak postwar landscape; or from sexual desire realized as insane violent energy. The melodramatization of action achieves a continual push and pull between rushing energy and emotional extension. For example, in *Anna*, Anna's fiancé Andrea fights with his rival Vittorio in the underground mill on his farm. Vittorio pulls a gun; the editing alternates between the immobile Anna screaming and sobbing and the two men fighting, until a gunshot is heard and an overflow of water rushes in from the underground workings of the mill. The orchestrated sounds of water, fighting, sobs, and the gunshot subside as the main musical theme rises on the soundtrack. The emotions of this climax are sustained through Anna's halting, devastated walk away from the mill, collapsing on the roadside, to awake in a hospital staffed by nuns, where she too will live out the rest of her days in service.

Populism: most of the contemporary-set films discussed here would have been classed as *neorealismo popolare*. As well as the aim to appeal to a popular audience, this indicates interest in this period in the ordinariness of, and easy identification with, the people to whom melodramatic events occur, who suffer an undeserved victimhood and with whom the spectator is encouraged to sympathize.

Faith: sympathetic recognition of the common condition of suffering encourages belief that something better awaits beyond the current state of things. Such faith characterizes both spiritual and more politicized visions of redemption in this era.

MELODRAMA, NEOREALISM, AND POPULAR AUTHENTICITY

Costume dramas such as *Appassionatamente* (9154, Giacomo Gentilomo) *Romanticismo* (1950, Clemente Fracassi), and *Senso* or *Beatrice Cenci* (1956, Riccardo Freda) portray the lavish lifestyles of past aristocracies, but the interest of Italian cinema during this period is more likely to be in the problems of everyday life. Its general address is exemplified in Vittorio De Sica's remark regarding *Ladri di biciclette / Bicycle Thieves* (1948) that "my film is dedicated to the suffering of the humble" (1978, 88). A humble status usually in itself guarantees a sympathetic portrayal in contrast to acquisitive or exploitative antagonists. This creates a shared ethic between the commercially successful melodramas of this period and neorealism, the internationally prized but less conventionally commercial films of postwar Italian cinema.

Neorealism can be seen as a radicalization of official attempts (whether by the Vatican or the state) to employ cinema's popularity to create a unifying national culture (see Bayman and Rigoletto 2013). In the years of reconstruction, neorealism is either everywhere—Alberto Farassino (1989) states that neorealism simply *is* Italian cinema of 1945 to 1949, affecting all filmmaking through its lower-class, rough-edged focus—or nowhere, representing a critical ideal against which actual films have fallen short. If one takes the former view, neorealism overlaps with popular melodramatics throughout this era, challenging assumptions that melodramatic emotion is incompatible with or even betrays (as contemporary criticism put it) realism (see Chiarini 1978).

Such overlap reveals issues raised by the Resistance struggle and featured not only in *Roma città aperta / Rome Open City* (1945, Roberto Rossellini) but also in the spy story *Due lettere anonime / Two Anonymous Letters* (1945, Mario Camerini). Here, a woman is courted by a collaborator, who betrays his rival, a Partisan, for her affections. She shoots the collaborator dead after discovering his deceit, as the streets of Rome flock with crowds celebrating the city's Liberation. The film ends on a close-up of her shedding a tear behind prison bars, having bidden farewell to her good-hearted Partisan suitor. Such connection would link neorealist concerns to *Avanti a lui tremava tutta Roma / Before Him All Rome Trembled* (1946, Carmine Gallone), starring Anna Magnani (of *Rome Open City*) as the leading lady in an opera troupe preparing a performance of *Tosca*. The

Occupation is here interwoven with allegory, for the opera is set in a Rome threatened by Napoleonic troops. German soldiers interrupt the performance to seize prisoners; the performers escape to a hideout, and when they hear of the Liberation sing out "Vittoria!" before the film cuts to the same line being performed onstage to an audience of Allied troops. The Liberation is similarly operatic in *O' sole mio* (1946 Giacomo Gentilomo), an adventure starring Tito Gobbi as a popular singer during the uprising that forced the ejection of the Nazis from Naples.

In each of these films, just as in the canonically neorealist *Rome Open City* and in other politically radical wartime adventure films including *Il sole sorge ancora* (1946, Aldo Vergano) and *Achtung! Banditi!* (1951, Carlo Lizzani), the occupation is understood through categories of suffering and evil. They work from a narrative of victimhood and betrayal, in which the Liberation is an inherently exciting resolution to dramatic conflicts generated by military repression. Melodrama figures as an eruption to the surface of a previously repressed popular energy, equated with irrepressible virtue as it overcomes vice, which in turn expresses fears of malaise, scarred innocence, and absent nurture after the war. *Sciuscià / Shoeshine* (1946, Vittorio De Sica)—alongside *Rome Open City* heralding neorealism—shows the plight of two Roman shoeshine boys dragged into the criminal underworld, then incarcerated, and finally led to fratricidal murder. The boys' manipulation by black-marketeers and then their abandonment to depersonalizing correctional institutions equals an emotionalization of political discourse. As their lawyer says in his (unsuccessful) closing arguments to the court, "return these innocents to their homes, their families, their schools, and their jobs . . . if you find them guilty, then we, all of us, are also guilty; for in pursuing our passions we have abandoned our children to themselves: they are always more and more alone." There are no heroes nor catharsis, but a society understood as needing reordering according to principles of sympathy and forgiveness (principles whose contemporary context was politically radical but whose Christian overtones are marked).

Contrary to the presumed opposition between realism and melodrama, this is a populist, passionate, and dramatic realism. It recalls Pedro Almodóvar's assertion that "when melodrama focuses on unemployment, they call it neorealism" (as cited in Fofi 2007, 188). In terms of broader aesthetic theory, it is an example of the common interest of realism and melodrama in truth, showing how realism's concern with the everyday transmutes into melodrama's preoccupation with mundane disappointments and realism's goal of immediacy becomes melodramatic intensity. The achievement of realist aims through melodrama points to the impossibility of schematizing any specific set of techniques or themes as intrinsically realist or melodramatic. They are instead relative terms whose effect emerges in implicit comparison to the other cultural artifacts that form their context: "in excess of . . ." for melodrama and "more like life than . . ." for realism. Realism may seek the news values of *cronaca*—an item in a newspaper (Leavitt 2013)—yet in neorealism this is less often a dispassionate observation than it is a search for sensational and shocking events, communicated with headline directness. Such realism is in tune with nineteenth-century *verismo*, whether of Emile Zola's novels or the Italian short stories of Giovanni Verga and Luigi Capuano. Its goal is a presentation of life in its most brutal and vivid aspects, unencumbered by heroics or by an idealized vision of humanity, or by the aesthetic principles of harmony or elegance.

This also corrects commonplace assumptions that melodrama consists only of domestic dramas of private emotion in contrast to realism as social critique. However, drama is created through the protagonists' environmental struggles: over the national territory in Resistance films, fish in the sea in *La terra trema* (1948, Luchino Visconti), fieldworkers striking against eviction in *Il mulino del Po / The Mill on the Po* (1945, Alberto Lattuada), or, as in *Il cammino della speranza / The Path of Hope* (1950, Pietro Germi), peasant emigration the length of the peninsula from Sicily into France. Indeed, Aprà (1976) considers the integration of personal drama with the land as neorealism's "real innovation" (24). Such politicization of spatial representation accords to melodrama's polarity between vice and virtue. Natural public and communal working space is represented as vital and good, whereas enclosed, private space is barren and isolating. The environment is also an element of elevation and intensification, with dramatic climaxes marked by storms whipping up (*Il mulino del Po*), the crashing waves of the sea (*La terra trema*, among many others), or the disorienting fury of a blizzard (*Il cammino della speranza*).

In philosophizing the neorealist use of space, Deleuze (1986) identifies an *espace quelconque* (any-space-whatever), when characters wander displaced and disoriented through the ruined spaces of postwar breakdown. Deleuze aims here to name something new, which he calls a fundamental break with action cinema and the beginning of a new art cinema starting with *Bicycle Thieves* and *Germania anno zero / Germany Year Zero* (1948, Roberto Rossellini). However, failed action is as much a characteristic of melodrama as of European art cinema. These films refunction for the purposes of art cinema what is in fact a common melodramatic figure of the disoriented protagonist lost in an alienating environment. Displaced wanderings are preludes to melodramatic crises in, among others, the prostitution film *La tratta delle bianche / The White Slave Trade* (1952, Luigi Comencini) and the crime films *La città si difende / Four Ways Out* (1951, Alberto Lattuada), *Il cammino della speranza* and *Senza pietà / Without Pity* (1948, Pietro Germi). In these films, a partially reconstructed but dehumanized commercial industrialism highlights the threat of exploitation, crime, or administrative bureaucracy.

Millicent Marcus (1989) suggests that neorealism presents its negative characters melodramatically and its positive characters through realism. Thus the Nazis in *Rome Open City* are presented in studio sets with artificial lighting, and Silvana in *Bitter Rice* is lured into escapist fantasies by her choice of reading material (specifically the sensational *fotoromanzo* romances of *Grand Hôtel*) and consequently betrays her fellow agricultural workers for the lures of a gangster who seeks to steal their harvest. Although Marcus is right to note how neorealist villains may act in false or artificial ways, this is not the end of melodrama in these films. The explosive blast of a bomb going off during nighttime curfew in *Rome Open City*, or the jagged darkness falling on Umberto D's face as he is confronted with the stripped walls of his empty room in De Sica's eponymous film of 1952, are both realistically motivated but increase their affective or symbolic charge through melodramatic expressiveness. The dichotomy noted by Marcus is, rather, a moral polarization between reactionary and artificial on one hand and popular emotional authenticity on the other. Films of the Resistance, crime stories, or tales of urban decay find villainy in a willingness to deceive and innocence in susceptibility to trickery. Villains espouse empty rhetoric and choose the luxuries of glamour, fashion, and wealth. This distaste for ostentation and display would also appear to be an implicit reaction to the pomp of Fascism, setting up idle richness, foreign exoticism, or escapist fantasies as wickedness in opposition to the popular condition. In this period, traditional Catholic ideas of essential peasant goodness (Patriarca 2010, 121) compete with the Communist expiation of a *popolo* who spent twenty years of Fascism "led astray by a corrupt ruling class" (197). The *dramatis personae* of modern Italian history are thus characterized by questions of authenticity, seen through conflicts around hidden virtue, betrayal, and suffering.

Recognizing authenticity is as important to neorealism as identifying virtue is to melodrama, and the two aims are often combined. Neorealist revelation occurs through plots that pit the genuine feeling represented as inherent to popular life against betrayal by the unfeeling agents of Fascism and exploitation. Dependence on their material environments ensures the natural veracity of "ordinary" protagonists' existence at the same time as it confirms the elemental nature of their emotional states. Goodness is recognized in work productivity, family reproduction, local community, and the struggle to maintain a modest existence. Nobility lies with abandoned children, unemployed veterans, maids, housewives, fishermen, and manual laborers, whose struggles occupy the films' moral center.

Melodrama ensures that realist goals of social relevance are supplied with emotional and expressive meanings, working to clarify how one ought to feel about the world and its injustices. Melodramatized emotion is also a guarantor of sincerity. Giovanna pleads with bandits for sympathy in the Communist Party–influenced *Caccia tragica / Tragic Pursuit* (1947, Giuseppe De Santis), imploring "we don't have anything, all we have is the ability to love each other." The lonely young protagonist of *Ti ho sempre amato*! (1953, Mario Costa), a rather conservative, Catholic-influenced film, is told, "anyone who truly loves is not capable of trickery." Authenticity is in these films a moral quality of importance to the reconstitution of shared values after the war, achieved by the combination of realist verification with melodramatic longing. Authenticity is part of the protagonist's status as representative of an entire social category constituted by suffering and named in Italian simply "il popolo."

MELODRAMA BEYOND NEOREALISM

The boom in melodramas was over by the mid-1950s, but Italian cinema would continue to employ melodrama, especially for emotionally charged subjects. It is not, however, the case that all tales of domesticity and crisis necessarily use melodrama. As Italian cinema developed through the 1950s, melodrama became a structuring absence for a burgeoning art cinema in which expression of the emotional life of characters on screen was losing its priority. *Storia di Caterina* episode from/ *Love in the City* (1953, Michelangelo Antonioni et al.) is about a woman encountering the indifference of social institutions: it plays out in long shots, often of Caterina's back, denying any access to her emotional life; similarly, the final reunion of the mother with her baby and her subsequent trial and acquittal are communicated solely through a series of newspaper headlines.

This creates what we might call a kind of melodrama *mancato* or *manqué*—a form of "failed" melodrama—a category that can exist only in a culture in which melodrama is terrifically important. The melodrama *mancato* can be felt precisely in those dramatic situations one would by convention expect to find increased emotionality and pathos. The deliberate removal of melodramatic expressivity charts a development of artistic interests away from the direct melodramas of De Sica and Zavattini in *I bambini ci guardano / The Children Are Watching Us* (1944) and *Sciuscià* to the observational style of *Storia di Caterina*. It also charts the progress of Rossellini through his Ingrid Bergman trilogy, from the melodramas *Stromboli* (1950) and *Europa '51* (1952) to the ill-tempered detachment of an apparently divorcing couple in *Viaggio in Italia / Voyage to Italy* (1954). The films are dedramatized; conflicts are not played out to their resolution. Indeed, the narration appears not to care about bringing us closer to the inner processes that constitute personhood. Rather, it seems as though the body is no longer a natural, physical key to the emotional truth of a situation. Such absences are brought to their apex in the films of Michelangelo Antonioni, where conflicted protagonists face moments of crisis and yet the spectator can never know what, if anything, those protagonists may actually feel, nor if the presentation of their lives has any meaning beyond a series of formal exercises.

The circumstances of the later 1950s are characterized by changed cultural attitudes toward emotion. This development moves from a sympathetic, morally polarized affirmation of experience to one in which meaning is opaque. Intense feeling drives neither the dramatic experience nor an understanding of the individual's rights within society. Since the late 1950s, Italian films that embrace melodrama do so in a knowing way that sometimes approaches pastiche. Such melodramas display a growing awareness of melodramatic expressivity itself, from the already anachronistic melodrama of *Rocco e i suoi fratelli / Rocco and His Brothers* of 1960—in which the histrionic actions of a family of southern immigrants are indices of their fatal attachment to a bygone world—to the postmodern homage to melodrama, *Io sono l'amore / I Am Love* (2009, Luca Guadagnino).

Melodrama continues as a mode in Italian cinema,[1] and although the contemporary era exhibits a more psychologically aware approach to conflicts, it also is more inhibited in its expressions of emotionality than postwar melodramatic cinema. Films such as *Mio fratello è figlio unico / My Brother Is an Only Child* (2007, Daniele Luchetti) or *La meglio gioventù / The Best of Youth* (2003, Marco Tullio Giordana) chart Italy's modern political history as collective trauma, felt in family conflicts and to be worked through by attention to the personal realm. As such, they testify to the continued importance of melodrama to a common understanding of shared experience. Terrorism and social strife in these films are misguided fanatical excesses that clash with the impulse to reconciliation achieved by successful negotiation of intimate and familial relations. But contemporary Italian melodrama also confirms a changed approach to unrepressed psychic energies, which are pathologized and put in conflict with the well-adjusted interpersonal attentiveness exhibited by the films' heroes. It is only in postwar neorealism that an uninhibitedly expressive melodrama is the adequate, and irrepressible, means of public engagement in social critique.

MELODRAMA AND THE PROMISE OF SALVATION

Rome Open City ends with the shooting of a priest, the hero of the story. A group of local boy parishioners, who form part of a Partisan band, watch his death from behind the wire fence of the Nazi headquarters and walk away, downcast. A panorama of the city opens out before them, the dome of St. Peter's Basilica dominates the skyline, and the musical theme, associated with defiant hope, comes to its climax. A story of betrayal and defeat has become one of sacrifice and rebirth within the contemporary urban landscape, guided toward the Vatican. Alternatively, *Senza pietà* ends in the death of its central couple, a black GI and his clandestine girlfriend; escaping from military and civilian authorities as well as a criminal gang, their jeep tumbles down a hill. Their hands reach out of the smashed jeep window, falling into a final clasp on the rocky shore and, as a choral version of "All God's Chillun Gotta Row (to Get to Heaven)" comes to its conclusion, the camera pans up to the sky, with a cut back to the crashing waves closing the film. In *Cielo sulla palude / Heaven Over the Marshes* (1949, Augusto Genina), the passage to the afterlife, as the film's title suggests, is explicit in an account of the recently canonized Maria Goretti. A fellow laborer violently rapes her. On her deathbed she promises to pray for him from heaven, before a darkness envelops her and a solo violin enters the soundtrack in place of her silence. Each of these endings, different in tone and political outlook, places the resolution to the drama on both a realist and a sacred plane. They signal how Italian melodrama involves the presence of the divine in important ways, not applicable in Protestant cultures. Italian cinema is distinctive in its employment of the atmosphere and accoutrements of Catholicism. It challenges claims that melodrama, despite its recognition of this-world suffering, must find transcendence in secular terms (Brooks 1976), or even that melodrama does not offer its characters transcendence at all (Elsaesser 2007; Goimard 1999).

Arguing what has become a foundational point in melodrama theory, Peter Brooks (1976) concludes that the proliferation of melodrama in Revolutionary France responds to the loss of the traditional Sacred, replacing Church authority with the law and humanized values. Responding to a crisis of morality and needing to reidentify virtue for a secularized world, "melodrama represents both the urge toward resacralization and the impossibility of conceiving sacralization other than in personal terms" (16). Yet, as Richard Allen shows (chapter 2), the opposition between the personal and the Sacred on which Brooks bases his argument is simply "not tenable." Allen charts the development of selfhood in the later

Middle Ages through the art historical concept of the "Christianity of Pathos." The Passion of Christ provides a "mise-en-scène of empathic suffering," producing a kind of melodramatic imagination *ante litteratum*. In a related manoeuver, John Champagne (2015) repositions the crisis of the traditional Sacred from the French Revolution back to sixteenth-century Italy and the Counter-Reformation. The aesthetic of individual passions is part of a Counter-Reformation strategy to oppose Protestant mistrust of the passions and the theatricality of Church ritual.

Christianity indeed offers a more appropriate evolutionary antecedent for melodrama than classical Greco-Roman tragedy, in comparison to whose heroic world Elsaesser (1987) and Goimard (1999) find melodrama a humbled dramatic form. Christianity, like melodrama, operates on the basis that pathos has a moral (and dramatic) force, its initial distinctiveness granting an ethical value to suffering. In opposing Ancient Stoicism, medieval scholastics saw tears as the penetration of God into the individual soul. Compassion, persecution, martyrdom, sacrifice, pity, penitence, charity—each relate the believer to a moral order through his or her capacity to feel. Christianity deals in situations of absolute moral polarity; at the center of its story is a family drama of son, Father, and *mater dolorosa* beset by persecution and undone by betrayal. From accounts of conversions to lamentations, parables, and moral tales, its narratives present states of innocence and sin, nostalgia for a lost paradise and the inevitability of suffering and sacrifice. The Italian films discussed here provide contemporary settings to stage similar explorations of human weakness.

Martin Riesebrodt (2010) defines religion as "primarily a promise of salvation" (89), and it is this promise that the films previously mentioned hold out. The ending of *Nel gorgo del peccato / In the Whirl of Sin* (1954, Vittorio Cottafavi) reveals that the film's voice-over belongs to the protagonist's mother, after she has been shot dead by a gangster jealously desiring her son's wife. Her narration, occurring over opening and closing images of clouds in the sky, is literally a heavenly voice; her martyrdom enables her son to live in married bliss because her murder has put their tormentor in jail. Alternatively, in *Noi peccatori / We Sinners* (1953, Guido Brignone), a war veteran rediscovers the loving wife he has spurned and who has lost the use of her legs after being hit by a truck. They are reunited in church at the culmination of the Our Lady of Pompeii procession as choral music rises and they genuflect in front of an altarpiece showing the Holy Family. Mysteriously, she walks again, and her moist eyes glint like the jeweled altar toward which she looks, indicating a divine aspect to the emotion that generates tears.

Italian melodrama encourages its spectator to imagine that a different life lies beyond the limitations of physical reality. The presence of good and evil, the active participation of fate, destiny, and the *deus ex machina* indicate the hidden workings of a divine design or the miraculous at work in melodrama's narrative dynamics. Melodramatic strategies such as musical accompaniment, chiaroscuro and artificial lighting effects, and striking compositional designs are properties that literally come from beyond the narrative world. The dramatic context of sanctified suffering draws an exalted status from such expressive strategies. They also allude to Church conventions. Roberta Lietti (1995) notes how the composition of climactic moments in Italian melodramas position the characters like figures in religious iconography. Gloom or shafts of light, stained glass, candles, incense, and glittering ornamentation are all essentially lighting effects that give churches a sacred atmosphere and that converge with melodramatic effects. In liturgies and mystery plays, musicians were positioned above the congregation on the higher level representing paradise (Jay Grout 1965); in melodrama an orchestral soundtrack has a privileged narrational role.

Chiaroscuro stages conflict as a Manichean battle between dark and light and recall Augustine's belief in the divinity of light, which is both material and immaterial, cast literally from a higher plane (Gill 2013). Melodramatic strategies act as artistic realizations of the doctrine of immanence—the belief that a transcendent God can make the divine present within the stuff of life. The presence of the Sacred, from protagonists who find their salvation in faith to artistic strategies that render immanence, explains how, in postwar Italy, Vatican Catholicism could itself be a method for overcoming the crisis of secular authority represented by the Fascist state's downfall, rather than a moment of crisis in the authority of the traditional Sacred, as Brooks argues of melodrama in general. The Vatican was indeed a daily resource for political and social reconstruction. Millions of Italians joined and voted for the Christian Democrats (DCI) as the permanent party of government, joined and enrolled their children in its cultural associations, read the DCI presses, and even watched their films in parish cinemas—*sale parocchiali*. Constituting a third of Italy's screens in the 1950s, these played a determining role in national film culture (Forgacs and Gundle 2008, 209). These films coincide with a resurgence of sightings of and devotional acts to the Virgin Mary in the postwar years (as satirized in *La dolce vita*, 1959, Federico Fellini). The cult of suffering motherhood finds further expression in the domestic melodrama (Günsberg 2005), and even more in the cycle of films of female martyrdom of which *Heaven over the Marshes* is the best known (see Grignaffini 2002). That crisis should be conceived in personal terms in these films does not then necessitate a break with the wider institutional or devotional system of faith. This system is instead the one employed both within postwar melodramas and in the broader postwar sociopolitical sphere as a means of triumphing over crisis.

MELODRAMMA

With its history of epics, diva films, comedy, melodrama, neorealism, and modernism, Italian cinema draws on a diversity of traditions rather than a single system of "classical" rules associated with Hollywood. If Catholicism acts to infuse reality with a sense of what lies beyond, opera, as a determinant of both melodrama and Italian cinema, confers on that reality an expressive elevation. In fact, *melodramma* means in Italian both opera and melodrama, indicating the setting of drama to music. The first decades of cinema coincide with the dominance of *verismo* opera. The works of composers including Giacomo Puccini, Pietro Mascagni, and Ruggero Leoncavallo acted as a bridge between realist literature, opera, and mass culture. Mascagni, for example, was involved in scoring the orchestral accompaniment for the prestige production of *Rapsodia satanica / Satan's Rhapsody* (1917, Nino Oxilia). It is to *verismo* opera that the films of *neorealismo popolare* bear most resemblance. The *veristi* display a populism that seeks "rustic or in some way 'brutal' subjects," giving them a theatrical and unpsychologized, "low-life" character (Corazzol 1993, 39–40). Different from the more detached narrational attitude of French literary naturalism, *verismo* opera creates "almost a new, 'low' style of the tragic and melodramatic" (43), which includes shouting and breathiness in loud vocal climaxes and the contribution of the orchestra "defining scenic events . . . almost functioning as a narrator" (42). Music clarifies inner predicaments and conflicts and, as Thomas Elsaesser (1987) argues of Hollywood melodrama, confers a "musicality" on the bare bones of plot and "low" character types. A further link with opera lies in the Italian cinematic star system, which emerged from the popular success of the operatic divas, whose gestural performance style is in turn a fundamental aspect of film drama. Exotic superproductions of operas such as *Aïda* (1871) spurred the spectacular staging characterizing the first epic feature films in Italian cinema, in which the drama is given a panoramic setting, be it historical, mythological, or contemporary, and which was directly borrowed by D. W. Griffith and so passed into Hollywood.

The influence of opera on Italian film melodrama shows how histrionic sensibilities offer methods to get at reality and the truth. This is most obvious in *cineopera*, the genre of films that include *Avanti a lui tremava tutta Roma*, mentioned earlier for its Resistance themes and companionship with *Rome, Open City*. The film is not exceptional in using opera to understand questions of national history. *O' sole mio*, also out in 1946, covers the Resistance to the Nazis in Naples; the romanticized history of the publishing house in *Casa Ricordi* charts its fortunes across the nineteenth century through the development of Italian opera, and includes reconstructions of the barricades that formed part of the struggle for the Risorgimento. Nor is it exceptional that opera should confer expressive grandeur on popular subjects: *Melodie immortali* (1952, Giacomo Gentilomo), a biopic of Pietro Mascagni, emphasizes his music as a product of his lower-class status and affinity with the suffering masses of Milan; Giuseppe Verdi, in the Matarazzo-directed biopic, insists "I come from the people, a peasant who makes music." Although Italian Marxist Antonio Gramsci saw this operatic national identity as less critically acute than the literary realism of French and English novels, *Senso* offers a Gramscian understanding of the operatic gestures denoting the failure of the national aristocracy, praised by Guido Aristarco as a new realism that went beyond neorealism to uncover the motive forces of history.

Scholarship on Italian film in fact proposes that melodrama is itself operatic. Gian Piero Brunetta (1995) notes the similarity of melodramatic plots and characterizations to those of operatic libretti (135). Sam Rohdie (1992) argues that in *Rocco and His Brothers* confrontations develop through vocal expressivity, including cries, screams, sobs and grunts, that would seem the logical development of a rustic, low-life *verismo* operatic aria. Furthermore, Guido Fink (1987) notes the importance in *Senso* of foregrounded stage setting to create dramatic climax, arguing that "moves, entrances, exits, violations of . . . ritual limits and taboos, end up acquiring the same weight in the 'perimeter of the scene' and on the luminous rectangle of the screen" (51–2). This sense of characters inhabiting not a real world but a stage setting is exemplified in the midpoint of *Senso* when the Countess betrays her cousin, a fighter for national liberation, by giving the battalion's funds he has entrusted to her to her lover, an occupying Austrian soldier seeking exemption from military service by bribery. At the moment of her betrayal, she turns to camera, saying to the soldier "wait," before the crescendo from Bruckner's seventh symphony crashes onto the soundtrack, their dialogue halts, and she leads her lover through three sets of heavy wooden doors, haltingly opening each in turn. Attention is thus directed to the role of the setting in the repeated scheme of release, followed by enclosure.

Luchino Visconti's work is emblematic of the combined practices running through this essay: an opera director as well as a filmmaker, who along with his anti-Fascist comrades directed what is credited as the first neorealist film, *Ossessione* (1943), and later some of the most successful melodramas of the 1950s, including *Senso* and *Rocco and His Brothers*. He appropriately characterizes Italian sensibilities in his claim to "love melodrama because it is located at the borders of life and theatre . . . theatre and opera, the world of the baroque: these are the motives which tie me to melodrama" (as cited in Bacon 1998, 62). This statement aptly places the melodramatic experience in relation to operatic and baroque, rather than classical, forms. Italian melodrama supports Linda Williams's contention that cinematic melodrama should be thought not as exceeding a classical norm but as the norm itself (see chapter 12). Indeed, melodrama has been named by Grignaffini (1996) as the "*macrogenere*" of Italian cinema.

Visconti characterizes melodrama as dependent on a border: that *between* excess *and* restriction. In *Senso* the Countess confronts a border both physical (the successive doors) and moral (her betrayal of the national cause for the pursuit of private passion). Similar boundaries or restrictions, whether social, personal, physical, or aesthetic are present throughout the examples discussed in this chapter. The opening image of *Catene* places its title—"Chains"—across a wide sunlit sky, and the film reaches resolution when the fugitive husband and unjustly outcast wife return to the reassuring confines of the family. To address the title of this book, it is as if melodrama was being bound at the very same time of its unbinding. The intensity of melodramatic conflict seems to reside in the moment that Prometheus strains at his bonds rather than at their fastening or discarding.

CONCLUSION: THE LIMITS OF EXCESS

Peter Brooks sees melodramatic excess as a gesture toward the ineffable, and its exaggerations as indicators of a lost world of exalted significance. But I have worked from the hypothesis that rather than a glimpse of something hidden, lost, and ineffable, excess should be understood as a relation between elements that are

286 Cultural and Aesthetic Debates

Figure 16.1 Anna (Silvana Mangano) in *Anna* (1951, Alberto Lattuada), about to turn away from her former lover who has asked her to return to him.

uncovered and made manifest within the drama. A final example, the ending of *Anna*, clarifies this relation. On recovering in the hospital where Anna works as a novice nun, her ex-fiancé asks her to return to him. Later, Anna undertakes a long walk through the dark cloisters of the hospital grounds, hiding from sight until she halts at the hospital gates, looking toward him waiting expectantly outside. She cries while caressing the bars of the gate, an ambulance siren wails, and she turns back to the hospital. In the operating theater, she responds to a surgeon who tells her that it is necessary sometimes to know how to lose: "I have not lost, professor. I have not lost." She dons her gloves and mask as the musical accompaniment comes to its final crescendo, and the door to the operating theater is closed.

As a paradigmatically melodramatic climax, this film confirms restriction. Anna's tearful caress of the bars suggests sacrifice and imprisonment (figure 16.1). The abrupt truncation of her rekindled romance confirms her destiny as a cloistered presence amidst the archways of the grand modernist building. Already dressed in a habit, she puts on her hospital gown and mask and bows her head in silent subservience. Yet it is through these very restrictions that the finale is felt as excessive. The soundtrack provides an enveloping musical commentary in place of her silence that is orchestrated with tight close-ups of her tearful face amidst the grand design of the hospital grounds. Her fondling of its gates indicates the continued aliveness of her inner being; her repeated resolve that she "has not lost" requires that her situation be read in terms other than those of everyday reality. The choral crescendo suggests holiness, but the ambulance sirens appear as inhuman screams at her predicament. Chiaroscuro evokes otherworldly forces, but Anna's face recalls the Madonna.

Although the operatic and sacred elements are particular to Italian melodrama, the importance of restriction to excess is relevant to melodrama *tout court*. First, excess is located in the *body*, as the instrument charged with expressing the very emotion that overwhelms it. Anna may pant and cry, or fondle the bars of a gate in substitution for sexual abandon, but her world is visually restricted to the inhuman empty, blank, confines of the imprisoning concrete hospital, her professional and moral boundaries imposed by the wimple shrouding her face and the mask over her mouth. This points to a second tension, that of a *populist* sympathy, which depends upon the fellow feeling of the mass Italian audience with the protagonist's subjection to an unfair or unfeeling environment. Dealing with states of crisis, melodrama is populist because it offers grand expressivity to those trapped within situations of marked ordinariness rather than heroic grandeur. Third, the *musicality* of melodrama—described by Elsaesser (1987) as including musical accompaniment along with aspects of lighting, mise-en-scène, and editing—confers an importance to situations of everyday mundanity or ordinary disappointment, without reducing the restrictions of everydayness or ordinariness. Finally, restriction lies in Brooks's main point, that what melodrama seeks to communicate with lies *beyond*—seen, for example, in Anna's nostalgia for a past life, the continued presence of her unrealized desire, her faith in service to a higher cause, or even her resemblance to popularly recognizable icons of female sacrifice.

Melodramatic conventions provide the measure by which to judge excess, not as deviations from a classical norm but through the boundaries that indicate the presence of the exceeded norms within the artworks themselves. This perspective allows us to maintain the commonsense connection of melodrama to excess, and to see its aesthetic and ethical value as lamentation, alongside its dramatic heightening of conflict. Excess is then a product of the melodramatic work's own internal tensions; emotional expressivity provides the outlet to overcome them. Through such analysis, melodrama studies may also overcome *its* internal tensions, and in particular its tendency toward unnecessary binary oppositions, whether between realism and melodrama, sacred and personal, or excess and norm.

NOTES

This essay develops some of my arguments in *The Operatic and the Everyday in Post-war Italian Film Melodrama*, Edinburgh: Edinburgh University Press, 2014. I thank Valerio Coladonato for his help in sourcing materials.

1. See O'Leary (2011), Cardone (2012), Bauman (2013), O'Rawe (2014), and Champagne (2015).

17

Costumes as Melodrama

Super Fly, *Male Costume,* and the Larger-Than-Life

DRAKE STUTESMAN

Clothing is one of the most public symbols of personal style, and if the viewer is sometimes confused or disturbed by the style of dress, perhaps this in itself signifies an important purpose.

(Foster 1997, 219)

Mute performance is one of illegitimate theatre's most evocative forms of expression.
(Moody 2000, 85)

I am an invisible man.

(Ellison 1952, 1)

THE COSTUME

Melodrama is inherent to costume as costumes, because they are identified *as costumes*, are associated with extreme display. Meant to visually convey information, costumes put on "mute performances" and, though they may mimic clothes, they are different because they are staged. They are expected to fire the imagination in settings that are understood as "imaginative"—that is circus, opera, dance, pageant, parade, film, theater, and more—and so are expected to reveal characters (rich, poor, country, city) and genre (comedy, science-fiction). To fulfill those expectations, costumes, though not always excessive in appearance, represent, in relation to clothes, an excess of subtle tricks. Designers describe a costume as "built," and they build it by ingeniously conforming to and deviating from cultural clothing codes to "telegraph," as designers call it, meaning to the audience (Landis 2003, 9). Costumes, especially film costumes (because of demands such as lighting and close-up), are complexly fabricated, even when they appear to be innocuous.

Though we respond to flagrant costumes and laugh at the too small hat or the too large shoes or marvel at the voluminous superhero cape and the star's long train, we also respond, often without knowing, to what isn't obvious. By fractionally moving a seam or infinitesimally toning color, a costume can induce a piercing subliminal impression. Something as modest as a shift in size or position of a padded shoulder can provoke an inexplicably overwhelming emotional *frisson* of transgression or power.[1] Because they support the story line both legibly and subtly, a narrative can be read from the costumes and, loaded with so much communication, they also can convey an underlying motif, which may stand apart from the story and inform the audience about what the dialogue cannot carry.[2]

Melodramatic tropes, especially the use of display as a crucial form of expression, appear in the costumes of *Super Fly*, the 1972 African American crime film about New York's narcotics trade that was identified with melodrama from the outset. Vincent Canby (1972), one of the seventies' most influential film critics, marked *Super Fly* as a "tough, unsentimental melodrama of the superior sort that recognizes fate in circumstances, and circumstances in character." At base, *Super Fly*'s most obvious melodramatic characteristic lies within its drug story. There is a melodramatic inner story—that of an individual fighting an oppressive social system.[3] *Super Fly*'s reliance on presentation also places it as melodrama.

The film's approach to the costumes of its lead, Youngblood Priest (Ron O'Neal), parallels the ways in which nineteenth-century male stars of melodramatic theater valued costume's possibilities. Melodrama scripts typically included vivid descriptions of costume. In a theater where "talk was an accessory" (Rahill 1967, 297–98), costume's ability to create an excess of meaning, either overtly or covertly, was one way that melodrama could "speak." Throughout the nineteenth century, the towering actors who made careers in melodrama, such as Ira Aldridge, Henry Irving, and Herbert Beerbohm Tree, took costume seriously.[4] Figures 17.1a through 17.1c illustrate the three men in roles they made famous: Aldridge as Zanga, Irving as Cardinal Wolsey, and Tree as King John. Even illustrations of the two canonical roles (Wolsey, King John) deploy melodramatic tropes.[5] The three actors pose in gestures that give their roles gravitas, but they go further, using their costumes to reveal their characters' inner pain, contradiction, and fatality. Reviewers avidly noted this. Critic Clement Scott in 1892 meticulously described Irving's use of brash colors for his Wolsey costume[6] and rhapsodized about Irving's ability to make a costume blast, stating that on first entrance, he was a " 'living picture' that exactly fascinated the eye." Scott felt that the costume spoke volumes, not only about the role but about how Irving played the role. "We see at once, *at first glance*, how Mr. Irving intends to read his character" (as cited in Richards 2005, 138–39; emphasis added).

Contemporary images in paintings, studio photographs, and drawings show that these actors did not just wear their costumes but actively worked with them to catch that "first glance." In figures 17.1a through 17.1c, the actors are depicted as swimming in fabric, wearing gigantic robes layered in tunics and capes, but even in these still images the men loom in their monumental clothing and despite or, arguably, because of those clothes project emotion and virility. Their character is apparent, as Scott's impassioned statement declares, before a line is spoken.

Figure 17.1 (a) Ira Aldridge in voluminous costume as Zanga, in Edward Young's *The Revenge* (1832). (b) Henry Irving's striking cassock, as Cardinal Wolsey (1892). (c) Herbert Beerbohm Tree as King John by Charles Buchel (1900). His copious robe suggests protection but his tunic's wrinkles droop with his worry. (d) The English King Charles II, by John Michael Wright (1661), in his Coronation clothes whose excessive rich fabrics and fur denote taste and supremacy. Courtesy of the Royal Collection Trust. © Her Majesty Queen Elizabeth II (2017).

The costumes expose life beneath the pose. Aldridge, the African American actor who became the "unequaled" rage of European theater (Lindfors 2007, 138), works his capacious gown and tunic as Zanga (figure 17.1), the cruel, enslaved prince in the melodrama *The Revenge*, a role he first played in 1832 at the Theatre Royal in Hull. By holding up the heavy folds, he makes his arm muscular but gives it an air of malice and stature. We see Irving similarly handling his cassock, which heaps on the floor (figure 17.1b). The *mozzetta*, his short cape, is starched or stitched with wrinkles so they won't disappear, suggesting experience and exhaustion to an audience who know the Cardinal's fate. An unwieldy long wrap has been added, so full that Irving must heft it over his arm. Given his expression, it is a chore he seems to relish, and Irving leans toward the viewer in a larger-than-life posture.[7] At the time, the *Observer* extolled that it was "hard to imagine a more wonderful figure than he makes in his [Wolsey] robes" (as cited in Richards 2005, 139).[8] Tree also poured over his costumes. Both men consulted artists specializing in historical painting but were known for interpreting, to suit themselves, a period costume's delicate shades and specific cuts (225). Tree, painted in 1900, as the beleaguered King John (figure 17.1c), wears a costume designed by Percy Anderson, a fur-lined, royal robe that rolls around him as if a protective wall; but his tunic, clinging to his body, sags and points to his worry and vulnerability.[9] These stage giants are not swallowed by their giant clothes. They make them their own. Though playing characters brought down by circumstance, the actors handle their costumes in such a way that it brings out the emotional complexity of their lives (Zanga's frustration, Wolsey's exhaustion, John's panic). A painting of Charles II in 1661 in his Coronation regalia (figure 17.1d), shows that this expression of power and masculinity through frontal display of excessive materiality and excessive sartorial splendor was deeply engrained in European culture. The actors, two centuries later, with their large costumes and pronounced body language, were tapping into these expected clothing codes. During the reign of Charles II, this masculine costume display had already penetrated the stage, not as an aristocratic exhibition but as a theatrical one. In this era, it was known that royals lent or gifted their personal clothes to esteemed actors to wear in plays. Charles even lent his coronation suit (de Marly 1982, 35). The actors requested these clothes partly because royal dress, made of silks, metal threads, jewels, and the like, carried light so well. But it also underscores how clothing and costume can merge when they are used to "stage" meaning (either political or theatrical). This exchange demonstrates the way that wearing clothes (as staging) reflects a relationship between the theatrical stage and the political stage, a relationship between performance and politics that continued into cinema.[10] In this respect, *Super Fly*'s Priest costumes—with their complex roots in early nineteenth-century America and its gestations of black theater, black dandyism, and civil rights politics—also link to melodrama's involved and energized use of costuming.

On first release in 1972, *Super Fly*, a small budget film directed by Gordon Parks Jr., appeared on only a few screens in the United States.[11] But in two months it swept the country and grossed $11 million. The low-key score with emotional lyrics by Curtis Mayfield grossed $20 million on record release (*Ebony*, July 1973, 91).

Super Fly went from a niche audience to a mainstream success and has become, over subsequent decades, a cult film with iconic status that ranges from cool to kitsch.[12] Though *Super Fly* is labeled a Blaxploitation film, it predates this subgenre. Unlike the "cheap imitations" made after 1972, it and two other films, *Sweet Sweetback's Baadasssss Song* (1971, Melvin Van Peebles) and *Shaft* (1971, Gordon Parks), set the genre's formula: a focus on black male leads and, as Ed Guerrero's (1993) analysis of the cinematic black male summarizes, a "retribution motif [along with] . . . corrupt white cops . . . [and] romanticized inner city" (94). Made by black directors and, by and large, with a black cast and crew,[13] the three films created a cinematic phenomenon—low budget, black-centered and black-made, urban crime stories that successfully appealed to a wide, diverse audience and, virtually overnight, grossed enormous profits. Guerrero saw that the formula also included an emphasis on costumes, which he saw as "aggrandized sartorial fashions of the black underworld" (94). *Super Fly*'s unique use of costume for Priest, however, sets it apart from *Sweet Sweetback's Baadasssss Song* and *Shaft*, as well as other films of its type, because the costumes are a careful and distinctive use of the important melodramatic tropes of material presentation, material excess, and the promotion of virility through that excess.

Though a crime story, the film is well known for Priest's exceptional outfits. When the film was released, few had seen anything like them on screen before. Even today, they are impossible to ignore. The costumes are large—for example, near floor length coats—have uniform white and brown tones or singular, striking patterns that stand out from multicolored backgrounds, and they appear as matching mono-hued suits cut close to the body in elegant lines. They are unusual in part because they stand out so dramatically, as both masculine and bold, and in part because these spectacular costumes, designed by Nate Adams, appear in a contemporary crime story shot on location in New York's hardest streets.[14] They create a new amalgamation of crime paradigm, material excess, emotional pathos, and melodramatic narrative.

Super Fly is about an affluent black drug dealer based in Harlem and selling throughout New York who is determined to leave the drug trade, which he feels demeans him. He struggles against his friends' opinions that he can't do better than the riches of dealing, that racism will keep him trapped in crime, while he struggles with his own feelings of ambition, avarice, selfishness, and anger. The story concerns Priest's last big score during which he faces his problems, fights oppressors, and gains money, love, and freedom. The script highlights racism as the force driving African American lives, and it is Priest's determination to get out of crime that drives the film. The film's trajectory is not the heist itself, which unfolds only at the very end and doesn't steer the script. As Darius James's commentary on black exploitation cinema makes explicit, *Super Fly*'s "true and artful portrait of a successful drug dealer fighting for his own redemption" (1995, 80) eclipses the crime story because the film portrays Priest as a black man whose identity has been obscured by the criminal life foisted on him. The script, by Phillip Fenty, is in many ways structured around the lingering Jim Crow of 1970s America. Fenty writes explicit dialogue about Priest's desire to get out of crime, about dealing as a cul-de-sac of racism, and about the African American need for legal work, legal citizenship, legal rights, and legally endorsed property—and for a guarantee that these rights will be backed by the justice system and the Constitution. *Super Fly*'s redemptive theme occurs through its recontextualizing of crime, positing it as neither drug trade nor theft but as blocking the black individual from self-definition. What redeems Priest is his refusal to be an "invisible man" and his relentless pursuit of his real self. This deeper story is exposed in his costumes. They function melodramatically as a means to "speak" visibility. They dominate the film's visuals.

Adams dressed Priest in strong tones, an almost monochromatic palette of starkly colored whites, browns, grays, and blacks, using clean lines and form-fitting cuts to create conspicuous silhouettes. The costumes are finely tailored, sumptuous, and excessive. The few patterns are big, in crisscross or loop forms, and perfectly mitered, with patterns meeting exactly at the seams. The costumes fit close to Priest's body and, to show that body, are often worn with closed fastenings. Like the costumes for Irving, Aldridge, and Tree, they are built to be looked at and make, as Irving's once did, a " 'living picture' that exactly fascinated the eye" (Clement Scott in Richards 2005, 138–39). This look is different from that of the other males. Adams dressed these actors in loud colors and cluttered textures, showing, for example, a man in a peach-colored suede pants and top and another in a shirt with large colored squares (figure 17.2). Adams dressed some in less kempt clothes, such as a wrinkled suit (figure 17.2) or a jacket with a rough fur collar (figure 17.3), and dressed others in dull solids, which is how the white police are always clothed (figure 17.4). Only Priest conforms to a svelte, tightly cut, single-hued look, and only he wears maxi-coats or matching suit-and-overcoat ensembles. Priest's immaculate appearance also contrasts intensely with the city

Figure 17.2 Priest, second from right, wears a dark unmarked coat, white turtleneck, and dark pants. The other costumes show wear (first on right, second on left, third on left) and patterns (second on left; third on right; first on left [hat]; fourth on right [tie]).

Costumes as Melodrama 295

Figure 17.3 To set Priest apart, Nate Adams costumed him in clean lines and monotone colors, in precisely cut silhouettes with squared shoulders. In contrast, his partner Eddie's lines are looser, with rough fur collar and sloping shoulders. His jacket lining shows and its closing is uneven.

Figure 17.4 The white cops in plain shirts and ties in solid colors.

streets, especially in scenes shot among tenements and derelict lots in Harlem. Priest's costumes—more complete, more together, and more stunning than those of the other men—are the focus of this analysis and demonstrate that costumes are a melodramatic performance in themselves. In their giant grandeur and their contrasts (to both mise-en-scène and actors), the costumes insist that they be seen. They tell an intense emotional story that follows the trajectory of the hero's fight, within himself and as a man in the world, against being made small.

This fight for self, the core of *Super Fly*'s story line, can be traced through Priest's costume changes. Priest first appears naked, lying in bed, chest exposed, staring into space. He is in a plush apartment, in bed with a woman after sex, and taking hits of cocaine. Over that shot, Curtis Mayfield sings "I gotta get away / The pain is getting worse day by day / The way it's always been." The disconnection between the despairing words and the visual abundance of this scene sets up Priest's inner motive, of needing to escape, but the costumes establish a deeper theme, less easy to articulate. When Priest leaves the bed, his body is seen in a close-up from waist to calf, in a dark profile. He is wearing white briefs that he has just put on. Then, still in close-up, he pulls on his dark pants (figure 17.5). Priest's first full outfit, as he walks out into the street, is dark pants, dark jacket, ribbed white turtleneck, and floor length, sleek brown fur coat. He wears a light gray, broad brim fedora with a black rim and wide black headband (figure 17.6).

Figure 17.5 Priest as a naked black man getting into costume and getting into the "life."

Figure 17.6 Priest's long protective fur coat promotes grandeur and wealth as well as insularity and vulnerability, much as Beerbohm Tree's *King John* costume did.

Later the jacket is revealed as having a small white trim around large external pockets, small epaulettes, white buttons on the cuffs, and a zipper closing.

With these two opening displays, Priest is introduced *first* as a man, naked, young, then as a man who enters into his clothes (puts on his pants). In this sense, his real self (the nude man) must enter the costume he wears not only as the fictional character of the dealer, but as a black man and a black male body. This is an essential part of the script: Priest wants to be recognized as a man, as the person whom he chooses to be. He wants to "wear" himself as he likes. On the brink of getting out of the drug life, Priest appears in the opening of *Super Fly* as a man *in* "the life"—with expensive taste, a glamorous routine, and a stylish, distinct, strong, put-together look. That he is encased in an almost floor length fur coat has more than one objective. Its length, shielding Priest, implies self-protection. Its fur (not a synthetic or weave) gives him a naturalness that enhances the first impression of him as a naked, and thus natural, man; but the expensive fur also signifies that Priest shields himself through money. The tropes of the lengthy fur power garment over a visibly vulnerable body echo the devices used by Tree's *King John* costume in 1900.

Priest has twelve costume changes. Through them, he shows a progress toward certainty and an increasing willingness to come forth, by revealing his clothed body and wearing more complexly detailed clothes. He progressively moves from protective long coats (his second outfit is also a maxi-coat, a luxurious white wool with a large pale gray diamond design, figure 17.12), to form-fitting jackets, as Priest, literally, reveals more of himself. The most striking jacket is a soft cream and brown suede (figure 17.7) with a large, dynamic pattern, which fits his torso like a shirt. This stark jacket has a severe, stencil-like dark-light contrast, which is the strongest pattern Priest has worn thus far. He wears it when he starts his final deal, and its crisp, declarative forms represent his resolution, now shaped into a

Figure 17.7 Priest's sharply defined cream and brown pattern on his suede jacket reveals that he is deciding to leave the "life."

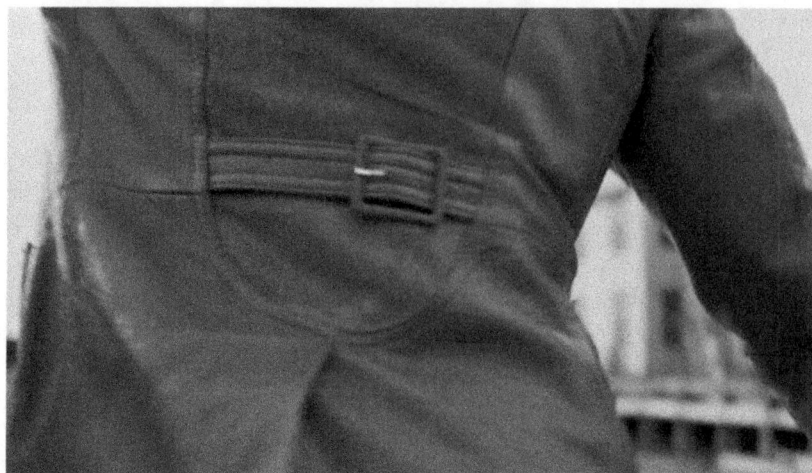

Figure 17.8 Priest's final costume, a leather outfit with complex details of tinted suede saddling and buckles, signifies his willingness to reveal himself as he escapes his criminal life.

specific plan to get out of the drug game. His final costume, worn in the last scenes, is a tight leather suit with suede highlights, in two-tone browns. In this ensemble, Priest tricks his betrayer, steals the big score, blocks the corrupt police, and leaves the trade (with his faithful lover). The leather suit, as the scenes evolve, divulges more and more details of its subtleties as seen in the buckled straps and tinted suede saddling that appears on the back, front, sleeves, and legs (figure 17.8). The suit is a compact balance of solids and detailing, and it suggests a man who is now able to reveal his complexities as he enters into what his friend has scoffingly called "that other world"—beyond the dealer life and its racist confines.[15]

Adams dressed the cast in 1970s African American men's fashion, a style in the mode of the decade that tended toward extravagant cuts, flash extras, and saturated color. Some of these features can be seen in an advertisement for the fashion label Eleganza, which offers, for example, a short cape, two-tone jumpsuit, and a wide collar with matching belt (figure 17.9).

Many 1970s African American clothes, especially Eleganza lines, came in opulent colors such as purple, magenta, or acid green, and Adams costumed the nonprincipals in these richer tones. The avoidance of color in Priest's almost achromatic blacks, whites, grays, and browns accentuates his presence but also hints that he is a man who will decide how to "color in" his liberated self. The cooled down palette and sleek silhouettes follow certain *haute couture* rules—the cuts show strong attention to tailoring, and the outfits are well coordinated. The lines are contoured, the colors don't clash, the patterns are balanced with solids, and the accessories, such as hats, conform to the overall outfit. This doesn't authorize the costumes as "right" because of being in "good taste"; rather, these effects create stability, which "telegraphs" information. Adhering to classic guidelines, Adams keeps Priest in a visual scheme that reads as tight, well organized, well balanced, and contained—all traits that Priest needs to stay on track and, as he says, "get . . .

Figure 17.9 Eleganza, a fashion label carrying African American styles in *Ebony*, July 1973, 91.

out of this whole scene." The costumes keep the viewer's eye focused. They aren't busy; the eye isn't confused.[16] Aside from their lack of opulent color, Priest's costumes deviated from the 1970s style in other key ways. The fashion of the period was notoriously eclectic, often haphazard in its design mixes, and just as often considered coarsely "antifashion," undirected, and tasteless. There is nothing undirected about Priest's costumes; they stand out as cohesive. Priest arguably fights the power of prejudice to determine who he is by dressing, not as racism sees him (insignificant) but as he sees himself (significant). The costumes say visually that Priest, as a person, commands attention, has confidence, and is different. But his style doesn't represent him as a man whose dress is self-created (that is, he hasn't created something idiosyncratically personal); rather, it deeply situates him in the African American community whose vogues permeated society and historically emphasized a standout male look.[17] This look wasn't just for the young or the radical. In his account of black 1970s fashion, Michael McCollom (2006) shows how typical and how fundamental this attire was, noting that his "very Black middle-class" father "had several [tuxedos, ranging] from a 60's Sutach-embroidered shawl collared style to a 70's Cranberry velvet two-button with grosgrain trim" (11). But for its gangsters, *Super Fly* takes this black fashion sense further.

This kind of black male splendor has deep roots in African American businesses and theater, especially visible in the style of the "Black Dandy," a vogue that began in the 1820s among young free black men in northern cities. The dandy, as a type of dresser, is typically figured as a male fashion plate and associated with extremes—extreme attention to dress, to affectation, to style. However, the late eighteenth-century "Supreme Dandy," Beau Brummell, addressed this idea by questioning what dressing itself meant. Brummell is known for the way in which he radicalized the dandy practices because he saw the dandy not as a fashionista but as a basis for male individualism. He overturned the idea that the dandy's sartorial focus was style alone, instead focusing on his look not as a way of dressing but as a way of framing himself. He advocated simplicity and structure as the way to showcase virility. For Brummell, it was less about the look, less about the clothes, but more about setting himself in a context of his choosing (as cited in Rogers 2012, 9).[18] This same agenda underpins the Black Dandy. It also appears in Priest's costumes.

Clothing has always played a key role in African American history and in American racism.[19] From colonial times, clothing had, for African Americans, a kind of confrontation built into its display. Until the nineteenth century, it was illegal for slaves to wear good clothes, though it's arguable that a law banning this practice signified that it was common (Walker 2009, 96). Grace Hale's 1998 study of segregation notes how fraught this censure was. "Clothing, more than any other consumer goods, conveyed a lasting meaning" and, by the 1820s, expensive clothing worn by blacks "incited white fears of upwardly mobile African Americans and the unhinging of class and racial identities which such 'New Negroes' signified" (190). A slave owner in 1822 ranted that the black "Dandies who measure their importance by their Dress" forget "their grade or station" (White 1999, 5). The Black Dandy was a man with a sartorial look that announced a presence, a deliberately provocative act that could fly in the face of racism's control. Unlike restrictions on other forms of ownership and basic rights, "clothing could cross the color line" (Hale 1998, 190); a person with money could purchase goods. Sumptuary laws had, in 1800s America, all but disappeared. This confrontational display of black identity through a display of clothing, already at work in 1830s black dandyism, is visible in *Super Fly*'s use of costume as an assault on control and as a flaunting of personhood.

By 1827, the Black Dandy was caricatured as "Zip Coon" in a racist song mocking the northern, moneyed, urban black dandy who was contrasted with, but remained cousin to, "Jim Crow," a southern, poor, black, country hick, dressed in rags (figure 17.10).

Costumes as Melodrama 301

Figure 17.10 *Zip Coon* (1827), a racist parody of the era's solvent Black Dandy.

Zip Coon was the start of a racial confrontation in which clothes were centralized, representing a twofold white fear of the Black Dandy. First, it was a fear of black audacity; second, it was a fear of the former slave, now a commonly present urbanite of the Jacksonian era,[20] who expressed full self-possession in fine, eye-catching clothing. This, in turn, reflected the growing black affluence of the 1820s and 1830s as black theaters, schools, businesses, and newspapers strengthened and prospered (Lewis 1996, 262; Cockrell 1997, 29). The Zip Coon's black dandyism, despite the ridicule, was a complicated cipher for whites. Overtly it was a racist affront, but covertly it reflected white-on-white rage. The contempt of poor whites for Zip Coon's sartorial "entitlement" sublimated their hatred of the upper class, which was impossible to express directly (Cockrell 1997, 93–94). The Black Dandy was enviably overt in his defiance, and his money gave him power, which poor whites lacked. Barbara Lewis (1996) connects the Black Dandy's publicly staged clothes with early black American theater companies, arguing that, beginning in the late 1820s, they saw the Black Dandy as a straight-up defiance of racism and used it to shape their theatrical ambitions (260).

Priest's costumes are a confluence of these multiple elements: black politics, dandyism, black masculinity, melodrama, and, especially, the silent ways in which hidden agendas are declared. None of the above can be separated from any analysis of costume design and melodrama in *Super Fly*, but they are, at times, not in tune. Black politics, as expressed in early seventies *black* cinema, has a complex and distinct history located in racial prejudice, white exclusivity, and black exclusion from theater, films, and film companies. The history of black cinema is composed as much by its own political and artistic trajectory as it is by a history woven into or expelled from white hegemonic representations.[21] Black male identity experiences the same struggle between separatism and integration. Melodrama similarly has been at the center of, parallel to, but in theory excluded from "legitimate" forms of staging. Much the same can be said of dandyism. But in *Super Fly* these positions overlap and form, perhaps, another kind of history in which they all play a part.

Super Fly's costumes shape the urban crime story's claim to "realism" as few film costumes, perhaps no other, have done. They stand out but, in doing so, point to the more complex story of self-realization that drives the film. By differentiating how narrative information is communicated, the distinction between epiphoric and diaphoric metaphor suggests how costume tells that story. Whereas an epiphor directly connects two disparate but easily comparable objects, a diaphor offers a comparison the basis of which is not immediately apparent. As such, a diaphor can carry layered and complex meanings.[22] Epiphoric film costumes are obvious. They reveal crucial information about plot, character, mise-en-scène, and so forth. But a film's costumes also can be diaphoric. They act as subliminal links, often conveying complexities not evident in the script that may reveal subversive counterdramas or, perhaps, elements of drama that can't be conveyed through words. Peter Brooks (1995) describes gesture as a "sign for a sign," which, like a metaphor, then exists in a state of translation (72). It can't be decoded or reduced to a specific denotation. It must be deciphered, allowing it to remain a thing in itself, not just a substitute for something else. Gesture's communication is not a replacement for words. Brooks situates the melodramatic gesture in a "gap in language" where it is both "grandiose and ineffable" (72). It tells, as costume does, more than the sum of its codes.

This use of the complex diaphor, which both connects and disguises, can be found in the idea of the excess of melodrama as provocatively realistic. The tactic of nineteenth-century British illegitimate theater described by Jane Moody (2000, 7), of taking lurid stories and embedding them in sharp contemporary debates on topics such as slavery and social mobility, is also at work in *Super Fly*. Illegitimate theater was categorized as "illegitimate" because it countered classical drama with what were seen as the lowbrow genres of melodrama, burletta, and extravaganza. *Super Fly* is a kind of latter day version of illegitimacy, categorized as Blaxploitation, a seventies lowbrow genre considered down-market and predictable in its exploitation of sensationalism. Like illegitimate theater, black cinema also was barred from performing in proscribed ways.[23] But illegitimate theater exhibited, through its disruptive forms and melodramatic excesses, a politics that often was too explosive or too emotional for critical discussion. Melodrama as a confrontation with social misery is obvious in *Super Fly*.[24] However, the links between black power and black male sartorial splendor as both threatening and enviable has an underlying presence in the film. This splendor exposes racial politics through its excess. The costumes uncover Priest's life in ways that the script cannot. They reveal the protagonist's destiny and display his inner sense of self. They visually represent his movement toward his goal. He never wavers in that commitment, much as his costumes never waver in their assertive stance but evolve, as Priest's resolution evolves, through visual changes in texture and silhouette. Costumes imply as much as they reveal. Their displays are "ineffable" as much as they are "grandiose." In the midst of violence, dereliction, and corruption, Priest's costumes *display* a grandiose (assured) but ineffable (complexity of identity) sense of self as unsplintered, secure, gigantic, beautiful; a sense of self that is entirely whole, a full "I am." The costumes reveal him as a man who knows what he wants and who he is. Priest's move from crime and demoralization to freedom from crime challenges and overcomes the racial status quo forced on him. *Super Fly*'s small story is set in a larger story about racism, the black male, the black male body, and black male options.

THE BODY

There is "a central paradox" in the relationship between costume and the body. Truly more about what it hides than what it shows, the costume acts as a "kind of magic screen onto which the repressed narrative" of human life "may be projected" (Chabon 2008, 20).[25] Without the body, attire is only an object of material culture. It no longer is an active part of life. This is in part what Chabon means. The *life* of the wearer is crucial to how the costume is constructed and the costume's true role; and its "deepest meaning" is to reveal the vulnerable person (20). Melodrama reflects this relationship in its staging of gesture. What was once staged as a *tableau vivant*, or a "wordless depiction of dramatic character" (Moody 2000, 85), is seen still in the conflation of costume with body. What was apparent in the theatrical garments/poses of Tree, Aldridge, and Irving is apparent in some of cinema's most famous costumes, which are inextricably associated with the wearer's larger-than-life gesture. Examples include Marilyn Monroe's white dress, designed by William Travilla, in *The Seven Year Itch* (1957), blowing upward while she, with pleasure, struggles, to no avail, with both arms straight down, to keep it from fully revealing her legs and underwear; John Travolta in *Saturday Night Fever* (1977), who stands, in his white three-piece suit, designed by Patrizia von Brandenstein, with his legs splayed, his butt out, and his arm pointing straight in the air; Keanu Reeves in *The Matrix Reloaded* (2003), his Kym Barrett designed black coat's chest and collar tight on his torso and its wide, ankle-length skirt whirling around his body. These costumes, recognized in silhouette around the world and widely copied, have become so famous they are identified in shorthand as "the white dress," "the white suit," and "the black coat." There is something "super" in each one of these items. Each shows a supernal sense of sexual youth, pleasure in being, beauty, defiance, rootedness, flux, and determination; what these costume images offer is greater than the image itself, implying a diaphoric tableau, both ineffable and grandiose, with multiple layers of meaning, often not easily put into words. *Super Fly*, as the name implies, is an excess of "fly," black urban slang for extreme cool. The word "super" associates Priest with an even-greater supra status. He is beyond just fly, he is in the realm of super fly, and "super" is always associated with an idealized or heroic place.

How is it that costume plays such a role in creating and choreographing a larger-than-life iconicity, not in terms of the costume itself but in what it represents as a symbiotic part of being/clothing/identity—so much so that the image (of the gesturing and costumed person as persona) becomes cultural parlance? This parlance, of the costume/body, cannot be replaced by words. The costume and its bodily action speak more than words can contain.

In *Super Fly* the melodramatic costumes can't be separated from the politics of the time. In the script, racism controls the Harlem drug trade, and the story of Priest's escape from that trade is also, in diaphoric metaphor, his triumph over that racism. His Black Dandy costumes, as exemplars of that triumph to come, are part of an earlier black tradition of defying racism through clothing. As Helen Bradley Foster (1997) argues, American slaves used clothes as a means to express selfhood; though they "did not even legally own their bodies, [the enslaved] still managed to reveal themselves as individual and communal beings by their dress" (4). She adds that such use of clothes was politically proactive. "The distinctive ways in which the enslaved wore their clothing and the special manner in which they viewed their clothing were important demonstrations of their refusal to accept cultural annihilation." They "set up their cultural boundaries with demarcations of style, and, in refusing to give up their style, they freed themselves" (220).

American black male stereotypes, Sandra Gunning (1996) argues, are fused with the "hypersexualized and criminalized" black male body. This version of that body "has always functioned as a crucial and heavily overdetermined metaphor in an evolving discourse on the nature of a multiethnic, multiracial American society" (3). Within *Super Fly*, the black male and the black male body manifest differently than in other crime melodramas because the costume plays such a strong part in representing the self.

In this film, the black male body is the key focus. Priest first appears as a naked man, impressing the viewer with nakedness as its particular goal: to be natural and to be thus a natural black man. African Americans' history of not "legally own[ing] their bodies" is present in *Super Fly*; to own his own body is what Priest wants, and to this end the film changes presentation of the black body from one that has been hyperized and overdetermined for centuries to one that is self-contained and self-determined. This goal is as much the melodramatic arc of the character as the crime story. Priest wants to choose his place in society and hates his position as a criminal; to this end the film uses costumes to manifest this new context. They take on the role of the diaphoric tableau as seen in the costume/body relationships of the "Marilyn dress," "Travolta suit," and "Matrix coat." Adam's costumes put forward a new tact, a new definition of citizen and man. It is the undetered assertiveness of the costumes—always tailored, clean and unmarked, visually dominant, and expressing maleness—that show that the body wearing them, like the costumes themselves, cannot be suppressed.

This is so foregrounded in *Super Fly* that it contrasts sharply with the role of costumes in *Shaft*. Unlike *Super Fly*, *Shaft* was a studio film (produced by MGM). Originally, Shaft was scripted as a white character, but due to the success of *Sweet Sweetback's Baadasssss Song*, he was rewritten as black. Shaft, played by Richard Rowntree, is a detective who, like the typical cinema private eye from Sam Spade to Easy Rawlins, lives between law and crime, and that is part of his appeal. Shaft and Priest have more in common than their positions on opposite sides of the law (as cop and criminal). But Shaft is placed in a white world, living in a West Village townhouse, and Priest is placed in a black world, predominately Harlem.²⁶ But what really keeps the two leads apart is their attire. Adams's use of Priest's splendor is different in intention from the strategies of *Shaft*'s costume designer, Joseph G. Aulisi. Rowntree, as a typical American macho P.I., wears a worn, creased leather coat, a riff on the classic disheveled trench coat of cinema's white male P.I. (figure 17.11). Shaft is not a dandy, but Priest is. As Brummell had done, Priest uses

Figure 17.11 John Shaft in leather trench coat in *Shaft* (1971).

clothing to pronounce his individualism and, as the Black Dandy had, to declare his blackness (figure 17.12). Shaft, conversely, is dressed in a costume that conforms to whiteness; only his trench coat's leather has a touch of difference.[27] The black actor's appearance in the role of dandy is atypical, and critics Donald Bogle and Guerrero are uneasy with Priest's costumes. Bogle (2016) dislikes them outright, referring to Priest as an "urban ballerina" (217). Although Guerrero (1993) finds them "exaggerated but polished," contributing to the film's "magnetic appeal," he finds Priest "traipsing" (96). Both words, "ballerina" and "traipse," in a context of filmic machismo suggest that these critics find the costumes unmanly. But the

Figure 17.12 Youngblood Priest in white long coat ensemble in *Super Fly* (1972).

very disruptive quality of the costumes shifts *Super Fly* and its formulaic crime melodrama into new territory, distinguishing it as African American. Priest's "sartorial fashion," by its very compact tailoring, is distinct from the more comically garish "pimp costumes" of the Blaxploitation films to come. Like the Black Dandy, Priest has an agenda of male self-determination, and his costumes carry that message.

Super Fly's costumes display Priest's splendor as a new and gorgeous platform for black masculine mystique and black masculine self-reinvention. It's arguable that the *Super Fly* costumes stage a melodrama about race and identity that in 1972 could not be overtly stated or, in another manner of silencing, was ignored. "*I am a man*" was the bitter line on many signs during the 1960s fight for civil rights, and Adam's costumes develop this political meaning at a deep level. As melodramatic stagings or enactments, the costumes announce a presence, a direction. They claim a life style and a triumph, telling through their own melodramatic expressiveness the story of Priest, who reclaims his own identity through his ambition, his determination; as costumes, they demonstrate his opposition to how society has defined him.

NOTES

1. Seemingly ordinary clothes, such as a T-shirt, are often crafted. Costume designer Jeffery Kurland (*Radio Days*, 1987, Woody Allen; *Ocean's Eleven*, 2001, Steven Soderbergh) explains: "I've never just bought an item and then put it on screen. With the character being created by a team—the writer, the actor, and the costume designer—one can't just go 'find' some clothing and expect to be right. Everything is filtered through a creative process. So even if an item is purchased, in the end, it too must be created, just as the writer creates the screenplay and the actor creates the character" (as cited in Landis 2003, 69). Period costumes also often have to be reworked, as designer Eiko Ishioka (*The Cell*, 2000, Tarsem Singh; *Bram Stoker's Dracula*, 1992, Francis Ford Coppola) explains: "Period pieces . . . require thorough research . . . [but] I will 'recook' the historical cues to create my own tableau" (as cited in Landis 2003, 48).
2. See also Stutesman (2005) and Bruzzi (2011).
3. Elsaesser (1991) argues that the contribution of eighteenth-century sentimental drama and fiction to melodrama was their "focus on suffering and victimization—the claims of the individual in an absolutist society" (73). *Super Fly* is arguably a melodrama about that claim.
4. Actresses Ellen Terry, Gaby Deslys, Sarah Bernhardt, Madame Celeste, Madame Vestris, Charlotte Cushman, and others also wore extreme costumes.
5. David Mayer (2004) notes that "illustrations of melodramatic performance are largely alike in depicting actors making large expressive gestures . . . often standing with legs apart, arms flung wide from their bodies, and fingers spread" (151).
6. Scott regaled Irving's Wolsey costume as "not scarlet at all, but an indescribably geranium-pink, with a dash of vermillion in it" (as cited in Richards 2005, 139).
7. Costumes probably designed by Charles Cattermole, made by London's premier costume house, Nathan's.

8. Richards (2005) records that the *Observer* noted Irving's focus on hues (139).
9. Percy Anderson designed many costumes for Tree's company in London and was well known, with his influence extending to designers such as Leon Baskt.
10. Numerous bonds existed between theater and aristocracy during the reigns of Charles II and James II because the London stage was part of the royal household (De Marly 1982, 35).
11. Bogle (2016, 217) lists the budget as $100,000, Guerrero (1993, 96) as $500,000 and Travis Mayfield, Curtis Mayfield's son, quotes his father as saying it was a budget, of "less than $300,000" (2016).
12. In 2013, for the film's fortieth anniversary, New York's Museum of the Moving Image held a screening and panel with Shelia Frazier, Nate Adams, and others.
13. *Sweet Sweetback's Baadasssss Song* (1971) had a black director, Melvin Peebles, who wrote and edited the film, Mr.B's Fashions of L.A and an unknown costume designer, both white and black producers, and a mostly black cast and crew. *Shaft* (1971) had a black director, Gordon Parks Sr., a white screenwriter, Ernest Tidyman, a white costume designer, Joseph G. Aulisi, and a mixture of whites and blacks among the producers, cast, and crew. *Super Fly* (1972) had a black director, Gordon Parks Jr., a black screenwriter, Philip Fenty, a black costume designer, Nate Adams (who played "Dealer"), and a white executive producer, Sig Shore (who played a cop), and mostly black producers, cast, and crew. All three films had black composers.
14. Despite many efforts, Nate Adams could not be contacted.
15. Eddie tells Priest, "You've got the fantasy of getting out of the life and getting that other world on its ear—what the fuck else you gonna do except hustle?"
16. John Dunn and Rita Ryack used a similar trick in costuming *Casino* (1995, Martin Scorsese), also set in the 1970s. They dressed their male leads in mono-colors so that they stood out from the busy 1970s backgrounds. The shirt, tie, and suit all came from exactly the same dye. (John Dunn speaking on a panel at the "Film Costume / Designing Realities" conference, New York University, October 17, 2015).
17. The 1940s zoot suit, for example, with its knee-length coat, giant shoulders, and wide-legged peg pants, was excess *par excellence*, cut in classic lines and at "times . . . seemed . . . the epitome of African American panache and modernity" (Peiss 2011, 94).
18. Brummell's agenda, much like Priest's costumes, was determined by clean-lined simplicity. He dressed the dandy in "simple, structured tailoring . . . absolute cleanliness" to form his context for a "new virility" (Rogers 2012, 10).
19. Until the 1860s, clothing was the preeminent black-owned trade, responsible for tailoring, importing luxury materials, and handling most high-end white and black custom. These artisan-merchants were a major influence in the rise of the American fashion industry. African Americans also dominated the lucrative secondhand clothing market, which affected most social strata (see Walker 2009, 141).
20. Cockrell (1997) states that there "is no doubt there really were dandies of color during the Jacksonian period; the newspapers were full of disdainful reports" (93).
21. For a history of black cinema from 1910 to 1950, see Henry Sampson (1995).
22. Epiphor is exemplified by the expression "my feet are blocks of ice." It is exaggerated and unreal, but the meaning is precise and obvious. Gertrude Stein exemplifies diaphor in her line, "Toasted Susie is my ice cream." Its meaning is not obvious.

There are multiple interrelations between the various subjects, and multiple meanings, and multiple emotions, are distinctly present.
23. In Britain in the eighteenth century and into the nineteenth, it was illegal for these theaters to stage spoken (and thereby the classical) drama. In the 1970s, it was virtually impossible for African Americans to play film roles outside of those prescribed by studios and their social prejudices. Scott (2015) states that from "1930–1960, African American activists fought Hollywood" for fair black representation (186).
24. Scenes show conditions of bad housing and addiction but also show thriving Harlem neighborhoods.
25. Chabon (2008) focuses especially on the superhero costume, but his discussion of how the costume hides/reveals the body is relevant to all costuming because the costume is there to convey meaning. Peter Brooks (2015) reviews Eugène Sue's 1842–1843 French crime serial, *The Mysteries of Paris*, as creating a "melodramatic presentation of reality" that brings "to light emotions and issues so often repressed" (46). This polarized combination matches the effect Chabon finds in super costumes.
26. Though Priest's address is unknown, his friends come by his apartment often, suggesting they live near the Harlem hangouts where many scenes are set.
27. Claiming the leading role of a black P.I., however, was radical in itself because it was unusual. Aulisi connected Shaft with that claim by dressing him in a trope associated with the white detective character.

18

Melodrama and Apocalypse

Politics and the Melodramatic Mode in Contagion

DESPINA KAKOUDAKI

Contemporary criticism in film studies has made an important case for expanding our understanding of melodrama, for considering it not as a genre but as something much greater, more culturally diverse, more versatile, and therefore more elusive. Over the decades, a wide range of texts have been described as melodramas, from grand epics to private family stories, from action serials and thrillers to women's films and "weepies," from westerns to crime, action, and disaster films. Each era forgets or revises the previous incarnations of the label, or resists the label altogether. After the end of the studio system and the demise of well-known (if unevenly applied) production and marketing categories, we find melodramas identified as dramas, thrillers, or sagas, connected to studio pedigrees and particular directors or actors, or branded as "Oscar pictures." Even when a director, producer, or actor describes a film as a melodrama in interviews, as Todd Haynes (as cited in Davis 2015) did in his descriptions of *Carol* (2015), no one in Hollywood overtly *markets* a film as a melodrama anymore.

Although the generic label of melodrama may be limited or avoided, the workings and logic of melodrama have expanded their reach to such an extent that contemporary mainstream Hollywood cinema is arguably fundamentally melodramatic. This, in effect, proves that melodrama is more than a genre but also displaces it yet again— melodrama is now everywhere. In defining the contours of the melodramatic mode, we confront a new problem in this ubiquity. Films that don't advertise themselves as melodramas are structured by their uses of the melodramatic mode because melodrama is in the bloodstream of contemporary cinema. Its radical dispersal makes melodrama both essential to cinematic storytelling and invisible *as* melodrama.

But what if the work of melodrama is denaturalized, either because the text offers an overdetermined or amplified melodramatic structure, or because the text disguises its dependence on melodrama? To discover the structural properties of the melodramatic mode in contemporary cinema, I propose that we need to see it where its impact might be clearest, which is in texts that are not using the melodramatic mode solely as their baseline. Stated axiomatically, the melodramatic mode is now the default narrative modality in mainstream cinema, where it functions as a way to tell a story, and in fact to tell it well. Recognizing the function of melodrama allows us to trace the narrative tendencies of contemporary cinema in general, and to revise long-standing misconceptions of melodrama as an aberrant narrative style, as excessive, or as unconventional. This may sound contradictory here because I plan to focus on certain off-beat uses of the mode, in texts that either exaggerate or resist its workings. But my examples must be seen in the context of the mainstreaming of melodramatic narration, not against an imagined other form of narration that would be an antithesis or counterpoint to melodrama. I hope to show that Hollywood cinema has absorbed the melodramatic mode so thoroughly because of the structural coherence, order, and sense of balance melodrama creates in a narrative. This is true both for conventionally linear narratives and for more experimental ones. The more genre mixing and mashing we see in mainstream cinema, the more these new hybrid forms depend on the underlying ordering structure of melodrama to function as narrative.

My examples are drawn from a particularly melodramatic genre, the disaster film. Since its resurgence in the 1990s, the disaster film has become a staple of contemporary Hollywood, deftly merging melodrama as action and as pathos with its cutting-edge spectacles, computer-generated imagery (CGI), primordial dangers, and adrenaline-fueled escapes and rescues (Keane 2001). As I argue elsewhere, disaster films are quintessential melodramas, using the melodramatic mode to highlight urgent political and social issues and to present spectacles of civic and personal conflict, suffering, struggle, resolution, reconciliation, and community (Kakoudaki 2002). In many ways, disaster films are descendants of the spectacular nineteenth-century stage action melodramas, with their literal and metaphorical cliff-hanger scenes and the extravagant stagecraft that brought horse-drawn carriages, boats, trains, buildings engulfed by fire, and even the eruption of Mount Vesuvius on stage (Booth 1965, 1967; James Pain in Mayer 1994; Daly 2011); as well as the early twentieth-century screen action/thriller serials, with their fast-paced adventures, escalating dangers, fearless heroines, and death-defying stunts (Singer 2001).

In addition to their affinities with earlier melodramatic forms and their extreme situations, heroism, visual spectacle, and special effects, disaster films bring traditional melodramatic principles into modern texts. Although they feature events drawn from contemporary headlines, thus claiming their timeliness and political relevance, disaster films also retain echoes of the vocabulary of nineteenth-century "blood and thunder" melodrama. Many of the moral questions staged in nineteenth-century melodrama, revolving around altruism, greed, egotism, charity, or sacrifice, can be evoked in disaster films in ways highly plausible to contemporary experience. The threat of absolute destruction in a disaster film sets up a life and death situation that demands big emotions and significant actions, and launches not just the drive for survival but the moral imperative for proving one's character and mettle. Disaster films often present nature as actor, sometimes with what Peter Brooks calls expressionist purpose, when nature externalizes the moods and feelings of the characters, but most often as a nonhuman agent or almost-agent that embodies and amalgamates social forces and tensions. Natural catastrophes in these films sometimes stand in for transcendental levels of danger, the closest we can get in the twenty-first century to nineteenth-century stage melodrama's depiction of evil, as enacted by cruel and single-minded villainous characters, whose only motivation sometimes seems to be their ability to hurt others. Human villains of that scale cannot be sustained in contemporary film outside of supervillains, Nazis, or sociopaths, and even with such characters we often get a modicum of psychological motivation or causal explanation about their actions and moral stance. Instead, nonhuman agents such as weather patterns, earthquakes, icebergs, tsunamis, and comets supply a categorical threat in disaster films without undermining a rationalist vocabulary for action, causality, and plausibility.

By translating the terms of older melodrama into modern narrative patterns, disaster films can help us define the presence and operation of the melodramatic mode in contemporary cinema. If melodrama, as David Grimstead (1987) has argued, spells out the moral and ethical tensions of a particular historical moment, then the disaster film functions as a weathervane (pun intended) of current concerns about action and politics. The tension between what happens, the historical and material realities we face, and what ought to happen, our desires for justice or retribution, constitutes the genre's political potential, visible in the disaster film's staging of contrasts between global threats and local actions, between the desire for global connectivity and the fear of a borderless and uncontrollable world.

THE MELODRAMATIC MODE: ON SUFFERING AND CHOICE

To understand how the apocalyptic and disaster film genre use the melodramatic mode, we have to explore an essential contiguity between melodrama and apocalypse. It is visible in the way the melodramatic mode constitutes events, especially the urgent, important, or life-threatening events that often power the emotional engines of melodrama. For instance, we have to recognize that the traumas disaster films showcase are real for many people every day. Even a cursory look at a newspaper today provides so many, too many, stories of injustice, pain and suffering, the scale and frequency of which is unfathomably more expansive and dispersed than even the exaggerated plots of Hollywood disaster films. Each story is a personal and cultural apocalypse, the end of someone's world. People sail through dangerous waters to save their families from war zones; people are persecuted, killed, or poisoned by their own governments; people are discriminated against, bullied, and raped; people lose their loved ones because someone walked into a building with a gun; people risk everything in order to cross a border; people die from preventable diseases; people see their homes disappear under rising sea levels; people starve or sleep in the street; people run away to escape their own abusive families. And this list does not include the personal traumas we experience: the death of a parent, the loss of memory, the sudden instability of a job, poverty, illness, betrayal, bankruptcy, depression. We may not describe these experiences as *apocalyptic* because we reserve that term for something singular or global, or something that cannot be endured. Our own survival stops us from using the concept of the apocalypse to describe such events, but they transform the world radically, they change everything.

I provide this snapshot of everyday traumatic events and personal apocalypses to showcase how melodrama reworks apocalyptic events into a specific mode of narration. One might describe everyday events as traumatic or tragic, and actual events may fuel, inspire, or inform a melodramatic narrative in fiction or film, but we would not describe these real-life events as melodramas. Even when a film features actual situations, the melodramatic effect does not hinge on the fact of the participants' suffering or the fact of pain or abuse but on the context created in order for that suffering to play a narrative role. Sometimes the melodramatic treatment helps make sense of the event, sometimes it accentuates a lack of meaning, and sometimes it creates the grounds for moral retribution or recognition (Brooks 1995; Gledhill 2002). Melodrama works by recruiting the event into a story, using the pain or suffering involved to create a particular aesthetic, dramatic, or narrative effect.

At a basic level, the moment an event is described or recounted, something happens—linguistic elements transform the bare facts into narrative patterns. Considered as a narrative or a dramatic form, the melodramatic mode is one of these possible patterns. It could be argued that "bare facts" or "events" do not exist before or outside narrative because the act of narration itself constitutes the facts. This is precisely why it is important to trace how the melodramatic mode constitutes facts and events in particular ways. For example, I did not write "people die" in my list, which would state an absolute existential fact; or "people get sick and die," which is narrative in some measure but with no melodramatic hook. In the phrasing "people die from preventable diseases," the melodramatic tension emerges when the word "preventable" adds injustice to the mini-story. The preventability of the diseases opens the phrase to melodramatic interpretation: these people did not have to die. If only, say, the resources of Western medicine could become available and affordable in the developing world, people would not die of asthma, AIDS, malaria, or malnutrition. An implicit choreography of action emerges, of withholding treatment or arriving "too late" or "in the nick of time" to save someone. And there it is: the small addition of "preventable" provides the foundational condition for a complete melodramatic structure, with villains, suffering, injustice, action, and pathos (Williams 2001).

This tendency to construct the possibility for choice is a primary feature of the melodramatic mode, especially in the American context. In contrast to tragedy, where events are structured so as to be inevitable and where human choice is thus revealed to be an illusion, melodrama requires the possibility of some form of openness, some wiggle room for options or alternative outcomes, in order to produce tension and suspense. The operations of chance, coincidence, accident, or fate, and the upheavals or surprises we may find in melodramatic texts emerge in this space of possibility and function as its most spectacular manifestations, active reminders that (in melodrama) anything might happen. Melodrama also uses the structural positioning or timing of an event to alter its narrative and emotional impact. In a melodramatic story, whether a character dies *just as* another character is arriving, apologizing, or bringing a medical kit is of high emotional importance. The existential incomprehensibility of the fact that people die is translated into a different issue of timing or choice, or into the sense that someone did not have to die at that precise moment, or from that particular disease. Melodrama's play with time dramatizes profound questions about human experience. Is it better for someone to die at a different moment? Is it less painful to have a loved one die after everything humanly possible has been done to save him or her? Is that a consolation? Death is unfair, unfathomable. We use a specific emotional vocabulary to give death a human (and narrative) dimension, as when we say "But at least she had a long life" or "But at least he didn't suffer at the end" or "But at least I was there." Perhaps there is an inherent melodramatic recuperation in the sentiment "But at least we tried everything," and it is this implicit underlying feeling that the idea of "preventable" activates in order to interpret death wistfully as avoidable and therefore unjust. As the final event of life, death is not related to timing or justice, it is just a given. Or, in existential terms, all death is unjust. But the death from a preventable disease at a particular moment in a melodramatic story is additionally unjust in specific terms, not in abstract existential terms.

In this rudimentary description, the melodramatic mode thus offers a way to navigate the tension between our awareness of the conditions of human life and our very human desire for overcoming or counteracting these conditions in our literary and dramatic forms. Things may just happen, events may just occur or follow each other in life, but in literary, narrative, and dramatic forms they connect, they are ordered so as to provide meanings or patterns, and they may be interpreted beyond the basic facts of their occurrence. What melodrama does with this interpretive function is quite complex, using plotting, timing, the ordering of events, and the treatment of choice to produce heightened forms of meaning. In my example, the phrasing "people die from preventable diseases" activates the melodramatic mode because it translates existential fact into something that has narrative *and* moral extension, transforming death from something unpredictable and inevitable in reality to something that involves questions of timing, justice, or action.

My focus on the arrangement and timing of events foregrounds the melodramatic mode as a structural baseline, not an overlay, tone, addition, or corruption of an otherwise presumably realist narrative structure. This distinction is essential if we are to recognize the fundamental operations of the melodramatic mode, and to resist descriptions that treat melodrama in terms of excess, as if it adds (too much stuff) onto a structure that could exist or be understandable without it. Premise, situation, timing, characterization, event, narrative unfolding, impact, expressiveness, emotional articulation—all these features of a text are constituted by its baseline modality. Each mode (the epic, tragic, lyric, pastoral, realist, or melodramatic mode) arranges textual elements and tendencies differently, and this operation is discernible in how a text sets up, comments on, enhances, or resolves its situations, what stance it might take toward events or worldview, what forms of expressiveness it engages. An epic modality would have a different treatment of causes and consequences than a pastoral one, and each mode presents different emotional tendencies, resolutions, and types of expressiveness. To contrast melodrama and realism, for example, the realist modality might add the types of expressiveness that tend to be understated or melancholy, or that refuse to see or show range in terms of emotion or action; the melodramatic mode might add more overt, demanding, acted out, or externalized emotion, and insert options or a range of actions or outcomes.

To recognize the melodramatic mode, then, we have to see it not as overlay but as substrate, as the foundation upon which all the other narrative and dramatic elements are built. To study how the melodramatic mode is activated in a text we can follow just one of its tendencies, its penchant for constructing space for alternative outcomes, which also draws the traumatic or tragic events of everyday life into a melodramatic premise. When the bare facts of suffering are transposed into a narrative context where actions and tensions are negotiable, and in ways they are not in real life, the story creates the impression of choice, the impression of alternative outcomes. If the actual event does not afford such transposition, then a secondary plotline might add that dimension. The magic trick of melodrama in this vein is that one story line asks the difficult questions, and the other story line asks and answers slightly different, limited, or answerable questions. These second answers do not match the first questions, but they are close enough to be satisfying or to provide the semblance of resolution. Films such as *Philadelphia* (1993, Jonathan Demme) and *Amistad* (1997, Steven Spielberg), for example, work in this mode, both using a two-layer narrative structure. On one implicit and largely invisible narrative layer, the films posit difficult and almost unsolvable social and political questions: Why can't we cure AIDS? Why can't we stop homophobia? Why can't we stop discrimination against gay people? Why can't we end slavery? Why are people dehumanized, tormented, and treated as property? Then in the second and more visible narrative layer, both films move to a court setting where these issues are rephrased into questions that *can* be adjudicated and solved: Did this law firm discriminate against this gay lawyer? Should these particular people be treated as property? In both cases, the judicial outcome is satisfying and presents social justice as a possible, desirable, and in fact available political outcome within the context of the film, despite the fact that these specific court decisions do not resolve the larger social questions.

The court settings of *Philadelphia* and *Amistad* offer a distinct, spatialized version of what many melodramas do in their layered narration. In both films, the desire for change is satisfied in the films' resolutions and in the courts' decisions, even though these are limited, individual, and local solutions to a much bigger social or political problem. The political potential of melodrama emerges from this slippage between two levels of question. Asking the first, broader, and more difficult questions can be a political statement, in which the story challenges foundational aspects of our reality, things we take as a given. Answering the second, more specific, and more local questions can be satisfying, politically resonant, provocative, or merely palliative. Yet the unanswerable questions about injustice, discrimination, racism, and slavery remain, even after the two films resolve what they could resolve. If we recognize the operations of this layered narrative style, we see how politically powerful melodramas can be. The confrontations they facilitate with difficult issues, such as patriarchy, racism, gender relations, capitalism, family trauma, abuse, or institutional injustice, to name just a few, resonate far beyond their sometimes limited resolutions.

CONTAGION: MELODRAMA AND THE QUESTION OF RESPONSIBILITY

We see the operations of this layered narrative approach and its impact for melodramatic narration in a film such as *Contagion* (2011, Steven Soderbergh), which presents a global virus outbreak and the government and medical response it entails. *Contagion* participates in the self-conscious tone that emerged in action and disaster films after the events of 9/11, when scenes of danger and destruction increasingly were staged in terms of political relevance and responsibility rather than for vicarious pleasure or spectacular, gratuitous violence. In general, the disaster film translates melodrama's desire for moral legibility into a choreographic alternation between responsibility and response (Kakoudaki 2002). Some films use the categorical situation to demand accountability on behalf of governments and organizations, or to assign political, social, and moral responsibility for the catastrophe. Others focus on the heroism of government and military agencies, emergency personnel, and professional first responders. Most disaster films also traffic in the spectacular visual presentation of threat, in thrilling sequences of exaggerated scale that depict annihilated cities and continents. The vicariousness of this spectacular tendency is usually mitigated through a focus on family or civic values, themes of sacrifice and altruism, and scenes of poignant or solemn consideration.

Contagion presents the threat of a global pandemic in tones that aim to be chilling in their realism, instead of thrilling or exciting. The film traces the spread of a disease from the first infected patient to populations on a global scale and presents the interaction among local, federal, and international agencies, such as the Centers for Disease Control and the Epidemic Intelligence Service, the World Health Organization, and the Department of Homeland Security. The film works solidly within the response-centric focus of films since the 1990s. In interviews, the director, screenwriter, and many of the actors mention their connection to real processes and people. Soderbergh describes the desire to make an "ultra-realistic" film. Screenwriter Scott Z. Burns consulted with scientists such as W. Ian Lipkin, who worked on SARS and the West Nile virus, and Lawrence Brilliant, who helped eradicate smallpox (MoviesOnline). The response scenarios depicted on screen mirror contingency plans and actual responses from recent events such as the 2009 flu pandemic. Yet despite its measured tones and focus on real-world details, the film stages a number of major and minor melodramas throughout, and closes with an intense apocalyptic sequence that provides an origin story for the outbreak. Why does the film need these melodramatic and apocalyptic excursions?

Although *Contagion* follows the multistory ensemble-cast style of many disaster films, it starts and ends with the family as ground zero. We meet the soon-to-be first victim of the disease, Beth Emhoff (Gwyneth Paltrow), in an airport bar in Chicago, on what the film tells us is "Day 2" of the epidemic. She is on her way back to her family in Minneapolis after a business trip to Hong Kong, snacking on peanuts from the bar's shared bowl and talking to her lover on the phone. They have just met for a brief sexual encounter that infects him with the virus she carries. In the fast-paced montage sequence that follows, the film shows a number of people getting sick: in Hong Kong, London, and Tokyo. Both Beth and a Japanese businessman we see in these scenes are reviewing papers from a company called AIMM Alderson, the logo clearly visible on the screen. Close-ups of people's hands produce a sense of insecurity about all the people we share the world with, the people who have touched door handles or sneezed on the bus next to us. But in addition to showing the practical effects of our connected world, where a person can traverse half the globe and infect myriad spaces and people in hours, the opening scene sets up the subplot of Beth's adulterous affair, adding a moral dimension to the story that is not necessary for the contagion narrative. Why do we need to know she just had sex with someone on her way back to her family? Isn't the phobic visual treatment of touch and proximity enough? If the virus can spread when one touches a credit card, why is sex needed at all to picture its transmission? Even in this early moment, we see that the film complicates its process-driven premise by providing a second layer of melodramatic explanation. Beth's adultery produces a sense of discomfort that functions as an excess meaning, and one that will reveal its narrative function later in the film.

In a standard narrative technique for mainstream Hollywood melodrama, the family story creates an intimate and local foil for communicating the impact of the disaster, and functions as a counterpoint to the professional heroes and official processes that dominate the film. Extending the "networked world" theme and reflecting the diversity of contemporary families, this is a blended family, for Beth and her husband Mitch (Matt Damon) have brought their kids from previous relationships into their life together. The family becomes a battleground. Mitch finds out about Beth's affair after she dies, an added betrayal that intensifies the impact of the tragedy for him. The infection restructures familial relationships across strict bloodlines: Beth and her son Clark die, Mitch and his daughter Jory survive. Mitch wonders if Jory has inherited his unexplained immunity to the new virus. He has to fight crowds for food and supplies, insists on keeping her completely isolated from her boyfriend until a vaccine can be found, and battles the deteriorating social conditions in their town.

Indeed, the film progresses through a networked narrative style that features quick and aggressive editing, oscillating between political plans, official efforts to curb the infection, scientific experiments to identify the virus and develop a vaccine, and scenes from Mitch's family life. In addition to the melodramatic treatment of loss in this family setting, we have numerous additional mini melodramas that are not always recognizable as such, partly because they are delivered to us piecemeal, interrupted, and dispersed. For example, the unscrupulous Alan Krumwiede

(Jude Law) makes millions selling fake herbal remedies that promise to cure the infection, using social media to sell both fear and hope. Counter to the sacrifices of most other characters, Alan is only out for himself. His story line includes meetings with a hedge fund manager also trying to profit from the outbreak, and a more personal three-act melodrama involving his former boss, an online magazine editor. She dismisses him as a conspiracy theory quack at the beginning of the film, later seeks him out in despair to buy some of his herbal cure, and then dies from the infection along with her unborn baby. We have silent scenes in which Dr. Ally Hextall (Jennifer Ehle) tests vaccine versions on monkeys, and then finds the poor animals dead in their cages. Her understated relief mirrors ours when one monkey survives. She impatiently injects herself with the vaccine prototype without waiting for proper trials and testing, so that she can meet her ill father without any protective gear, eager to touch and kiss him. Dr. Ellis Cheever (Laurence Fishburne) violates orders by warning his girlfriend to leave Chicago just before the city is officially quarantined, and later gives his priority vaccine dose, available to him as a CDC official, to the son of the building's janitor. A researcher refuses to shut down his experiments and destroy virus samples, and then manages to grow the virus in bat lung cells, thus ensuring the first step toward developing a vaccine. A World Health Organization official is kidnapped by one of her colleagues and kept in a remote village in Hong Kong as a guarantee that the village will receive priority doses of the vaccine. And so on.

These actions create stereotypical victims, villains, and heroes, but also create complex human figures out of the detached professionals that begin the film, remaking them into people whose actions combine duty and belligerence, professionalism and self-interestedness. In fact the film includes even smaller melodramas, so minimalist as to be contained in one line, one image or gesture. As Dr. Cheever administers the vaccine to his girlfriend, now wife, she says, "If we weren't married, I'd have to wait almost a year," implying that they got married expressly for this reason. The implied mini drama anticipates a sensational soap opera plotline or scandalous newspaper headline, "Married for the Vaccine!" When Dr. Hextall meets her sick father in the hospital, she says "You're here because you stayed in your practice treating sick people after everyone else went home," identifying his noble self-sacrifice in one sentence. When the kidnapped WHO official finds out that the village was given placebos instead of the real vaccine in order to release her, she runs out of the airport to warn them. When Dr. Erin Mears (Kate Winslet), a CDC officer who has been coordinating response efforts in Minneapolis, realizes she is sick, she creates lists of the people she met so that they can be treated. On her death bed, she overhears the man on the next cot begging for a blanket, and with effort takes off her own overcoat to give to him, a final gesture of sacrifice interrupted by her death.

By focusing on recognizably melodramatic sacrificial actions and complex depictions of human motivation, these mini melodramas transform the standard response scenarios that otherwise structure the film and infuse it with pathos and sentimentality. It is especially interesting to trace the functions of melodrama here, because the film expressly undermines this dimension of pathos in its narrative style and unfolding. In contrast to more overtly melodramatic disaster films, such as *San Andreas* (2015, Brad Peyton), that prioritize the melodramatic through-line, build toward emotional scenes, and use them to forward the narrative and resolve conflicts, *Contagion* distributes and interrupts its melodramatic elements. The film's editing is confident, secure in the knowledge that we can follow the myriad story lines and supply the missing emotions that would flesh out these dispersed melodramas. The film uses the archive of known plotlines creatively; it knows we know how to expand the narrative hint into a fuller story arc. But the editing style also ensures that none of the melodramatic plotlines will stay on screen long enough to take over the story.

In this, *Contagion* alters the terms and effects of the disaster film as a quintessential network narrative. The typical aims of network narratives revolve around revealing the inherent connectivity of the world. Stories inch closer together and intersect dramatically, as in *Amores Perros* (2000, Alejandro G. Iñárritu) or *Crash* (2004, Paul Haggis); or reveal an inherent parallelism or causal connectivity about a global issue, as in *Traffic* (2000, Steven Soderbergh) or *Babel* (2000, Alejandro G. Iñárritu) (see Bordwell 2006; Azcona 2010; Ciafone 2014). In *Contagion*, on the other hand, there is a self-consciousness about the concept of the network narrative. Yes, a pandemic connects us all around the world, but conversely our connectivity is what makes us sick, what facilitates the virus's fast transmission and global range. Here the effect of the interrupted narrative style is not to bring the disparate stories together but to undercut the process by which emotion can be developed, so that the film's foundational dependence on the melodramatic mode will remain hidden. As each story line interrupts the others, the film separates the emotional scenes with impersonal expository scenes, quick montages of official action, shots of empty landscapes and destroyed urban environments, and official events that add a detached, cooler, or even clinical tone. The effect is a form of compartmentalization, in which the film belies its dependence on melodrama. Yet, as I propose, the narrative would not work or have emotional resonance without the pervasive deployment of melodramatic narrative strategies. And because it resists melodrama, *Contagion* shows us what the melodramatic mode does, how it functions to organize the narration even in texts that resist it.

The mix of registers is most acutely felt when we consider the ending of the film, or in fact its multiple endings. The first ending is both official and personal: while people around the world are being vaccinated, Dr. Hextall puts on protective gear, enters a secure part of the lab, and deposits a sample of the virus in frozen storage. The threat is now identified, labeled as MEV-1, boxed up, and put away next to other contained threats such as SARS and H1N1. In a visual parallel, we see large boxes with the same label, MEV-1, on military trucks that deliver the vaccine to inoculation stations. Dr. Hextall closes the lab door and lingers at the porthole window with a slight smile, satisfied. The second ending returns us to Mitch who has created a prom setting in the living room so Jory can finally dance with her boyfriend, now vaccinated. All the required props are there: a new dress, corsage, banners, tiny lights, music. Looking for his camera, Mitch discovers Beth's last pictures from Hong Kong, from her night at the casino only days before she died, and he cries alone in the closet looking through them. Each picture replays images that the film has now shown us at least three times, first as a timeline of the infection created by the WHO officials, then as footage from security cameras, then as implied flashbacks of uncertain origin that replay Beth's last night in Hong Kong. The song "All I Want Is You," by U2, resonates over the traumas of the film, for Mitch and also for Jory, dancing in the living room with her boyfriend: "But all the promises we make / From the cradle to the grave / When all I want is you." Making promises is replaced by breaking promises in a later verse of the song. The teary father gazes at the dancing couple, the daughter aims a shy and grateful glance back at him. Despite the virus and the mayhem, the future combines a continuity of traditions, the prom, with the kinds of open endings only young love can allegorize. Why would the resilience of the human body and the success of international cooperation and medical science have to be celebrated in terms of an old-fashioned, gendered, heterosexual, American ritual? The silent pathos of the lost love, of Beth's remembered image, betrayal, life, and death, is what makes the prom scene appear fitting and recuperative instead of overwrought or merely conventional. Time starts again. Young love erases, forgets, rewinds the broken promises and the losses of love.

The third and final ending of the film indeed rewinds the story, taking us back to the origin of the outbreak. A bulldozer with the AIMM Alderson company logo prominent on its side is tearing down tall trees. Bats fly out of the trees, displaced, and one feeds on a cluster of bananas, flies over the twilight forest, and then settles inside a large covered building, a pigsty. The bat drops a banana piece, which is then eaten by a young piglet. In the daytime, men arrive and take stock of the pigs, selecting our piglet and others, putting them in cages and onto a truck. From the piglet in the cage we cut abruptly to a close-up of the dead piglet on a platter, as a chef is preparing it for cooking, rubbing and shoving garlic or spices in the pig's mouth. The chef is interrupted, wipes his hands quickly on his apron, and then we see him on the casino floor shaking hands with . . . Beth! The words "Day 1" appear on the screen, and we have arrived, finally, at the beginning, at the first moment of transmission that only Mitch has unknowingly seen in the badly lit pictures on the small digital camera. The film's insistence on closing the causal loop creates a circular pattern: Beth is an executive of the company that destroyed the forest and displaced the bats. She was there to celebrate the groundbreaking ceremony for a new factory, perhaps to celebrate that very bulldozing of these very trees.

Here again we see the melodramatic transformation of scientific causality into a narrative of responsibility. The film presents a well-documented chain of contagion, modeled on the Nipah virus that was transmitted from bats to pigs, and from pigs to humans, in Malaysia in 1999. Zoonotic viruses and animal to human transmissions have been well documented in recent years. The film could have just used this process to model virus transmission routes for viewers, as it explains other complex scientific concepts. But instead, the film uses the scene to tie up its loose political ends and present a narrative of responsibility that we did not know was needed. This origin story is, in fact, a morality tale, a circle of global processes and effects: the medical, governmental, and scientific responses that save the day present the advantage of a networked and connected world. At the same time, it is global processes that cause the outbreak, by enacting Western corporate interests and neoliberal policies upon the natural landscape of faraway places (Murray and Heumann 2009; Reber 2010). The first victims of this corporate global agenda are the plants, the trees that are cut down, then the animals that are killed or displaced, then the animals raised for human consumption, and then the people who work with and consume these animals. In a connected world, the effects of imperialist economic actions do not remain in their original place but instead jump easily from forests to fancy casinos, from the East to the West, from the South to the North, and from bats to pigs and then to people. This didactic causal chain is quite strict in its indictment of one company. The tendency toward melodramatic forms of closure in the film collapses the relation of cause and effect, bringing the end figuratively and literally to the beginning. And in the process, it creates a narrative of moral responsibility that scapegoats Beth in more ways than one. Because of her participation in the corporate plan, Beth carries a form of moral liability for the contagion, not just as the first victim or the transmitter but also as the metaphorical cause. This is the redirected culmination of the adultery subplot. Her sexual affair undermines Beth's moral standing; in the melodramatic layering of the story, she then has to also embody the proverbial sins of the virus and the corporation, the two impersonal and disembodied entities that cause the disease but cannot be held responsible. Their faults become her fault.

Why does the film need this clear and circular causal mapping of the disease? The melodramatic use of Beth as the culprit reveals that it is difficult for the text to sustain a critique of the corporation, of environmental destruction, and of global capitalism, without a specific, individual, and personalized villain. In its fundamental tendency to personalize and embody, the melodramatic mode here offers an important insight, that in fact abstract or diffuse entities such as corporations and governments are made of people, who decide and act while also disguising their actions as the impersonal and unemotional actions of the corporation. In the virus origin story, the film presents corporate actions as part of a mathematical equation in which environmental destruction equals death. But then somehow this cannot stand alone as a statement of political or historical fact. In the film's expressive dimension, the indictment of global corporate capitalism also hides under the indictment of Beth, in a basic melodramatic gesture that personifies moral positions or abstractions into particular embodied characters. It's not slavery, it's Simon Legree. It's not capitalism, it's one company, it's one executive, it's Beth. The effect is further complicated by the film's choice of villain. Even a film as thoughtful as *Contagion* cannot fully revise two major blind spots of American cultural and cinematic populism: the inability to fully criticize capitalism, and the inability to fully accept women's professional success and sexual freedom. Beth's opportunistic sexual encounter in Chicago aligns her with the opportunism of self-involved characters like Alan, and personifies the opportunism of the corporate executives who can only see the short-term benefits of bulldozing the jungle, and, indeed, the opportunistic randomness of viral infection.

This connection, in which Beth's adultery grounds all the other forms of accountability the film cannot deliver, brings us surprisingly close to the deployment of virtue as a moral quality in nineteenth-century stage melodrama—surprising because morality or "virtue" seem out of place in a film full of procedures, scientific analyses, and material conditions. Despite the difference in style and scale, *Contagion* resorts to an implicit, formative, and clearly traditional moral move that seems out of synch with its technical and scientific references and edgy style. In the quest to assign moral accountability, the film creates a series of personified wrongdoers, because the disease itself offers no such option. In melodramatic terms, viruses make for excellent if frustrating villains. They are so simple and efficient that they have just one action, they infect their hosts and then replicate and infect more hosts. As melodramatic villains, anthropomorphized here for added effect, viruses have no discernible motives other than survival, they cannot be dissuaded, they simply must do what they do, as if acting out of pure selfishness. Their single-mindedness renders them utterly inhuman and as irrepressible as a natural force. Viruses also disable the moral vocabulary we might like to employ to understand actions and causality: viruses have effects but no motivating causes; they have actions but no intentions; they have results but no goals; they are destructive but not out of malice; they are deadly but not evil. And the impersonality of the virus makes even victory feel hollow, because a virus does not care that some hosts survive, it does not resent being defeated by a vaccine. One cannot gloat over or punish a virus. The virus will not say, as the film clearly wishes it would say, "Rats! Foiled Again!" The virus mutates or remains unscathed in a different host species and becomes a potentiality, capable of beginning again in the future. Viruses also evoke political concerns. In the 1990s they were implicitly associated with technology, especially computers and networks, and the loss of control that accompanies the digitization of data and the automation of processes. In the 2000s and 2010s a virus is pretty scary in itself as a reference to actual pandemics, but because it is invisible and could be lurking anywhere, it is also a good conduit for many contemporary fears: the invisible threat of ideology or political extremism; the sleeper terrorist cell; the suddenly violent or murderous classmate, coworker, or neighbor; the person who does not look like an enemy, who is only identified as such after the violent act, and whose motives may never be understood.

To return to my layered approach to melodramatic narration, most of *Contagion* engages with specific and solvable questions about the global response to the virus, delivered in the cool tones and procedural style of up-to-date response scenarios. When we recognize the film's melodramatic investments, however, we see how they add complex implicit and explicit meanings, an integrated and foundational sense of order in the way the story unfolds, and a narrative of ethical and political responsibility. In addition to presenting the human impact of the pandemic, the film's melodramatic layers and multiple endings build up to an intensely apocalyptic denouement, arriving at the origins of the infection and the real villains of the film, the corporations that have caused the destruction of the forest. And yet, even when we see that this specific company, AIMM Alderson, created the conditions for the transmission of the virus, there is no way to prosecute or hold them accountable, sue them for the costs of the global pandemic, change their corporate agenda or protocol. The implicit and unsolvable question that the narrative choices of *Contagion* point toward is whether predatory capitalism is in fact the only truly global engine, far more dispersed and operational than our lagging political and social processes. Despite the film's imagery of proximity and responsibility, these institutions remain distanced from the effects of their opportunistic and destructive actions.

The operations of the melodramatic mode in *Contagion* and other end-of-the world narratives reveal the political and ethical paradoxes of our cultural moment. The disaster genre's depiction of global context is, in fact, one of its most meaningful contributions to political discourse. Narratives of the threat of total destruction always activate the concept of the Earth as one entity. The fear of nuclear annihilation that emerges after WWII produces a singular weapon, The Bomb, a singular planet, Earth, a singular "human race," and a singular purpose, survival. In recent years, this sense of connectivity encompasses questions of economic globalization, the Internet as a global mode of communication, global surveillance through satellite imagery and GPS navigation, remote controlled wars through the use of drones, cyberwarfare, and concerns about pandemics, the production and transportation of food, environmental destruction, and climate change.

Our current dilemma is that we have modes of global communication and experiences of shared global danger, yet we have no means of global governance. We cannot make a decision, vote, or act as Earth citizens, completely beyond the geographical boundaries of the region, or the political boundaries of the nation. Even in our disaster films, the depiction of global threats and global solutions is asymmetrical, with threats often coming into the First World from other places, and solutions going from the First World to other places. A neocolonial logic revises both historical legacies and contemporary realities, forgetting the ways in which the First World's voracious energy consumption, colonial agendas, and stranglehold on capital affect and disrupt political, economic, and social realities in the rest of the world. Disaster films showcase the processes and effects of globalization implicitly, and unevenly. In cinematic spectacles of destruction, sometimes the dream of global fairness becomes a nightmare equilibrium, in which the developed world's economic immunity is shattered when everybody is subject to a much more precarious common denominator of life conditions. The films produce heroic narratives of saving the world in order to evade the active and evolving fears that accompany our desire for connectivity, and our implicit recognition of the neocolonial politics of the twenty-first century.

19

Even More Tears

The Historical Time *Theory of Melodrama*

JANE M. GAINES

As film melodrama theory explains, tears are a consequence of "discrepancies" between points of view or between knowledges (Neale 1986, 7, 10). Recall the ending of *Madame X* (1966). The young lawyer (Keir Dullea) has just defended a nameless woman (Lana Turner) accused of murder. She lies dying on a cot adjacent to the courtroom where the jury will momentarily return with their verdict. He leans over her and asks if she has a son. Sharing the mother's point of view, *we* know something that *she* knows and that the young man at her side *does not know*. We know that *she is his mother*. Here is knowledge *discrepancy:* one knows, the other doesn't, and we, the sympathetic viewer, cannot bear it. However, this is not all. To make things worse for the characters, knowledge *discrepancy* is marked by temporal *irreversibility*. The clock, we say, "cannot be turned back." Her life is over. Terminal events such as death and life prison sentences cannot be reversed. Here, then, are the basics of the theory that viewers are brought to tears by narrative structures controlling information and events in time (Barthes 1977, 119).[1] By proposing "even more tears" in this chapter, I acknowledge other structures that may order the *narratives* of our lives but that also order our lives themselves even more profoundly.

In *Madame X*, events have been organized in such a way that the viewer witnesses the mother as unjustly condemned. A caring mother has made an unfortunate mistake and has been accused of abandoning her husband and child. Thrust out of her home, spiraling downward into addiction, the woman has retaliated by murdering the villain who took advantage of her. The viewer has thus been led to see the trial of the sympathetic mother as a miscarriage of justice, and reinforcing this, the jury is still out when she dies. Because of the injustice, the viewer may want someone to intervene to prevent the judgment or, if not, to ameliorate the situation. Things "being what they are," however, this situation is hopeless. Because she is dying, there will be neither mother-son reunion nor triumph of innocence. Nothing can be done to alter events in either the world of the film or the world of the viewer. Any action would be futile against death and the court. Here then is a dramatic situation to confirm Franco Moretti's (1983) analysis that tears come when we feel that conditions should be changed but that such change is completely impossible. He concludes that "tears are the product of powerlessness" (162). Thus the theory of tears in melodrama hinges on two narrative devices—discrepancy and irreversibility—that construct futility in the face of total impossibility.

But not exactly argues Steve Neale (1986), revising Moretti's thesis. The spectator may be powerless, but this is not because change is impossible. Neale states that tears come because spectators are powerless to delay or to intervene to change a course of narrative events that hypothetically could be changed (11). We cry whether the ending is happy or sad. We cry at the irreversibility of time when it's "too late," but we also cry when we are relieved to find that it is *not* finally too late. Sad or happy, it doesn't really matter because what is on the line is our *wish*, withheld or rewarded by narrative time. Neale believes our crying sustains our desire for the fulfillment of a fantasized union with the mother (19). The fulfillment of the wish may be delayed by the sad ending, but satisfaction can always come again later, perhaps in another moving picture (22). For three decades Neale's highly influential essay has been basic to theorizing the way moving picture stories bring viewers to tears. In the intervening years, few have challenged or amended this theory, even after the waning in film studies of psychoanalysis and its specialized notion of desire. But is that all that can be said about crying?

Linda Williams (2001) contributes significantly to rethinking tears in her reading of *Way Down East* (1920, D. W. Griffith). Although she takes up temporal irreversibility, she challenges Moretti's reading of tears as the "product of powerlessness." Williams grants that tears may "flow from" the powerlessness of failure to arrive on time, too late to rescue innocence, but concurs that tears equally may be a response to the successful rescue that is not too late. Here Williams goes beyond Neale's link between tears and desire, pointing to something additional needed to explain melodrama—a theory of happy tears to shore up melodrama's "investment" in the possibility that *time can be reversed*. If time can be reversed, innocent virtue can be reaffirmed. Or, given the reverse of time, the action required in response to the pathos of suffering has a chance of success (32).

Consider, for instance, the ice floe sequence in *Way Down East* (figure 19.1). Melodrama goes overboard, so to speak, in an effort to rectify an injustice. Anna is both cast out on the ice in the storm and thrown against the irreversibility of time signified by the river's course. But this sequence might also suggest that irreversibility is deployed to heighten the opposite—reversibility. After prolonged cross-cutting between Anna on the ice and her rescuer (Richard Barthlemess), Anna is saved by such a reverse in the "nick of time" at the edge of the falls. Her rescue, however, is more than just a rescue. The narrow victory at the edge of the falls shows that melodrama, against all odds, strives to "reverse time," as Williams argues (32). Thus Griffith's "cut back" is recruited to turn back events in time, ideally in the service of proving innocence.[2] Melodrama, Williams explains quoting Peter Brooks (1976), wants above all "to return to the time of origins and the space of innocence" (35). To put it another way, melodrama wants to affirm the origin of virtue in individual goodness and singular heroic acts. As a rhetoric invoked on behalf of innocence, melodrama clearly will go to the extreme. To melodramatize the reversal, that

Figure 19.1 Poster featuring the ice flow sequence from D. W. Griffith's *Way Down East* (1920).

turning back of time, the film sets the innocent Anna, wrongly accused, against the blizzard and the frozen river. However, the fury of the storm, the rapid current of the river, and the insert footage of Niagara Falls with its treacherous drop, tip us off that something even more is on the line. Here the staging of a significant battle in the war "against time" is even more important. Witnessing Anna's rescue at the edge of the falls, we understand why such a near miss might be called "death-defying" and then realize how it underscores Williams's analysis of this sequence as a triumphant defeat of time (2001, 31). We grasp that the stubborn irreversibility of time itself is defied. As Williams argues, Anna's rescue indicates that the hoped-for reversal of events not only "defies" time but also champions temporal reversal as time's defeat "by time" (35).

I have always been struck by this analysis of the ice floe rescue as the "defeat of time," and it has led me beyond the either-or of reversal-irreversibility to something much larger that I suspect is at work here. Williams's explication of time's defeat tips me off that this is not all, and Neale's insistence on the spectator's powerlessness to intervene points to something that grips every one of us. Indeed, the premise of a victory over time is where I begin to have a creeping suspicion that deeper philosophical issues are at stake.

Two clues to what else is operative can be seen in *Letter from an Unknown Woman* (1948, Max Ophuls). In the beginning, Stefan reads the letter from Lisa as he learns not only *what* he has lost but that he *never knew* what it was that he had all along. When he hears her words in voice-over—"By the time you read this letter, I may be dead."—we realize with him that no act can intervene to reverse the event that has already taken place. What has taken place is the last and final event in a life. Why death? For one reason, if there was ever any uncertainty about the hardened irreversibility of time, the question is settled once and for all by death. Death, as we often say, "comes only once." Moretti (1983) goes a step further in his structural analysis, positing that the function of the protagonist's death is always to prove that time is irreversible (162). But it is not only irreversibility that is at work here. Stefan is convulsed with regret when his new knowledge closes the gap and rectifies the *discrepancy* between what one character knew and what the other didn't. The enormity of that knowledge discrepancy—between Lisa's devotion to him and his total ignorance of her (as well as the existence of the son he has fathered)—now stands revealed. But Lisa's death dramatizes another gap even wider than that between Stefan's obtuseness and Lisa's obsession, and I do not mean that between the living and the dead, although that too. There is yet another kind of discrepancy at work, one that cannot be rectified with more knowledge. Not ever. Two additional factors, two clues, need to be taken into account here, both pointing to a larger scheme of things and, as we will see, implicating the viewer. First, it is not only that Lisa has died but that with her death her fantasy also languishes, and it is her vain hope for the future that is our first clue. Second, Lisa dies caring for her young son under a cholera quarantine. Within the fiction, the death of the innocent child is indicative of this something larger at work to which I will shortly turn. Just note here that the death of mother and child marks a convergence between that which is "never to be" and that which "could have been." And what explains the distance between these temporalities? What I mean by "even more tears" is that in the death of an innocent, accompanied as it is by so many hopes dashed, there is much more lost than life. To get at how much more, we need to turn to the philosophical question of *historical time* and its attendant discrepancies.

The question of the irreversibility of events in time is more philosophically difficult than it first appears. One indication of this is French Annales School founder Ferdinand Braudel's (1980) rant against the one-way direction of events in time. The historical researcher is frustrated by what he calls "historical time, so imperious because it is irreversible" (48). Braudel sounds rather like the character who cannot get back to the time before, cannot reverse the course of events. This is to say that the historian too grapples with the stubborn unidirectionality of historical time, its pattern exemplified by the event that, once over, cannot come again later as the same event that it was, no matter how much this may be wished. Common sense, as wise as it is useless, weighs in here: "what's over is over," and "what's done can't be undone." On a par with melodrama, common sense is indicative of how we cope with the inexorability of historical time.

HISTORICAL TIME: THE RELATIONSHIP OF THE THREE MODES OF TIME

Historical time is a structural relationship—one of especially frustrating unevenness—that explains my earlier reference to this other discrepancy that I will take up as temporal "asymmetry."[3] By *asymmetry*, I mean the imbalance that characterizes the relationship between past, present, and future. If we thought for a minute that past, present, and future—as modes of historical time—were arranged as straightforwardly as one, two, and three, we might think again about the melodramas of our lives. In the present, we can neither divine what is ahead nor escape what has already happened. One time must pass, giving way to another that cannot yet have arrived. Past events weigh on present choices as future events loom ahead, never there in the present, always elsewhere. Now consider the way fiction stages such temporal disjuncture. Fiction borrows this same asymmetry, and, conversely, humans navigate the imbalance in the events of their lives with help from—what else?—the scenarios of popular fictions. Here, however, I propose to connect film melodrama theory with another academic tradition wherein temporal asymmetry has been given the fullest consideration. Thus to ask how moving image melodrama is past, present, or future oriented is to turn to the philosophy of history.[4] The one time as it relates to another is a problem taken up by theorists of history such as Reinhart Koselleck (2004) and Louis Althusser (1979). Elsewhere (Gaines, forthcoming) I consider what I call the "melodrama theory of historical time," using moving image melodrama to explore a philosophical question, but here I do the opposite. Using theories of history to elucidate melodrama structure, I propose the *historical time theory* of melodrama.

Basic to historical time in contemporary theories of history are Martin Heidegger's three modes as temporal "ecstasies" (1996, 308–21). We learn from Heidegger that these modes of time may be felt to coexist, for instance, as when the past "comes again," held over in custom or tradition like the legacy of slavery in our current times. More important for melodrama theory, the past, the present, and the future are in circular relation such that we invariably understand each one in terms of the others (Carr 1987, 198). The present, for example, is always modified by the past and the future, just as the past is modified by the present, and so forth. Let us now add Louis Althusser's deeper insight to the question of melodrama's long gone "space of innocence" (Brooks 1976, 29). What this insight contributes to an explanation of pathos is the understanding of levels of historical time as "never together." For in Althusser (1979), paradoxically, the "absence" of the one time depends on the "presence" of the other (103). Here the temporal asymmetry underpins the knowledge discrepancy illustrated in the final scene from *Madame X*. The innocent time can never come again because past and future, by popular as well as philosophical definition, are not now and *never can be* together; in fact, there is no presence of one without the absence of the other. It is thus not only points of view that are at odds in the heart-wrenching meeting of mother and son. Modes of time are also structurally estranged. The past, in which she left home and family, could never have known the future of her crime. In the present of their reunion, her grown son, that future, has no access to the absent past where his mother is hidden.

At some points, Koselleck's theory of history is reminiscent of melodrama theory. "It is not only because events, once transpired, cannot be repeated, that past and future cannot be reconciled," he reflects (2004, 38). Like Braudel, Koselleck can find no way to connect the two modes at either end of time's line. Is it no wonder then that melodrama, obsessed with trying to reconcile positions that are flat out irreconcilable, can so productively utilize the breach between temporal modes to pathos-producing ends. Now consider the unbridgeable separateness of past and future realms, neither directly accessible from the other. Then see that where theories of history posit past and future as irreconcilable (the past and future as never together), moving image melodrama dramatizes familial rifts as unresolvable; time being "what it is," characters are neither able to revisit past events nor to access events that lie ahead. Viewers are led from one now to the next now in which events can occur, but not into the future now where events cannot yet occur. However, future events may be imagined and past events hazily recalled, so there is always recourse to the plot reordering device—the flashback to the past or flash forward to the future. In fiction, as we know, there is the additional capacity to erase an entire event or to take imaginative license with temporal givens. Yet the modality of melodrama often borrows the constraints of "imperious" time to evoke pathos. Such effects of temporal boundedness we know without even knowing that we know them, in life as in the drama's narrativization of life's events. If we don't notice this charting across the three modes of time, it is of course because of the inseparability of time-telling from the tale, something remarked on by Paul Ricoeur (1980), who once observed that storytelling's way of placing narrative "in" time is a way of "taking it for granted" (17). This is exactly what the story must do if its goal is to imitate life. As viewers or readers, however, so interwoven are our lives with the dramatization of those lives that we miss what melodrama takes from and then gives back to us as narrative enigmas exacerbated by the resolute structure of historical time.

ALWAYS TOO LATE OR NEVER TOO LATE?

This structure finds expression in the "too late" narrative device. Or we could say that the lopsidedness of historical time can be exemplified in the rescue attempt that is "too late." Here, a historical time approach emphasizes a convergence of times that may have been obscured by the concept of "all at once." Given its fullest theorization in Mikhail Bakhtin (1981), "too late" as "failure to meet" is ruled by "chance time," the only time that belongs exclusively to the present (94). Crucially, the time of chance is open to any unpredictable intervention—in that "split second" when meeting and "failure to meet" or to rescue is on the line. But the problem is not exactly too late so much as the "wrong time," as Bakhtin clarifies when he says that intervention may occur *either* too late or too early to change the course of events (94). Too late clearly confirms irreversibility when events are felt to occur one after the other, chained together in time, the deciding event confirming that what's "over is over." But it would be a mistake to blame this linear chain as film theory historically did for a time, following Jean-Luc Comolli's critique of "linear" historiography.[5] More useful for a historical time theory of melodrama is Althusser's diagnosis that accompanies his critique of "continuous and homogenous time." Forget "continuous time" he counters. Historical time is actually much more "complex and peculiar" (1979, 103). Althusser, in his essay on historical time, posits the "absence" of one level as the "presence" of another, the *there* dependent upon the *not there* (104). Again and again, too late threatens characters with "no going back." Too late also confirms that a renunciation is forever, a love lost never returns, and the estranged cannot be reunited over the grave. Yes, melodrama's too late relies on the horizontality of time's one-way passage, but that passage also splits into the structuralist coexistence of presence and absence, present and past, *there* and *not there*, each dependent on the other for meaning.

Whereas earlier I focused on Neale's discussion of how the spectator's powerlessness to intervene to reverse the irreversibility of events produces tears, after Althusser, I now see something else. Neither the "chain" nor "line of time" metaphor is adequate to represent the shift of positions in which the present takes the place of the time that was once the future, and the past is abandoned, no longer either the present that it once was nor the future that it had been so long before. This is why I think that irreversibility needs to be conjoined with temporal asymmetry, the concept I borrow from the philosophy of history (see Danto 2007). If still in doubt about the asymmetrical disjuncture of the three modes of time, think of Hamlet's exasperation expressed in the metaphor "time is out of joint."

For example, think of mixed race Sarah Jane throwing herself, sobbing, on her mother's coffin at the end of *Imitation of Life* (1960). Annie will never know that Sarah Jane has belatedly returned to cry out her love for her mother and to blame herself for her death. "It is too late. Sarah Jane is in tears. The spectator is in tears," Neale says (1986, 19). Here on another level is a reenactment of the relativity of historical time. The one mode of time cannot know or be the other that has replaced it, yet each modifies the other. In too late, the present moment's differentiation between "then," "now," and "next" flashes up as a convergence of three times. Sarah Jane thus enacts a more elongated *triangulation* of time when she arrives belatedly. For "at that moment," the "now" conjoins the "before now" with the "never to be." We may glimpse in those once alive but now dead the "former present" status of the past. Annie's contrite daughter Sarah Jane comes back, coincidentally, just at that moment when it is too late, and in so doing brings the one time (the past that "once was" the present) to bear on another (the present), the time that stands between past and future. In what I call the "two times that cannot meet," we have the total irreconcilability of past and future.[6] Here indeed are the concerns of the contemporary philosophy of history as it contemplates the "now" relative to the "before now" as indicative of the disjuncture of historical time (see Jenkins 2003, 5). Reframed in these terms, melodrama's basic concern would seem to be the innocent "past now" to which the characters cannot return, except of course by the intervention of the "chance time" coincidental event that so astonishingly reverses events in time. Yet in moving pictures such as *Imitation of Life*, that intervention never comes. Or a sad event is shown to have never happened after all.

Just when we start to think that the threat of too late against the wish to "turn back time" must be fundamental, we remember narratives in which finally it wasn't too late. Most striking are those in which characters thought to be dead "return to life" as in *The Rosary* (1913, Lois Weber) or *Seventh Heaven* (1927, Frank Borzage). Then there is the narrative of reform. Think of characters who, when given a second chance, demonstrate that it is "never too late" as in the alcoholic husband reformed and reunited with his family in *The Drunkard's Reformation* (1909, D. W. Griffith). Just as when we begin to see melodrama's investment in the threat of too late hanging over every moral decision, every failure to act, or every action taken too slowly, at least one critic stops us. American melodrama demonstrates that it is "never too late"—never ever. Arguing for the "therapeutic" function of motion picture film and literary melodrama, Lauren Berlant (2008) finds in these fictions the conviction that "there is always a tomorrow" (269). Consider in this regard a tearful Stella Dallas at the scene of her daughter's wedding, relegated to watching it from the sidewalk. Turning away from the window, she strides toward the camera, a lilt in her walk, her handkerchief between her teeth, her tears now gone. If *Stella Dallas* (1937) is to be believed, there is "always a tomorrow"—the promise of things to come, the worldview of the optimism Berlant thinks is the job of women to keep alive for everyone (7). There is "always a tomorrow," and yet, says Neale (1986), there isn't because "it is in reality *always* too late" (20). One indication of the depths probed here, the very problem of existence itself, is the abundance of so much commonsense wisdom: "Never say never," "What's over is over," or, leaving a hair's breadth of room to encourage false hope, "It's not over until it's over."

MELODRAMA'S COMPOSITE TENSE

Tears may indeed be the consequence of realizing "too late" that time cannot be reversed or, conversely, the result of seeing "too late" dramatically averted. As I am arguing, this thesis needs further expansion, and I have hinted that this is because for the characters (but especially for the viewers) much more hangs in the balance. Here is what I mean. It may be that *irreversibility* dooms characters to lose *even more* than the loved ones they mourn. So much more. Also lost are the events planned for and dreamed of in a highly anticipated future, events yet to be realized. Misery is especially acute when what is lost is not only past happiness but, in addition, happiness "yet to be." To return to my earlier point, this is why the loss of the child, especially if born dead, is so poignant. Much more than a lifetime is lost. As a consequence of the death of the child, there can be neither present nor past nor the infinite possibilities of future events. The future, however, may be as bleak as it is promising. Conversely, the mother's benevolent act of infanticide snatches the child from the terrible future of slavery, as in Toni Morrison's novel *Beloved*, or infant death saves Anna Moore's child from the future of illegitimacy in *Way Down East*.

So I propose that the unreached future needs to be part of our equation, but that is not all because, following Koselleck's theorization of historical time, human history is invested in *more than one future* time. Let me illustrate this with the kinds of words and phrases used to dramatize our three modes. For example, "suddenly" or "at just that moment" denote Bakhtin's intervention of the "chance" event in the present, the only mode of time in which chance occurs (1981, 92).[7] Other phraseology hints at both the absolute distinction *and* the modification of one time by another. Consider, in this regard, certain melodramatized tenses as symptomatic of human time dilemmas, tenses held over from Victorian theatrical and literary melodrama but recognizable today despite the archaic usage. For example, there is "never to be" or the redundant "ever after" and "forever and always." Melodrama even utilizes composite tenses that look two ways at once from the vantage of the present, confirming the relativity of time's modes, as I have been arguing. The present, for instance, might be tinged with the backward view in the composite "what had been but is no longer" or "what once was but can never be again." Yet these phrases also seem to gesture toward a future that, however wished for, "never was." In the archaic "nevermore" or "never again," one finds a nuanced awareness of the loss of hope in the "former future" that eerily remembers that *both* the past and the present "once were" themselves "futures." Such phrases confess that melodrama as a modality is obsessed with the problem of the way that the "former" present (the past) impinges on the "present" present, which is also the "former future" of an earlier present now past. Acknowledging that "former future" is Koselleck's term, let's bring the philosophy of history back to bear on melodrama narrative again (see Tribe 2004, xi).

Here we need Koselleck's (2004) formulation of the "present" as the very time that was "once anticipated," a feature of a new temporality in the modern moment focused on futurity as never before, mapped over the last three hundred years. Especially relevant, the previously anticipated present is for him a "former future" (2). Stated another way, any given present was once a future (Tribe 2004, xi). Koselleck's "former future," the present, may also face ahead in expectation of another future, what might be called the "future" future, or the future "to be," to distinguish it from the "former future." We always forget, of course, that the "present" present was a once-wished-for time forthcoming, a "former future" that this present can no longer be. So think of the enormity of the loss if characters, arriving too late, relinquish in their missed moment not only the once anticipated present, the "former future," but in addition the future ahead that is always so full. Here is the loss of not one but two futures—the one that came and wasn't and the one that can never be. Never. Ever.

THE LOSS OF THE FUTURE AND THE "FORMER FUTURE" IN SILENT ITALIAN MELODRAMA

Now let's consider in dramatic terms the devastation of the loss of the "former future" that the present can no longer be, beyond which the "future" future also drops off. One such melodramatization of the familiar dilemmas of historical time is Francesca Bertini and Gustavo Serena's *Assunta Spina* (1913). Early in the narrative, Assunta, played by the Italian diva Bertini (figure 19.2), is scarred when she accidentally steps before the knife wielded by her jealous lover Michele. In that moment, their "former future" or "what was hoped to be" in this present is gone. As a consequence of his deed, Michele is sent to prison. In the intervening years, Assunta takes up half-heartedly with Don Frederigo. At the end of the melodrama, she arrives "too late" to stop the avenging knife of her former lover Michele, who, released "too soon" from prison, discovers Assunta's infidelity and kills Don Frederigo. Assunta, arriving "too late" at the scene, is arrested for the murder. From the point of view of the present as a "former future" that is, immediately interpreted from the viewpoint of the once "hoped for," we see that not only has the once anticipated but now dreaded reunion of Assunta and Michele been canceled, but that another set of expectations replaces them, expectations for a future too terrible to have been imagined—the unexpected future in which Assunta will take Michele's place in prison. We have here an even more striking temporal *triangulation*, the "suddenly" moment of chance time along with the glimpse of the happy situation that "once was" and the dead-end future of "never to be."

Nearly ten years later, Italian director-producer Elvira Notari, in '*A Santanotte* (1922), staged another such triangulation of time's three modes, twisting the lives of Nanninella, Toré, and Carluccio—the heroine and her two rival lovers (see Tomadjoglou 2013). When Nanniella's father falls from a cliff, Toré, her favorite, is accused, and she rejects her lover as the murderer of her father. But the wrongly imprisoned Toré breaks out of jail on the day of Nanninella's wedding to villain Carluccio. Just then she hears Toré, still her favorite, singing outside her window. At that very moment, Carluccio confesses that he knows Toré is innocent of the murder of her father, and Nanninella, realizing that she has falsely accused Toré (and has just married the villain), drives a knife into her bosom.[8] In a single present moment when our three "ecstasies" are triangulated, a past mistake reaches forward to steal the future time. This mistake, her past failure to recognize her lover's innocence, robs them of the anticipated "former future," the present that "might have been" at the start of the film. They lose as

Figure 19.2 Portrait of Francesca Bertini, actress in and coproducer with Gustavo Serena of *Assunta Spina* (1913) Italy.

well the "future" future, that is, all of the time ahead of them. That is, they lose "even more"—not one but two futures.

To draw an early hypothesis about Italian silent melodrama, we might say that its goal is to ensure that suffering is maximally prolonged (as well as widely distributed) as a consequence of a miscarriage of justice or, even more likely, as an irrational act. Melodrama borrows the totally irreconcilable difference between past and future modes, relying on the temporal asymmetry of "never together" for its own dramatic ends. At the same time, the problem of existence, in its most familiar form, endlessly restages commonsense wisdom based on the irreversibility of linear time: "there is no going back." Two kinds of metaphors are operative: one set straightens out events along the reversible-irreversible time line, but the other has more difficulty signifying the felt coexistence of times Althusser theorized.

What is so puzzlingly paradoxical, so peculiar here? It is the lover Toré's unanticipated break from prison and his wished-for *presence* that triggers Nanninella's self-inflicted *absence* from the world of the living. She kills herself because she thinks that what they had had "before now" is "no longer." But her act is ill-timed because both the revelation of his innocence and his *presence* to her are, in the vernacular, "one breath away." Just at the moment that she is killing herself, he is singing outside her window. The knowledge *discrepancy* is especially unbearable. Not only does she not see him (as we do) but she *does not hear him* (although he is singing his heart out). Melodrama has tried to *reverse* the "this, then this" lock-step time "march" that condemned Toré. And it has succeeded. After all, Toré miraculously breaks out of prison. And yet he does not intervene *because he does not know*. Let me step back to say that it may yet be difficult for us to see this arrangement of time as in any way weird or peculiar because we are acculturated to the shuffling of these three modes. Take a minute to think about Nanninella's narrative. In the "present" present, which is also her "former future," her wedding day, she has both married the wrong man and killed herself.

Most pressing for a historical time theory of melodrama, however, is the way in which both *Assunta Spina* and *'A Santanotte*, with the young couple as centerpiece, posit the secure future as endangered by passion. Here, then, is the wish for a return to the "space of innocence," but there is no returning. To acknowledge the present as a "former future," a time that "once was" anticipated, is to make the loss even worse. The lovers lose not only what they had first expected—that they would be together—but lose the dream of the time ahead on which their lives together was premised. Or, as I am arguing, they lose not one but two futures. There is something of this in Neale (1986, 19), whose emphasis I have supplemented by aligning fantasy with anticipation of a future time in an effort to demonstrate the existential enormity of the human relation to historical time. So I posit the impact of this larger loss—not only *no future time* but the death of all fantasy on which everything in perpetuity is pinned—for all that we ever have of the future is a fantasy of it anyway. This is to suggest that we cry "even more" after the temporary reprieve of happiness, or the intervention of coincidence, because the play with time confirms that against it we have no power and can only hope for postponement (Neale 1986, 21).

Italian silent film melodrama may qualify the thesis that moving picture melodrama wants to get back to the "space of innocence" with the retort that there is "no getting back to" the time before. Indeed, Angela Dalle Vacche (2008), in her seminal study of the Italian diva, explains that she is unlike the Hollywood female star whose narrative followed an "inclination toward change." If the American star's trajectory was one way, we can expect that "divisimo," as a mix of "suffering and rebellion," would help to illustrate the greater difficulties of the ever-askew modes at the same time that these modes, at odds, confirm the diva's precarious existence (as well as ours) in the world outside the fiction (6).

Left to its own devices, melodrama would override narrative cause and effect logic that stipulates "this leads to that." Yet if a narrative in the classical sense, melodrama subscribes to a cause and effect pattern with a heavy investment in the need for resolution.[9] What will matter finally is less the temporal moment than the outcome, the final consequence of events. Outcomes must above all appear to flow from the actions of agents of cause and effect and follow from earlier events. In the middle, however, we can expect the cross-cut "play" with temporal chunks—the "game" of suspense that produces, as Roland Barthes (1977) says, so much "anxiety and pleasure" (119). Thus the narrative may return to *irreversibility* (this followed by that and that's the end) even after having staged a *"reversibility* of moments" (1981, 100). Such is the case with our two Italian narratives in which there is no final intervention to stop the too terrible but inevitable outcome. Perhaps we can here appreciate what reversibility is up against, why the intervening event that "turns back time" has been so often criticized as "unmotivated" or unjustified and the American happy epilogue as "tacked on" (Bordwell 1982, 6).

THE POLITICAL VALENCE OF MELODRAMA: THE FUTURE AS THE PAST OR NOT

So I arrive at a critical question for all who have considered whether melodrama was *either* progressive *or* reactionary, or both, and if both, as containing the seeds of "containment and resistance," as has been so often argued following Frankfurt School–informed criticism (Gaines 2000, 107). Now I am asking this question somewhat differently. Instead, I want to know whether melodrama is more past oriented (looking back to) than future directed. The question as to whether melodrama can be read as progressive or reactionary has often been referred to the *contents* of the imagined and hoped for future[10] (although not the dreaded future). Melodrama is finally reactionary, the argument goes, because the future toward which it gestures, on which all hopes are pinned, is no different from the past. Here then melodrama is seen as holding a conservative worldview in which "the future is the past." In this analysis, the future may hold the "better," but this "better" is only relative to "the good" of social tradition; and if the future holds the "better," this can't mean an abstract "betterment" but can only be the wish for the old and established known. So here we have the "yearning for the future" that will be "as it was" in the past, the paradoxical wish for the new to be the old, a paradox to join the others in which melodrama both follows reality too closely (in its disreputable subject matter) and abandons reality (in its stylistic excesses).

Framed this way, the question as to whether melodrama is progressive or reactionary, is forward-looking or tradition-bound, is quite unresolvable. Why? Here may be the wish for the future to be as the past, but remember that the future is so wonderously full, enlarged as it is by fantasy. Given this discussion of historical time, with emphasis on futures *plural*, consider as well how the present as the once anticipated "former future" and the next future, the one ahead, add up to something much more consequential. We might then argue that melodrama evidences *a wish for both* the future and the past. Indeed, knowing as we do how easily silent era endings were altered to accommodate national sensibilities such as that of the Russians for sad but "inevitable" endings, we might have suspected that either-or had been built in all along (Tsivian 1989, 24). Further, how else do we explain melodrama as wanting to override stubborn, separate temporalities, to have both the past and the future at once. Melodrama, in its flawed attempts to rectify past mistakes, to reverse time, to tack on the happy end that "awards" a future to uncertainty or resolves differences with unjustifiable coincidences, might then be understood as demonstrating a willingness to buck the givens of historical time. The mode, it could be argued, exhibits a high "tolerance" level for the irreconcilability of past, present, and future (Singer 2001, 46). Melodrama tolerates irreconcilability, all the while taking irreconcilability as a dramatic point of departure, the underlying structure upon which to peg so much anguish as well as so many thrills.

EPILOGUE

In the end, it may be futile to try to say exactly why we cry. We cry "in" despair, "because" it's over, "at" the sound of a voice, and sometimes "with" the happy or sad characters on screen. Although I maintain that the interrelation between the three temporal modes is a useful way into the problem, I also have shown how their always-at-odds relation causes anxiety; how their discrepant asymmetry—their "never together"—so frustrates human plans. Here is where we need to figure the future (as dreaded or hoped for) into our equations in the study of melodrama. To return to Linda Williams's (2001) addendum to Neale and Moretti, tears are not the consequence of powerlessness but signify expectation, a "hope of fulfillment." Tears, the reverse of powerlessness, she thinks may even be a "source of power" in the future (32). Or, on the authority of Bette Davis as Charlotte Vale, crying expresses the tiniest of "hopes" tinged with sadness. As Charlotte confesses to Jerry on the Rio balcony in *Now, Voyager* (1942), "these are tears of gratitude . . . an old maid's tears of gratitude for the crumbs offered." Responding to his dismissal of her confession, she goes on: "You see, no one ever called me darling before." Here tears come at the *triangulation* of a long sad past, momentary near happiness, and future wish, however tentative. It is that someone so worthy of love wasn't loved in the past but now is and in the future just might be. But such swelling must be attributable to Max Steiner's score and its orchestration as well, in which violins strain to tell us what Charlotte is feeling and that cue us to feel too (Gorbman 1987, 65–66).

Then again, a theory of tears may elude us because we have been focusing on the wrong thing. What these theories have in common is the loss of object or person. However, as Jacques Derrida (2005) frames the problem, there are many ways to weep, and they do not all entail loss of something: "One is either weeping intransitively, period, or one is weeping tears, transitively, (bemoaning the loss of) something or someone." With so much "intransitive" weeping, just weeping, it is difficult to know just "what" it was or "to whom" such crying is appealing (119). It may be that the weeping is just weeping, just uncontrollable sobbing, especially because at some historical moments the present is felt to be so unbearable and the future, as it is said, is felt to be all that we "have." But, of course, by definition, no one can ever really "have" the future.

NOTES

1. This is also part of the definition of suspense.
2. Eisenstein (1977, 200) uses the term *cut back* to identify the device he saw in Griffith's *After Many Years* (1908).
3. Danto (2007) is the original source of this term.
4. For an introduction to the relevance of the new philosophy of history for film and media studies, see Gaines (2013).
5. Thompson and Bordwell (1983) summarize the French Marxist critique of "linear" historiography initiated by Jean-Louis Comolli in the journal *Cahiers du Cinéma* 1971–72. Influenced by Althusser, the article included a critique of "evolutionary" assumptions, "teleological" tendencies, the notion of "influence," "firsts," and the idea of the "origin" of cinema (5–6).
6. See my forthcoming book, *Pink-Slipped*, chapter 5.
7. Silent cinema would recruit this language for intertitles, perhaps the most famous of which is its use in *The Battleship Potemkin* (1924, Sergei Eisenstein,) to signal the appearance of the Czar's armed soldiers at the top of the Odessa Steps: "Suddenly."
8. This scene is streamed on https://wfpp.cdrs.columbia.edu/pioneer/ccp-elvira-notari/.
9. Linda Williams (2001) has challenged the "dominance" of classical narrative, displacing it with melodrama as "the dominant" or effectively the "norm" (23). See also chapter 12.
10. David Grimstead argues that melodrama's conception of the "promise of human life" is finally no "revolutionary future" but instead the turn back to a "golden past" (as quoted in Gledhill 2002, 21).

Bibliography

Abbott, Willis J. 1912. "Famous Women of History," December 31. In Robinson Locke Collection, Billy Rose Theatre Division, New York Public Library of the Performing Arts, New York City, vol. 131: 150.
Abel, Richard. 2006. *Americanizing the Movies and "Movie-Mad" Audiences 1910–1914*. Berkeley: University of California Press.
Affron, Charles. 1982. *Cinema and Sentiment*. Chicago: University of Chicago Press.
Althusser, Louis. 1969. "Footnote to 'The Piccolo Teatro:' Bertolazzi and Brecht." In *For Marx*, trans. Ben Brewster. Harmondsworth: Penguin.
———. 1979. *Reading Capital*. trans. Ben Brewster. London: Verso. First published 1966.
Altman, Rick. 1989. "Dickens, Griffith, and Film Theory Today." *South Atlantic Quarterly* 88, no. 2 (Spring): 321–55.
———. 1999. *Film/Genre*. London: BFI.
———. 1998. "Reusable Packaging: Generic Products and the Recycling Process." In *Refiguring American Film Genres: History and Theory*, ed. Nick Browne, 1–41. Berkeley: University of California Press.
Anderson, Mark. 2009. *Japan and the Specter of Imperialism*. New York: Palgrave Macmillan.
Anker, Elisabeth. 2014. *Orgies of Feeling: Melodramatic Politics and the Pursuit of Freedom*. Durham, N.C.: Duke University Press.
"Announcing the Photoplay Magazine Medal of Honor." 1921. *Photoplay* (June): 29.
Aprà, Adriano. 1976. "Capolavori di Massa." In *Neorealismo d'Appendice. Per un Dibattito sul Cinema Popolare: Il Caso Matarazzo*, ed. Adriano Aprà and Claudio Carabba, 9–37. Rimini: Guaraldi Editori.
Archer, William. 1923. *The Old Drama and The New*. London: William Heinemann.
Artaud, Antonin. 2010. *The Theatre and Its Double*, trans. Victor Corti. Richmond: Oneworld Classics. First published 1938.
Atkinson, Brooks. 1970. *Broadway*. New York: Macmillan.

Aubert, Charles. 1985. *The Art of Pantomime*, trans. Edith Sears. New York: Dover Publications. First published 1927.

Bachman, Erik, and Evan Calder Williams. 2012. "Reopening the Matarazzo Case." *Film Quarterly* 65, no. 3 (Spring): 59–65.

Bacon, Henry. 1998. *Visconti: Explorations of Beauty and Decay*. Cambridge: Cambridge University Press.

Bahadur, Satya Prakash. 1972. *Ramayana of Goswami Tulsidas*. Delhi: Jaico.

Bakhtin, Mikhail M. 1981. *The Dialogic Imagination*, trans. Caryl Emerson and Michael Holquist, ed. Michael Holquist. Austin: University of Texas. First published 1975.

———. 1986. *Speech Genres and Other Late Essays*, trans. Vern W. McGee, ed. Caryl Emerson and Michael Holquist. Austin: University of Texas Press.

Baldasty, Gerald. 1999. *E. W. Scripps and the Business of Newspapers*. Urbana: University of Illinois Press.

Baldelli, Pio. 1999. "Il cinema popolare degli anni '50." In *Appassionatamente: Il Mélo nel Cinema Italiano*, ed. Orio Caldiron and Stefano Della Casa, 129–39. Turin: Lindau.

Baldwin, Neal. 2001. *Henry Ford and the Jews*. New York: Public Affairs.

Bank, Rosemarie K. 1982. "The Second Face of the Idol: Women in Melodrama." In *Women In the American Theatre*, ed. Helen Kirch Chinoy and Linda Wilson, 240–45. New York: Crown.

Bao, Weihong. 2015. *Fiery Cinema: The Emergence of an Affective Medium in China, 1915–1945*. Minneapolis: University of Minnesota Press.

———. 2005. "From Pearl White to White Rose Woo." *Camera Obscura* 20, no. 3: 193–231.

Barasch, Moshe. 1976. *Gestures of Despair in Medieval and Early Renaissance Art*. New York: New York University Press.

Barnouw, Eric, and S. Krishnaswamy. 1980. *Indian Film*, 2nd ed. New York: Oxford University Press.

Barthes, Roland. 1977. "Introduction to the Structural Analysis of Narratives." In *Image/Music/Text*, trans. Stephen Heath, 79–124. New York: Hill and Wang.

Basinger, Jeanine. 2000. *Silent Stars*. Middletown, Conn.: Wesleyan University Press.

Bauman, Rebecca. 2013. "You Don't Exist: *I Am Love* as Political Melodrama." *Studies in European Cinema* 10, no. 2/3: 103–17.

Baxandall, Michael. 1980. *The Limewood Sculptures of Renaissance Germany*. New Haven: Yale University Press.

Baym, Nina. 1978. *Women's Fiction: A Guide to Novels By and About Women in America, 1820–1870*. Ithaca: Cornell University Press.

Bayman, Louis. 2014. *The Operatic and the Everyday in Post-war Italian Film Melodrama*. Edinburgh: Edinburgh University Press.

Bayman, Louis, and Sergio Rigoletto. 2013. "The Frame and the Museum: Framing the Popular." In *Popular Italian Cinema*, ed. Louis Bayman and Sergio Rigoletto, 1–29. Basingstoke: Palgrave MacMillan.

Bazin, André. 2005. "The Evolution of the Language of Cinema." In *What Is Cinema?* vol. 1, trans. Hugh Gray, 23–40. Berkeley: University of California Press.
———. 2003. *Qu'est-ce que le cinéma?* Paris: Les Éditions du CERF. First published 1958–1962.
Beach, Frank L. 1969. "The Effects of Western Movement on California's Growth and Development, 1900–1920." *International Migration Review* 3: 25–28.
Belasco, David. 1912. "Belasco Contract Christmas Present to this 'Movie Heroine.'" *Worchester Massachusetts Gazette*, December 12. In David Belasco scrapbooks, r.12. Robinson Locke Collection, Billy Rose Theatre Division, New York Public Library of the Performing Arts, New York City.
Belting, Hans. 1981. *The Image and Its Public in the Middle Ages: Form and Function of Early Paintings of the Passion*, trans. Mark Bartusis and Raymond Meyer. New Rochelle, N.Y.: Aristide D. Caratzas.
———. 1994. *Likeness and Presence: A History of the Image Before the Era of Art*. Chicago: University of Chicago Press.
Benjamin, Walter. 1968. "The Work of Art in the Age of Mechanical Reproduction." In *Illuminations*, trans. Harry Zohn, ed. Hannah Arendt, 217–51. New York: Schocken. First published 1936.
Bentley, Eric. 1964. *The Life of the Drama*. New York: Athenaeum.
Berlant, Lauren. 2008. *The Female Complaint: The Unfinished Business of Sentimentality in American Culture*. Durham, N.C.: Duke University Press.
Berry, Chris, and Mary Farquhar. 2006. *China on Screen: Cinema and Nation*. New York: Columbia University Press.
Bevington, David. 2012. *Medieval Drama*. Indianapolis: Hackett.
Bhaskar, Ira. 2012. "Emotion, Subjectivity and the Limits of Desire: Melodrama and Modernity in Bombay Cinema, 1940s–1950s." In *Gender Meets Genre in Postwar Cinemas*, ed. Christine Gledhill, 161–76. Urbana: University of Illinois.
Bhaskar, Ira, and Richard Allen. 2009. *Islamicate Cultures of Bombay Cinema*. New Delhi: Tulika Books.
Blair Parker, Lottie. 1898. *'Way Down East*. Typescript of final version, elaborated by Joseph R. Grismer, performed at Manhattan Theatre. In Robinson Locke Collection, Billy Rose Theatre Division, New York Public Library of the Performing Arts, New York City.
Boehnel, William. 1936. "'The Petrified Forest' on Music Hall Screen." New York: *World-Telegram*, February 7.
Bogle, Donald. 2016. *Toms, Coons, Mammies, and Bucks: An Interpretative History of Blacks in America*. New York: Continuum. First published 1994.
The Bombay Times and Journal of Commerce. 1859. Bombay, India.
Booth, Michael. 1965. *English Melodrama*. London: Herbert Jenkins.
———, ed. 1967. *Hiss the Villain: Six American and English Melodramas*. New York: Benjamin Blom.
———. 1991. *Theatre in the Victorian Age*. Cambridge: Cambridge University Press.
———. 1981. *Victorian Spectacular Theatre 1850–1910*. London: Routledge and Kegan Paul.

Bordwell, David. 1973. *Filmguide to La Passion De Jeanne D'Arc*. Bloomington: Indiana University Press.
———. 1981. *The Films of Carl-Theodor Dreyer*. Berkeley: University of California Press.
———. 1982. "Happily Ever After, Part Two." *The Velvet Light Trap* 19: 2–7.
———. 1997. *On the History of Film Style*. Cambridge, Mass.: Harvard University Press.
———. 2006. "Nordisk and the Tableau Aesthetic." In *100 Years of Nordisk Film*, ed. Lisbeth Richter Larsen and Dan Nissen, 81–95. Copenhagen: Danish Film Institute.
———. 2006. *The Way Hollywood Tells It: Story and Style in Modern Movies*. Berkeley: University of California Press.
Bordwell, David, Janet Staiger, and Kristen Thompson. 1985. *The Classical Hollywood Cinema: Film Style and Mode of Production to 1960*. New York: Columbia University Press.
Boucicault, Dion. 1926. *The Art of Acting*. New York: Dramatic Museum of Columbia University. First published 1882.
———. 1987. *The Colleen Bawn; or, The Brides of Garryowen*. In *Selected Plays of Dion Boucicault*, ed. Andrew Parkin, 191–256. Washington, D.C.: Catholic University of America Press.
Brandlmeier, Thomas. 1995. "Franz Osten (Ostermayr), A Bavarian in Bombay." *Griffithiana*, 53 (May): 77–93.
Brandon, Ruth. 1991. *Being Divine*. London: Mandarin.
Branscombe, Peter. 2001. "Melodrama." In *The New Grove Dictionary of Music and Musicians*, vol. 16, 2nd ed., ed. Stanley Sadie and John Tyrrell, 360–62. London: Macmillan.
Bratton, Jacky. 1994. "The Contending Discourses of Melodrama." In *Melodrama: Stage, Picture, Screen*, ed. Jacky Bratton, Jim Cook, and Christine Gledhill, 25–37. London: BFI.
Braudel, Ferdinand. 1980. "History and the Social Sciences: The Longue Durée." In *On History*, trans. Sarah Matthews, 25–54. Chicago: University of Chicago Press.
Braudy, Leo. 1997. *The Frenzy of Renown*. New York: Vintage. First published 1986.
Brewster, Ben, and Lea Jacobs. 1997. *Theatre to Cinema, Stage Pictorialism and the Early Feature Film*. Oxford: Oxford University Press.
Brooks, Peter. 1976. *The Melodramatic Imagination: Balzac, Henry James, Melodrama, and the Mode of Excess*. New Haven: Yale University Press. Reprinted 1985 and 1995.
1994. "Melodrama, Body, Revolution." In *Melodrama: Stage, Picture, Screen*, ed. Jacky Bratton, Jim Cook, Christine Gledhill, 11–24. London: BFI.
———. 2015. "The Mysteries of Paris." *New York Review of Books*. (December): 46–47.
———. 1984. *Reading for the Plot: Design and Intention in Narrative*. Cambridge, Mass.: Harvard University Press.

Brunetta, Gian Piero. 1995. *Cent'Anni di Cinema Italiano 2: dal 1945 ai Giorni Nostri*. Rome: Laterza.

———. 2003. *The History of Italian Cinema: A Guide to Italian Film from Its Origins to the Twenty-First Century*, trans. Jeremy Parzen. Princeton: Princeton University Press.

Bruzzi, Stella. 2011. " 'It will be a magnificent obsession': Femininity, Desire, and the New Look in 1950s Hollywood Melodrama." In *Fashion in Film*, ed. Adrienne Munich, 160–80. Bloomington: Indiana University Press.

Buckley, Matthew S. 2012. "Introduction." *Modern Drama* 55, no 4 (Winter): 439–36.

———. 2009. "Refugee Theatre: Melodrama and Modernity's Loss." *Theatre Journal* 61, no. 22 (May): 175–190.

———. 2006. *Tragedy Walks the Streets: The French Revolution in the Making of Modern Drama*. Baltimore: John Hopkins University Press.

Bugliosi, Vincent. 1996. *Outrage: The Five Reasons Why O. J. Simpson Got Away with Murder*. New York: Norton.

Buñuel, Luis. 2000. "Carl Dreyer's *The Passion of Joan of Arc* (1928)." In *An Unspeakable Betrayal: Selected Writings of Luis Buñuel*, trans. Garrett White, 121–22. Berkeley: University of California Press.

Cameron, Kate. 1936. " 'Petrified Forest' A Thrilling Picture." (New York) *Daily News*, February 7.

Canby, Vincent. 1972. "Superfly." *New York Times*. Undated cutting.

Canetti, Elias. 1994. *El suplicio de las moscas*, trans. Cristina García Ohlrich. Madrid: Anaya.

Cardone, Lucia. 2012. *Il melodramma*. Milan: Il Castoro.

Carr, David. 1987. "Review of *Futures Past: On the Semantics of Historical Time*." *History and Theory* 26, no. 2 (May): 197–204.

Casadio, Giuseppe. 1990. *Adultere, Fedifraghe, Innocenti: La Donna del 'Neorealismo Popolare' nel Cinema Italiano degli Anni Cinquanta*. Ravenna: Lango Editore.

Caulibus, John of. 2000. *Meditations on The Life of Christ*, trans. and ed. Francis X. Taney Sr., Anne Miller, and C. Mary Stallings-Taney. Asheville, N.C.: Pegasus Press. First published c. 1300.

Chabon, Michael. 2008. "Secret Skin: An Essay in Unitard Theory." In *Superheroes: Fashion and Fantasy*, ed. Andrew Bolton, 20–21. New York: Metropolitan Museum of Art/Yale University Press.

Champagne, John. 2015. *Italian Masculinity as Queer Melodrama*. Basingstoke: Palgrave MacMillan.

Chaplin, Charles. 1964. *My Autobiography*. New York: Simon & Schuster.

"Charlotte Cushman." 1874. Unsourced. November 4. Robinson Locke Collection, Billy Rose Theatre Division, New York Public Library of the Performing Arts, New York City, vol. 131: 20.

Chatterjee, Sudipto. 2007. *The Colonial Staged: Theatre in Colonial Calcutta*. Calcutta: Seagull Books.

Cheah, Pheng, and Bruce Robbins. 1998. *Cosmopolitics: Thinking and Feeling Beyond the Nation*. Minneapolis: University of Minnesota Press.

Chen, Jianhua. 2009. *Cong geming dao gonghe: Qingmo zhi minguo shiqi wenxue dianying yu wenhua de zhuanxing* [From Revolution to Republicanism: Transformations in Literature, Cinema and Culture from late Qing to the Republican Period]. Nanning: Guangxi shifan daxue chubanshe.

Chen, Xiangyang. 2012. "Women, Generic Aesthetics, and the Vernacular: Huangmei Opera Films from China to Hong Kong." In *Gender Meets Genre in Postwar Cinemas*, ed. Christine Gledhill, 177–90. Urbana: University of Illinois Press.

Chiarini, Luigi. 1978. "Neorealism Betrayed." In *Springtime in Italy: A Reader In Italian Neorealism*, ed. David Overbey, 207–13. London: Talisman Books.

Ciafone, Amanda. 2014. "The Magical Neorealism of Network Films." *International Journal of Communication* 8: 2680–2704.

Cioran, Emil M. 1995. *Tears and Saints*, trans. Illinica Zarifopol-Johnson. Chicago: University of Chicago Press.

Cockrell, Dale. 1997. *Demons of Disorder: Early Blackface Minstrels and Their World*. Cambridge: Cambridge University Press.

Cohen, John S., Jr. 1933. "Douglas Fairbanks, Jr., and Parachutes in 'Parachute Jumper.'" (New York) *Sun*, January 26.

Colligan, Mimi. 2013. *Circus and Stage: The Theatrical Adventures of Rose Edouin and GBW Lewis*. Clayton, Victoria: Monash University.

"Confessions of a Motion Picture Press Agent." 1918. *Independent*, August 24.

Cook, Pam. 2012. "No Fixed Address: The Woman's Picture from *Outrage* to *Blue Steel*." In *Gender Meets Genre in Postwar Cinemas*, ed. Christine Gledhill, 29–40. Urbana: University of Illinois.

Cooper, Mark Garrett. 2010. *Universal Women*. Urbana: University of Illinois Press.

Corazzol, Adriana Guarnieri. 1993. "Opera and *Verismo*: Regressive Points of View and The Artifice of Alienation." *Cambridge Opera Journal* 5, no. 1 (March): 39–53.

Cott, Nancy. 1987. *The Grounding of Modern Feminism*. New Haven: Yale University Press.

———. 1978. "Passionlessness." *Signs* 21: 219–36.

Cox, John. 2000. *The Devil and the Sacred in English Drama 1350–1642*. New York: Cambridge University Press.

Creelman, Eileen. 1936. "Leslie Howard and Bette Davis in Sherwood's Drama, 'The Petrified Forest'." (New York) *Sun*, February 7.

Crewe, Regina. 1936. "'The Petrified Forest:' Tense Melodrama in Cinema Form, with Liberal Spice of Humor." *New York American*, February 7.

Cullingford, Elizabeth Butler. 1997. "National Identities in Performance: The Stage Englishman of Boucicault's Irish Drama." *Theatre Journal* 49, no. 3: 287–300.

Dadek, M. Zeynep. 2015. "Arabesk Film and Culture in Turkey." PhD, diss., New York University.

Dalle Vacche, Angela. 2008. *Diva: Defiance and Passion in Early Italian Cinema*. Austin: University of Texas Press.

Daly, Nicholas. 2007. "The Many Lives of the Colleen Bawn: Pastoral Suspense." *Journal of Victorian Culture* 12, no. 1: 1–25.

———. 2011. "The Volcanic Disaster Narrative: From Pleasure Garden to Canvas, Page, and Stage." *Victorian Studies* 53, no. 2: 255–85.

Danto, Arthur C. 2007. *Narration and Knowledge*. New York: Columbia University Press.

Darr, Alan Phipps, and Giorgio Bonsanti. 1986. *Donatello e i Suoi: Scultura fiorentina del primo Rinascimento*. Milan: Arnoldo Mondadori Editore.

Davis, Nick. 2015. "The Object of Desire: Todd Haynes Discusses *Carol* and the Satisfactions of Telling Women's Stories." *Film Comment* 51, no. 6 (November/December): 30–35.

de Marly, Diana. 1982. *Costume on Stage 1600–1940*. Totowa: Barnes and Noble Books.

De Sica, Vittorio. 1978. "Why *Bicycle Thieves*?" In *Springtime in Italy: A Reader In Italian Neorealism*, ed. David Overbey, 87–89. London: Talisman Books.

Deacon, Desley. 2008. "Location! Location! Location! Mind Maps and Theatrical Circuits in Australian Transnational History." *History Australia* 5, no. 3: 81.1–81.16.

deCordova, Richard. 1990. *Picture Personalities*. Chicago: University of Illinois Press.

Del Mar Azcona, María. 2010. *The Multi-Protagonist Film*. Chichester, UK: Wiley-Blackwell.

Deleuze, Gilles. 1986. *Cinema 1: The Movement Image*. Paris: Athlone.

Deleuze, Gilles, and Félix Guattari. 1987. *A Thousand Plateaus: Capitalism and Schizophrenia*, trans. Brian Massumi. Minneapolis: University of Minnesota Press.

Derrida, Jacques. 2005. *On Touching—Jean-Luc Nancy*. Stanford: Stanford University Press.

D—G (George Daniel). 1830. "Remarks" on *Luke the Labourer*. In Cumberland's Minor Theatre 2, no. 3: 3–6.

Dissanayake, Wimal, ed. 1993. *Melodrama and Asian Cinema*. Cambridge, UK: Cambridge University Press.

Doane, Mary Ann. 1987. *The Desire to Desire*. Bloomington: Indiana University Press.

———. 1990. "Information, Crisis, Catastrophe." In *Logics of Television: Essays in Cultural Criticism*, ed. Patricia Mellencamp, 222–39. Bloomington: Indiana University Press.

Doxtater, Amanda. 2010. "Perilous Performance: Dreyer's Unity of Danger and Beauty." http://english.carlthdreyer.dk/aboutdreyer/working-method/perilous-performance.aspx. Last accessed June 23, 2017.

Dreyer, Carl Theodor. 1950. "Dreyer 1950." Unpublished introduction to screening of *La Passion de Jeanne d'Arc* at Danish Film Museum. In Dreyer's *Udklips mapper*, Dreyer Collection, Danish Film Institute.

———. 1915. "Esther." Unpublished scenario #1352a. Nordisk Films Kompagni Archive, Danish Film Institute, Copenhagen.

———. 1964. *Om Filmen*. Copenhagen: Gyldendals Ugleboger.

Dreyer, Carl Theodor, and Donald Skoller. 1991. *Dreyer in Double Reflection*. New York: Da Capo Press. First published 1973.

Drum, Jean, and Dale D. Drum. 2000. *My Only Great Passion: The Life and Films of Carl Th. Dreyer*. Lanham, Md.: Scarecrow Press.

Duckett, Victoria. 2015. *Seeing Sarah Bernhardt: Performance and Silent Film*. Urbana: University of Illinois Press.

Dudden, Faye E. 1995. *Women in the American Theatre: Actresses and Audiences 1790–1870*. New Haven: Yale University Press.

Dyer, Richard. 1991. "*A Star Is Born* and the Construction of Authenticity." In *Stardom: Industry of Desire*, ed. Christine Gledhill, 132–40. London: Routledge.

——. 1979. *Stars*. London: BFI.

Eaton, Walter Prichard. 1910. "Women as Theatre-Goers." *Woman's Home Companion* 37 (October): 79.

Eforgan, Estel. 2010. *Leslie Howard: The Lost Actor*. London: Vallentine Mitchell.

Egan, Linda. 2001. *Carlos Monsiváis: Culture and Chronicle in Contemporary Mexico*. Tucson: University of Arizona Press.

Eisenstein, Sergei E. 1977. "Dickens, Griffith, and the Film Today." In *Film Form*, trans. and ed. Jay Leyda, 195–255. New York: Harcourt Brace Jovanovich.

——. 1988. *Eisenstein on Disney*, trans. and ed. Jay Leyda. London: Methuen.

Ellison, Ralph. 1952. *The Invisible Man*. New York: Random House. First published 1947.

Elsaesser, Thomas. 2007. "A Mode of Feeling or a View of the World? Family Melodrama and the Melodramatic Imagination Revisited." In *Il melodramma*, ed. Elena Dagrada, 23–45. Rome: Bulzoni.

——. 1987. "Tales of Sound and Fury: Observations on the Family Melodrama." In *Home Is Where the Heart Is: Studies in Melodrama and the Woman's Film*, ed. Christine Gledhill, 43–69. London: BFI. First published 1972.

——. 1991. "Tales of Sound and Fury: Observations on the Family Melodrama." In *Imitations of Life: A Reader on Film and Television Melodrama*, ed. Marcia Landy, 68–91. Detroit: Wayne State University Press. First published 1972.

Eltis, Eos. 2013. *Acts of Desire; Women and Sex on Stage, 1800–1930*. Oxford: Oxford University Press.

Engberg, Marguerite. 1993. "The Erotic Melodrama in Danish Silent Films 1910–1918." *Film History* 5, no. 1: 63–67.

Fahs, Alice. 2011. *Out on Assignment*. Chapel Hill: University of North Carolina Press.

Farassino, Alberto, ed. 1989. *Neorealismo: Cinema Italiano 1945–49*. Turin: Editori Stampatori.

Feuer, Jane. 1986. "Narrative Form in American Network Television." *In High Theory/Low Culture*, ed. Colin MacCabe, 101–14. Manchester: Manchester University Press.

Fink, Guido. 1987. " 'La Signora Contessa è in Camera Sua.' Teatralità del Cinema Italiano del Dopoguerra." *Quaderni di Teatro* 9, no. 35 (February): 51–62.

"First National Completes Interesting Survey." 1920. *Wid's Daily*, October 18: 17.

Fischer-Lichte, Erika. 2008. *The Transformative Power of Performance: A New Aesthetics*. New York: Routledge.

Fitzgerald, Percy. 1892. *The Art of Acting in Connection with the Study of Character, the Spirit of Comedy and Stage Illusion*. London.
Fofi, Goffredo. 2007. "Bread and Tears (and Jeers): An Introduction to Matarazzo's Cinema," trans. Helen Claudia Doyle. *Cinegrafie* 20: 185–89.
Forgacs, David, and Stephen Gundle. 2008. *Mass Culture and Italian Society from Fascism to the Cold War*. Bloomington: Indiana University Press.
Foster, Helen Bradley. 1997. *"New Rainments of Self": African American Clothing in the Antebellum South*. New York: Berg.
Freedberg, David. 1989. *The Power of Images*. Chicago: University of Chicago Press.
Fulton, Rachel. 2002. *From Judgment to Passion: Devotion to Christ and the Virgin Mary, 800–1220*. New York: Columbia University Press.
Gaines, Jane M. 2000. "Dream/Factory." In *Reinventing Film Studies*, ed. Christine Gledhill and Linda Williams, 100–13. London: Arnold.
———. 2012. "The Genius of Genre and the Ingenuity of Women." In *Gender Meets Genre in Postwar Cinemas*, ed. Christine Gledhill, 15–28. Urbana: University of Illinois Press.
———. 2016. "On Not Narrating the History of Feminism and Film." *Feminist Media Histories* 2, no. 2. http://fmh.ucpress.edu.ezproxy.cul.columbia.edu/content/2/2/6. Last accessed February 21, 2017.
———. Forthcoming. *Pink-Slipped: What Happened to Women in the Silent Film Industries?* Urbana: University of Illinois Press.
———. 2013. "What Happened to the Philosophy of Film History?" *Film History* 25, no. 1: 70–80.
Gangar, Amrit. 2013. *The Music That Still Rings at Dawn, Every Dawn: Walter Kaufman in India, 1934–1946*. Mumbai: Goethe Institut/Max Mueller Bhawan.
Gangar, Amrit, and Christoph von Ungern-Sternberg. 2005. "Naushad, Haas and the Genesis of *City of Love*: An Interview with Naushad Ali." *Osian's Cinemaya* 651 (April-June): 46–48.
Gänzl, Kurt. 2002. *William B. Gill: From the Goldfields to Broadway*. New York: Routledge.
Garcia, Gustav. 1888. *The Actor's Art: A Practical Treatise on Stage Declamation, Public Speaking, and Deportment for the Use of Artists, Students and Amateurs*. London.
García Riera, Emilio. 1971. *Historia documental del cine mexicano*, vol. 2. Guadalajara: Universidad de Guadalajara.
Gentile, Guido. 1989. "Testi di devozione e iconografia del Compinato." In *Niccolò dell'Arca: Seminario Di Studi*, ed. G. Agostini and L. Ciammetti, 167–95. L. Bologna: Nuova Alfa editorial.
Gerould, Daniel C., ed. 1983. *American Melodrama*. New York: Performing Arts Journal Publications.
———. ed. 2002. *Pixérécourt: Four Melodramas*, trans. Daniel Gerould and Marvin Carlson. New York: Martin E. Segal Theater Center.
———. 1991. "Russian Formalist Theories of Melodrama." In *Imitations of Life: A Reader on Film and Television Melodrama*, ed. Marcia Landy, 118–34. Detroit: Wayne State University Press.

Gerould, Katherine Fullerton. 1921. "Movies." *Atlantic Monthly* (July): 22–30.

Gerow, Aaron. 2010. *Visions of Japanese Modernity: Articulations of Cinema, Nation, and Spectatorship*. Berkeley: University of California Press.

Gibbs, Anna. 2002. "Disaffected." *Continuum: Journal of Media and Cultural Studies* 16, no. 3: 335–41.

Gill, Meredith. 2013. " 'Until Shadows Disperse:' Augustine's Twilight." In *The Sensuous In The Counter-Reformation Church*, ed. Marcia B. Hall and Tracey E. Cooper, 252–73. Cambridge: Cambridge University Press.

Gledhill, Christine. 1992. "Between Melodrama and Realism: Anthony Asquith's *Underground* and King Vidor's *The Crowd*." In *Classical Hollywood Narrative: The Paradigm Wars*, ed. Jane Gaines, 129–67. Durham, N.C.: Duke University Press.

———. 2011. "Mary Pickford: Icon of Stardom." In *Flickers of Desire: Movie Stars of the 1910s*, ed. Jennifer M. Bean, 43–68. New Brunswick, N.J.: Rutgers University Press.

———. 2002. "The Melodramatic Field: An Investigation." In *Home Is Where the Heart Is: Studies in Melodrama and the Woman's Film*, ed. Christine Gledhill, 5–39. London: BFI. First published 1987.

———. 1989. "On 'Stella Dallas' and Feminist Film Theory." *Cinema Journal* 25, no. 4 (Summer): 44–48.

———. 2003. *Reframing British Cinema, 1918–28: Between Restraint and Passion*. London: BFI.

———. 2000. "Rethinking Genre." In *Reinventing Film Studies*, ed. Christine Gledhill and Linda Williams, 221-43. London: Arnold.

———. 1991. "Signs of Melodrama." In *Stardom: Industry of Desire*, ed. Christine Gledhill, 207–29. London: Routledge.

———. 1994. "Speculations on the Relation Between Soap Opera and Melodrama." In *American Television: New Directions in History and Theory*, ed. Nick Browne, 123–44. Chur, Switzerland: Harwood Academic.

Glenn, Susan A. 2000. *Female Spectacle: The Theatrical Roots of Modern Feminism*. Cambridge, Mass.: Harvard University Press.

Gluck, Carol. 1987. *Japan's Modern Myths: Ideology in the Late Meiji Period*. Princeton: Princeton University Press.

Goimard, Jacques. 1999. "La Parola e la Cosa." In *Lo Specchio della Vita. Materiali sul Melodramma nel Cinema Contemporaneo*, ed. Vittorio Spagnoletti, 9–95. Turin: Lindau.

Gorbman, Claudia. 1987. *Unheard Melodies: Narrative Film Music*. Bloomington: Indiana University Press.

Gottlieb, Sidney (ed.). 2015. *Hitchcock on Hitchcock: Selected Writings and Interviews*, vol. 2. Oakland: University of California Press.

"Great Moment." 1931. *Exhibitors Herald* (July 9): 5.

Grignaffini, Giovanna. 2002. "Beata vergine e madre." In *La scena madre: scritti sul cinema*, 227–39. Bologna: Bononia University Press.

———. 1996. "Il femminile nel cinema italiano. Racconti di rinascita." In *Identità Europea nel Cinema Italiano dal 1945 al Miracolo Economico*, ed. Gian Piero Brunetta, 357–89. Turin: Edizione della Fondazione Giovanni Agnelli.

Grimstead, David. 1971. "Melodrama as Echo of the Historically Voiceless." In *Anonymous Americans: Explorations in Nineteenth-Century Social History*, ed. Tamara K. Hareven, 80–98. Englewood Cliffs, N.J.: Prentice-Hall.

———. 1968. *Melodrama Unveiled: American Theater and Culture, 1800–1850*. Chicago: University of Chicago Press.

———. 1987. *Melodrama Unveiled: American Theater and Culture, 1800–1850*. Berkeley: University of California Press.

Grossberg, Lawrence. 1997. *Bringing It All Back Home: Essays on Cultural Studies*. Durham, N.C.: Duke University Press.

———. 1992. *We Gotta Get Out of This Place: Popular Conservatism and Postmodern Culture*. New York: Routledge.

Guerrero, Edward. 1993. *Framing Blackness: The African American Image on Film*. Philadelphia, Pa.: Temple University Press.

Gunn, Anna. 2013. "I Have a Character Issue." *New York Times*, August 24.

Gunning, Sandra. 1996. *Race, Rape, and Lynching: The Red Record of American Literature, 1890–1912*. New York: Oxford University Press.

Gunning, Tom. 1989. "An Aesthetics of Astonishment: Early Film and the (In)Credulous Spectator." *Art and Text* 34 (Spring): 31–45.

———. 1986. "The Cinema of Attractions: Early Film, Its Spectator and the Avant-Garde." *Wide Angle* 8, no. 3/4: 63–70.

———. 1993. "Now You See It, Now You Don't: The Temporality of the Cinema of Attractions." *Velvet Light Trap* 32 (Fall): 3–12.

Günsberg, Maggie. 2005. *Italian Cinema: Gender and Genre*. Basingstoke, UK: Palgrave MacMillan.

Gupt, Somnath. 2005. *The Parsi Theatre: Its Origin and Development*, trans. and ed. Kathryn Hansen. Calcutta: Seagull Books.

Hagerdon, Roger. 1995. "Doubtless to Be Continued: A Brief History of Serial Narrative." In *To Be Continued: Soap Operas Around the World*, ed. Robert Allen, 27–48. London: Routledge.

Hale, Grace Elizabeth. 1998. *Making Whiteness: The Culture of Segregation in the South, 1890–1940*. New York: Vintage Books.

Hall, Roger A. 2001. *Performing the American Frontier, 1870–1906*. Cambridge: Cambridge University Press.

Hallett, Hilary A. 2011. "Based on a True Story." *Pacific Historical Review* 80, no. 2 (May): 177–210.

———. 2013. *Go West Young Women! The Rise of Early Hollywood*. Berkeley: University of California Press.

Hamilton, Clayton. 1910. "The Career of Camille." In *The Theory of the Theatre*, 369–71. New York: Henry Holt.

———. 1911. "Organizing the Audience." *Bookman* (October): 34.

Hampton, Benjamin. 1971. "The Pickford Revolution." In *History of the American Film Industry*, chapter 8. New York: Dover. First published 1931.

Hansen, Kathryn. 1999. "Making Women Visible: Gender and Race Cross-Dressing in the Parsi Theatre." *Theatre Journal* 51, no. 2: 127–47.

———. 2006. "Ritual Enactments in a Hindi 'Mythological': Betab's *Mahabharat* in Parsi Theatre." *Economic and Political Weekly* 41, no. 48 (December 2): 4985–91.

———. 2009. "Staging Composite Culture: Nautanki and Parsi Theatre in Recent Revivals." *South Asia Research* 29, no. 2: 151–68.

———. 2011. *Stages of Life: Indian Theatre Autobiographies*. Ranikhet: Permanent Black.

Hansen, Miriam Bratu. 1983. "Early Silent Cinema: Whose Public Sphere?" *New German Critique* 29: 147–84.

———. 2000. "Fallen Women, Rising Stars, New Horizons: Shanghai Silent Film as Vernacular Modernism." *Film Quarterly* 54, no. 1 (Autumn): 10–22.

———. 1999. "The Mass Production of the Senses: Classical Cinema as Vernacular Modernism." *Modernism/Modernity* 6, no. 2: 59–77.

———. 2000. "The Mass Production of the Senses: Classical Cinema as Vernacular Modernism." In *Reinventing Film Studies*, ed. Christine Gledhill and Linda Williams, 332–50. London: Arnold.

———. 2010. "Vernacular Modernism: Tracking Cinema on a Global Scale." In *World Cinemas, Transnational Perspectives*, ed. Nataša Durovicová and Kathleen Newman, 287–314. New York: Routledge.

Harootunian, Harry. 2000. *Overcome by Modernity: History, Culture, and Community in Interwar Japan*. Princeton: Princeton University Press.

Hart, Darryl G. 2002. *That Old Time Religion in Modern America*. Chicago: Ivan R. Dee.

Hayward, Jennifer. 1997. *Consuming Pleasures: Active Audiences and Serial Fictions from Dickens to Soap Opera*. Lexington: University of Kentucky Press.

"Hedda Gabler." 1907. *Current Literature* (January): 152.

Heidegger, Martin. 1996. *Being and Time*, trans. Joan Stambaugh. Albany, N.Y.: SUNY Press.

Heilman, Robert. 1968. *Tragedy and Melodrama: Versions of Experience*. Seattle: University of Washington Press.

Higham, Charles. 1981. *Bette*. London: New English Library.

Hill, Joseph. 1970. *Women in Gainful Occupations, 1879 to 1920*. Census Monograph IX. Westport, Conn.: Greenwood Press. First published 1929.

Hilmes, Michele. 1997. *Radio Voices: American Broadcasting 1922 to 1952*. Minneapolis: University of Minnesota Press.

Holmes Collection. 1915. "Action Is the Spice of Life." *New York Telegraph*, November 21; "A Charming Dare-Devil," *Pictures and the Picture-Goer*, March 15. In Robinson Locke Collection, Billy Rose Theatre Division, New York Public Library of the Performing Arts, New York City, vol. 1, envelope 737.

Home and School Speaker, a Practical Manual of Delsarte Exercises and Elocution Containing Instructions for the Cultivation and Preservation of the Voice and Use of Gestures. 1897. Chicago: W. B. Conkey.

Hori, Keiko. 2000. "*Konjiki yasha* no ranpon—Bertha M. Clay wo megutte." *Bungaku* 1, no. 6 (November/December): 188–201.

Howe, Herbert. 1924. "Is Mary Pickford Finished?" *The Preview*, March 25. In Pickford Core Clipping File, Margaret Herrick Library, Academy of Motion Picture Arts and Sciences, Beverley Hills, Calif.
———. 1922. "The Real Pola Negri." *Photoplay* (November): 38.
Howes, Marjorie. 2011. "Melodramatic Conventions and Atlantic History in Dion Boucicault." *Eire-Ireland* 46, no. 3/4: 84–101.
Huang, Nicole. 2005. *Women, War, Domesticity: Shanghai Literature and Popular Culture of the 1940s*. Leiden, Netherlands: Brill Academic.
Huang, Xuelei. 2014. *Shanghai Filmmaking: Crossing Borders, Connecting to the Global, 1922–1938*. Leiden, Netherlands: Brill Academic.
Hughes, Elinor. 1934. "Bette Davis at Last Shows She Is Learning How to Act." *Boston Herald*, June 3.
Hyslop, Gabrielle. 1985. "Deviant and Dangerous Behavior." *Journal of Popular Culture* 19, no. 3: 65–78.
———. 1992. "Pixérécourt and the French Melodrama Debate: Instructing Boulevard Theatre Audiences." In *Melodrama*, ed. James Redmond, 61–85. Cambridge: Cambridge University Press.
International Jew, the World's Foremost Problem. 1920. Reprint of articles appearing in the *Dearborn Independent*, May 22–October.
Ito, Ken K. 2008. *An Age of Melodrama: Family, Gender, and Social Hierarchy in the Turn-of-the-Century Japanese Novel*. Stanford: Stanford University Press.
Iwamoto, Kenji. 1998. "From *Rensageki* to *Kinodrama*." *Review of Japanese Culture and Society* 10 (December): 1–13.
James, Darius. 1995. *That's Blaxploitation: Roots of the Baadasssss 'Tude (Rated X by an All-Whyte Jury)*. New York: St. Martin's Press.
James, Henry. 1941. *A Small Boy and Others*. New York: Charles Scribner's Sons. First Published 1913.
James, Louis. 1976. "The Modality of Melodrama." In *English Popular Theater 1819–1851*, ed. Louis James, 83–87. New York: Columbia University Press.
Jansen, Katherine Ludwig. 2001. *The Making of the Magdalen: Preaching and Popular Devotion in the Later Middle Ages*. Princeton: Princeton University Press.
Jasraj, Madhura Pandit. 2015. *V. Shantaram: The Man Who Changed Indian Cinema*. New Delhi: Hay House India.
Jay Grout, Donald. 1965. *A Short History of Opera*. New York: Columbia University Press.
"Jazzy, Money-Mad Spot Where Movies Are Made." 1921. *Literary Digest*, March 6: 71–72, 75.
Jenkins, Keith. 2003. *Refiguring History*. New York: Routledge.
Jiecheng and Jianyun (given names). 1923. "Guer jiuzuji benshi" [Synopsis of *Orphan Rescues Grandfather*], *Chengxing* [The Morning Star] 3, special issue on *Guer jiuzuji*, 6–8.
Johnson, Claudia Durst. 1984. *American Actress*. Chicago: Nelson-Hall.
Jones, Andrew. 2011. *Developmental Fairytales, Evolutionary Thinking and Modern Chinese Culture*. Cambridge, Mass.: Harvard University Press.

Jowett, Garth, I. C. Jarvie, and Kathryn Fuller-Seeley, ed. 1996. *Children and the Movies*. Cambridge: Cambridge University Press.

Kabraji, Kekhushro Navroji. 1888. *Bholi Jan athva Dhananum Dhan*, 2nd ed. Bombay: Ranina Union Press.

Kaisar-i Hind. Bombay. 1887.

Kakoudaki, Despina. 2011. "Representing Politics in Disaster Films." In *International Journal of Media & Cultural Politics* 7 no. 3: 349–56.

———. 2002. "Spectacles of History: Race Relations, Melodrama and the Science Fiction/Disaster Film." *Camera Obscura* 17, no. 2: 109–53.

Kanfer, Stefan. 2011. *Tough Without a Gun: The Extraordinary Life of Humphrey Bogart*. New York: Faber and Faber.

Kaplan, Ann E. 1992. *Motherhood and Representation: The Mother in Popular Culture and Melodrama*. New York: Routledge.

———.1987. "Mothering, Feminism and Representation: The Maternal in Melodrama and the Woman's Film 1910–1940." In *Home Is Where the Heart Is: Studies in Melodrama and the Woman's Film*, ed. Christine Gledhill, 113–37. London: BFI.

———. 1991. "Problematizing Cross-Cultural Analysis: The Case of Women in the Recent Chinese Cinema." In *Perspectives on Chinese Cinema*, ed. Chris Berry, 141–55. London: BFI.

———. 2006. "Problematizing Cross-Cultural Analysis: The Case of Women in the Recent Chinese Cinema." In *Asian Cinema: A Reader and Guide*, ed. Dimitris Eleftheriotis and Gary Needham, 156–67. Honolulu: University of Hawai'i Press.

Karnes, Michelle. 2011. *Imagination, Meditation, and Cognition in the Middle Ages*. Chicago: University of Chicago Press.

Kau, Edwin. 1989. *Dreyer Filmkunst*. Copenhagen: Akademisk Forlag.

Keane, Stephen. 2001. *Disaster Movies: The Cinema of Catastrophe*. London: Wallflower Press.

Kemble, Marie-Thérèse. 1815. *Smiles and Tears*. London: John Miller.

Kermode, Frank. 1983. *The Classic: Literary Images of Permanence and Change*. Cambridge, Mass.: Harvard University Press. First published 1975.

Kesavan, Mukul. 1994. "Urdu Awadh and The Tawaif: the Islamicate Roots of Hindi Cinema." In *Forging Identities: Gender, Communities and the State*, ed. Zoya Hasan, 244–57. New Delhi: Kali for Women.

Kinoshita, Chika. 2005. "In the Twilight of Modernity and the Silent Film: Irie Takako in *The Water Magician*." *Camera Obscura* 20, no. 3: 91–127.

Klaprat, Cathy. 1985. "The Star as Market Strategy: Bette Davis in Another Light." In *The American Film Industry*, ed. Tino Balio, 351–76. Wisconsin: University of Wisconsin Press.

Klebanoff, R. 2000. "Passion, Compassion, and the Sorrows of Women: Niccolò dell'Arca's Lamentation over the Dead Christ for the Bolognese Confraternity of S. Maria della Vita." In *Confraternities and the Visual Arts in Renaissance Italy*, ed. Barbara Wisch and Diane Cole Ahl, 146–72. New York: Cambridge University Press.

Kleinhans, Chuck. 1978. "Notes on Melodrama and the Family Under Capitalism." *Film Reader* 3: 40–47.

Koselleck, Reinhart. 2004. *Futures Past: On the Semantics of Historical Time*, trans. Keith Tribe. New York: Columbia University Press.

Landis, Deborah Nandoolman, ed. 2003. *Screencraft: Costume Design*. Burlington: Focal Press.

Lansing, Carol. 2008. *Passion and Order: Restraint of Grief in the Medieval Italian Communes*. Ithaca: Cornell University Press.

Law, Kar. 1997. "Archetypes and Variations: Observations on Six Cantonese Films." In *Cantonese Melodrama, 1950–1969*, ed. Li Cheuk-to, 15–22. The Tenth Hong Kong International Film Festival. Hong Kong: Urban Council.

Leach, Joseph. 1972. *Bright Particular Star*. New Haven: Yale University Press.

Leavitt, Charles. 2013. "Cronaca, Narrativa, and the Unstable Foundations of the Institution of Neorealism." *Italian Culture* 31, no. 1: 28–46.

Lee, Alfred McClung. 2000. *The Daily Newspaper in America*. London: Routledge. First published 1937.

Lee, Haiyan. 2006. *Revolution of the Heart: A Genealogy of Love in China, 1900–1950*. Stanford: Stanford University Press.

Lefebvre, Henri. 2004. *Rhythmanalysis: Space, Time and Everyday Life*, trans. Stuart Elden and Gerald Moore. London: Continuum.

Lewis, Barbara. 1996. "Daddy Blue: The Evolution of the Dark Dandy." In *Inside the Minstrel Mask: Readings in Nineteenth-Century Blackface Minstrelsy*, ed. Annemarie Bean, James V. Hatch, and Brooks McNamara, 260–62. Middleton: Wesleyan University Press.

Li, Cheuk-to, ed. 1986. *Cantonese Melodrama 1950–1969*. Hong Kong: Urban Council.

Li, Daoxin. 2006. "China's Hollywood Dream [Zhongguo de Haolaiwu Mengxiang]." *Journal of Shanghai University* 5: 35–40.

Li, Suyuan, and Jubing Hu. 1997. *Zhongguo wusheng* dianyingshi [History of Chinese Silent Film]. Beijing: Zhongguo dianying.

Li, Yu. 2005. *Xian Qing Ou Ji*. Beijing: China Society Press.

Lietti, Roberta. 1995. "Stilemi iconografici in *I figli di nessuno*: Il racconto delle immagini nel melodramma di Raffaello Matarazzo." *Comunicazioni sociali* 17, no. 2/3 (April–September): 193–213.

Lindemann, Albert S. 2000. *Anti-Semitism Before the Holocaust*. Edinburgh Gate: Pearson Education.

Lindfors, Bernth, ed. 2007. *Ira Aldridge, The African Roscius*. Rochester, N.Y.: University of Rochester Press.

Liu, Lydia. 1995. *Translingual Practice: Literature, National Culture, and Translated Modernity—China, 1900–1937*. Stanford: Stanford University Press.

Lukács, György. 1971. *History and Class Consciousness: Studies in Marxist Dialectics*, trans. Rodney Livingstone. Cambridge, Mass.: MIT Press. First published 1923.

Lutgendorf, Philip. 2006. "Is There an Indian Way of Filmmaking?" *International Journal of Hindu Studies* 10, no. 3: 227–56.

Ma, Jean. 2015. *Sounding the Modern Woman: The Songstress in Chinese Cinema*. Durham, N.C.: Duke University Press.

Mack, Robert, ed. 2006. "Introduction." *The Vicar of Wakefield*, vii–xxxviii. Oxford: Oxford University Press.

Mâle, Émile. 1986. *Religious Art in France: The Late Middle Ages, A Study of Medieval Iconography and Its Sources*, trans. Marthiel Mathews, ed. Harry Bober. Princeton: Princeton University Press. First published 1908.

Mantle, Burns. 1935. " 'The Petrified Forest' Is Exciting: Leslie Howard an Engaging Hero of Desert Romance at the Broadhurst." (New York) *Daily News*, January 9.

Marcus, Millicent. 1989. *Italian Film in the Light of Neorealism*. Princeton: Princeton University Press.

Marfatia, Meher. 2011. *Laughter in the House! 20th-Century Parsi Theatre*. Mumbai: 49/50 Books.

Marks, Martin M. 1997. *Music and the Silent Film, Contexts and Case Studies*. New York: Oxford University Press.

Marsan, Jules. 1900. "Le mélodrame et Guilbert de Pixérécourt." *Revue d'Histoire littéraire de la France*, 7e Année, no. 2: 196–203.

Martín-Barbero, Jesús. 1993. *Communication, Culture and Hegemony. From the Media to Mediations*, trans. Elizabeth Fox and Robert A. White. London: Sage.

———. 1987. *De los medios a las mediaciones: comunicación, cultura, hegemonía*. Mexico: Gustavo Gili.

Martineau, Jane, ed. 1992. *Andrea Mantegna*. New York: Metropolitan Museum of Art.

Marvell, Andrew. 2000. "To His Coy Mistress." In *Americans' Favorite Poems*, ed. Robert Pinksy and Maggie Dietz, 183–84. New York: Norton.

Massumi, Brian. 2002. *Parables for the Virtual: Movement, Affect, Sensation*. Durham, N.C.: Duke University Press.

Mayer, David. 2004. "Encountering Melodrama." In *The Cambridge Companion to Victorian and Edwardian Theatre*, ed. Kerry Powell, 145–63. New York: Cambridge University Press.

———. 1994. " 'The Last Days of Pompeii' by James Pain." In *Playing Out the Empire: Ben-Hur and Other Toga Plays and Films, 1883–1908. A Critical Anthology*, ed. David Mayer, 90–103. Oxford: Clarendon.

———. 1997. "Learning to See in the Dark." *Nineteenth Century Theatre* 25, no. 2 (Winter): 92–114.

———. 1999. "Which Legacy of the Theatre? Acting in the Silent Film: Some Questions and Some Problems." In *Screen Acting*, ed. Peter Kramer and Alan Lovell, 10–24. London: Routledge.

———. 2006. "*Why Girls Leave Home:* Victorian and Edwardian Melodrama Parodied on Early Film." *Theatre Journal* 58 (December): 575–93.

Mayer, David, and Matthew Scott. 1983. *Four Bars of "Agit:" Music for Victorian and Edwardian Melodrama*. London: Theatre Museum and Samuel French.

Mayer, David, and Yuri Tsivian. 2006. "How *The Two Orphans* Became *Orphans of The Storm*." In *The Griffith Project*, vol. 10: *Films Produced 1919–1946*, ed. Paolo Cherchi Usai, 123–37. London: BFI.

Mayfield, Todd, and Travis Atria. 2016. *Traveling Soul: The Life of Curtis Mayfield*. Chicago: Chicago Review Press.

McArthur, Benjamin. 1984. *Actors and American Culture, 1880–1920*. Philadelphia, Pa.: Temple University Press.

McCollom, Michael. 2006. *The Way We Wore: Black Style Then and Now*. New York: Glitterati.

McConachie, Bruce. 1992. *Melodramatic Formations: American Theatre and Society, 1820–1870*. Iowa City: University of Iowa Press.

McDonald, Keiko I. 2000. *From Book to Screen: Modern Japanese Literature in Film*. Armonk, N.Y.: M. E. Sharpe.

McFeely, Deirdre. 2012. *Dion Boucicault: Irish Identity on Stage*. Cambridge: Cambridge University Press.

McHugh, Kathleen. 2005. "South Korean Film Melodrama: State, Nation, Woman and the Transnational Familiar." In *South Korean Golden Age: Melodrama, Gender, Genre, and National Cinema*, ed. Kathleen McHugh and Nancy Abelmann, 17–42. Detroit: Wayne State University Press.

McNamer, Sarah. 2011. *Affective Mediation and the Invention of Medieval Compassion*. Philadelphia, Pa.: University of Pennsylvania Press.

McTeague, James H. 1993. *Before Stanislavsky: American Professional Acting Schools and Acting Theory 1875–1925*. Metuchen, N.J.: The Scarecrow Press.

McWilliam, Rohan. 2000. "Melodrama and the Historians." *Radical History Review* 78: 57–84.

Mead, Rebecca J. 2004. *How the Vote Was Won: Woman Suffrage in the Western United States, 1868–1914*. New York: New York University Press.

———. 1998. " 'Let the Women Get Their Wages as Men Do.' " *Pacific Historical Review* 67, no. 3: 317–47.

Mehta, Kumudini A. 1960. "English Drama on the Bombay Stage in the Late Eighteenth Century and in the Nineteenth Century." PhD diss., University of Bombay.

Meisel, Martin. 1983. *Realizations: Narrative, Pictorial, and Theatrical Arts in Nineteenth-Century England*. Princeton: Princeton University Press.

"The Menace of German Films." 1921. *Literary Digest*, May 14: 28–30.

Merrill, Lisa. 1999. *When Romeo Was a Woman*. Ann Arbor: University of Michigan Press.

Merritt, Russell. 1983. "Melodrama: Postmortem for a Phantom Genre." *Wide Angle* 5, no. 3: 24–31.

Metz, Christian. 1982. *The Imaginary Signifier: Psychoanalysis and the Cinema*. Bloomington: Indiana University Press. First published 1977.

Miller, Barbara Stoler, trans. and ed. 1977. *The Gitagovinda of Jayadeva: Love Song of the Dark Lord*. Delhi: Motilal Banarasidas.

Mishra, Yatindra. 2009. "The Bai and the Dawn of Hindi Film Music (1925–1945)," trans. Anamika and Madhu B. Joshi. *The Book Review* 33, no. 2 (February): 46–47.

"Miss Cushman." 1876. *Spirit of the Times: The American Gentleman's Newspaper*, February 26. Robinson Locke Collection, Billy Rose Theatre Division, New York Public Library of the Performing Arts, New York City, vol. 131: 25.

Mittell, Jason. 2006. "Narrative Complexity in Contemporary American Television." *The Velvet Light Trap* 58 (Fall): 29–40.
———. 2015. *Complex TV: The Poetics of Contemporary Television Storytelling*. New York: New York University Press.
Moncrieff, William Thomas. 1828. *The Lear of Private Life; or, Father and Daughter*. Richardson's New Minor Drama. vol. 1. London: T. Richardson.
Monsiváis, Carlos. 1997. *Mexican Postcards*, trans. and ed. John Kraniauskas. London: Verso.
———. 1994. "Se sufre pero se aprende (El melodrama y las reglas d ela falta de límites)." In *A través del espejo: El cine mexicano y su público*, ed. Carlos Monsivás y Carlos Bonfil, 99–244. Mexico City: Ediciones el Milagro.
Moody, Jane. 2000. *Illegitimate Theatre in London 1770–1840*. New York: Cambridge University Press.
"Morals and the Movies." 1921. *The Nation*, April 21: 581.
Moretti, Franco. 1983. *Signs Taken for Wonders: Essays in the Sociology of Literary Forms*, trans. Susan Fischer, David Forgacs, and David Miller. London: Verso.
Morreale, Emiliano. 2011. *Così Piangevano: Il cinema melò negli anni cinquanta*. Rome: Donzelli editore.
Moses, Montrose, and John Mason Brown. 1934. *The American Theatre as seen by its critics: 1752–1934*. 2nd ed. New York: Norton.
"Motion Picture Industry." 1921. *Exhibitors Herald*, October 22: 41.
"'Movie' as an Industry." 1917. *Literary Digest*, October 16: 55.
"Movie Morals." 1917. *New Republic*, August 25: 100–101.
MoviesOnline. 2011. "Stephen Soderbergh Interview, *Contagion*." http://www.moviesonline.ca/2011/09/steven-soderbergh-interview-contagion/. Last accessed May 1, 2017.
Mulvey, Laura. 1996. "Americanitis: European Intellectuals and Hollywood Melodrama." In *Fetishism and Curiosity*, 19–28. London: BFI.
Munsterberg, Hugo. 1971. *American Traits*. Port Washington, N.Y.: Kennikat Press. First published 1901.
Murray, Robin L., and Joseph K. Heumann. 2009. *Ecology and Popular Film: Cinema on the Edge*. Albany, N.Y.: SUNY Press.
Nasaw, David. 2000. *The Chief*. New York: Houghton Mifflin.
———. 1993. *Going Out*. New York: Basic Books.
Ndalianis, Angela. 2005. "Television and Neo-Baroque." In *The Contemporary Television Series*, ed. Michael Hammond and Lucy Mazdon. 83–101. Edinburgh: Edinburgh University Press.
Neale, Steve. 1986. "Melodrama and Tears." *Screen* 27, no. 6 (November/December): 6–22.
———. 1993. "Melo Talk: On the Meaning and Use of the Term 'Melodrama' in the American Trade Press." *The Velvet Light Trap* 32: 66–89.
Neergaard, Ebbe. 1950. *Carl Dreyer: A Film Director's Work*. New Index Series 1. London: BFI.

———. 1940. *En Filminstruktørs Arbejde: Carl Th. Dreyer Og Hans Ti Film*. København: Atheneum Dansk Forlag.
———. 1960. *Historien Om Dansk Film*. København: Gyldendal.
Neergaard, Ebbe, and Erik Ulrichsen. 1963. *Dreyer: Ebbe Neergaards Bog Om Dreyer: I Videreført Og Forøget Udgave Ved Beate Neergaard Og Vibeke Steinthal*. København: Dansk Videnskab.
———. 1963. *The Story of Danish Film*. Copenhagen: Danske Selskab.
Negri, Pola. 1970. *Memoirs of a Star*. Garden City, N.Y.: Doubleday.
Neville, Henry, and Hugh Campbell. 1895. *Voice, Speech, and Gesture: A Practical Handbook to the Elocutionary Art*. London.
Newcomb, Horace. 1974. *TV: The Most Popular Art*. New York: Anchor Press.
Newman, Michael Z. 2006. "From Beats to Arcs: Toward a Poetics of Television Narrative." *The Velvet Light Trap* 58: 16–28.
Nicoll, Allardyce. 1955. *A History of English Drama, 1660–1900*, vol. 3, *Late Eighteenth Century Drama, 1750–1800*. Cambridge: Cambridge University Press.
Nodier, Charles. 2002. "Introduction to Pixérécourt's *Théâtre Choisi* [1843]." In *Pixérécourt: Four Melodramas*, trans Daniel Gerould and Marvin Carlson, ed. Daniel Gerould, xi–xix. New York: Martin E. Segal Theater Center. First published 1843.
Noverre, Jean Georges. 1760. *Lettres sur la danse et les ballets*. Paris.
O'Leary, Alan. 2011. *Tragedia all'italiana: Italian Cinema and Italian Terrorisms 1970–2010*. Oxford: Peter Lang.
O'Rawe, Catherine. 2014. " 'Boys Don't Cry:' Weeping Fathers, Absent Mothers and Male Melodrama." In *Stars and Masculinities in Contemporary Italian Cinema*, chapter 3: 69–93. Basingstoke, UK.: Palgrave MacMillan.
O'Sullivan, Sean. 2010. "Broken on Purpose: Poetry, Serial Television, and the Season." *Storyworlds: A Journal of Narrative Studies* 2: 59–77.
———. 2006. "Old, New, Borrowed, Blue: *Deadwood* and Serial Fiction." In *Reading Deadwood: A Western to Swear By*, ed. David Lavery, 115–29. London: I. B. Tauris.
Palsetia, Jesse S. 2001. *The Parsis of India: Preservation of Identity in Bombay City*. Leiden, Netherlands: Brill.
Park, Robert. 1925. "The Natural History of the Newspaper." In *The City*, ed. Robert Park, Ernest Burgess, and Roderick McKenzie, 80–98. Chicago: University of Chicago Press.
Parsons, Louella. 1920. "In and Out of Focus: Josephine Quirk; She Is Following Horace Greeley's Advice and Going West." Unsourced. November 21. In Parsons Scrapbook no. 4. Margaret Herrick Library, Academy of Motion Picture Arts and Sciences, Beverley Hills, Calif.
" 'Passion' Sets Record." 1921. *Exhibitors Herald*, July 23: 56.
Patriarca, Silvana. 2010. *Italian Vices: Nation and Character from the Risorgimento to the Republic*. Cambridge: Cambridge University Press.
Patten, Robert L. 1978. *Charles Dickens and His Publishers*. Berkeley: University of California Press.

Payne, David. 2005. *The Re-enchantment of Nineteenth-Century Fiction: Dickens, Thackeray, George Eliot and Serialization*. New York: Palgrave Macmillan.

Pearson, Roberta S. 1992. *Eloquent Gestures: The Transformation of Performance Style in the Griffith Biograph Films*. Berkeley: University of California Press.

Pedwell, Carolyn, and Anne Whitehead. 2012. "Affecting Feminism: Questions of Feeling in Feminist Theory." *Feminist Theory* 13, no. 2: 115–29.

Peiss, Kathy. 2011. *Zoot Suit*. Philadelphia, Pa.: University of Pennsylvania Press.

Petro, Patrice. 1989. *Women and Melodramatic Representation in Weimar Germany*. Princeton: Princeton University Press.

Pickford Core Clippings. n.d. "Tess." *Moving Picture World*. Margaret Herrick Library, Academy of Motion Picture Arts and Sciences, Beverley Hills, Calif.

Pickford Oral History Transcript. Butler Library: Columbia University, New York City.

Pickford, Mary. 1954. *Sunshine and Shadow*. Garden City, N.Y.: Doubleday.

Pisani, Michael V. 2014. *Music for the Melodramatic Theatre in Nineteenth-Century London and New York*. Iowa City: University of Iowa Press.

Pixérécourt, René-Charles Guilbert de. 2002. "Final Reflections on Melodrama." In *Pixérécourt: Four Melodramas*, trans. Daniel Gerould and Marvin Carlson, ed. Daniel Gerould, 315–18. New York: Martin E. Segal Theater Center. First published 1843.

———. 2002. *Pixérécourt: Four Melodramas*, trans. Daniel Gerould and Marvin Carlson, ed. Daniel Gerould. New York: Martin E. Segal Theatre Center.

Postlewait, Thomas. 1996. "From Melodrama to Realism: The Suspect History of American Drama." In *Melodrama, the Cultural Emergence of a Genre*, ed. Michael Hays and Anastasia Nikolopoulou, 39–60. New York: St Martin's Press.

Poulton, M. Cody. 2001. *Spirits of Another Sort: The Plays of Izumi Kyōka*. Ann Arbor: University of Michigan, Center for Japanese Studies.

Pribram, E. Deidre 2012. "Circulating Emotion: Race, Gender and Genre in *Crash*." In *Gender Meets Genre in Postwar Cinemas*, ed. Christine Gledhill, 41–53. Urbana: University of Illinois Press.

———. 2016. *A Cultural Approach to Emotional Disorders: Psychological and Aesthetic Interpretations*. New York: Routledge.

———. 2014. "Feeling Bad: Emotions and Narrativity in *Breaking Bad*." In *Breaking Bad: Critical Essays on the Contexts, Politics, Style, and Reception of the Television Series*, ed. David Pierson, 191–207. Lanham, Md.: Lexington/Rowman & Littlefield.

Probyn, Elspeth. 2004. "Everyday Shame." *Cultural Studies* 18, no. 2/3 (March/May): 328–49.

Qureshi, Regula Burckhart. 1986. *Sufi Music of India and Pakistan: Sound, Context and Meaning in Qawwali*. Cambridge: Cambridge University Press.

Rahill, Frank. 1967. *The World of Melodrama*. University Park: Pennsylvania State University Press.

Rangacharya, Adya. 1996. *The Natyashastra: English Translation with Critical Notes*. Delhi: Munshiram Manoharlal.

Rao, Vidya. 1990. " 'Thumri' as Feminine Voice." *Economic and Political Weekly* 25, no. 17 (April): WS31–WS39.

"Real Perils of Pauline." 1921. *Literary Digest*, December 4: 147–49.

Reber, Dierdra. 2010. "Love as Politics: *Amores Perros* and the Emotional Aesthetics of Neoliberalism." *Journal of Latin American Cultural Studies* 19, no. 3: 279–98.

"Review of The Petrified Forest." 1936. *Variety*, February 12.

Richards, Jeffrey. 2005. *Sir Henry Irving: A Victorian Actor and His World*. London: Hambledon and London.

Ricoeur, Paul. 1980. "Narrative Time." *Critical Inquiry* 7, no. 1 (Autumn): 169–90.

Riesebrodt, Martin. 2010. *The Promise of Salvation: A Theory of Religion*. Chicago: University of Chicago Press.

Rifbjerg, Klaus. 1964. "Om Neergaard om Dreyer." *Vindrosen, Gyldendals litterære Magasin* 11: 65–68.

Robinson, David. 1990. *Music of the Shadows: The Use of Musical Accompaniment with Silent Films, 1896–1936*. Pordenone, Italy: Le Giornate del Cinema Muto.

———. 1995. *Musique et cinéma muet*. Les Dossiers du Musée D'Orsay 56. Paris: Réunion des Musées Nationaux.

Rogers, Nigel. 2012. *The Dandy: Peacock or Enigma?* London: Bene Factum.

Rohdie, Sam. 1992. *Rocco and His Brothers*. London: BFI.

Roland Core Clippings. n.d. "Ruth Roland Rides Again." Unsourced. Margaret Herrick Library, Academy of Motion Picture Arts and Sciences, Beverley Hills, Calif.

Rosse, Michael David. 1995. "The Movement for the Revitalization of 'Hindu' Music in Northern India, 1860–1930: The Role of Associations and Institutions." PhD diss., University of Pennsylvania.

Rousseau, Jean-Jacques. 1791. *Essai sur l'origine des langues*. Paris.

Rowell, George. 1971. *Victorian Dramatic Criticism*. London: Methuen.

Russell, Catherine. 1993. "Insides and Outsides: Cross-Cultural Criticism and Japanese Film Melodrama." In *Melodrama and Asian Cinema*, ed. Wimal Dissanayake, 143–54. New York: Cambridge University Press.

Ryan, Mary. 1990. *Women in Public: Between Banners and Ballots, 1825–1880*. Baltimore, Md.: Johns Hopkins University Press.

Saitō, Ayako. 2011. "Shiraito, yomigaeru." In *Oudan suru eiga to bungaku*, ed. Toeda Yūichi, 41–94. Tokyo: Shinwasha.

Sampson, Henry. 1995. *Blacks in Black and White: A Source Book on Black Films*. Lanham, Md.: The Scarecrow Press.

Sanderson, Rena. 1998. "Gender and Modernity in Transnational Perspective." *Prospects* (January): 280–305.

Satō, Tadao. 1982. *Currents in Japanese Cinema*. Tokyo: Kodansha International.

Scaramazza, Paul, ed. 1974. *Ten Years in Paradise*. Arlington, Va.: Pleasant Press.

Schechner, Richard. 2001. "Rasaesthetics." *The Drama Review* 45, no. 3: 27–50.

Schneider, Dorothy, and Carl J. Schneider. 1994. *American Women in the Progressive Era, 1900–1920*. New York: Anchor.

Schraeder, Paul. 1996. "Notes on Film Noir." In *Movies and Mass Culture*, ed. John Belton, 153–70. New Brunswick, N.J.: Rutgers University Press.

Schwartz, Michael. 2009. *Broadway and Corporate Capitalism: The Rise of the Professional-Managerial Class, 1900–1920*. New York: Palgrave.

Sconce, Jeffrey. 2004. "What If? Charting Television's New Textual Boundaries." In *Television After TV: Essays on a Medium in Transition*, ed. Lynn Spigel and Jan Olsson, 93–112. Durham, N.C.: Duke University Press.

Scott, Ellen C. 2015. *Cinema Civil Rights: Regulation, Repression, and Race in Classical Hollywood Era*. New Brunswick, N.J.: Rutgers University Press.

Seki, Hajime. 1997. "*Konjiki yasha* no juyō to media mikkusu." In *Media, hyōshō, ideorogī: Meiji sanjūnendai no bunka kenkyū*, ed. Komori Yōichi, Kōno Kensuke, and Takahashi Osamu, 158–94. Tokyo: Ozawa Shoten.

Shackle, Christopher. 2007. "The shifting sands of love." In *Love in South Asia: A Cultural History*, ed. Francesca Orsini, 87–108. New Delhi: Cambridge University Press.

Shantaram, V. 1987. *Shantarama*. transcrib. and ed. Madhura Jasraj, trans. [Marathi into Hindi] Moreshwar Tapaswi. Delhi: Rajpal and Sons.

Sharma, Sunil. 2005. *Amir Khusraw: The Poet of Sultans and Sufis*. London: Oneworld.

Shastri, Gopal. 1995. *Parsi rangbhumi*. Vadodara, India: Sadhana Shastri.

Shaw, George Bernard. 1932. *Our Theatres in the Nineties*, 3 vols. London: Constable and Company.

Shepherd, Simon. 1994. "Pauses of Mutual Agitation." In *Melodrama: Stage, Picture, Screen*, ed. Jacky Bratton, Jim Cook, and Christine Gledhill, 25–37. London: BFI.

Shepherd, Simon, and Peter Womack. 1996. *English Drama: A Cultural History*. Oxford: Blackwell.

Sherwood, Robert Emmet. 1962. *The Petrified Forest*. New York: Dramatists Play Service. First published 1934.

Shingler, Martin, and Christine Gledhill. 2008. "Bette Davis: Actor/Star." *Screen* 49, no. 1: 67–76.

Shukla, Sonal. 1991. "Cultivating Minds: 19th century Gujarati Women's Journals." *Economic and Political Weekly* 26, no. 43: WS63-WS66.

Siddons, Henry. 1807. *Practical Illustrations of Rhetorical Gesture and Action, adapted to the English Drama from a work on this same subject by M. Engle, Member of the Royal Academy of Berlin, Embellished with numerous engravings, expressive of the various passions, and representing the modern costume of the London theatres*. London.

Sikov, Ed. 2007. *Dark Victory: The Life of Bette Davis*. New York: Henry Holt.

Singer, Ben. 2001. *Melodrama and Modernity: Early Sensational Cinema and Its Contexts*. New York: Columbia University Press.

Smith, Andrew B. 2003. *Shooting Cowboys and Indians*. Boulder: University of Colorado Press.

Sørensen, Peer E. 2009. *Vor Tids Temperament: Studier I Herman Bangs Forfatterskab*. Copenhagen: Gyldendal.

Southern, R. W. 1953. *The Making of the Middle Ages*. New Haven: Yale University Press.

St. Johns, Adela Rogers. 1969. *The Honeycomb*. Garden City, N.Y.: Doubleday.
Stamp, Shelley. 2000. *Movie Struck Girls*. Princeton: Princeton University Press.
Stanton, Stephen, ed. 1957. *Camille and Other Plays*. New York: Hill and Wang.
"A Star at Last." 1921. *Variety*, September 23: 9.
Stebbins, Genevieve, and Steele MacKaye. 1977. *Delsarte's System of Expression*. New York: Dance Horizons. First published 1885.
Stevenson, Jill. 2013. *Sensational Devotion: Evangelical Performance in Twenty-First-Century America*. Ann Arbor: University of Michigan Press.
Stowe, Harriet Beecher. 2005. *Uncle Tom's Cabin*. Mineola, New York: Dover Publications. Reprint edition. First published 1852.
Sturm, Hertha, and Marianne Grewe-Partsch. 1987. "Television—The Emotional Medium: Results from Three Studies." In *Emotional Effects of Media: The Work of Hertha Sturm*, ed. Gertrude J. Robinson, 25–36. Montreal, Canada: McGill University.
Stutesman, Drake. 2005. "Storytelling: Marlene Dietrich's Face and John-Frederics's Hats." In *Fashioning Film Stars: Dress Culture Identity*, ed. Rachel Mosley, 27–38. London: BFI.
Taj, Imtiaz Ali. 1969. *Urdu ka klasiki drama*, vol. 5, *Raunaq ke Drame. Hissa Avval*. Lahore: Majlis Taraqqi-i Adab.
Taussig, Michael. 1993. *Mimesis and Alterity: A Particular History of the Senses*. New York: Routledge.
Taylor, Charles. 2007. *A Secular Age*. Cambridge, Mass.: Harvard University Press.
———. 2002. "Modern Social Imaginaries." *Public Culture* 14 (Winter): 90.
Teo, Stephen. 2006. "Chinese Melodrama: The *Wenyi* Genre." In *Traditions in World Cinema*, ed. Linda Badley et al., 203–13. New Brunswick, N.J.: Rutgers University Press.
Thomas, Rosie. 2006. "Indian Cinema: Pleasures and Popularity." In *Asian Cinemas: A Reader and Guide*, ed. Dimitris Eleftheriotis and Gary Needham, 280–94. Honolulu: University of Hawai'i Press.
Thompson, Kristin. 1986. "The Concept of Cinematic Excess." In *Narrative, Apparatus, Ideology: A Film Theory Reader*, ed. Philip Rosen, 130–42. New York: Columbia University Press.
———. 1999. *Storytelling in the New Hollywood: Understanding Classical Narrative Technique*. Cambridge, Mass.: Harvard University Press.
Thompson, Kristin, and David Bordwell. 1994. *Film History: An Introduction*. New York: McGraw-Hill.
———. 1983. "Linearity, Materialism and the Study of Early American Cinema." *Wide Angle* 3: 4–15.
Thompson, Warren S. 1955. *Growth and Changes in California's Population*. Los Angeles: Haynes Foundation.
Thomsen, Bodil Marie. 2006. "On the Transmigration of Images: Flesh, Spirit and Haptic Vision in Dreyer's *Jeanne d'Arc* and von Trier's Golden Heart Trilogy." In *Northern Constellations*, ed. C. Claire Thomson, 43–57. Norwich, UK.: Norvik Press.

Thorburn, David. 1976. "Television Melodrama." In *Television as a Cultural Force*, ed. Richard Adler and Douglass Cater, 77–94. New York: Praeger.

Thorsen, Christian Isak. 2009. *Isbjørnens Anatomi: Nordisk Films Kompani Som Erhvervsvirksomhed I Perioden 1906–1928*. København: Det Humanistisk Fakultet, Københavns Universitet.

Tibbetts, John C. 2001. "Mary Pickford and the American 'Growing Girl.'" *Journal of Popular Film and Television* 29, no. 2: 50–62.

"Time to Clean Up the Movies." 1921. *Literary Digest*, October 15: 28–29.

The Times of India. 1861–1904. Bombay. Accessed through ProQuest Historical Newspapers Database.

Tomodjoglou, Kim. 2013. "Elvira Notari." In *Women Film Pioneers Project*, ed. Jane M. Gaines, Radha Vatsal, and Monica Dall'Asta. New York: Center for Digital Research and Scholarship, Columbia University Libraries. http://wfpp.cdrs.columbia.edu. Last accessed May 1, 2017.

Tompkins, Jane. 1985. *Sensational Designs: The Cultural Work of American Fiction 1790–1860*. New York: Oxford University Press.

Tribe, Keith. 2004. "Translator's Introduction." In Reinhart Koselleck, *Futures Past: On the Semantics of Historical Time*, vi–xx. New York: Columbia University Press.

Tsivian, Yuri. 1989. "Some Preparatory Remarks on Russian Cinema." In *Silent Witnesses: Russian Films 1908–1919*, ed. Paolo Cherchi Usai et al., 24–40. London: BFI.

Ungern-Sternberg, Christoph von. 2005. "Willy Haas, A German-Jewish Scriptwriter Exiled in India." *Osian's Cinemaya* 651 (April-June): 42–45.

Vardac, Nicholas A. 1949. *Stage to Screen: Theatrical Method from Garrick to Griffith*. Cambridge, Mass.: Harvard University Press.

Vasudevan, Ravi. 2010. *The Melodramatic Public: Film Form and Spectatorship in Indian Cinema*. Ranikhet, India: Permanent Black.

Vicinus, Martha. 1989. "Helpless and Unfriended." In *When They Weren't Doing Shakespeare*, ed. Judith L. Fisher and Stephen Watt, 174–86. Athens: University of Georgia Press.

Walker, Alexander. 1995. *Bette Davis*. London: Claremont Books.

Walker, Juliet E. K. 2009. *The History of Black Business in America: Capitalism, Race, Entrepreneurship*, vol. 1, *To 1865*. Chapel Hill: University of North Carolina.

Walker, Michael. 1982. "Melodrama and the American Cinema." *Movie* 29/30: 2–38.

Wallen, Denise A. 1998. "Such a Romeo as We Had Never Ventured to Hope For." In *Passing Performances*, ed. Robert A. Schanke and Kim Marra, 41–62. Ann Arbor: University of Michigan Press.

Welter, Barbara. 1966. "The Cult of True Womanhood, 1820–1860." *American Quarterly* 2: 151–74.

Weltmann, Manuel. 1969. *Pearl White: The Peerless Fearless Girl*. South Brunswick, UK.: A. S. Barnes.

White, Pearl. 1919. *Just Me*. New York: Georg H. Doran.

White, Shane, and Graham White. 1999. *Stylin': African American Expressive Culture from Its Beginnings to the Zoot Suit*. Ithaca: Cornell University Press.

Whitfield, Eileen. 1997. *Pickford*. Lexington: University of Kentucky Press.

Williams, Carolyn. 2012. "Melodrama." In *The Cambridge History of Victorian Literature*, ed. Kate Flint, 193–219. Cambridge: Cambridge University Press.

Williams, Linda. 1991. "Film Bodies: Gender, Genre and Excess." *Film Quarterly* 44, no. 4 (Summer): 2–13.

——. 2012. "Mega-Melodrama! Vertical and Horizontal Suspensions of the 'Classical.'" *Modern Drama* 55, no. 4 (Winter): 523–43.

——. 1998. "Melodrama Revised." In *Refiguring American Film Genres: History and Theory*, ed. Nick Browne, 42–88. Berkeley: University of California Press.

——. 2009. "Melodrama Revised." In *Emotions: A Cultural Studies Reader*, ed. Jennifer Harding and E. Deidre Pribram, 336–50. London: Routledge.

——. 2014. *On The Wire*. Durham, N.C.: Duke University Press.

——. 2001. *Playing the Race Card: Melodramas of Black and White from Uncle Tom to O. J. Simpson*. Princeton: Princeton University Press.

Williams, Raymond. 1988. *Keywords: A Vocabulary of Culture and Society*. London: Fontana. First published 1976.

——. 1973. *The Long Revolution*. Harmondsworth: Pelican. First published 1961.

——. 1966. *Modern Tragedy*. London: Chatto and Windus.

——. 1997. *Problems in Materialism and Culture*. London: Verso. First published 1980.

Winship, Mary. 1921. "Oh, Hollywood! A Ramble in Bohemia." *Photoplay* (May): 7, 109–11.

Winter, Marion Hannah. 1975. *The Pre-Romantic Ballet*. London: Dance Horizons.

Winter, William. 1906. "Great Actresses and Great Women: Charlotte Cushman." *Saturday Evening Post* (September 29). Robinson Locke Collection, Billy Rose Theatre Division, New York Public Library of the Performing Arts, New York City, vol. 131: 151.

Wordsworth, William. 1905. "On The French Revolution, As It Appeared To Enthusiasts At Its Commencement." In *The Complete Poetical Works*, 234. London: Macmillan. First published 1805.

Wu, Jian, ed. 1997. *Chinese Popular Songs in the 1930s and 1940s* [Jie Yu Hua: Zhongguo Sansishi Niandai Liuxing Gequ]. Beijing: North Literature and Art Press.

Yajnik, R. K. 1934. *The Indian Theatre*. New York: E. P. Dutton.

Yeh, Emilie Yueh-yu. 2009. "Pitfalls of Cross-Cultural Analysis: Chinese *Wenyi* Film and Melodrama." *Asian Journal of Communication* 19, no. 4 (December): 438–52.

——. 2013. "A Small History of Wenyi." In *The Oxford Handbook of Chinese Cinemas*, ed. Carlos Rojas and Eileen Cheng-Yin Chow, 225–49. Oxford: Oxford University Press.

——. 2012. "*Wenyi* and the Branding of Early Chinese Film." *Journal of Chinese Cinemas* 6, no. 1: 65–94.

Yomota, Inuhiko. 2001. "*Kyōka, shinpa, nihon eiga*." In *Izumi Kyōka*, ed. Tsubouchi Yūzō, 400–409. Tokyo: Chikuma shobō.

Yoshimoto, Mitsuhiro. 1993. "Melodrama, Postmodernism, and Japanese Cinema." In *Melodrama and Asian Cinema*, ed. Wimal Dissanayake, 101–26. New York: Cambridge University Press.

———. 2006. "National/International/Transnational: The Concept of Trans-Asian Cinema and the Cultural Politics of Film Criticism." In *Theorizing National Cinema*, ed. Valentina Vitali and Paul Willemen, 254–61. London: BFI.

Young, Karl. 1933. *The Drama of the Medieval Church*, vol. 2. Oxford: Clarendon Press.

Zhang, Zhen. 1998. "An Amorous History of the Silver Screen: Film Culture, Urban Modernity, and Vernacular Experience in China, 1896–1937." PhD diss., University of Chicago.

———. 2005. *An Amorous History of the Silver Screen: Shanghai Cinema, 1896–1937*. Chicago: University of Chicago Press.

———. 2010. "Ling Bo: Orphanhood and Postwar Sinophone Film History." In *Chinese Film Stars*, ed. Yingjing Zhang and Mary Farquhar, 121–38. New York: Routledge.

———. 2012. "Melodrama as Global Vernacular: *Daybreak* and Beyond." Paper given at Symposium in Memory of Miriam Hansen. Columbia University.

———. 2013. " 'Orphan Island' Revisited: Notes on Star-Crossed Love, Disfigured Face and the Periodization of Wartime Shanghai/Chinese Film History." Paper given at Chinese-Language Cinema during World War II conference, Taiwan National University of Arts, November 29–30.

———. 2012. "Transplanting Melodrama: Observations on the Emergence of Early Chinese Narrative Film." In *A Companion to Chinese Cinema*, ed. Yingjin Zhang, 25–41. Malden, Mass.: Wiley-Blackwell.

Zheng, Junli 1936. "Xiandai Zhongguo dianying shilue" [A Concise History of Modern Chinese Film]. In *Zhonghuo jindai yishu fazhanshi* [A History of the Development of Art in Modern China], ed. Li Puyuan et al., 1–132. Shanghai: Liangyou.

Zheng, Peiwei, and Guiqing Lui. 1996. *Zhonguo wusheng dianying juben* [Chinese silent film scripts], vol. 2. Beijing: Zhongguo dianying chubanshe.

Zhong, Dafeng, Yingjin Zhang, and Zhen Zhang. 1997. "From *Wenmingxi* [Civilized Play] to *Yingxi* [Shadow Play]: The Foundation of Shanghai Film Industry in the 1920s." *Asian Cinema* 9, no. 1 (Fall): 46–64.

Zhou, Jianyuan. 1923. "Daoyan" [Introduction]. *Chengxin* [The Morning Star] 3, special issue on *Guer jiuzuji*, 3–4.

Zwicker, Jonathan E. 2006. *Practices of the Sentimental Imagination: Melodrama, the Novel, and the Social Imaginary in Nineteenth-Century Japan*. Cambridge, Mass.: Harvard University Press.

Contributor Biographies

RICHARD ALLEN is dean of the School of Creative Media, City University Hong Kong. He is author of *Projecting Illusion* (1995) and *Hitchcock's Romantic Irony* (2007), co-author of *Islamicate Cultures of Bombay Cinema* (2009), and co-editor of numerous books on the philosophy of film and the films of Hitchcock, including *The Hitchcock Annual*. He is currently completing *Bollywood Poetics*.

HANNAH AIRRIESS is a PhD candidate in the Department of Film and Media at UC Berkeley. Her dissertation focuses on the figure of the "salaryman" in postwar Japanese studio film, specifically examining the way workplace cinema tracks shifting notions of the individual's relationship to political economy and new categories of labor in the era of high economic growth (1955–1972). Her other research interests include East Asian transnational cinemas and global melodrama.

LOUIS BAYMAN is lecturer of film studies at the University of Southampton. His research specialisms include popular cinema, Italian studies, and melodrama, and he has a range of publications on these topics, including *The Operatic and the Everyday in Postwar Italian Film Melodrama* (Edinburgh University Press, 2014.

IRA BHASKAR is professor of cinema studies at the School of Arts and Aesthetics, Jawaharlal Nehru University, New Delhi. Her publications include work on historical poetics, melodramatic forms and histories, and trauma and memory studies. She has co-authored *Islamicate Cultures of Bombay Cinema* and is currently editing a volume of Ritwik Ghatak's screenplays—*Ghatak's Partition Quartet*. She is also working on her book on "Trauma, Memory and Representation in Indian Cinema."

MATTHEW BUCKLEY is associate professor of English at Rutgers University. His publications include *Tragedy Walks the Streets: The French Revolution in the Making of Modern Drama* (2006), and articles in *Modern Drama, Theatre Journal, Victorian Studies, Studies in Romanticism* and elsewhere. In 2012, he edited a special issue of *Modern Drama* (55:4) devoted to recent scholarship on stage, film, and television melodrama; in 2014, he founded the Melodrama Research Consortium, which aims to advance collaborative, interdisciplinary research on melodrama's global history. His current project, *Becoming Melodramatic*, explores melodrama's origins and their implications for our understanding of narrative culture in modernity.

HELEN DAY-MAYER, a theatre historian, studies the nineteenth-century stage, its performers, repertoire and effects, and their numerous confluences with early motion pictures. She formerly taught drama at the Universities of London and Manchester. She is co-founder of The Victorian and Edwardian Stage on Film Project at the University of Manchester.

AMANDA DOXTATER is assistant professor of Scandinavian studies at the University of Washington. Her contribution is part of a current monograph project examining the intersections of film melodrama and Scandinavian art-house cinema in the work of Carl Th. Dreyer. She has published on Henrik Ibsen's staging of the falling body in *The Master Builder*, on representations of ethnicity and globalization in recent Swedish cinema, and on the figuration of precarious childhood in Ruben Östlund's 2011 film, *Play*.

JANE GAINES is professor of film, Columbia University, and the author of two award-winning books, *Contested Culture: The Image, the Voice, and the Law*, and *Fire and Desire: Mixed Race Movies in the Silent Era*. For research on the forthcoming *Pink-Slipped: What Happened to Women in the Silent Film Industries?* she received an Academy of Motion Picture Arts and Sciences scholars grant. She continues to write on the history of intellectual property (with implications for contemporary piracies), documentary theory, costume and body, and, most recently, has taken up a critique of the "historical turn" in the field. In 2013, Columbia University Libraries published the international collaborative online Women Film Pioneers Project: wfpp.cdrs.columbia.edu, which she initiated.

CHRISTINE GLEDHILL was professor of cinema studies at Staffordshire University and more recently visiting professor at University of Sunderland and New York University. She has written and edited work on feminist film criticism, melodrama, British cinema, genre, film acting and stardom, including edited collections, *Home is Where the Heart Is: Essays on Melodrama and the Woman's Film* (1987) and *Gender Meets Genre* (2012), and the monograph, *Reframing British Cinema, 1918–1928: Between Restraint and Passion* (2003). With Julia Knight at University of Sunderland she established the Women's Film and Television History Network, co-organized the first *Doing Women's Film History* conference (2011) and co-edited *Doing Women's Film History: Reframing Cinemas Past and Present* (2015).

HILARY A. HALLETT is an associate professor of history at Columbia University where she teaches modern American culture and politics with a focus on gender, film and popular culture in transatlantic perspective. Her first book was *Go West, Young Women! The Rise of Early Hollywood* (2013). In 2016, she edited a special issue, "The History of Celebrity," in *Feminist Media Histories*. In 2016–2017, she was a fellow at the New York Public Library's Cullman Center for Scholars and Writers, to work on her current project, *The Siren Within: Elinor Glyn and the Invention of Glamour*, (forthcoming, 2018).

KATHRYN HANSEN is a cultural historian with special expertise in Indian theatre. Her recent book, *Stages of Life: Indian Theatre Autobiographies*, presents the life stories of four artists in the Parsi theatre. It is centrally concerned with first-person narratives as a form of cultural memory. *Grounds for Play: The Nautanki Theatre of North India*, her first monograph, won the A.K. Coomaraswamy Book Prize. She is Professor Emerita of Asian Studies at the University of Texas at Austin, where she served as Director of the Center for Asian Studies and Interim Director of the South Asia Institute. Among her interests are gender and performance, folklore and orality, and early cinema in South Asia.

DESPINA KAKOUDAKI is associate professor of Literature at American University, where she teaches courses in film, literature, and the history of science and technology. She is the author of *Anatomy of a Robot: Literature, Cinema, and the Cultural Work of Artificial People* (2014), and coeditor of *All About Almodóvar: A Passion for Cinema* with Brad Epps (2009). She has published articles on robots and cyborgs, affective computing, race and melodrama in action and disaster films, and the military role of the pin-up in WWII. She is currently working on a new book on melodrama in contemporary cinema.

DAVID MAYER, emeritus professor of Drama and research professor, University of Manchester, UK, studies British and American popular entertainment of the 19th and early 20th century. Recent writings explore links between the Victorian stage and early motion pictures. He is co-founder of "The Victorian and Edwardian Stage on Film Project", a contributing member to the [D.W.] "Griffith Project (Le Giornate del Cinema Muto)". His books include *Harlequin in his Element: English Pantomime, 1806–1836* (1968), *Henry Irving and "The Bell"* (1984), *Playing Out the Empire: Ben-Hur and other Toga-Plays and Films* (1994), *Stagestruck Filmmaker: D.W. Griffith and the American Theatre* (2009), and *Bandits! or, The Collapsing Bridge: an Early Film and a late-Victorian Stage* (2015). In 2012 he received the Distinguished Scholar Award from the American Society for Theatre Research. A Guggenheim Fellow, he has also received research fellowships from Yale and Harvard Universities, the Harry Ransom Humanities Research Center, the Leverhulme Trust, and the British Academy.

CARLOS MONSIVÁIS (1938–2010) was a Mexican cultural critic, writer, journalist and political activist. Considered one of the leading intellectuals of his time, he cast his ironic gaze on nearly every aspect of Mexican life, from politics and football to poetry and art. An insightful analyst of Mexican popular culture, and especially the cinema of the "golden age," he was a master of the essay/chronicle as is evident in books such as *Días de guardar* and *Aires de familia*.

E. DEIDRE PRIBRAM is the author of *A Cultural Approach to Emotional Disorders: Psychological and Aesthetic Interpretations* (2016) and *Emotions, Genre, Justice in Film and Television: Detecting Feeling* (2013). She writes on cultural emotion studies, media studies, gender, and popular culture. She is professor in the Communications Department of Molloy College, Long Island, New York.

MARTIN SHINGLER is senior lecturer in Radio and Film Studies at the University of Sunderland (UK). He is the author of *Star Studies: A Critical Guide* (2012) and the co-author of *On Air: Methods and Meanings of Radio*, with Cindy Wieringa (1998) and *Melodrama: Genre, Style & Sensibility*, with John Mercer (2004). Since 1995, he has published numerous essays on the work of Bette Davis. He is currently writing a book entitled *When Warners Brought Broadway to Hollywood, 1923–39* for Palgrave/Macmillan and is co-editing a series of books on film stars for BFI/Palgrave.

DRAKE STUTESMAN teaches at New York University and the Pratt Institute. She edits the peer-reviewed, cinema and media journal, *Framework*. Her work has been published by, among others, the British Film Institute, Museum of Modern Art (New York), Museum of Contemporary Art (Los Angeles), Koenig Books, and *Bookforum*. Recent work includes a book on the hat (Reaktion Books) and essays on silent cinema (*Silver Screen* series, Rutgers UP), Japanese film (*Fashion & Consumption*), methods for costume scholarship (*The Costume for Performance Anthology*, working title, Bloomsbury Press) and the 1960s (*Fashion, Film and the 1960s*, Indiana UP). She is writing a biography of costume designer, Clare West, and a monograph on milliner/couturier, Mr. John.

KATHLEEN M. VERNON is associate professor and chair of the Department of Hispanic Languages and Literature at Stony Brook University where she teaches courses on Spanish and Latin American cinema and culture. She has published widely on various aspects of Spanish-language cinema from the 1930s to the present, with special focus on melodrama, film music and sound, and women's cinema. She is currently completing a book entitled *Listening to Spanish Cinema*.

LINDA WILLIAMS is professor emerita in the Department of Film and Media, and the Department of Rhetoric, at the University of California, Berkeley. She teaches courses on surrealism, pornography, women's films, documentary, racial melodrama and serial television. Her most recent single-authored books are, *Playing the Race Card: Melodramas of Black and White from Uncle Tom to O.J. Simpson* (Princeton, 2001), *Screening Sex* (Duke, 2008) and *On The Wire* (Duke, 2014).

PANPAN YANG is a PhD student in the joint program in Cinema and Media Studies and East Asian Languages and Civilizations at the University of Chicago. She holds an MA in Cinema Studies from New York University. She is particularly interested in how animation reanimates film theory and has published articles on Chinese animation. Her other interests embrace global melodrama and early Chinese cinema.

ZHEN ZHANG is associate professor in Cinema Studies and History at New York University. Her scholarly publications include: *An Amorous History of the Silver Screen: Shanghai Cinema 1896–1937*, *The Urban Generation: Chinese Cinema and Society at the Turn of the 21st Century*, and the forthcoming co-edited volume, *DV-Made China: Digital Subjects and Social Transformations*. She is founder and co-organizer of Reel China Documentary Biennial since 2001, and founder and director of the Asian Film and Media Initiative since 2012.

Index

Page numbers in italics indicate figures.

A Little Friend (1925). *See* Zhang Shichuan
Abandoned One (1923). *See* Duyu, Dan
Abbas, K. A., 262
Achtung! Banditi! (1951, Carlo Lizzani), 277
acting: *abhinaya*, use of body, gestures and
  face to express emotion, 266; acting
  and nonacting, boundary between, 187,
  188; American acting theory, and "the
  natural," xviii, 146; authenticity, 192–93;
  Before Stanislavsky (James McTeague)
  145, 146; British traditions, 148; early
  stage and film, viewed now, 99–100, 108,
  113n2/6; Enlightenment theories, 104–5;
  gestural, 3, 107, 243, 266, 284; gestural,
  nineteenth century, xiii, 99, 104–5, 108,
  109, 110, 112, 113n6 (*see also* gesture);
  handbooks, and emotional expression,
  xxii, 6; melodramatic, 108–9, 111, 146,
  224; naturalism, new codes of, 7; physical
  (*see* Delsarte, François), 106–7, 112;
  restrained, for middle-class audiences, xvi;
  silent film, 100; styles and early cinema,
  7, 105; technique [in the West], 113n2;
  "think the thought," 146. *See also* cross-
  dressing; Davis, Bette, Day-Mayer, Helen
  and Mayer, David, chap. 6; emotion; *Fog
  Over Frisco*; Howard, Leslie; *The Petrified
  Forest*; Rousseau, Jean-Jacques; voice
—*Actor's Art, An* (1888), 106, 349 (*see* Garcia,
  Gustav); *Art of Acting, The* (1882), xxiii,
  344 (*see also* Boucicault, Dion); *Art of
  Pantomime, The* (1927, Aubert, Charles),
  107, 342; from early melodrama to silent
  film, 104–5; gesture in, xxiv, 104–5; *Home
  and School Speaker* (1897, anon.), 106,
  352; manuals, 112; melodramatic acting,
  mistaken conception, 6; and music,
  110–11; nineteenth century, xxiv, 105–8,
  109; *Practical Illustrations of Rhetorical
  Gesture and Action* (1807, Henry Siddons)
  105–6, 362. *See also* Delsarte, François;
  Fitzgerald, Percy; Neville, Henry
actor(s): actor-characters (*varieté
  melodrama*), 188, 191; Australian, 55;
  body/bodies of, 6, 105–6, 108, 113n4,
  146–47, 197, 291 (*see also* Priest in *Super
  Fly*); travelling to India, 49; demands on,
  xxiii (*see also* Boucicault), 6, 56–57, 104,
  312; and double (identity) roles, 103–4;
  melodramatic stage acting, demands of,
  104; gestural vocabulary, 110; passim;
  -managers: Boucicault, Dion, 50, Jahangir
  Khambata, 65, Madame Vestris and
  Charles Mathews, xvi; music and, 109–11,
  112; nature as, in disaster films, 312;
  nineteenth century, late, 102; silent film,
  100, 112; spectators and, 188, 191; tools,
  104, 112; on tour, 53, 101; visible, with
  electric stage lighting, 109; voice, 104,
  113n3 (William S. Hart), 113n7; in

actor(s) (*continued*)
  Western societies, 100. *See also* acting, manuals; costume; cross-dressing; gesture
  — as star, xvi, xix; Alla Nazimova, 130. Bruce Lee, 96; *See also*; Cushman, Charlotte, 116, 119; Rose Edouin, star calibre, 55; fictional roles and real lives, xxiii; K. M. Balivala and *Bholi Jan*, 57; Roscoe Arbuckle; socials, vehicles for female impersonators, 65; Western commodity culture in China, 223. *See also* acting; actor(s), female/male; Davis, Bette; Hollywood; Howard, Leslie; Sevilla, Ninon
actors, female: actor-manager, Vestris, Madame, xvi; (actor)-writer-producers (*see* Roland, Ruth and White, Pearl), 125; Balivala, K. M., and, 57; costumes, extreme, 307*n*4; Davenport, Fanny, 101; family system and, 54; and feminist theory, 165; "foreigners," 129; lionized, 120; Marguerite, role of, in *La Dame aux camellias*, 117–18; professional feats of, 116; in socials, 64; *Tess* and 123; turn-of-the nineteenth century, 5; western stars, 125; women in acting profession, 64–65. *See also* Bernhardt, Sarah; Cushman, Charlotte; Davis, Bette; Del Río, Dolores; Edouin, Rose; Falconetti, Marie; Fenton, Mary; Garcia, Sara; Holmes, Helen; Magnani, Anna; Mangano, Silvana; Nazimova, Alla; Pickford, Mary; Swanson, Gloria; White, Pearl; women
actors, male: Balivala, K. M., 57; costume and, 290–92; double (identity) role, Irving, Henry, 103–4; towering nineteenth-century, 290–92. *See also* Aldridge, Ira; Bogart, Humphrey; costume; Forrest, Edwin; Gassman, Vittorio; Howard, Leslie; *Petrified Forest, The*; Robinson, Edward G.; Travolta, John; Tree, Herbert Beerbohm; Valentino, Rudolph
actress(es) (see actors, female), 5, 57, 116, 117, 118, 120, 123, 125, 129, 165, 307*n*4
Adams, Nate, 308*n*12/13/14/16. *See also* costume; *Super Fly*
affect, *l'affect* (Gilles Deleuze and Guattari, Félix, 234); aesthetic perception and, 4; Chinese, 234; -defined mass culture, xvii; *dianran nuhuo* ("igniting the fire of indignation"), and emotion, 238–40, 241; excess as, 239; felt (Peter Brooks), xxii; *Feminist Theory*, special issue on feminism and affect, 238; melodrama studies and, 237
— affective: in image, the, 239; meme, as, 85, 93; sensational replacing, 241
— affective piety, 46; Christian, and American melodrama, 33; gender in, 34, 44. *See also* Allen, Richard; emotion; Pribram, E. Deidre
Airriess, Hannah: chap. 4 (69–82): English melodrama fiction and Meiji-era serials in turn-of-century Japan, 8; Japan's melodramatic imagination, 70–79; popular serialisation, 211. *See also Konjiki yasha*; *Taki no shiraito*; "vernacular modernism"
Aldridge, Ira, 290: costumes to be looked at, 294, 303; as Zanga in *The Revenge*, 290, 291, 292
All That Heaven Allows (1955). *See* Sirk, Douglas
Allen, Richard, chap. 2 (31–47), xxvii: "affective piety," 32–34, 35, 39, 44, 46, 47; art history, 3; Christianity of Pathos, the, 3, 34–38; European melodrama, new histories of, 7–8; Christ's Passion to melodrama, from, 39–43; Sacred, the traditional and selfhood, 3, 272*n*17, 281–82; women, emotion and empathy, 43–46. *See also* Bhaskar, Ira; Champagne, John; Monsiváis, Carlos; Italy; *Way Down East*
Almodóvar, Pedro: camp melodramas, 214; on unemployment in melodrama, 277
Althusser, Louis, xxi; critique of "continuous and homogenous time," 331, 339*n*5; time, absence/presence, 330, 331, 336; time and theorists of history, 329. *See also* Comolli, Jean-Louis; Thompson, Kristin and David Bordwell; historiography; time
Altman, Rick: the 1950s, 137; and the "classical," 217*n*3; early cinema shorts, wordless adaptations of stage melodramas, 208; and the elephant of melodrama, 212; genres, open to invention, 172; *melodrama/melodramatic*, concepts of problematized, 137 (*see also* Hughes, Elinor). *See also* woman's film, the

America. *See* acting; actors; blockbuster; *Contagion*; Cushman, Charlotte; emotion; girls; Griffith, D. W.; Hallett, Hilary A., chap. 7; Kakoudaki, Despina, chap. 18; Lubitsch, Ernst; *The Petrified Forest*; Pickford, Mary; serial(s) television; Shingler, Martin, chap. 8; Simpson, O. J.; Stutesman, Drake, chap. 17; *Super Fly*; *Uncle Tom's Cabin*; Valentino, Rudolph; White, Pearl; Williams, Linda, chap. 10; women

American Crime Story: The People vs O. J. Simpson (2017, FX, Ryan Murphy). *See* Simpson, O. J.

Amistad (1997, Steven Spielberg), 316. *See also* disaster film(s)

Amores Perros (2000, Alejandro G. Iñárritu), 320. *See also* disaster film(s)

Amrit Manthan (1934, V. Shantaram), 256–58, 257, 258, 271n4

Amrohi, Kamal, 264. *See also Mahal*

anagnorisis/recognition, xix

Anand, Chetan, use of expressionist aesthetics, 254–56, 262. *See also Neecha Nagar*

Anderson, Mark, 7

Anderson, Percy, 292, 308n9. *See also* costume; Tree, Herbert Beerbohm

Anna (1951, Alberto Lattuada), 275, 285, 286–87; box office success, 274; *chiaroscuro* lighting, 287; climax, 286. *See also* Mangano, Silvana

Antonioni, Michelangelo, 280. *See also Storia di Caterina*

Appassionatamente (1954). *See* Gentilomo, Giacomo

Arbuckle, Roscoe, 131–32. *See also* girls; women

Archer, William, 100

Aristarco, Guido, 284

art: Sarah Bernhardt and *art nouveau* (Victoria Duckett), 107; Christ's Passion in art, public, 40; historical artworks, 3 (*see also* Allen, Richard, chap. 2); illustrations, cartoons, in newspapers, 126, 132; melodrama as a form of, 9, 11 (*see also* Buckley, Matthew, chap. 1), 63, 207–8, 210; modern, 17–18; and popular culture, xviii, 11 (*see also* Doxtater, Amanda); the Renaissance, 36; Sinicizing, 88. *See also* Hansen, Miriam

Artaud, Antonin: actor (*La Passion de Jeanne d'Arc*), 185; modern era as different, the, 28; theater as plague, 28

artists: Australian on the 1867 Lewis tour to Calcutta, 53; nineteenth-century costume paintings, 290–92; print, 60; vocabulary of expressive gestures, developing 37, 44

'A Santanotte (1922, Elvira Notari), 334–36, 339n8

Assunta Spina (1913, Francesca Bertini, 335, and Gustavo Serena), 334, 336

asymmetry: temporal, 9 (*see also* time). *See also Hunduan Lanquiao*, 229–30

Aubert, Charles, 107. *See* acting, manuals

Aulisi, Joseph G., 305, 308n13, 309n27. *See also* costume; *Shaft*

Aurat (1913). *See* Khan, Mehboob

auteur, inapplicable to televisual serial poetics, 177; Dreyer, Carl, Th., as international, 1950, 189; use of genre to identify *auteurs*, 217

Avanti a lui tremava tutta Roma/*Before Him All Rome Trembled* (1946, Carmine Gallone), 276; *cineopera*, 284

Aventurera/*Adventuress* (1950). *See* Gout, Alberto

Babel (2000, Alejandro G. Iñárritu), 320. *See also* disaster film(s)

Bakhtin, Mikhail: conventions, shared xxiii; chance event in the present, 333; critique, the outsideness of xxv; the dialogic process xxiv; and the genericity of emotion xxiii–xxiv; meaning ix; theory of genre ix, historical time 331. *See also* Williams, Raymond

Balivala, K. M., 57; and actresses, 57; in *Bholi Jan*, 57; and Maurice Freyberger, 57; Victoria Theatrical Company, director, 57, 62

— and Kabraji, playhouse pioneers, 56–57, 59; and *The Colleen Bawn*, 57, 62; printed English scripts, 62

Balukhatyi, Sergei, 199

Balzac, Honoré de, 2, 205, 206 (*see also* Brooks, Peter); *Splendeurs et misères des courtisanes*, 188, 191 (*see also* Dreyer, Carl Th., "Esther")

bambini ci guardano, I/The Children Are Watching Us (1944) (*see* De Sica, Vittorio)
Bao Tianxiao, popular writer of Mandarin Ducks and Butterflies literature. *See East Lynne*
Barbero, Jesús Martín, 164–65, 167n6
Barthes, Roland, 325, 337
Bayman, Louis, chap. 16 (273–87): bases of a popular form, 273–76; beyond neorealism, 279–81; Catholic ethos, and neorealist films and popular melodramas, 4, 33; Italian postwar cinema and political crisis, 10; melodrama, neorealism and popular authenticity, 276–79; melodrama and the promise of salvation, 281–83. *See also Catene; Roma città aperta*
Beatrice Cenci (1956, Riccardo Freda), 276
Beaumarchais, Pierre-Augustin Caron de, 25
Before Him All Rome Trembled (*see Avanti a lui tremava tutta Roma*)
Belasco, David, 120, 145, Gerould, Daniel on, 140–41; and modern melodramas, 140, 146; naturalism or melodrama, xvi. *See also* Mary Pickford, 120–21, 125; sensational and immoral plays, 120–21 (*see also* Munsterberg, Hugo). *See also* acting; Pickford, Mary
— *Madame Butterfly* (1900), 121 (*see also Madame Butterfly*, 1932); *Du Barry* (1901), 121; *The Girl of the Golden West* (1905), 121. *See also* Gerould, Daniel; *A Good Little Devil* (1913), 125
Bella Donna (1912, Charles Frohman, James Bernard Fagan, playwright, from the 1909 novel by Robert Smith Hichens). *See* Nazimova, Alla
Bella Donna (1923, George Fitzmaurice, from the 1912 play), 129. *See also* Negri, Pola
beloved:
— in the Sufi tradition, 33, 47n1
— in the *Vaishnav bhakti* tradition of Krishna devotion, 33. *See also bhakti* (devotion), 268, 271n9; *Gopinath*, 262; *Pati Bhakti*, 65–66
— the Virgin Mary as Christ's in *Song of Songs*, 36
Beloved, the, the Divine Being in Sufism, 268, 269. *See also* Sufi; *Veer Zaara*

Beloved (1987, Toni Morrison), 333
Belting, Hans, 35–36. *See* Christ, *Passion of*
Benda, Georg Anton (1722–1795), 25
Benjamin, Walter, 28
Bentley, Eric, 20
Bergman, Ingrid: *Casablanca* 158; trilogy (1950–1954, Roberto Rossellini), 280
Berlant, Lauren, 332
Bernhardt, Sarah: costumes, extreme, 307n4; greatest international star of late nineteenth century, 117; "spiraling," 107. *See also Dame aux camellias, La*
Bertini, Francesca, 335. *See also Assunta Spina*
The Best of Youth. See also meglio gioventù, La
Betab, 65: *Qatl-e Nazir* (1901), 65; *Kasauti* (1903), adapted from *Dorangi Duniya* (*see* B. N. Kabra, 65); *Mahabharat*, Parsi theater, 66, melodramatic devices, 66; *Zahri Samp* (1933), 65–66. *See also* socials
Bevington, David, 43
Beyond the Rocks (1922, Sam Wood), 131
bhakti/devotion; Vaishnavism, 271n9. *See* beloved; *Pati Bhakti*; *Gopinath*; music; the Sacred
Bhargavi Neelayam (1964, A. Vincent), 265
Bhaskar, Ira, chap. 15 (253–72): 4, 8–9; affective piety, 46; aural aesthetics, 262–67. *See also* music; German expressionism and Indian cinemas, 253–61; Meera, female devotee, in Krishna devotion, 33. *See also* beloved; Sufi poetry and song, 4; the Sacred, 253, 270; selfhood, felt, 260. *See also Amrit Manthan; Kunku; Mahal; Neecha Nagar; Shejari*
Bhavnani, Mohan, 254; *Prem Nagar* (*City of Love*, 1941). *See* Haas, Willy
Bholi Gul (1892). *See* Kabra, B. N.
Bholi Jan athva Dhananum Dhan/Innocent Belle (1887. *See* K. M. Kabra and K. M. Balivala, adapted from *The Colleen Bawn*) 8, 49, 57–62, 63, 64, 354; *Bholi*, various spellings, 58. *See also* Balivala, K. M.; socials
Bianchi, Giorgio. *See La nemic/The Enemy*
Bicycle Thieves/Ladri di biciclette (1948). *See* De Sica, Vittorio

Birth of a Nation (1915, D. W. Griffith), 92, 97n9, 181, 215

Bishop's Carriage, The (1913). *See* Pickford, Mary

Bitter Rice/Riso Amaro (1949). *See* De Santis, Giuseppe

Blair Parker, Lottie: 'Way Down East, 1899, playwright, 99, 110, 111, 343. *See also* 'Way Down East

Blasco Ibañez, Vicente, author, *Four Horsemen of the Apocalypse* (1916)

A Blind Orphan Girl (1925). *See* Zhang Shichuan

blockbuster: action film, the contemporary, in the mold of blood and thunder melodramas, 215–16; *Gone with the Wind* as a "*wenyi* blockbuster," 223, 233; Hollywood pictures in 1930s Shanghai,"never-seen-before," 225–26

body, the 303–7 (*see also* Stutesman, Drake): in acting, 6, 105–6, 113n4 (*see also* Day-Mayer, Helen and David Mayer, chap. 6), 197, 199; *any*, in the place of victim or oppressor/perpetrator, xxii, 5; black male, in *Super Fly*, 294, 296, 297, 303 (*see also* Stutesman, Drake); in *Contagion*, 321; and costume, 292–93, 309n25 in *Feminist* Theory, special issue on feminism and affect, 238–39 (*see also* Gibbs, Anna); gendered, 44; gesture carried away from, 100, 107; in *La Passion de Jeanne d'Arc*, 185, 187, 188, 195, 196, 197, 199, 200n1; in *Lydia*, 200n2; Marie Falconetti as Jeanne, 194–95; and mind, 16, 105 (*see* Rousseau, Jean-Jacques), 112; in *The Petrified Forest*, 146–47; rhythms of and camera movement, xxiv; sensate, material, 242; suffering, 34, 36; and voice, 264, 265; *abhinaya* 266 (*see also* Bhaskar, Ira)

— bodily: action, the costume and, 304; in contact (*see* music, *danzón*); functions, 214; levels, 107 (*see also* Henry Neville); movement xvi, xvii, 106 (*see* Delsarte, François); nonverbal communication, 240 (*see* Massumi, Brian. *See also* Fitzgerald, Percy); sensation, 238; skills, 112; stance, 100; thrills, xv; ways, affect in, 239

— China (*see* Yang, Panpan): bodily excess, 225–27, 235; bodily trauma, 220; *dianran nuhuo* ("igniting the fire of indignation"), and the spectator's body, 234 (*see also l'affect*); *Hunduan* ("one's soul is disconnected from the body"), 229

— Christ as human, 3; of Christ, 35, 36; idealised in the Italian tradition, 36; in the "Pietà," 36–37

— Italy (*see* Bayman, Louis): affective elements grounded in the body, 275; the body in melodrama *mancato*, 280 (*see also* films of Michelangelo Antonioni); bodily expressivity, 275; excess located in the body, 287 (*see also* Anna)

— Japan: of scholarship, 86; works, *wenyi* and melodrama, 90, 92

Boehnel, William, theater critic, 144–45, 149. *See also The Petrified Forest*

Bogart, Humphrey, 149, 150n8; Alexander Walker on, 148; in *Casablanca*, 158; in *Petrified Forest, The*, 139, 142, 150n8

Bombay Talkies, 254, 264

Booth, Edwin, 101

Bordwell, David, the "modernity thesis," against, 217n6; new norms, variants of the old, 217n2; tableau aesthetic, Nordisk's, 201n14

— *La Passion de Jeanne d'Arc*: cinematic performance space and, 191; corporeality trumped by psychology, incommensurate with melodrama, 201n21

— Staiger, Janet, and Kristin Thompson, *The Classical Hollywood Cinema: Film Style and Mode of Production to 1960*, 9, 208–9, 225, 226; "classic," use by others of, 217n5; "classical" (Bordwell), xix, 208, 210–11, 212; on Frank Borzage's "old melodramatic situations . . . with true characterizations" (Bordwell), 213; genres (Bordwell), 217n7; the "modernity thesis" (Bordwell), 212

realism, melodrama as lack of, 213; recalcitrant genre, melodrama as, 212

— and Kristin Thompson, 47n5; (Bordwell) causes, character motivation and narrative logic, xxi, xxii; classical American cinema endures, 208, 217n2. *See also* Thompson, Kristin and David Bordwell

Borzage, Frank, on melodrama (1922), 213; *Seventh Heaven* (1927), 332

Boucicault, Dion, 50, 51, 106; acting school, NY, 106 (*see also*); *Art of Acting* (1926), xxiii, 344; language and, 62; Maurice Freyberger and, 54; melodramas of, 49, 54; military-themed fare, 56; *Octoroon*, 53, 55; plays, 56, 212 (data on *The Colleen Bawn*, 67); plays starring Rose Edouin, 53. See also acting: manuals; *Bholi Jan*; *Colleen Bawn, The*; Kabra, K. N.; Lewes, George B. W.

boundaries between: excess and restriction, 286; entertaining spectacle and ritual sacrifice, in *La Passion de Jeanne d'Arc*, 187; melodrama and realism, 11; melodrama scholarship and the desire for liberating narratives, 29; professional and the moral, the (in *Anna*), 287; performer and role, 191; Western thinking and other practices and traditions, 4

Boytler, Arcady. See *mujer del puerto, La*

Brame, Charlotte M., rewrite of *East Lynne* as *A Woman's Error*, 91

— pseudonym, Clay, Bertha M.: *Dora Thorne* (1880), the basis of *Chikyōdai* (Kikuchi Yūhō), 75; *Weaker Than a Woman* (1870/1890), similarities to *Konjiki yasha* (Ozaki Kōyō), 75, 76. See *East Lynne*; *Konjiki yasha*; Kikuchi Yūhō

Braudel, Ferdinand, 329, 330

Breaking Bad (AMC, 2008–2013), 180, 182, 246, 247–50, 251n4; Anna Gunn editorial, 250; and complexity, 179; gendered marital relations, 247–48; quality works, 177, serial shows, 245. *See also* Buckley, Matthew

Brignone, Guido: *Core 'ngrato/Ungrateful Heart* (1951), 274; *Noi peccatori/We Sinners* (1953), 282

Broken Blossoms (1919, D. W. Griffith), 92, 97n9, 154

Brooks, Peter, xxvii, 11, *Les Mystères de Paris*, readership for, 170, 309n25; gesture, a "sign for a sign," 302

— *The Melodramatic Imagination: Balzac, Henry James, Melodrama, and the Mode of Excess* (1976): xxiii; 2–4; affect, felt, xxii; an age of mass culture, 206; "central poetry" of the nineteenth-century world, melodrama as, 16; characters' personalised virtues and vices, recognition of, 5; the "classical," melodrama's challenge to, 207; dramatic excitement of significance itself, xxii; emotion, plastic figurability of, 147, 150n10; excess, inherent feature of stage melodrama's "text of muteness," 6, 212, 214, 286; familiar dramaturgical motifs, 4; "fundamentally expressionist drama," melodrama as, 254, 264, 312; individual energy and socio-economic forces that power modernity, xxi; "the ineffable," 233, 286; "interesting"/"exciting," tension between, xiv; melodrama, a flexible *mode* of aesthetic perception and affect, 4; melodrama as a genre [hitherto], 206; melodrama as "peculiarly modern form," 69, 205; "melodramatic imagination," 86; "moral occult," 31, 32, 47, 72, 205–6, 219, 226, 253; origin of melodrama, the French Revolution and aftermath, and the final liquidation of the traditional Sacred, 3, 19, 20, 23, 25–26, 31–32, 46–47, 83, 115, 215, 227, 253, 281, 283, 326; sensation, supposedly gratuitous/critical search for meaning, tension between, xxii; space of innocence, melodrama's, 326, 330; theatrical melodrama, 20–21; what lies beyond, Brooks's main point, 287. *See also* Allen, Richard; Buckley, Matthew; Elsaesser, Thomas; Nodier, Charles; Yang, Panpan; Williams, Linda

Brummell, Beau, 300, 305, 308n18. *See also* costume, Black Dandy; *Super Fly*

Brunetta, Gian Piero, 284

Buckley, Matthew, chap. 1 (15–29): aesthetics of expressionism, 245; affect and emotion, 241; contradictory emotion, 249–50; melodrama's sources, historicisation of, 3; narratives, central role in modern; 206; Williams, Linda, on, 206

— melodrama: as affective meme, 85, 93; as "distillate form," 72, 75; as drama of morality, myth of, 3; European, histories of, 7; French, 240; as post-French Revolution, myth of, 3, 215; 242;

presumed moral substrate of, xxi; and the "traditional Sacred" (Peter Brooks), relationship to, 31. *See also* Pribram, E. Deidre, emotions and melodrama past

Buñuel, Luis on tears in *La Passion de Jeanne d'arc*, 195

Burns, Scott Z. *See Contagion*

Bustillo Oro, Juan, 157; *Cuando los hijos se van*/When the children leave home, 1941, 156–57; Sara Garcia in, and on, 157

Byron, Joseph, 1899 photographs, *'Way Down East*

Caccia tragica/*Tragic Pursuit* (1947). *See* De Santis, Giuseppe

Cai Chusheng. *See Spring River Flows East, The*

Cai Guorong, screenplay writer: *wenyi* having two strands, 88

Camille (1853, 1921). *See La Dame aux camélias*

Camerino, Mario. *See Due lettere anonime*/ *Two Anonymous Letters* (1945)

Cameron, Kate, 144, 145, 149

Cammino della speranza, La/*The Path of Hope* (1950). *See* Germi, Pietrotti

Canby, Vincent, 290

Canetti, Elias, 164

Caprice (1913). *See* Pickford, Mary

Capuano, Luigi. *See verismo*

Carol (2015, Todd Haynes), 311

Casablanca (1942, Michael Curtiz), 158. *See also* Bergman, Ingrid; Bogart, Humphrey

Casa Ricordi (1954, Carmine Gallone): costume drama, 274; and opera, 284. *See also* Italian melodrama

Castle of Otranto, The (1764, Horace Walpole), xi

Castle Spectre: A Dramatic Romance, The (1797), xii. *See also* Lewis, "Monk"

Catene/*Chains* (1949. *See* Raffaello Matarazzo; title from a *fotoromanzo* story; story adapted from a *sceneggiata*, "Lacreme napulitane"/Neapolitan Tears), 273–75; border between excess and restriction, 276, 286; box office record, 274. *See also* Lombardo, Gustavo; melodrama, unbinding; Visconti, Luchino, *Senso*

Chabon, Michael, 303, 309n25

Chains. *See Catene* (1949); Matarazzo, Raffaello

Champagne, John, 273, 287n1, 282

Chaplin, Charles/Charlie, 129, 345; considered "classical" by Renoir, 217n5; on Pickford, Mary, 121

Charles II, King, 291, 292, 308n10

Chekhov, Anton, xvi

Chen Yunshang, 227, in Huacheng Company's *Gone with the Wind*, 228, 232

Chi è senza peccato …/*Who Is Without Sin?* (1953). *See* Matarazzo, Raffaello

Chikyōdai. *See* Yūhō, Kikuchi

Child of Love (1780). *See* Kotzebue, August von. *See also* Inchbald, Elizabeth

The Children Are Watching Us. *See bambini ci guardano*

China. *See* body, the; *Gone with the Wind*; *Hundian Lanqiao*; language; Lewis, George B. W.; music; *Orphan Rescues Grandfather*; sacred/Sacred, the; *The Spring River Flows East*; *Waterloo Bridge*; Yang, Panpan, chap. 13; Zhang, Zhen, chap. 5

Christ, 32; body of, 3, 34, 35, 36, 44; as both man and God, 35, 39; Christ-God, 3, 35; *Christ on the Road to Calvary* (1599–1600, Tabacchetti and Giovanni d'Enrico) 42; *Crucification* (1528, Peter Dell the Elder), 41, 41; death of 34, 43, 44; and the Devil, 35, 41, 42, 43; divinity of, 39, 40; *Entombment* (1465–1470, Andrea Mantegna) 37, 38; female devotion to, 44; incarnation of, 33, 35; *Meditations on the Life of Christ* (c.1300, John of Caulibus), 35, 40; melodrama and, 31–34, 39–43, 44, 45–47; nun's marriage to, a, 44; suffering of, 32, 34, 35, 36, 37, 39, 41, 44; *The Wakefield Buffeting, The* (mid-fourteenth century), 43. *See also* lamentation; Lamentation; Allen, Richard, women, emotion, and empathy

— Passion of, xxii, 32 passim; melodrama and, 40–41, 43; *The Passion of the Christ* (2004, Mel Gibson), 47n2; representation and, 3, 32–33, 35–36, 39, 40–43. *See also* Allen, Richard; Christianity of Pathos

Chun Kim. *See Mother's Happiness*
Cielo sulla palude/Heaven Over the Marshes (1949. *See* Augusto Genina), 281; *Heaven over the Marshes*, 283
Cioran, Emil M., 154
città si difende, La/Four Ways Out (1951). *See* Germi, Pietro
Clay, Bertha M, pseudonym. *See* Brame, Charlotte M.
Coburg productions:
— *The Lear of Private Life; Or, Father and Daughter* (1820, adapted by William Moncrieff), adapted from *The Father and Daughter. See also* interest; sensation
— 1828 publicity posters, xiii: *The French Buccaneer; or, The Rock of Annaboa*; *St Valentine's Eve; or, The Fair Maid of Perth* (founded on the Walter Scott novel, *The Fair Maid of Perth*)
Coelina (1800). *See* Pixérécourt, René-Charles Guilbert de
Colleen Bawn, The (1860, Dion Boucicault, based on *The Collegians*, 1829, Gerald Griffin), 8, 50–52, 60, 61, 66, 344; *Bholi Jan* and, 58–62; class and gender in, 59; conventions of melodrama in, 52; (*see* Rose Edouin), 53, 54, 55; Dion Boucicault and Alice Robertson in, 50; Dion Boucicault operatic libretto for, 55; "—*Galup,*" 61; Gujurati version, Bombay, 1887, 49, 58; in India, 49, 52, 55–56; Kabra and Baliva and, 62–63; the Lewises (*see*), 55; in London and Dublin, 50; Maurice Freyberger, scene painter, 54; into Parsi theater, 57; pastoral vision, 58; Queen Victoria and, 50; sensation scene (Lundgren, Egron Sellif), 55; story outline, 50–52; *Times of India* on, 49, 55, 56. *See also Bholi Jan*; Hansen, Kathryn; Lewis, George B. H.; *Lily of Killarney, The*; Parsi theater
Collegians, The (1829, Gerald Griffin), 50
Coma (1978, Michael Crichton), xiv
Comencini, Luigi. *See tratta delle bianche, La/ The White Slave Trade*
Comolli, Jean-Luc, 331, 339n5
compadre Mendoza, El. See de Fuentes, Fernando

Conklin, Peggy, 142, 150n8; in *The Petrified Forest*, stage version, 142 (Bette Davis in the film version, 143)
Contagion (2011, Steven Soderbergh) 10, 317–24; and capitalism, 322; distribution and interruption of melodramatic elements, 320; editing style, 320; endings, 320–21; mini melodramas in, 319; narrative technique, 318; networked narrative style, 318, 320; scientific research, 317; and women's success and sexual freedom, 322. *See also* disaster film, the
Cooper, Patience, goddess of Indian silent cinema, 65, 66. *See also* Betab; *Pati Bhakti*; socials
Core 'ngrato/Ungrateful Heart (1951). *See* Brignone, Guido
Costa, Mario: *Perdonami!/Forgive Me!* (1953), 274; *Ti ho sempre amato!* (1953), 279
costume, xvii, xix, 10, 289–92; Agha Hashr socials, 66; 1970s African American clothes, 298–300; the "Black Dandy," 300–302; the body and, 196, 303–4; costume/ body relationships, 305; diaphoric, 302, 308n22; drama, 149n1, 274, 276; Eiko Ishioka, designer, on period costumes, 307n1; Eleganza, 298–99; epiphoric, 302, 308n22; as extra, 225; extreme, and female actors, 307n4; fetishism and, 163 (*see also* Monsaváis, Carlos, chap. 9); Jeffery Kurland, on his role as designer, 307n1; John Shaft (Richard Rowntree) in *Shaft*, 305–6; and Li Yanfang in male role, 231; nineteenth century, 290–93, 291; in *Super Fly*, 293, 294, 296–300, 302–3, 304–5, 306–7 (*see also* body); superhero, 309n2; as Western melodramatic element, 225;
— designer(s): *See also* Adams, Nate; Anderson, Percy; Aulisi, Joseph G.; Barrett, Kym, 304; Dunn, John, 308n16; Ryack, Rita, 308n16; Travilla, William, 303; von Brandenstein, Patrizia, 304. *See also* acting; Aldridge, Ira; Beerbohm, Herbert; Brummell, Beau; Irving, Henry; *Senso*; Stutesman, Drake, chap. 17
Cottafavi, Vittorio. *See Nel gorgo del peccato/ In the Whirl of Sin*
Cox, John, 42

Crash (2004, Paul Haggis), 320. *See also* disaster film(s)
Creelman, Eileen, on *The Petrified Forest*, 143–44
Crewe, Regina, on *The Petrified Forest*, 144, 149
Crinkle, Nym (1934), xviii
cross-dressing: female impersonators in socials, 64, 65; Li Yanfang as male protagonist in the Yue female-only opera version of *Waterloo Bridge*, 230; in melodramatic scenarios and film stars, 5; in scenarios by Carl Th. Dreyer, 190. *See also* Balivala, K. M.; Cushman, Charlotte; Sundari, Jayshankar; Pickford, Mary; serial(s)
Cuando los hijos se van/When the children leave home (1941). *See* Bustillo Oro
Curtiz, Michael. *See Casablanca*
Cushman, Charlotte, 118–20; extreme costumes, 307n4; first American female theater star, 1857, 116; in London, 1856, 118; male audience interruption of *Romeo and Juliet* (1860), 118; "My journal: The Actress," 120; "power and energy of manhood," 118, 121; publicity and, 119–20; sexual difference, crumbling power of, 120. *See also* actors, female; cross-dressing
— and Susan Cushman 118; with, in *Romeo and Juliet*, 118, *119*

Dalla Vacche, Angela, 337
Dallas (CBS, 1978–1991), 176, 178, 179. *See also* serial television melodrama
Daly, Augustin. *See Under the Gaslight*
Dame aux camélias, La (1852, Alexandre Dumas fils; U.S. debut as *Camille*, 1853, 117–18, 363; U.K. production as *Heartsease*, 1875), 117–18
— *Camille* (1921, Ray C. Smallwood), 130. *See also* Nazimova, Alla; Valentino, Rudolph
Dangerous (1935). *See* Green, Alfred E. *See also* Davis, Bette
Danzón (1991). *See* Novaro, Maria
Darwin, Charles, xxii, 106. *See* acting
Davenport, Fanny, 101
David Copperfield. *See* Dickens, Charles

Davis, Bette, 149, 158; *Dangerous* (1935, Alfred E. Green), 143, 150n9; *Fog Over Frisco* (1934, William Dieterle), 137, 145 (*see also* Hughes, Elinor); *Of Human Bondage* (1934, John Cromwell), 143
— acting skills: British traditions, 148; histrionic, 143, 147, 150n9; Jane Gaines on Davis's tears in *Now, Voyager*, 338; modern melodramatic, 146, 147–48; vibrant new talent, 143
— in *The Petrified Forest*, 139, 143, 145, 146–48, *147*, 150n9; Alexander Walker on, 148
Davis, Phoebe. *See 'Way Down East*
Day of Reckoning, The (1850, adapted by James Robinson Planché from the French *drame, L'Enfant de Paris*, by Emile Souvestre), xvi
Daybreak. *See Tianming*
Day-Mayer, Helen and David Mayer, chap. 6 (99–113), Performing/Acting Melodrama: acting manuals and theories, 105–8; the actor as "natural," xvi; character, double role, 103–4; "excess," challenging early melodrama as, 6; gesture, 100, 102, 104–10, 111–12; history, 100–101; melodrama, denigration of, 11, 100, 113n1; moral clarity, 102; psychology, psychiatry, psychoanalysis, 243; Rousseau, Jean-Jacques, 104–5; twenty-first-century view of early melodrama, 99–100; villain, casting of, 102; voice, 102, 113n3; *'Way Down East*, 99, 110–12; a Western framework, 101; the word (spoken), restriction of, xvii. *See also* acting; actors; Blair Parker, Lotte; Mayer, David; *Way Down East*; melodrama, devices
de Cordova, Richard, 117
de Fuentes, Fernando: femininity virilized, 162: *Doña Bárbara* (1943); fetish objects in, *Allá en el rancho grande*/Out on the Big Ranch (1936), 163; independent women, *La selva de fuego*/Jungle Fire (1945), 162, 167n4
— revolution-themed epic mode, 156, 167n4: *compadre Mendoza, El*/Godfather Mendoza (1935), 156; *Vámanos con Pancho Villa*/Let's go with Pancho Villa (1936)

Dell, Peter (the Elder). *See* Christ
Delsarte, François, 106–7; Delsartian acting, 107 (*see also* acting, manuals: *Home and School Speaker*); Stebbins, Genevieve and Steele MacKaye, and, 106. *See also* acting, gestural; acting, manuals: body, the; Darwin, Charles; Day-Mayer, Helen and David Mayer; MacKaye, Steele; Neville, Henry
DeMille, Cecil B., 129. *See also* Swanson, Gloria
De Santis, Giuseppe: *Caccia tragica/Tragic Pursuit* (1947), 279; and *fotoromanzi*, 278; *Riso amaro/Bitter Rice* (1949), 274
Derrida, Jacques, 339. *See* tears
De Sica, Vittorio: *Ladri di biciclette/Bicycle Thieves* (1948), 276; melodramas of, 280; nighttime curfew in *Umberto D* (1952), 278
— and Cesare Zavattini, *bambini ci guardano, I/The Children Are Watching Us* (1944), 280; direct melodramma, 280; *Sciuscià/Shoeshine* (1946), 277 *Les Deux orphelines*, 1874, Adolphe Dennery and Eugène Corman, 92. *See also* Griffith, D. W., *Orphans of the Storm*
D—G (George Daniel). *See Luke the Labourer; Or, The Lost Son*
Dharti ke Lal (1946, K. A. Abbas), 262
Dick Tracy (1937 film serial), 173. *See also* Hagerdon, Roger; serial(s)
Dickens, Charles: *David Copperfield*, *Omoide no ki* based on, 75; influence on late Meiji narratives 75; and melodramatic form, 101; in *Oliver* Twist: parodying alternation of overwrought tragedy and comedy, 171–72; and seriality 170–171; *The Tale of Two Cities*, adapted as *The Only Way*, xvi; [fantasized] threat by female playwrights, 118
disaster film(s), 10, 311, 312–13, 317, 318, 320, 324; multistory ensemble-cast, 318; spectacular tendency, 317. *See also Contagion*
Dissanayake, Wimal, 87, 219
Diderot, Denis, affective aesthetics, 22, 25; *drame bourgeois* of, 215
Doane, Mary Ann, 172, 212
Dog of Montargis, The; or The Forest of Bondy (1816). *See* Pixérécourt, René-Charles Guilbert de

dolce vita, La (1960, Federico Fellini), 283
Doxtater, Amanda chap. 11 (185–201). *See also* Dreyer, Carl Th.; melodramatic practices and *La Passion de Jeanne d'Arc*, 11; "Esther," Dreyer scenario, 191–92; Falconetti, Marie, *varieté* actress, 195–99; *Jeanne d'Arc* and performance space, 192–95. *See also* "Lydia," Dreyer scenario, 185 passim; sensational forms, xvi; shaping Dreyer's persona: (*see*) melodramatic negation and "authenticity," 188–90; *varieté* stage space and performing bodies, 190–91. *See also Lydia*; Neergaard, Ebbe; Nordisk
Dreyer, Carl Th., authenticity, 189, 190–91, 192–93, 201n15; "Esther" (scenario), 188, 191–92, 201n18 (*see also* Holger-Madsen; pathos); *Gertrud* (1964), 190, 201n17; immolation scene, 186, 200n4; *Leaves from Satan's Book* (1921), 189, 200n4; and melodrama, 188, 189, 200n7 (*see also* Williams, Linda); melodrama to *auteur*, 189, 200n3/11/12/13; *Mikaël* (1924), 190, 200n6 (*see also* Gledhill, Christine); and Nordisk, 189–90, 200n10, 201n16; *Ordet* (1955), 190; on *La Passion de Jeanne d'Arc*, 185, 199n1; performance, 191, 193, 194, 201n19/20; presence of melodramatic practices, 11, 185–86, 188–90, 200n2; *The President* (1919), 189; "The Real Talking Film," (1933), 193 and the real tears of Marie Falconetti, 195–96, 201n24; scenarios by, 190; theater reviews, 190; and *varieté* melodrama, 190–91, 193–84. *See also Lydia*; Neergaard, Ebbe; Nordisk; *Passion de Jeanne d'Arc, La*; Rifbjerg, Klaus
Drum, Jean and Dale D. Drum, 195–96, 197
Drunkard's Reformation, The (1909). *See* Griffith, D. W.
Du Barry (1901). *See* Belasco, David
Duckett, Victoria, 107
Due lettere anonime/Two Anonymous Letters (1945, Mario Camerini), 276
Dukhiyari Bachu. See Kabra, K. N.
Dumas père, Alexandre, 101. *See also* melodrama, history: melo-drame
Dutt, Guru. *See Sahib Bibi aur Ghulam*

Duyu, Dan: *Abandoned One* (1923), 95; *Sea Oath*—a.k.a. *Swear by God* (1921), twin genealogy of *wenyi* in, 88
Dyer, Richard, xxii, xxiii
Dynasty (ABC, 1981–1989), 176. See also serial(s)

East Lynne (1861, Ellen Wood), adaptation of, in colonial India 49—Rose Edouin in, 55; rewritten by Charlotte M. Brame, 91 [as a two-part serial, *A Woman's Error* (November 1872 to March 1873)]
— Chinese adaptation: translation of the Japanese, and newspaper publication by Bao Tianxiaoa; adaptation as a "Civilized Play" (Zhengqiu Zheng); *Konggu lan* ("Orchid in an Empty Valley," 1926, Zhang Shichuang), 91, 97n8; screenplay, 1925, by Bao Tianxiao, developed with Zhengqiu Zheng and Zhang Shichuan
— Indian serialized adaptation (from 1880, K. N. Kabra); and as *Bholi Gul* (1892, B. N. Kabra), 63, 65; stage adaptations, *Dukhiyari Bachu*, and *Dukhi Gul* (1883, Edal Mistri), 63)
— Japanese serialisation (around 1900, by Ruiko Kuroiwa), *No no Hana* ("Flowers of the Wilderness"), 91
Edouin, Rose, 52, 53–55, 54; in Australia, 49; and *The Colleen Bawn*, 53, 54, 55; in *East Lynne*, 55; family, 52, 53–54, 56; in India, 54, 55–56; Lewis, Mrs G. B. W., née, 53; in male roles, 55; in plays by Dion Boucicault, 53; Director, the Lewis Dramatic Troupe, 49. See also *ColleenBawn, The*; Lewis, George B. W.
Eisenstein, Sergei: cut back, 339n2 (*see also* Griffith, D. W.); *Eisenstein on Disney* (1988), 236n8; and intertitles, 339n7; -like montage, 185
Eisner, Lotte, 254
Eleganza, 298, 299
Ellison, Ralph, 289; referenced, 294
Elsaesser, Thomas, xxvii; 1950s genre of family melodrama, 205; the American dream of liberal justice, 216; Catholicism and melodrama, 281; eighteenth-century sentimental fiction focus on suffering and victimization, 307n3; excess of characters' emotions, critique of middle-class ideologies, 6; "melodramatic imagination" across Western popular culture, 206; melos, 205; the musicality of Hollywood melodrama, 284, 287; and Peter Brooks, 206, 207, 212. See also Brooks, Peter; Buckley, Matthew; Williams, Linda
emotion: aesthetic feeling, reintroduction into critical dialogue, xxv, 209; and affect (*see* Pribram, E. Deidre), 238–40; Christianity of Pathos; emotion of Black politics, 303; Christianity of Pathos. See Allen, Richard, chap. 2; emotion, virility and pathos in *Super Fly*, 290, 295; emotional vocabulary for death, 315; emotionality (Pribram, E. Deidre), 180; emotionality in Italian melodrama and neorealism, 273 passim; excess of emotions, 6, 205; feminism and the Oedipal family, 5; intensity of in transnational cinemas, 7, 9; melodrama's emotional effects, 5, 27; melodrama's genres as repositories of emotional knowledge (Jane Gaines), xxiv; in the O. J. Simpson story, 181; overemotional "other" (*see* Buckley, Matthew), 17; and the Sacred in Indian cinemas (*see* Bhaskar, Ira, chap. 15), 9; in seriality, 180; in social and political processes, ix; women and, 44
— early twentieth century: American melodrama and worldwide appeal, xix; Chinese classical opera audiences and, 225; emotion-producing theatrical devices, in Hollywood, xix–xx; the *folletín*/serial novel, in Mexico, 152; *Gone with the Wind* and *The Spring Flows East*, 234; Hollywood melodramas, 115, 116; *The Petrified Forest in* Shingler, Martin, chap. 8; *'Way Down East* (Lottie Blair Parker) and *Way Down East* (D. W. Griffith), 99, 110–12; *wenyi*, 223, 224. See Zheng Zhenqiu and D. W. Griffith, similar ability to arouse emotional response, 93. See also Bakhtin, Mikhail; Balukhatyi, Sergei; Brooks, Peter; Buckley, Matthew; melodrama: devices; Pribram, E. Deidre, chap. 14
— eighteenth century: early stage practices, xiii; the Gothic xi-xii; *Lovers' Vows*, xi

— nineteenth century: *The Lear of Private Life; Or, Father and Daughter*, xiv–xv; the "natural" vs emotional expressiveness, xvi; *scènes à faire*/emotionally logical climaxes, xvi; *Smiles and Tears*, xiv, xix, xix–x; twenty first-century reading of nineteenth-century performance, 100 passim; Victorian domestic melodrama in India, 63, 66. *See also* acting: manuals; Day-Mayer, Helen and David Mayer;
enlightenment and modernity, overlapping or divergent visions of, 84
Enlightenment, the: gesture/body and mind, a living machine, 104–5; melodrama and loss of pre-Enlightenment moral authority (Peter Brooks), 69; values, 214–15
Euripides, in the genealogy of melodrama, 25; melodramatic form, 101
Europa '51. See Rossellini, Roberto

Falconetti, Marie. *See* Dreyer, Carl Th.; *Passion de Jeanne d'Arc, La*
Famous Players, 122; -Lasky, 141
Farassino, Alberto, 276
Father and Daughter, The (1800, Amelia Opie), xiv-xv. *See also*: Coburg productions; *Smiles and Tears*
Fenton, Mary, first major actress of Parsi theater, 65. *See also* socials
Fernández, Emilio: and John Ford, 158; *Pueblerina* (1949), 163; revolutionary epics, 162; *Salón México* (1949), 163, 164
Feuer, Jane, 183n4
figli di nessuno, I/Nobody's Children (1951). *See* Matarazzo, Raffaello
Fischer-Lichte, Erika, 194, 201n19; on the work of Marina Abramović, 201n27
Fitzgerald, Percy, 108; *The Art of Acting in Connection with the Study of Character, the Spirit of Comedy and Stage Illusion*, 349. *See also* acting, manuals
Flash Gordon (1936 serial). *See* Hagerdon, Roger. *See also* serialization
Florian, Jean-Pierre Claris de (1755–1794), 25
Fog Over Frisco (1934, William Dieterle). *See* Davis, Bette; Hughes, Elinor
Ford, Henry. *See* Hollywood
Ford, John, 158
Forgive Me!. See Perdonami!
Forrest, Edwin, 101, 118
Foster, Helen Bradley, 304
Four Horsemen of the Apocalypse, The Los cuatro jinetes del apocalipsis (1916), Vicente Blasco Ibañez, author; adapted for screen (1919–1921, June Mathis), 130
— (1921, Rex Ingram). *See* Valentino, Rudolph
Four Ways Out seecittà si difende, La
Fracassi, Clemente: *Romanticismo* (1950), 276; *Sensualità* (1952), 274
Freda, Riccardo. *See Beatrice Cenci*
French Revolution: supposed origin of melodrama: Richard Allen on, 31–32, 282; Japan and, 69, 71, 72; Matthew Buckley on, 3, 19, 20–21, 26, 28, 242; and origins of modernity, 205; orphan figure from, the, 83, 92. *See also* Brooks, Peter
Freud, Sigmund, xxii, 103
Freyberger, Maurice. *See* Balivala, K. M. *See also Bholi Jan*; Boucicault, Dion

Gaines, Jane, M., chap. 19 (325–39), xxvii, 9: always too late or never too late?, 331–32; *'A Santanotte*, 334–36; *Assunta Spina*, 334, 336; historical time: relationship of the three modes of time, 329–30; *Imitation of Life*, 331–32; "linear" historiography, critique of, 331, 339n5; loss of the future and the "former future" in silent Italian melodrama, 334–37; melodrama, either progressive or reactionary? 337; melodrama's composite tense, 332–34; melodrama's genres as repositories of emotional knowledge, xxiv; melodrama's theory of historical time, 329; *Now, Voyager*, 338–39; past and future, total irreconcilability of, 332, 339n6; the philosophy of history, 329, 339n4; the political valence of melodrama: the future as the past or not, 337–38; *Stella Dallas*, 332; tears, 325, 338–39. *See also* Dalle Vacche, Angela; Eisenstein, intertitles; Koselleck, Reinhart; tears; women
Gallone, Carmine. *See Avanti a lui tremava tutta Roma/Before Him All Rome Trembled*; *Casa Ricordi*

Garcia, Gustav, 105, 106. *See also* acting: manuals

Garcia, Sara, emblematic icon of all-sacrificing mother, 165. *See also* Bustillo Oro, Juan, *Cuando los hijos se van*

Gassman, Vittorio. *See Anna*; *Mambo*

Gay, John (1685–1732), 25

Geertz, Clifford, 31. *See* Brooks, Peter

Genina, Augusto: *Maddalena* (1954), maternal melodrama, 274. *See also Cielo sulla palude*/*Heaven Over the Marshes*

Gentilomo, Giacomo: *Appassionatamente* (1954), 276; *Melodie immortali* (1952), 284 (*see also* Mascagni, Pietro); *O' sole mio* (1946), 277, 284

Germania anno zero/*Germany Year Zero* (1948). *See* Rossellini, Roberto

Germi, Pietro: *cammino della speranza, Il*/*The Path of Hope* (1950), prostitution, 278; crime films: *La città si difende*/*Four Ways Out* (1951), 278; *Senza pietà*/*Without Pity* (1948), 278, 281

Gerould, Daniel: *American Melodrama*, 79; citing Sergei Balukhatyi, 199; *The Girl of the Golden West*, 140–41; "heroine, the inevitable idealization of," 122; melodrama, always "an art of wholesale borrowing," 70, 79; melodrama as universally appealing, xix; melodramas, relocatable theatrical commodities, 79 (*see also* serial(s), Meiji literature); stereotyped characters, mid-century, 140; *Uncle Tom's Cabin*, xviii; United States and melodrama, "democratic revolution in thought and feeling," xviii. *See also* Belasco, David; Pixérécourt, René-Charles de

Gerow, Aaron, 71–72

Gertrud (1964, Carl Th. Dreyer), 190, 201*n*17

gesture(s), xxi, 153: in acting, 6, 100, 104–12 (Day-Mayer, Helen, and David Mayer, chap. 6), 307; in acting handbooks, xxii; authentic than words, thought of as more, xxiii; in *Breaking Bad*, 247; Carl Th. Dreyer and Marie Falconetti, 194–95; communicative form, xxiv (Bakhtin, Mikhail); in *Contagion*, 319, 322;

economy of (Leslie Howard's skill), 142; in *The Girl of the Golden West*, 141; in Italian melodrama, 275, 264; larger-than-life, by actors in some cinema costumes, 303; melodramatic, as "ineffable" in a "gap in language" (Peter Brooks), 302; in the *Natyashastra*, 266; in the Passion of Christ, 3; in religious painting, expressive vocabulary of, 37; in *Shejari*, 260; of suffering, 32. *See also* acting; acting, manuals; body; Fitzgerald, Percy; Lambranzi, Guido; Pearson, Roberta

Ghatak, Ritwik. *See Subarnarekha*

Ghosh, Girish Chandra, Bengali dramatist, 56. *See also* George B. W. Lewis

Gibbs, Anna, 238

Giketsu Kyōketsu ("Loyal Blood, Valiant Blood," 1894–1895). *See* Kyōka, Izumi

Giordana, Marco Tullio. *See meglio gioventù, La*

girl(s): "attractive," action actresses as, 116–17; *A Blind Orphan Girl*, 95; chorus, 217*n*7; country, Jeanne [du Barry], 129; extra, 130; the Girl in *The Girl of the Golden West*, 140; "good," in *Nosotros los pobres*, 159; growing, stories, 123 (*see* Pickford, Mary); "matinee," 120; modern American, 5; modern Americanism and its, 125; the modern, in vernacular modernism (Miriam Hansen), 85; "movie-struck," 117; Parsi, at a benefit for Mrs. Lewis, 56; *Poor Little Rich Girl, The*, 133*n*2; pretty, Hollywood the most powerful threat to millions of, 132; Shanghai and *Gone with the Wind*, 222; society, in *The Great Moment*, 129; in *Tess of the Storm Country*, 123; in *'Way Down East*, 99, 110; *Why Girls Leave Home*, 108; young, practice of marrying older men to, 258; young women stars as, 117. *See also* Hallett, Hilary A; White, Pearl; Zhang, Zhen

Girl of the Golden West, The (1905). *See* Belasco, David

Gish, Lillian: "wishy-washy" suffering victims, 122; in *Way Down East*, 83, 111, 112. *See also* Hallett, Hilary A; women

Gledhill, Christine, Prologue (ix–xxv), affect, 240; Americanizing melodrama, xvii–xix; Bakhtin and the genericity of emotion, xxiii–xxix; British acting between restraint and passion, 148; cross-media, 81*n*1, 87–88; cultural-critical division, xv–xvi; historicizing melodrama, x–xiv, 70; Hollywood, xix–xxi, 46; ideology and critique, xxiv–xxv; mapping the entire "melodramatic field" in *Home Is Where the Heart Is*, 212–13; melodrama and cinema, xvii; melodrama and realism, 171, 215; melodrama's genres, 5; melodrama's presumed overidentifications, 200*n*6; melodramatization of television serials, 174; modality, 219, 237; moral feeling, xiv–xv; neoclassical hero, fate of in premodern tragedies, 115; personalization, rethinking, xxi–xxiii, 243; reinvention, 136; shifts in characterisation and performance, by the 1890s, 146

— and Linda Williams, Introduction (1–11)

Gluck, Carol, 73

Glyn, Elinor, writer. *See The Great Moment* (1921). *See also Beyond the Rocks*

Gobbi, Tito. *See O' sole mio*

Goimard, Jacques, 281, 282

Goldsmith, Oliver. *See The Vicar of Wakefield*

Gone with the Wind (1939, Victor Fleming; novel, 1936, (*see also*) Margaret Mitchell, 224), 8, 231, 234; in China, *Luanshi Jiaren* ("a beauty at a turbulent time"), 219–20, 221–23, 221; excess and, 224, 225–26; Latin American reception, 158; music and, 231–32, 232; Shanghai girls and, 222–23; transnational travel in a cross-cultural context, 224; Vivien Leigh, 221, 222; "*wenyi* blockbuster," 223–24. *See also* Chinese melodramas; *Spring River Flows East, The*

— Chinese remakes, 227–29, 231, prints extant: Huadian Company (Mei Lingxiao), 227–28; 1941, American films banned, 227–28; 1943, Kugan drama troupe, 228

— 1940, Huacheng Company remake (dir: Zhang Shankun), 234; musical interludes sung by Chen Yunshang, 232, 232; starring Chen Yunshang, 227, 228

Gopinath (1948, Mahesh Kaul), 262

Gout, Alberto: *Aventurera*/Adventuress(1950), 163, 167*n*7; *Mujeres sacrificadas*/Self-sacrificing women (1952), 163; *Sensualidad*/Sensuality(1951) 163

Gramsci, Antonio, 284

Great Moment, The (1921, Sam Wood), 129. *See also* Glyn, Elinor; Swanson, Gloria

Green, Alfred E.: *Dangerous* (1935), 143. *See also* Davis, Bette; *Parachute Jumper* (1933), 149*n*3

Grein, J. T., xvi, xviii

Griffith, D. W.: *After Many Years* (1908), Eisenstein on, 326, 339*n*2; cinematic language, Tian Han on, 93; and "classical" cinema, 209; comparisons with Zheng Zhengqiu, 93; *Drunkard's Reformation, The* (1909), 332; European melodrama, debt to, 80; "fever" in 1920s Shanghai, 8, 79, 84, 91–92, 93–94, 95, 97*n*9; Italian opera staging, and, 284; and Lillian Gish, 122; martyrdom of virtue in, 40; melodrama, indebted to early stage, 92–93; melodrama and religion in America, 34; orphan drama 91–92; tragic cast to melodramatic plots, 154; *wenyi* films, and, 80. *See also Birth of a Nation, The*; *Broken Blossoms*; *Orphans of the Storm*; *Way Down East*

Grignaffini, Giovanna, 283, 286

Grimstead, David: melodrama and historical moral tensions, xvii, 313, 339*n*10

Grossberg, Larry, 238

Gu Wuwei. *See Who's His Mother?*

Guadagnino, Luca. *See Io sono l'amore*

Guan Haifen. *See Student's Hard Life, A*

Guerrero, Ed, 293, 306, 308*n*11

Gunning, Sandra, 304

Gunning, Tom, 212

Gunsmoke (CBS 1955–1975), 173, 174

Guy, Alice, 112

Haas, Willy, writer, 254, 256: *Prem Nagar* (*City of Love*, 1941); *Neecha Nagar*, 1946. *See also* Bhavnani, Mohan

Hagerdon, Roger, 173

Hale, Grace, 300

Haley, Alex. *See Roots*

Hallett, Hilary A., chap. 7 (115–33): *Camille* (1853), 117–18; *Camille* (1921). See also starring Alla Nazimova, and Rudolph Valentino, 130; Charlotte Cushman, 118–20 (*see also* cross-dressing); cliff-hanging serial stars (Helen Holmes, Ruth Roland, Pearl White), 123–27; film as industry, 121–22; melodramas and early American film, 121–27; melodramatic women on the nineteenth-century stage, 117–21; the "modern American girl," 5, 132; *Passion* (*see* starring Pola Negri), 127–29; post [WW1] war melodramas, 127–32; scandal, first, and the Hays Code, 131–32; sensational-romantic melodramas, 123–27, 129 (*Tess*, 123); women in early Hollywood, 5. *See also* actors, female; girls; Pickford, Mary; women

Hammond, Percy, 142

Hampden, Walter, 101

Hampton, Benjamin, "Pickford Revolution" (1931), 116

Hansen, Kathryn, chap. 3 (49–67), 8. *See* Dion Boucicault and sensation drama, 50–52; George B. W. Lewis and Rose Edouin, The Lewises, Australia to India, 52–56; K. N. Kabra and K. M. Balivala and Parsi theater, 56–66; research sources, 50, 67. *See also Bholi Jan*; *The Colleen Bawn*; socials

Hansen, Miriam: and American popular culture, xix; Chinese cinema, influence of Hollywood on early, 76; "classical" Hollywood cinema and melodrama's global status, 81; the classical, "transvalued," 210; "cultural respectability, sexual and gender related," 117; "global vernacular," 80; melodrama as single genre, sees, 211; melodrama's universal appeal, xix; "vernacular modernism," 80, 85, 173, 212. *See also Konjiki yasha*; *Weaker Than a Woman*; Williams, Linda, chap. 12; Yang, Panpan; Zhang, Zhen

Haolaiwu, in magazine titles, 220, 221

Harris, Henry, and "melo-drame," xii

Harootunian, Harry, 74, 81n3

Hart, William S. Hart, first recorded actor's voice, 113n3

Harvey, John Martin, in *The Only Way* (*The Tale of Two Cities* renamed), xvi

Hashr, Agha, writer, 65, 66; *Nek Parveen* ("The Good Parveen," 64) *or Silver King*, 66; *Yahudi ki Larki* (1913), 66. *See also* socials

Haynes, Todd, 311

Hayward, Jennifer, 170, 183n8

Hearst, William Randolph: and female protagonists, the rage for, 126; and E. W. Scripps: production values, 126; and national news, 125–26; *The Perils of Pauline*, co-producer, 125

Hearts Adrift (1914). *See* Pickford, Mary

Heartsease (1875). *See Dame aux camellias, La*

Heaven Over the Marshes. See Cielo sulla palude

Heidegger, Martin, 329–30

Heilman, Robert, 20, 33, 215, 217n1

Hipócrit/Hypocrite (1949). *See* Morayta, Miguel

historiography: critique of linear, 339n5; modernization of melodrama makes past plays "old-fashioned," 149

history, baton model of theatrical, xvi

historical: approaches, xxvii; change, x (*see also* Williams, Raymond); differences, subsumed, 87; genericity, xxv; hindsight, 32; periodized "genre" studies, 87; significance, 17–18, 20; understanding, 72; view of, longer, 75. *See also* time, historical

— historically informed perspective, 223

— historicizing, x–xiv, 3

Hitchcock, Alfred, 350; *Alfred Hitchcock Presents* (NBC, CBS, 1955–1965), 183n2; "Why I Make Melodramas" (1937), 217n8

Holcroft, Thomas. *See A Tale of Mystery*

Holger-Madsen, *Den hvide Djoevel*/*The Devil's Protegé* (1916, from "Esther," scenario by Carl Dreyer, adapted from *Splendeurs et misères des courtisanes*, Honoré de Balzac), 188. *See also Lydia* (1918); *The Temptation of Mrs Chestney* (1916), 190; *Which is Which?* (1917, from "Hans rigtige Kone," scenario by Carl Th. Dreyer), 190. *See also* Nordisk

Holmes, Helen, 123–25, 124; in cliff-hanging serials, 123; lead of *The Hazards of Helen* (Kalem 1914–1917) 123. *See also* Roland, Ruth; White, Pearl

Hong, Shen, pioneer filmmaker, 90
Hori, Keiko, 75
Howard, Leslie, 141, 143, 150n6; *Lesley Howard: The Lost Actor* (2010, ed. Estelle Eforgan), 141. *See also Gone with the Wind*; Davis, Bette, *Of Human Bondage*
— acting style, 141, 148; British tradition, 148; Jeffery Richards on, 141, 142; modern melodramatic, 146, 147–48
— *The Petrified Forest*: and, 150n7; in, 139, 141, 144, 146, 147, 148, 149; Alexander Walker on, 148; Bert Mantle on, 142; critics on: Kate Cameron on 144, 149; Percy Hammond on, 142; Regina Crewe on, 144, 149
Howe, Julia Ward, "better about womankind" (1857), 118. *See* Cushman, Charlotte
Huang, Nicole, 221. *See Gone with the Wind*
Huang, Xuelei, 90, 91, 97n8. *See also East Lynne*; *Konggu lanxun*
Hughes, Elinor, critic: *Fog Over Frisco*: action film as melodrama, 137–38; on Bette Davis in, 145. *See also The Petrified Forest*; with "implausible stock types," 138
Hunduan Lanqiao (1941, Mei Qian), song-and-dance remake of *Waterloo Bridge*, 229–30, 230, print extant, 231; echoed in *The Spring Flows East*, 234; gendered narrative asymmetry in, 229–30; songs from 231. *See* music; Zheng Junli in, 233
Hugo, Victor, "melo-drame," 101

I Am Love. See Io sono l'amore
Ibsen, Henrik, xvi
Imitation of Life (1960). *See* Sirk, Douglas
In the Whirl of Sin. See Nel gorgo del peccato
Iñárritu, Alejandro G. *See Amores Perros*; *Babel*
Inchbald, Elizabeth:
— *Lovers' Vows* 1798, adapted from *Child of Love* (1780), August von Kotzebue, xi; Jane Austen's *Mansfield Park, and*, xi
— *Wives as They Were, and Maids as They Are*, 63. *See also* Kabra, K. N., *Sudhi Vachche Sopari*
India. *See* Balivala, K. M.; Betab; *bhakti*; Bhaskar, Ira, chap. 15; *Bholi Jan*; Cooper, Patience; *East Lynne*; Edouin, Rose; emotion; Hansen, Kathryn, chap. 4; Kabra, K. N.; language; Lewis, George B. W.; melodrama, devices, sound; melodrama, devices, mise-en-scène; melodrama genres; melodrama history, nineteenth century; music; the Sacred; Shantaram, V.; socials
Io sono l'amore/I Am Love (2009, Luca Guadagnino), 280
Irving, Henry, and costume, 290, 291, 292, 303, 307n6/7, 308n8; Clement Scott on (1892), 290, 294, 307n6; double role, 103–4. *See also* Fitzgerald, Percy
Ishioka, Eiko, costume designer, 307n1
Italy. *See* Bayman, Louis, chap. 16; body, the; *Catene*; De Sica, Vittorio; emotion; Gentilomo, Giacomo; Germi, Pietro; Matarazzo, Raffaello; melodrama: ethos, morality and religion; melodrama genres; music; Notari, Elvira; Rossellini, Roberto; the Sacred; tears; Visconti
Ito, Ken K. *An Age of Melodrama: Family, Gender, and Social Hierarchy in the Turn-of-the-Century Japanese Novel* (2008), 69, 74; Dickens, Charles, importance for, 75 (*see also* Brame, Charlotte M./Clay, Bertha M.; Roka, Tokutomi; Yūhō, Kikuchi; Hori, Keiko); *Konjiki yasha* ("The Golden Demon"), melodrama, use of term, 75, 82n4; popular fiction, reading of, 74–75; serialized, and melodrama, 74, 75; *risshin shusse* ("self-advancement"), 75. *See also* Brooks, Peter; Japan
Izumi Kyōka, 69, 77, 82n6; film adaptations by, Kenji Mizoguchi (*see*), 77; and *Resurrection* (1902, Leo Tolstoy), 77, 82n8; student of Osaka Kōyō, 77. *See also* Ito, Ken K.; *Taki no shiraito*
— *Giketsu Kyōketsu* (Loyal Blood, Valiant Blood 1894–1895, author; adapted as play, *Taki no shiraito* (The Water Magician), 1895 by Kawakami, Otojirō), 77, 82n7; Poulton, Cody M. on the novel, 79; serialized from 1894.

Jade Pear Spirit (1924, Zhang Shichun and Xu Hu), 92; adapted by Zheng Zhengqiu from Xu Zhenya "father" the Mandarin Ducks and Butterfly fiction, 97n10

James, Henry: Peter Brooks study of, 2, 205, 206; on *Uncle Tom's Cabin*, 76, 206
James, Louis, 32
Jameson, Frederic, melodrama as ideologeme, 71
Japan. *See* Airriess, Hannah, chap. 4; Brame, Charlotte M.; Dickens, Charles; *East Lynne*; Ito, Ken. K.; Izumi Kyōka; Kenji Mizoguchi; *Konjiki yasha*; Meiji literature; melodrama genres; melodrama history, nineteenth century; serial(s); Tokutomi Roka; Yūhō, Kikuchi; Yoshimoto, Mitsuhiro;
Journey to Italy. *See Viaggio in Italia*
Juddin Jhagro. *See* Jahingir Khambata

Kabra, B. N., 63, 65; *Bholi Gul*/The Innocent Gul (1892, Kabra, B. N., 63, 64. *See also East Lynne*); *Dorangi Duniya*, 65 (*see also* Betab). *See also* Kabra, K. N.
Kabra, K. N. (Kekhushro Navroji; honorific Kabraji), playhouse pioneer, 56, 57; importation of *The Colleen Bawn*, 57; *Sudhi Vachche Sopari* (1884), adapted from *Wives as They Were, and Maids as They Are* (*see* Inchbald, Elizabeth), 63; Victoria Theatrical Company, 57. *See also* Balivala, K. M., *Colleen Bawn, The*
— *Bholi Jan athva Dhananum Dhan*/Innocent Belle (1887, adapted from The Colleen Bawn)
— *East Lynne*, Parsi theater adaptations: *Dukhiyari Bachu*; *Bholi Gul*. *See* Kabra, B. N.
Kakoudaki, Despina, chap. 18 (311–24): *Contagion*: melodrama and responsibility, 317–24; Hollywood melodrama narrative as structural coherence, 312; the melodramatic mode: on suffering and choice, 313–17; ministory, 314; network narrative/world, 318, 320, 322, 323; spectacular qualities and chilling realism of *Contagion*, 10, 320
— disaster films as quintessential melodrama, 312–13; choreographic alternation between responsibility and response, 317; films, 320; global context for, 324; impact of the disaster, 318. *See also* Soderbergh, Steven

Kaplan, Ann, cross-cultural analysis, 86, 219; mother in *UncleTom's Cabin*, 44; the woman's film, 212
Kaufmann, Walter, composer, 254
Kaul, Mahesh. *See Gopinath*
Kemble, Marie-Thérèse. *See Smiles and Tears*
Kenji Mizoguchi: *See* adaptations of work by Izumi Kyōka, 77, 82n5; continual presence of melodrama, 72; documentary on, 82n8; on melodrama and *Resurrection* (Leo Tolstoy), 82n8; (*see also*) *Taki no shiraito* (1933); versions of *Onoga tsumi* (My Sin, 1926), 77
Khambata, Jahangir, actor-manager, 65
Khan, Mehboob: *Aurat* (1940); *Najma* (1943)
Khanna, Ranjana, 238
Kleinhans, Chuck, xxi
Knots Landing (CBS, 1979–1993). *See also* serial television melodrama
Konggu lan (1926). *See* Zhang Shichuan; *Konggu lanxun* (1938), 97n8
Konjiki yasha (The Golden Demon, Ozaki Kōyō, author), newspaper serial and novel, 74–75, 76; as film (1911; 1937, Shimizu Hiroshi), 77; and global circulation, 69, 79; late Meiji social and ethical coordinates, 76; popularity, 76; reference to *Weaker Than a Woman* (Clay, Bertha M., author), 75, 76; serialization, 74, 76, 79; as shinpa play, 77; translated into English, 79; transmedial exchange, 74, 76, 79. *See also* Anderson, Mark; Brame, Charlotte M.; *East Lynne*; Ito, Ken K.; Kyōka, Izumi; Meiji; Zwicker, Jonathan E.
Koselleck, Reinhart, one time as it relates to another, 329, possibility of reconciliation between past and future, 330, the "former future," 333. *See* Gaines, Jane, M., chap. 19
Kotzebue, August von, xi, 25; *Child of Love* 1780, xi (*see* Inchbald, Elizabeth, *Lovers' Vows*); *The Stranger* 1790/1798, xi
Kōyō, Ozaki, 74. *See also Konjiki yasha*; Kyōka, Izumi
Kunku (1937). *See* Shantaram V.
Kurland, Jeffery, 307n1. *See also* costume

Ladri di biciclette/*Bicycle Thieves* (1948). *See* De Sica, Vittorio
Lady Audley's Secret (1863), xxiii

Laila-Majnun, Sufi tradition, 33
Lambranzi, Guido, 107
lamentation, 35, 36, 37, 43, 287; *compianti/*
    groups 37, 42, 44; Mary Magdelene's,
    35; the Marys' and, 36; in *La Passion de
    Jeanne d'Arc*, 185. *See also* Christ
Lamentation: *Lamentation* (1304–1306,
    Giotto di Bondone), 37; *Lamentation over
    the Dead Christ* (1455–1460, Donatello),
    37, 38; *Lamentation over the Dead Christ*
    (1463, Niccolo' dell'Arca), 37, 44, 45;
    Mary's, 36, 43. *See also* Christ
Landeta, Matilde, *Trotacalles/Streetwalker*
    (1951), 163
language: 1940s China, drift between old
    and new languages, 232; grounding us in
    the social (Mikhail Bakhtin), xxiii; high-
    flown "poetic" (Mexico), 163, 165, 166;
    Indian languages, 49; Japanese-language
    scholarship, 77; late-romanticisim. *See*
    Lara, Agustin, 160; modern Shanghaiese,
    97n6; orphan-centred films, multi-
    language, 85, 96; Parsi eighteenth-century
    theater not defined by language (region
    or ethnicity), 56; possession or loss of,
    sign of evil or innocence, 42; verbal in
    eighteenth-century "illegitimate" theater,
    xii, 6; vernacular, "humanizing" the
    drama of Christ's Passion, 40; visceral
    in the novel, xxii. *See also* emotion;
    Lambranzi, Guido; Massumi, Brian;
    melodrama, devices; *Nosotros los pobres*;
    Rousseau, Jean-Jacques; *The Wakefield
    Buffetting*; Yue Opera's *Waterloo Bridge*
Lara, Agustín, 155, 160. *See also* music,
    bolero
Lasky, Jesse. *See* Famous Players-Lasky;
    Passion (1920)
Lattuada, Alberto: *See Anna*; *Il mulino del
    Po/The Mill on the Po* (1949), 278
*Lear of Private Life; Or, Father and Daughter,
    The. See* Coburg productions
Lee, Bruce, 96
Leigh, Vivien. *See Gone with the Wind*
Leoncavallo, Ruggero, composer, 283
Lessing, Gothold Ephraim, in the pre-
    Revolutionary geology of melodrama, 22,
    25, 101

Letter from an Unknown Woman (1948,
    Max Ophuls), 328
Lewes, George H., xvi, xviii
Lewis, Barbara, 302
Lewis, George B. W., in Australia, 49, 52, 54;
    and British patronage, 56; and China,
    52–54; and Girish Chandra Ghosh, 56; in
    India, 49–50, 52–54; the Lewis Dramatic
    Troupe/Company 49, 52, 54, 55, 56;
    military-themed fare, 56; Raj dignitaries,
    56. *See also* Boucicault, Dion: *The Colleen
    Bawn*
— the Lewises, 50, 52, in India, 52–54, 55–56,
    57, 62; Indian audiences, 56; monograph
    on, 49–50; Mrs G. B. W. Lewis, 53 (see
    also Edouin, Rose)
Lewis, Matthew Gregory "Monk," 22. *See
    also Castle Spectre: A Dramatic Romance,
    The Lietti, Roberta*, 282–83
Li Yanfang, 231. *See also Waterloo Bridge*
Li Yu (1610–1680). *See Xian Qing Ou Ji*
Lillo, George, 22, 25. *See also The London
    Merchant*
Lily of Killarney, The (1862). *See* opera
    inspired by *The Colleen Bawn*, libretto by
    Dion Boucicault
Lizzani, Carlo. *See Achtung! Banditi!*
Lombardo, Gustavo, 274. *See also Catene*
London Merchant, The (1731), xi. *See also*
    Lillo, George
loss, x; of Christ, 45; in *Contagion*, 318,
    321, 323; of hope in the former future,
    333; of language, 42; and melodrama,
    26, 244; in melodrama, 40, 64, 86,
    104, 241, nineteenth century, of the
    term melodrama, xvi; in silent Italian
    melodrama, 334–37; and time, 333, 334;
    of the Traditional Sacred, 3, 4, 207, 240,
    253, 281. *See also* Christ, Passion of;
    emotion; melodrama; sacred/Sacred;
    tears; time
Lost (ABC 2004–2010), 177, 179, 251n3/4
Love in the City (1953). *See Storia di
    Caterina*
Lovers' Vows (1798). *See* Inchbald, Elizabeth
Luanshi Jiaren. See Gone With the Wind
Lubitsch, Ernst: considered "classical" by
    Renoir, 217n5; era's boldest sex comedies,

129; *Passion* (1920), 127–28; women working with, 129. *See also* Negri, Pola; Pickford, Mary; Swanson, Gloria

Luchetti, Daniele. *See Mio fratello è figlio unico* (2007)

Luke the Labourer; Or, The Lost Son (1830, D-G (George Daniel); 1826, J. B. Buckstone, uncredited playwright), poster, xx; preface to, xv

Lundgren, Egon Sellif, artist. *See Colleen Bawn, The*

Lydia (1918, Holger-Madsen, from "Lydia," scenario by Carl Th. Dreyer), 185–86; conventional film criticism, 186; Fribert, *187*; Fribert's POV, *186*; immolation scene, 186, 187, 200n2; *Jeanne d'Arc*, link with, 188; Lydia, 190, 191, 197, 200n2; *varieté* in, 190. *See also Passion de Jeanne d'Arc, La*

Lyons Mail, The (1854, Charles Reade, playwright), 103–4. *See also* Irving, Henry, double role

Mack, Robert, xi. *See The Vicar of Wakefield*

MacKaye, Steele, 106, 107; *Paul Kauvar; Or, Anarchy* (1887), xviii. *See also* Delsarte, François

Madame Butterfly (1932, Marion Gering), 271n2. *See also* Belasco, David

Madame X (1966, David Lowell Rich), 325–26, 330

Maddalena (1954). *See* Genina, Augusto

Mahal (1949, Kamal Amrohi), 262–64, *263*, *264*; *Aayega Aanewala*, song in, 265; influence of song sequences on *Bhargavi Neelayam*. *See also* music, Sufi/*qawwali*; Wirsching, Josef

Mâle, Émile, Christianity of Pathos, 32

Magnani, Anna. *See Avanti a lui tremava tutta Roma*/*Before Him All Rome Trembled*; *Roma città aperta*

Mambo (1954, Robert Rossen), 274

Mandarin Ducks and Butterfly literature, 88; 1910s and 1920s, 90, 97n7; Griffith fever compounded by popularity of, 92

Mangano, Silvana. *See Anna*; *Mambo*

Mansfield Park. *See* Inchbald, Elizabeth, *Lovers' Vows*

Mantle, Burns, 142

Marcus, Millicent, 278–79

Marx Brothers burlesques, 209

Mary Magdalene, 32, 34, 35, 36, 43, 45

Mascagni, Pietro, composer, 283–84: *Rapsodia satanica*/*Satan's Rhapsody* (1917, Nino Oxilia); biopic of, *Melodie immortali* (1952, Giacomo Gentilimo)

Massumi, Brian: *l'affect* (Deleuze), note on translating *A Thousand Plateaus*, 234; on affect and emotion, 238–40; "affective in image reception, primacy of the," 239; on excess, 239; 251n1. *See also* emotion; Pribram, E. Deidre

Mavell, Andrew, 169

Matarazzo, Raffaello, 274; Catholic melodramas, 46; *Chi è senza peccato …*/*Who Is Without Sin?* 274; Giuseppe Verdi biopic, 284; *I figli di nessuno*/*Nobody's Children* (1951), 46, 274; *Tormento* (1950), 274; *Torna!* (1954), colour remake of *Catene*, 274–75. *See also Catene*/*Chains*; Lombardo, Gustavo

Mathews, Charles. *See The Day of Reckoning*

Mathis, June, 130. *See also* Hollywood, women working in; Nazimova, Alla; Valentino, Rudolph

Mayer, David, 6; baton model of history, the, xvi; on Brooks, Peter, 31; performance, illustrations of melodramatic, 307n5; realism, high art's claim on, 244. *See also* Day-Mayer, Helen and David Mayer

Mayfield, Curtis, music score, *Super Fly*, 292, 296, 308n11, 357

Mayo, Archie. *See Petrified Forest, The*

McCollom, Michael, 300

McHugh, Kathleen, postwar Korean melodrama as "transnational familiar," 85

McNamer, Sarah, the centrality of gender to the Christianity of Pathos 43, 44. *See also Planctus Mariae*

McTeague, James, *Before Stanislavsky*, 145, 146. *See also* acting; Day-Mayer, Helen and Mayer, David

meglio gioventù, La/*The Best of Youth* (2003, Marco Tullio Giordana), 280

Meisel, Martin, xvii, 109

meller, American film trade press term (1938–1960) for action movies, 137

Melodie immortali (1952). *See* Gentilomo, Giacomo

melodrama: 1, 2, 67; melos (Greek: song) and drama (Greek: action), 1, 20

melodrama as business: as commercial genre-producing system, xix; commercial production practices, 2; copyright laws, absence of, xiii, 87–88; flexible mode for commerce, nineteenth century, xiii; global mass culture, 88; Hollywood, 116, 127; Hollywood and marketing, 311; post-French/Industrial Revolution entrepreneurial opportunities, xii; transnational mode, 69, 95; Victorian plays for sale in Bombay, 62; as Western commodity culture, 223, 230; in young nineteenth-century American republic, xvii. *See also* Pickford, Mary

melodrama, critical concepts of, 101, 152, 172–73, 241; as affective meme, 16; Almodóvar, Pedro, on, 277; and Chinese dramatic and cinematic forms, 219; cinematic, as the norm, 286; contemporary criticism and, 311; critique and ideology, xxiv–xxv; culturalist view of "melodrama" as Western, 87; denigration, xv–xvi, 171, 113n1; drama of morality/sentiment, 27; elephant of, the Chinese, 235; elephant, the, and film scholars; as global vernacular, 79–81; as ideologeme (Frederic Jameson), 71; *mancato/manqué*/failed, 280; meaning, xxii; "meaning" (Mikhail Bakhtin), 9; *melodrama/melodramatic* problematised, 137; as modality, xiii–xiv, xvi, xviii, xxii, xxiv; mode of cultural mediation, significant, 70; as mode of excess, the problem, 214; "modern form" (*see* Peter Brooks), 69; nobility that melodrama commands, the 154; non-Western traditions as, 86; as Oscar pictures, post-Hollywood studio system, 311; as pre-existing "classical" cinema, 207; and realism, 20; redefinition, continual, 136–37; spectacle and sensation, xviii; and "structure of feeling" (*see* Raymond William), ix–x; texts described as, 311;

transmutation, problem of, 137; universal or Western?, 7; Victorian, 241; villain, central, 41; Visconti, Luchino on, 286; *wenyi and*, 84, 223–24; as Western form, 15, 73, 87. *See also* Brooks, Peter; the "classical"; Elsaesser, Thomas; Hughes, Elinor; Ito, Ken T.; *The Petrified Forest*; Yang, Panpan; Yeh, Emilie Yue-yu; Western

melodrama, devices, 6, 273, 287; Balivala, K. M., artistic director, 57; body and costume, nineteenth-century actors, 292; close-up, 162, 192, 201n21. *See* costume, particularly in *Super Fly* (*see* Drake Stutesman, chap. 17); *coup de théâtre*, xvi, 19–21, 197, 273; Dreyer, Carl Th, scenarios, 190; ending of *Senza pietà*, 281; expressionist lighting, 253–54, 260, 262, 264, 265; expressivity as spectacle, 273; filmic elements, xxi, xxiv; German expressionism and *bhava*/emotion 1940s Bombay cinema, 253 passim; gesture, 107, 108, 154; Griffith, D. W. developing cinematic language, 93; Huacheng Company's *Gone with the Wind*, 232–33; intertitles, 339n7; lyricism in Italian film melodramas, 275, 282, 283; merging aesthetic practices, ix, xvii; naturalism and, xvi; Nazis in *Roma città aperta*, 278; nineteenth-century stage technologies, xvii, 6–7, 108–9, 113n22; *La Passion de Jeanne d'Arc*, 185, 193–95; performative in *The Wire*, 247; pictorialism, nineteenth-century, xviii; and realism, xiv, 100 (scenic artist), 197, 243; and representation, 35–36; *scène à faire*, xvi, xix–xxi; *Senso*, 285; sound, xxi, 109, 157–58, 281; sound in Indian cinema, 253, 254, 256, 265, 275 (*see further*, Bhaskar, Ira, chap. 15); space, 191, 278; *Stella Dallas*, 332; in *varieté*, 191; and *verismo*, 283–84; Western drama as equally naturalism or melodrama, xvi. *See also* acting; emotion; language; mode; music

— editing: in *Contagion*, 318, 320; the musicality of melodrama (Thomas Elsaesser), 287; parallel, 94; *song picturization* in Bombay film, 272n11; temporal manipulation of the dialectic of pathos and action (D. W. Griffith), 93; of

theatrical space, 191, 193, 194, 197–99 in *La Passion de Jeanne d'Arc*
— mise en scene: and Carl Th. Dreyer, 190, 193; and the causal logic of narrative, xxi; displacement of expression from plot into subversive mise-en-scène, 4; of empathetic suffering, with the Passion of Christ, 32, 35, 37, 43, 46, 282; expressionist in 1940s Indian cinemas, 253, 262, 264, 270; frigid in *An Orphan*, 84; in *The Hazards of Helen*, 123; "ironic" in *All That Heaven Allows*, 86; metaphoric in *Mother's Happiness*, 95; in the musicality of melodrama (Thomas Elsaesser), 287; nineteenth century, viewed in the twenty-first, 100; serial television, 172; spectacular Chinese, 225; in *Super Fly*, 295, 302;Victorian and Edwardian stage, 109; Western definition, 89
melodrama: ethos, morality and religion. *See* loss
— ethos: ascetic in 1930s China, 226; Catholic, in postwar Italy, 3; egalitarian ethos, in young republican America, xvii; social, in *wenyi*, 89
— morality: Christian, realigned, 3; as drama of morality, 3, 24; dramatic recognition of good and evil, 215; and moral feeling, xiv–xv; moral foundation of, myth of (Matthew Buckley), 23–28; moralism often second to sensation and spectacle, 3
— religion: Christ's Passion, historical connection with, 40–41, 43, 47; Christian catechism in secular terms in Spanish and French theaters, turn of the century, 152–53; religious significance close to the surface, 32; as "silent pulpit," 23. *See also the Sacred*; suffering
melodrama genre(s): xiii, xviii, xix, xxii, xxiii, xxiv–xxv, 4–6, 10, 11, 15, 16, 21–22, 109, 136, 137, 199, 206, 209–10, 211, 212–14, 215–16, 217n7; American television serials, 172, 175, 180; Hollywood, 119, 303; Indian, 63, 245; Italian, 274, 275; Japan, 69, 72; Mexico, 162
melodrama history:
— forerunners and early appearances, ix–xiii; America and melodrama, 17; ballets d'action, 104; Beau Brummell, 300; Bunraku and Kabuki plays, 72; *crux scenica* 107, 113n4; *drame bourgeois* (Diderot), 215; eighteenth century, 3, 21, 22, 25, 100–101, 309n23; Euripides, 101; German rise of neoclassicism, 208; *melodrame*, xii, 215; melodrama devalued as form by 1900, 143, 149n2; Paris *boulevard*, 1790s, 215; Parsi theater, 56–57; pre-[French] Revolutionary genealogy of melodrama, 25; sentimental drama, 307; *sturm und drang* (Schiller), 215. *See also* Gledhill, Christine, *Prologue*; Buckley, Matthew, chap. 1
— nineteenth century: acting manuals, xxiv (*see also* Day-Mayer, Helen and David Mayer); British "illegitimate" theater, 302, 309n23; cross-media evolution, 10; diversity of theatrical subgenres, xiii, 3; English literature in Japan, 75; "immoral melodramas," 116; Japanese literature of, 69–70; mid-London theatrical life burgeoning, xv; "melodrama" in English parlance, 64; melodramas carried to India, 49; morality, 103, 323; orphan imagination (*see* Zhang, Zhen); Parsi theater, 90; pictorialism, xvii; Sarah Bernhardt, 117; secularization, 152; seriality, 6, 75, 76, 170, 177, 179; social ethics and slavery, 44 (*see also* America); (*see* socials), Indian, 64–66; towering English actors, 290–91; women participating, 5, 120; world, melodrama as a "central poetry" of (Brooks cited), 16
melodrama media:
— cinema and nineteenth-century pictorialism, xvii; Hollywood's melodrama, universal appeal of, xix;
— cross-media, 152; novel to play, xiii; novel to *shinpa* play and film, 75; early stage to screen, 208; hybridity and mixed programming, xiii; Indian, 65–66; novel to TV, 175; stage and novel or TV, 180; stage to newsprint to screen, 116; transmedial, 73, 75, 78, 81n1, 228. *See The Colleen Bawn; East Lynne; Giketsu Kyōketsu; Santa; Stella Dallas; Tess of the Storm Country; Uncle Tom's Cabin; Waterloo Bridge; 'Way Down East*

— literature: *See* Brooks, Peter; Elsaesser, Thomas
— newspaper serialization, Charles Dickens and Eugène Sue, 170–71. *See also Konjiki yasha,* 74; Meiji-era, 6, 76; serial(s); seriality
— stage, xiii; as archaic relic, 208–9, 212; *Coelina* (*see also*) as hybrid, 21; evil, depiction of, 313; in *Oliver Twist* (Dickens), 171; parody of in *Why Girls Leave Home,* 108; "text of muteness," 6; today, 99; *The Petrified Forest* on Broadway, reviews of, 141–43; *See* Coburg
— TV serials. *See* Linda Williams, chap. 10
melodrama unbound: 1930s Chinese spectatorship in the context of Confucian rules, 226; American slaves' refusal of cultural annihilation through style, 304; expanding boundaries of realism, the, xiv; global circuit of melodrama, 67; "legitimate" theater and popular entertainment, end of boundary, 1843, xv; mass culture, content- and affect-defined, xvii; melodrama and *wenyi,* 84; passionate melodramas in Hollywood and the [American] sexual order, 129; the *qawwali* narrative, 270. *See* bound; boundaries; *Prometheus unbound*
— unbinding: challenge of melodrama scholarship to traditional critical histories, 29; crossing disciplinary boundaries, ix; facilitating the intersection of cultural boundaries, xii; figure of the orphan, a trope for transnational cross-cultural analysis, 18; intersections of melos and drama in a non-Western lineage, 235; melodrama bound at the same time of its unbinding, 286; melodrama from its "default" Westernized myths and definitions, 89; melodrama from its identity as oppositional "other," 9; melodrama's willingness to buck historical time, 338; seeing melodrama in a cross-cultural context, 235
Mercier, Louis-Sebastien (1740–1814), 25
Merritt, Russell, *the terms melodrama/melodramatic,* problematized, 137
Mexico. *See* Christ; emotion, early twentieth century; language; melodrama genres; Monsiváis, Carlos, chap. 9; music; sacred/the Sacred; serials, novel; tears; woman
Mill on the Po, The. See mulino del Po, Il
Mio fratello è figlio unico/My Brother Is an Only Child (2007, Daniele Luchetti), 280
Mistri, Edal. *See* Kabra, K. N.
Mitchell, Margaret, *Gone with the Wind,* 1936 novel, Pulitzer Prize winner
Mittel, Jason, narrative complexity in TV serials, 177, 178, 180, 183n6, 245, 246, 250, 251n3; contemporary TV serial within melodramatic mode, 180
mode, melodramatic, xiii, xvi, xvii, 69, 83, 87, 115, 160, 188, 213–14, 217, 219, 311: American, 314; auditory, visual, and verbal expressiveness, xvii, 4, 31, 172; *Contagion,* and, 320, 324; contemporary cinema's bloodstream, in, 311–12, 313; critical responses to, 135; deficiencies, of defined, 138; excess, of, 18, 207, 214, 315; French Revolution, and, 215; genre-producing machine, as, 5; genre, relation to, 5, 66, 205; imagination, of, 2, 7, 20, 205; Indian distinctiveness, 254; intermodal history, of, 18, 213; Italian cinema, in, 280; Japan, prominent in, 74; modernity, of/and, 2, 24, 32, 71, 72, 76, 78, 80, 83, 205; modernization of, 315; moral legibility, and, 31; paradoxically conservative and innovative, 199; personalization of virtues and vices (Peter Brooks), 5; reach, broad of, 1, 21, 81, 213; realism, and, 10, 214; sensationalized, 120, 211; serial television, and, 180; significance, power and endurance, of, 11, 149; socio-political issues, and, 312; transformative power, of, 96; transgeneric, 6, 85, 213; transmedial, 73, 75, 76, 85, 206, 211; transnational, 83, 95; ur-mode of popular modernism, 211; vernacular modernism, of, 80; vilification of, 181. *See also* excess
—modality, melodramatic, xiii, 5, 17, 219, 315–16: acknowledgement of inarticulate desires, 237, 241, 244; aesthetic perception, as, 4; audiences engaged by, emotionally and intellectually, 143; changes in, 245; congruence with mainstream narrative forms, 314; cross-cultural, 70;

cross-generic, 4, 9; cultural mediation and contestation, and, 70, 72, 76, 78, 80; default in mainstream cinema, 312; disaster films' use of, 313; diverse systems, in, 22; effects, xiv; emotion, and, 241, 242, 251; performance, of, xiii, 146; redefinition of, 136; stylization, and, 267; time, relation to, chap. 19; tragedy, relation to, 20–21; *wenyi* akin to, 89
—modes: alternative, melodrama crowding out, 16; other (realism, comedy, romance), melodrama's relation to, 2, 5, 13, 156, 213, 214, 216, 315–316; reflexive and objective modes, melodrama's opposition to, 16; theatrical, and the French Revolution, 21, modernism, vernacular, xviii, 80–81, 85, 89–90, 211–12. *See also* realism, tragedy
Moncrieff, William, 358. *See also* Coburg productions
Monroe, Marilyn, 303–4; "the white dress," 305
Monsiváis, Carlos, chap. 9 (152–67); the aesthetics of consolation, 153–54; *bolero*, 151, 155, 160, 167n3; *cancion ranchera*, 160–61; Catholicism in Mexican popular culture, 1930s–1960s, 4, 164–65; cited by scholars of Latin American cinemas, 151; *Cuando los hijos se van*, 156–57 (*see also* Sara García); excess, 155, 156, 157, 160–61; introduction by Kathleen M. Vernon, translator, 151–52; machismo, 160; La *mujer del puerto*, 155–56; *Nosotros los pobres*, 158–60; *Santa*, 155; the secularization of tears, 154–55
— women: censorship and, 163; the close-up, 162; fetishism, 163–64; in Mexican films: Dolores del Rio, María Félix, 162; the new role for women (Jean Arthur, Joan Crawford, Bette Davis, Katherine Hepburn, Rosalind Russell) post WW2, 158, 162
— 1960s: feminisation of the workplace and subjection of, 165; feminism, 165; new female characters, 165–66; women film and video directors, 166
Moody, Jane, eighteenth-century "illegitimate theater": verbal language/muteness, xii, 40, 42, 289; costume, body, gesture, 303; diverse entertainment forms, xiii, lurid stories within sharp contemporary debate, 302–3; melodrama's detractors, xv–xvi; social injustice, 40
Monzaemon, Chikamatsu, eighteenth-century plays, 72
Morayta, Miguel: *Vagabunda*/Tramp (1950), 163; *Hipócrita*/Hypocrite (1949), 163
Moreno, Antonio. *See Santa*
Moretti, Franco, tears, 325–26, 338; death of the protagonist, time and knowledge, 328
Morrison, Toni. *See Beloved*
Mother's Happiness (1926, Shi Dongshan), remade as *Song for a Mother* (1937, Zhu Shilin, 97n13), as *A Mother Remembers* (1953, Chun Kim), 95
mujer del puerto, La/The woman of the port, 1933, Arcady Boytler, 155–56
Mujeres sacrificadas/Self-sacrificing women (1952). *See* Gout, Alberto
mulino del Po, Il/The Mill on the Po (1949, Alberto Lattuada), 278
Mulvey, Laura, American popular culture as "the modern," xviii, the woman's film, 212
Murolo, Roberto, Neapolitan singer, 274. *See also Catene, sceneggiata*
Murphy, Ryan. *See American Crime Story: The People vs O. J. Simpson*
music: *melos* 1, 64, 205, 215, 231, 235
— China: female-performed opera classes, 231; songs from remakes of Hollywood films, 231–33; *Waterloo Bridge* (see), 230–31 (*see* music, opera); Yan Huizhu, 229; Yue opera, female only. *See* Yang, Panpan
— eighteenth century, 21–22: expressive speech, musical underscoring, gesture, choreographed movement, songs and dances, xiii, xvii, xix, xxiv; French and German romanticism, xii; music in urban entertainments, xii; opera, 3, 21, 22; *Pygmalion*, 22
— India: *aalaap*, 265, 272n12; Agha Hashr socials, 66; Bhakti (devotion), and Sufi songs, 268; in *Bholi Jan* (*see also*), *ghazals, thumris, garbis, lavanis* as ragas and folk, 59, 272n14 (*see also The Colleen Bawn*); courtesans and singing women, 266, 272n15; K. N. Kabra, classical musician, 57; *Mahal*, 265; Mani Ratnam on song, 267; melodrama defined, 64; *qawwali*,

music (*continued*)
268–69, 272n20/22 (*see also Veer Zaara*); *Rama-Charita-Manas*, 271n6/7; sacred musical and poetic traditions, especially song, 8–9, 253, 262; *Shejari*, 260–61; *song picturization*, 264, 272n11; South East Asia and the *Natyashastra*, 265–67; *Subarnarekha*, 265; Sufi poetry and song, 4, 267, 268–69, 270. *See* Bhaskar, Ira
— Italy: melodrama emerging from opera, 10, 287; opera (*see* music, opera); opera-citing, 274, 276 (*see Roma città*; operatic expressivity in melodrama, 273); *sceneggiata*, 274 (*see also Catene*); Luchino Visconti, 285
— in melodrama: Mayfield, Curtis, lyrics and score for *Super Fly*, 292, 296, 308n11; as representation, 1, 4; strident, excess (Thomas Elsaesser), 6
— Mexico: *bolero*, 151, 155, 160, 167n3; *canción ranchera*, 160–61; *danzón*, 163, 167n5; song in *Nosotros los pobres*, 159
— nineteenth century and early Hollywood: musical accompaniment, musical character cues, xix; musicians travelled to India and the Far East [theatrical tours], 49, 53; voice, music, sound effects, xvii
— opera: *The Colleen Bawn* as, 50, 55; European opera taken to India, 62, 64; *Faust*, 192 (*see* Dreyer, Carl Th.); Italian, 283–84; Peking and other Chinese forms, 90, 225, 232, 233
My Brother Is an Only Child. *See Mio fratello è figlio unico*
Mystères de Paris, Les (1842–1843). *See* Sue, Eugène

Najma (1943). *See* Khan, Mehboob
Nazimova, Alla, 130: *Bella Donna* (1912, Broadway), success in, 129; *Camille* (1921), 130 (*see La Dame aux camélias*); as extra girl, 130 (*see* girl(s)); as Hedda Gabler, 130; in passionate melodramas, 117. *See also* Mathis, June; Valentino, Rudolph
Ndalianis, Angela, a new form of the baroque, 217n4
Neale, Steve: on the terms *melodrama/melodramatic*, 137; it is *always* too late, 332, 336, 338; spectator's powerlessness to intervene, 328, 331; tears, 194, 325, 326, 331, 338
Neecha Nagar (1946, Chetan Anand), 254–56, 255, 262. *See also* Haas, Willy
Neergaard, Ebbe: on Carl Th. Dreyer, 189, 200n11; on Dreyer and Marie Falconetti, 195, 201n22/24; first history of Danish cinema, 195, 200n12; on Nordisk, 200n11/12. *See also* Rifbjerg, Klaus
Negri, Pola, 128; and American-press rival, Gloria Swanson, 129; *Bella Donna* (*see also*); Mary Pickford on, 129; in passionate melodramas, 117; *Passion* (1920, *see also* Ernst Lubitsch), 128–29; *Woman of the World, A*, 129. *See also* actors, female
Nek Parveen or Silver King. *See* Hashr Agha
Nel gorgo del peccato/In the Whirl of Sin (1954, Vittorio Cottafavi), 282
nemica, La/The enemy (1952, Giorgio Bianchi), maternal melodrama, 274
Neville, Henry, 107; 1895 manual, 107, 109, 359. *See also* acting: manuals; Bernhardt, Sarah; Day-Mayer, Helen and David Mayer; Delsarte, François
Newcomb, Horace, popular television, 175, 178
Newman, Michael Z., prime-time television serial rhythm, 183n7
New York Acting School. *See* America. *See also* American, Academy of Dramatic Arts; Belasco, David
Nobody's Children. *See I figli di nessuno*
Nodier, Charles, on melodrama's origin, 19, 23, 32; (1843) on Pixérécourt, René-Charles Guilbert de (*see also*), 23, 24–25, 26. *See also* Brooks, Peter
Noi peccatori/We Sinners (1953). *See* Brignone, Guido
No no Hana. *See East Lynne*
Nordisk Films Kompagni, 185, 188–91, 200n2/3/10/11/12, 201n14/16/28; Dreyer in, 189–90, 199, 201n16; Dreyer's break with, 189, 190; *Leaves from Satan's Book* (1921, Carl Th. Dreyer), 189; *varieté* [melodrama], 188, 190–91, 192–93, 195, 196, 199, 200n5. *See also* Dreyer, Carl Th. *Lydia*; Neergaard, Ebbe

Nosotros los pobres/We the poor (1948, Ismael Rodríguez), 151, 158–60, 163
Notari, Elvira, 334, 339n8
Novaro, Maria, *Danzón* (1991)
Now, Voyager (1942, Irving Rapper), 338–39

Octoroon. See Boucicault, Dion; Edouin, Rose
Of Human Bondage (1934). See Davis, Bette
O. J.: Made in America (2017, ESPN, Ezra Edelson). See Simpson, O. J.
Oliver Twist. See Dickens, Charles
Omoide no ki. See Roka, Tokutomi; Dickens, Charles
O'Neal, Ron (Youngblood)Priest. See Pribram, E. Deidre; *Super Fly*
Onoga tsumi. See Yūhō, Kikuchi
Only Way, The. See Dickens, Charles
Ophuls, Max. See *Letter from an Unknown Woman*
Opie, Amelia. See *Father and Daughter, The*
Oprah Winfrey Show, The, 273
Orphan, An (1929, Chinese adaptation of *Way Down East*), 84
Orphan Rescues Grandfather (1923, Zhang Shichuan and Zhengqiu Zheng), 83–84, 85, 94, 94, 95, 96n1, 97n11; critics' use of melodrama and, 90, popularity of, 92, 94; twin genealogy of *wenyi* in, 88.
Orphans of the Storm (1921, D. W. Griffith, based on *Les Deux orphelines*, 1874, Adolphe Dennery and Eugène Corman, 92), 83, 154; in China 84, 85, 92, 95, 97n9
O' sole mio (1946). See Gentilomo, Giacomo
Ossessione (1943). See Visconti, Luchino
Osten, Franz, 254. See also *Prapancha Pash*; *Prem Sanyas*; *Shiraz*
O'Sullivan, Sean, serial television and the season, 178; script pace, 179
Ozu Yasujiro, 72

Parachute Jumper (1933). See Green, Alfred E.
Parivartan (1925, Radheshyam, Kathavachak), 66. See also socials
Parks, Gordon, Jr., 292, 308n13
Parks, Gordon, Sr., 293, 308n13. See also *Shaft*
Parsons, Louella, on women working in Hollywood, 127

Passion (1920, Ernst Lubitsch, title changed from *Madame du Barry*), 127–29. See also Negri, Pola
Passion de Jeanne d'Arc, La/*The Passion of Jeanne D'Arc* (1928, Carl Th. Dreyer), 185, 188, 192–99; 200n9; art house movie, 11, 201n23; "authentic," 188, 193, 194; conventional film criticism, 186; Dreyer on, 185, 189, 193, 199n1,201n15/25/26; *gogl* in, 189, 197, 198; immolation scene, 186, 187, 200n4; Luis Buñuel on Jeanne's tears, 195; and melodrama, 194, 201n21; tears in and over, 194–95, 197; *varieté* in, 188, 190–91, 193–94, 195. See also *Lydia*; Neergaard, Ebbe; Nordisk
— Falconetti, Marie: as Jeanne, 185, 187, 194–96, 197, 201n22; head shaved, 194, 196–97, 198, 201n24; *varieté* star, 188, 196. See also tears
Path of Hope, The. See *cammino della speranza, La*
pathos, 8, 10, 87, 200n6; 1950s family melodrama, and, 205; and action, 87, 214, 216, 275, 326; in Bholi Jan, 63; in Coelina, 92; costumes and, in Super Fly, 293; the disaster film, in, 312; emotionality, and, 242, 280; feminism and, 200n7, 212; Hollywood and, 6; in Meiji-era literature, 75, 77; and melodrama, xvi, xviii, 242, 330; of melodramatic timing, 9; mise-en-scène of, 35; and modernity, xxii; and moral drama, 25; orphan figure, and the, 86, 93, 94; personality types, performers, and, 11; in The Petrified Forest, 135–36; pre-Revolutionary genealogy of melodrama, Peter Brooks and, 20–21, 31, 32; in, 25; and recognition, 10, 191, 241; sensational-romance, heroine's path in, 116; of separation, 8, 39, 264, 272n10, 321; in serials and soap opera, 172, 173, 176; of suffering, 216, 326; and suffering virtue, 33; Thomas Elsaesser and, 205; time and, 9, 330. See also *The Lear of Private Life*; *Passion de Jeanne d'Arc, La*; see also Zhang, Zhen Christianity of: 3, 32–37, 41 passim (chap. 2), 282; Mary Magdalene, 32, 36, 43; Virgin Mary, 32, 36, 37, 43, 45, 283. See also Christ; Christ, Passion of

Pati Bhakti/Worship of the Husband (1922, (*see*) Harikrishna Jauhar with Patience Cooper), 64, 66. See also *bhakti*; socials
Patten, Robert L., monthly one-schilling parts, pre-publication, 170
Paul Kauvar; Or, Anarchy (1887). See Mackay, Steele
Pearson, Roberta, melodrama, devalued form by 1900, 143, 149n2
Pedwell, Carolyn, *Feminist Theory, on feminism and affect*, 238
People vs O. J. Simpson, The (2017, Ezra Edelson). See Simpson, O. J.
Perdonami!/Forgive Me! (1953). See Costa, Mario
Perils, of Pauline, The (1914, William Randolph Hearst, co-producer), 125, 126; "Real Perils of Pauline," *Literary Digest*, 1921, 126. See also serials; White, Pearl
peripetia/reversal, xix
Petrified Forest, The (1936) (*see* Archie Mayo, film version of the 1935 play by Robert E. Sherwood), 135, 138–40, 149, 150n4; acting, vehicle for, 135, 142, 145; artful direction, 144; as melodrama, 9, 135, 138, 141, 142, 143; philosophic crime thriller and tragic romance, 138, 142; reviews of stage and screen version, 135; stage to screen, speedy transition, 11
— on stage: 135; Peggy Conklin as Gabby Maple, 142; reviews of, 142–43: Burns Mantle, Percy Hammond; similarities to *The Girl of the Golden West*, 140, 141. See also Belasco, David; Howard, Leslie
— on screen: *139*, 143, 145, *147*; acting in, melodramatic, 146–48, 150n10; Alexander Walker, 148; Bette Davis as Gabby Maple, 143, 150n9; Eileen Creelman, 143–44, 149; Kate Cameron, 144, 145; reviews of: William Boehnel, 144–45. See also Davis, Bette; Howard, Leslie
Petro, Patrice, Weimar cinema, 254
Philadelphia (1993, Jonathan Demme), 316. See also disaster film(s)
Pickford, Mary, 5; *Bishop's Carriage, The* (1913), 122; Broadway, 1907 debut, 120; Broadway, last play, *A Good Little* Devil (1913) (*see also* Belasco, David), 125; business woman, 121, 122, 122, 123; *Caprice* (1913), 122–23; and cliff-hanging serials, 123; Famous Players, 122; and the "foreigners," 129; and Gloria Swanson, 129; as growing girl, 123, 133n2 (*see also Rebecca of Sunnybrook Farm*); *Hearts Adrift* (1914), 123; "Pickford Revolution" and the emerging star system, 116; *Rosita* (1923) (*see also* Ernst Lubitsch), 129; sensational-romantic melodramas, 122–23; star image, 121. See also *Tess of the Storm Country*; White, Pearl
Pixérécourt, René-Charles Guilbert de, xxi, 22, 24–25, 26, 360; adulation as "father of melodrama," 25; Charles Nodier on: as "silent pulpit" 23, 24, 26; drama of morality, 24; formula, 22; melodramatic form, *melo-drame*, 101; Frank Rahill on; "recipe" 21, 22, 24
— *Coelina* (1800), xii, 21, 22, 25, 92–93. See also orphan, the; *Tale of Mystery, A*
— *Dog of Montargis, The*; Or *The Forest of Bondy* (1816)40, 92
Planctus Mariae, 43
Podosi. See also Hindi version of *Shejari*, 271n7
Poor Children, The (1924). See Zhang Shichuan
Postlewait, Thomas, rationale for the denigration of melodrama, 113n1
Poulton, M. Cody, 69; on *Taki no shiraito*, 79. See also Izumi Kyōka
Prabhat Film Company, 256, 271n4
Prapancha Pash (*A Throw of the Dice*, 1929, Franz Osten), 254. See also Rai, Himanshu
Prem Nagar (*City of Love*, 1941). See Bhavnani, Mohan; Haas, Willy
Prem Sanyas (*Light of Asia*, 1925, Franz Osten), 254
Pribram, E. Deidre, chap. 14 (237–51): *Breaking Bad* (*see also*), 180, 182, 245, 246, 247–50; characters as culturally embedded beings, 180; drama driven by emotions rather than narrative logic, xxi; emotion and affect, 238–40; emotional expressiveness, 7; emotions and melodrama past, 240–44; emotions and melodrama present, 244–51; narrativity, 239, 243, 251n1; nonlinguistic

communication, 240; serialization, 180.
    See also The Wire, 245, 246–47; Buckley,
    Matthew; Massumi, Brian; Mittel, Jason;
    Pedwell, Carolyn and Anne Whitehead;
    Singer, Ben; Thorburn, David; Williams,
    Linda
Price, Gertrude, "female moving picture
    expert" in Hollywood, 127
Prometheus, 1, 286; *Prometheus Bound* and
    Prometheus Unbound, 1; and unbinding,
    11
Pueblerina (1949). *See* Fernández, Emilio
Puccini, Giacomo, composer, 283
Pulitzer, Joseph: and national news, 125–26
    (*see also* Hearst, William Randolph);
    Pulitzer Prize, 135, 224
Pygmalion. *See* Rousseau, Jean-Jacques

Queen Victoria, and *The Colleen Bawn*, 50;
    Golden Jubilee celebrations 1887, 57. *See
    also* Balivala, K. M.
Queen's Husband, The. *See* Sherwood, Robert
    Emmet

Rahill, Frank, on *The Petrified Forest*, 148; on
    Pixérécourt, René-Charles Guilbert de, 21,
    22; costume and meaning, 290
Rai, Himanshu, producer, 254
Rani, Devika, 254
Rappe, Virginia, death of, 131–32. *See also*
    girls
Rapsodia satanica/Satan's Rhapsody (1917,
    Nino Oxilia). *See also* Mascagni
realism: authenticity, as, 279; changing modes
    of, 214; costume in *Super Fly*, and, 302;
    critical investment in, xvi, 15, 20, 174, 197,
    211, 244; emotion, normatively opposed
    to, 46, 278; emotion, used to evoke in
    Zhengju, 97*n*11, 215, 277; expanding
    boundaries of, xiv; means of melodrama's
    modernisation, 136, 141, 149, 173,
    215; melodrama, and 34, 145, 213;
    melodrama, coexistence with, 171–72,
    217, 234; melodrama, opposed to, 209;
    melodrama's claim to, xiii; mode, as, 214;
    modern art, associated with, 19; modes,
    other (comedy, melodrama, romance and
    fantasy), relation to/combination with,
xiii, 2, 5, 143, 216, 235, 277, 283, 287, 317;
    neorealism, and 160, 276, 278, 281, 284;
    nineteenth-century novel, and, 21; poetic,
    in French cinema, 210; psychological, 243;
    repression, and, 244, 273, 316; rise against
    melodrama, 17, 244, 273; secondary status
    to melodrama, 18; silent film performance,
    and, 100; social against moral didacticism,
    155; sources, shared with melodrama, 16;
    spectacular, 197; unbinding melodrama
    from opposition to, 9, 10, 11, 213, 214,
    234, 273, 277, 287
Reade, Charles. *See The Lyons Mail*; Irving,
    Henry
Rebecca of Sunnybrook Farm (1917 film,
    Marshall Neilan; based on the 1903 novel
    by Kate Douglas Wiggin; starring Mary
    Pickford, 123, 133*n*2
Reeves, Keanu, 304; the "Matrix coat," 305
Resurrection (1899, Leo Tolstoy), and
    Japanese melodrama, 77, 82*n*8
Reunion in Vienna (1931). *See* Sherwood,
    Robert Emmet
Rich Man, Poor Man (1970, Irwin Shaw; ABC
    mini-serial, 1976), 175
Ricoeur, Paul, time in narrative, 330
Riemenschneider, Tilman, 1460–1531,
    Germany, sculptor and wood carver,
    followers of, 37; Peter Dell the Elder a
    pupil, 41. *See also* Christ
Riesebrodt, Martin, religion as promise of
    salvation, 282
Rifbjerg, Klaus, on Carl Th. Dreyer, 189, 197,
    200*n*13. *See also* Neergaard, Ebbe
Rigoletto, Sergio, 200*n*8, 276
Riso amaro/Bitter Rice (1949). *See* De Santis,
    Giuseppe
Robbins, Bruce, 96
Robinson, Edward G., American Academy of
    Dramatic Arts, 146; Juan Orol, fan of, 158
Rocco e i suoi fratelli/Rocco and His Brothers
    (1960), 280, 285; Sam Rohdie on, 284. *See
    also* Visconti, Luchino
Rodney King, 181, 182
Rodríguez, Ismael: *See Nosotros los pobres/
    We the poor*; the classic of classics, 158;
    Ustedes, los ricos/You the rich (1948) and
    Pepe el Toro (1953), 160

Roots (ABC, 1977, Alex Haley)
Rosita. *See* Pickford, Mary
Roland, Ruth, 125, *126*; cliff-hanging serial stars, 123; *The Timber Queen* (1922), own production company, 125; western serials, 125, 133n3. *See also* actors, female; serial(s); White, Pearl; women
Roma città aperta/Rome Open City (1945) (*see* Roberto Rossellini), 276, 278, 281 (*see also* Italian melodrama, salvation), 284; heralding neorealism, 277. *See also* Magnani, Anna
Romanticismo (1950). *See* Fracassi, Clemente
Romeo and Juliet (William Shakespeare): Rose Edouin as Romeo, 55; Charlotte Cushman as Romeo, *118*, *119*
Rome Open City. *See Roma città aperta*
Roots (1977, Alex Haley), 175; Linda Williams on, 183n3
Rosary, The (1913, Lois Weber), 332
Rossellini, Roberto:
— Ingrid Bergman trilogy (*Stromboli*, 1950; *Europa '51*, 1952; *Viaggio in Italia/Journey to Italy*, 1954), 280. *See also* melodrama: critical concepts, *mancato*
— *Germania anno zero/Germany Year Zero* (1948), 278. *See also Roma città aperta*
Rossen, Robert. *See Mambo*
Rousseau, Jean-Jacques: affective aesthetics, movement toward, 22, in the pre-Revolutionary geology of melodrama, 25; languages, on the origin of, and gesture, 104–5, 106; music-drama of, 215
— *Pygmalion* 1762/1775, 22; *scène lyrique*, alternated speech and mime to music, xii, and the verbally inexpressible, xii
Rowell, George, xvi. *See The Day of Reckoning*
Rowntree, Richard, John Shaft. *See* Pribram, E. Deidre; *Shaft*
Russell, Catherine, cross-cultural criticism and Japanese film melodrama, 72

sacred/Sacred, the, 33:
— traditional Sacred, the, 3: all-encompassing hierarchical authority in Middle Ages, 35; oversimplified understanding of relationship between, and the secular, 46; structures of religious and social order, 19

— collapse/crisis/liquidation/loss of the traditional Sacred, 3, 19, 23, 253, 281–82; melodrama as quest for lost moral legibility now "occulted," 205; scholars of melodrama on, 31–32
— post-Sacred/secular: affective piety repurposed, 32; "man as the centre of all things" (Peter Brooks), 32; modernity, 24; a new "drama of morality," 23; world finds its self-reflexive form, 24
— China: contest between "traditional Confucian" values and "modern Western," 227
— France: law and humanized values replace Church authority, 281
— India: Bhakti and Sufi traditions and melodrama, 33, 268; inherent connection between the Sacred and the profane, 268; the Sacred fully active in Indian melodrama, 4, 253; traditions of the Sacred, 267–71. *See also* Bhaskar, Ira; Hansen, Kathryn
— Italy: climactic use of characters like figures in religious iconography, 283; Catholic belief in reality infused with the divine, 273; melodrama and the promise of salvation, 281–83 (*see also* Bayman, Louis); Vatican Catholicism, 283
— Mexico: Christianity [and] symbology, 153; sacred values, 156; secularization, 152. *See also* Allen, Richard; Brooks, Peter; Buckley, Matthew; Champagne, John; French Revolution
Sahib Bibi aur Ghulam (1962, Ali, Abrar) (*see also* Dutt, Guru, 272n11), 264–65
St Valentine's Eve; or, The Fair Maid of Perth. *See* Coburg productions
Sairandhri (1933). *See* Shantaram, V.
Salón México (1949). *See* Fernández, Emilio
Sampson, Henry, black cinema history, 308n21
San Andreas (2015, Brad Peyton), 320. *See also* disaster film(s)
Santa (1903, novel, Federico Gamboa); 1931, film, Antonio Moreno (*see bolero*); 1943, film, Norman Foster, 155
Schiller, Friedrich: affective aesthetics, movement toward, 22; the

pre-Revolutionary genealogy of melodrama, 25; *sturm und drang* of, 215
Sciuscià/Shoeshine (1946). *See* De Sica, Vittorio
Sconce, Jeffrey: quality television, 175, 176, 177, 245, 251n2
Scott, Clement. *See* Irving, Henry
Scott, Ellen C., African American actors and roles proscribed by social prejudice, 309n23
Scott, Walter, *The Fair Maid of Perth*, novel. *See* Coburg Productions; "morbid fictions" of threat by female playwrights, 118
Scripps, E. W. *See* Hearst, William Randolph; newspapers, syndication
Sea Oath/Swear by God (1921). *See* Duyu, Dan
Sedaine, Michel-Jean (1719–1797), 25
Senso (1954, Luchino Visconti): border between excess and restriction, 286; costume drama, opera-citing, 274, 276; a Gramscian understanding of operatic gesture, 284; Guido Fink on, 284–85; successful *melodramma*, 285
Sensualidad/Sensuality(1951). *See* Gout, Alberto
Sensualità (1952). *See* Fracassi, Clemente
Senza Pietà. *See* Germi, Pietro
Serena, Gustavo. *See Assunta Spina*
serial(s), definitions, 169; melodrama, 173; villains, xvii
— film: 1930s America, 173; cliff-hanging, 123, 178 (*see also* Holmes, Helen; Roland, Ruth; White, Pearl); queens and melodramatic scenarios, 5; sensational-romantic, 116
— Meiji literature: convergence of with English melodramatic literature, 8 (*see also* Izumi Kyōka, Kikuchi Yūhō, Tokutomi Roka); drama of recognition and spectacular action and violence, 75, 78. *See also Konjiiki yasha* (Ozaki Kōyō, most important Meiji novel, 74, 76, 77); Meiji era (1890–1912), 70–72, 73; melodrama, the term, 74, 75 (Ken K. Ito); Mizoguch Kenji films, 72, 77; modernity and earlier sentimental literature, 75; serialisations and cross-media adaptations, 77; *shinpa* plays and silent film, 77

See Airriess, Hannah, chap. 4. *See also Taki no shiraito; Weaker than a Woman*
— novel: Brooks, Peter on, 170; folletín in Mexico, 152, nineteenth-century Britain and France, 170–171 (*see* Dickens, Charles and Sué, Eugène), 183n1; serialization in newspapers, 74, 91. *See East Lynne; Mandarin Duck and Butterflies* literature
— seriality/serialities, 6, 169–71, 174, 176, 177, 180, 247 (*see* Williams, Linda, chap. 10); and addiction, 183; commercial, 178; realism and, 173; and time, 246
— television serial drama: 6, 7, 173–79; accumulation, 175–76; comedy, 176, 183n4; "Complex TV," 177, 179, 245 (*see also* Mittel, Jason and Sconce, Jeffery); contemporary serial, 176–79; enduring diegetic worlds, 175; prime time, 174, 176, 183n7; *Rich Man, Poor Man*, 175; *Roots*, 175, 183n3; soap opera and melodrama, 174, 176; *time in*, 178, 179–80, 183n8; *Transparent* (2014-ongoing, Amazon), 177, 180. *See also Breaking Bad; Dallas; Lost;* Simpson, O. J.; *Sopranos, The; Stella Dallas; The Wire*. *See* Williams, Linda, chap. 10
Seventh Heaven (1927). *See* Borzage, Frank
Shaft (1971, Gordon Parks Sr.), 293, 305, 308n13; Shaft and costume, 305, 305, 306, 308n13, 309n27. *See also Super Fly*
Shakespeare, William (1564–1616): adapted for India, 49; "morbid fictions" of threat by female playwrights, 118; nineteenth century, mixed programmes, xiii; sentimental drama alongside, eighteenth century, new forms of, xi; tragedies, Charlotte Cushman cross-dressing in, 118; tragedies as melodramatic, 152
Shantaram, V. 256, 258, 260, 271n2/4; and expressionism, 260; *Kunku* (1937), 258–60, 259; *Sairandhri* (1933), 256, 271n4. *See also Amrit Manthan*; Prabhat Film Company; *Shejari*
Shaw, George Bernard, dramatist, xvi, detractor of melodrama, 100
Sheik, The. *See* Valentino, Rudolph
Shejari (1941, V. Shantaram), 260–62, 261; *bhavi* and the *Ramayana*, 260; Hindi version, *Podosi*, 271n7

Shepherd, Simon, xvii; and Peter Womack, xvi, 39; the term "melo-drame," xii
Sherwood, Robert, Emmet, 135, 141, 142, 144, 150n5/7, 362; stage to screen:
— *Reunion in Vienna* (1931; 1933 film, Sidney Franklin), 141
— *The Petrified Forest* (1934; (see) 1936 film, Archie Mayo); Burns Mantle, 142; Regina Crewe, 144; reviews for the text: William Boehnel, 144
— *The Queen's Husband* (1928; as *The Royal Bed*, 1931, Lowell Sherman), 141
— *Waterloo Bridge* (see 1930; 1931 film, James Whale)
Shi Dongshan. See *Mother's Happiness*
Shingler, Martin, chap. 8 (135–50): Elinor Hughes, theater critic, on *Fog Over Frisco*, 1935, 137–38; melodrama: in continual process of renewal, 9, 136–37; melodrama rendered as parody, early twentieth century, 10
— *A Petrified Forest*: acting in, 145–48; crime thriller and tragic romance, 138–45; melodrama applied to both stage (1835) and screen (1936) versions, 9. See also Davis, Bette; Howard, Leslie
Shiraz (1928, Franz Osten), 254. See also Rai, Himanshu
Shoeshine. See *Sciuscià*
Siddons, Henry. See acting: manuals
Simpson, O. J.: black and white perceptions, opposed, in one (serial) melodrama, 182; "made" in (a racist) America, 181; not raced, 182; *O. J.: Made in America*, 180–82 (Ezra Edelson, 2017), 181–82; "playing the Race Card," accusation by the prosecution, 181; trial serialized, 180–82: *American Crime Story: The People vs O. J. Simpson* (Ryan Murphy, 2017), 181; videoed beating of Rodney King, 180–81; viewers and the acquittal, 182
Singer, Ben, 87, 208, 338; Japanese cinematic melodrama, scholarship on, and, 69–70; melodrama, "a compensatory faith," 23; *Melodrama and Modernity* (2001) 211, 242–43, 244; melodrama as sensational modernity, 212; melodrama's excesses challenge "the classical," 207, 217n6;

sensationalism and action in turn-of-the-century American melodrama theater, 78; sensational-romantic serials, 116; serial films, 173, 312; spectacular realism in *La Passion de Jeanne d'Arc*, 197
Sirk, Douglas, *All that Heaven Allows* (1955), 86; *Imitation of Life*, 331–32; ironic ideological subversion, 4; ironic mise en scène, 86; stylistic excess, xxi; Universal cycle, 1970s rediscovery of, 86
Smiles and Tears (1815, Marie-Thérèse Kemble), xiv, 354. See also *The Father and Daughter*; Brooks, Peter, "interesting"
socials, Indian, 64–66. See also cross-dressing; Fenton, Mary; Hashr, Agha; *Pati Bhakti*
Soderbergh, Steven, on costume, 307n1. See also *Contagion*; *Traffic*
sole sorge ancora, Il (1946, Aldo Vergano), 277
Soler, Fernando: actor in *Cuando los hijos se van*/When the children leave home(1941), 157; director of *La hija del penal*/Born in Prison, 1949), 163
Song for a Mother (1937). See *Mother's Happiness*
Sopranos, The (HBO, 1999–2007), 177, 178, 179, 251n2/3
Sorensen, Peer, 200n6
Spring River Flows East, The/*Yijiang Chunshui Xiangdongliu* (1947, Zheng Junli and Cai Chusheng), two parts: affection and, 234; comparisons with *Gone with the Wind*, 233, 234; conflicts of modernity, 234; echoing *Waterloo Bridge*, 234; folksong in, 235; narrative coincidences, 235; "*wenyi* blockbuster," 233
Staiger, Janet. See Bordwell, David; Janet Staiger; and Kristin Thompson
Stanislavsky. See acting
Stebbins, Genevieve. See Delsarte, François
Stella Dallas (late 1930s, radio soap opera), 173; (1937 film, King Vidor), 332
Storia di Caterina, episode from *Love in the City* (1953, Michelangelo Antonioni et al.), 279–80. See also melodrama: critical concepts, *mancato*
Stowe, Harriet Beecher. See *Uncle Tom's Cabin*

Stranger, The (1790, 1798). *See* Kotzebue, August von
Stromboli (1950). *See* Rossellini, Roberto
Student's Hard Life, A (1925, Guan Haifeng), 95
Stutesman, Drake, chap. 17 (289–309): Adams, Nate, (*see* costume designer on *Super Fly*), 293, 294–95, 298, 305, 308*n*12; "Black Dandy," 300–302; the body, 303–7; the costume, 289–303; costume and towering nineteenth-century actors (*see* Ira Aldridge; Henry Irving; Herbert Beerbohm Tree), 290–92; costuming the black male hero of *Super Fly*, 10, 290, 292, 293, 294–99, 300, 302–3, 305–6, 307. *See also* costume; Shaft in *Shaft*, 305, 306, 308*n*13/27; costume; *Sweet Sweetback's Baadasssss Song*; Zip Coon
Subarnarekha (1962, Ritwik Ghatak), 265, song in. *See also* 272*n*12
Sudhi Vachche Sopari. *See* Kabra, K. N.
Sue, Eugène, 309*n*25; *Mystères de Paris, Les* (June 1842–October 1843), 170
Sundari, Jayshankar, female impersonator, 65. *See also* socials
Super Fly (1972, Gordon Parks Jr.), 292–300, 302–303, 304–5, 307, 308*n*13; African American crime film, 290; black male, 10, 293, 297, 302–3, 304; Curtis Mayfield songs, 292, 296, 308*n*11; "invisible man" (*see* Ellison, Ralph), 289, 294; as melodrama, 307*n*3; melodramatic tropes in, 290, 303, 309*n*24; presentation, reliance on, 290; script, 293–94; small budget success, 292, 308*n*11; Vincent Canby on, 290. *See also* Mayfield, Curtis; *Sweet Sweetback's Baadasssss Song*
— costume and body in, 10, 293, 294–95, 294, 295, 296, 296–300, 297, 298, 305–7, 306; Black Dandy, 304, 306–7; Eleganza 298, 299; Nate Adams, and, 293, 294, 298, 304. *See also* costume, Black Dandy; *Shaft*
Swanson, Gloria, 129; and American-press rival, Pola Negri, 129; *Beyond the Rocks* (1922), *131*; *The Great Moment* (1921, Glyn, Elinor), 129; Mary Pickford on, 129; in passionate melodramas, 117, 129. *See also* Lubitsch, Ernst; Valentino, Rudolph

Sweet Sweetback's Baadasssss Song (1971, Melvin Van Peebles), 293, 305, 308*n*13. *See also* Blaxploitation

Taki no shiraito (The Water Magician), original story by Izumi Kyōka (*see*); 1933 film, adaptation and direction by Kenji Mizoguchi, 77–78, 79; first film adaptation, 1912, 77; as melodrama, 78; readings of: Saitō, Tadao; Kinoshita, Chika, 78; success of novel, play, film, 77, 78
Tale of Mystery, A (1802, Thomas Holcroft,adapted from *Coelina*) (*see also* Pixérécourt, René-Charles Guilbert de), xii, 92
Tasca, Madame. *See* Boucicault, Dion
Taylor, Charles, 117; the "buffered" self, 34
tears, 325–26, 332, 338–39; and *Cuando los hijos se van*/When the children leave home, 157; and death, 328; discrepancies, consequence of, 325, 326; and fulfillment, hope of, 336; God, the penetration of into the individual, 282; high art, C19, and, 244; and *Imitation of Life*, 331; intensity of, 1931–1955, irreversibility, 326, 331, 332; "Lacreme napulitane"/Neapolitan Tears, 274–75; and lyricism, 275; and Marie Falconetti's in *La Passion de Jeanne d'Arc*, 194–95, 197, 201*n*24; Mary Magdalene's, 35, 43, 45; in melodrama, 33; Mexico, 157; Mother Mary's, 45; mothers and wives reduced to, 166; and the New Testament, 153; and *Nosotros los pobres*, 159; and *Now, Voyager*, 338–39; the secularisation of, 154–55; shared, 194; and *Stella Dallas*, 332; theory of, 339; the Valley of, 153; and the Victorian melodrama audience, 243; of the white race, 44; Yan Huizhu and *Waterloo Bridge*, 229. *See also* lamentation; *Lamentation*; Moretti, Franco; Neale, Steve; *Smiles and Tears*; Williams, Linda
terra trema, La (1948). *See* Visconti, Luchino
Tess of the d'Urbevilles (1891, Thomas Hardy). *See Way Down East*
Tess of the Storm Country (1909 novel by Grace Miller White; 1914 film, Edwin S. Porter), starring Mary Pickford, 123

— 1922 remake, Mary Pickford, independent producer, 123; optimistic spin on Thomas Hardy's Tess, 123. *See also Tess of the d'Urbevilles*

Thompson, Kristin, 217n2; narrative excess, 225, 233; narrative linearity, 235. *See also* Bordwell, David, Janet Staiger, and Kristin Thompson; Bordwell, David and Kristin Thompson; Yang, Panpan

— and Bordwell, David, ambiguous moral space, 253–54; "linear" historiography, 339n5

Thomsen, Bodil, on *La Passion de Jeanne d'Arc*, 201n21

Thorburn, David, American television melodrama, 245

Tianming/Daybreak (1933, Sun Yu), 76

Timber Queen, The (1922). *See* Roland, Ruth

Ti ho sempre amato! (1953). *See* Costa, Mario

time, 9, 325–39: in *Hamlet*, 331; chance, xxii, 314, "chance time" (Mikhail Bakhtin), 331, 332, 333, 339n7; composite tense, 333; historical time, 9, 328–38, 333 (Reinhart Koselleck), 334 (*see Assunta Spina*); *historical time theory* of *melodrama*, 329; irreversibility, temporal, 325, 326, 328, 329, 331, 333, 336, 337; melodrama's play with, 315; modes of, the three different 9, 329–30, 331, 333, 334 (*see also 'A Santanotte*); "reverse time" (Linda Williams), 326; and space in plays before cinema, xix; televisual/serial, 177–78; temporal asymmetry, 329, 330, 331, 336, 338; temporal "ecstacies" (Martin Heidegger), 329, 334

Tokutomi Roka, *Omoide no ki* (1901, Footprints in the Snow), based on *David Copperfield*, 75. *See also* Dickens, Charles

Tompkins, Jane, on *Uncle Tom's Cabin*, 44

Tormento (1950). *See* Matarazzo, Raffaello

Torna! (1954). *See* Matarazzo, Raffaello

Traffic (2000, see also Steven Soderbergh), 320. *See also* disaster film(s)

tragedy: alternation with comedy in Dickens, 171; cultural status of, 27–28; Greek (and Prometheus bound), 1, 101, 215, 282; Heilman, Robert, on, 215, 217n1; *Jeanne d'Arc*, as, 201n23; Latin-American context, in, 152; neoclassical, 180; realism and, 214; traditional Sacred, and; Williams, Raymond on 10, 13

— and melodrama: melodrama as failed or not, 206, 216; melodrama's evolution from/opposition to/difference from, 106, 153, 171, 214; melodrama's replacement of/overlap with, 207, 213

Tragic Pursuit. *See Caccia tragica*

trans: -action, 105, 106, 107; -atlantic, 50, 93; -create, 62, 260; -cultural, 15, 18, 84, 85, 95, 96, 107, 225; -denomination, 34; -figuration, 155; -gender, 180; -generic, 85, 87; -gress, 86, 94, 140, 160, 290; -lingual, 72, 91; -media, xxvii, 15, 69, 70, 73, 75, 76, 77, 78, 80, 81, 85, 89, 91, 97, 212, 225, 228; -mission/mit, 16, 196, 318, 320, 321, 322, 323; -mute, 70, 136, 137, 266, 277; -national, xvii, 4, 7, 8, 11, 21, 69, 70, 72, 79, 80, 81, 83, 84, 85, 86, 88, 89, 90, 93, 95, 96, 107, 212, 220, 224, 228, 232; -parent, 177, 180; -plant, 72, 86, 89, 91, 93, 228, 229; -port, 59, 171, 324; -pose, 32, 96, 316; -value, 210

Transparent. *See* serial television melodrama

tratta delle bianche, La/The White Slave Trade (1952, Luigi Comencini)

Travolta, John, 304; "the white suit," 305

Tree, Herbert Beerbohm, 290, 291, 292, 294, 297, 303, 308n9

Trotacalles/Streetwalker (1951). *See* Landeta, Matilde

Two Anonymous Letters. *See Due lettere anonime*

Uncle Tom's Cabin (1852, Harriet Beecher Stowe), 363; affective piety and 44–45; American melodrama, seminal catalyst for, xviii; Evangelical Protestantism and, 34; Henry James on, 76, 206; martyrdom and, 40, 47n4; seriality and, 181, 183n1; social justice, 215

Under the Gaslight (1867, Augustin Daly), 118, 172

Ungrateful Heart. *See Core 'ngrato*

Valentino, Rudolph: in *Beyond the Rocks*, 131; European brand of passionate

melodramas, 117; *Four Horsemen of the Apocalypse, The* (1921), 130; and Pola Negri, 129; *Sheik, The* (1921), 130
— in *Camille* (1921), 130 (*see La Dame aux camélias*; Mathis, June; Nazimova, Alla)
Vagabunda/Tramp (1950). *See* Morayta, Miguel
Vámonos con Pancho Villa/Let's Go With Pancho Villa (1936). *See* de Fuentes, Fernando
Van Peebles, Melvin. *See Sweet Sweetback's Baadasssss Song*
Vasudevan, Ravi, 90; on the link between "classical" Hollywood narration and *production*, xix
Veer Zaara (2004 Yash Chopra), 270
Verdi, Giuseppe. *See* Matarazzo, Raffaello
Verga, Giovanni, short story writer. *See verismo*
Vergano, Aldo. *See sole sorge ancora, Il*
Vestris, Madame. *See The Day of Reckoning*
Viaggio in Italia/Journey to Italy (1954). *See* Rossellini, Roberto
Vicar of Wakefield, The (1766 Oliver Goldsmith), xi, xiv
Vicinus, Martha: on *Heartsease*, 118; melodrama as how (things) ought to be, 213
Visconti, Luchino, 285–86; emblematic of combined practices, 285; *La terra trema* (1948), 278; melodrama, border between excess and restriction, 286; *Ossessione* (1943), 285 (*see* neorealism). *See also* Italian melodrama; *Rocco e i suoi fratelli*; *Senso*

Wagner, Richard, 28
Wakefield Buffeting, The (mid-fourteenth century), 43. *See also* Christ
Walker, Alexander, 148
Walker, Michael, melodrama continually developing, 136
Walpole, Horace. *See The Castle of Otranto*
Walpole, Hugh, 101
Waterloo Bridge: (1930, Robert Emmett Sherwood, playwright), 141, 236n7
— (1931, James Whale), 150n5, 236n7
— (1940, Mervyn LeRoy), 8, 229; *Auld Lang Syne* melody, 229; Chinese title: *Hunduan Lanqiao*, 229, 236n7; Yan Huizhu viewing, 229;
—(1940, Yue opera version), 230–31
— 1941: Hollywood films banned, 227; Chinese remake *Hunduan Lanqiao* (1941, Mei Qian), 229–30, 230; *The Farewell Waltz* (*Auld Lang Syne*) in, 231–32
— (1945, Xinguang Theater/Shanghai Radio), 231
— in history of Hollywood melodrama (and of China's) 231. *See also Spring River Flows East, The*
'Way Down East (1899, Lottie Blair Parker playwright), 99, 110–12 (see also *Way Down East*), 343; photographs of, 112
Way Down East (1920, D. W. Griffith, based on Lotte Blair Parker's play (*see also*), 111–12, and on Thomas Hardy's *Tess of the d'Urbervilles*), 123, 154, 327, in China (1922/1924), 92 (*see also Orphan, An*); basic components of melodrama, 83; Chinese title *Laihun*, 97n9; "cut back," 326, 339n2; "fallen woman," 45–46, 123, 333; inter titles, Blair Parker's words, 111; last-minute rescue, xiv, 40; play to film, 99; protagonist agency beyond passive stance, 47n4; Shanghai screening 92; Sinified version, 84; and tears, 326; and time, 326–28, 333. *See also* Christ, *Passion of*
Weaker Than a Woman. See Clay, Bertha M.; *Konjiki yasha*
We Sinners. See Noi peccatori
Weber, Lois. *See The Rosary*
Western: American and European traditions, universal applicability of, assumed, 86, 235; cultures, melodrama as intelligible picture of the world to, 101; film theory and transnational melodrama, 7–9; "hegemony, geopolitical space of" (Jameson), 71; mass society, individualism advanced by, 115; modern letters and arts, transplanted in China via Japan, 89; stories of "fearless faithful manhood," 120; subjectivity, influence of Christ's divine incarnation on, 33. *See also* melodrama, critical concepts; melodrama, unbinding; Yang, Panpan; Yeh, Emilie Yue-yu

White, Pearl, as "peerless fearless girl," 125; *The Perils of Pauline*, 125, 126. See also actors, female; girl(s); Hearst, William Randolph; Mary Pickford "a devoted fan," 125; serial queen, 116; Roland, Ruth; serial stars, 123;

White Slave Trade, The. See *tratta delle bianche*

Whitehead, Anne. See Pedler, Carolyn

Who's His Mother? (1926, Gu Wuwei), 95

Who Is Without Sin? See *Chi è senza peccato . . .*

Why Girls Leave Home (1908/1912), 108. See also girls

Williams, Carolyn, Victorian melodrama, 241

Williams, Linda: the black and white melodrama of race, 212; contradiction between egalitarian ideals and slavery, xviii; domestic melodrama, 49; dramatic *recognition* of good and evil, 234; feminists, and melodrama as sexist, 200n7; melodrama, 86, 136; melodrama as default mode of Hollywood cinema, 46, 47n3/4/5 (*see* Allen, Richard), 244, 286, 339n9; "Melodrama Revised," 87; *Playing the Race Card*, 183n3; suffering, sympathy for, 201n18. See also *Uncle Tom's Cabin*, xviii; 76, 215; *Way Down East*, 83, 326–28; tears

— chap. 10 (169–83): accumulation and prime time, 175–76; contemporary serial television melodrama, 176–79; melodrama, 171–73; O. J. Redux, 180–82; Rodney King, 181; serial television melodrama, 173–75; seriality, 169–71, 246; televisual time/serial time, 179–80; *The Wire* (*see also*), 182

— chap. 12 (205–17): Peter Brooks, 205–6, 207; "classical," categorised by Bordwell, Staiger and Thompson, xix, 9; "classical" Hollywood cinema, 209–212; the elephant of melodrama, 212–13; excess and "classicality," 207–9; family melodrama, objection to genre, xix; Matthew Buckley, 206; melodrama and justice, 213–17; melodrama and realism, 115; Thomas Elsaesser, 205, 206, 207; *The Wire* (*see also*), 215

— Gledhill, Christine, and, Introduction, 1–11

Williams, Raymond: critique xxv; culture x; historical change x; individual x–xi; interest xiv–xv; *Modern Tragedy*, x, passim; structural change/s x; structure/s of feeling, ix, x, xxiii

Winkelmann, Johann Joachim, German neoclassicism, 208

Wire, The (HBO, 2002–2008), 177, 179, 182, 245; American version of Greek tragedy, 215; Bodie in, 246–47, 251n3/4

Wirsching, Josef, 254; and *Mahal*, 264

Without Pity. See *Senza pietà*

Wives as They Were, and Maids as They Are. See Inchbald, Elizabeth. See also Kabra, K. N.; *Sudhi Vachche Sopari*

Womack, Peter. See Shepherd, Simon

woman: abandoned, 8; at centre of Indian socials, 64; death by fire, in *Lydia* and *La Passion de Jeanne d'Arc*, 185–87; -hood, erotically daring performances of, 130; -hood, so-called native American, 116, 117; "-hood, true," 116; -hood, white, 130, 181; Jeanne, -child, 196; -kind, Julia Ward Howe on, 118; melodrama still a suffering woman in a domestic context, 172; as mother in *Uncle Tom's Cabin*, 44; suffering, in *Gertrud*, 201n17; Tess, 123; woman's desire contained (*Najma*), 262; woman's desire as destructive (*Mahal*), 262. See also girls; Pickford, Mary; White, Pearl

— abandoned or orphan, 8; *Way Down East*, 83

— erring/fallen, 40, 45–46, 85, 116, 118; "age-old cross" of the, 40; Virginia Rappe portrayed as, 132; *Way Down East*, 40. See also *Hunduan Lanqiao*

— Mexico: in early sound cinema, 161–62; fallen woman in *Santa*, 155; fetishism and, 163–64; a new idea of woman, 165; woman suffering, 153

— woman's film, 78, 81, 88, 138; Rick Altman on, 172; and André Bazin, 210; familiar sentiments of, 216; feminists, 1980s, and pathos of, 212; as ghetto, 46; Mary Ann Doane on, 172; *Taki no shiraito as*, 78; woman's genre, melodrama as, 34

women: as action characters (*see* Cushman, Charlotte; White, Pearl); emotion, empathy and, 43–46; emotions associated with, 34; and feminization of the domestic sphere, 6; increasing importance in theater and early film, 5, 120–21 (*see* Hallett, Hilary A.); and Kabra, K. N., 57; in modernizing societies, fate of, 85; new role for, 158. *Seeking work in Hollywood*, 127, 133n4; working in Hollywood, 127 (*see* Mathis, June; Parsons, Louella; Price, Gertrude); women's contribution to modernising popular culture, 5
— melodrama and, 118; melodramatic, on the C19 stage, 117–21; as women's culture, 4. *See also* girls; *Gone with the Wind* in China; Pickford, Mary
Woman of the World, A (1925, Mal St Clair). *See* Negri, Pola
Wood, Ellen. *See East Lynne*
Woodman's Hut, The (1814), xiii
Wordsworth, William, 17

Xian Qing Ou Ji, author Li Yu, Chinese dramaturgical tradition and melodrama, 225, 235, 236n3

Yahudi ki Larki (1913). *See* Hashr, Agha
Yan Huizhu. *See Waterloo Bridge* (1940)
Yang, Panpan, chap. 13 (219–36); China's Gone with the Wind, 233–35; Chinese cinema's response to Hollywood, 8; Confucian culture, 226–27; the elephant, 235; excess, types of, 224–27; *Gone with the Wind* (*see also*), in China, 8, 219; Hollywood banned, original remakes, 227–31; Hollywood dream in the Orphan Island, 220; Japan and China, 227; melodrama at the crossroads of culture, 219–20; melos, melodrama and excess, 231–33; Shanghaiese, modern vocabulary, 97n6; *The Spring Flows East* (*see also*), 233; *Waterloo Bridge* (*see also*), 8; *wenyi*, melodrama and, 223–24; *wenyi*, transnational address of, 8. *See also* music; Zhang, Zhen
Yasujiro Ozu, 72
Yeh, Emilie Yue-yu, making Chinese terms, critical keywords, 88; Mandarin Ducks and Butterflies literature, 97n4; *wenyi*, 88, 89, 223; "Wenyi and the Branding of Early Chinese Film," 88. *See also* Yang, Panpan; Zhang, Zhen
Yijiang Chunshui Xiangdongliu (*see Spring River Flows East, The*). *See* tears
Yomota, Inuhiko, on Izumi Kyōka, 77, 82n6 69; early cinema and shinpa's "melodramatic imagination," 77
Yoshimoto, Mitsuhiro: "Melodrama, Postmodernism, and Japanese Cinema" (1993), 70–71, 78; on ideologeme, 71, 81n2; postwar melodrama as narrative of victimhood, 78
Yūhō, Kikuchi:
— *Chikyōdai*, based on *Dora Thorne*, 75. *See also* Brame, Charlotte M., 77
— *Onoga tsumi* (*My Sin*, 1912–1922, various media incarnations) (*see also* KenjiMizoguchi), 77

Zavattini, Cesare [screenwriter] 280. *See also* De Sica, Vittorio
Zhang, Zhen, chap. 5 (83–97); global circulation of melodrama, establishing the 79–80; Griffith, D. W./"Griffith fever," 8, 79–80; Mandarin Ducks and Butterflies fiction, 97n7; melodrama as quintessentially "Western" or "American," questioning, 72–73, 87; melodrama versus *wenyi*, 86–91; the orphan and abandoned woman, 8; permutations of the orphan drama, 91–95; vernacular, melodrama as global, 8, 80 (*see also* Hansen, Miriam); *wenyi* 88–91. *See also East Lynne*; *Orphan Rescues Grandfather*; *Orphans of the Storm*; Yang, Panpan
Zhang Shichuan: *Orphan Rescues Grandfather* (with Zheng Zhengqiu), 1923, 83; *A Blind Orphan Girl* (1925), 95; *A Little Friend* (1925), 95; *The Poor Children* (1924), 95
Zhang Shichuang: *Konggu Ian* "Orchid in an Empty Valley" (1926). *See also East Lynne*
Zheng Junli: male protagonist in *Waterloo Bridge* (1941) Yihua Company, 233; on Griffith fever following *Way Down East*, 91–92; *see also The Spring River Flows East*

Zheng Zhengqiu, 90, 97*n*9; comparisons between Zheng and Griffith, 93; *Konggu lan* writer with Bao Tianxiao, 91; *Orphan Rescues Grandfather* (with Zhang Shichuan), 1923, 83; use of "melodrama," 90. *See also* Griffith, D. W.; *East Lynne*; *Jade Pear Spirit*

Zhu Shilin. *See Mother's Happiness*

Zip Coon (1827), 300–302, 301, 308*n*20

Zola, Emile. *See verismo*

zoot suit, 164, 308*n*17

Zwicker, Jonathan E.: *Konjiki yasha*, reading of, 74–75; global circulation of nineteenth-century melodramatic literature and late Meiji narratives, 75; *Practices of the Sentimental Imagination* . . . (2006), 69, 75; serials, nineteenth-century Japanese, 76

FILM AND CULTURE
A SERIES OF COLUMBIA UNIVERSITY PRESS

EDITED BY JOHN BELTON

What Made Pistachio Nuts? Early Sound Comedy and the Vaudeville Aesthetic
Henry Jenkins
Showstoppers: Busby Berkeley and the Tradition of Spectacle
Martin Rubin
Projections of War: Hollywood, American Culture, and World War II
Thomas Doherty
Laughing Screaming: Modern Hollywood Horror and Comedy
William Paul
Laughing Hysterically: American Screen Comedy of the 1950s
Ed Sikov
Primitive Passions: Visuality, Sexuality, Ethnography, and Contemporary Chinese Cinema
Rey Chow
The Cinema of Max Ophuls: Magisterial Vision and the Figure of Woman
Susan M. White
Black Women as Cultural Readers
Jacqueline Bobo
Picturing Japaneseness: Monumental Style, National Identity, Japanese Film
Darrell William Davis
Attack of the Leading Ladies: Gender, Sexuality, and Spectatorship in Classic Horror Cinema
Rhona J. Berenstein
This Mad Masquerade: Stardom and Masculinity in the Jazz Age
Gaylyn Studlar
Sexual Politics and Narrative Film: Hollywood and Beyond
Robin Wood
The Sounds of Commerce: Marketing Popular Film Music
Jeff Smith
Orson Welles, Shakespeare, and Popular Culture
Michael Anderegg
Pre-Code Hollywood: Sex, Immorality, and Insurrection in American Cinema, 1930–1934
Thomas Doherty
Sound Technology and the American Cinema: Perception, Representation, Modernity
James Lastra
Melodrama and Modernity: Early Sensational Cinema and Its Contexts
Ben Singer
Wondrous Difference: Cinema, Anthropology, and Turn-of-the-Century Visual Culture
Alison Griffiths
Hearst Over Hollywood: Power, Passion, and Propaganda in the Movies
Louis Pizzitola
Masculine Interests: Homoerotics in Hollywood Film
Robert Lang
Special Effects: Still in Search of Wonder
Michele Pierson
Designing Women: Cinema, Art Deco, and the Female Form
Lucy Fischer

Cold War, Cool Medium: Television, McCarthyism, and American Culture
Thomas Doherty
Katharine Hepburn: Star as Feminist
Andrew Britton
Silent Film Sound
Rick Altman
Home in Hollywood: The Imaginary Geography of Cinema
Elisabeth Bronfen
Hollywood and the Culture Elite: How the Movies Became American
Peter Decherney
Taiwan Film Directors: A Treasure Island
Emilie Yueh-yu Yeh and Darrell William Davis
Shocking Representation: Historical Trauma, National Cinema, and the Modern Horror Film
Adam Lowenstein
China on Screen: Cinema and Nation
Chris Berry and Mary Farquhar
The New European Cinema: Redrawing the Map
Rosalind Galt
George Gallup in Hollywood
Susan Ohmer
Electric Sounds: Technological Change and the Rise of Corporate Mass Media
Steve J. Wurtzler
The Impossible David Lynch
Todd McGowan
Sentimental Fabulations, Contemporary Chinese Films: Attachment in the Age of Global Visibility
Rey Chow
Hitchcock's Romantic Irony
Richard Allen
Intelligence Work: The Politics of American Documentary
Jonathan Kahana
Eye of the Century: Film, Experience, Modernity
Francesco Casetti
Shivers Down Your Spine: Cinema, Museums, and the Immersive View
Alison Griffiths
Weimar Cinema: An Essential Guide to Classic Films of the Era
Edited by Noah Isenberg
African Film and Literature: Adapting Violence to the Screen
Lindiwe Dovey
Film, A Sound Art
Michel Chion
Film Studies: An Introduction
Ed Sikov
Hollywood Lighting from the Silent Era to Film Noir
Patrick Keating
Levinas and the Cinema of Redemption: Time, Ethics, and the Feminine
Sam B. Girgus

Counter-Archive: Film, the Everyday, and Albert Kahn's Archives de la Planète
Paula Amad
Indie: An American Film Culture
Michael Z. Newman
Pretty: Film and the Decorative Image
Rosalind Galt
Film and Stereotype: A Challenge for Cinema and Theory
Jörg Schweinitz
Chinese Women's Cinema: Transnational Contexts
Edited by Lingzhen Wang
Hideous Progeny: Disability, Eugenics, and Classic Horror Cinema
Angela M. Smith
Hollywood's Copyright Wars: From Edison to the Internet
Peter Decherney
Electric Dreamland: Amusement Parks, Movies, and American Modernity
Lauren Rabinovitz
Where Film Meets Philosophy: Godard, Resnais, and Experiments in Cinematic Thinking
Hunter Vaughan
The Utopia of Film: Cinema and Its Futures in Godard, Kluge, and Tahimik
Christopher Pavsek
Hollywood and Hitler, 1933–1939
Thomas Doherty
Cinematic Appeals: The Experience of New Movie Technologies
Ariel Rogers
Continental Strangers: German Exile Cinema, 1933–1951
Gerd Gemünden
Deathwatch: American Film, Technology, and the End of Life
C. Scott Combs
After the Silents: Hollywood Film Music in the Early Sound Era, 1926–1934
Michael Slowik
"It's the Pictures That Got Small": Charles Brackett on Billy Wilder and Hollywood's Golden Age
Edited by Anthony Slide
Plastic Reality: Special Effects, Technology, and the Emergence of 1970s Blockbuster Aesthetics
Julie A. Turnock
Maya Deren: Incomplete Control
Sarah Keller
Dreaming of Cinema: Spectatorship, Surrealism, and the Age of Digital Media
Adam Lowenstein
Motion(less) Pictures: The Cinema of Stasis
Justin Remes
The Lumière Galaxy: Seven Key Words for the Cinema to Come
Francesco Casetti
The End of Cinema? A Medium in Crisis in the Digital Age
André Gaudreault and Philippe Marion
Studios Before the System: Architecture, Technology, and the Emergence of Cinematic Space
Brian R. Jacobson

Impersonal Enunciation, or the Place of Film
Christian Metz
When Movies Were Theater: Architecture, Exhibition, and the Evolution of American Film
William Paul
Carceral Fantasies: Cinema and Prison in Early Twentieth-Century America
Alison Griffiths
Unspeakable Histories: Film and the Experience of Catastrophe
William Guynn
Reform Cinema in Iran: Film and Political Change in the Islamic Republic
Blake Atwood
Exception Taken: How France Has Defied Hollywood's New World Order
Jonathan Buchsbaum
After Uniqueness: A History of Film and Video Art in Circulation
Erika Balsom
Words on Screen
Michel Chion
Essays on the Essay Film
Edited by Nora M. Alter and Timothy Corrigan
The Essay Film After Fact and Fiction
Nora Alter

GPSR Authorized Representative: Easy Access System Europe, Mustamäe tee
50, 10621 Tallinn, Estonia, gpsr.requests@easproject.com

www.ingramcontent.com/pod-product-compliance
Lightning Source LLC
Chambersburg PA
CBHW081146290426
44108CB00018B/2451